3. ANTHONY GORDON

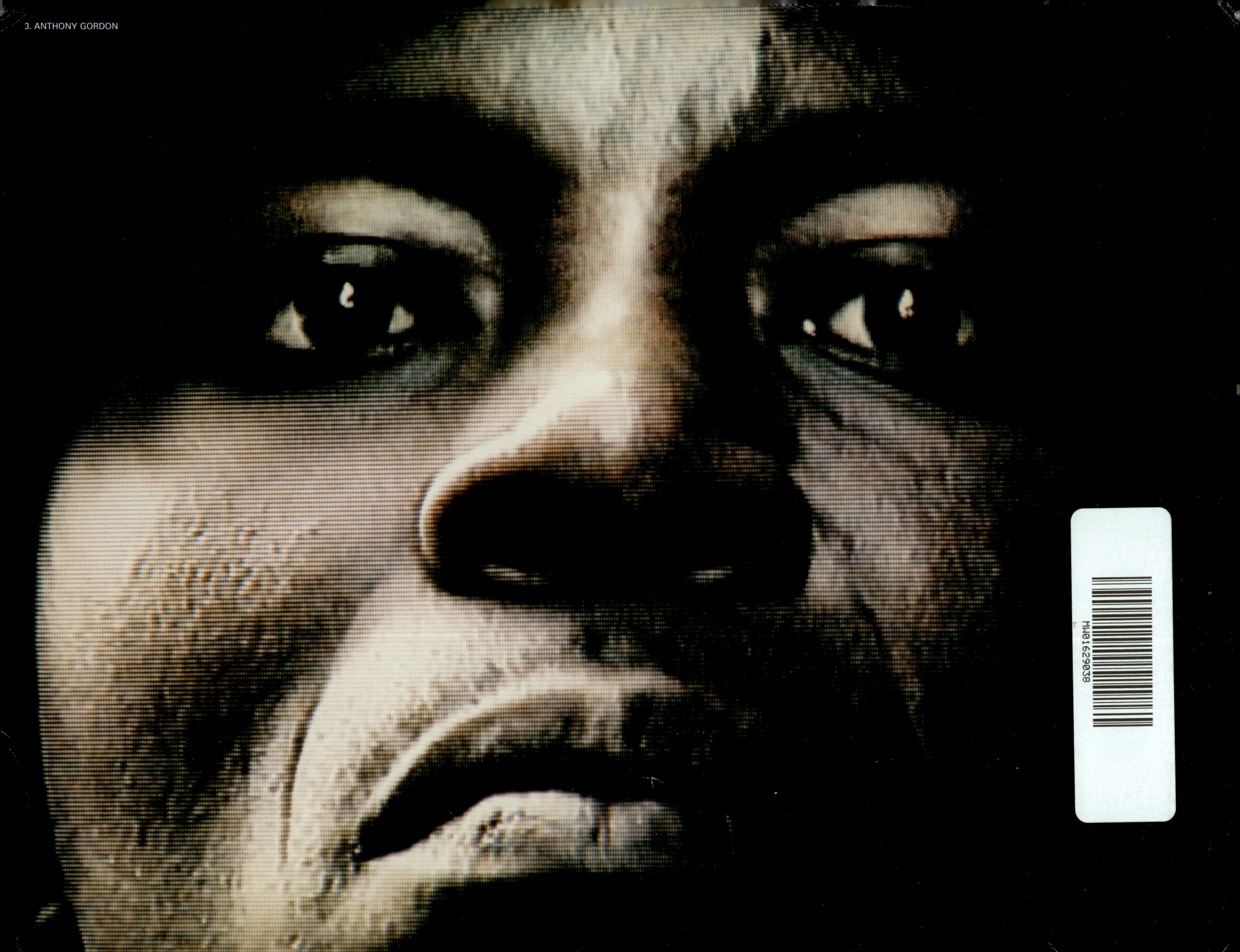

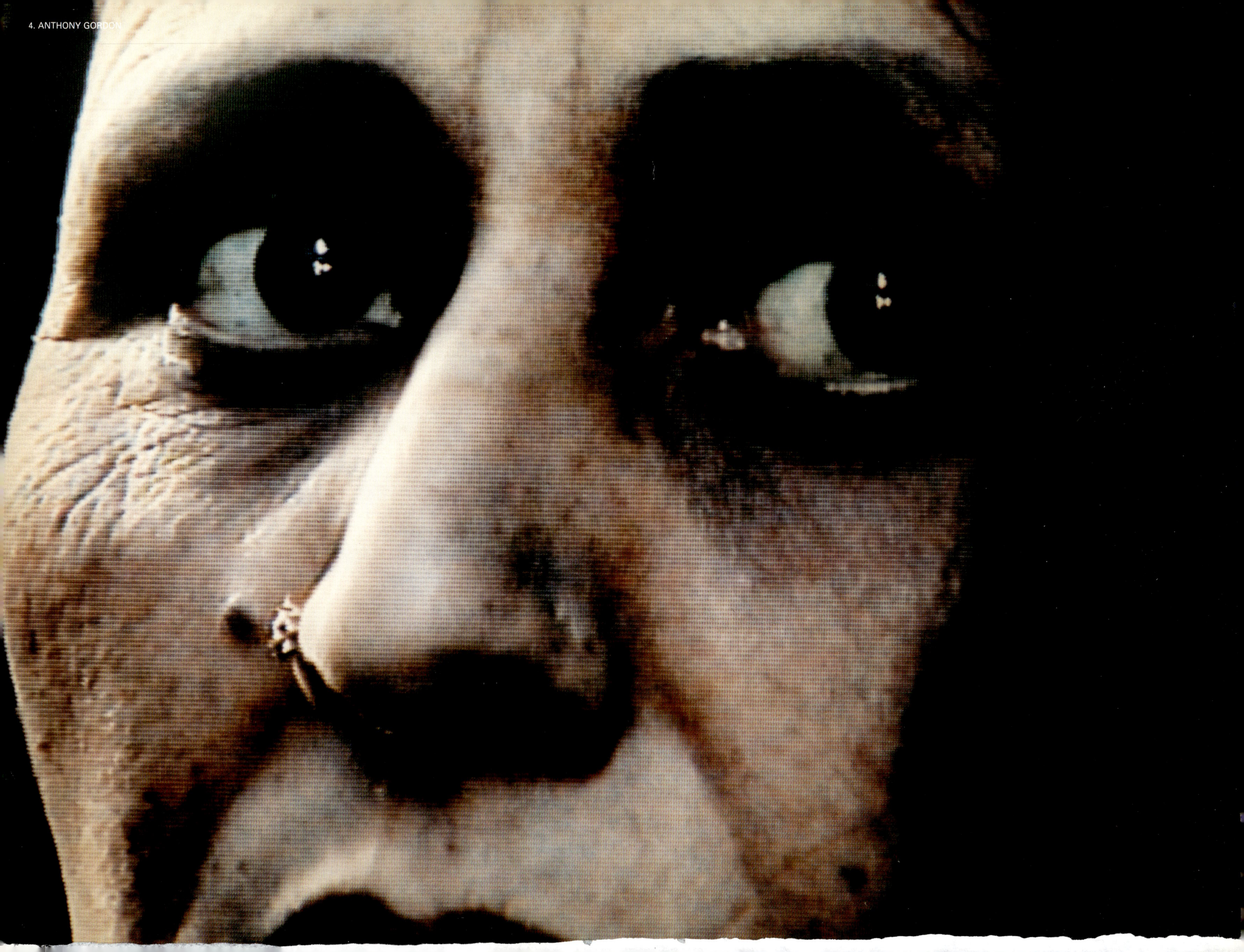

4. ANTHONY GORDON

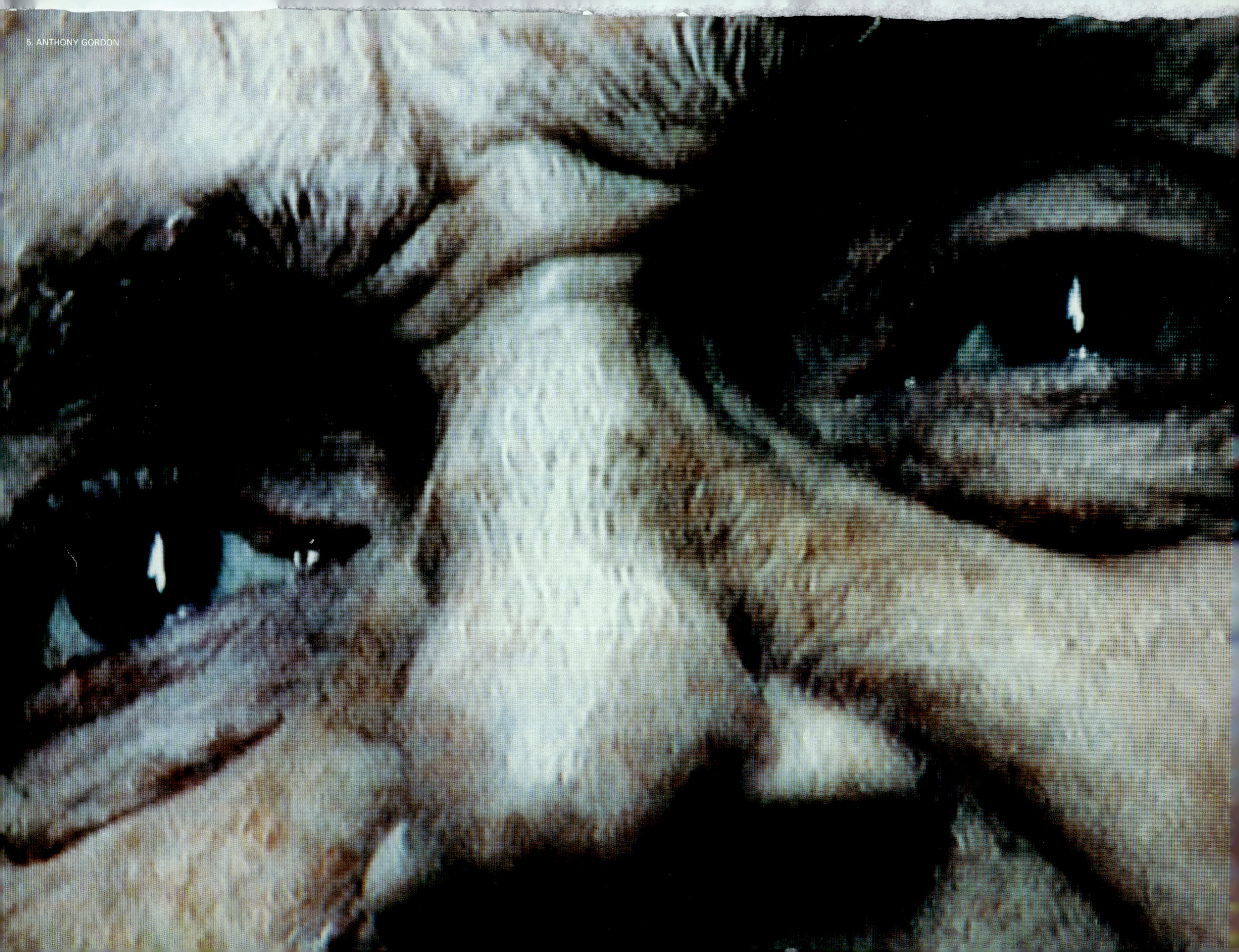

5. ANTHONY GORDON

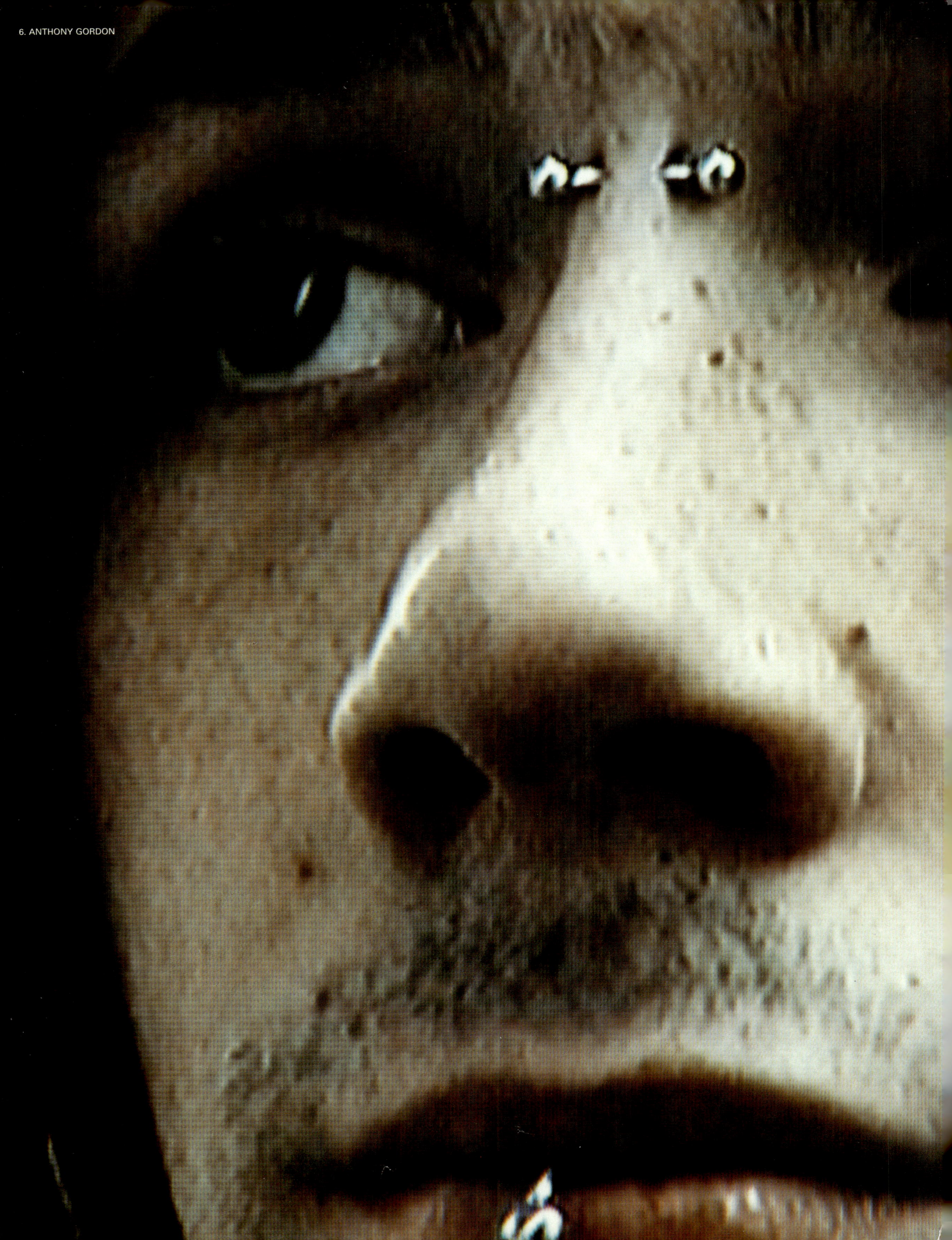

6. ANTHONY GORDON

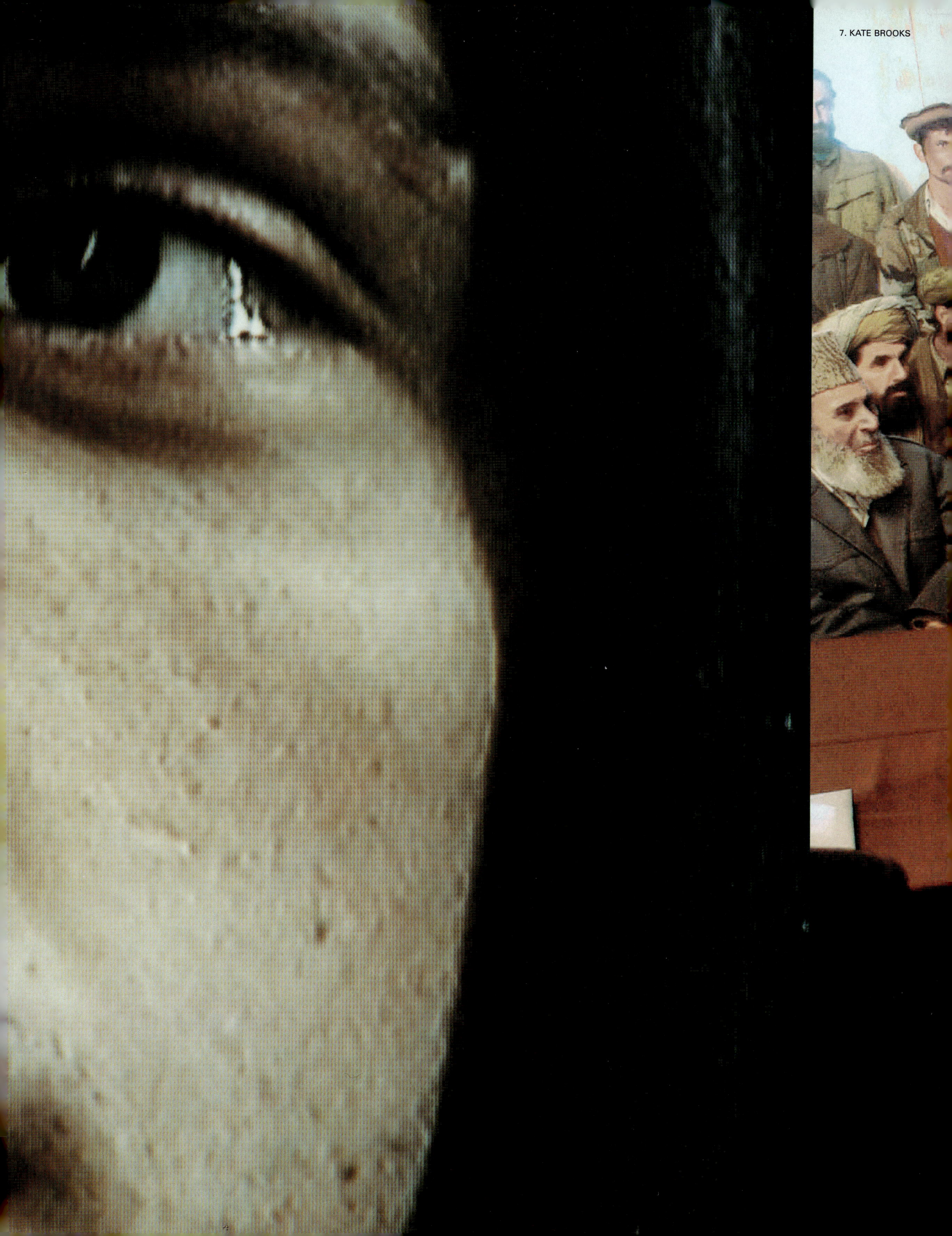

7. KATE BROOKS

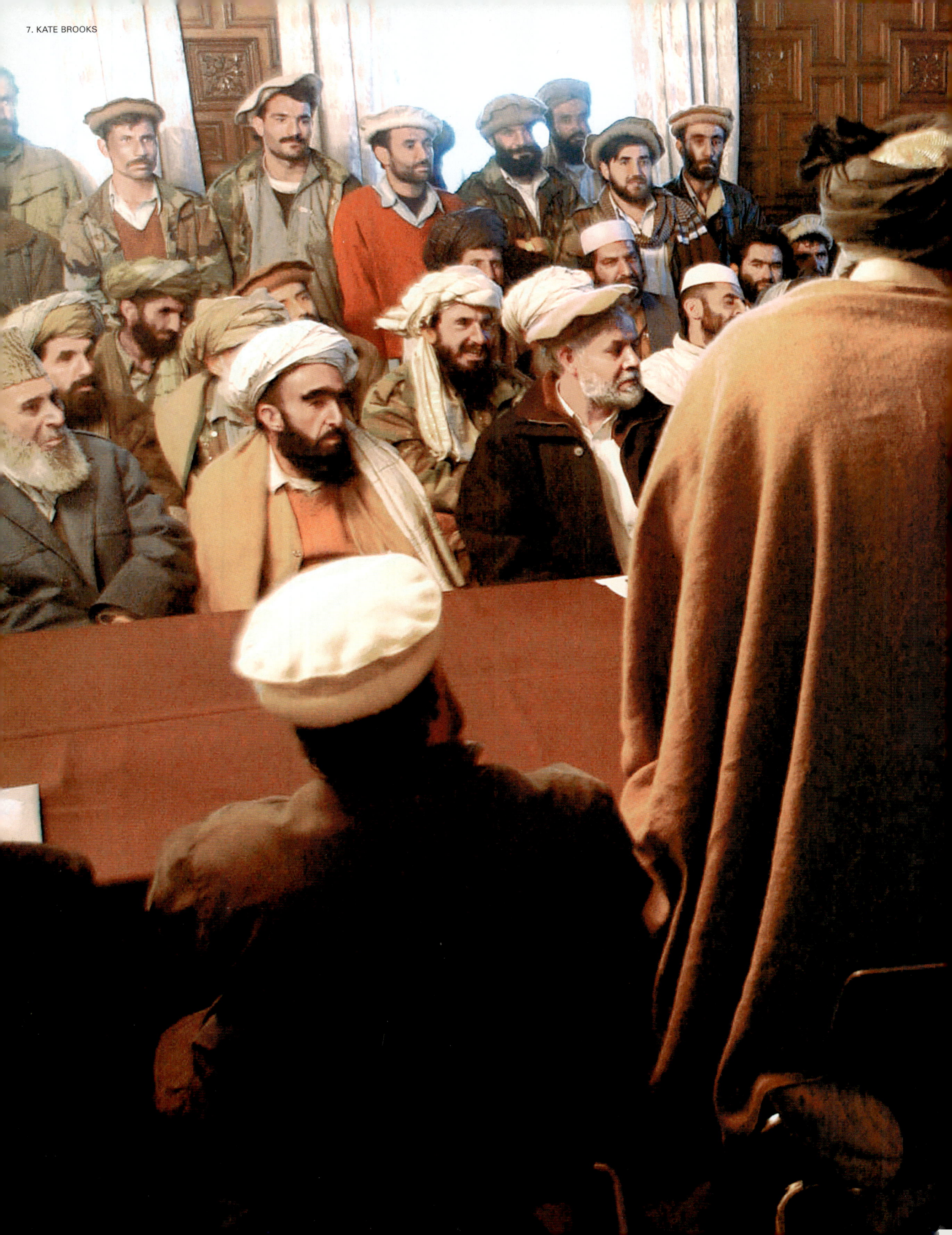

7. KATE BROOKS

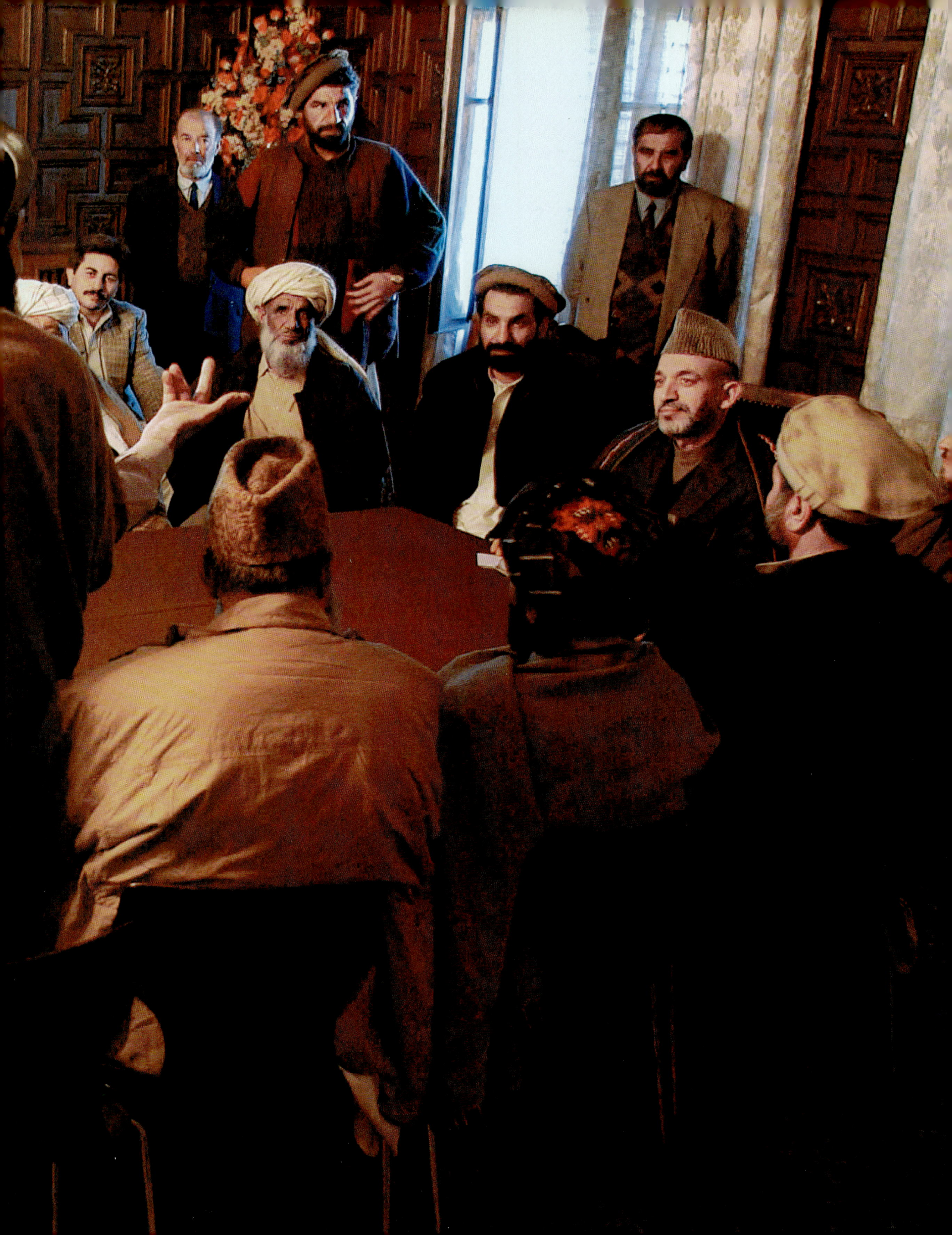

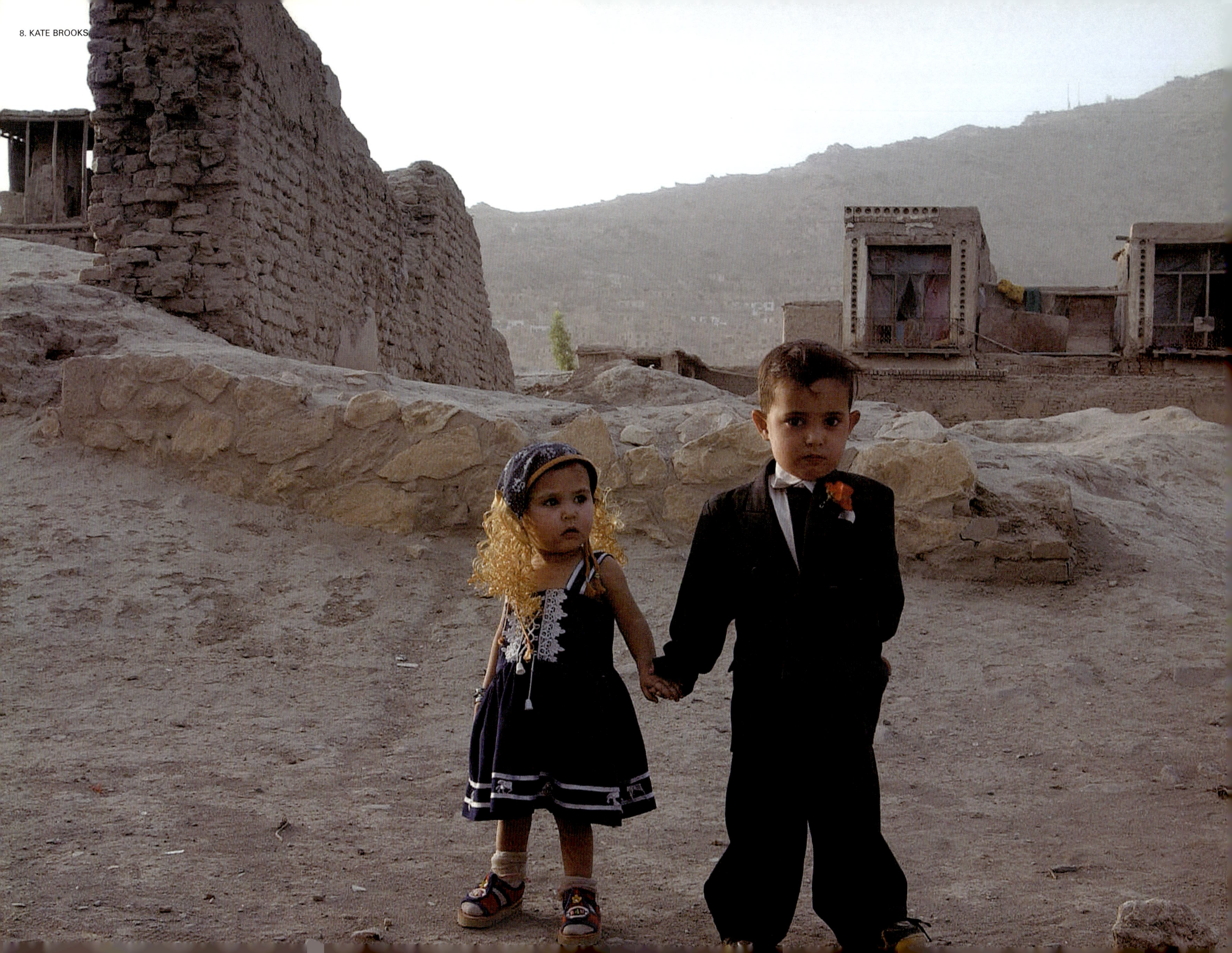

8. KATE BROOKS

9. JUDY WALGREN

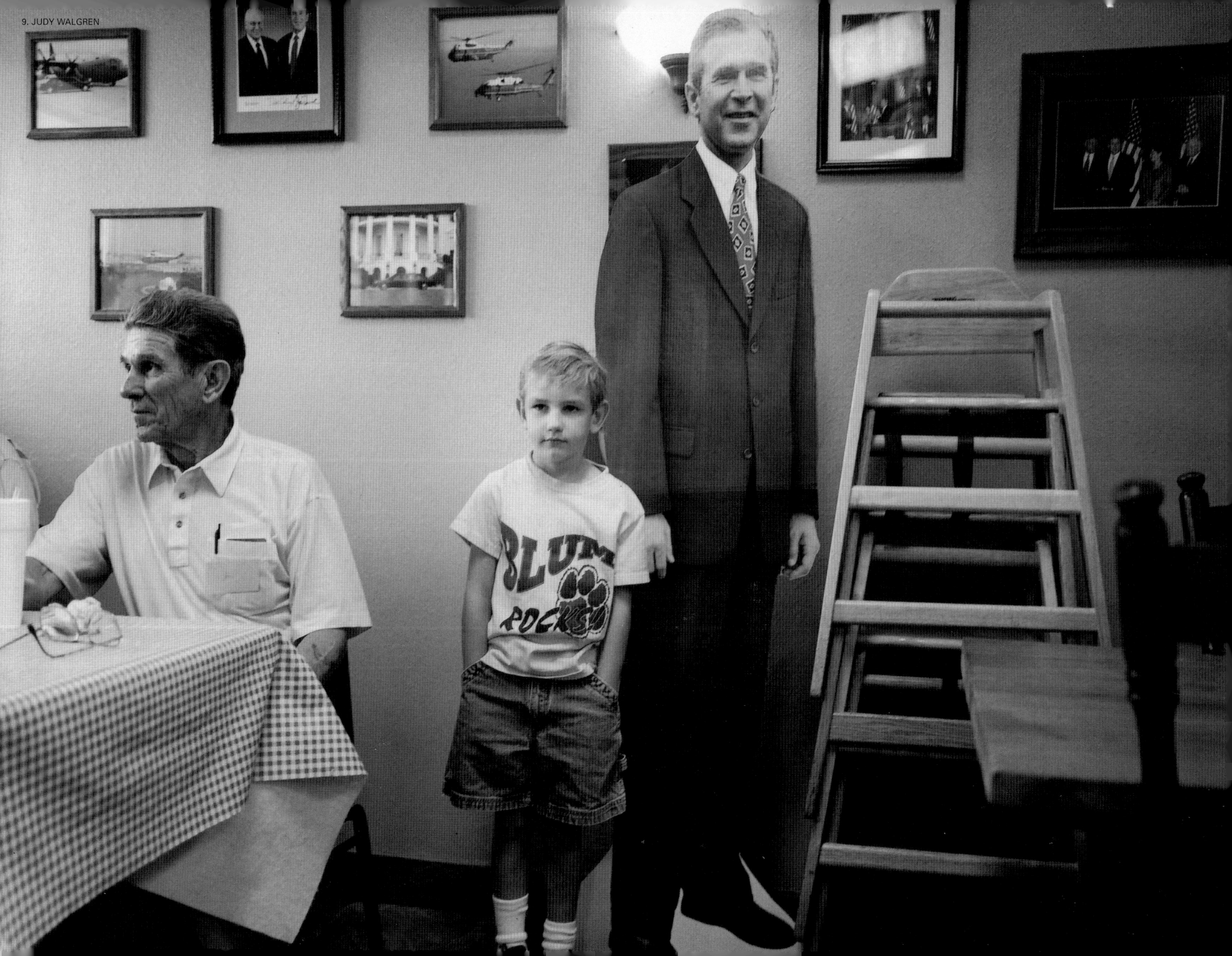

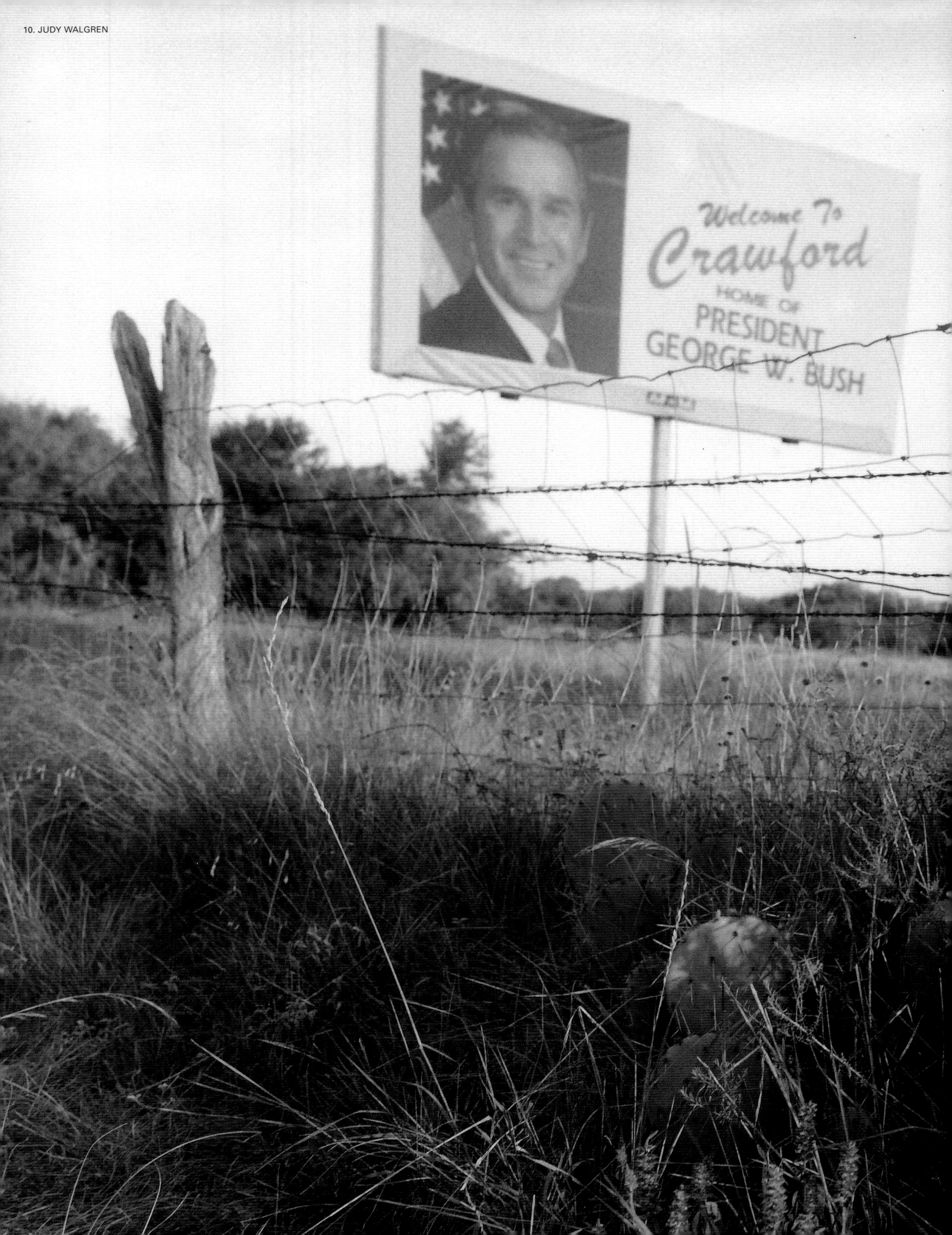
Welcome To
Crawford
HOME OF
PRESIDENT
GEORGE W. BUSH

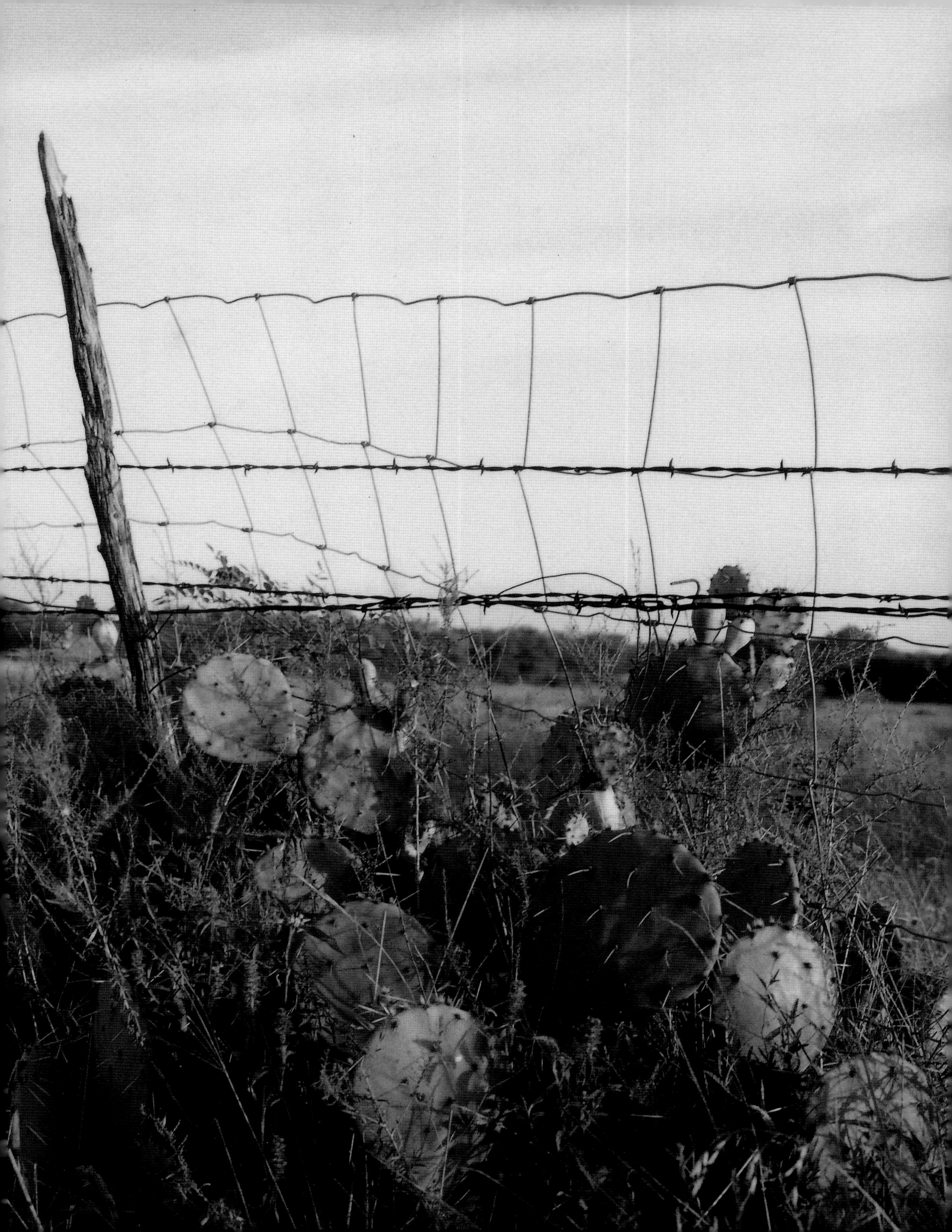

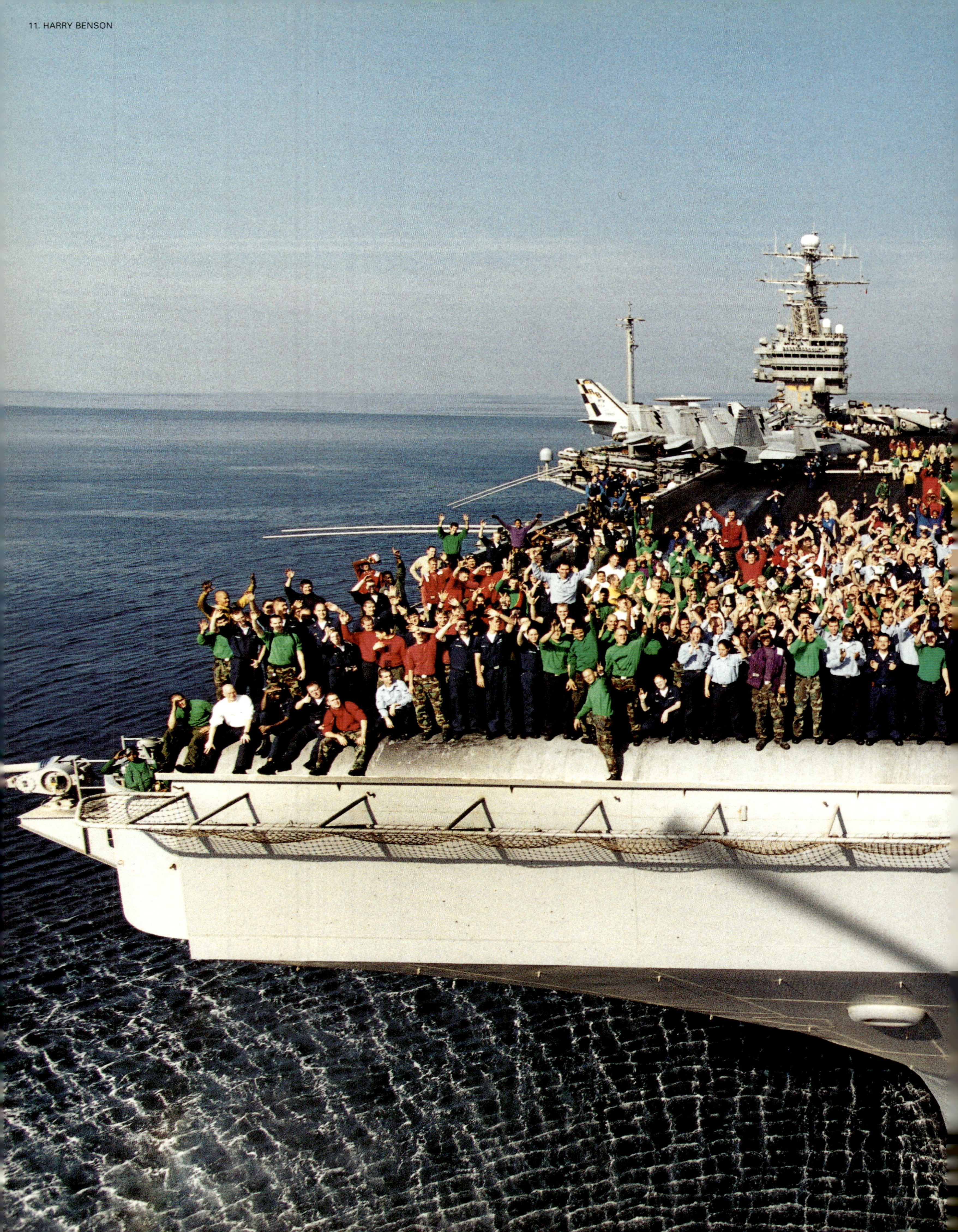

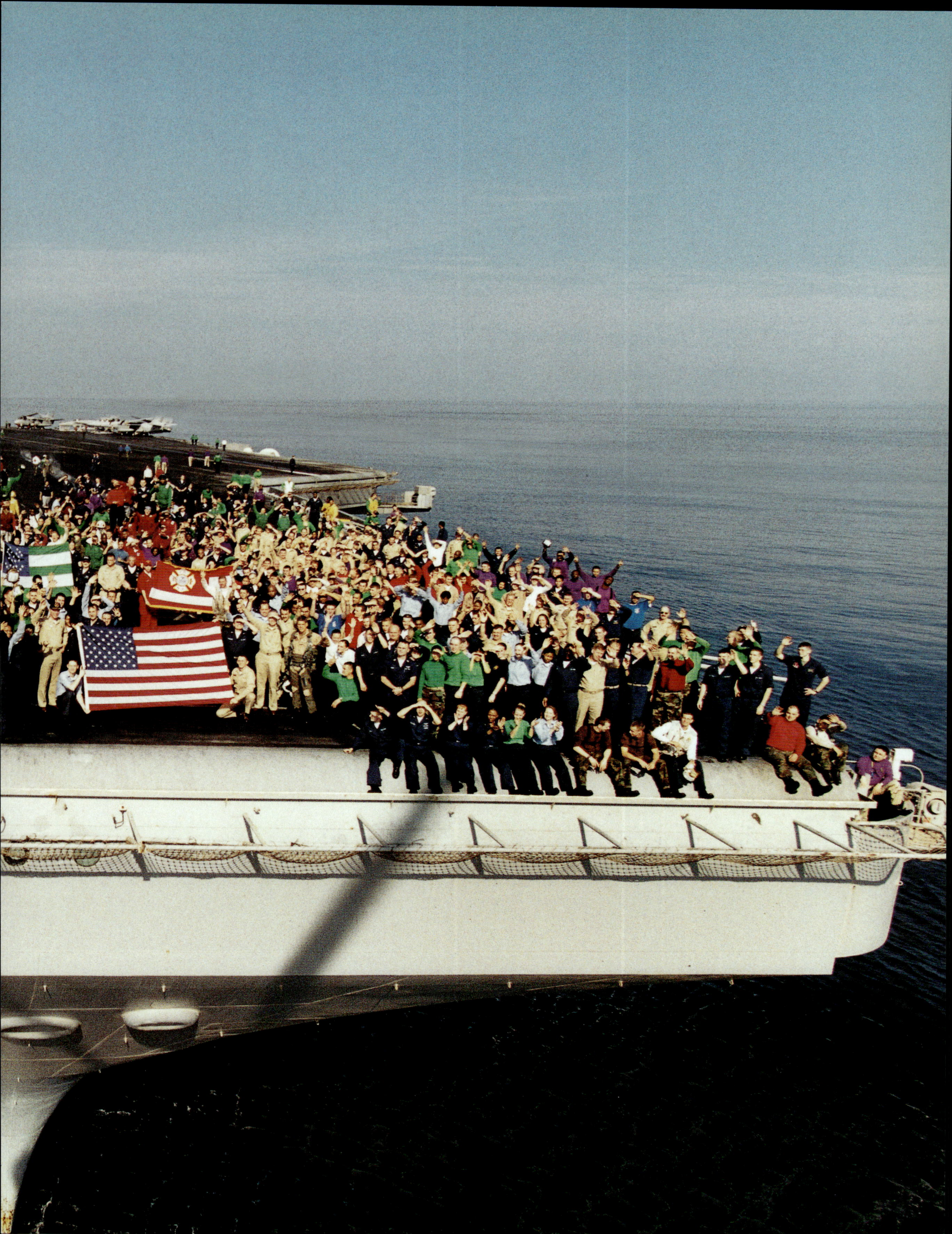

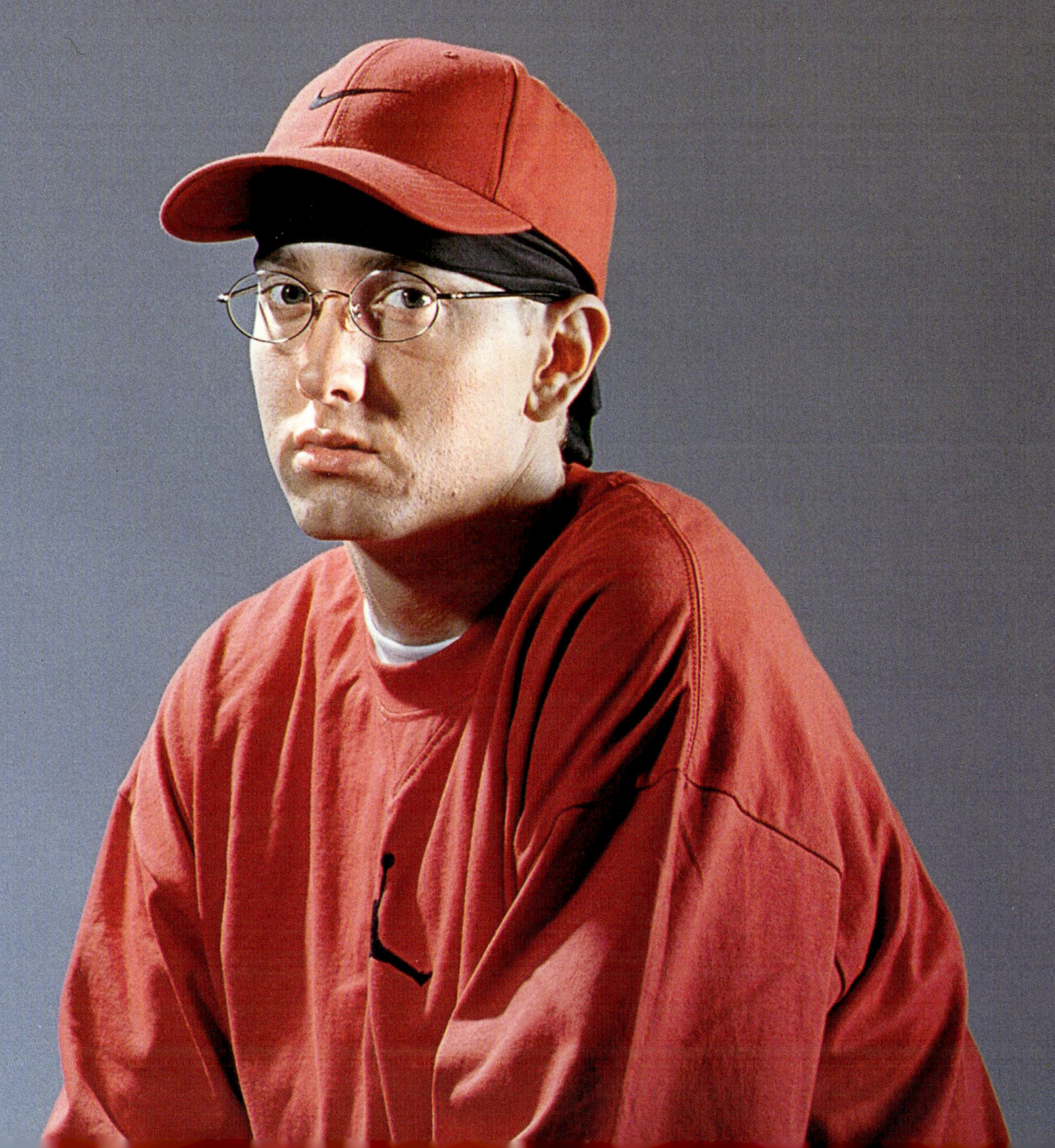

12. DAVID HARRY STEWART

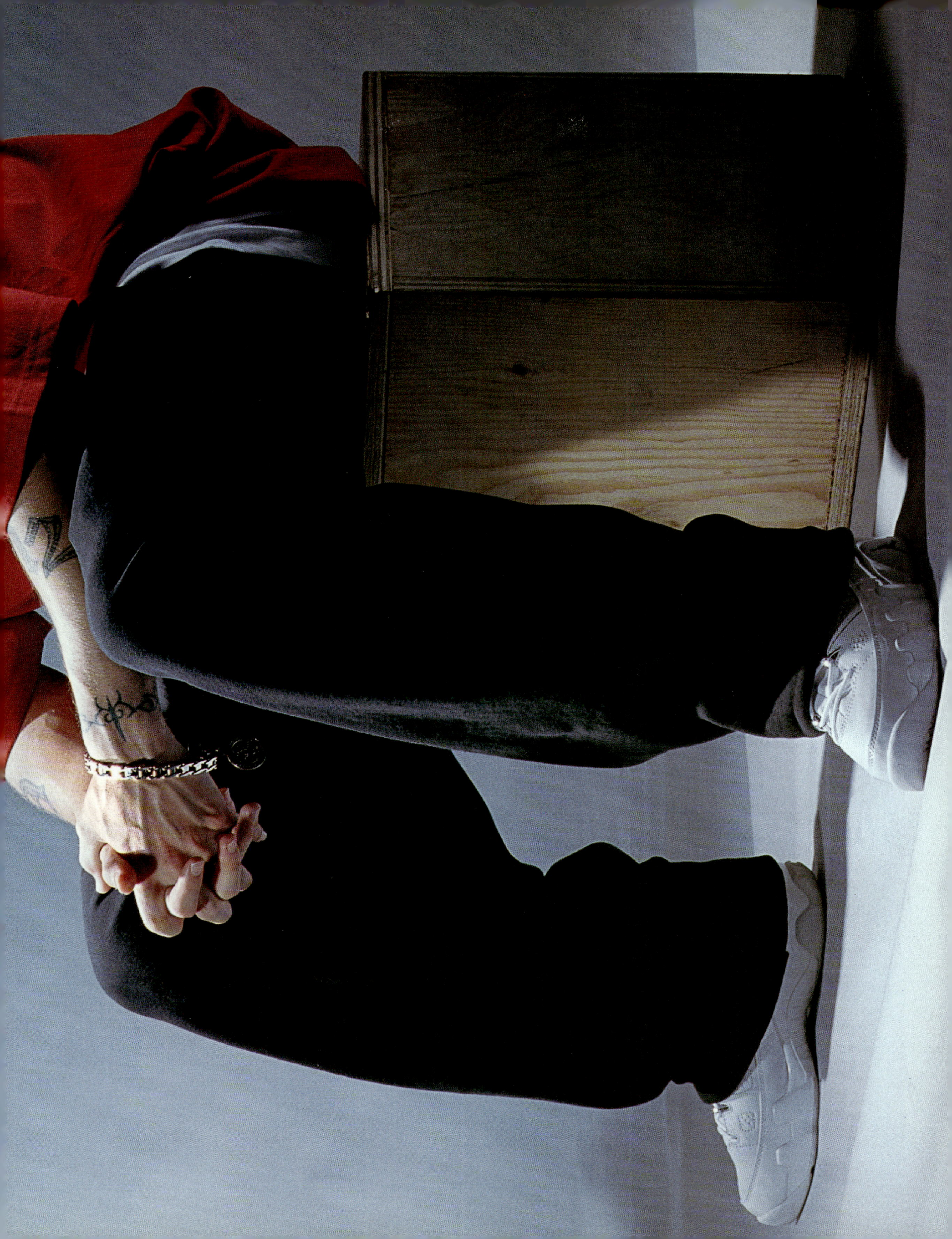

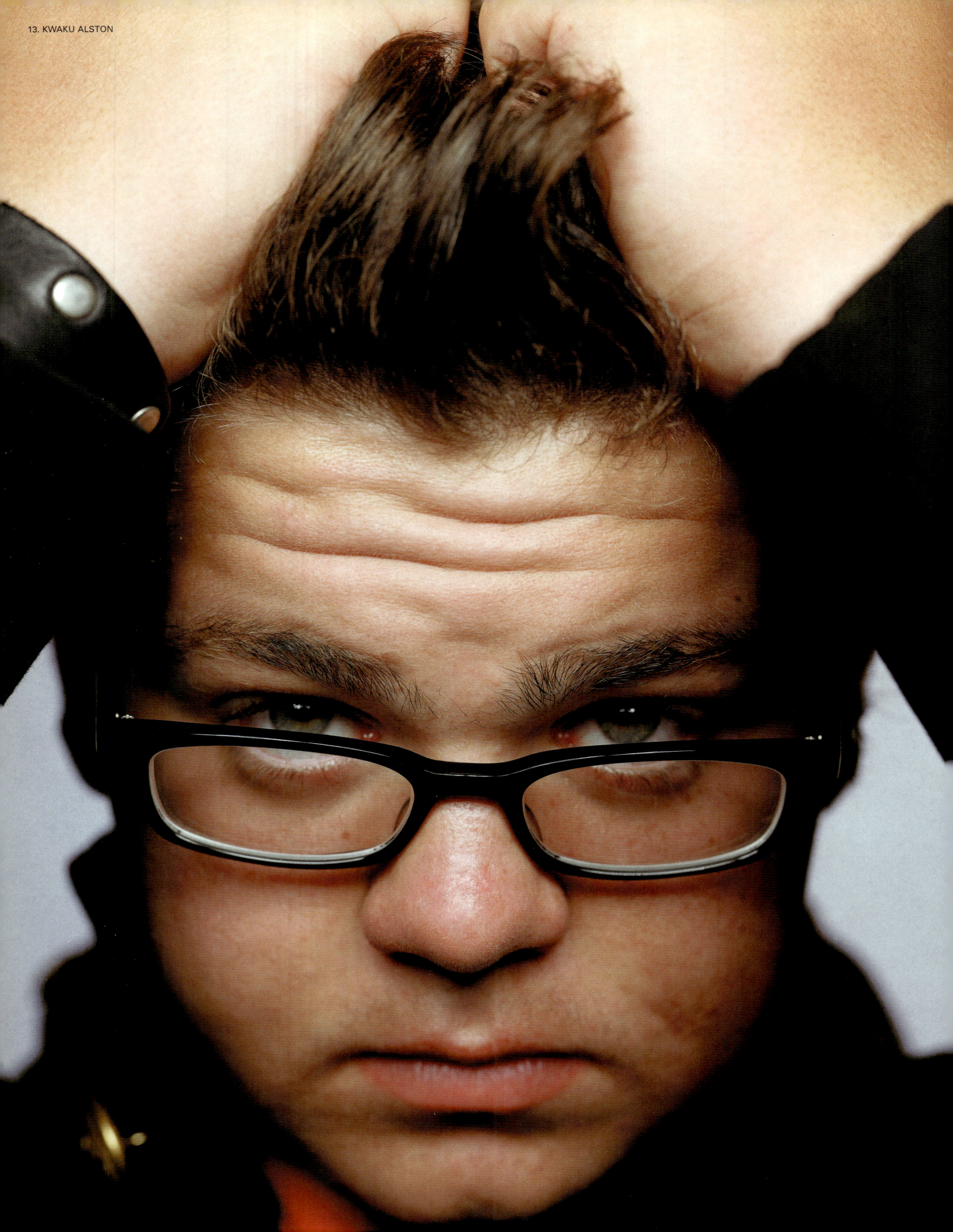
13. KWAKU ALSTON

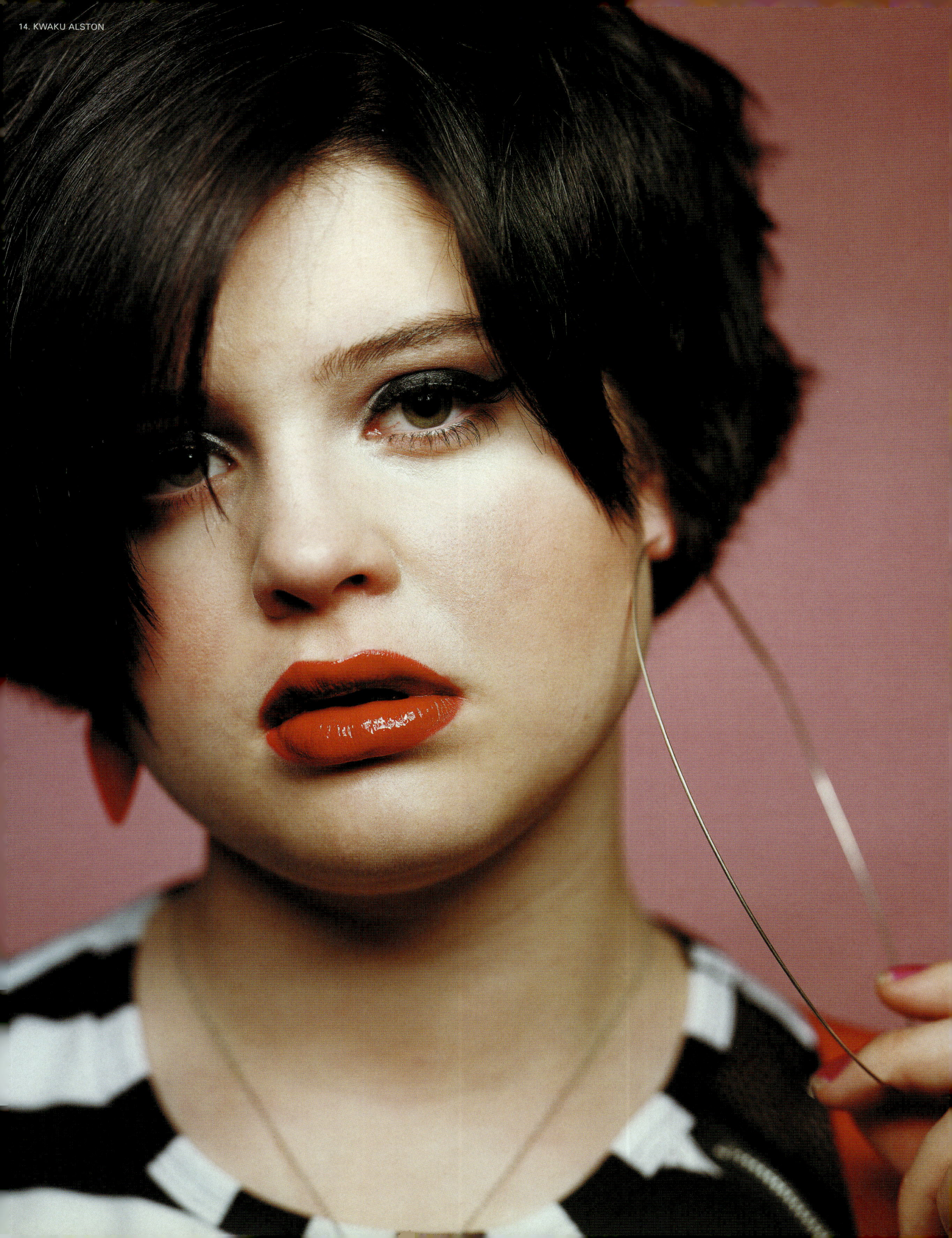

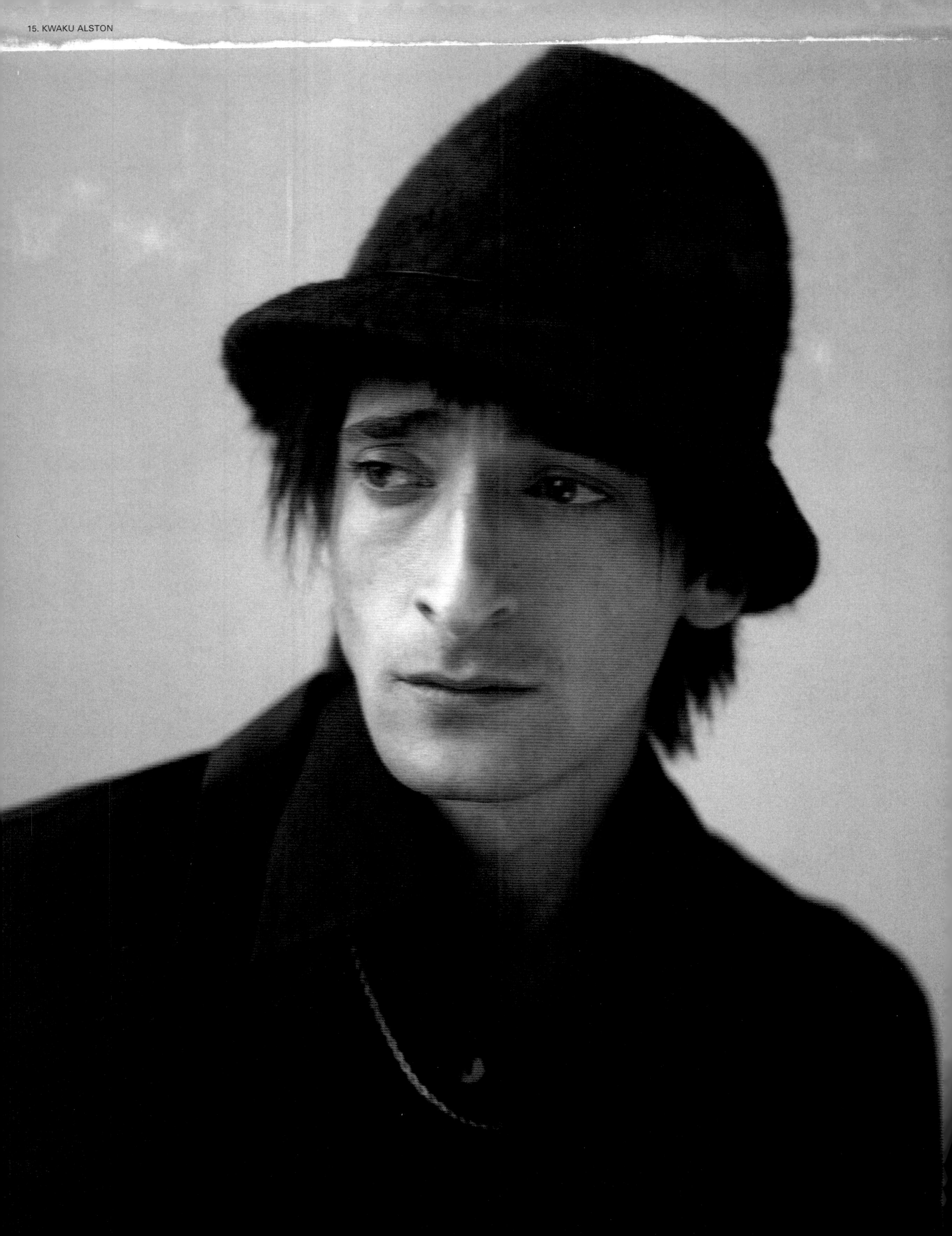

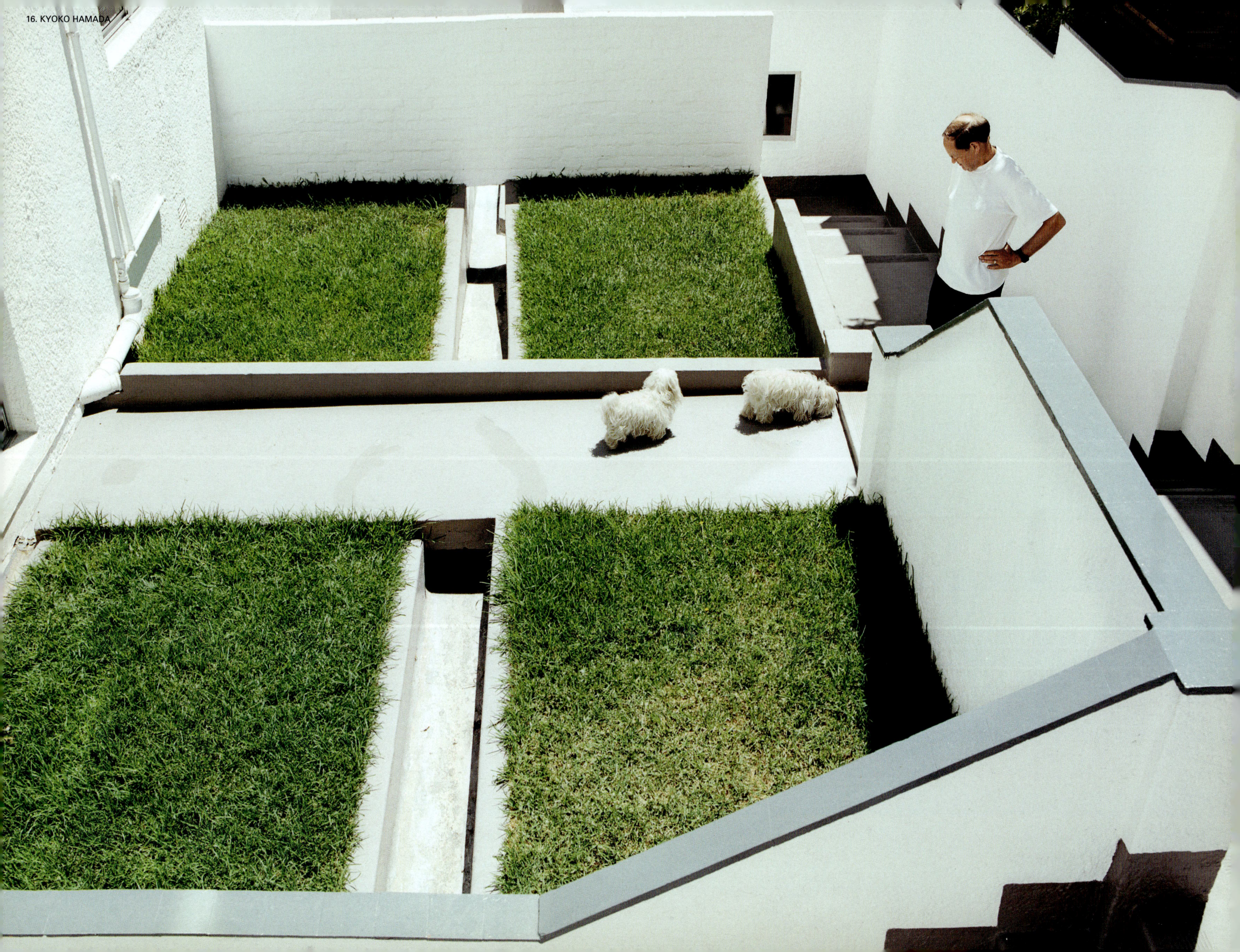

16. KYOKO HAMADA

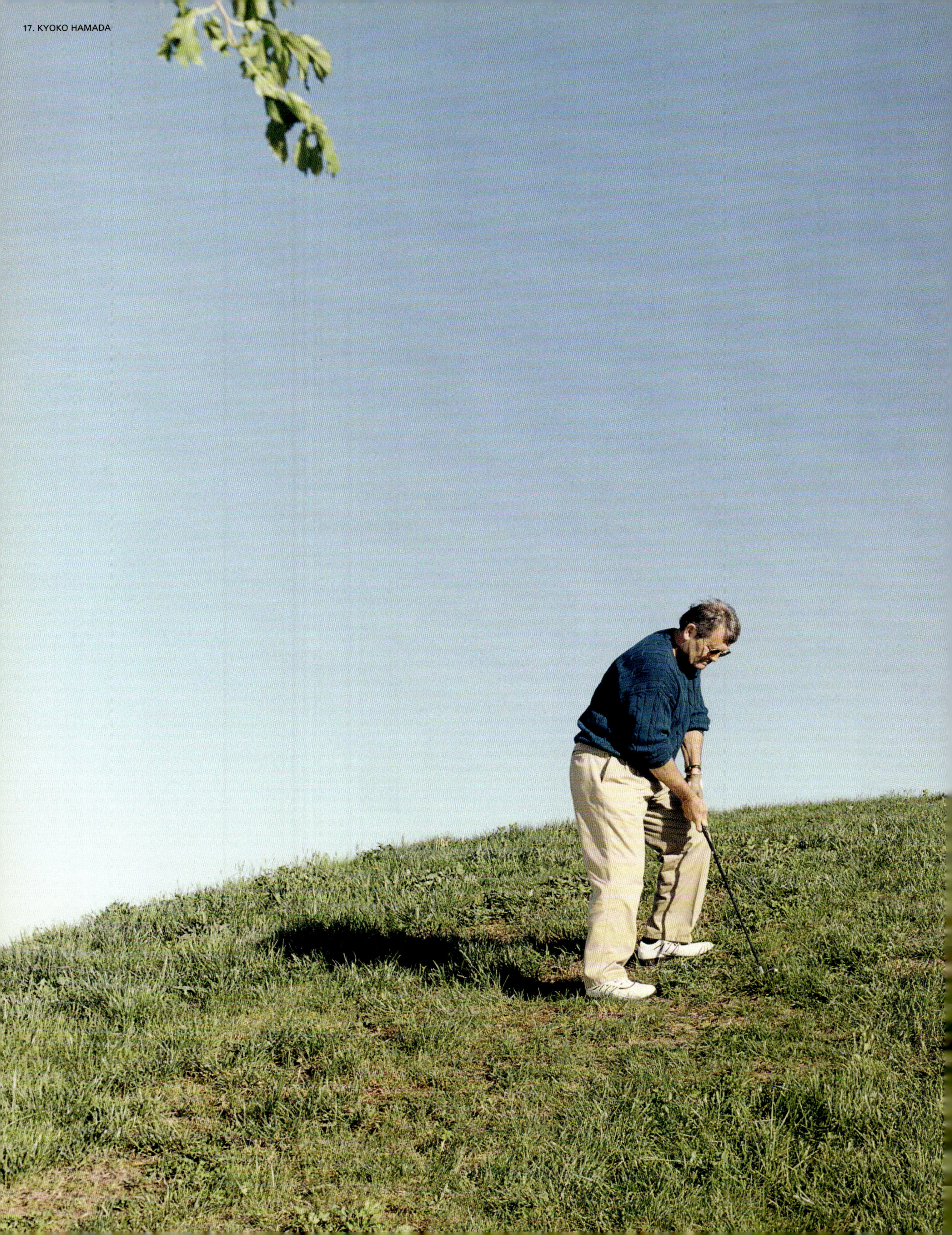

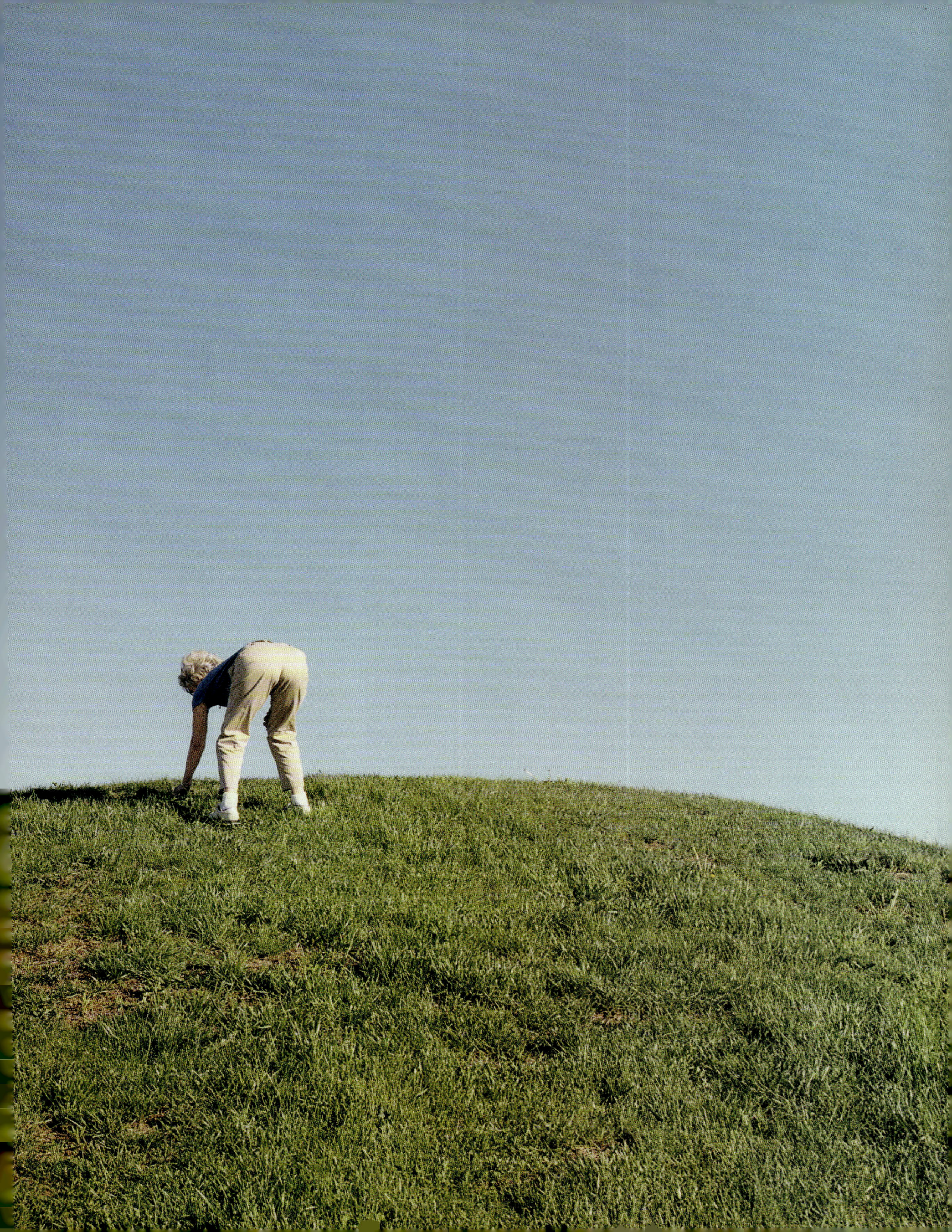

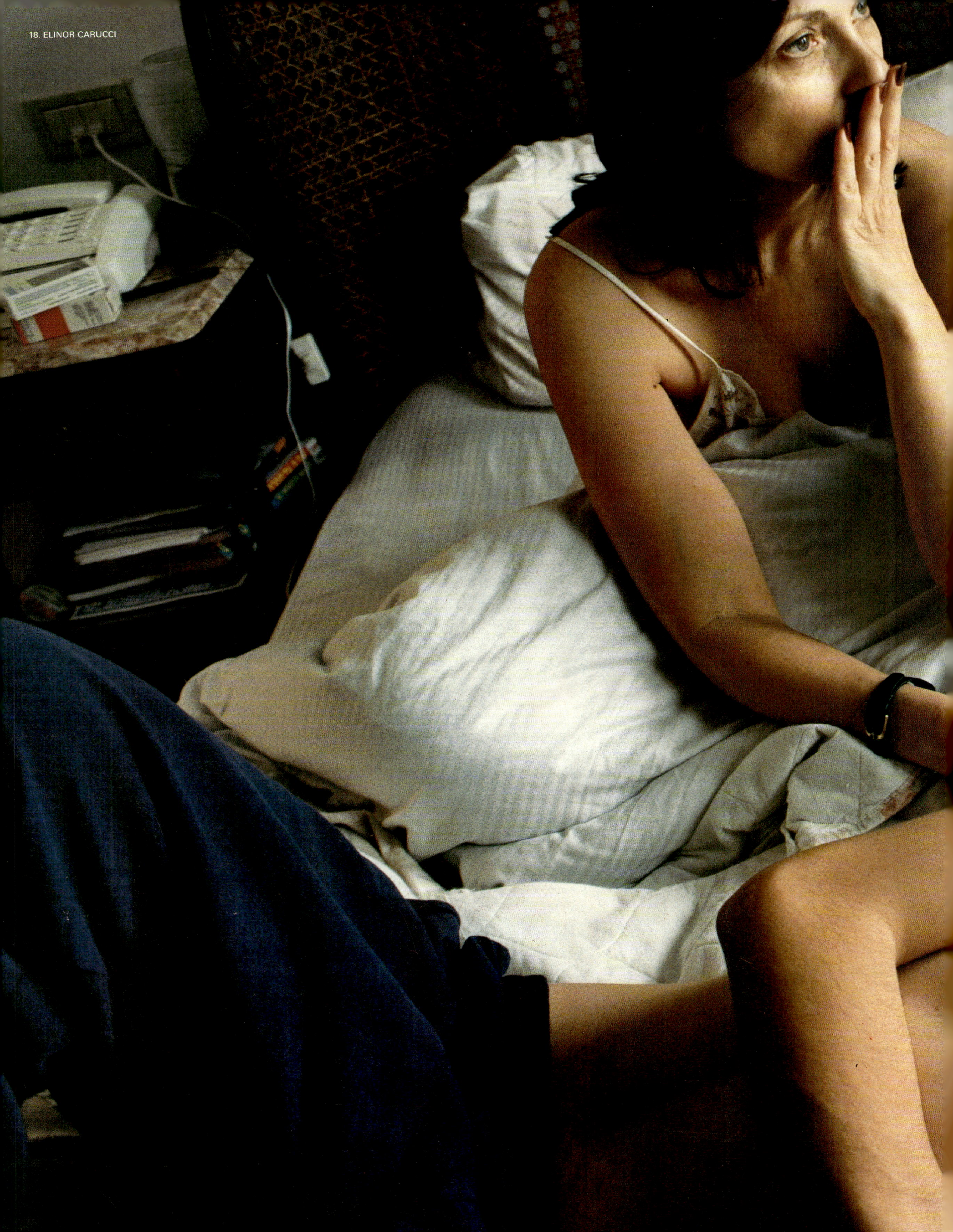

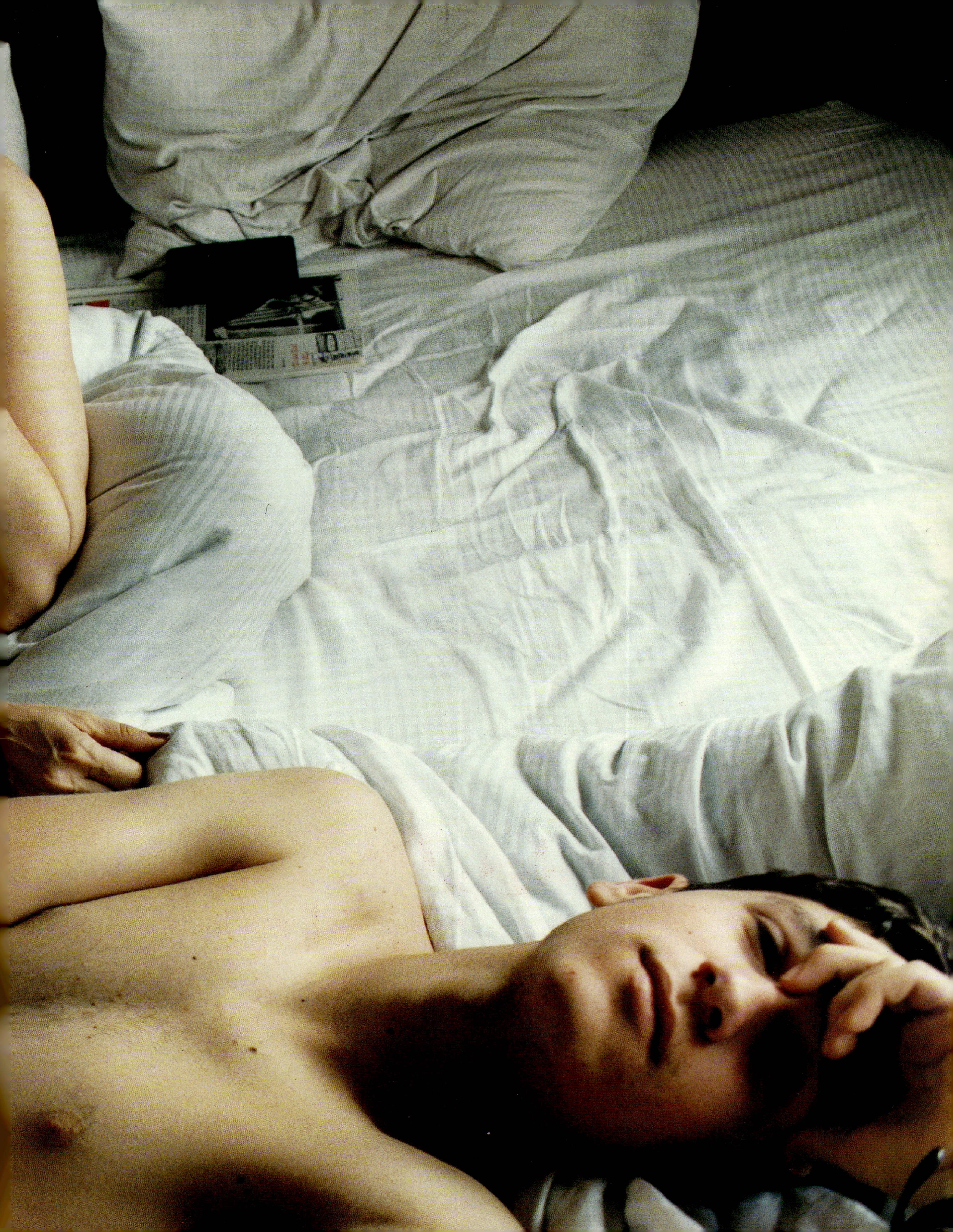

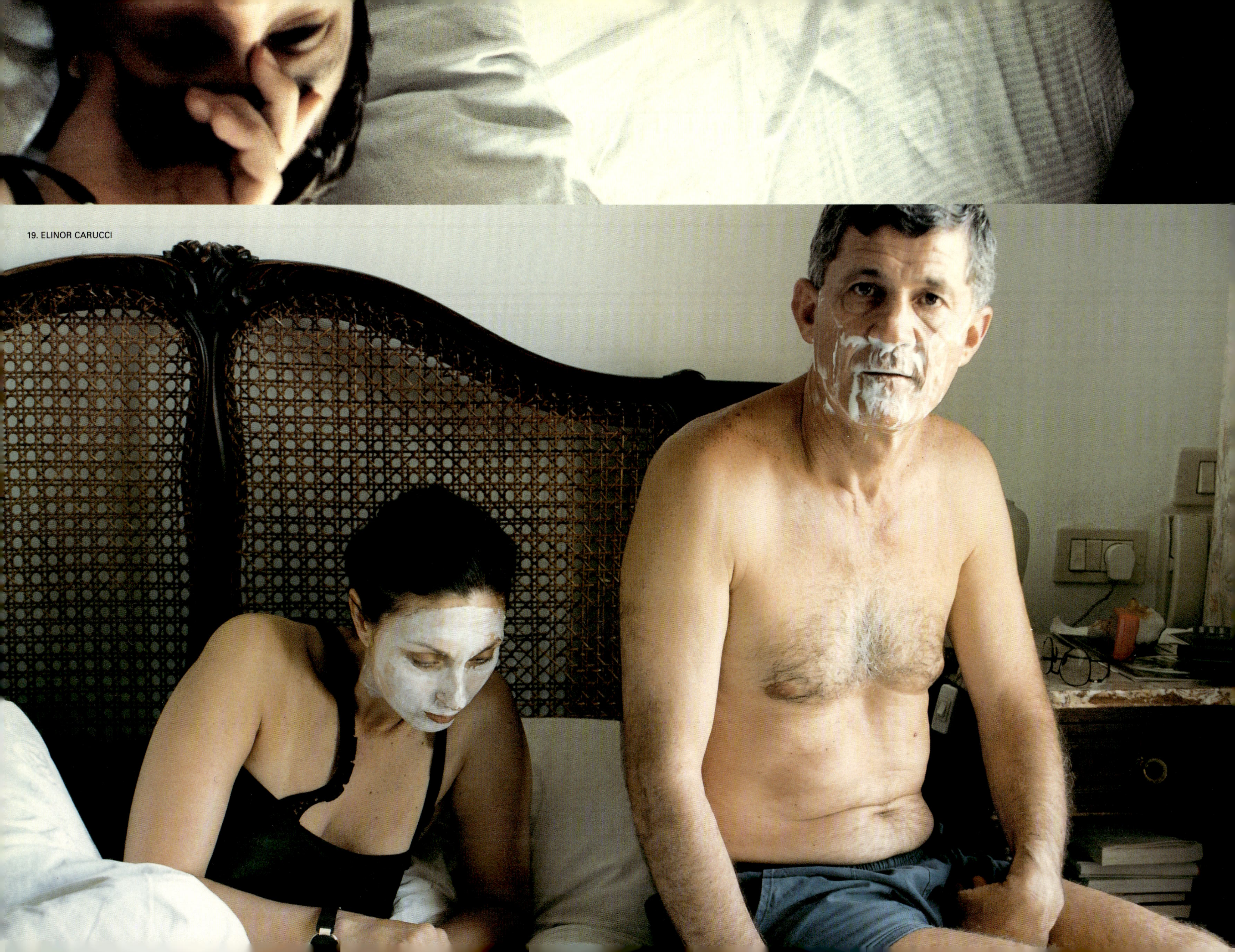
19. ELINOR CARUCCI

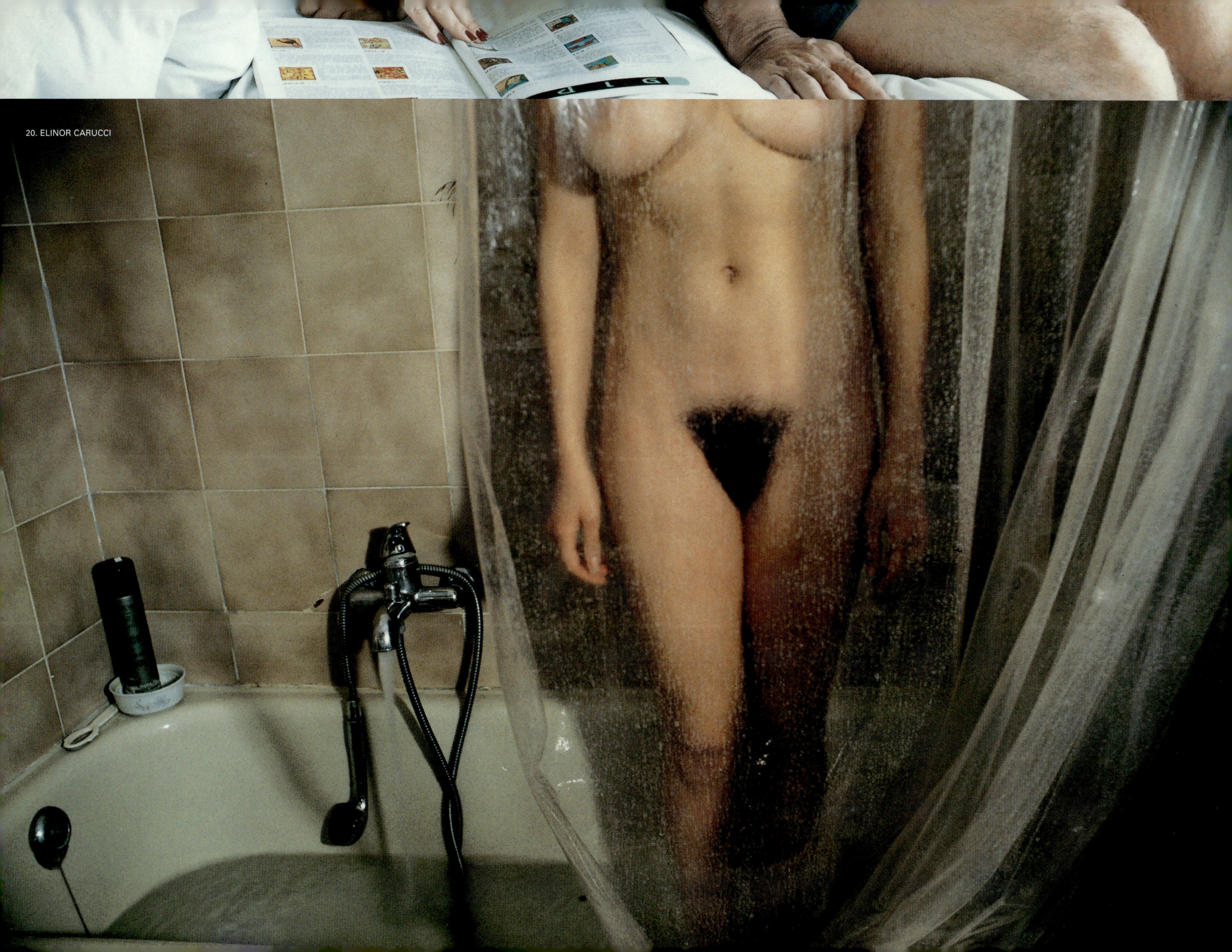

20. ELINOR CARUCCI

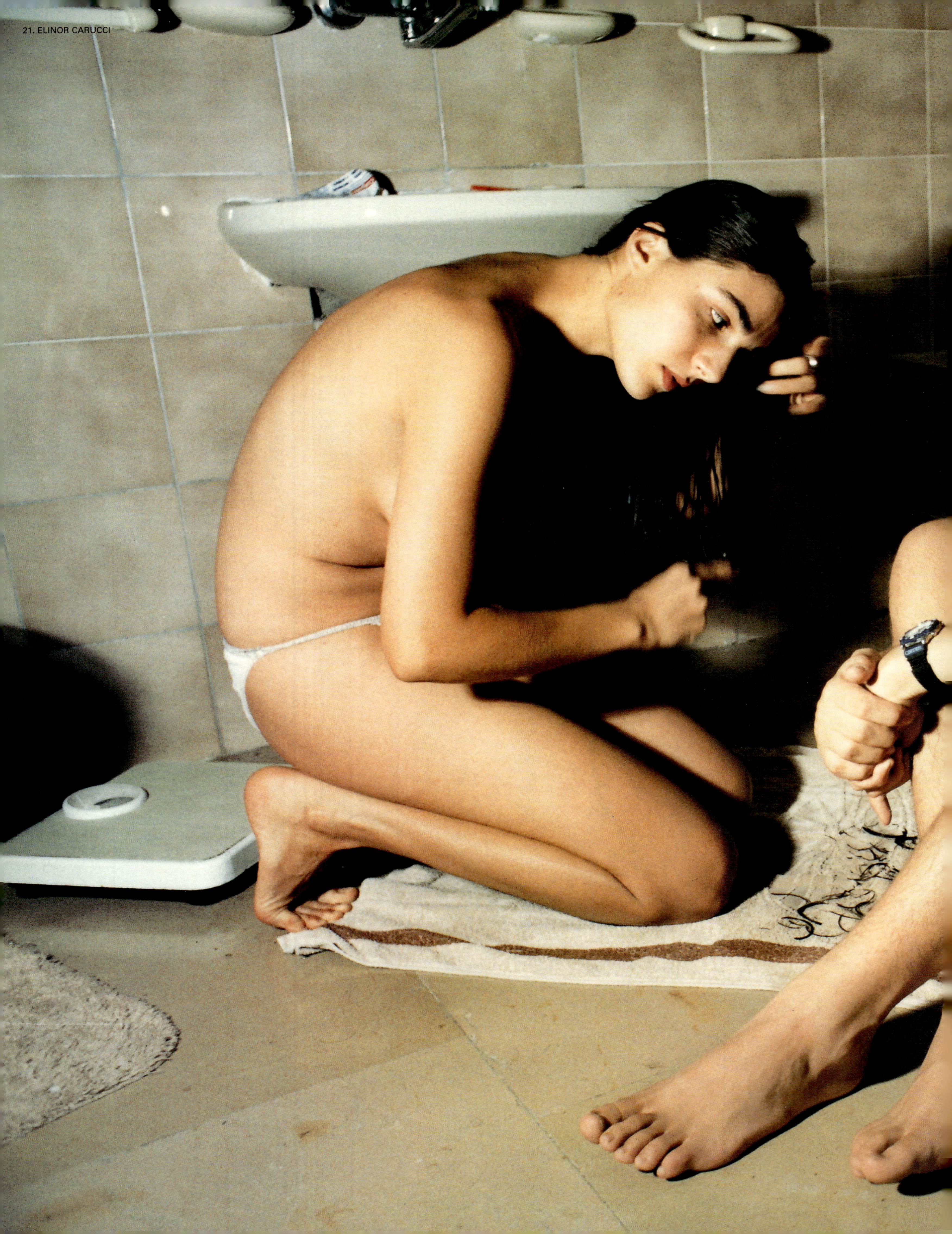

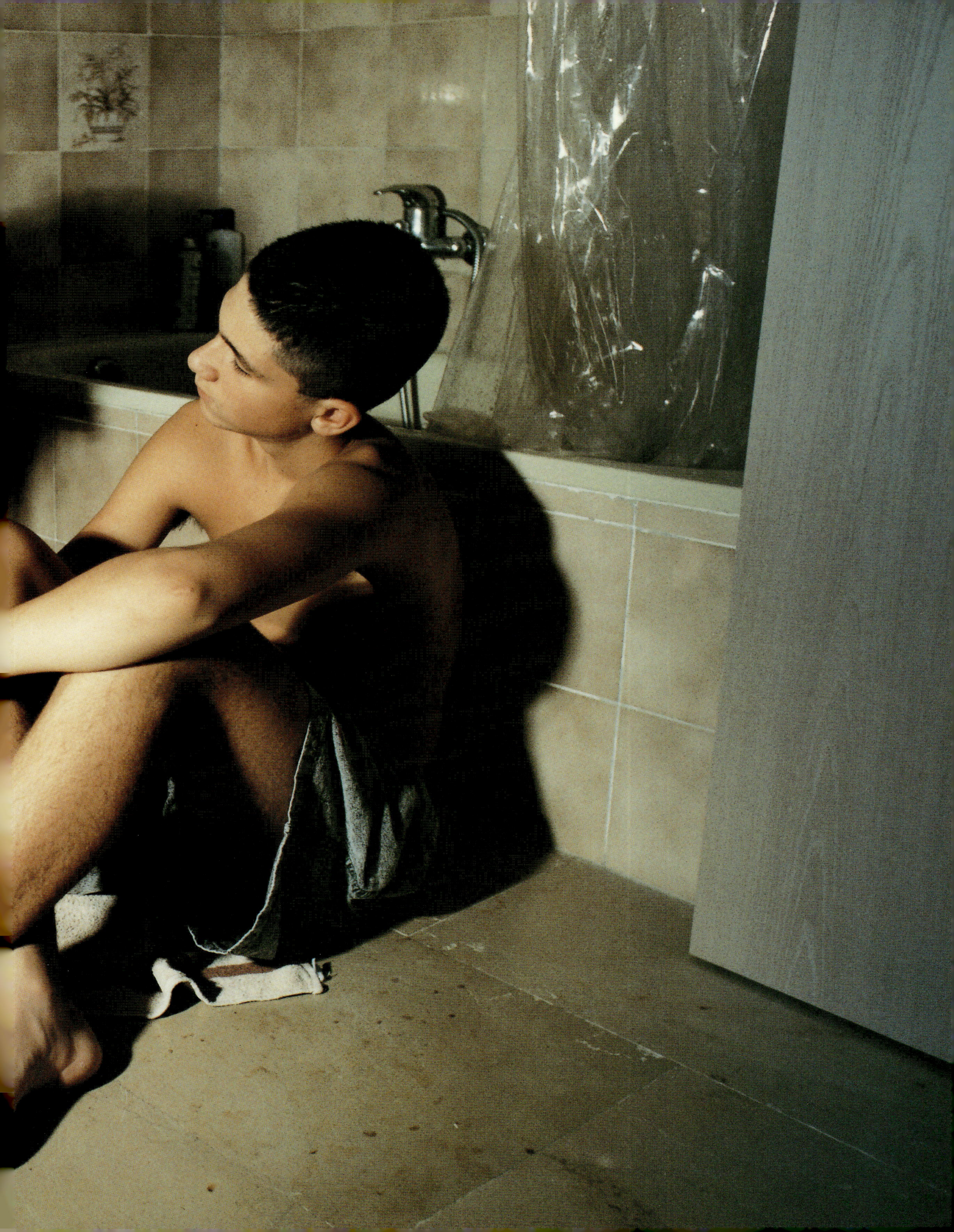

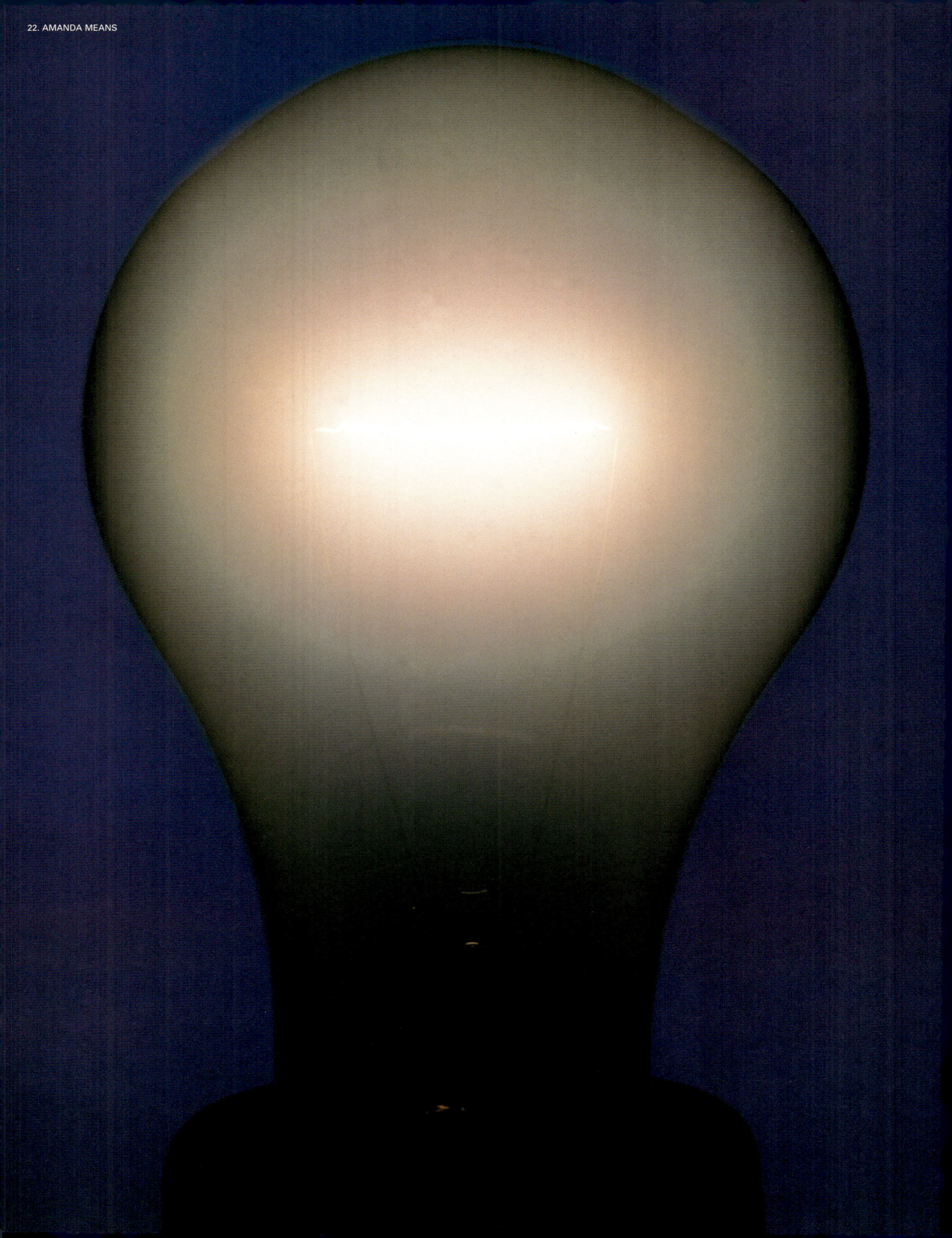

22. AMANDA MEANS

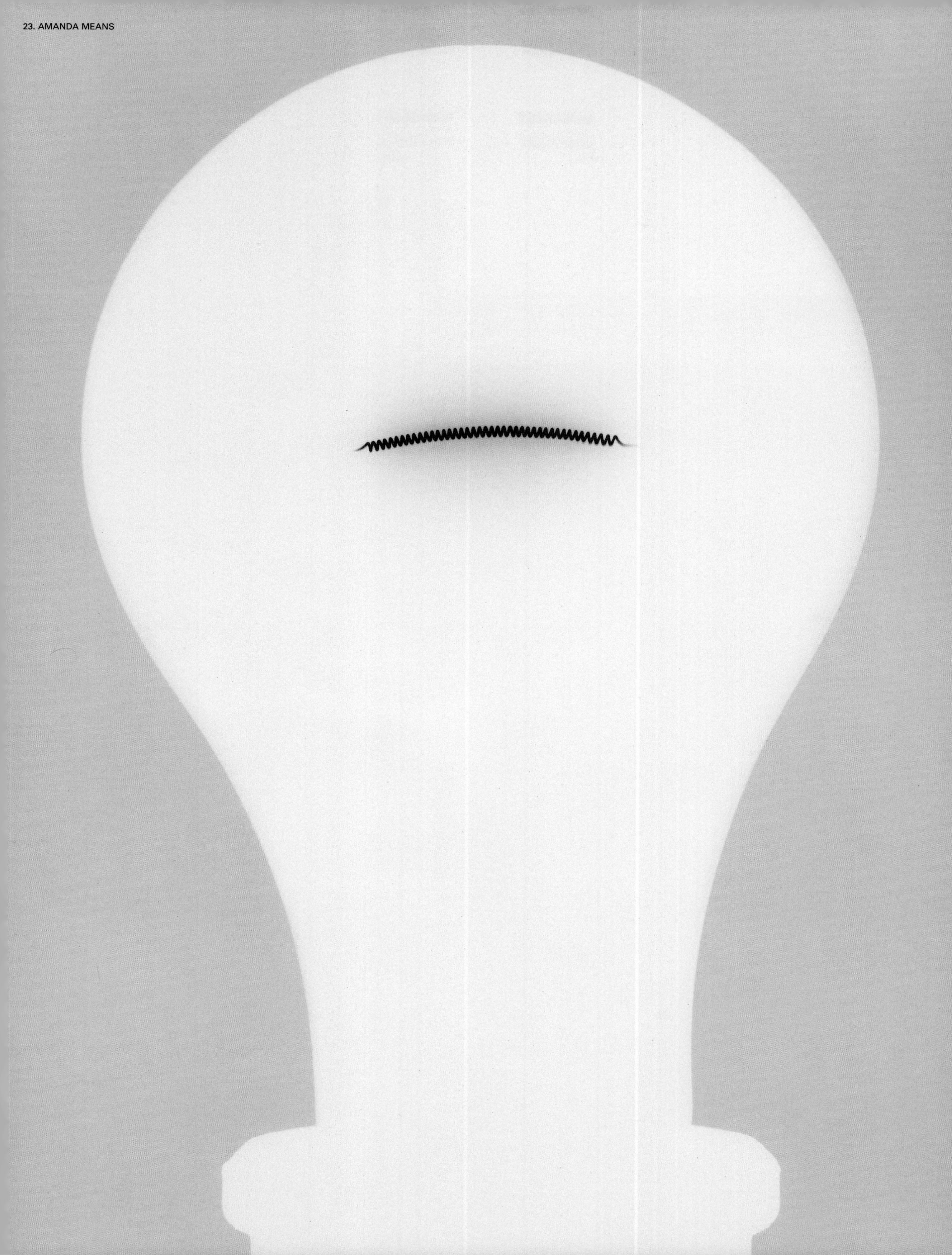

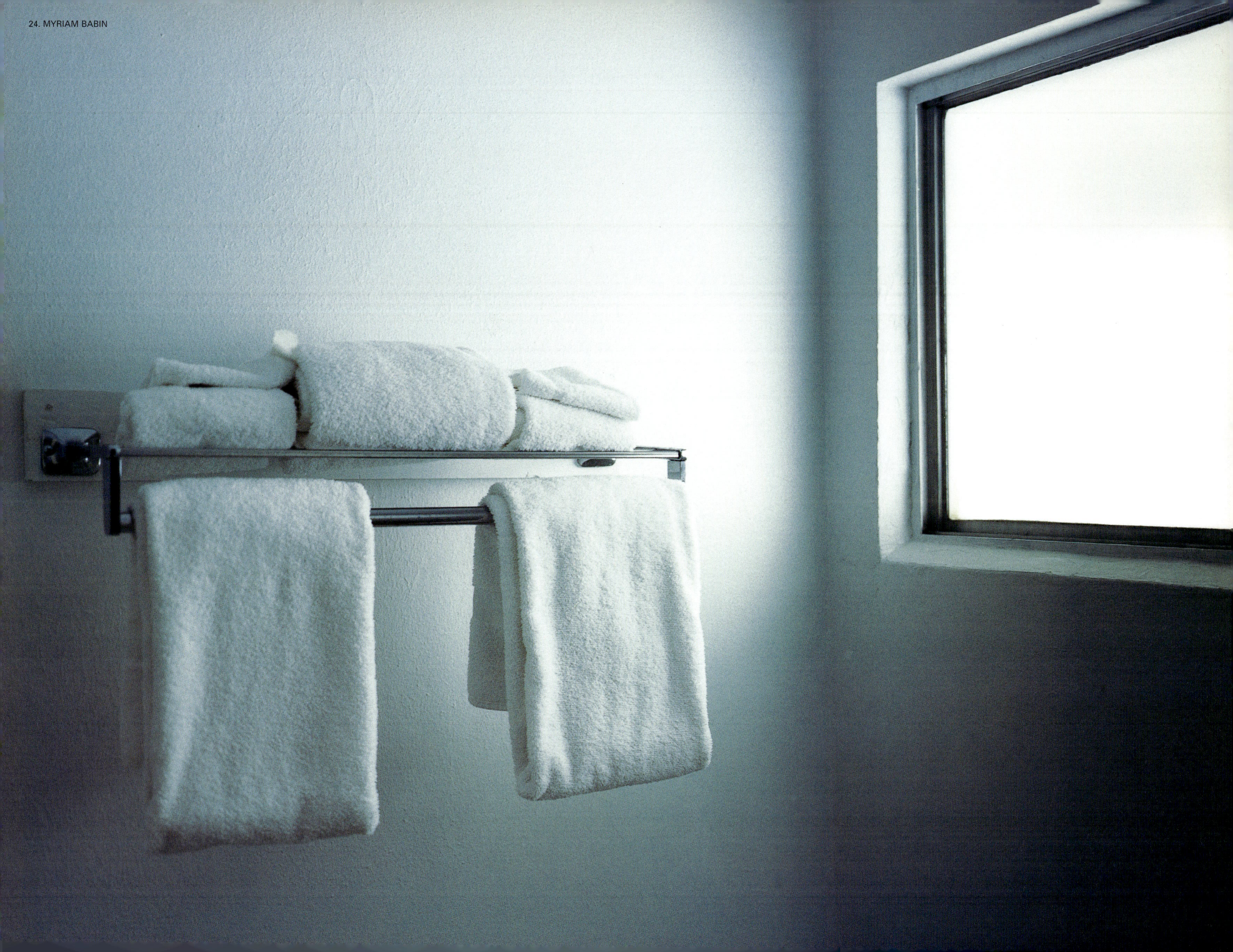

24. MYRIAM BABIN

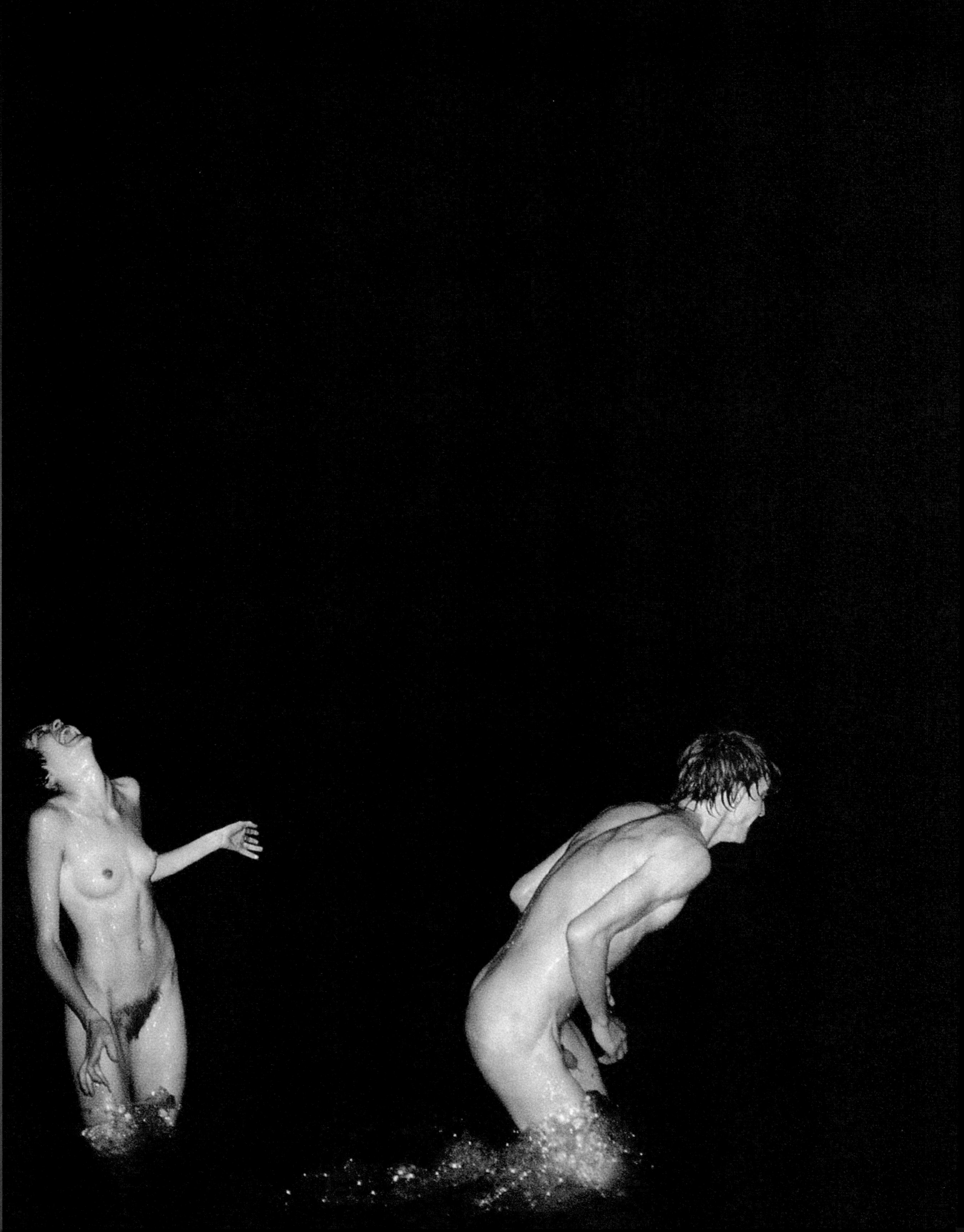

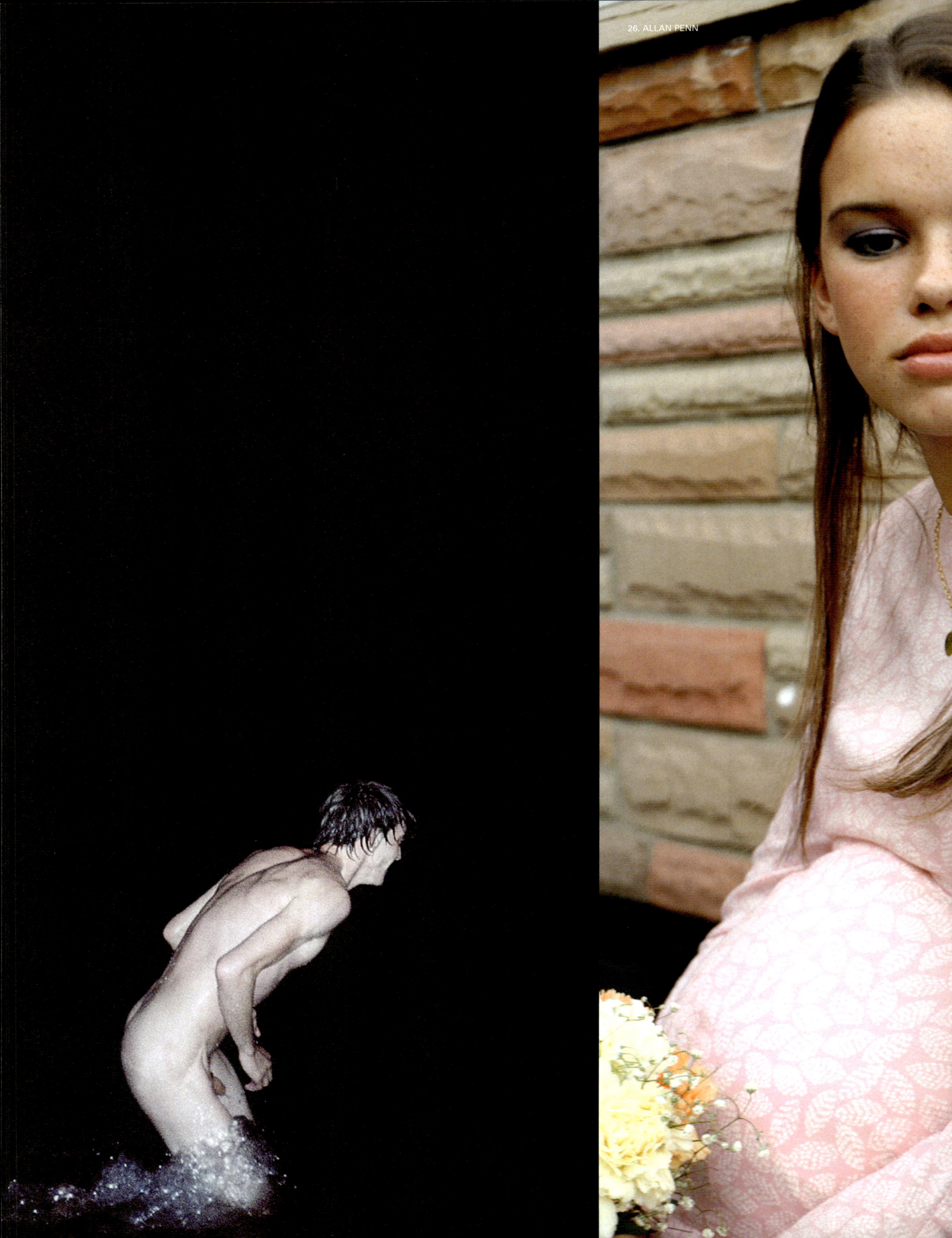

26. ALLAN PENN

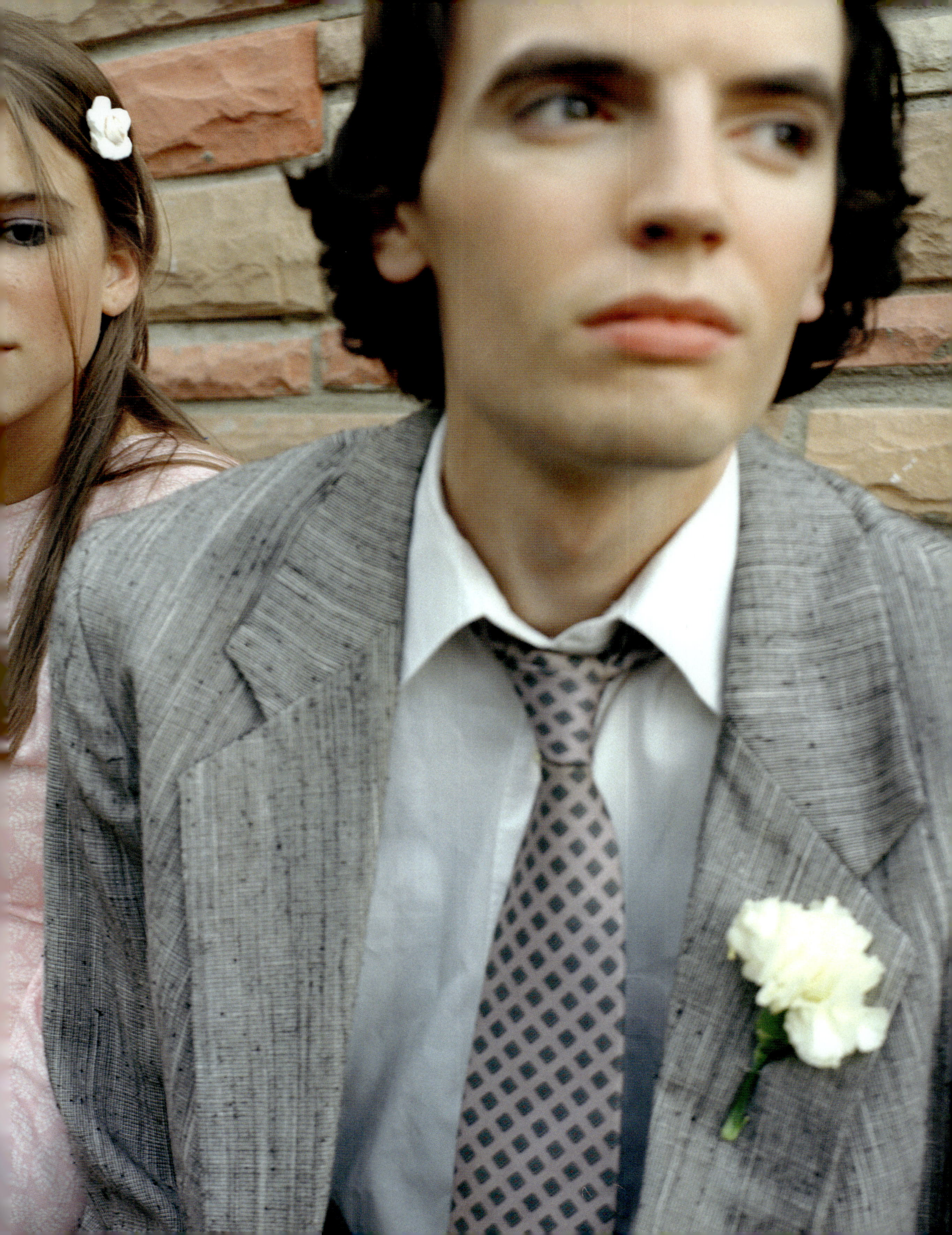

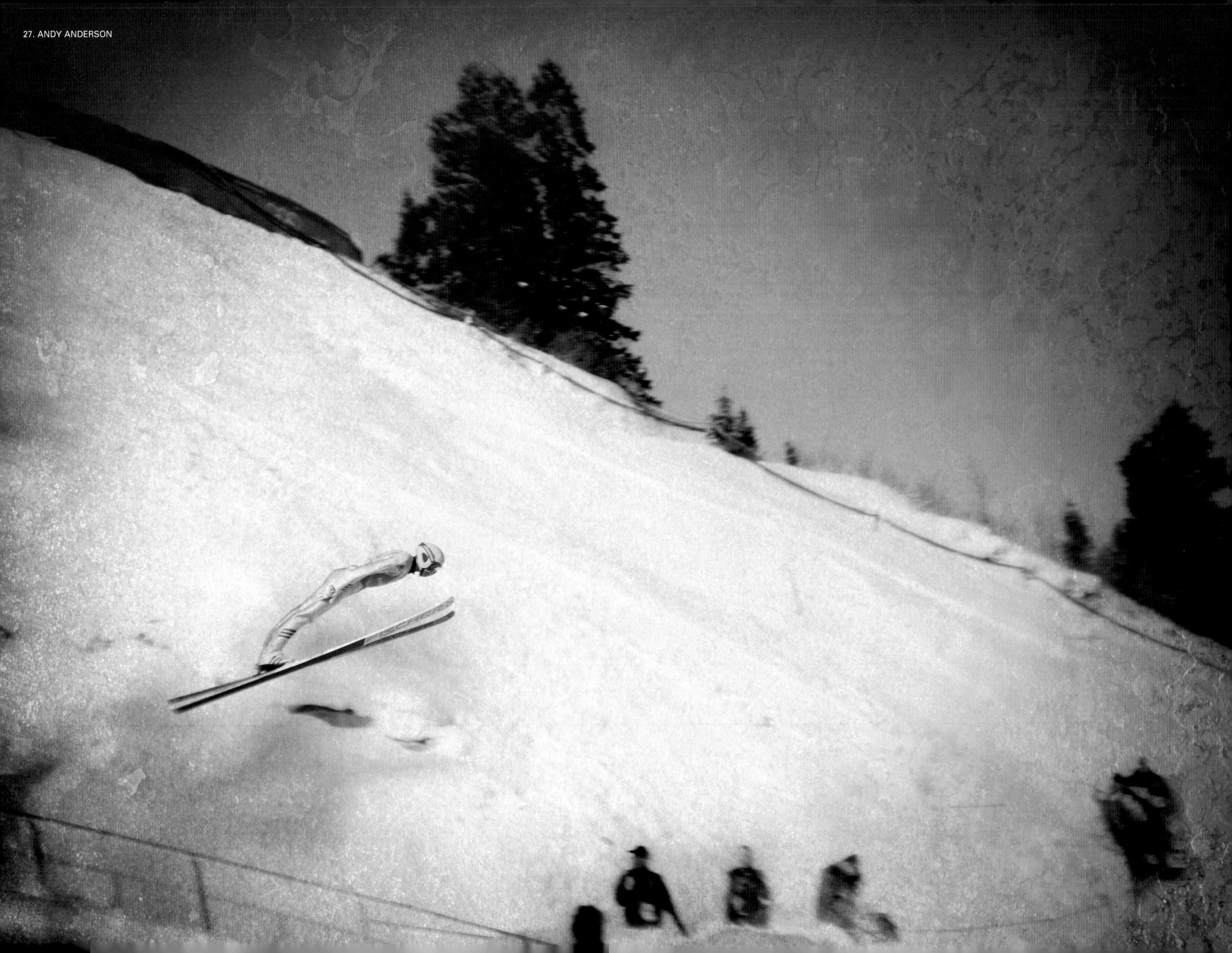

27. ANDY ANDERSON

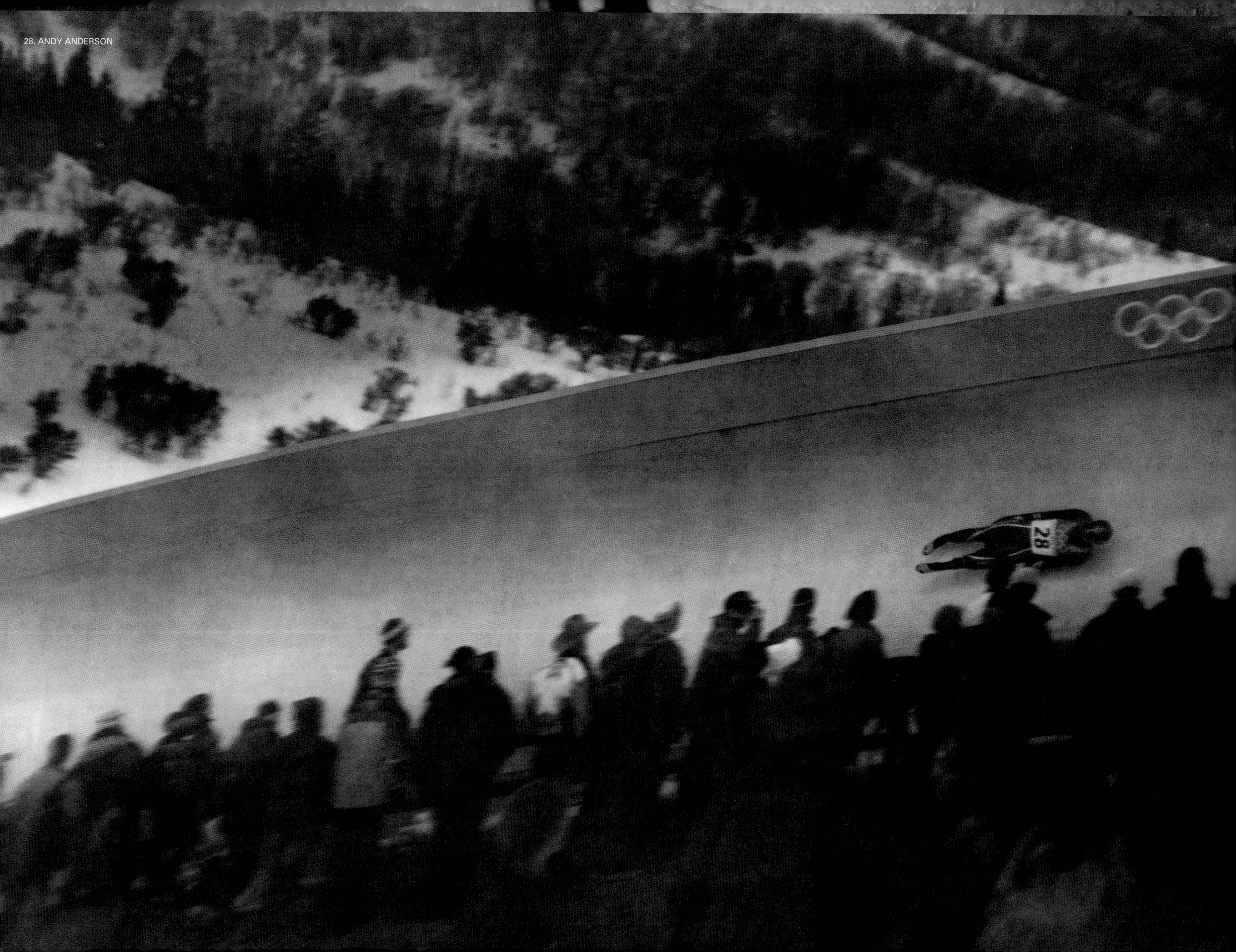

28. ANDY ANDERSON

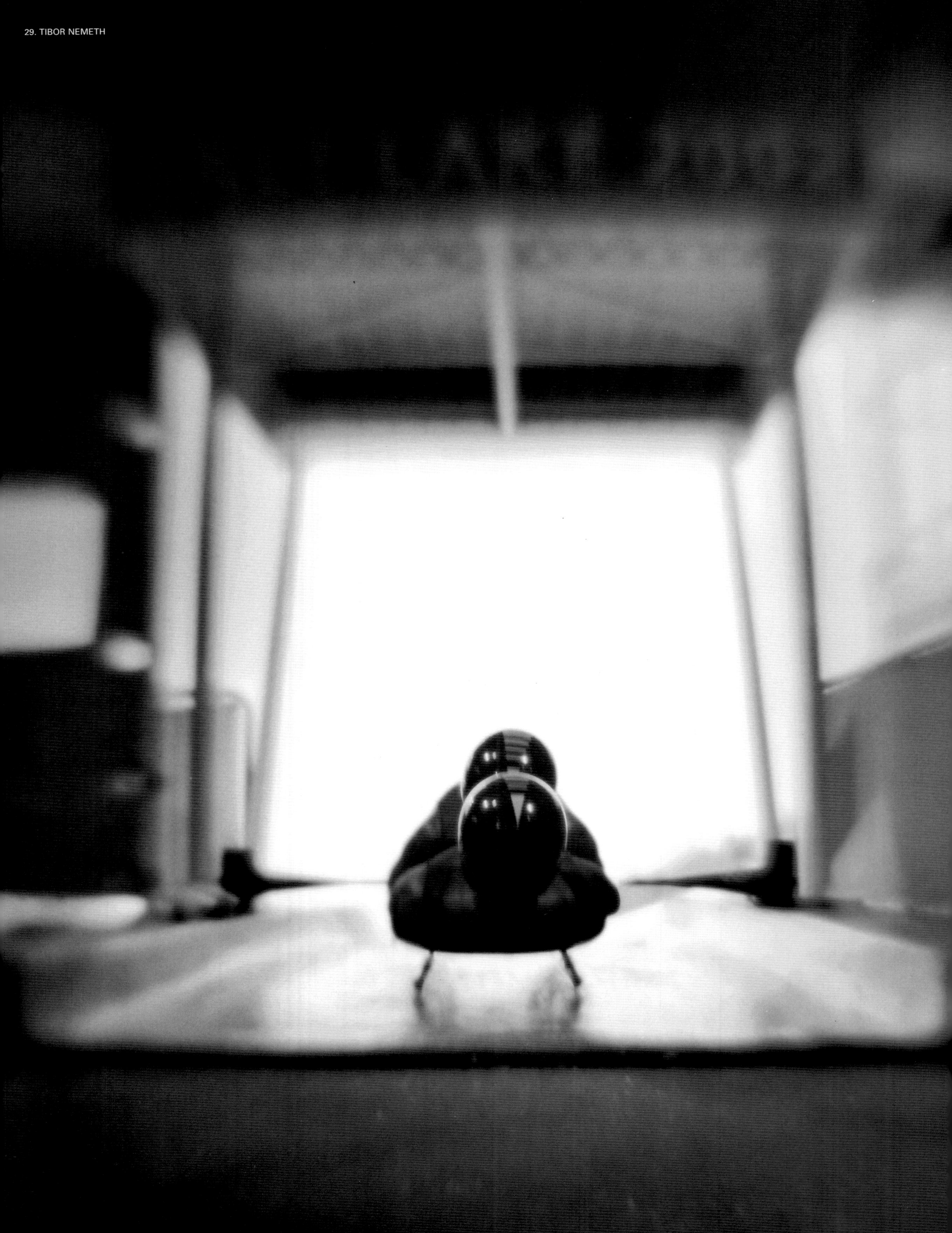

29. TIBOR NEMETH

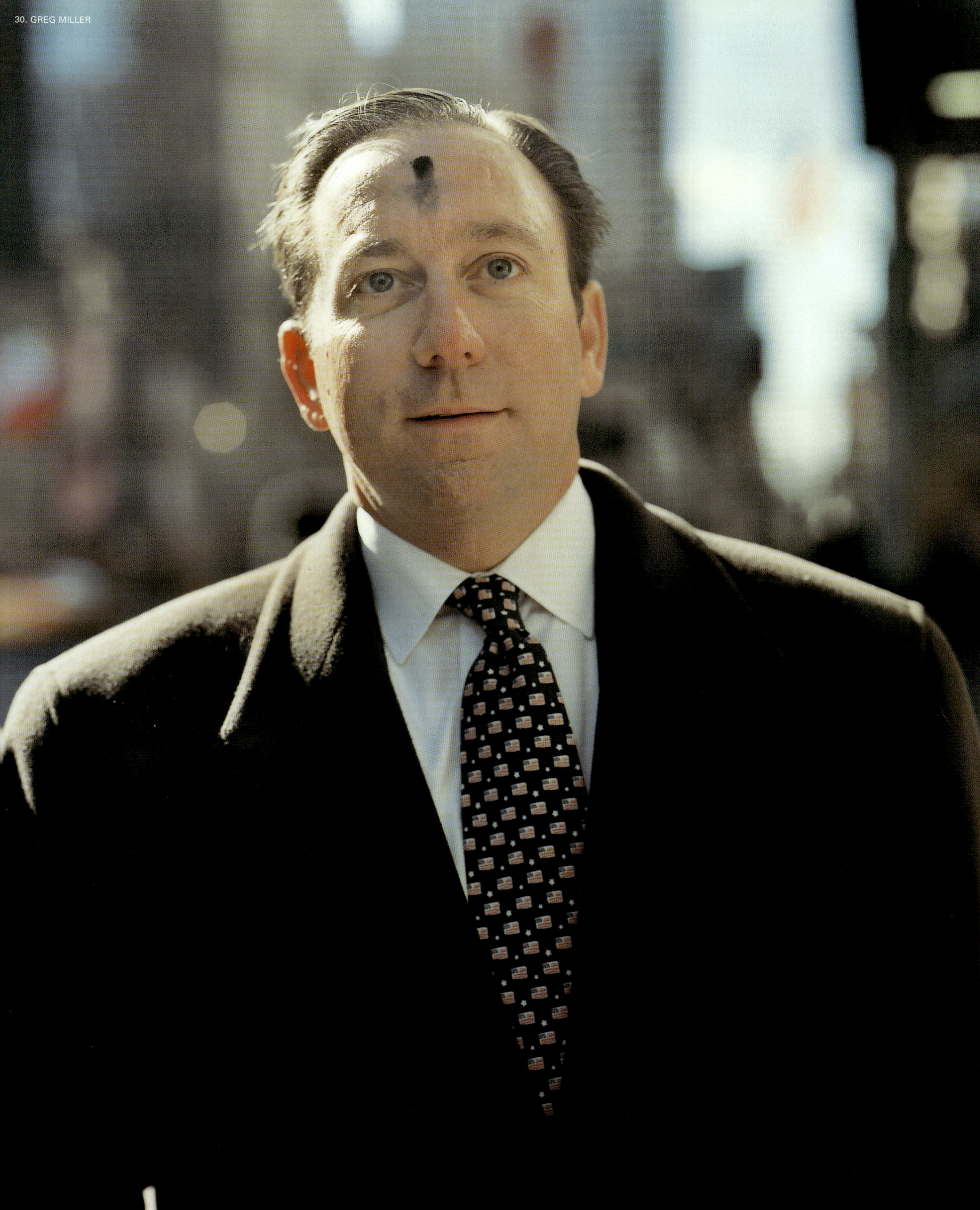

30. GREG MILLER

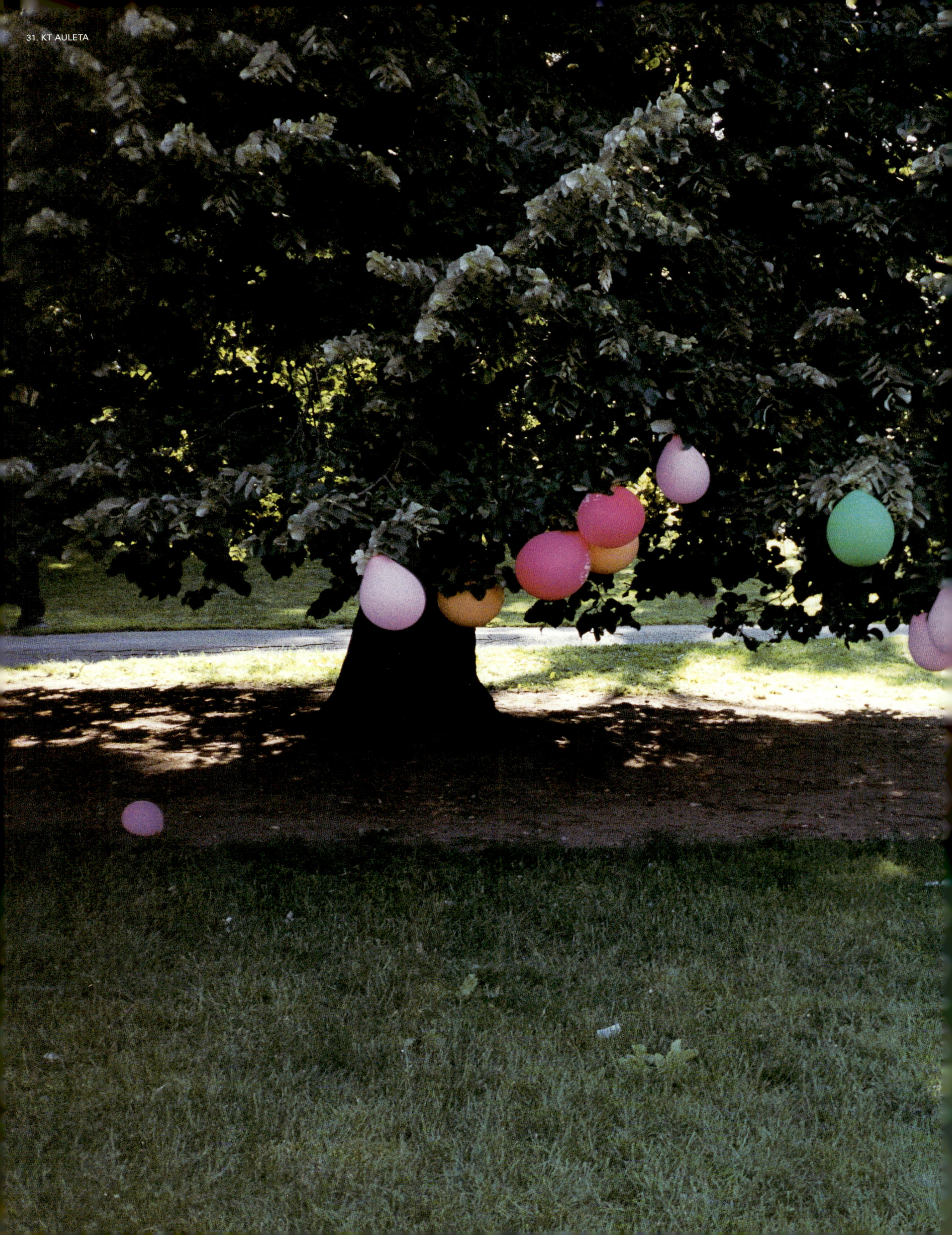

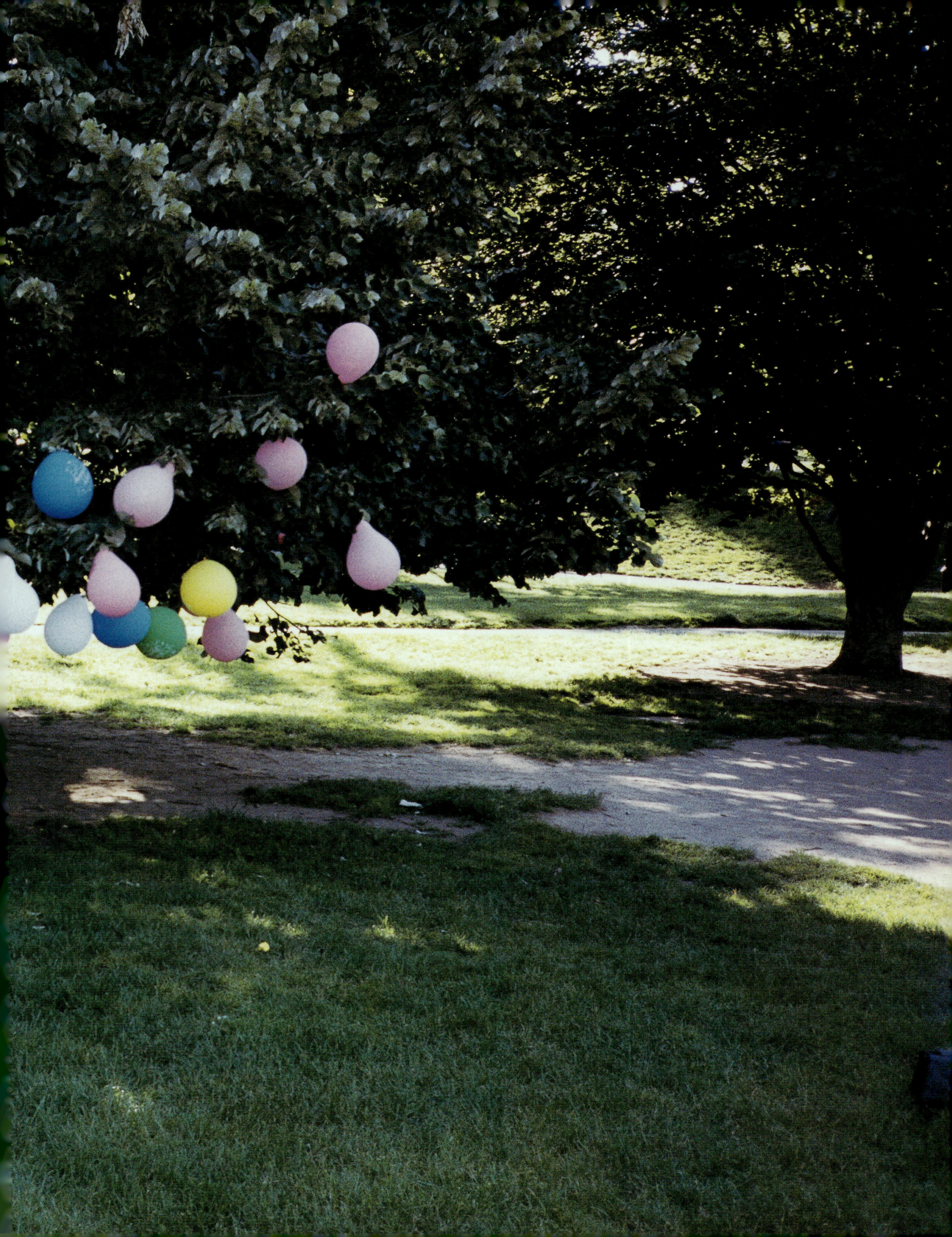

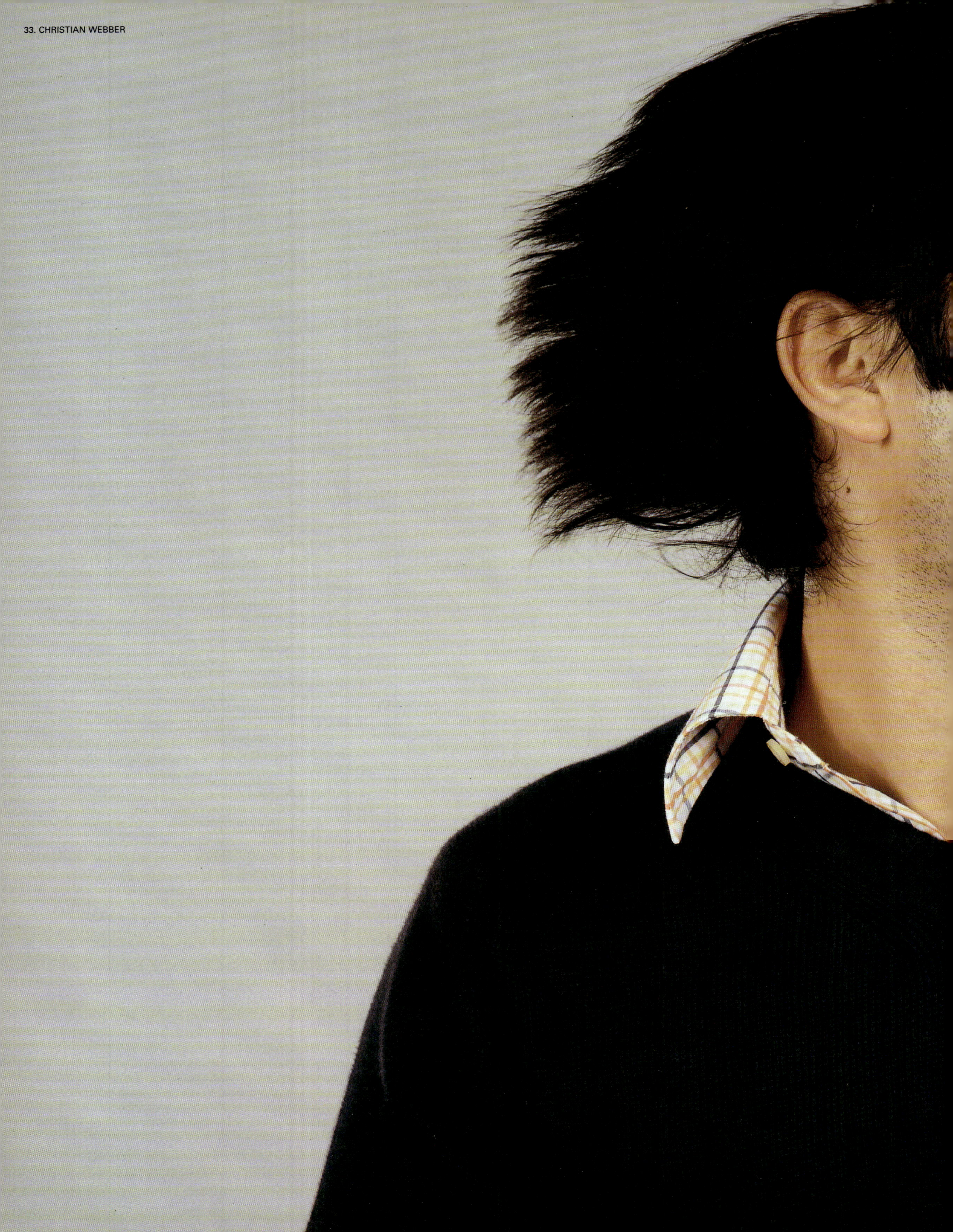

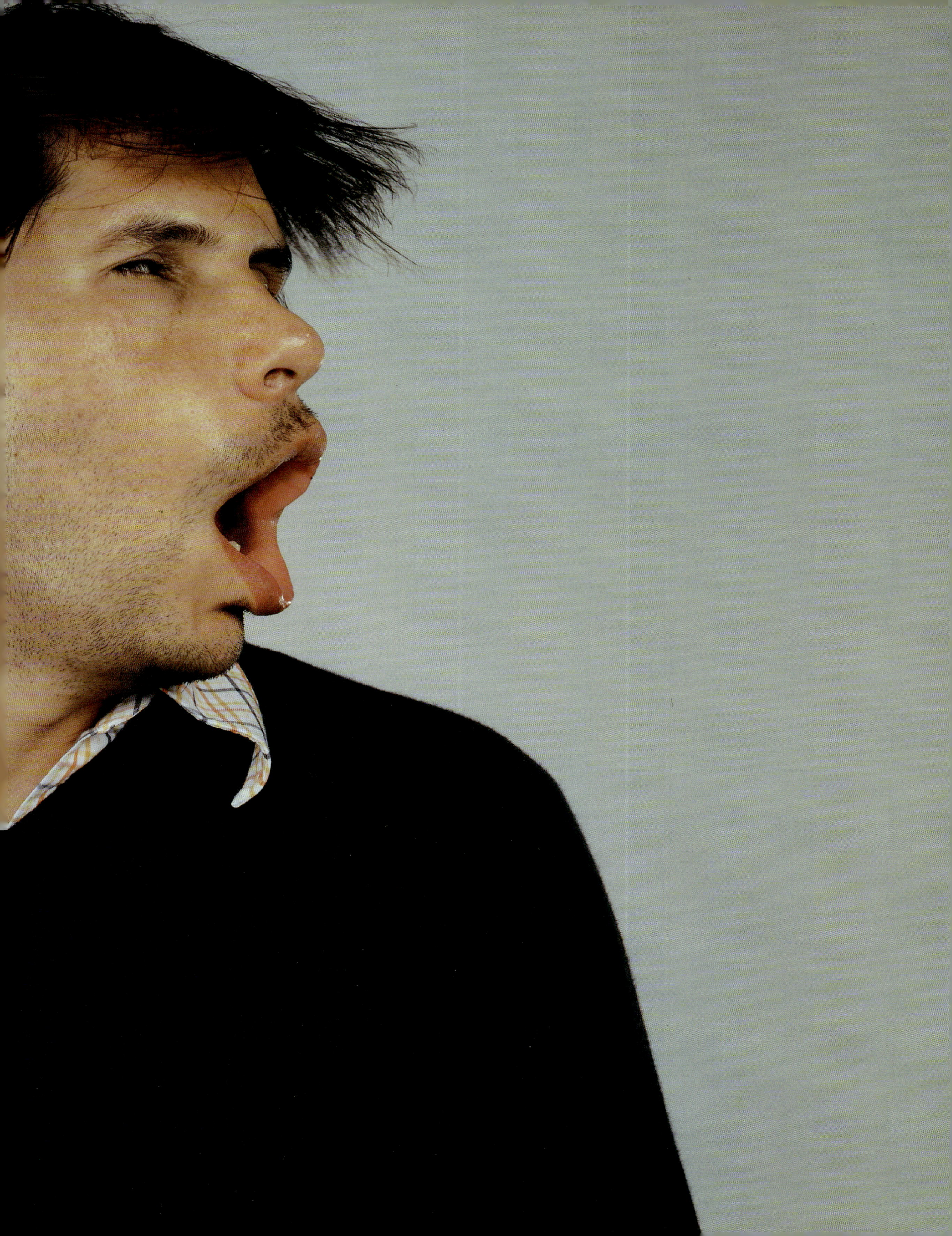

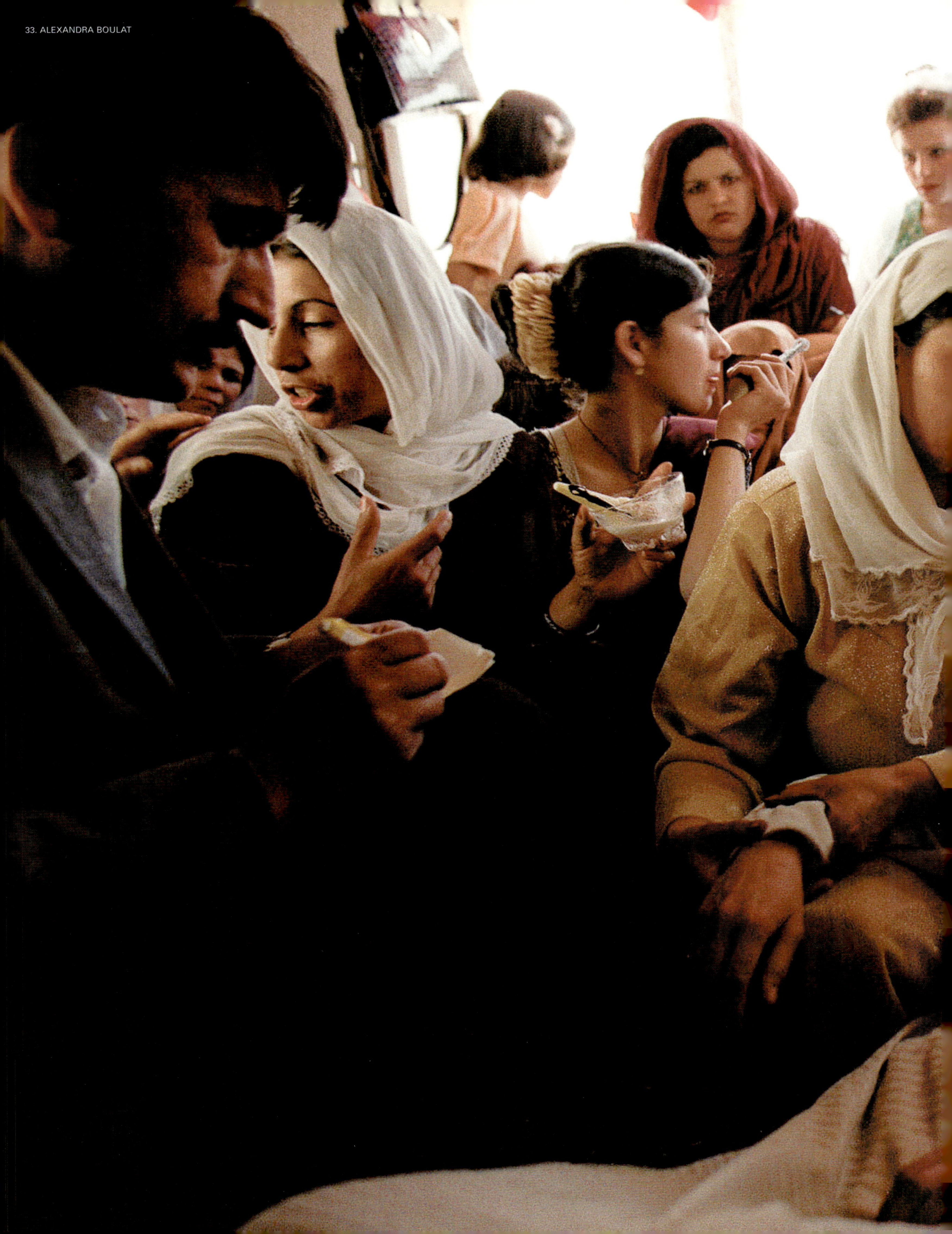

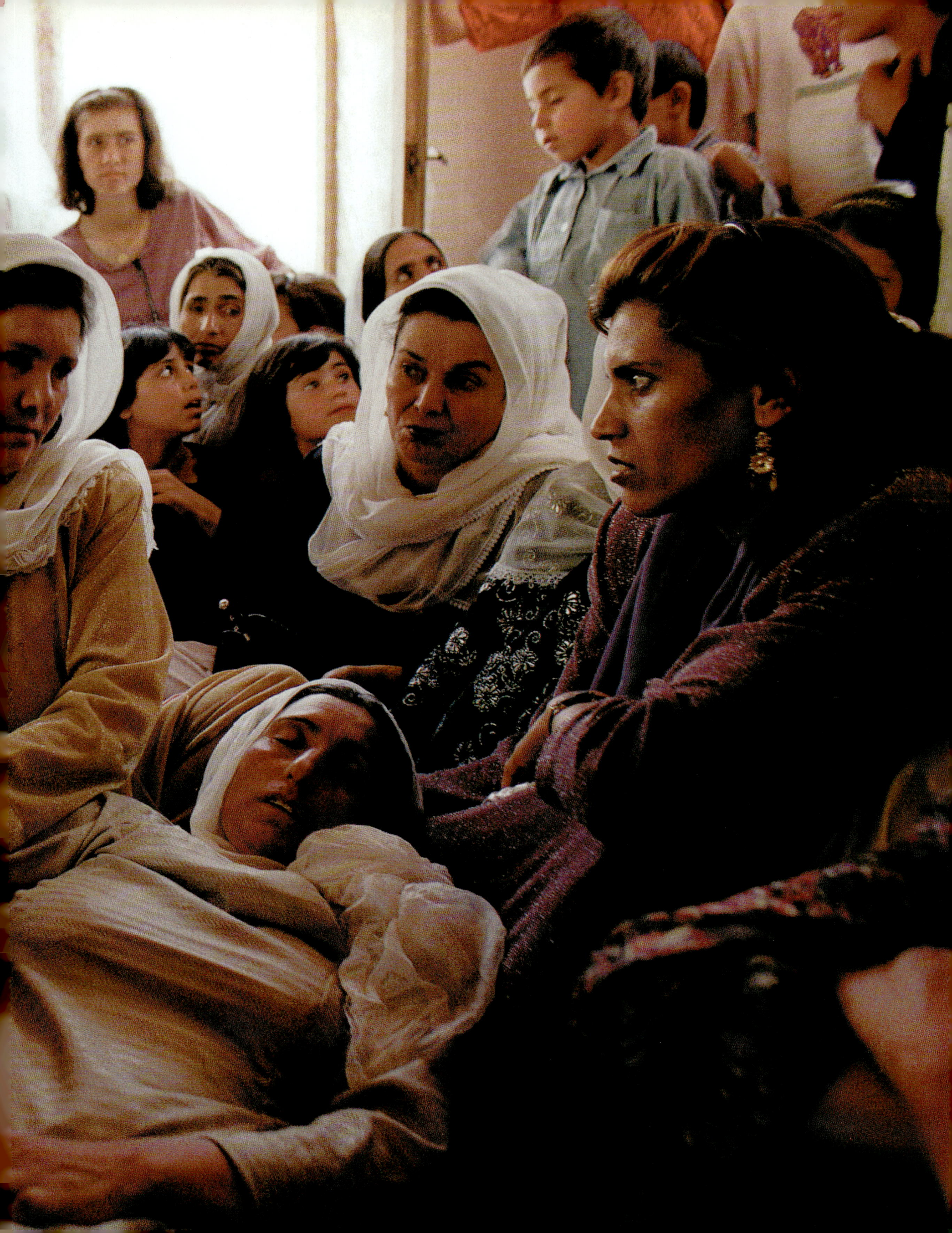

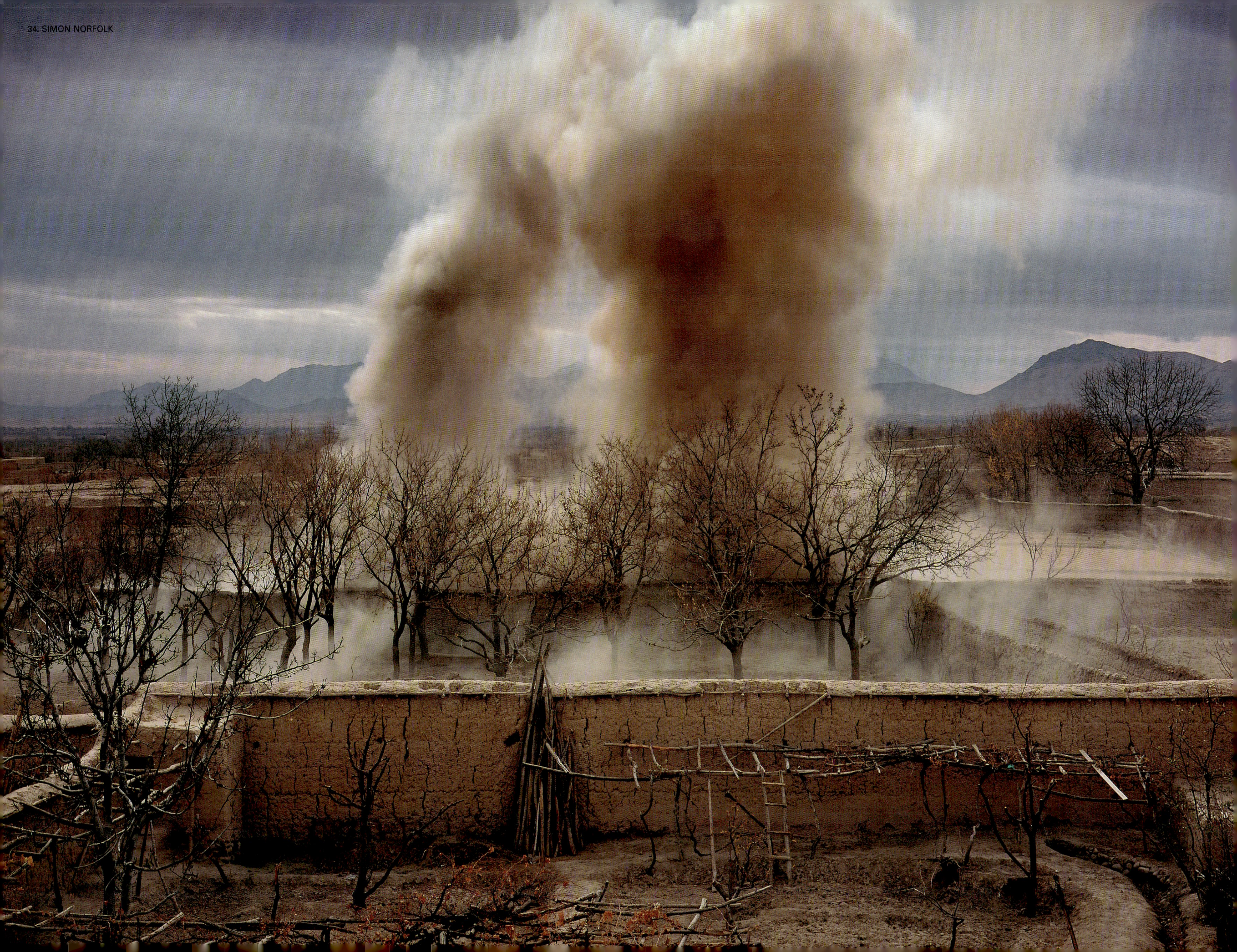

34. SIMON NORFOLK

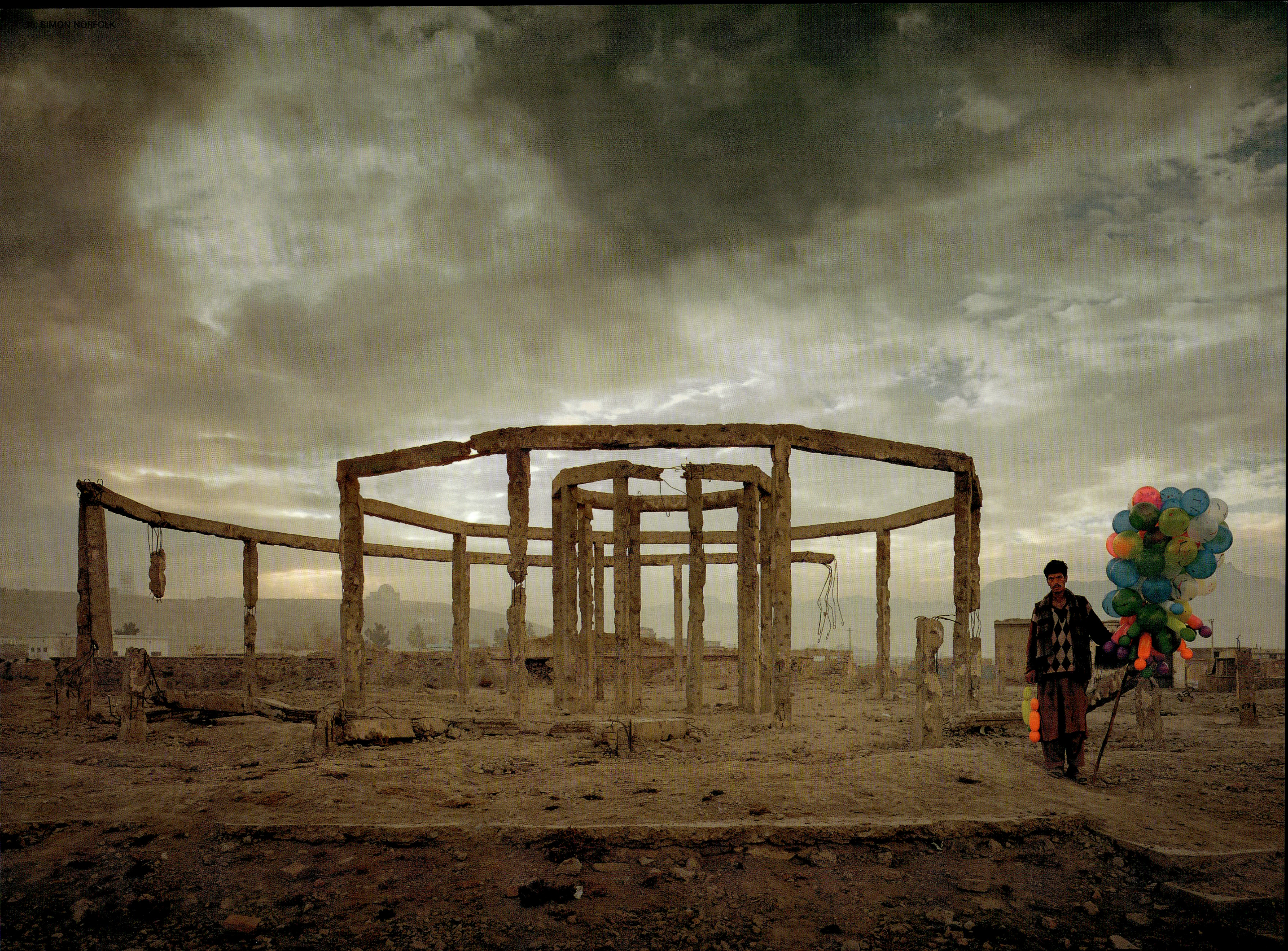

SIMON NORFOLK

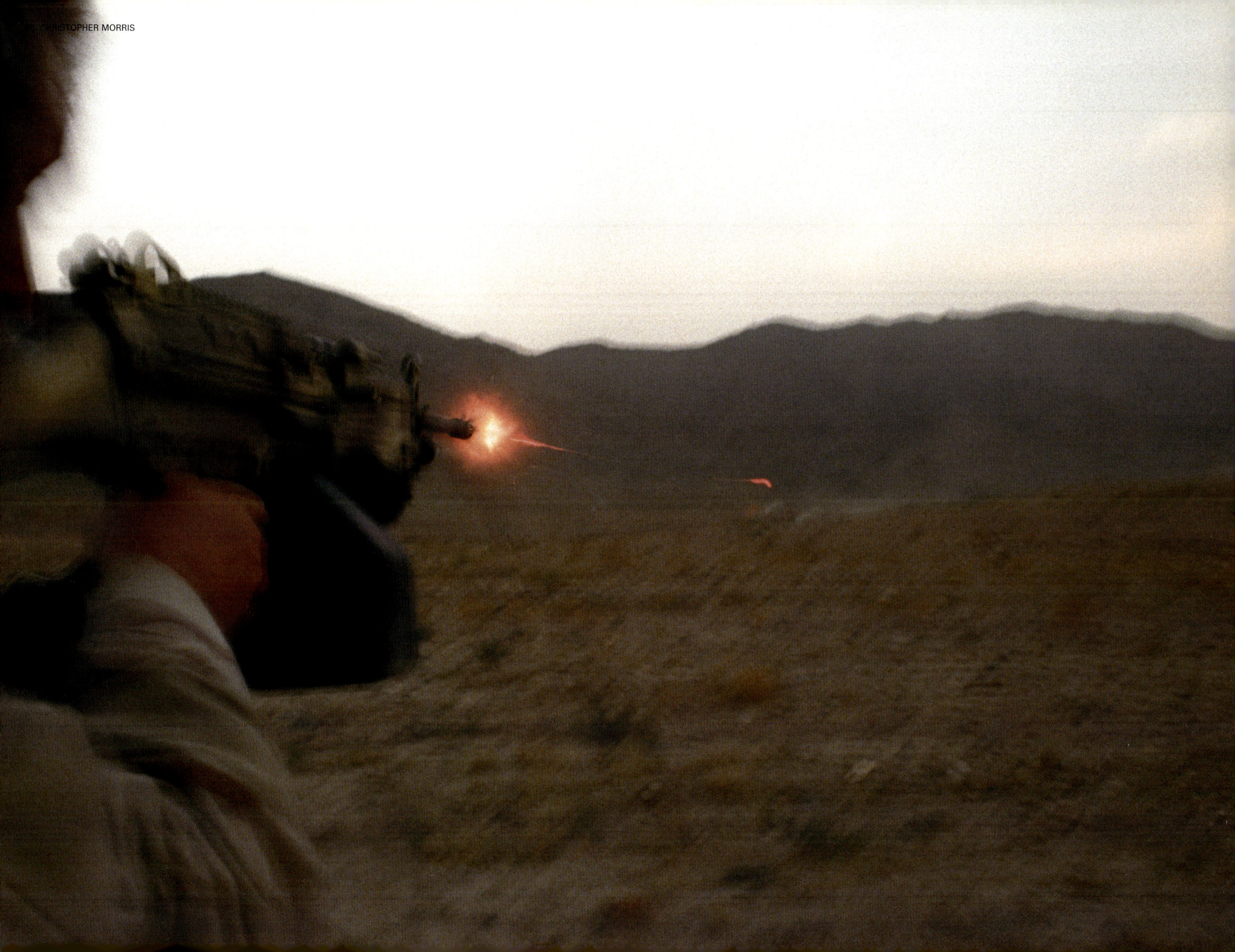

STOPHER MORRIS

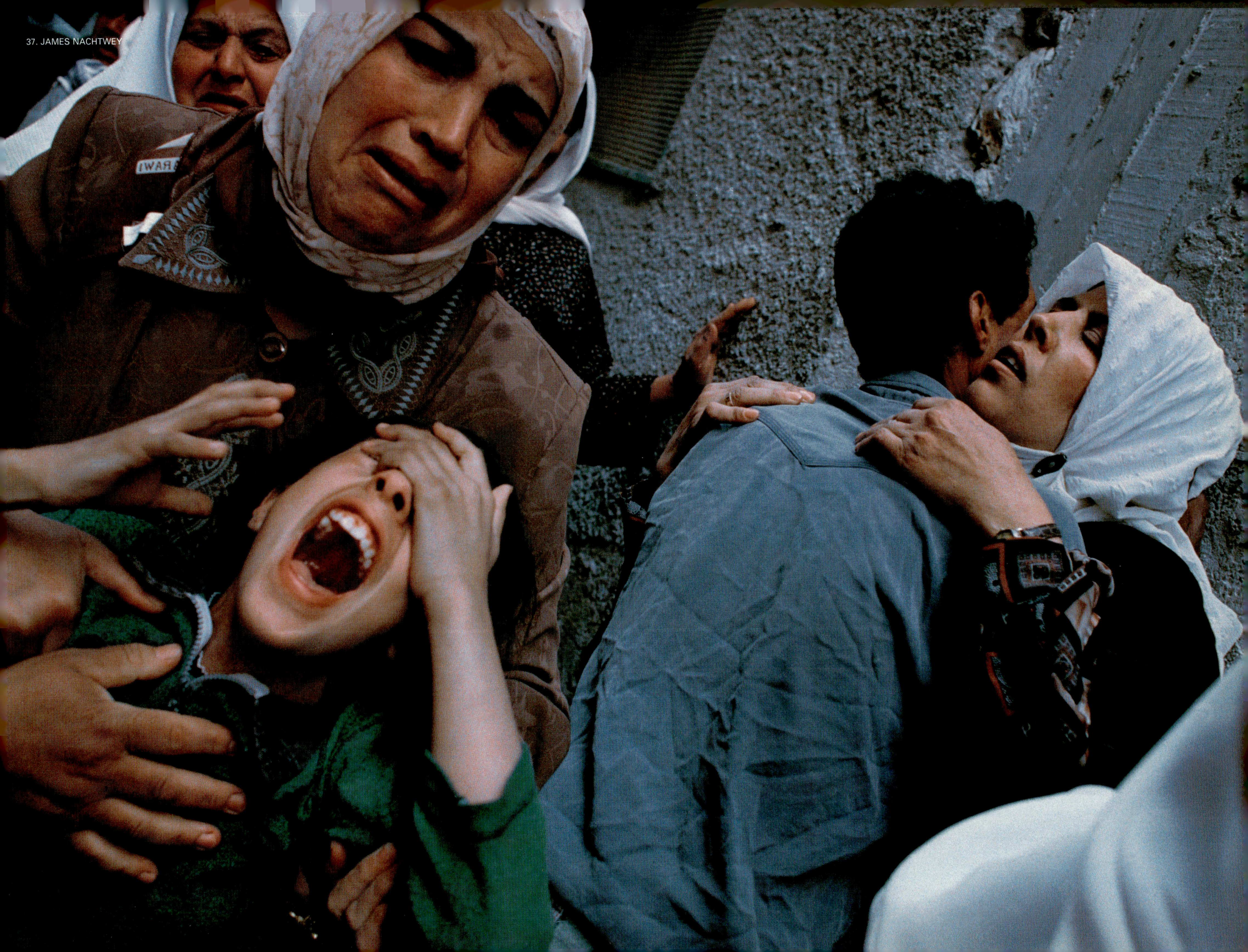

37. JAMES NACHTWEY

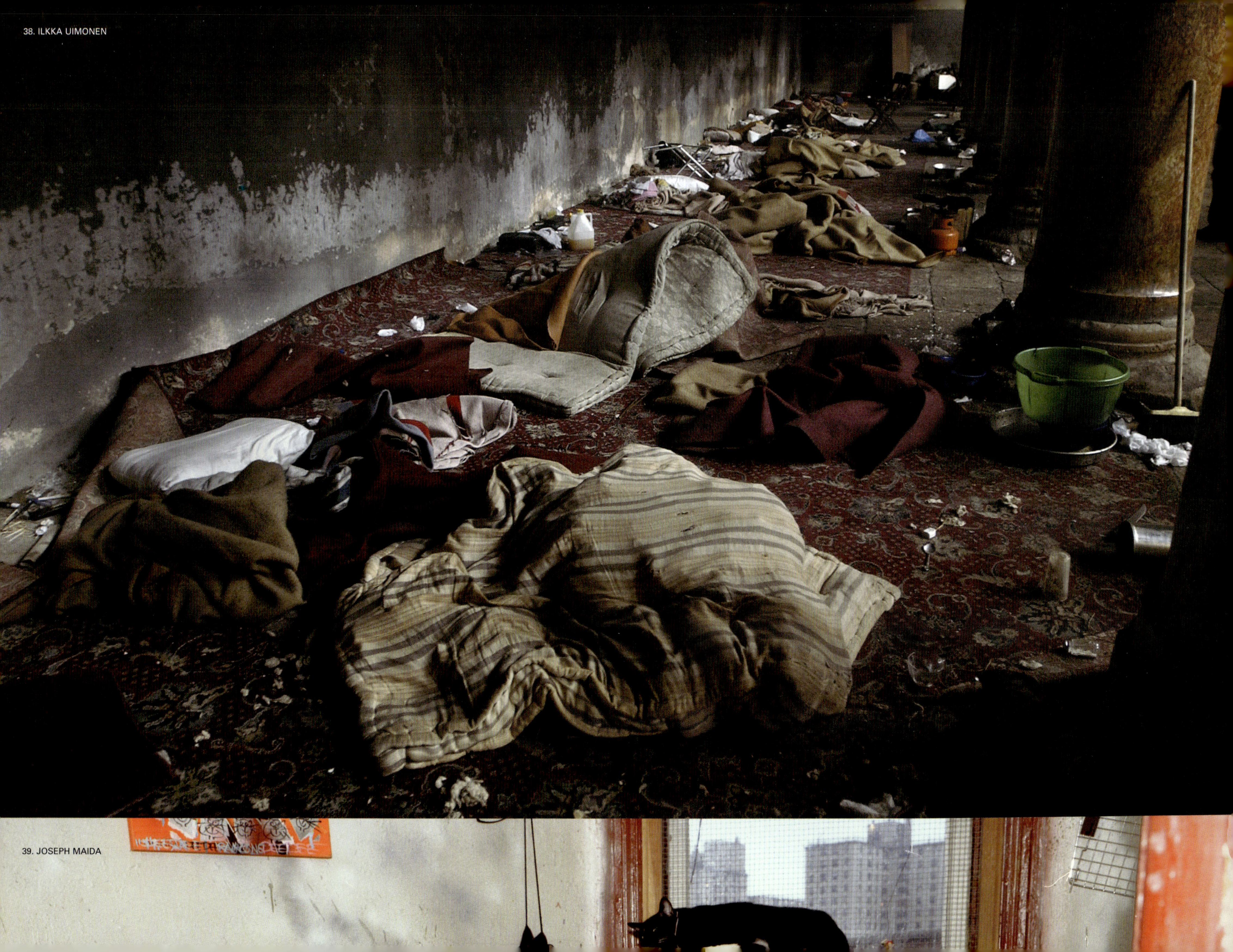

38. ILKKA UIMONEN

39. JOSEPH MAIDA

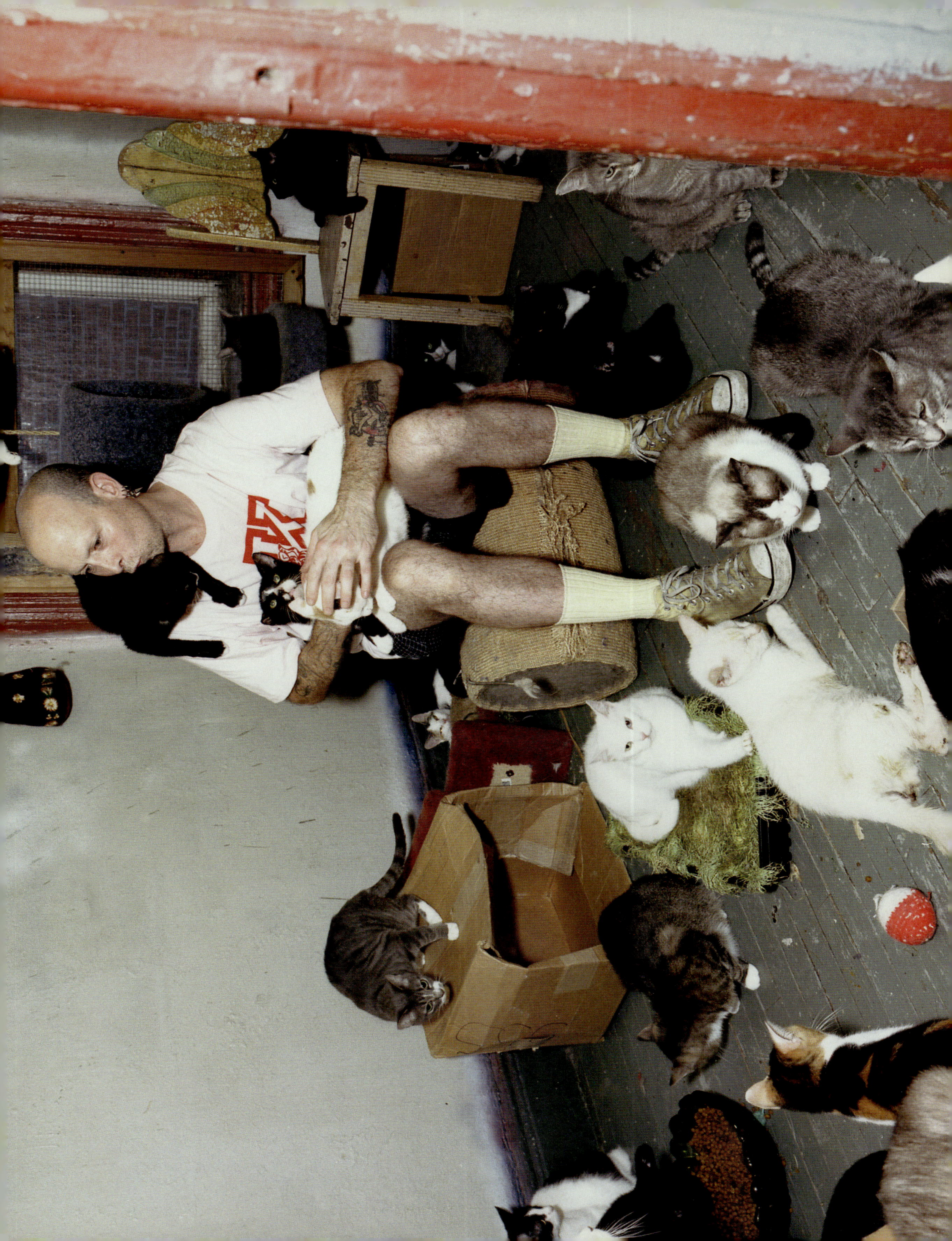

40. JOSEPH MAIDA

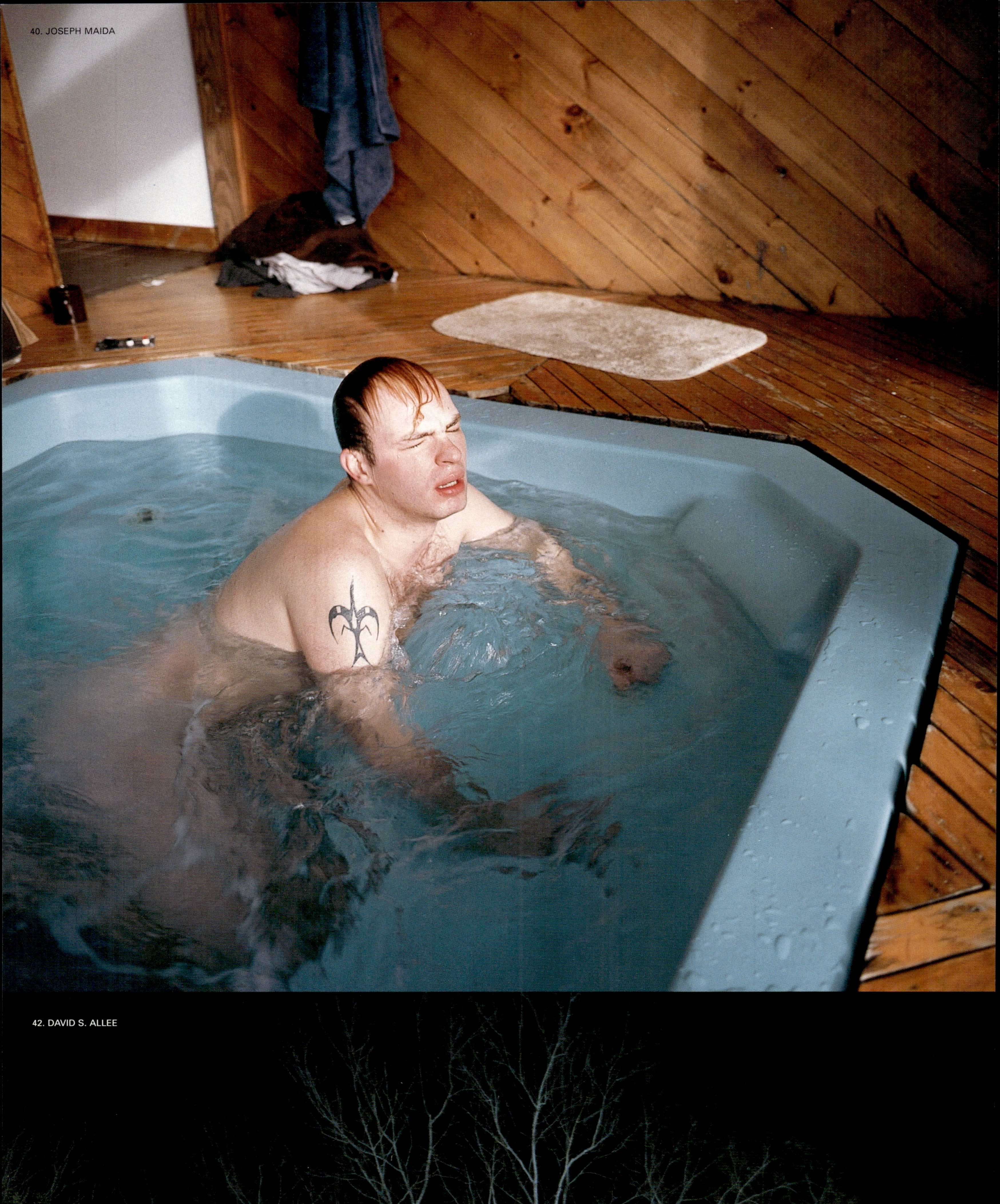

42. DAVID S. ALLEE

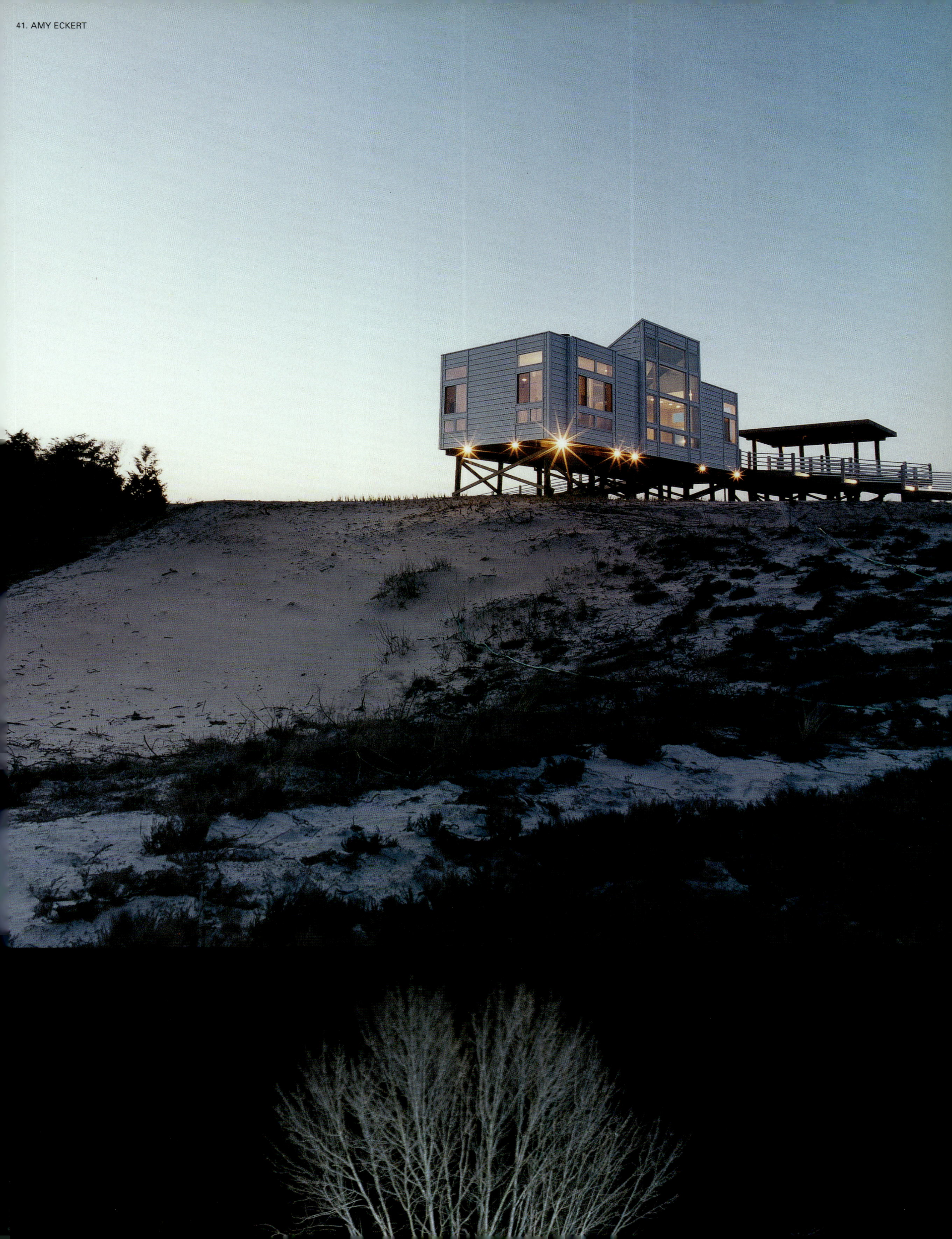

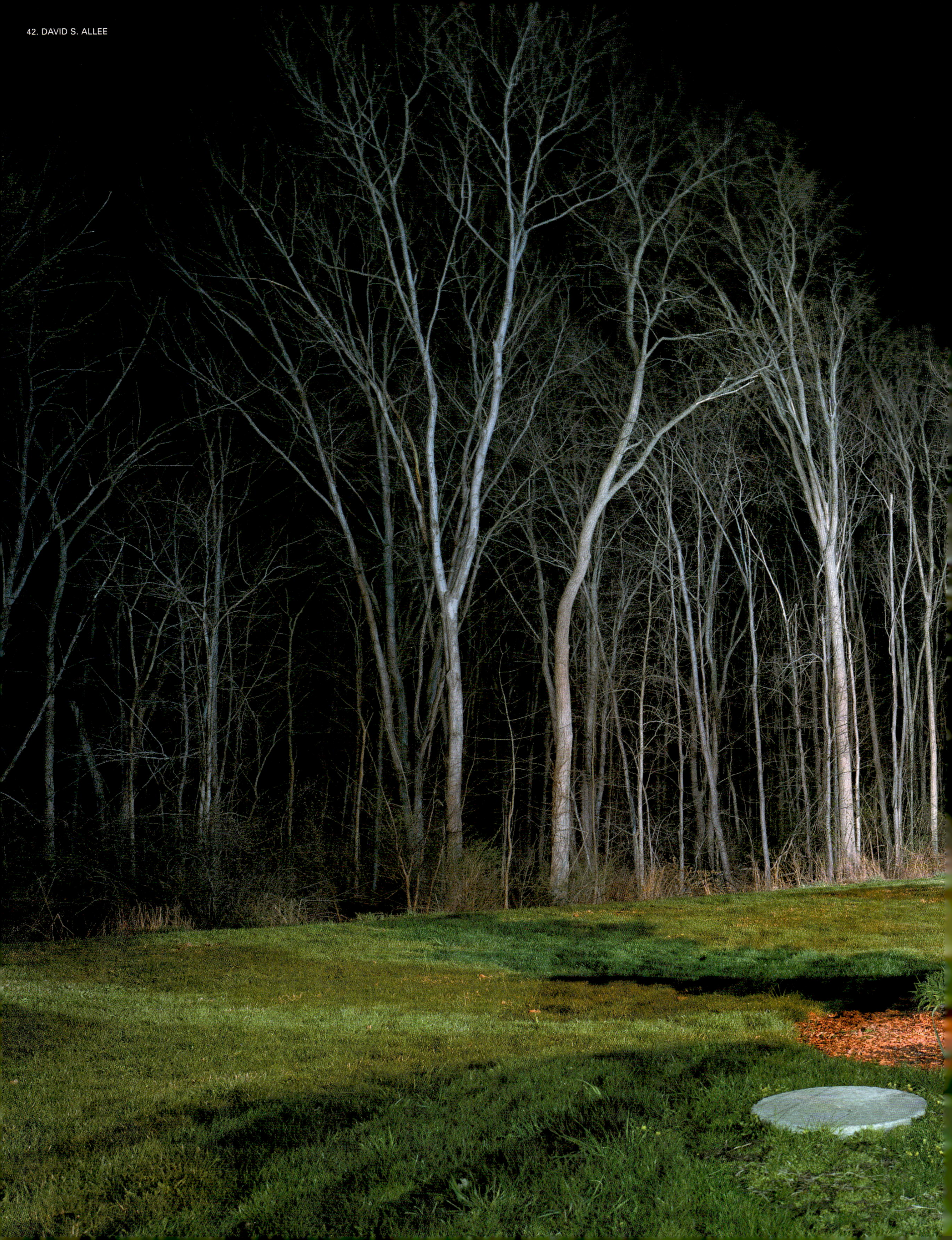

42. DAVID S. ALLEE

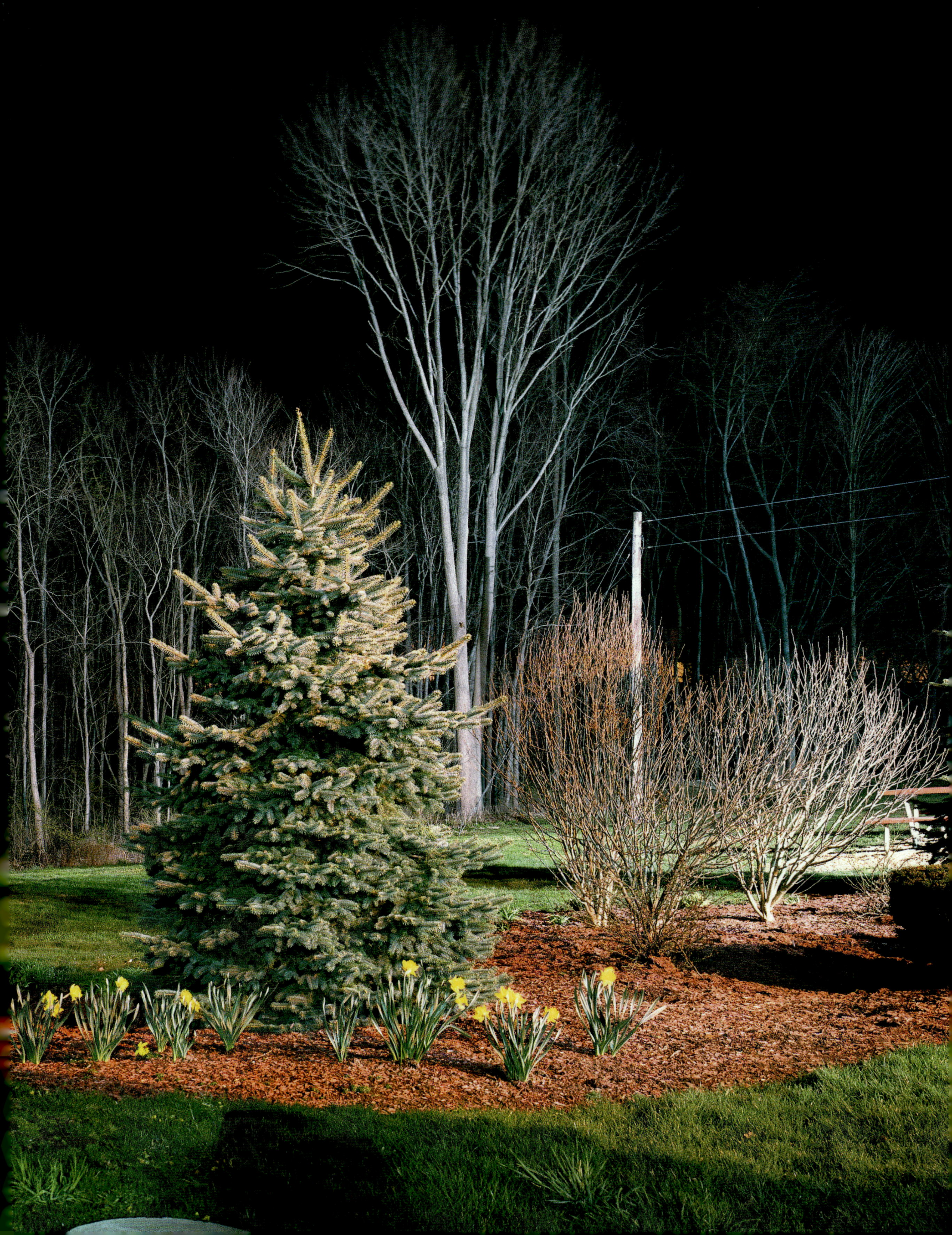

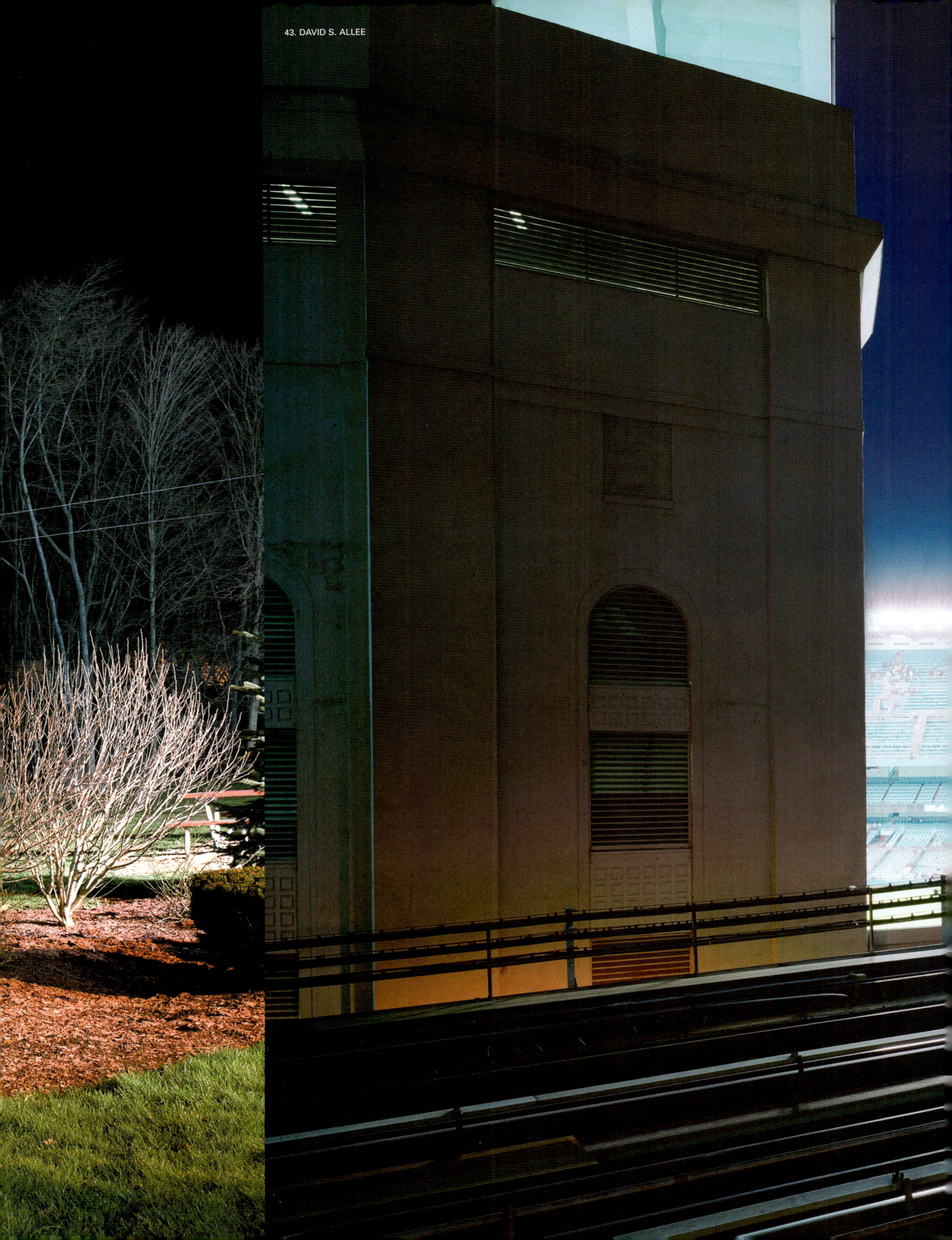

43. DAVID S. ALLEE

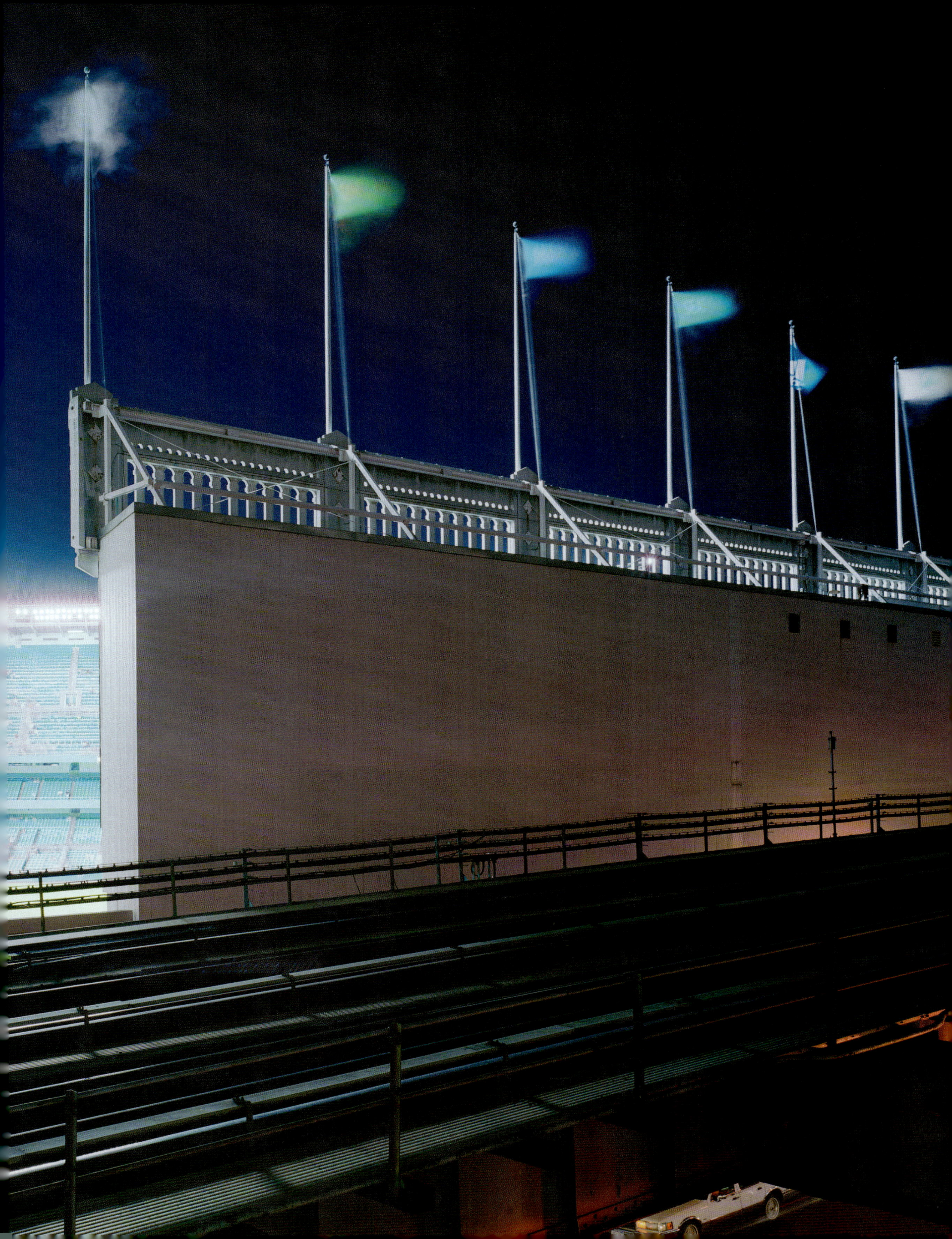

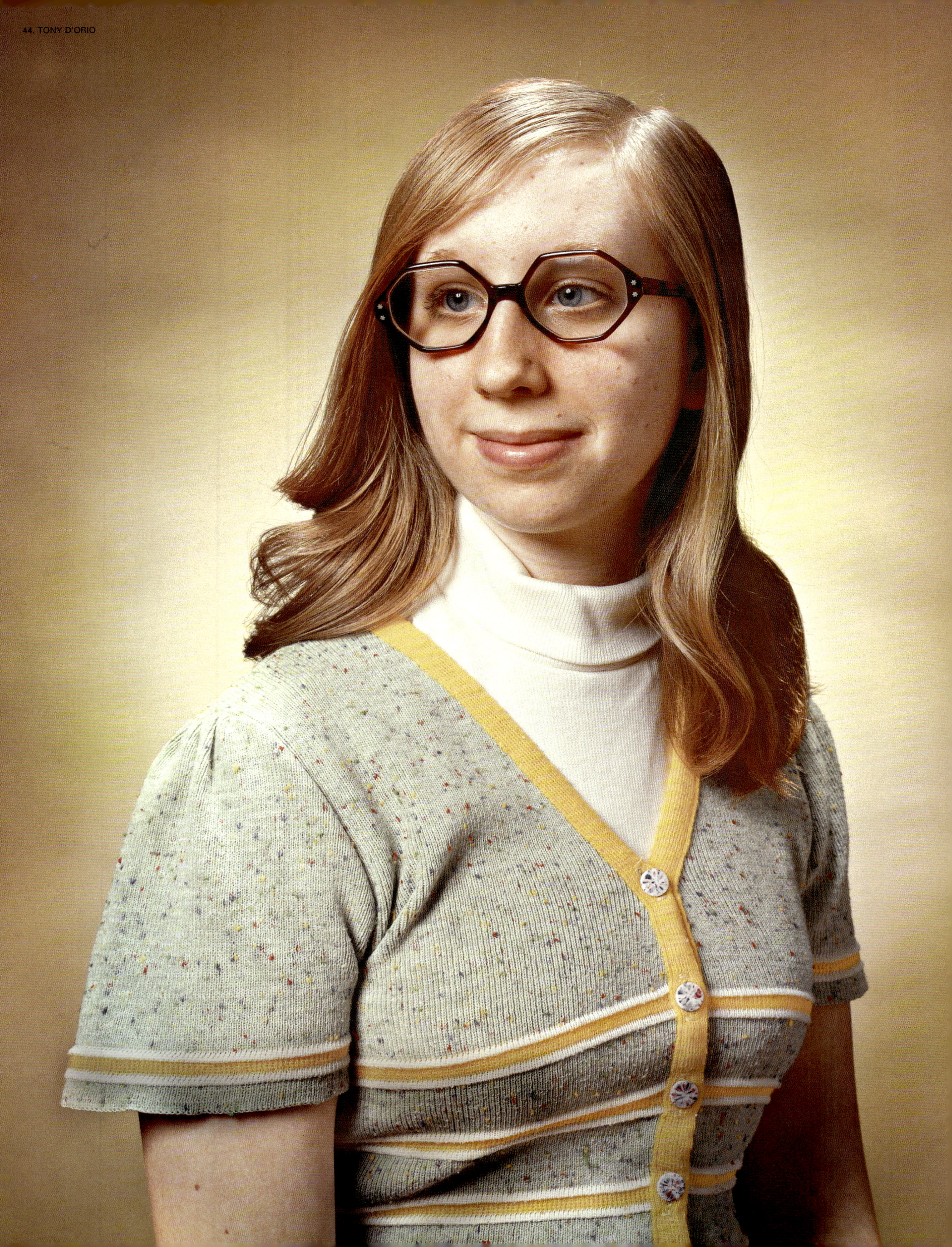

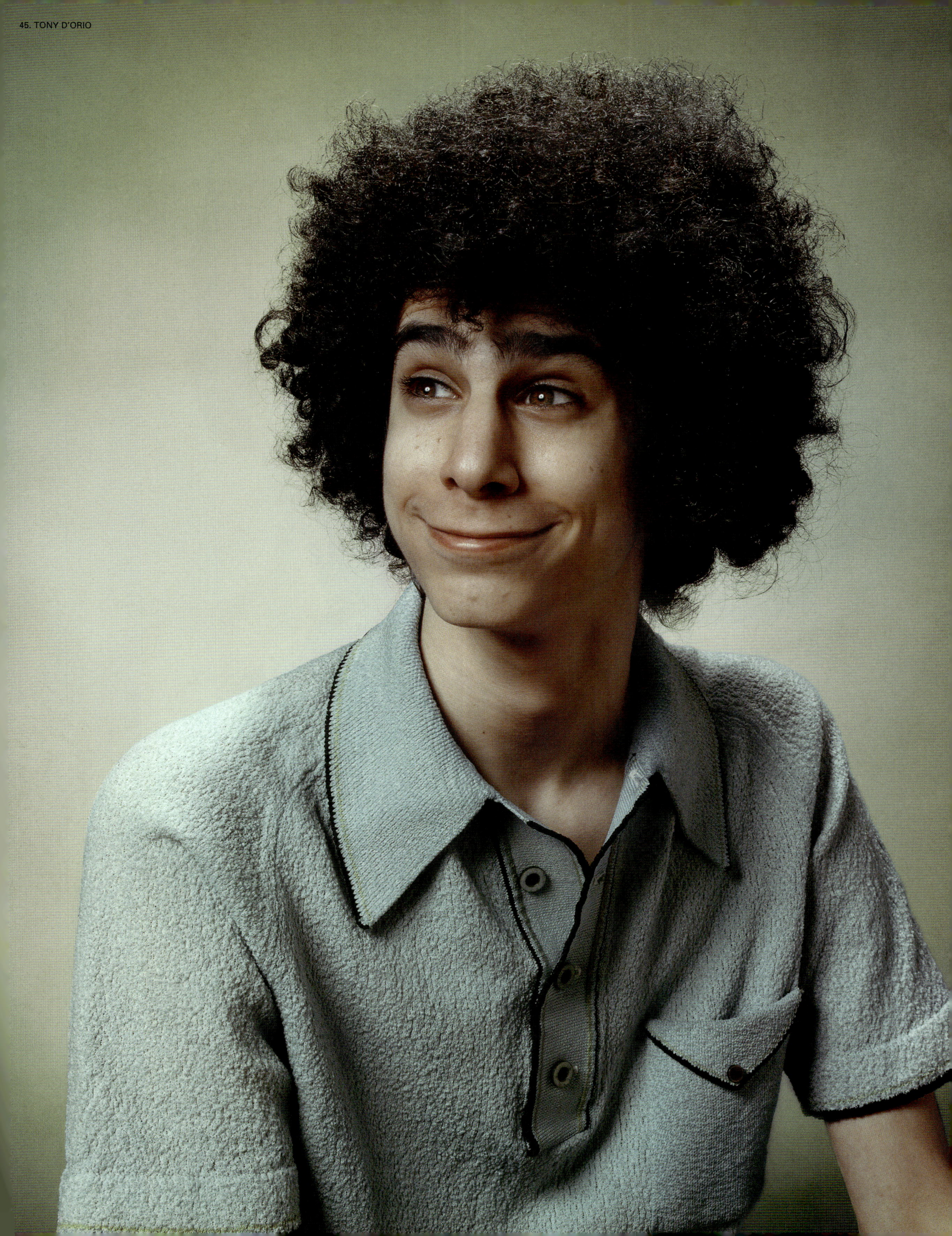

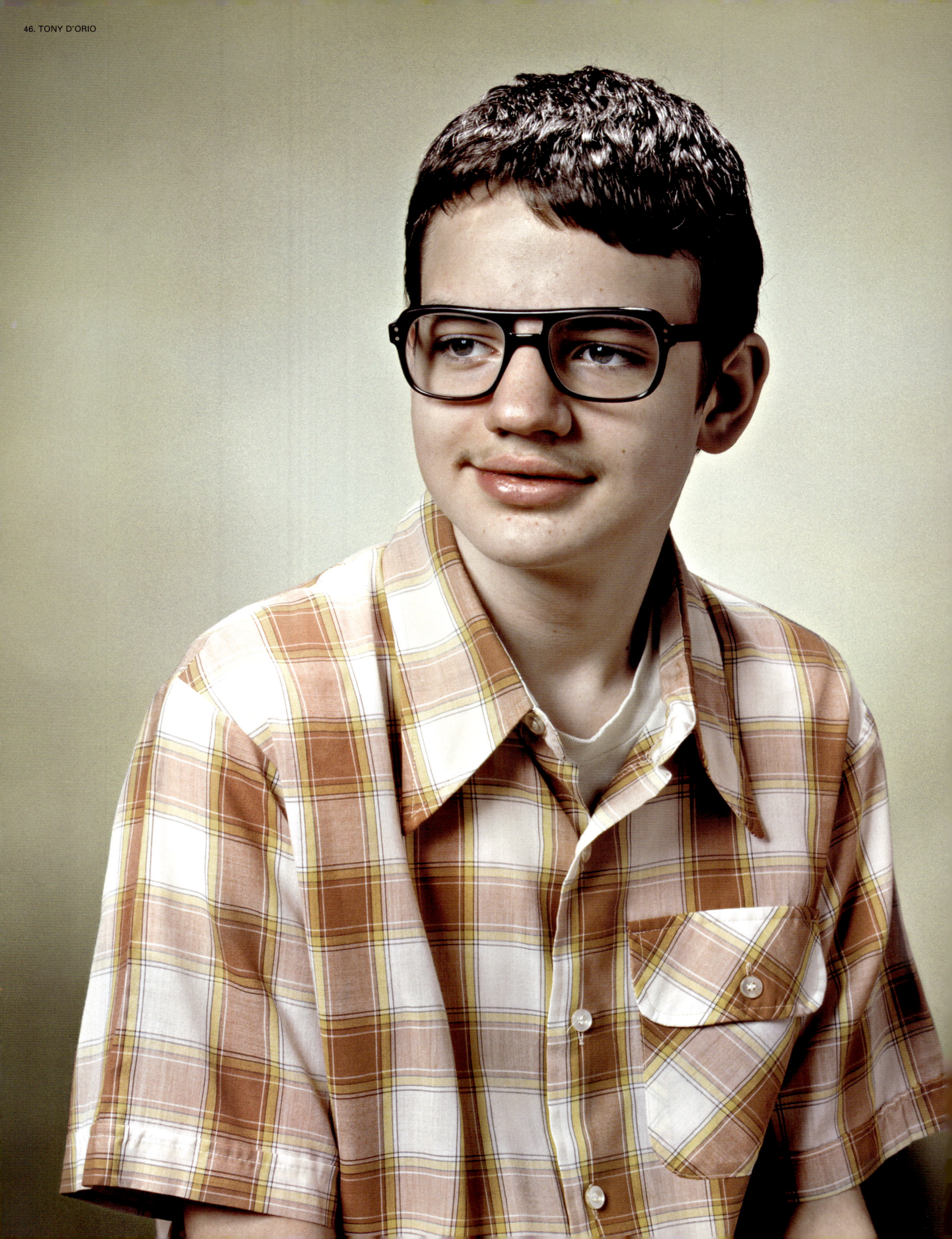

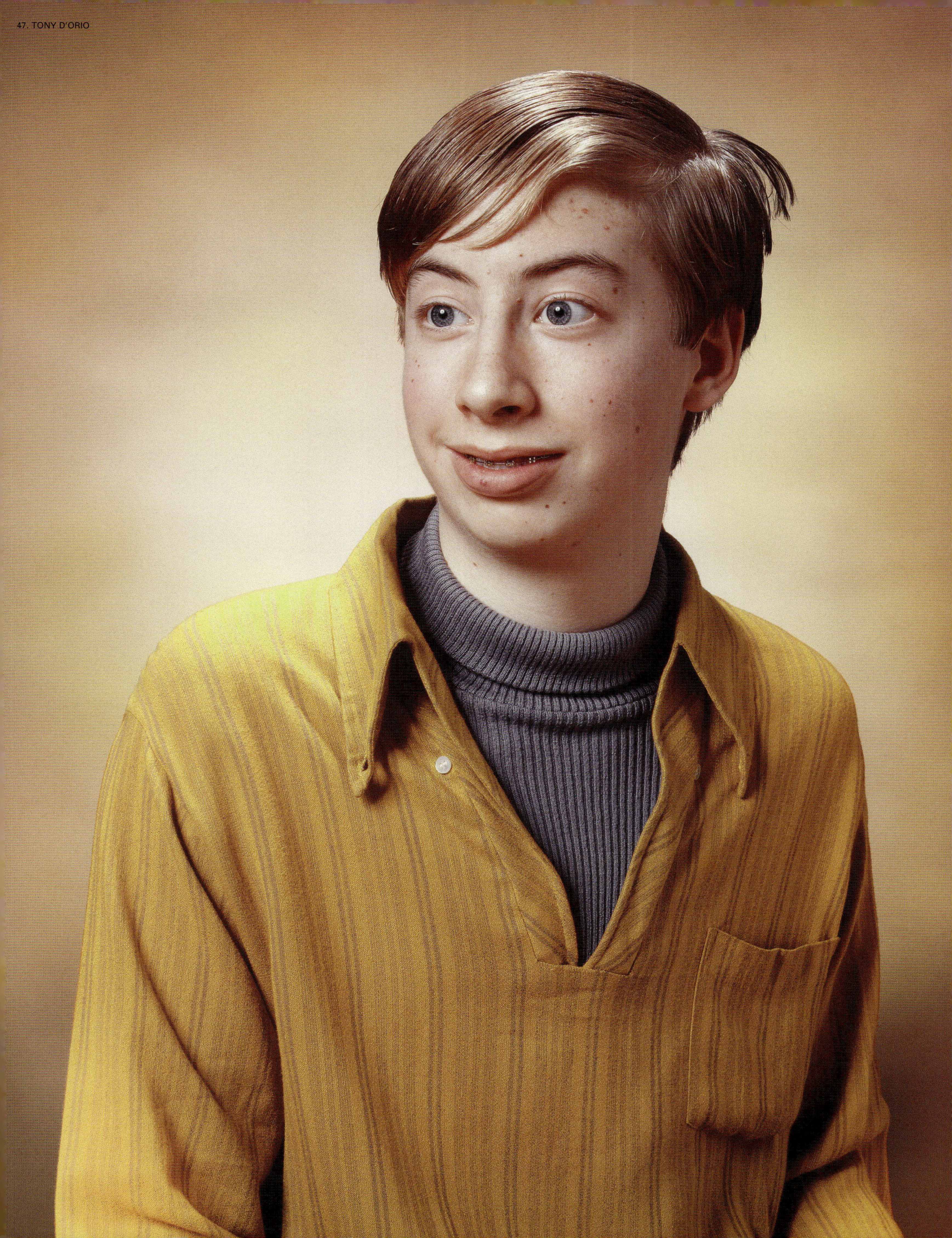

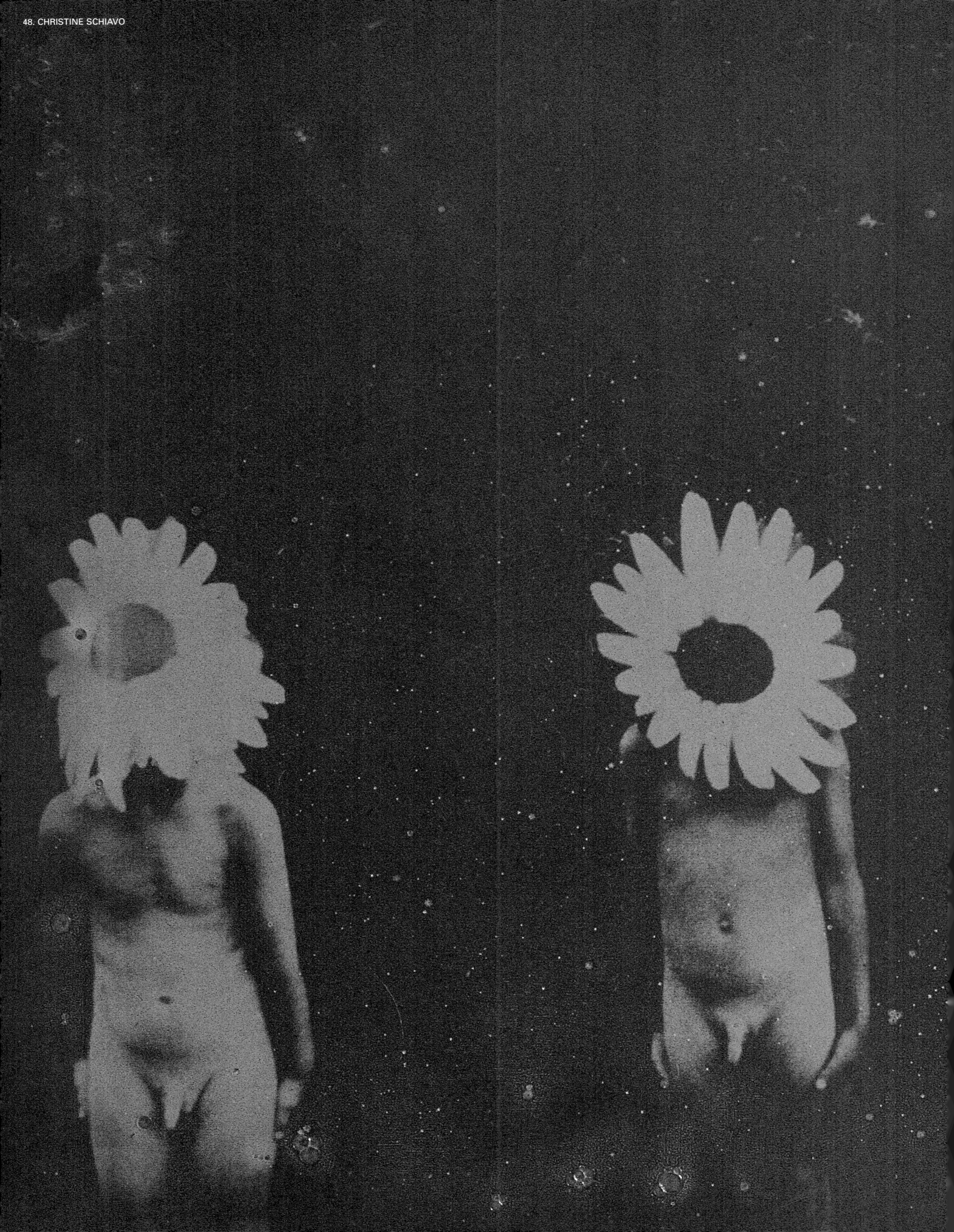

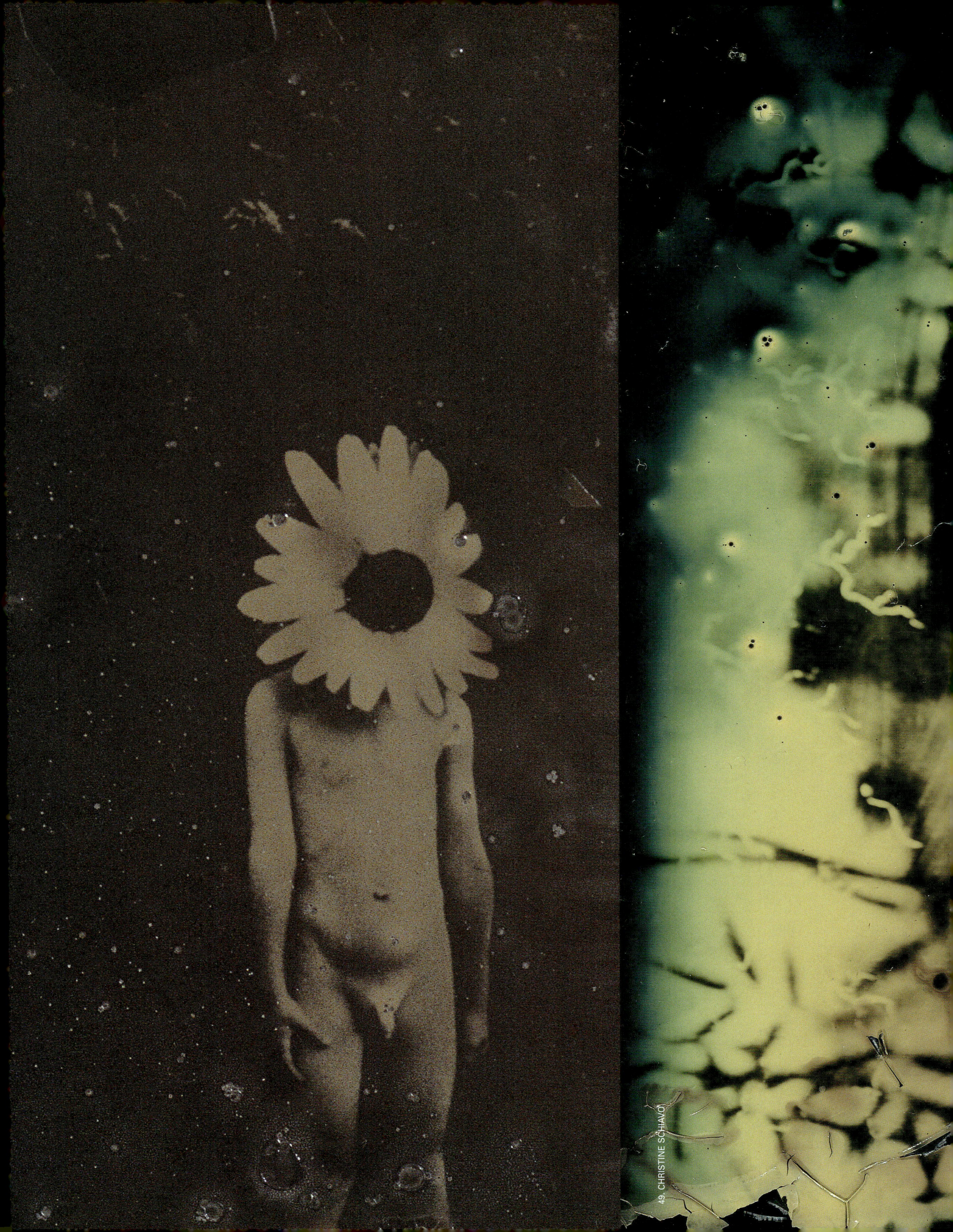

49. CHRISTINE SCHIAVO

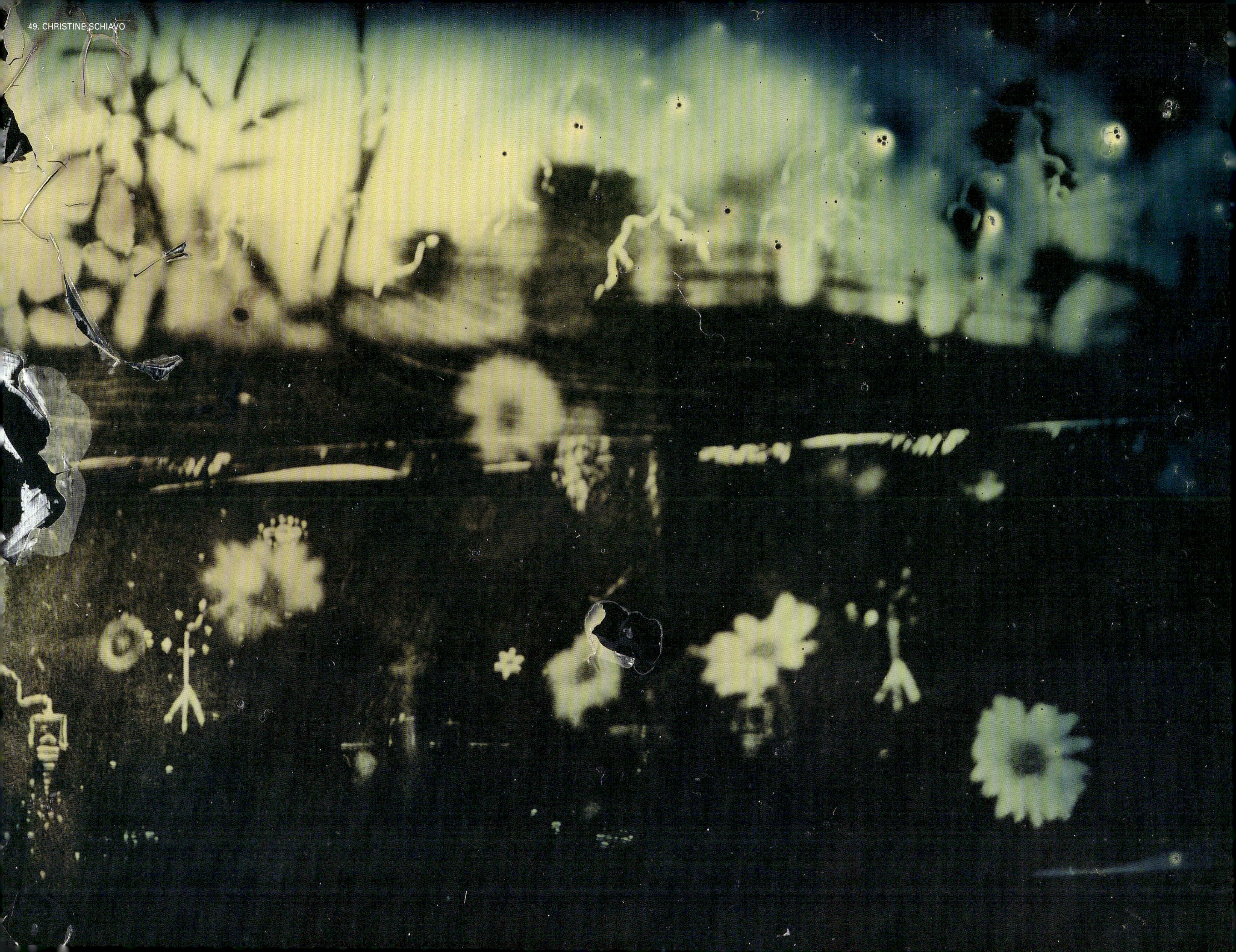

49. CHRISTINE SCHIAVO

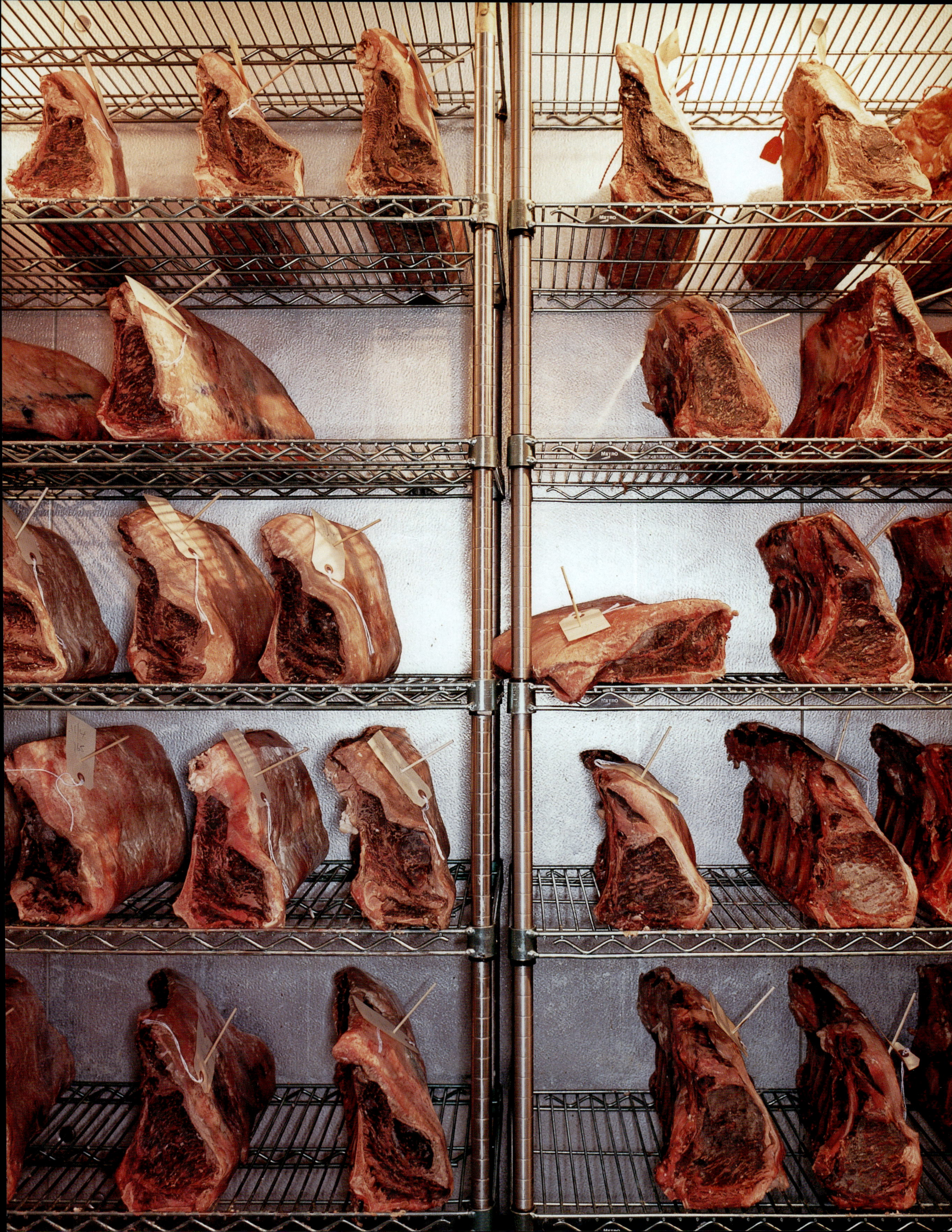
METRO
METRO

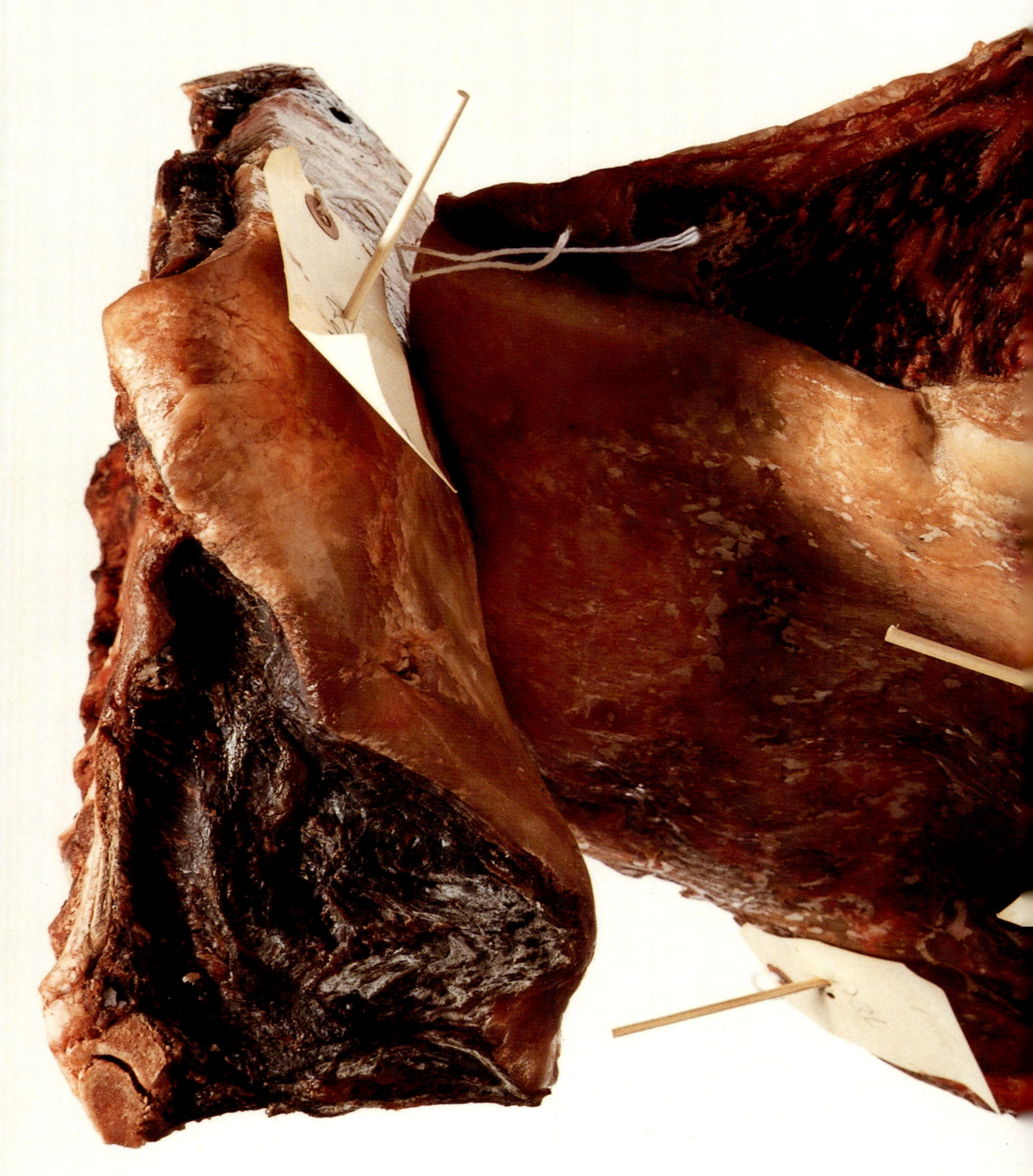

50-51. CRAIG CUTLER

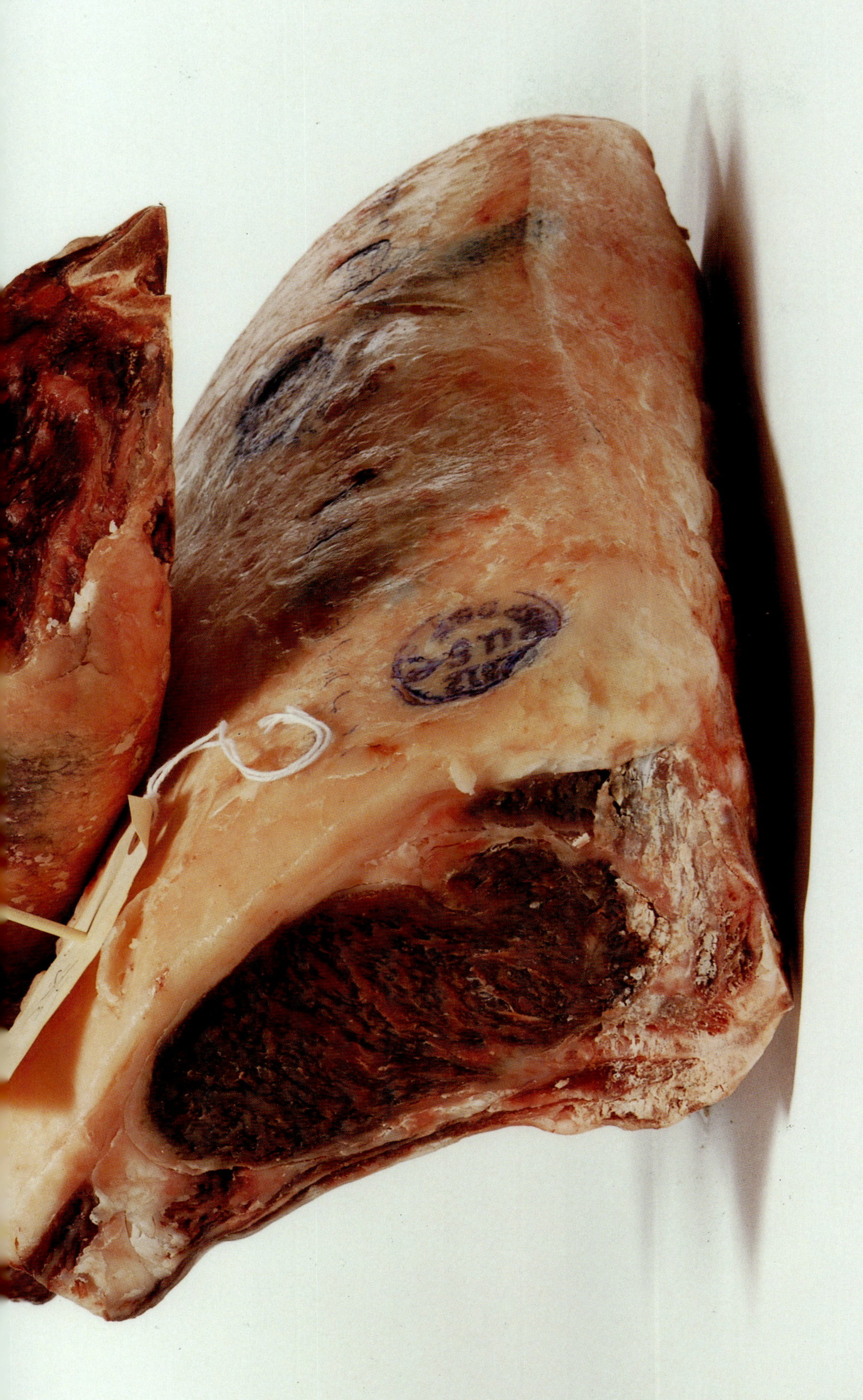

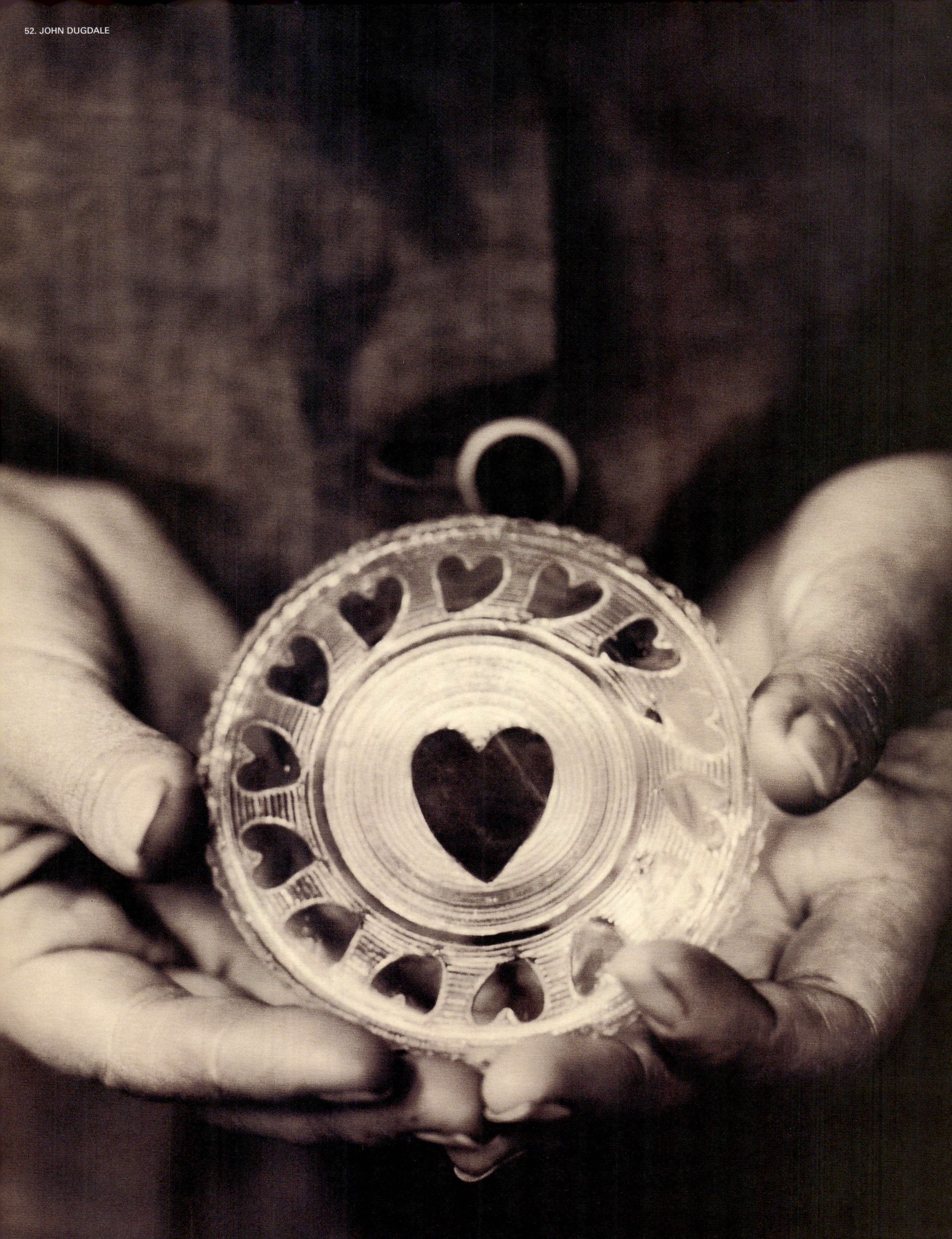

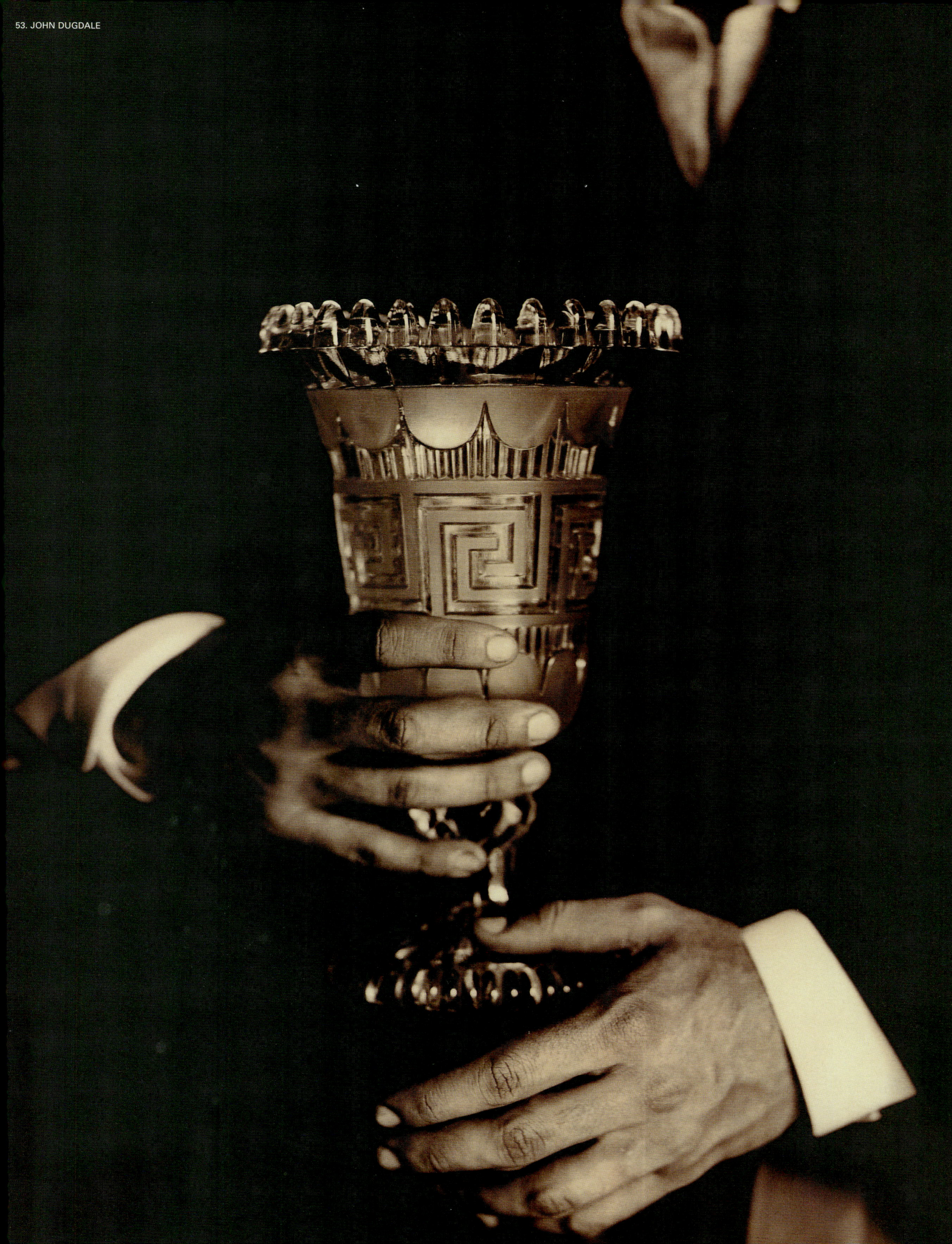

53. JOHN DUGDALE

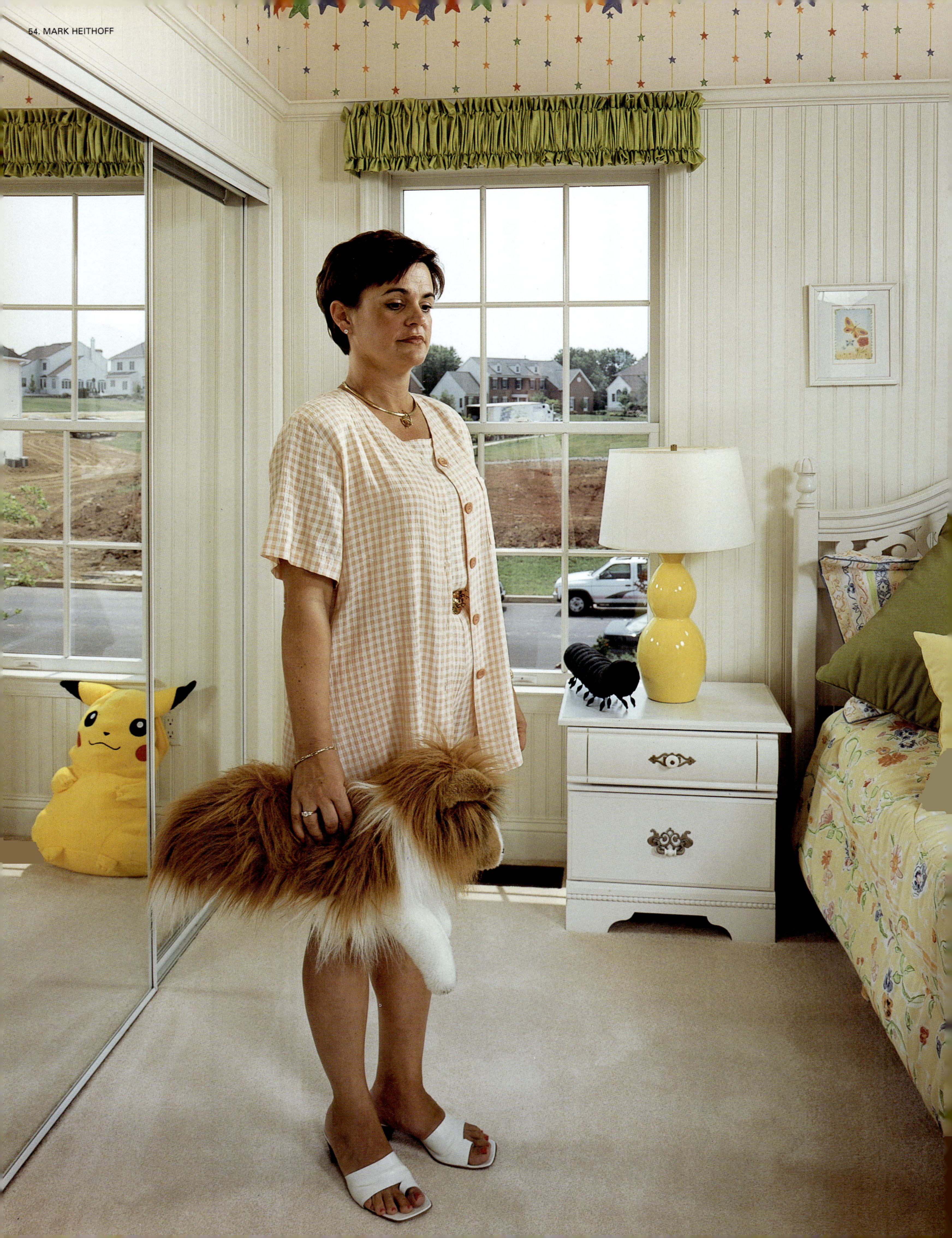

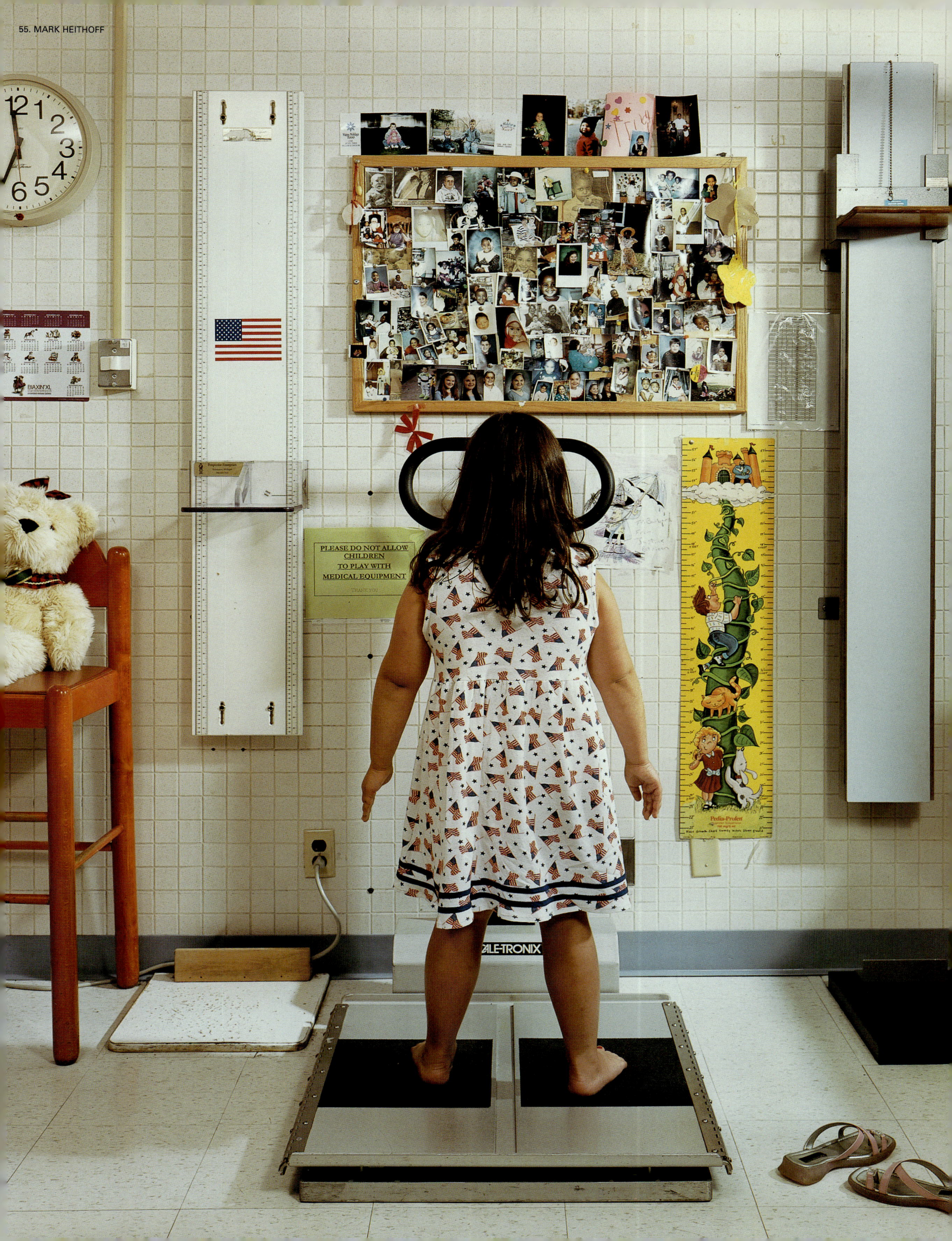

55. MARK HEITHOFF

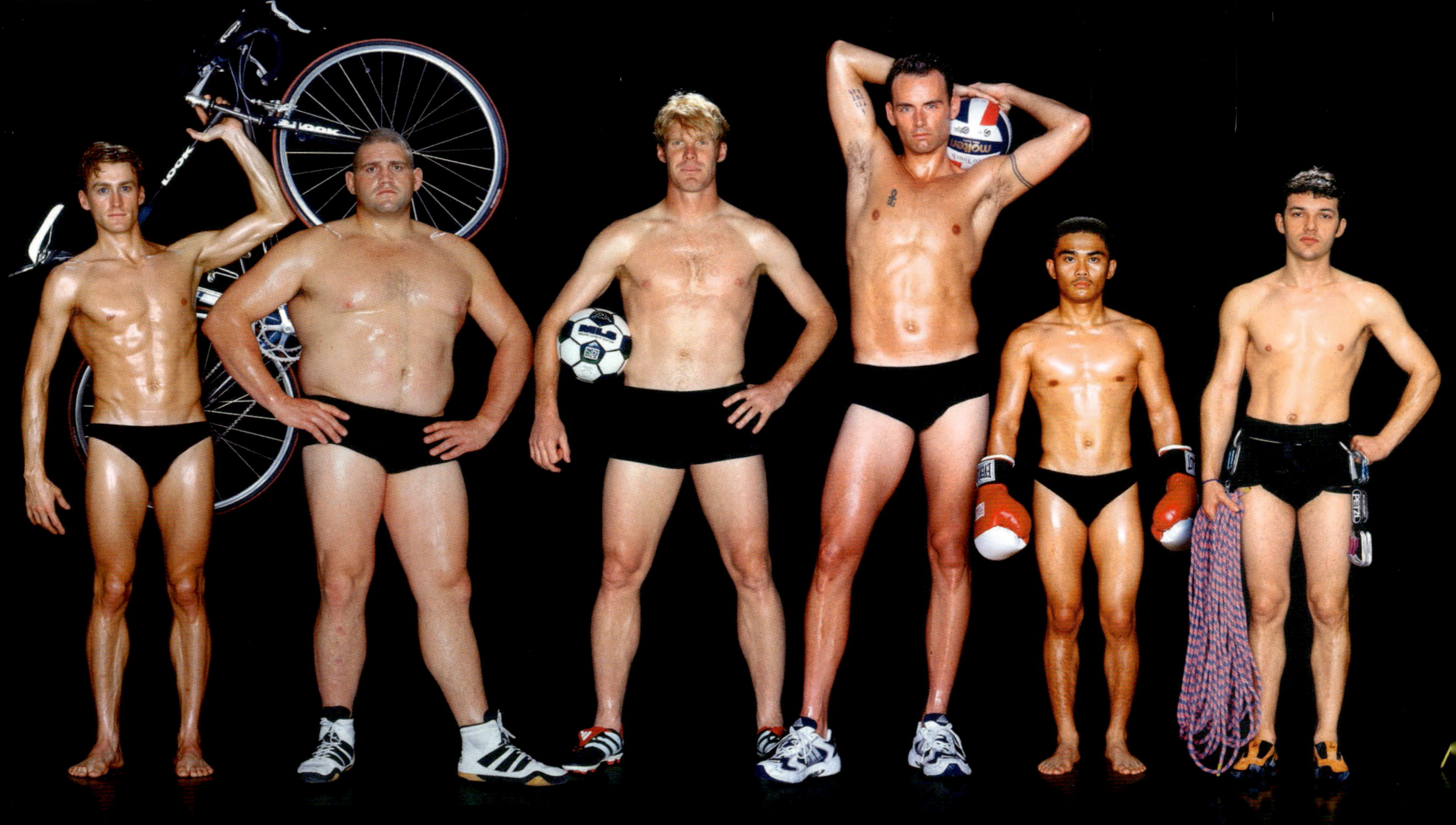

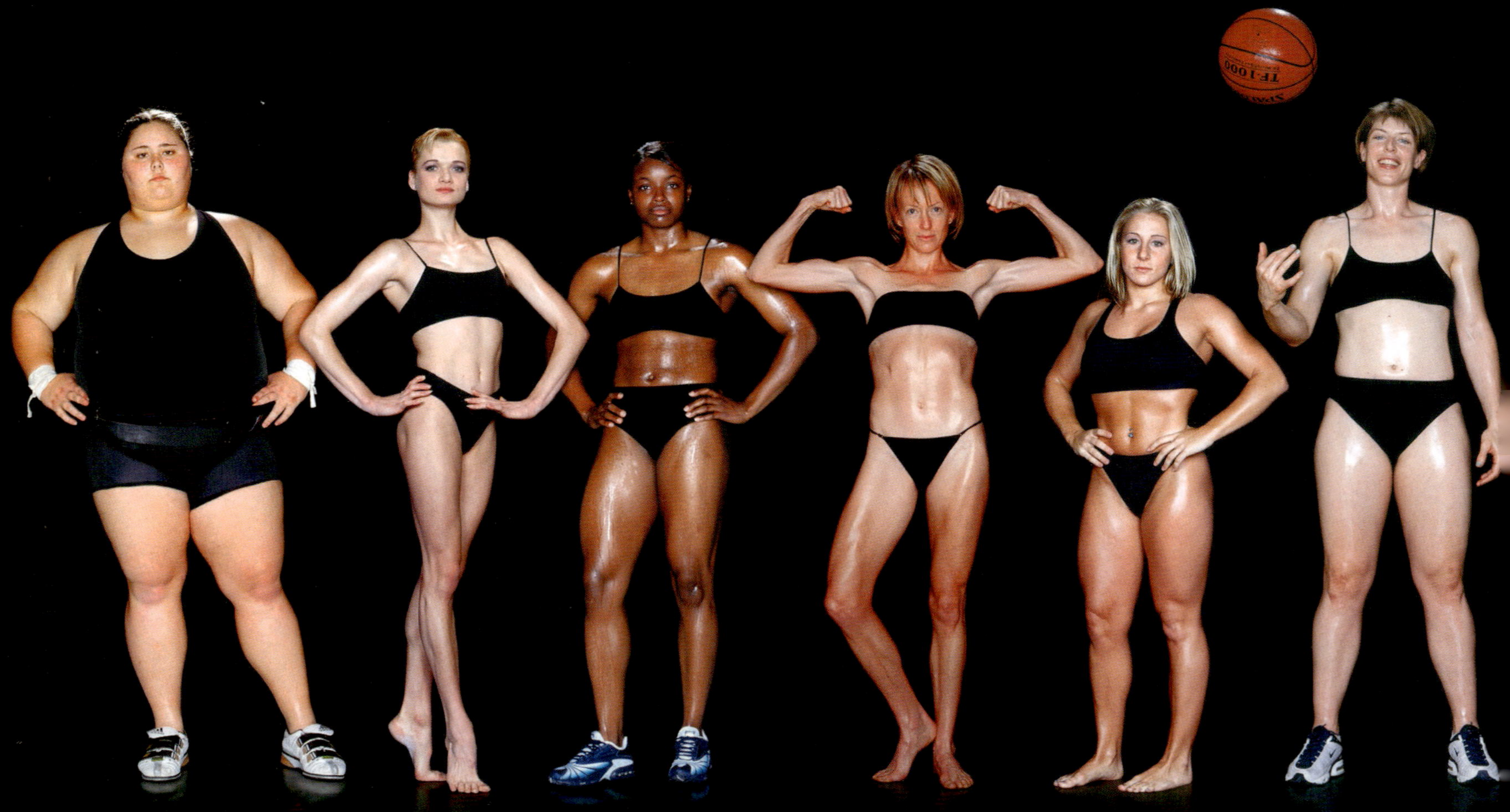

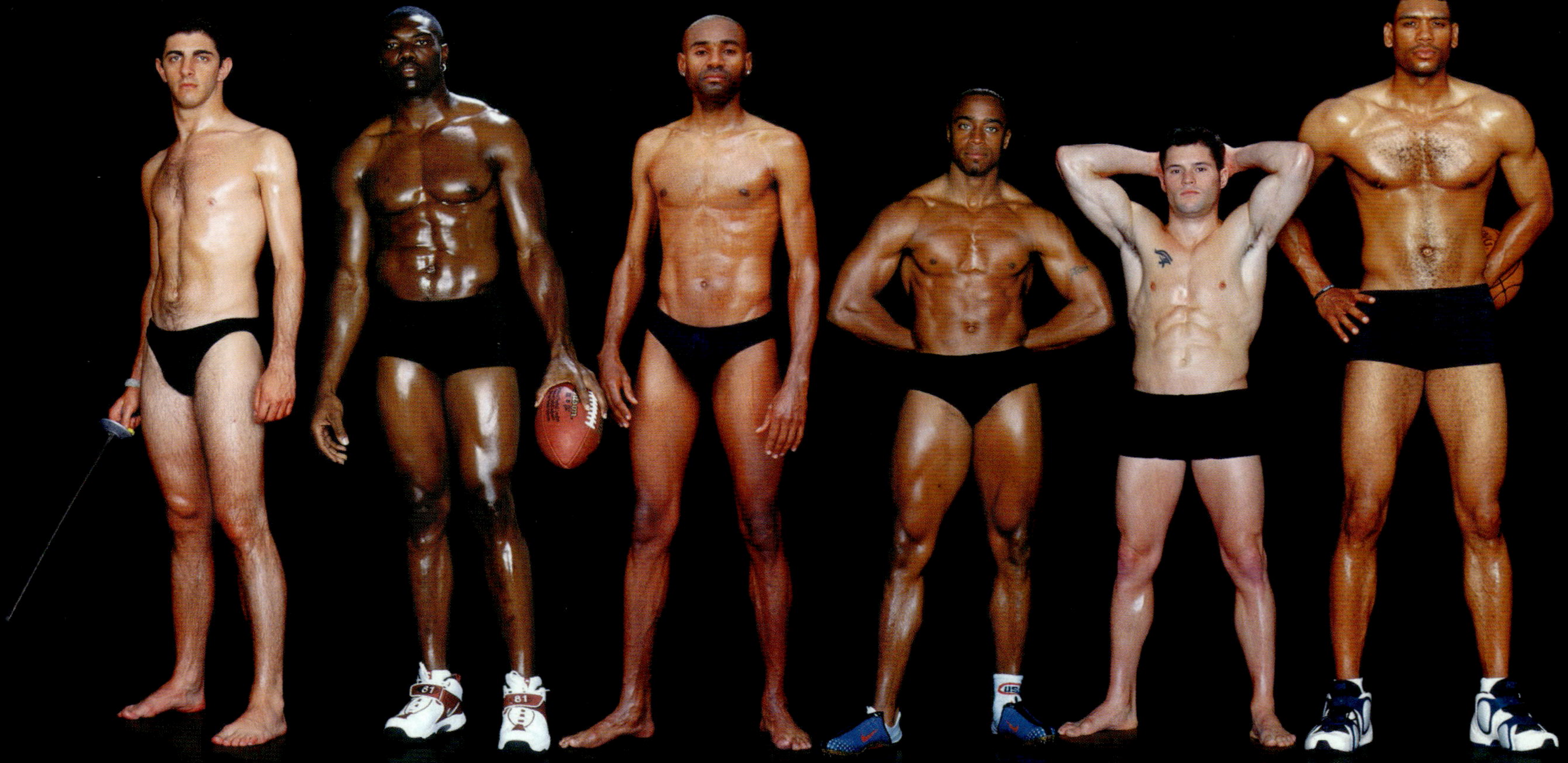

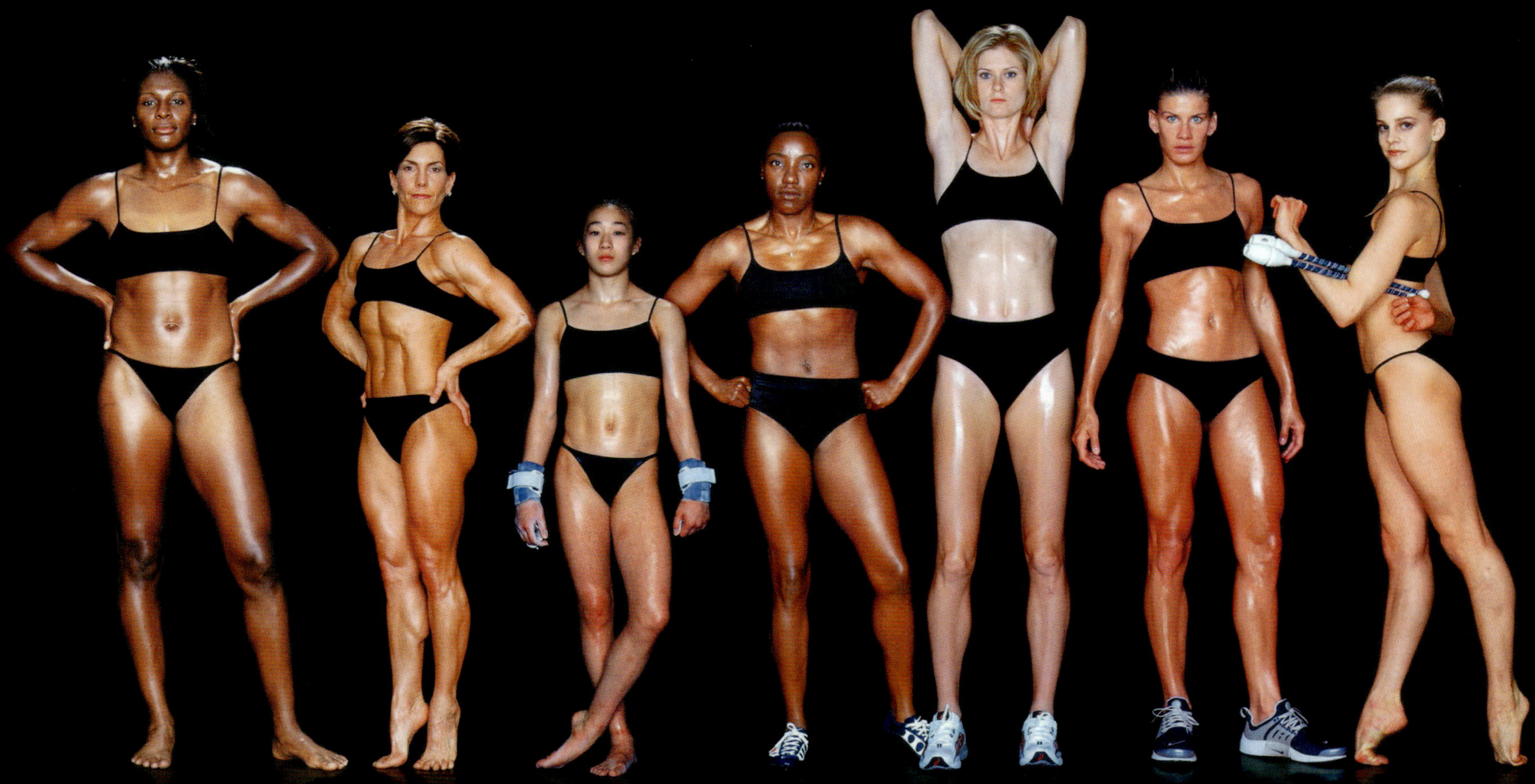

57. HOWARD SCHATZ

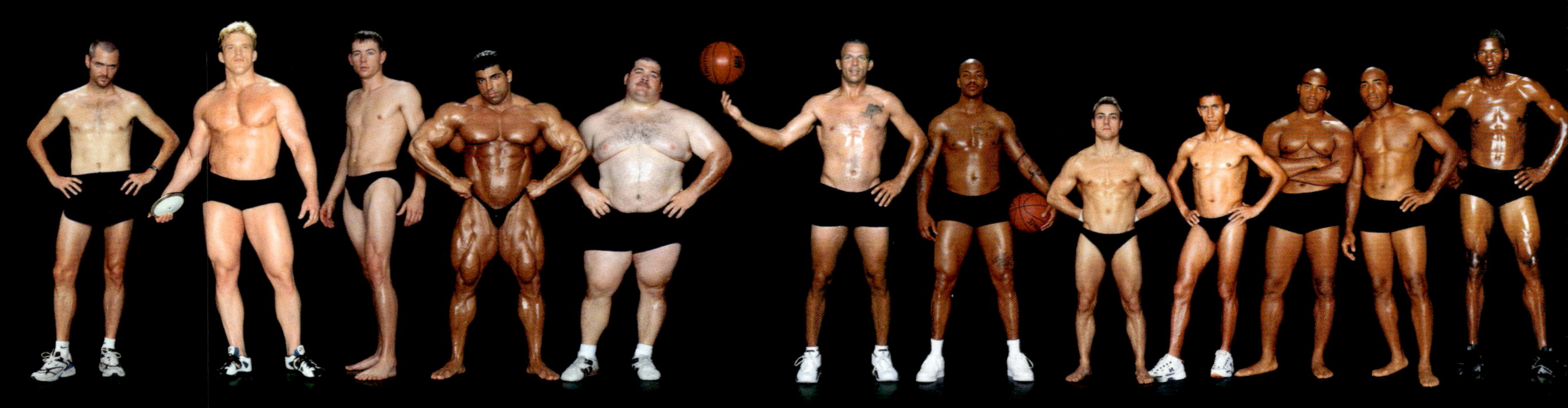

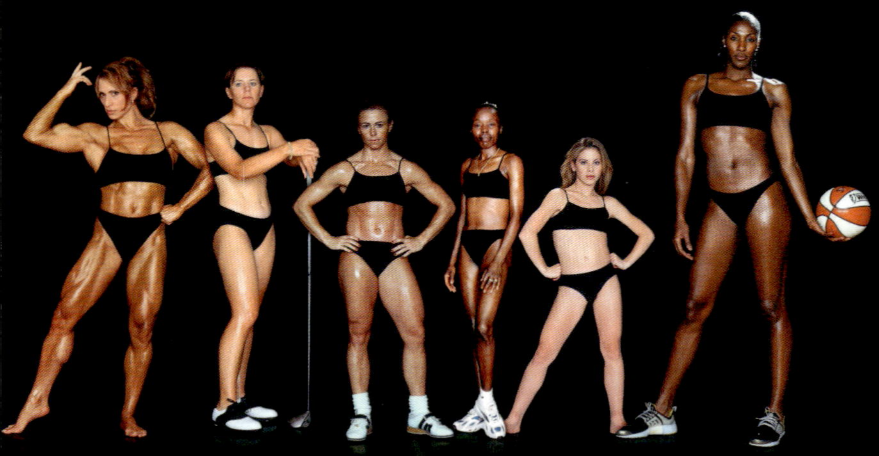

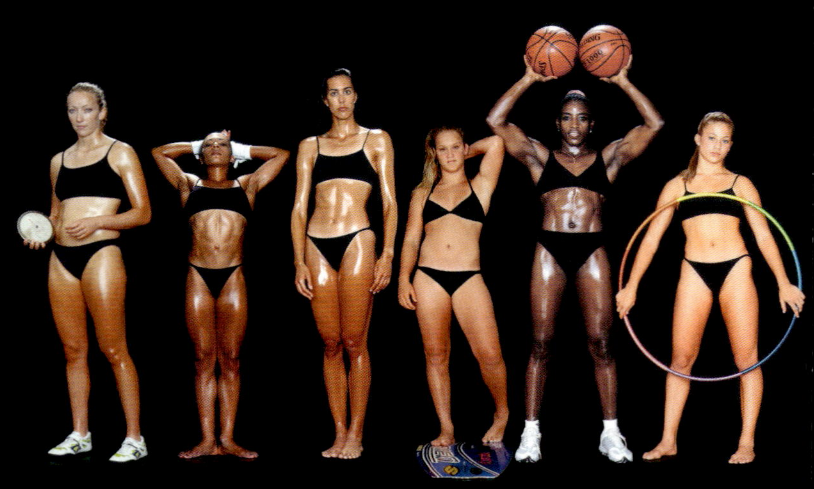

58. HOWARD SCHATZ

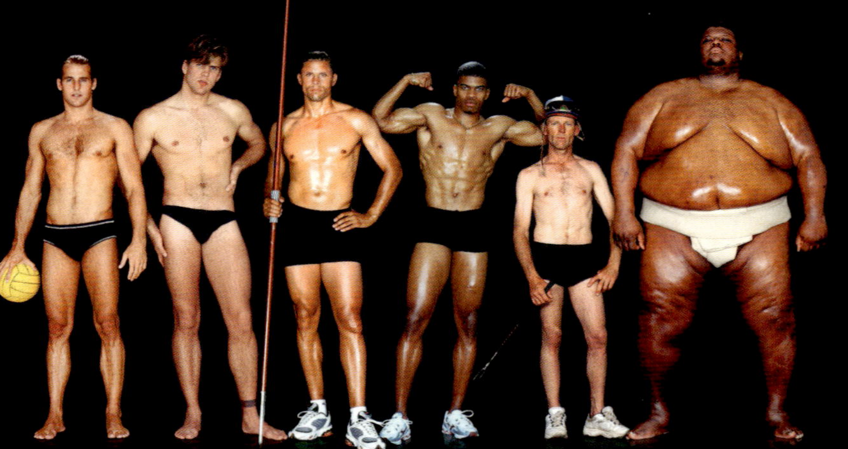

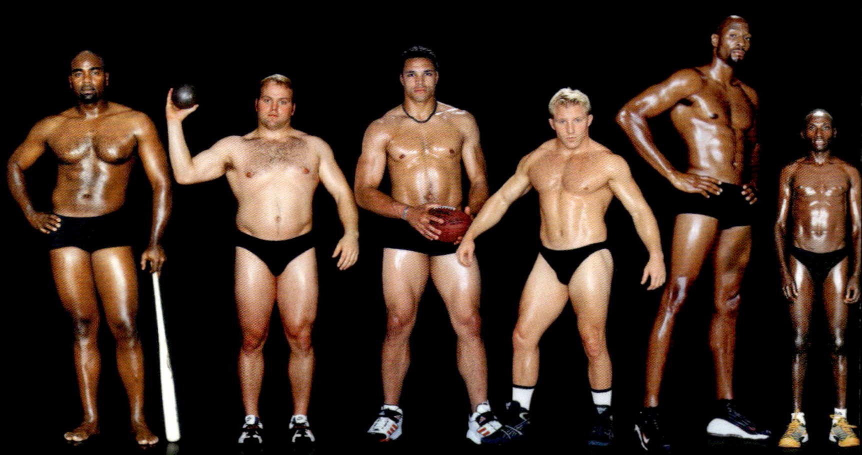

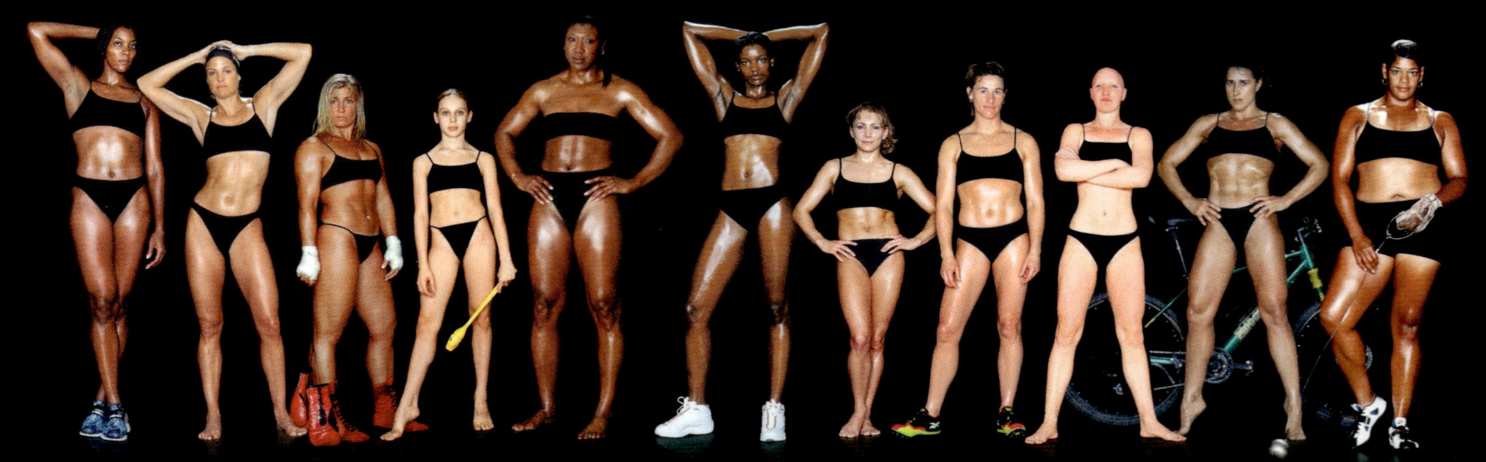

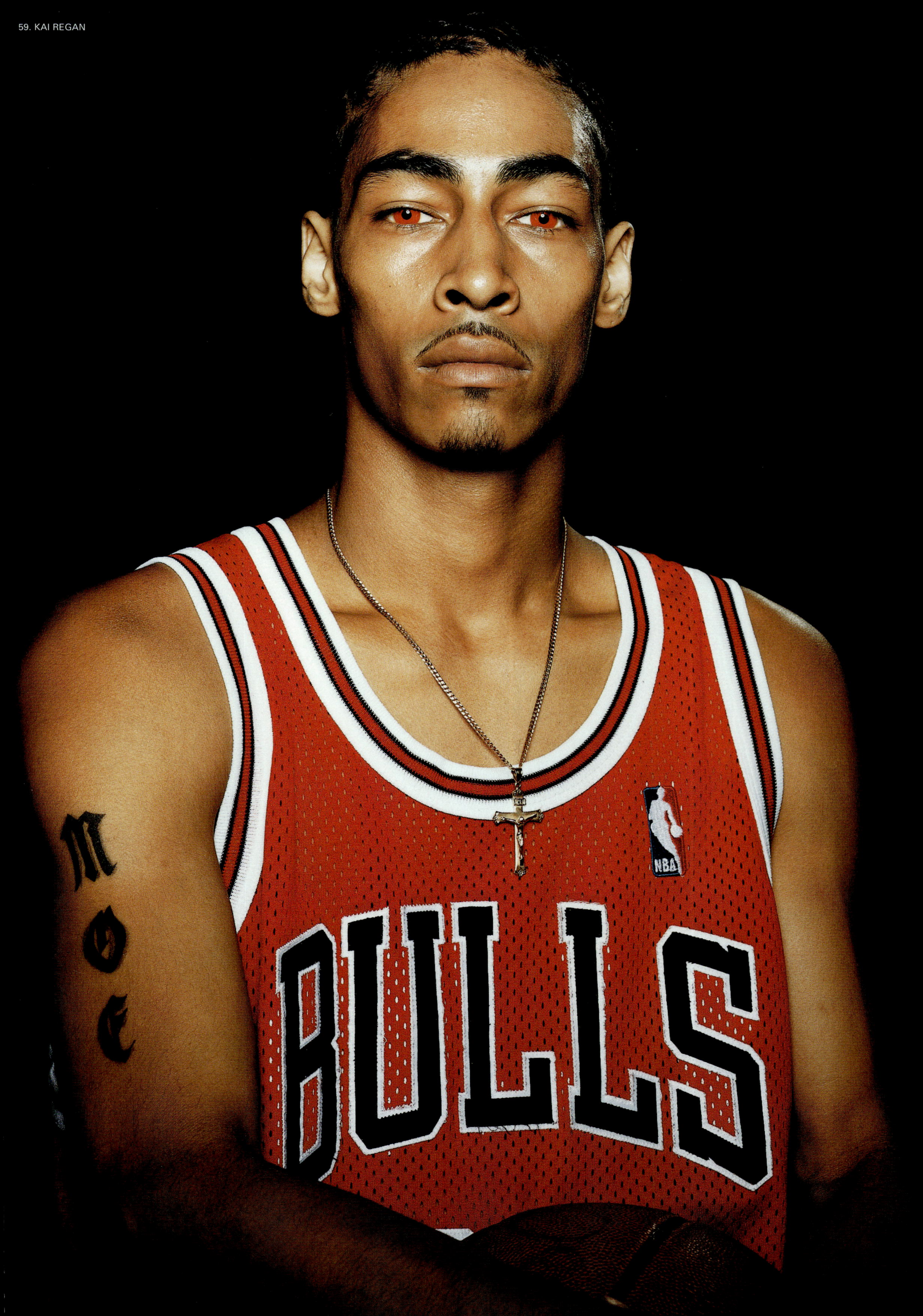

59. KAI REGAN

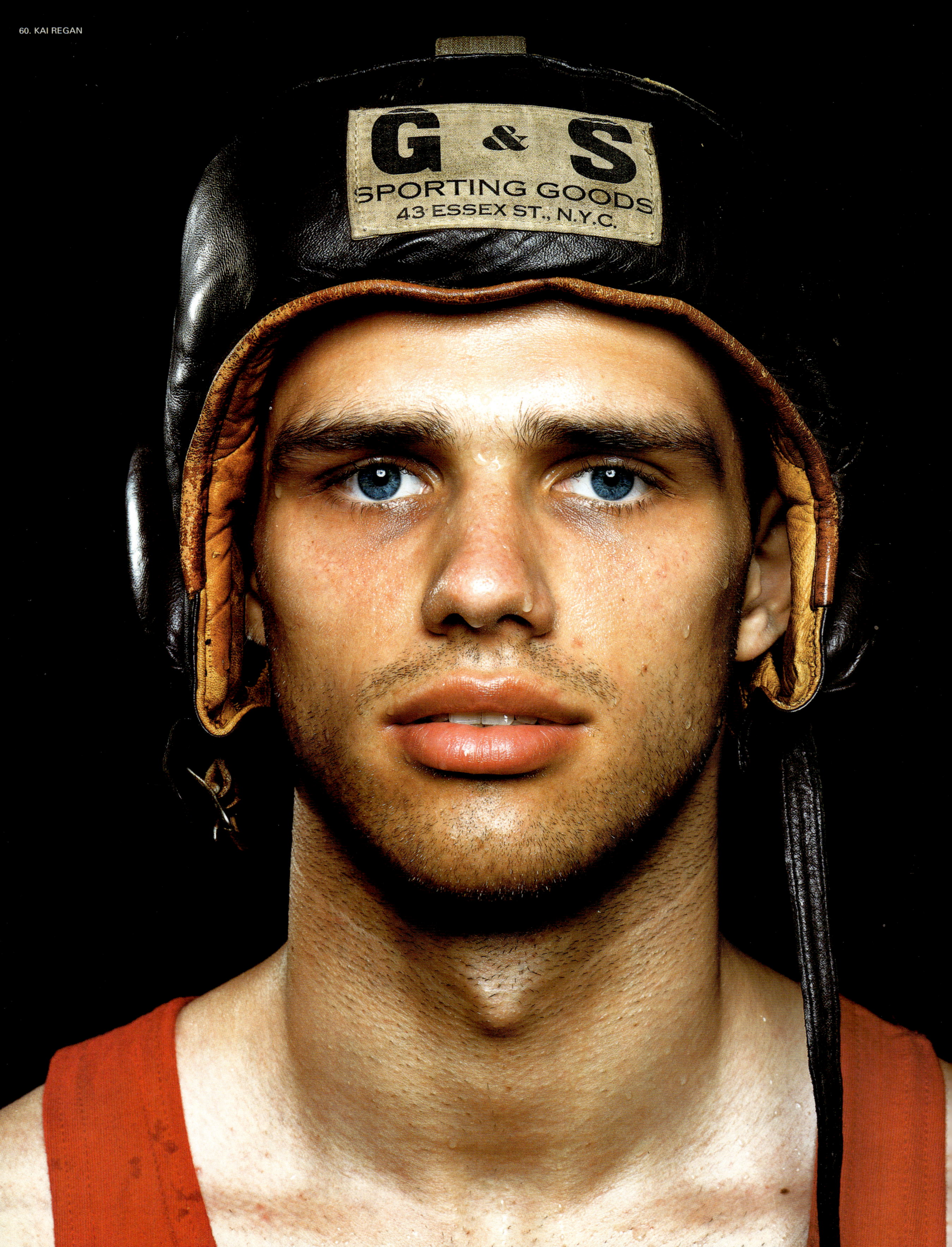
G & S
SPORTING GOODS
43 ESSEX ST., N.Y.C.

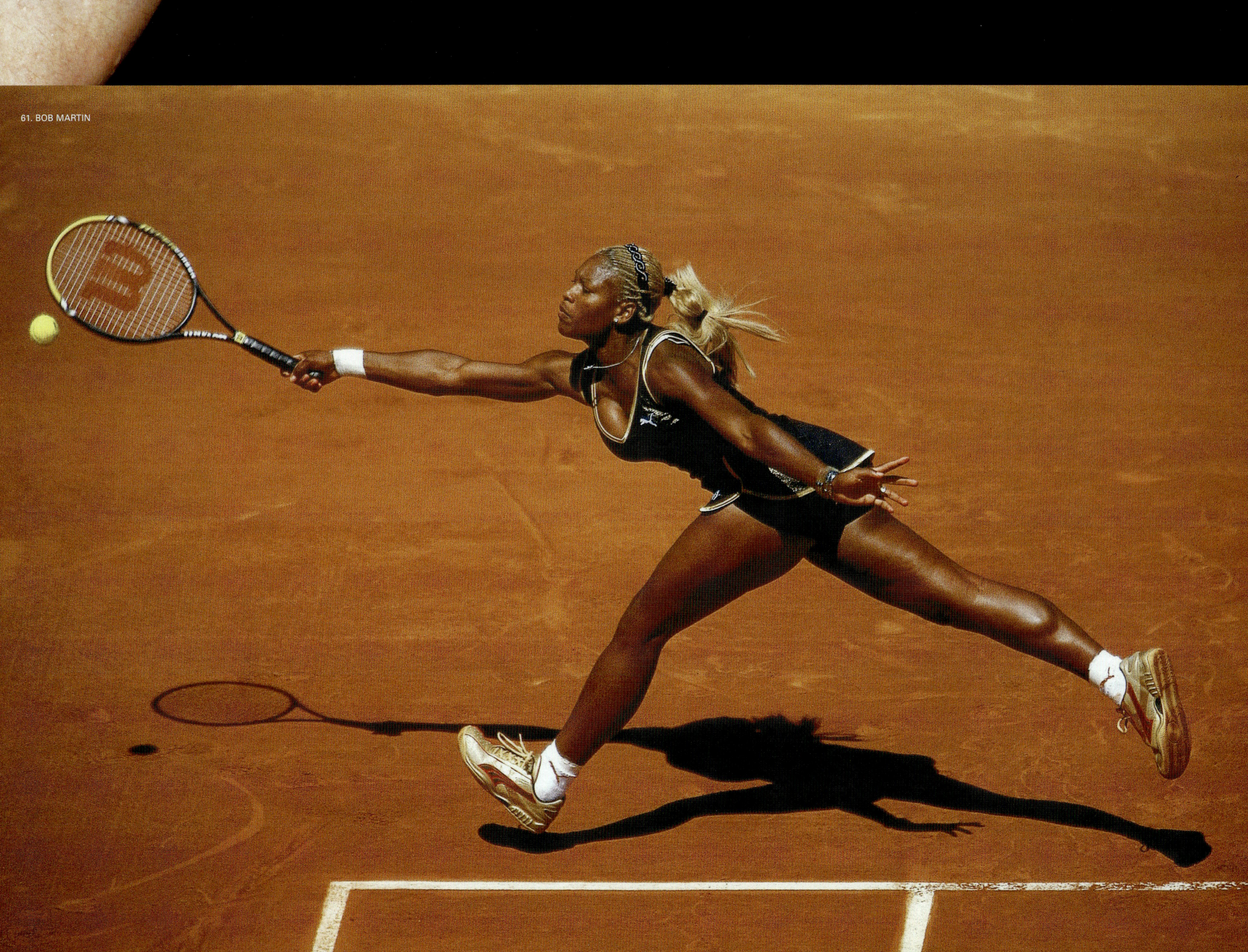

61. BOB MARTIN

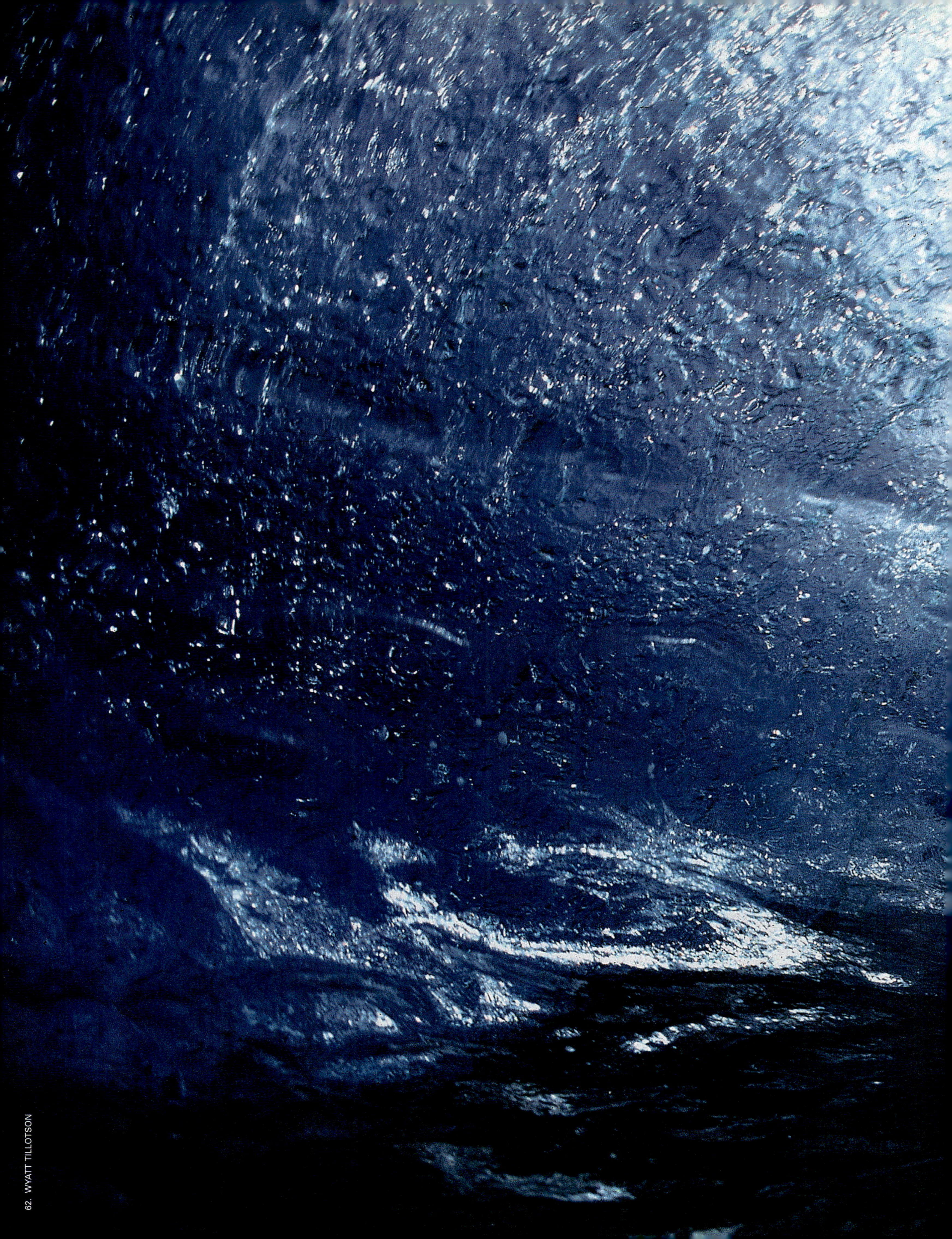

62. WYATT TILLOTSON

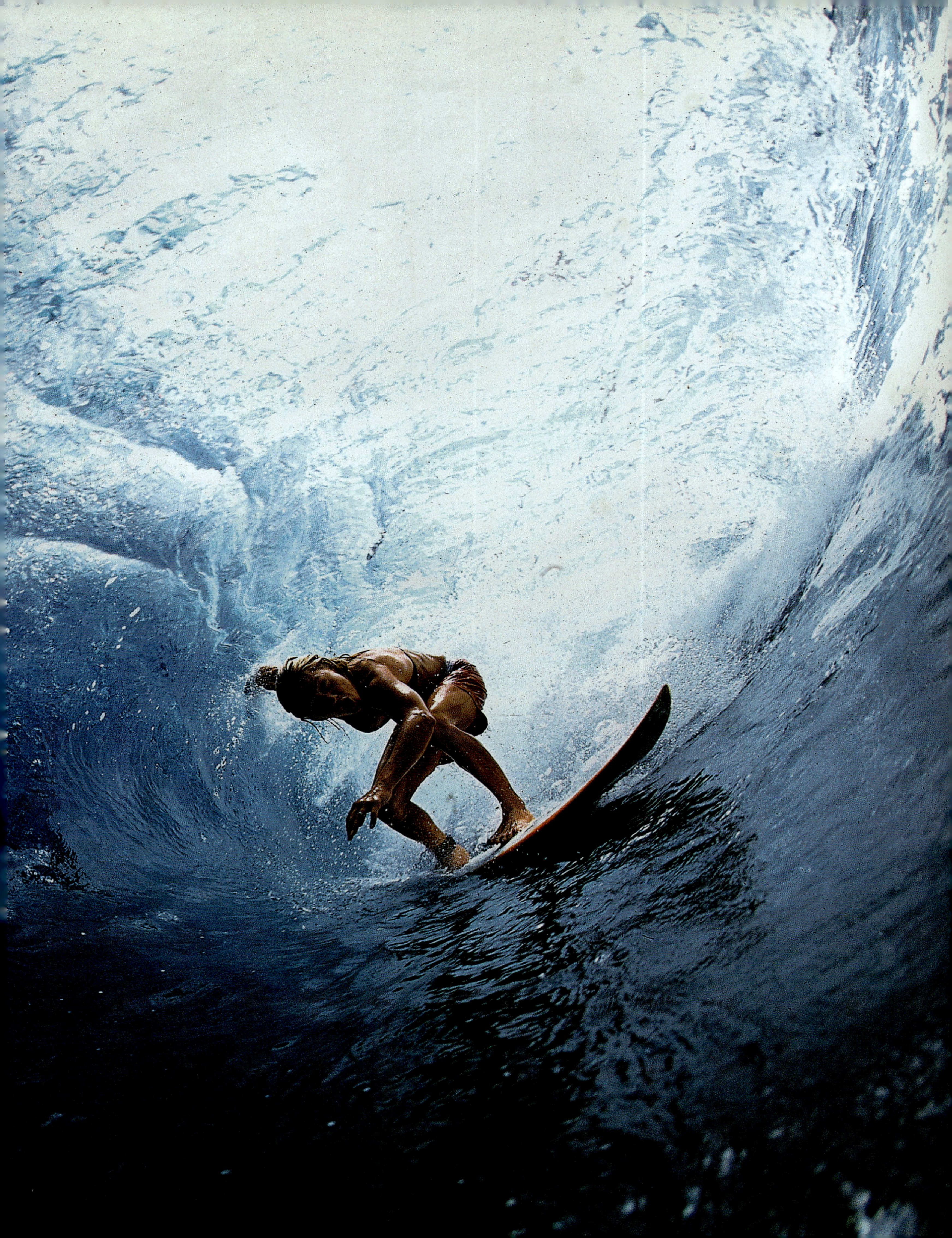

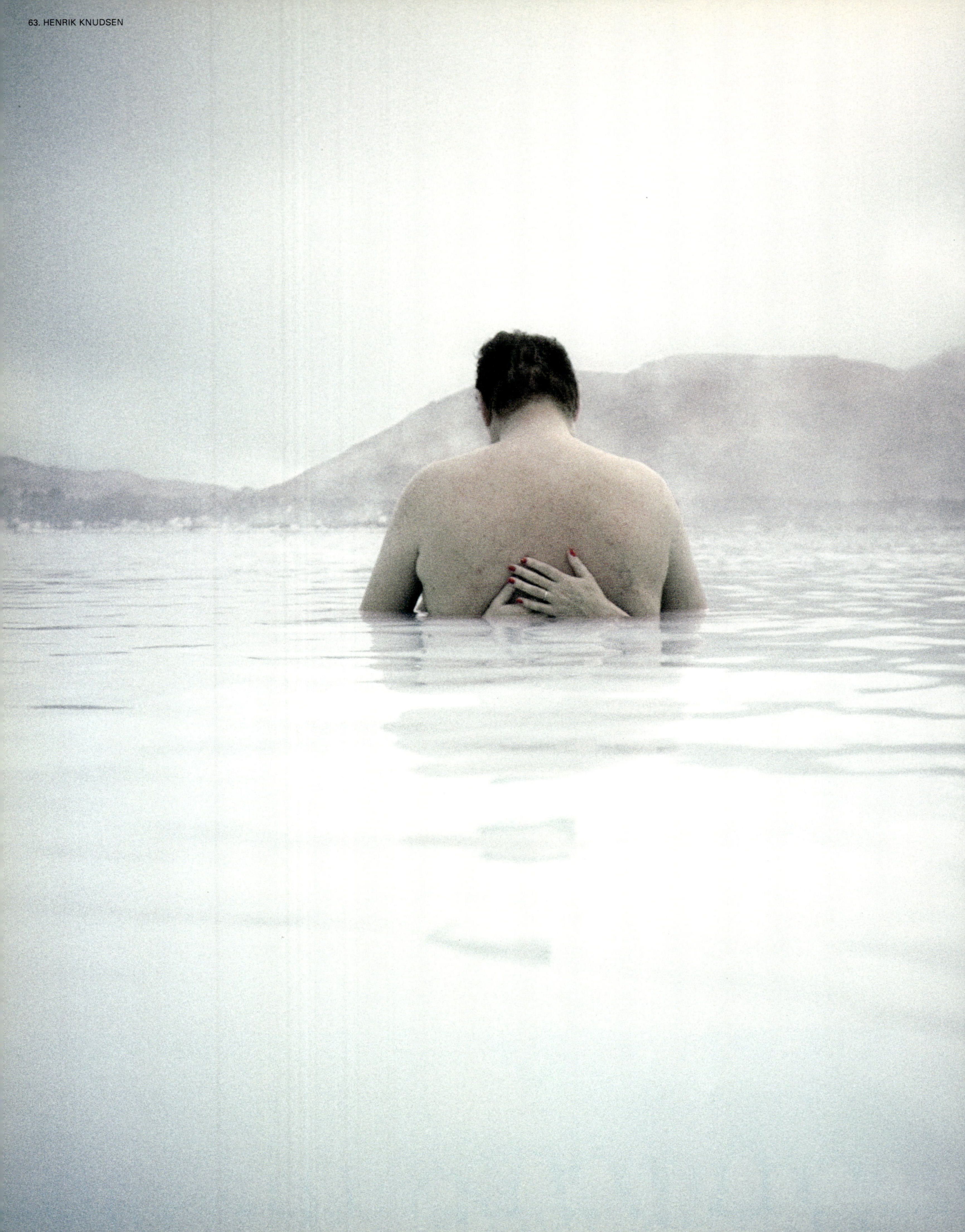

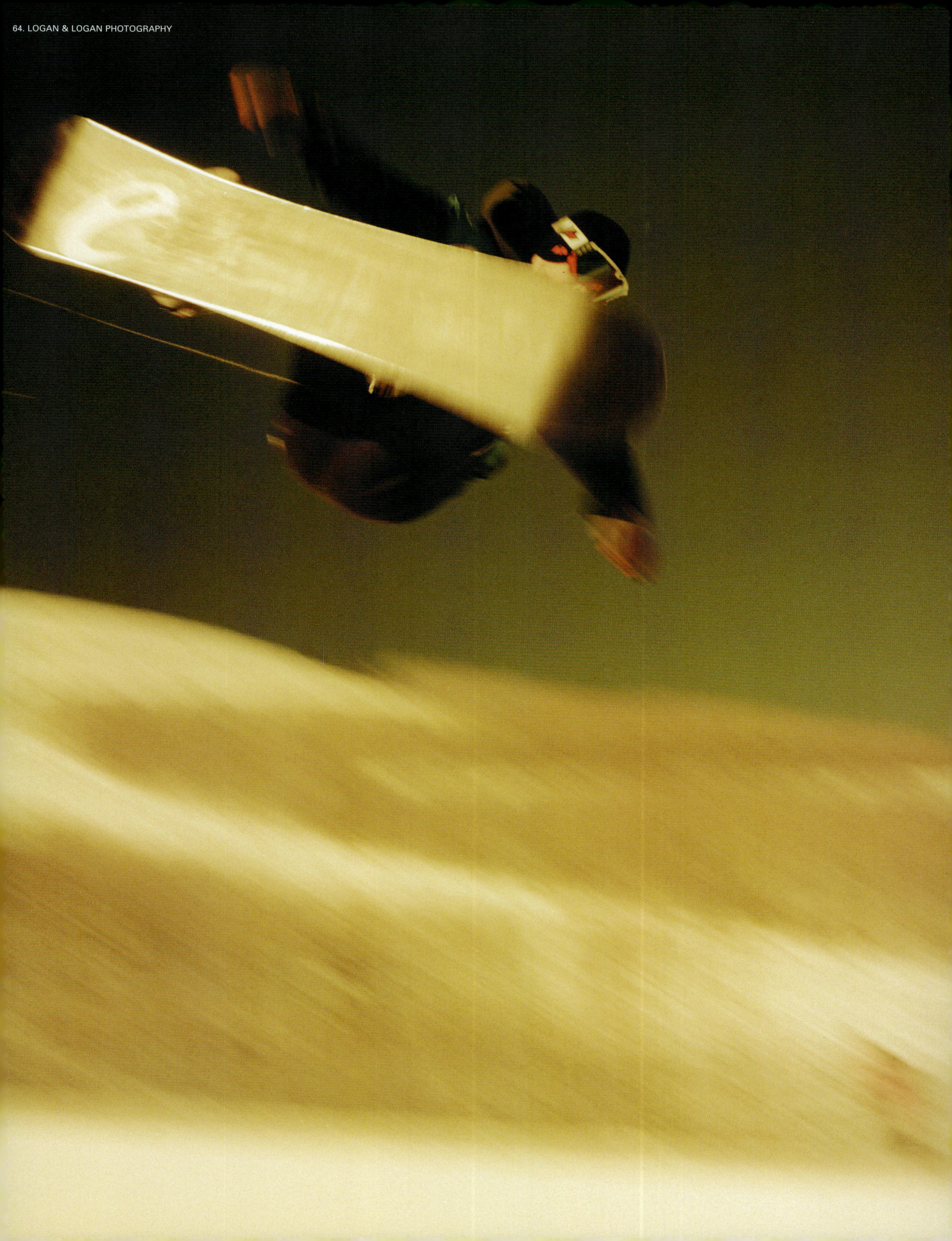

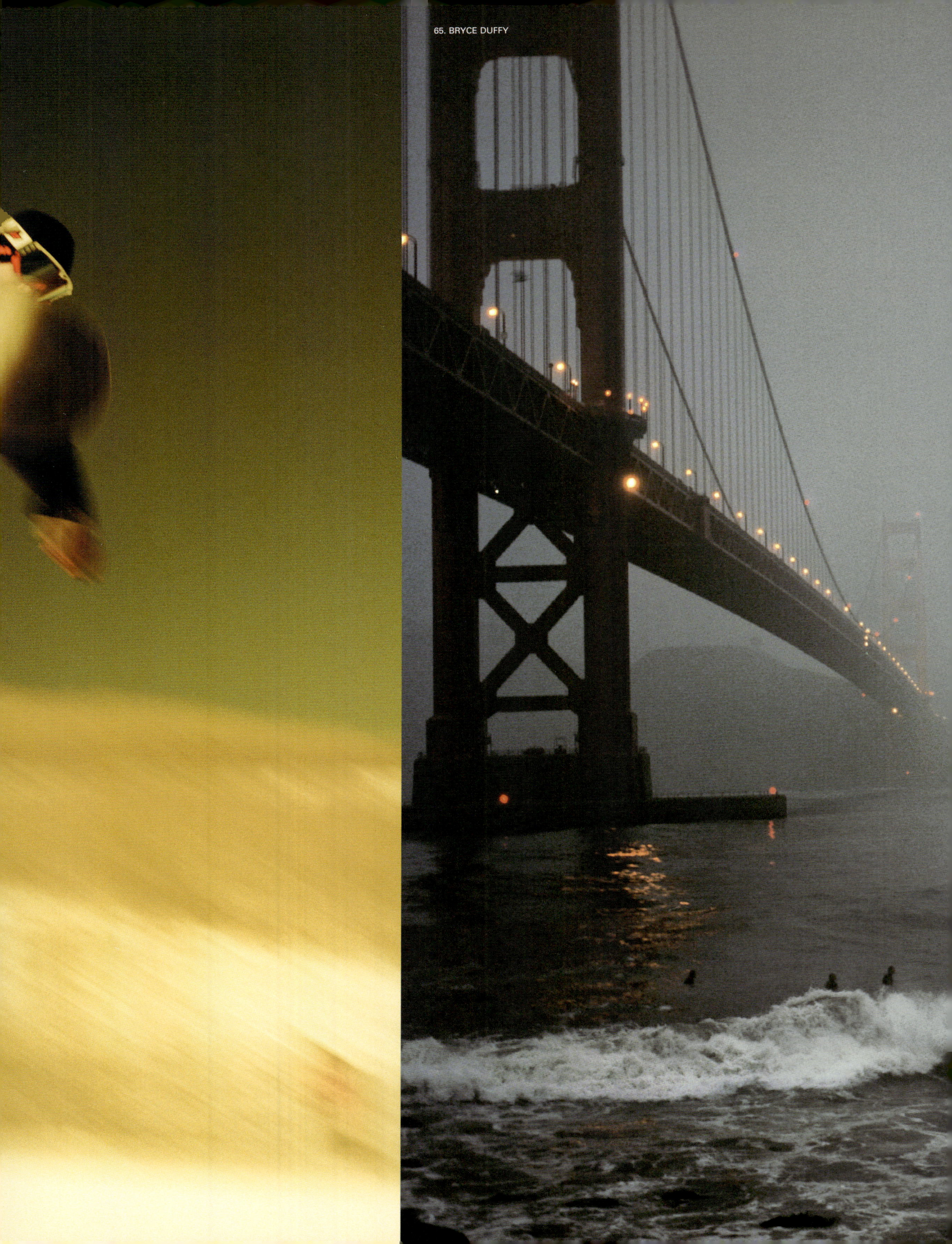

65. BRYCE DUFFY

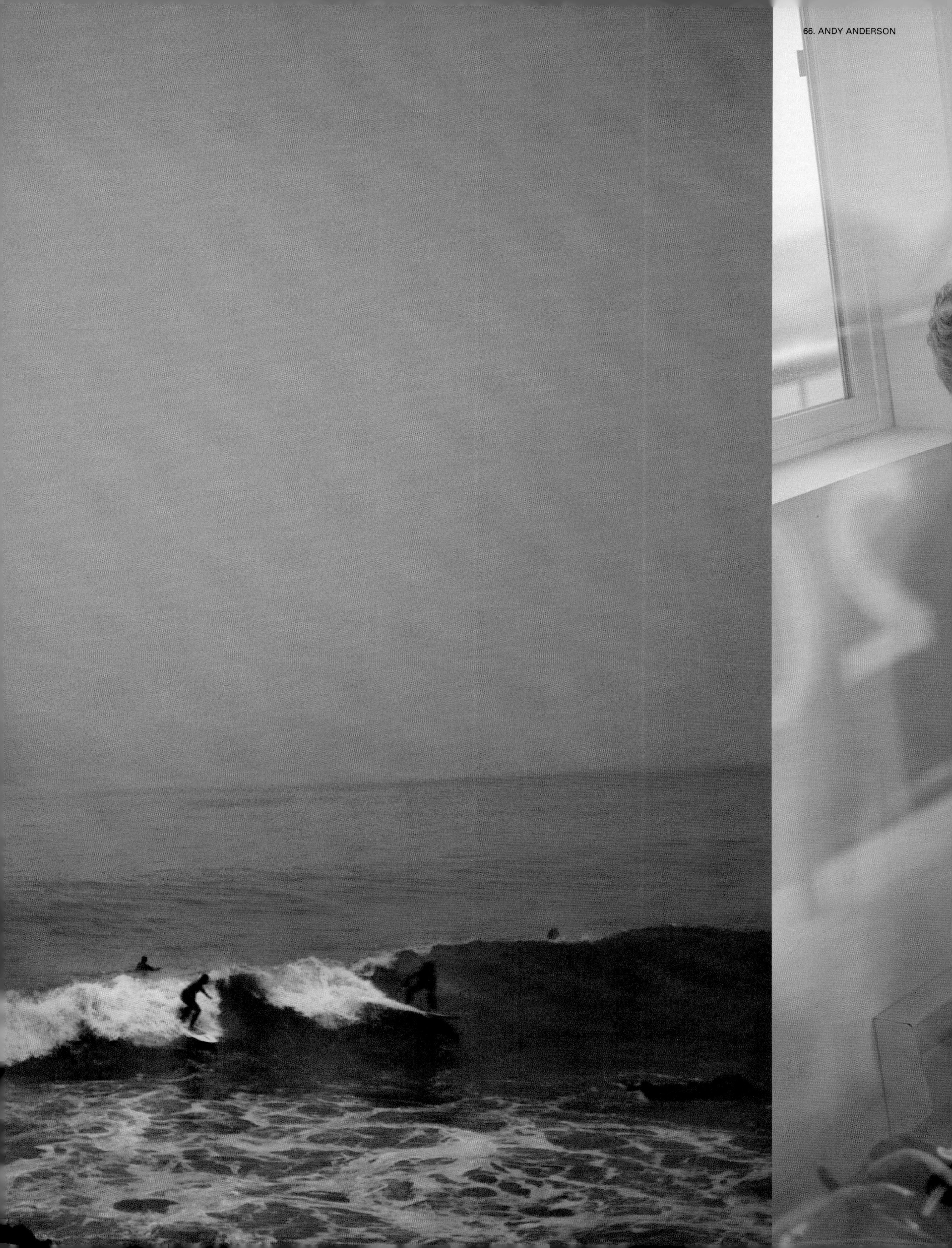

66. ANDY ANDERSON

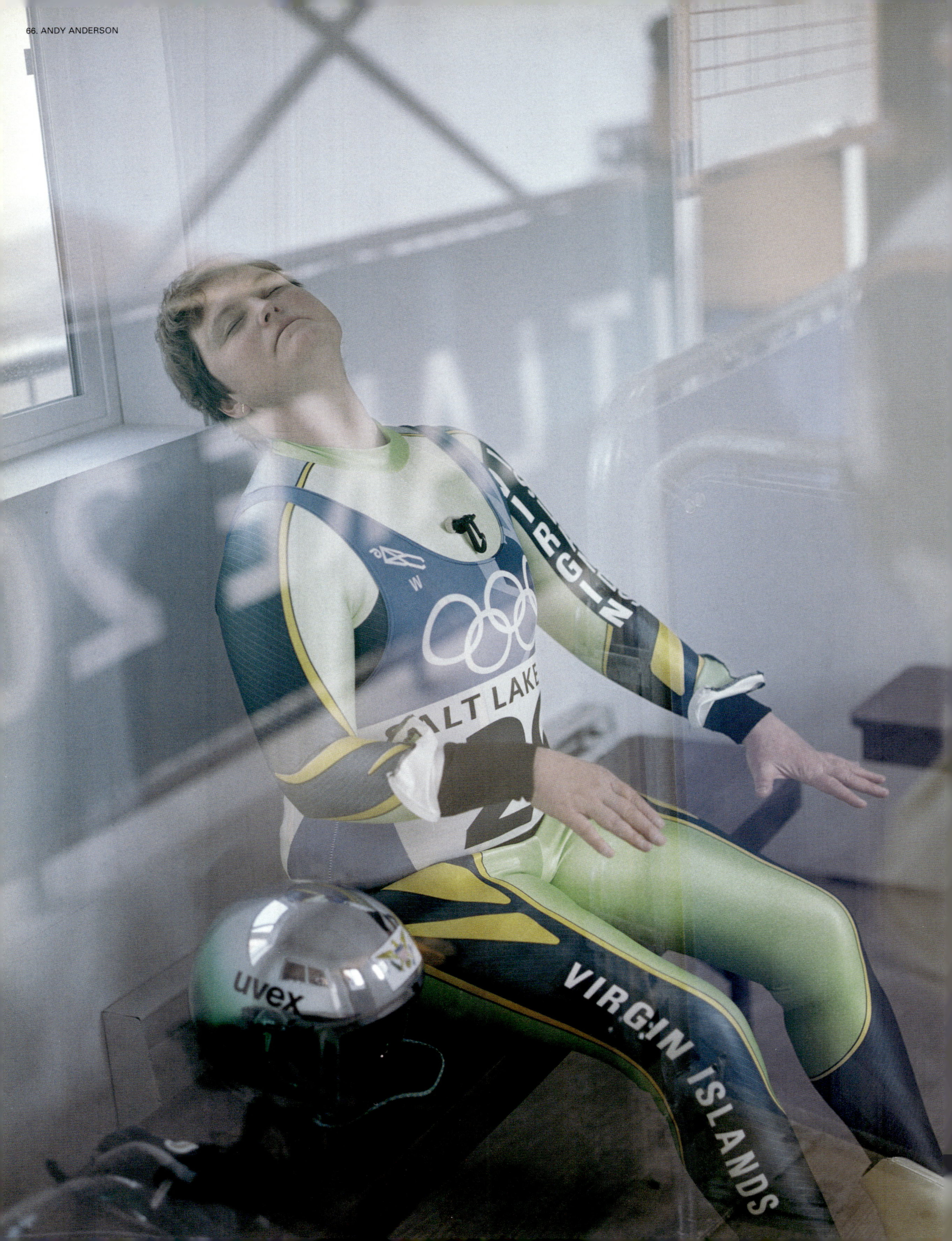

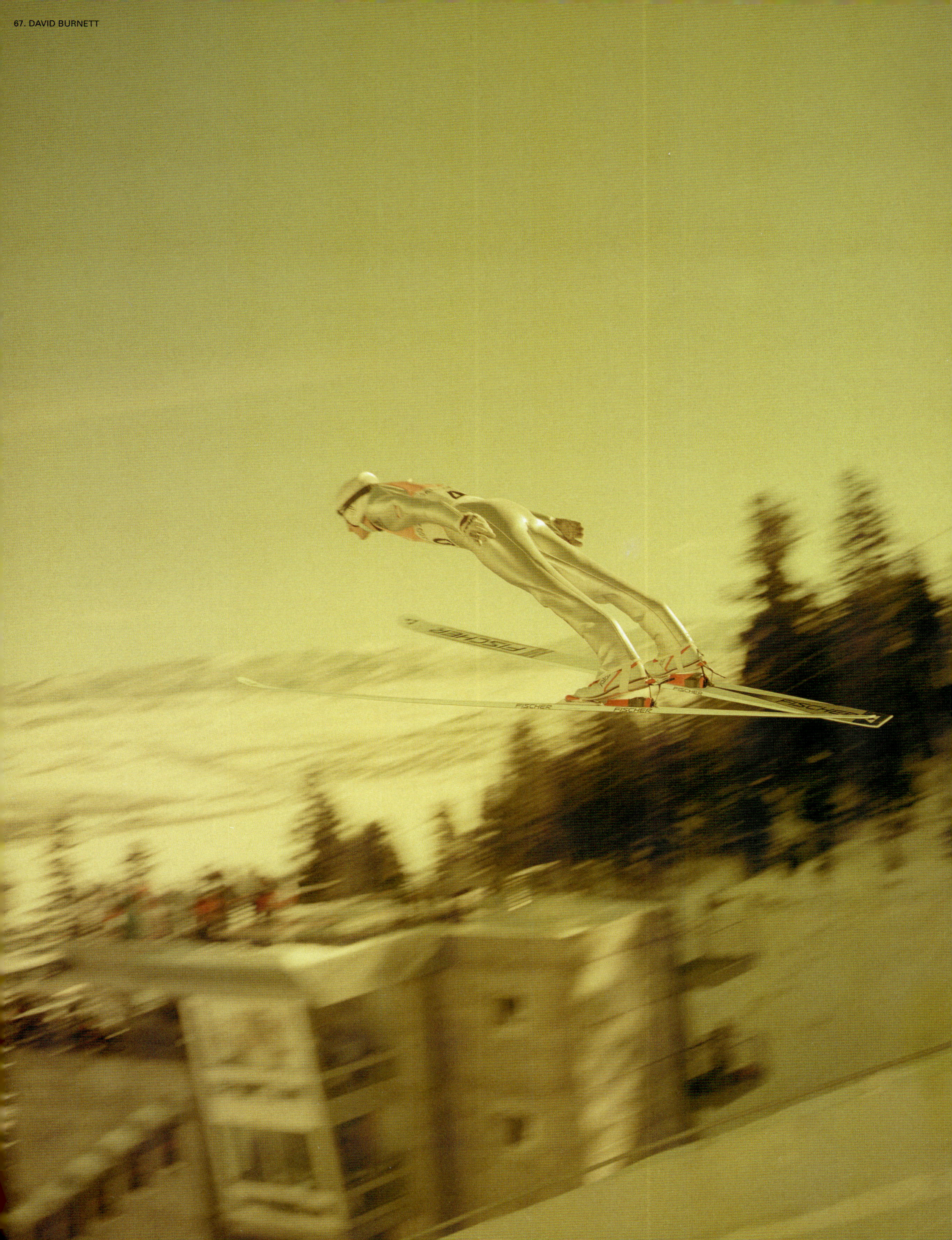

67. DAVID BURNETT

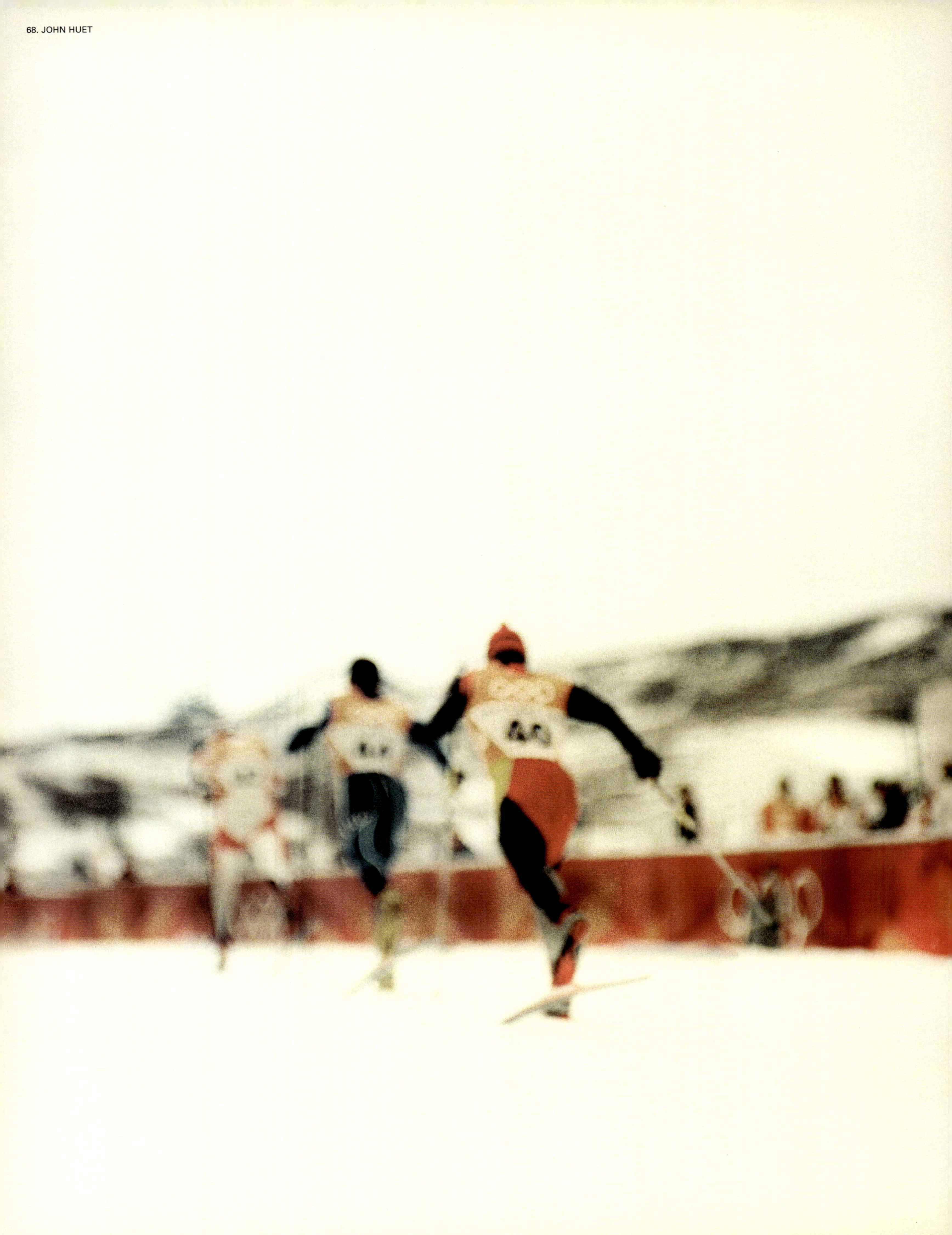
68. JOHN HUET

69. JOHN HUET

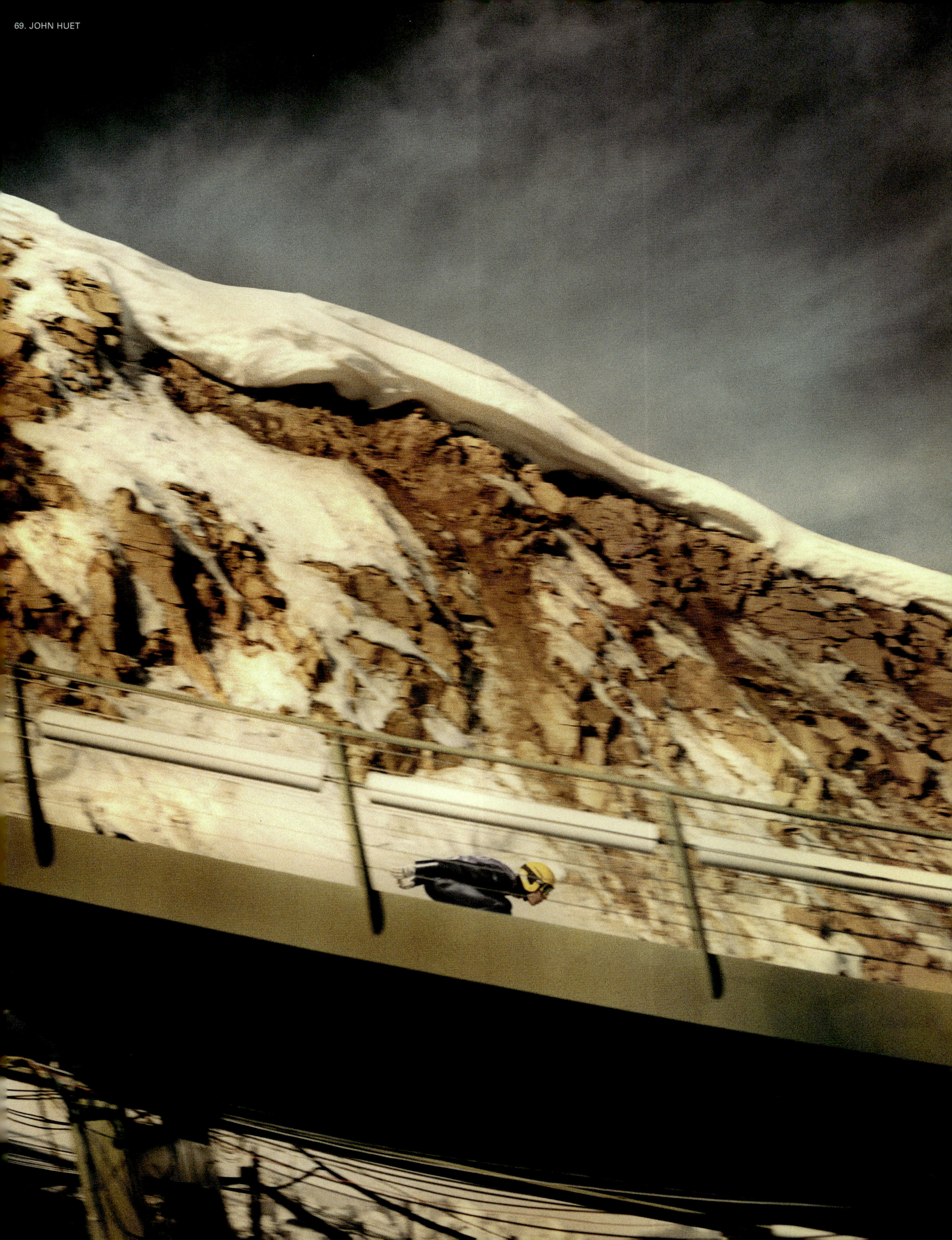

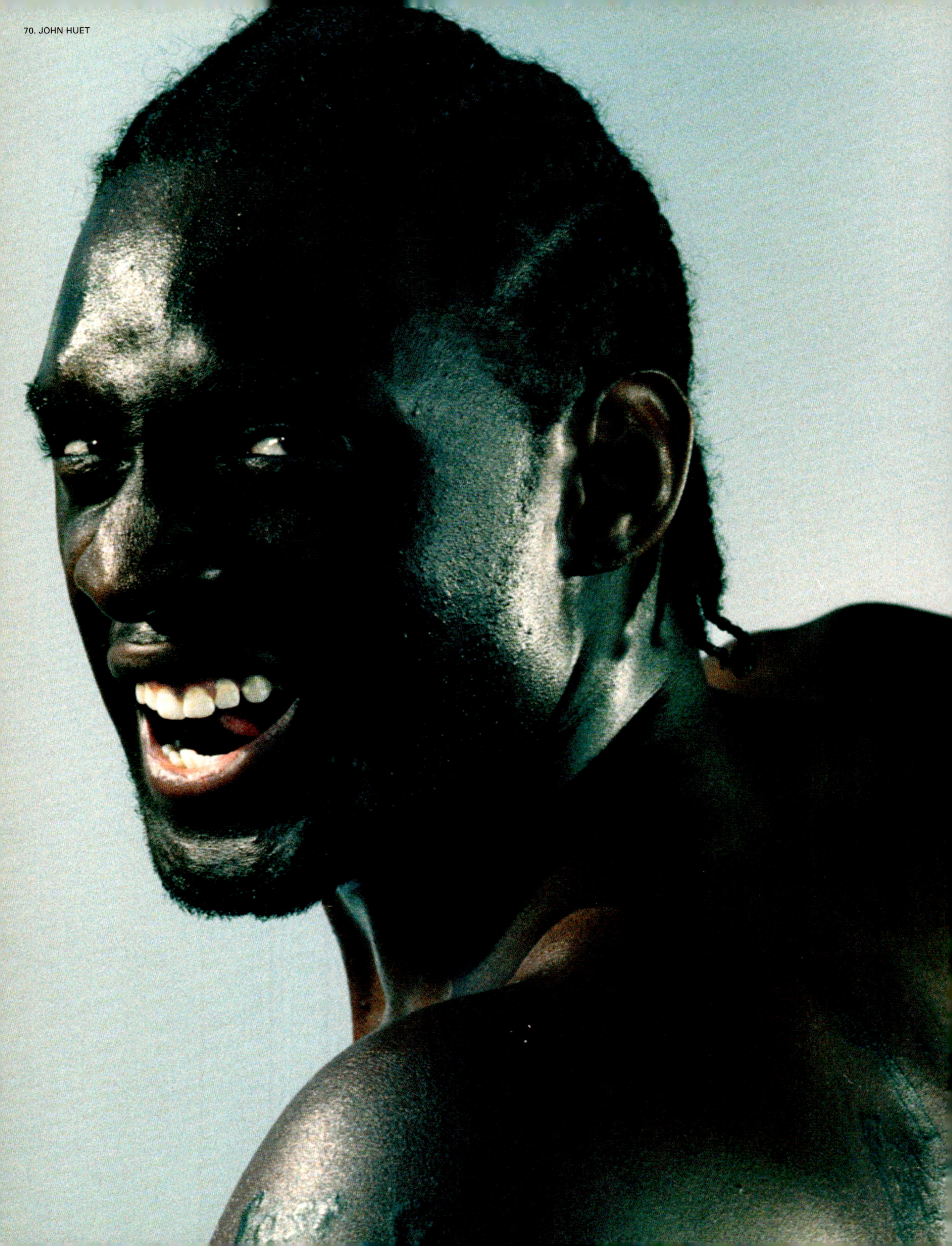

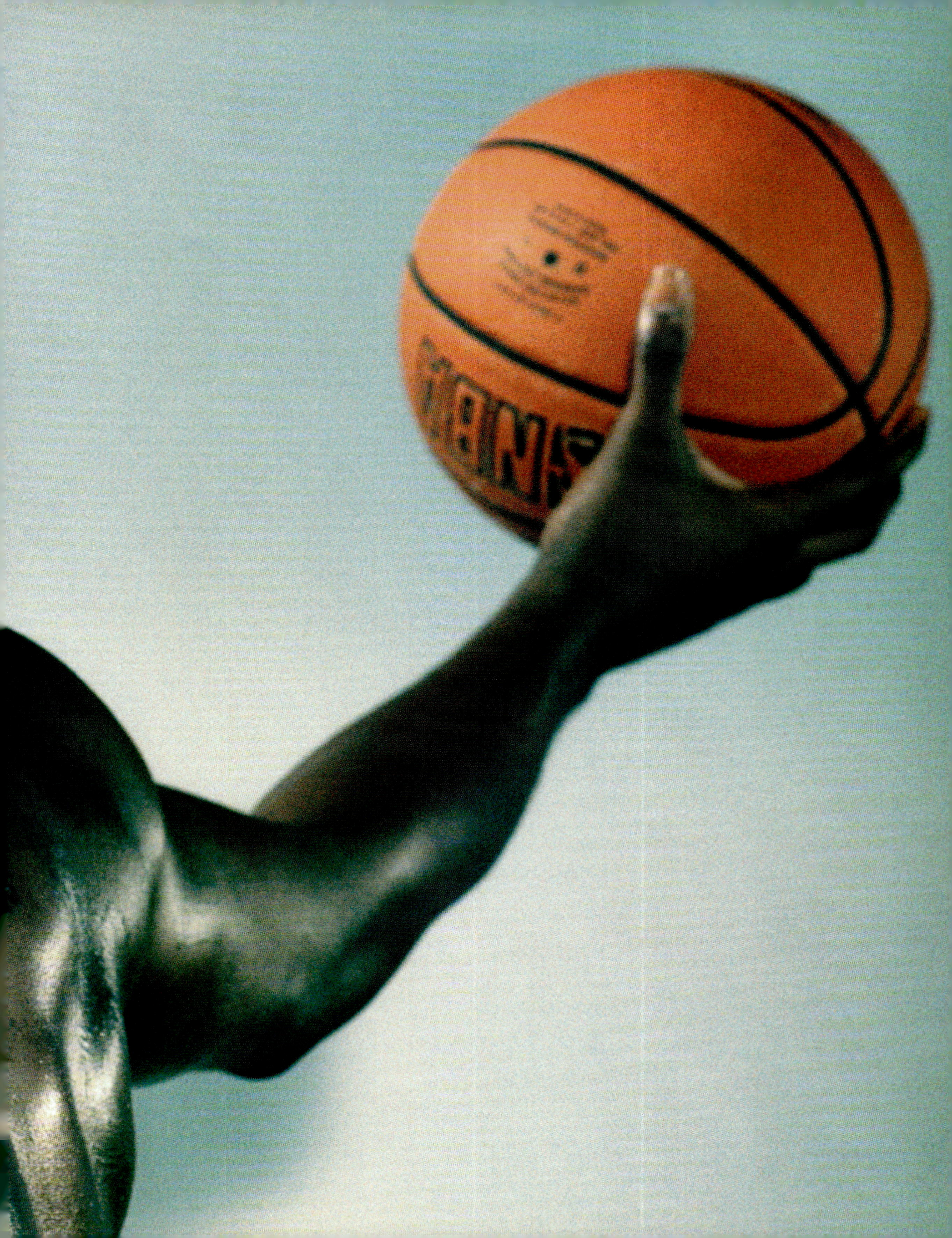

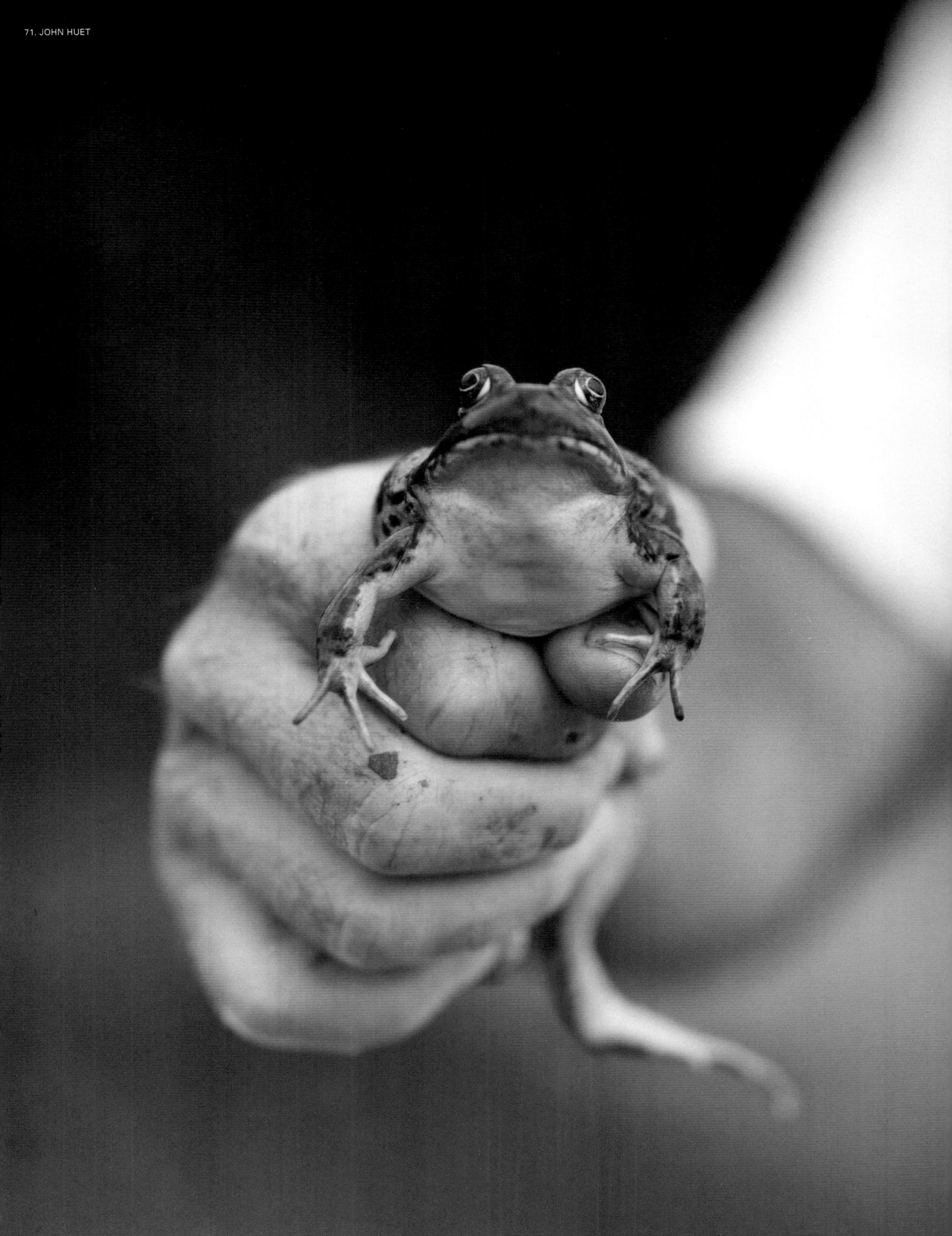

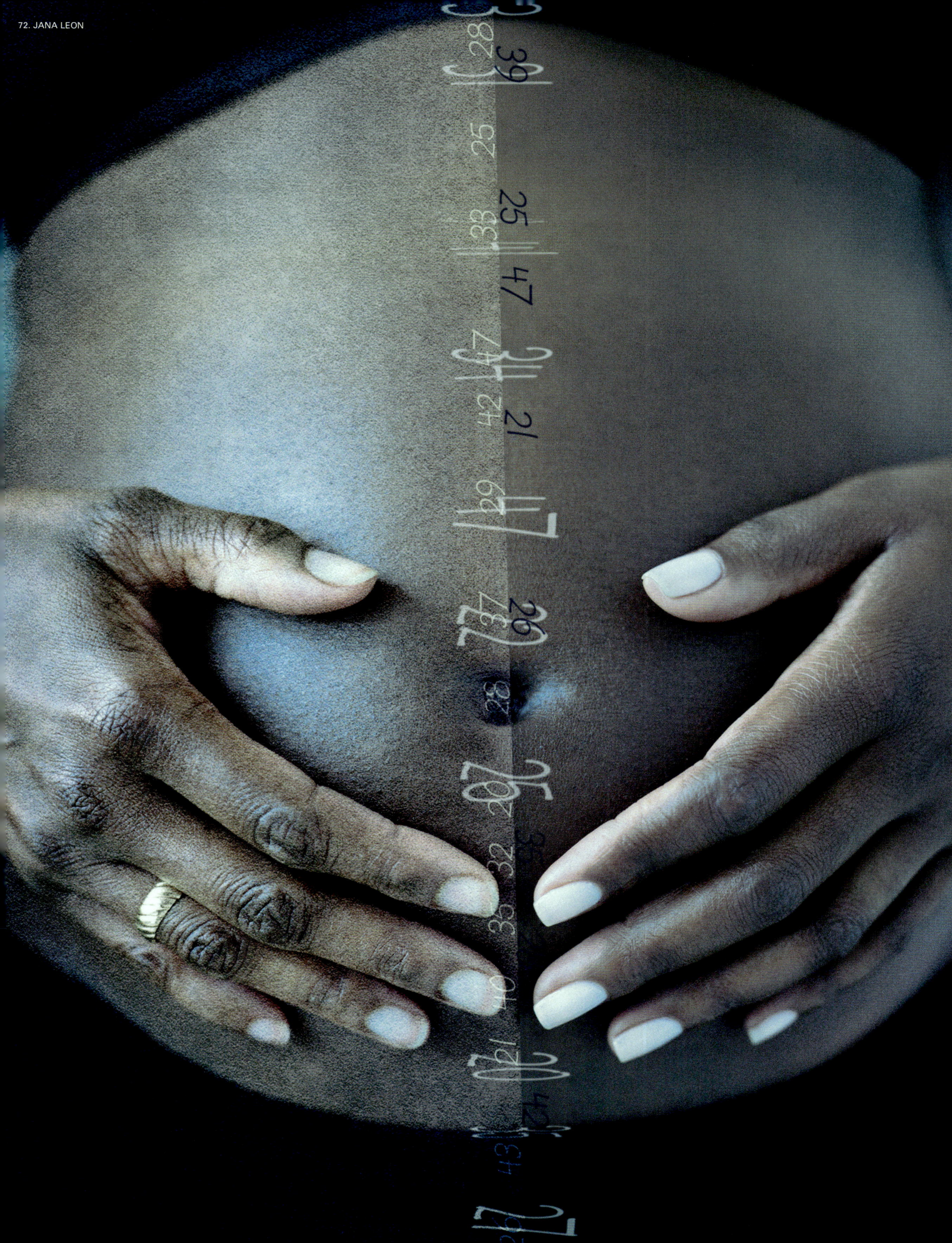

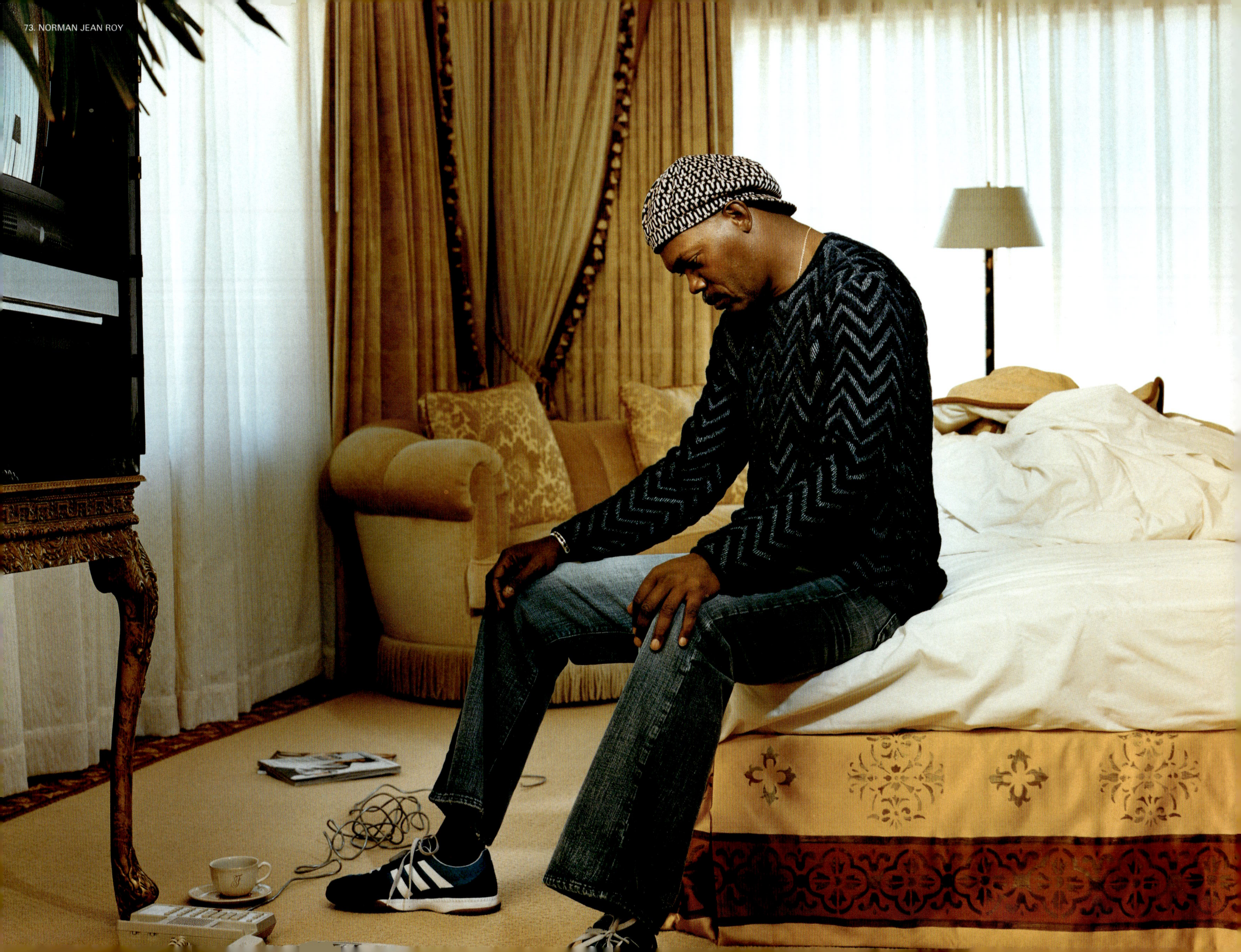

73. NORMAN JEAN ROY

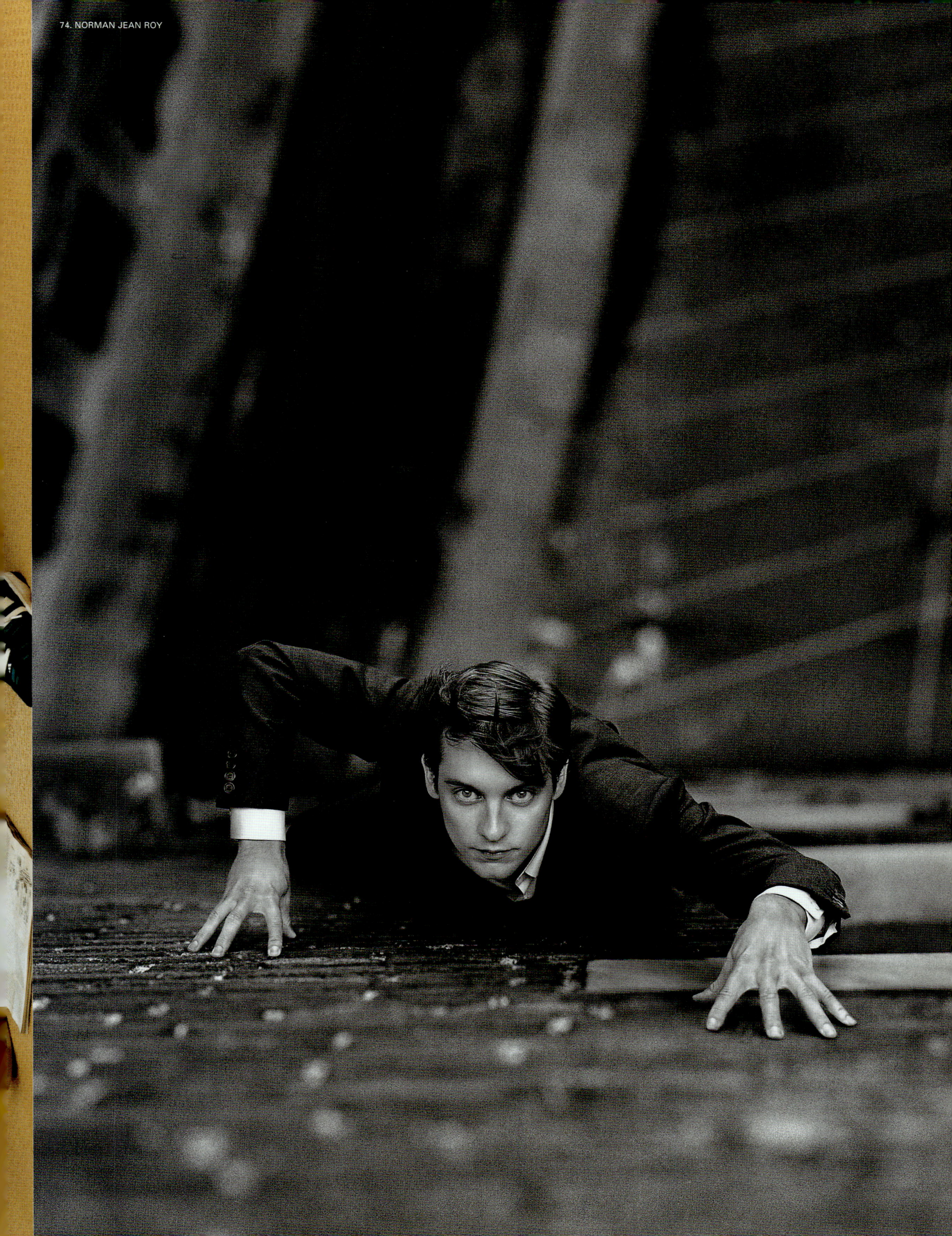

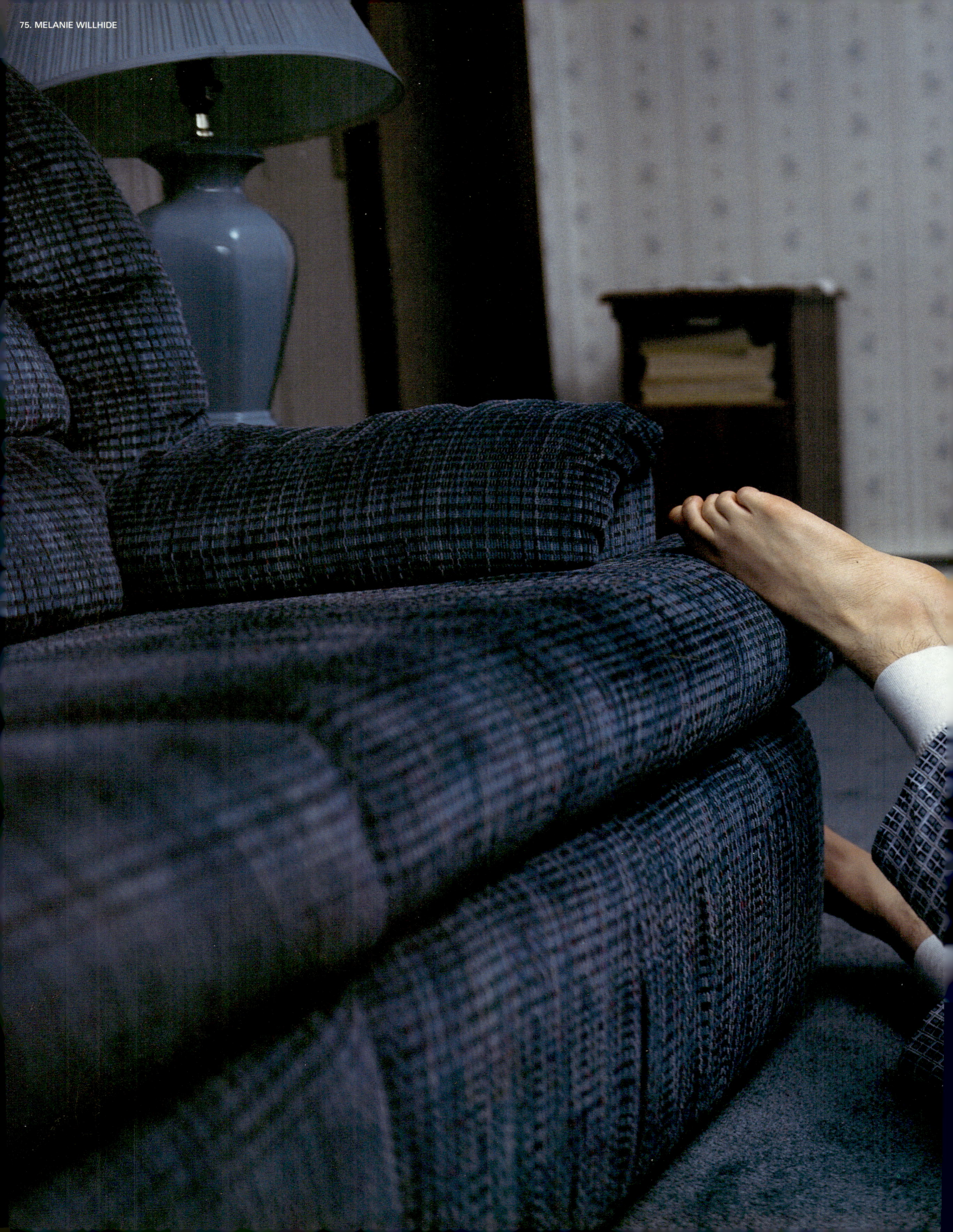

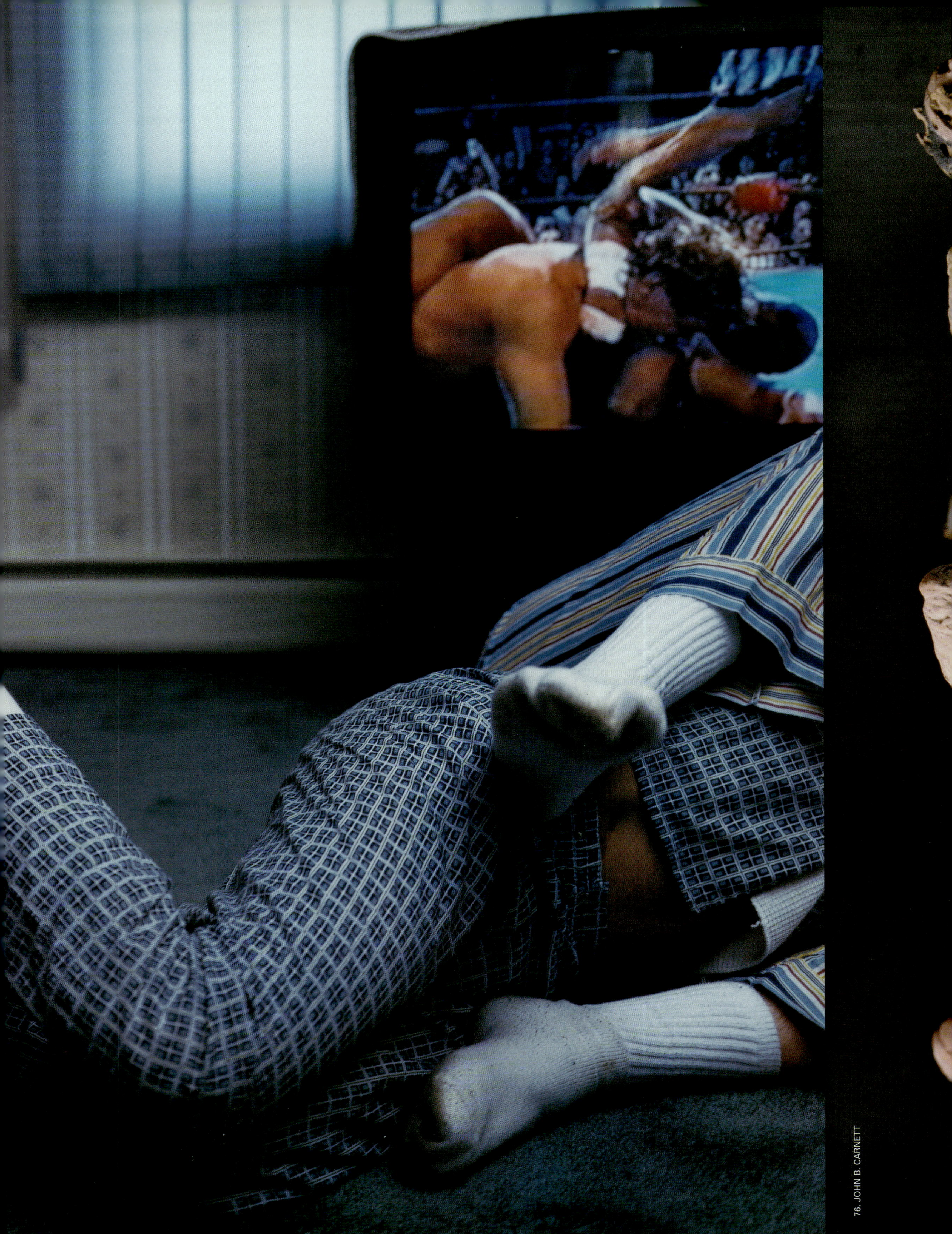

76. JOHN B. CARNETT

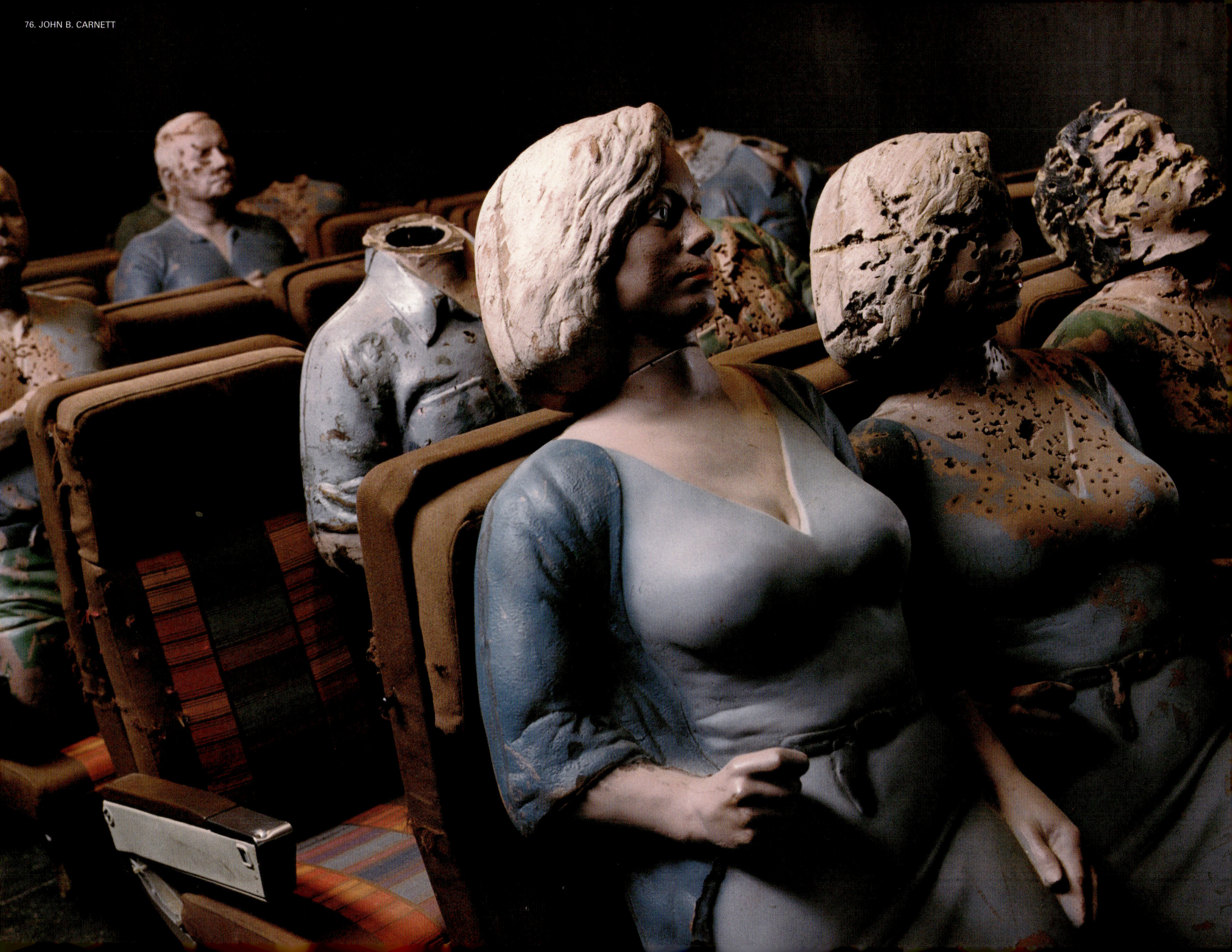

76. JOHN B. CARNETT

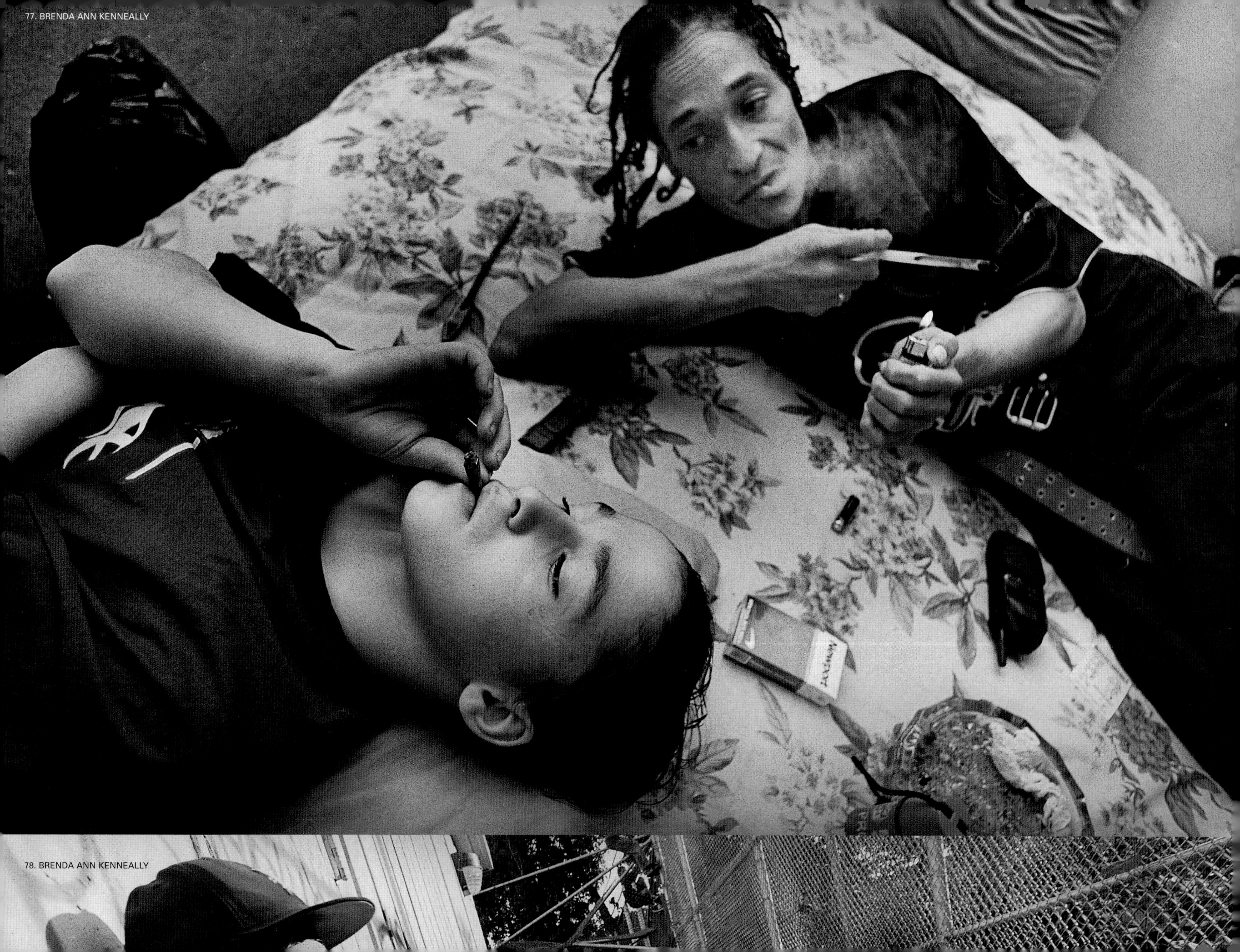

77. BRENDA ANN KENNEALLY

78. BRENDA ANN KENNEALLY

78. BRENDA ANN KENNEALLY

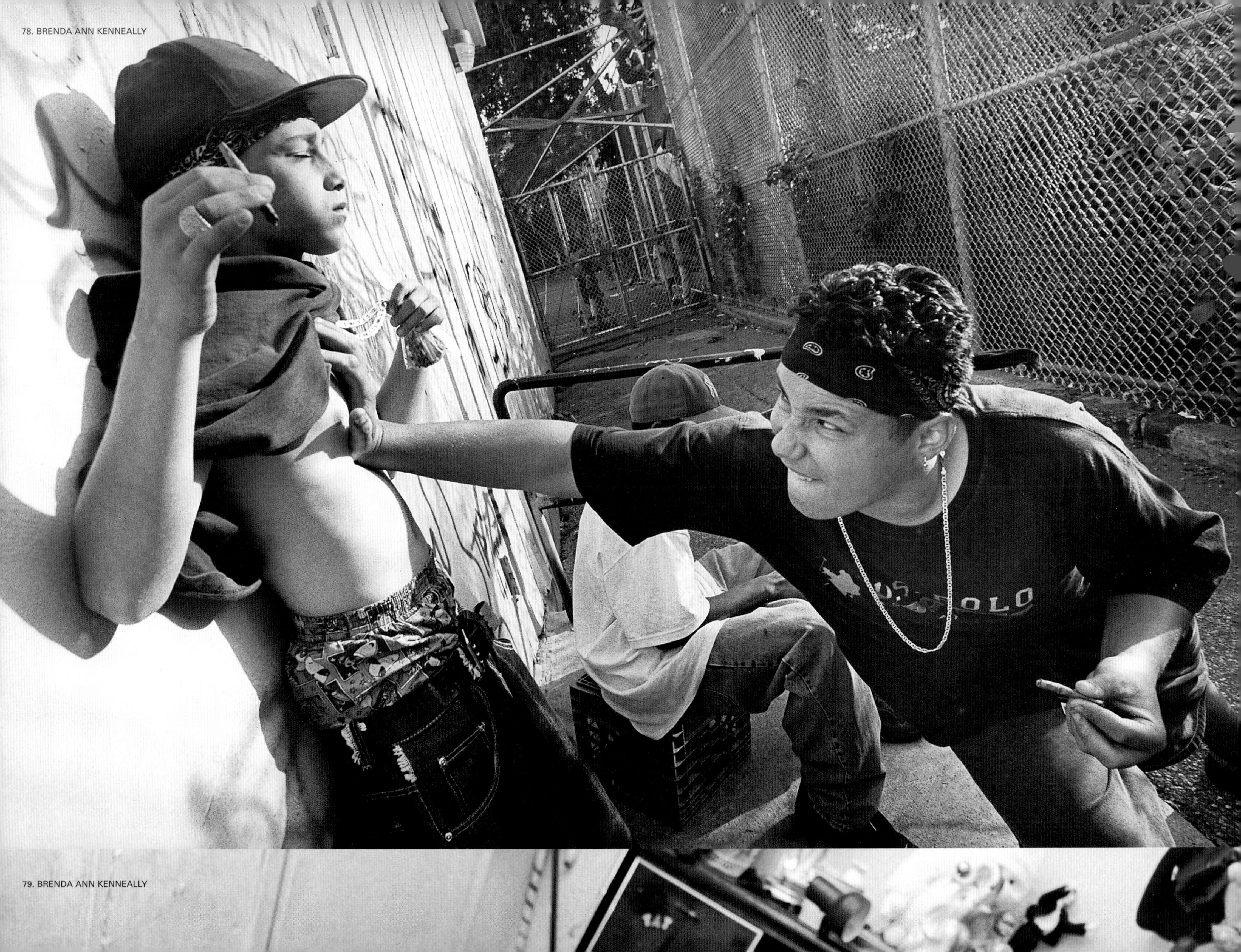

79. BRENDA ANN KENNEALLY

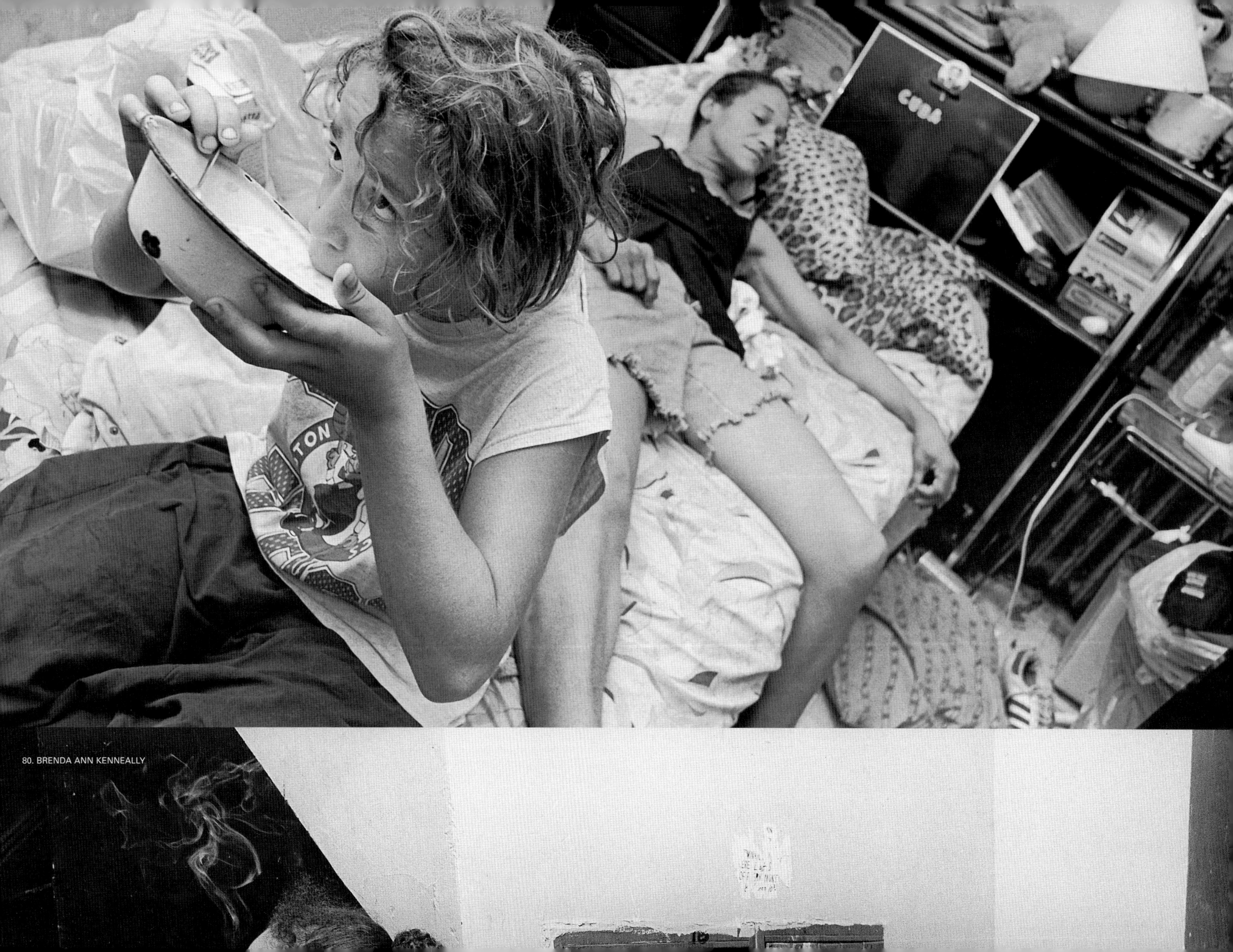

80. BRENDA ANN KENNEALLY

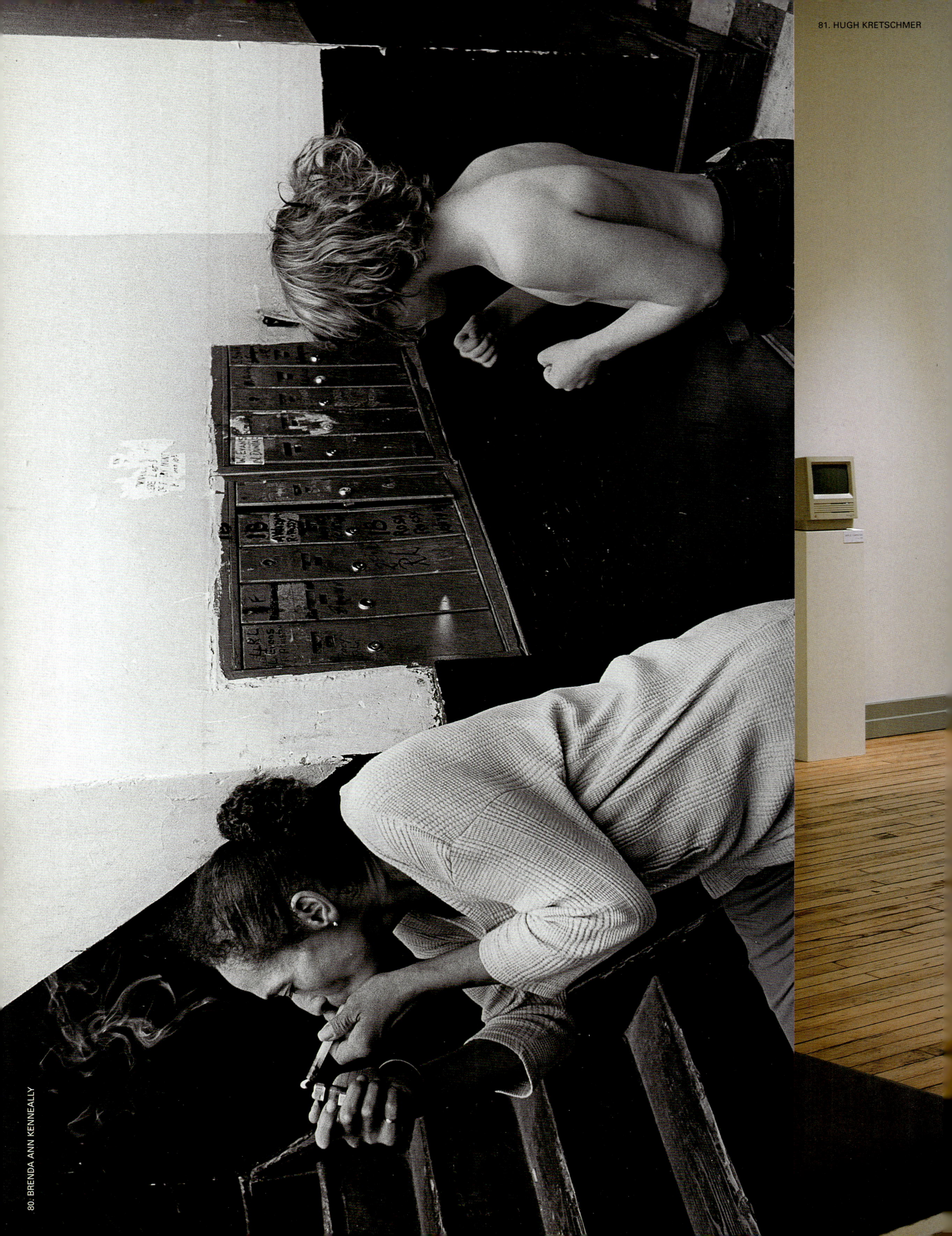

81. HUGH KRETSCHMER

80. BRENDA ANN KENNEALLY

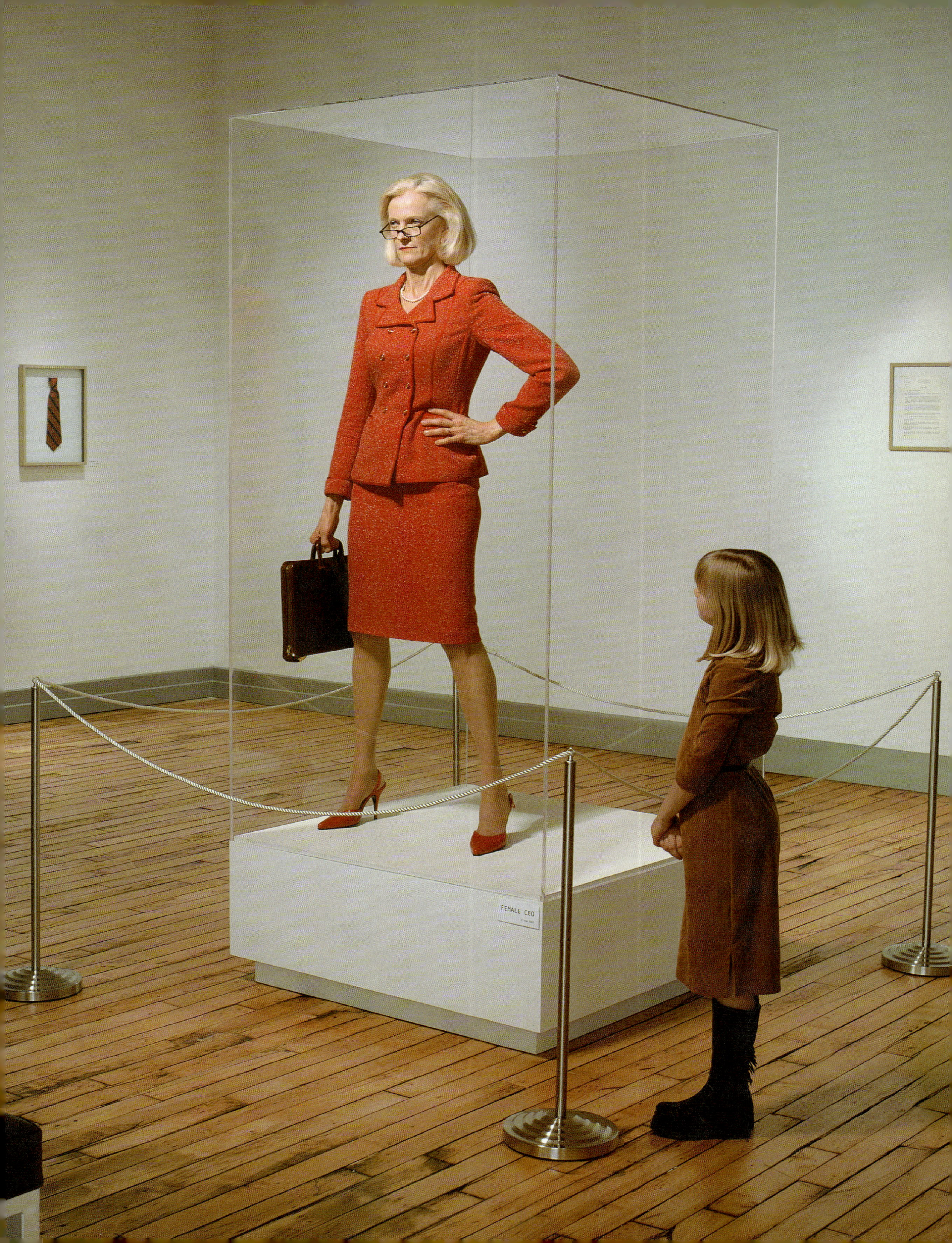
FEMALE CEO

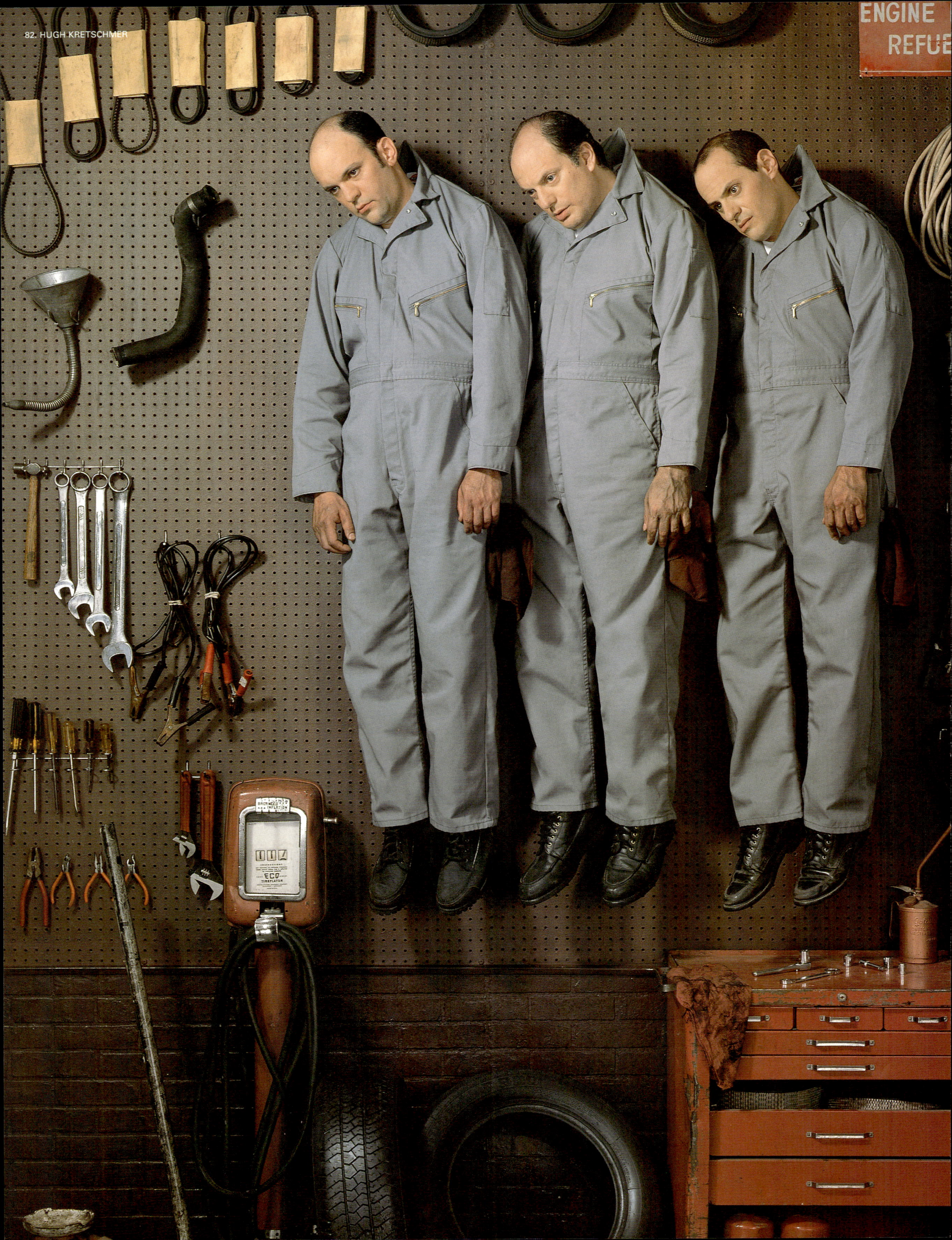
ENGINE
REFUE

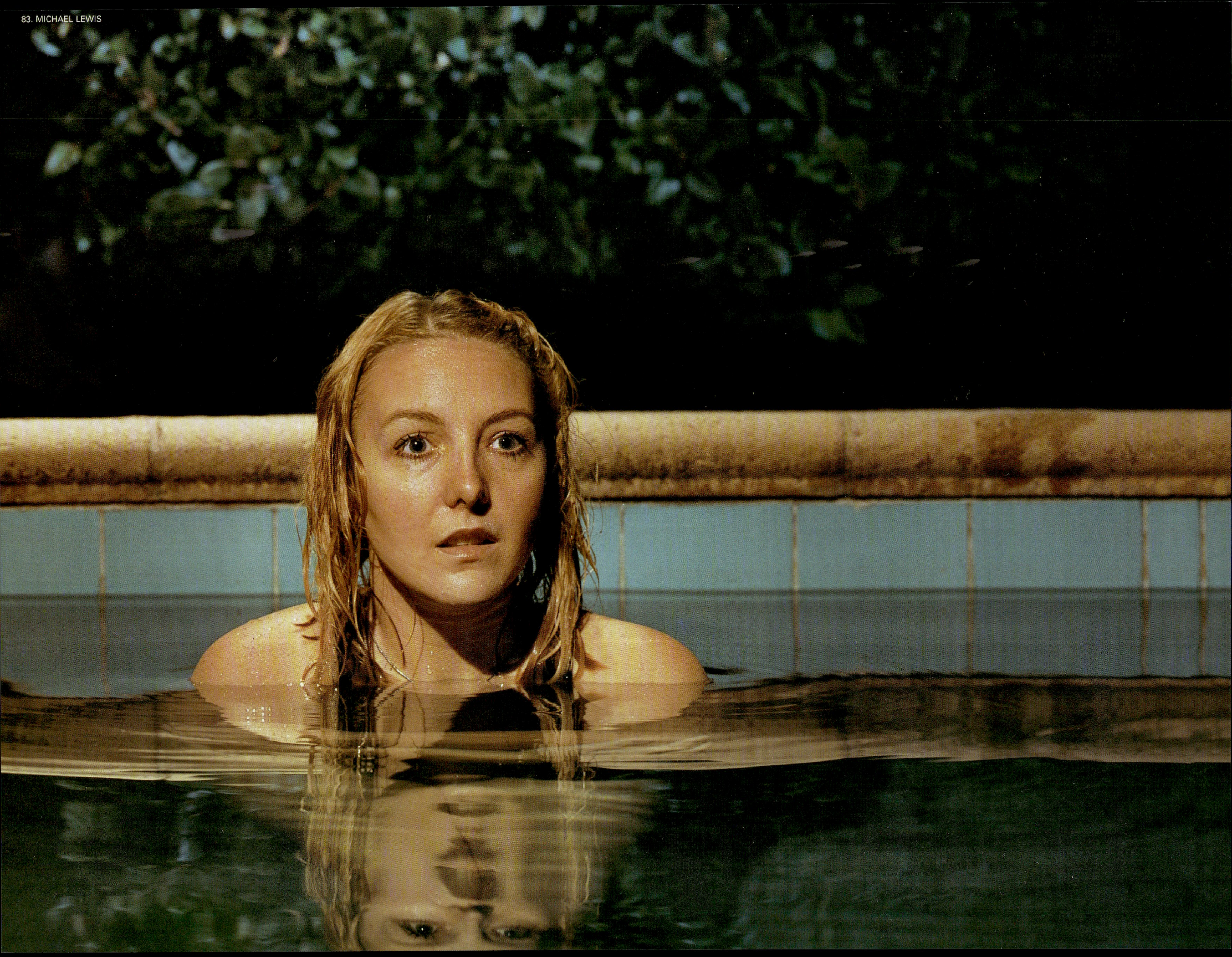

83. MICHAEL LEWIS

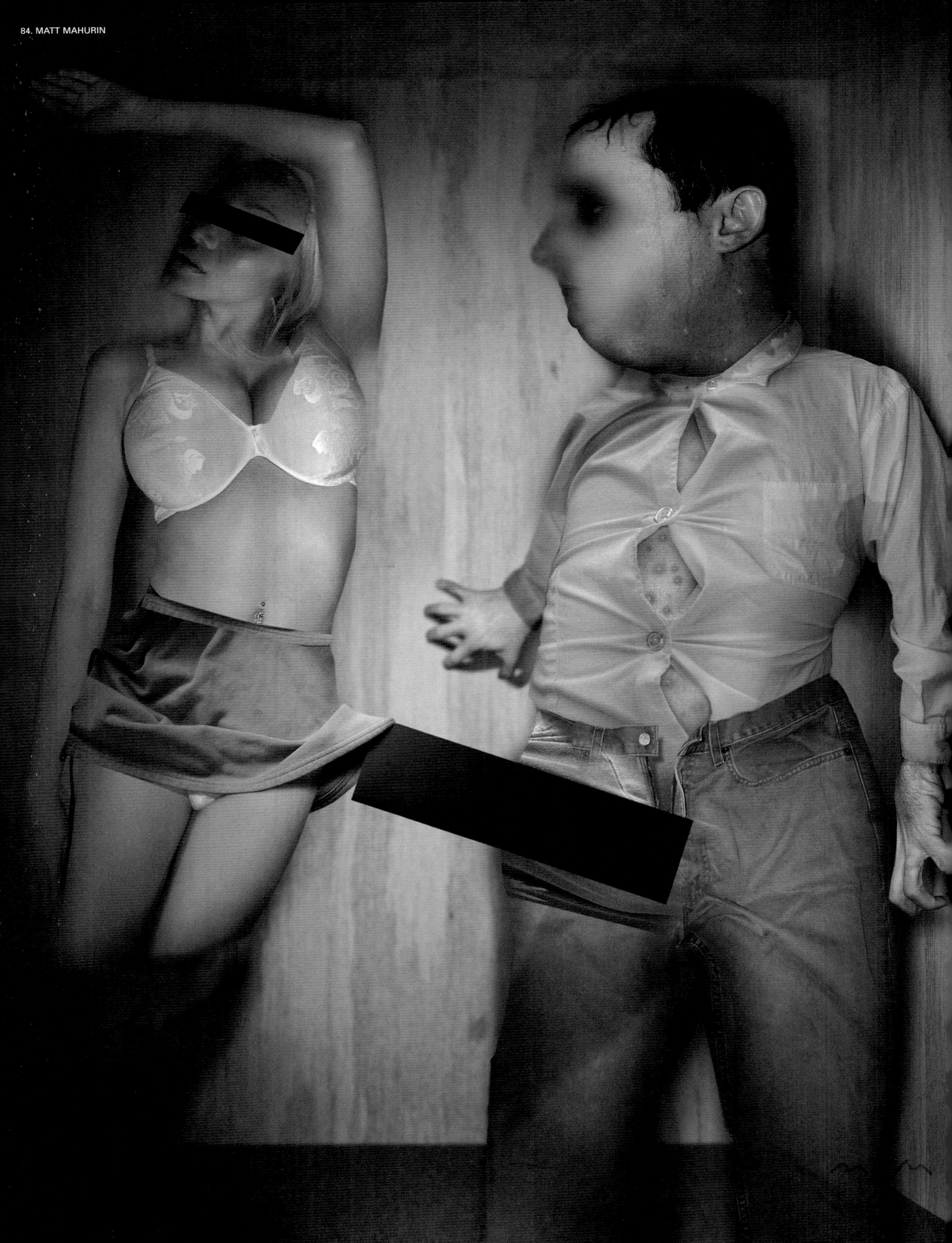

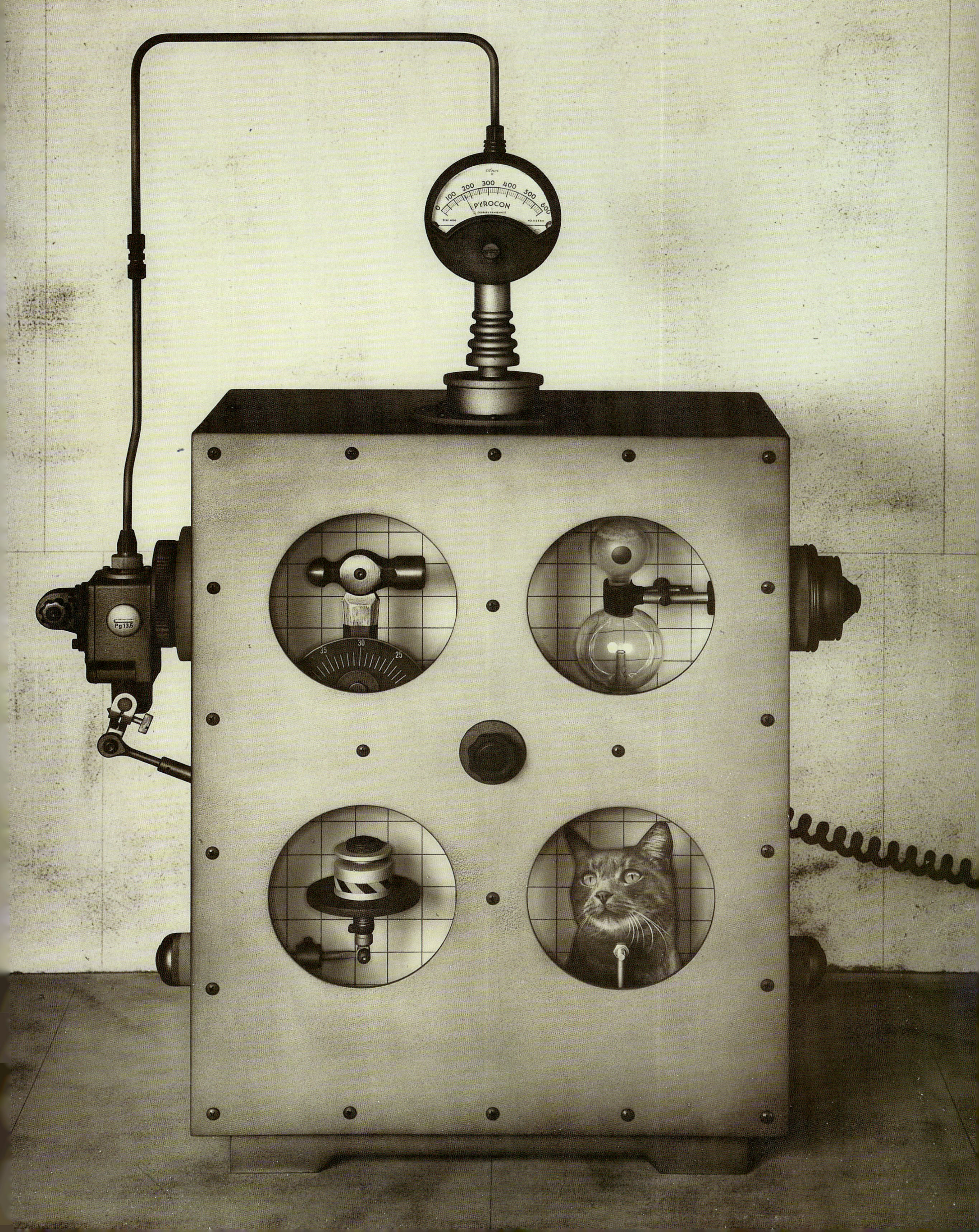

85. DAN WINTERS

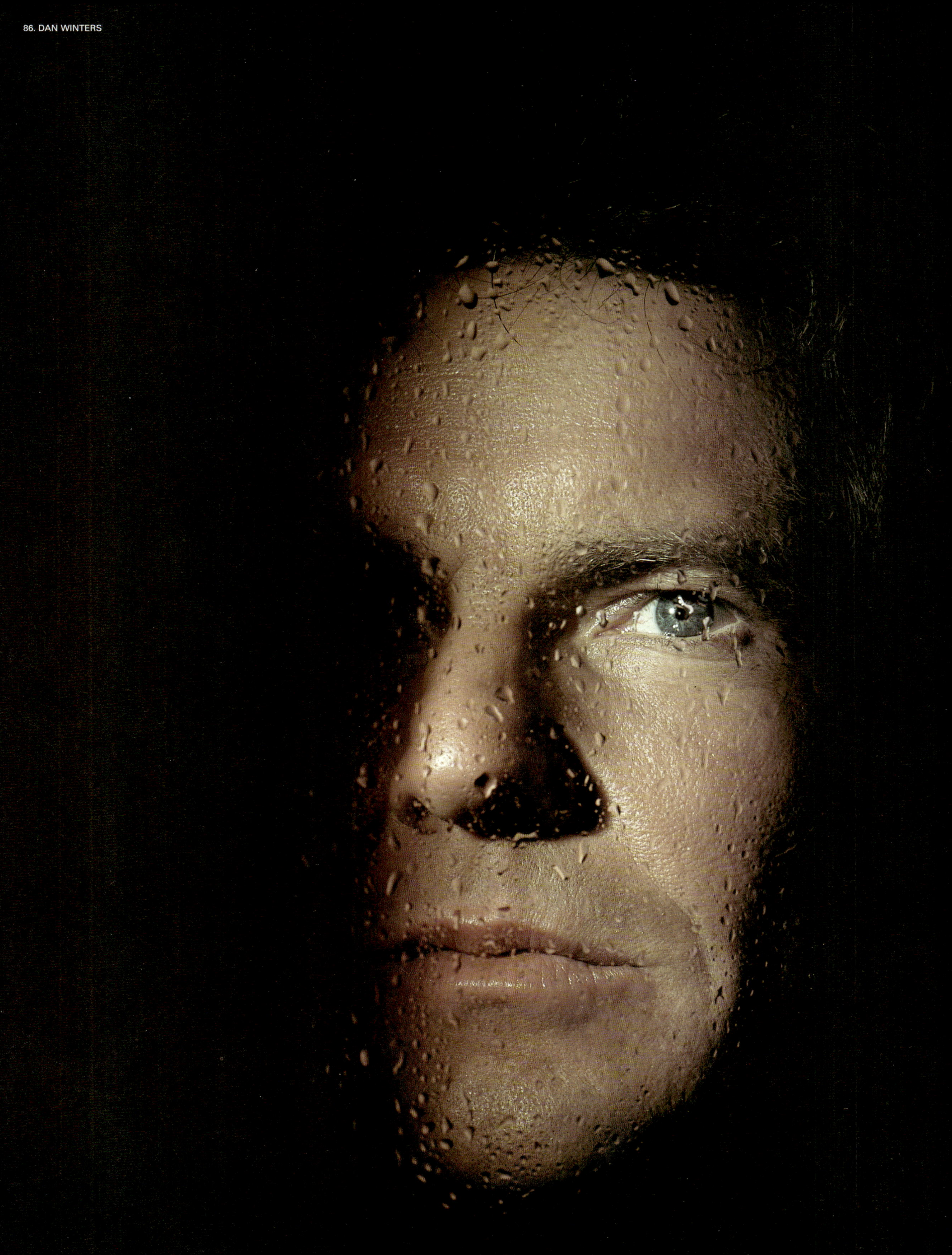

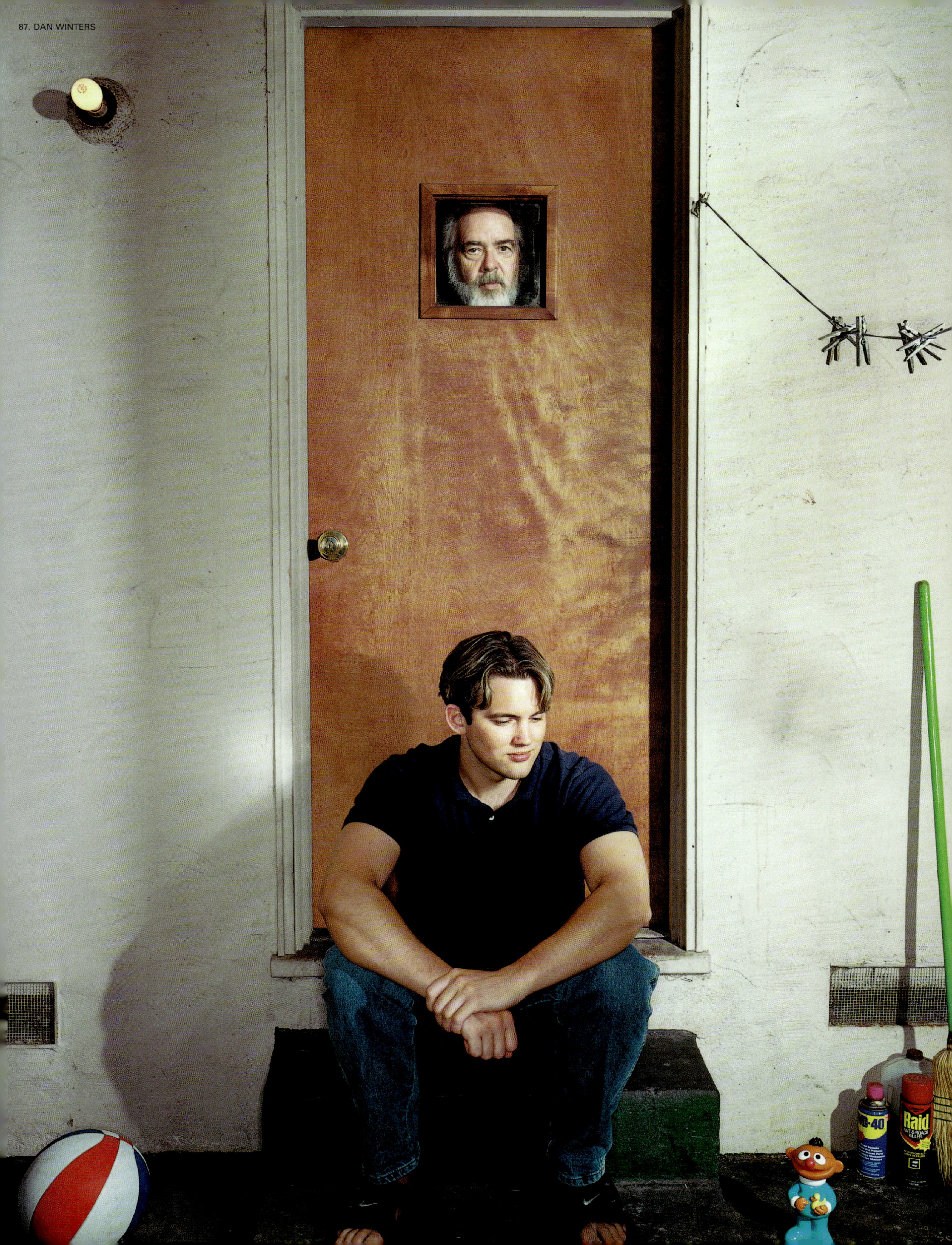

87. DAN WINTERS

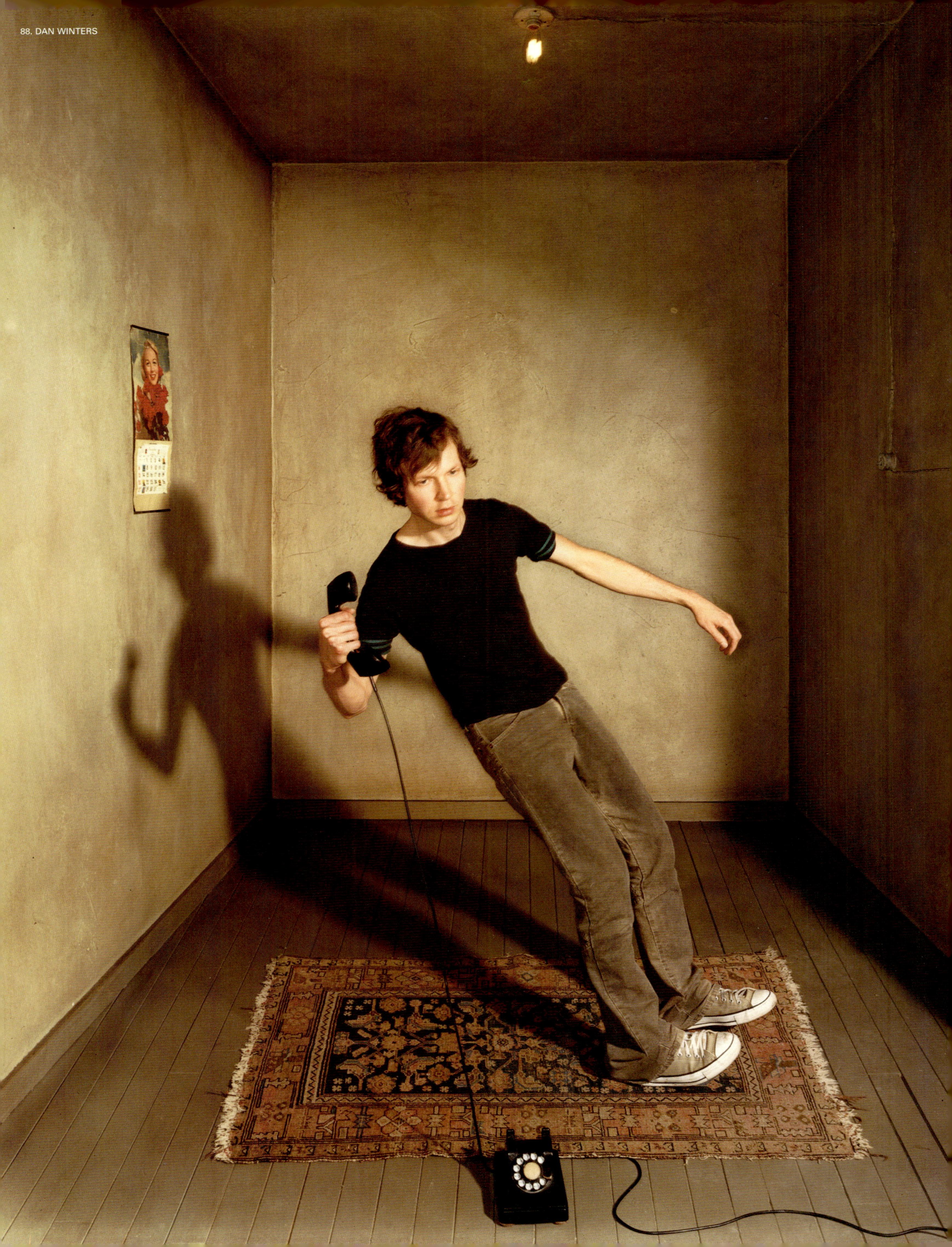

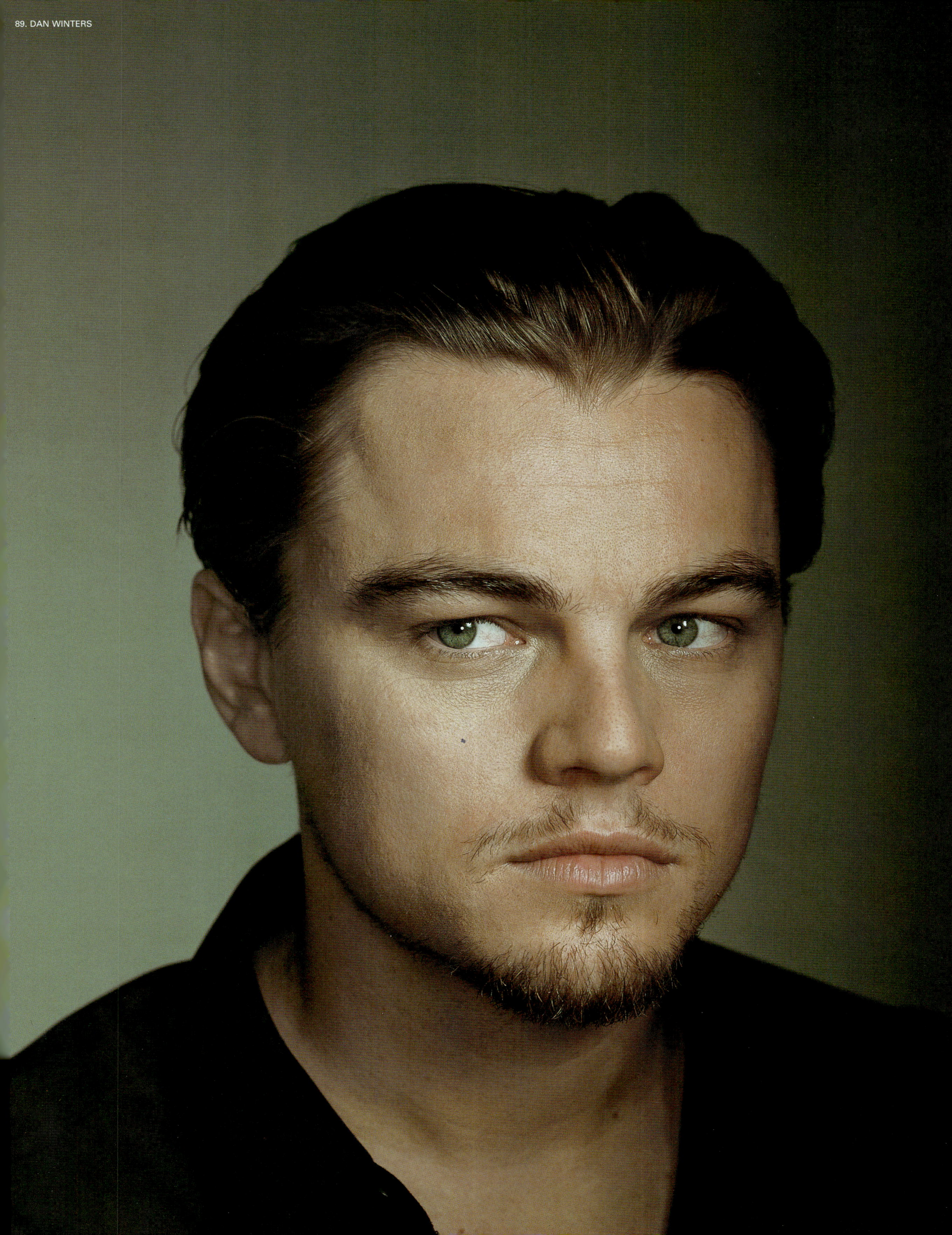

89. DAN WINTERS

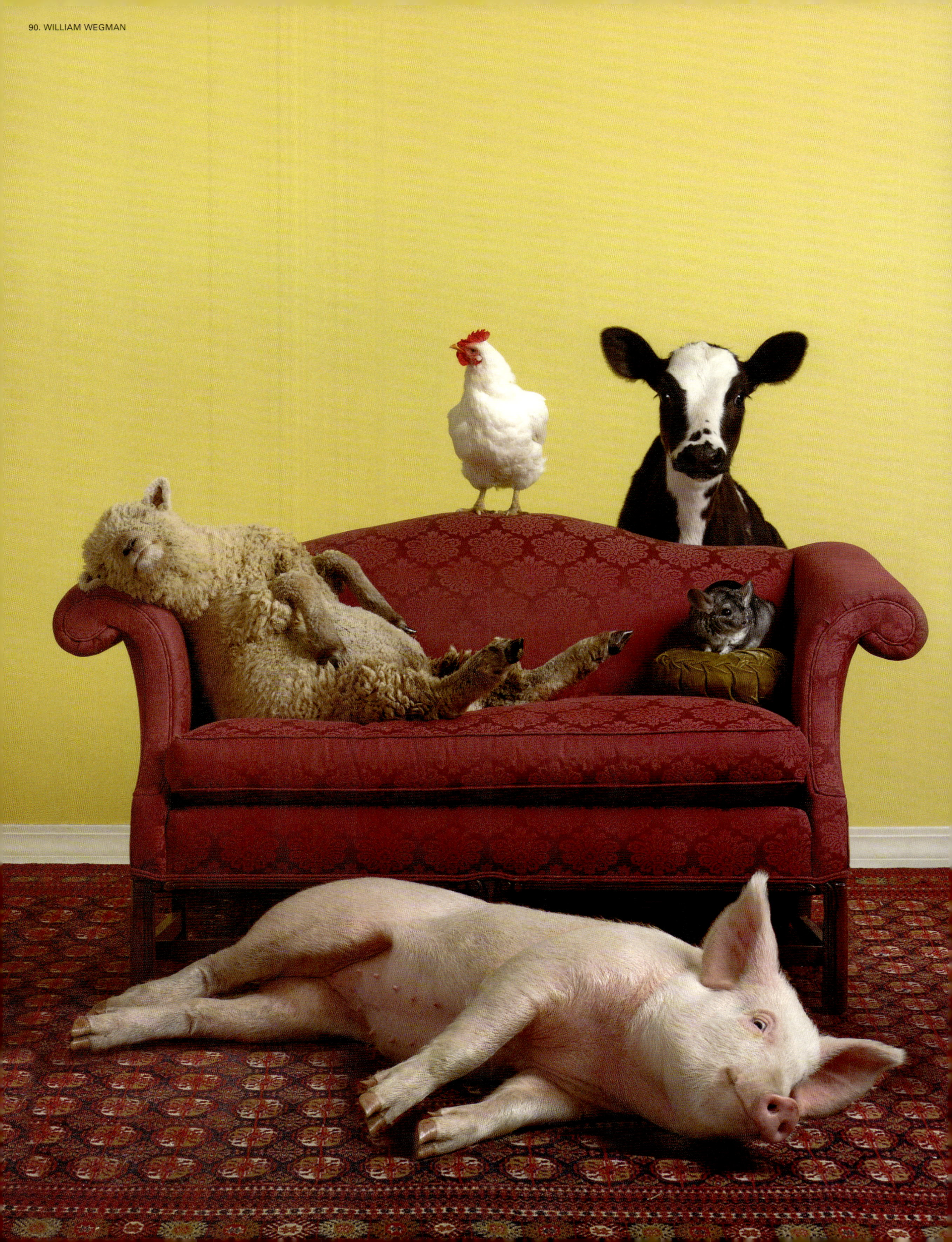

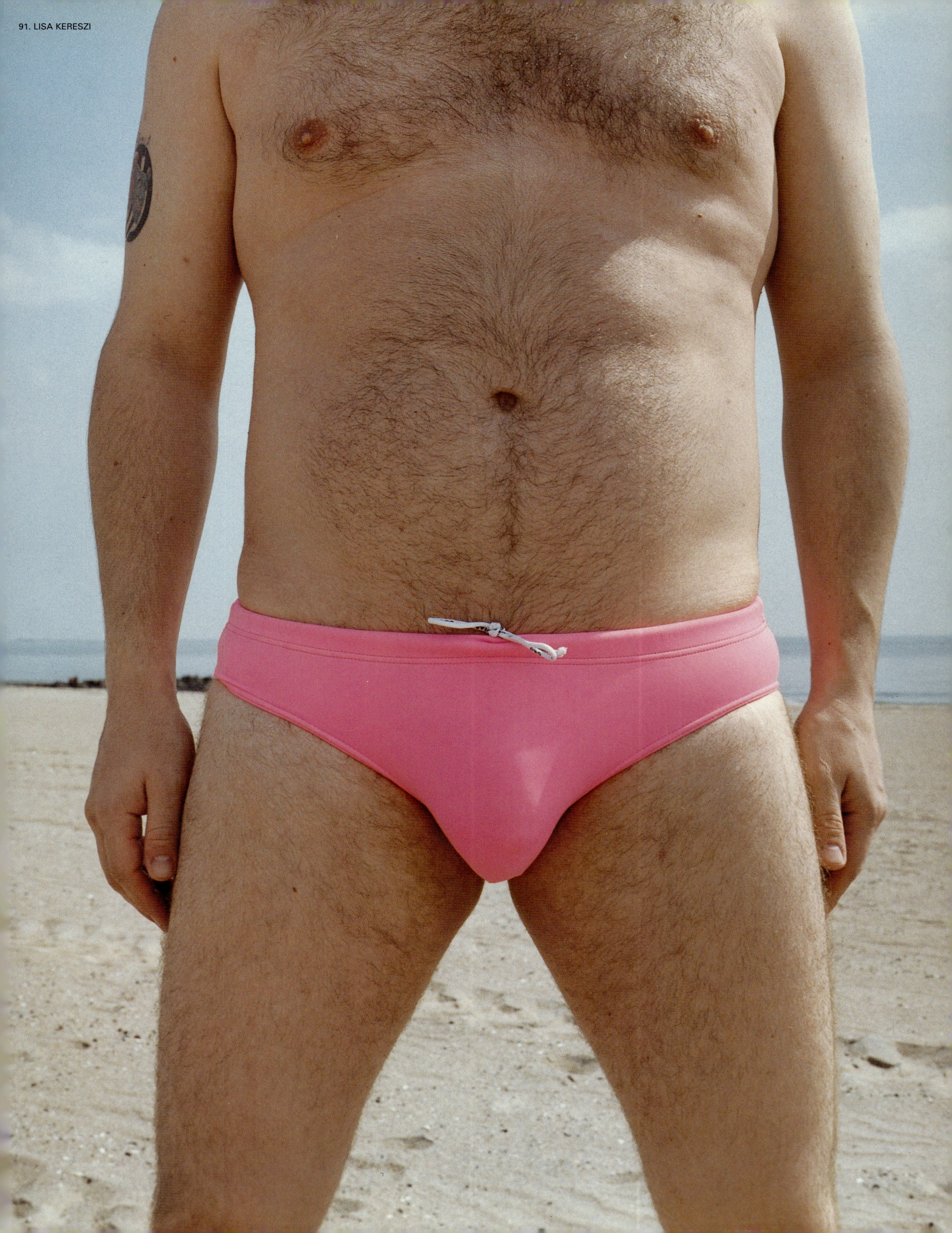

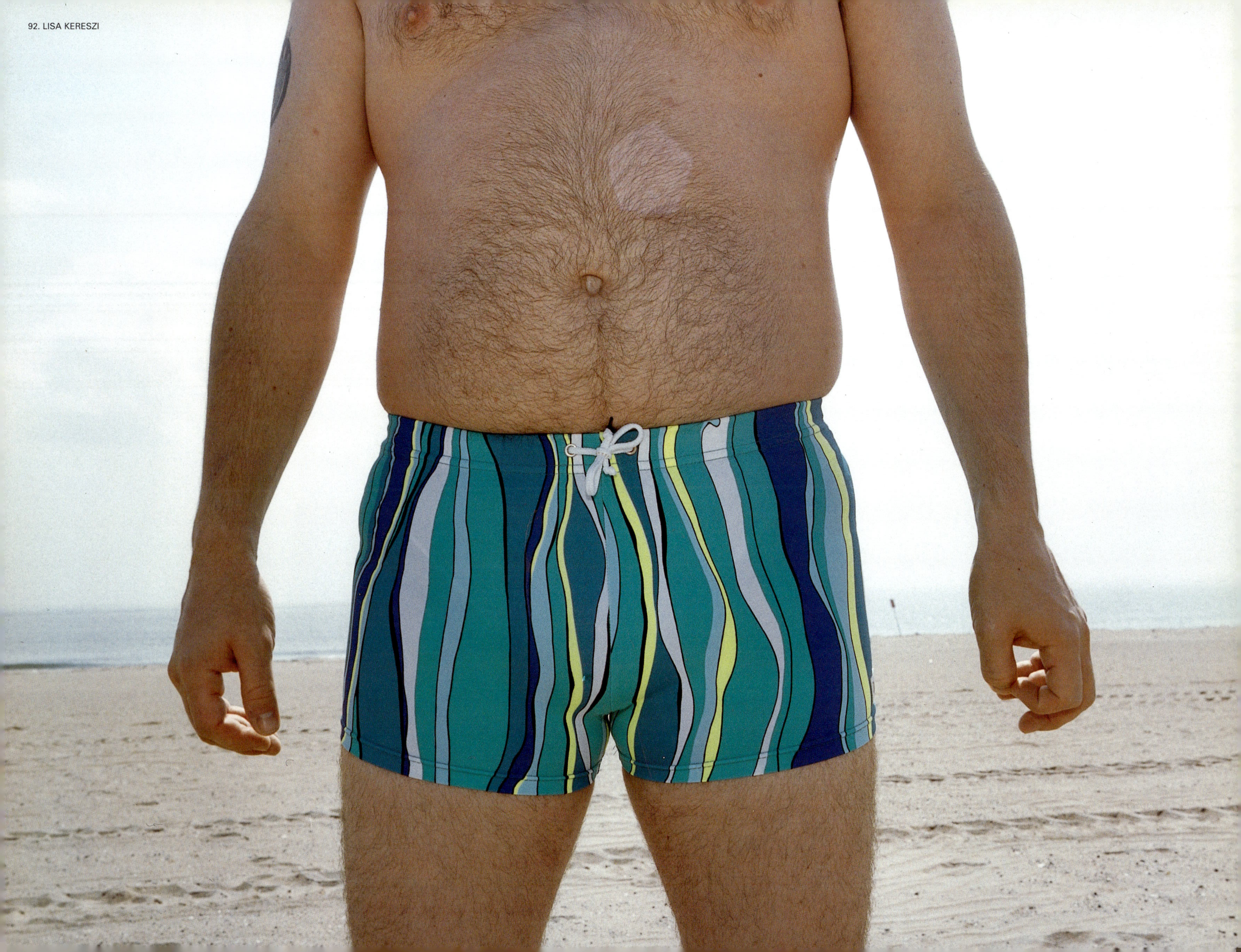

92. LISA KERESZI

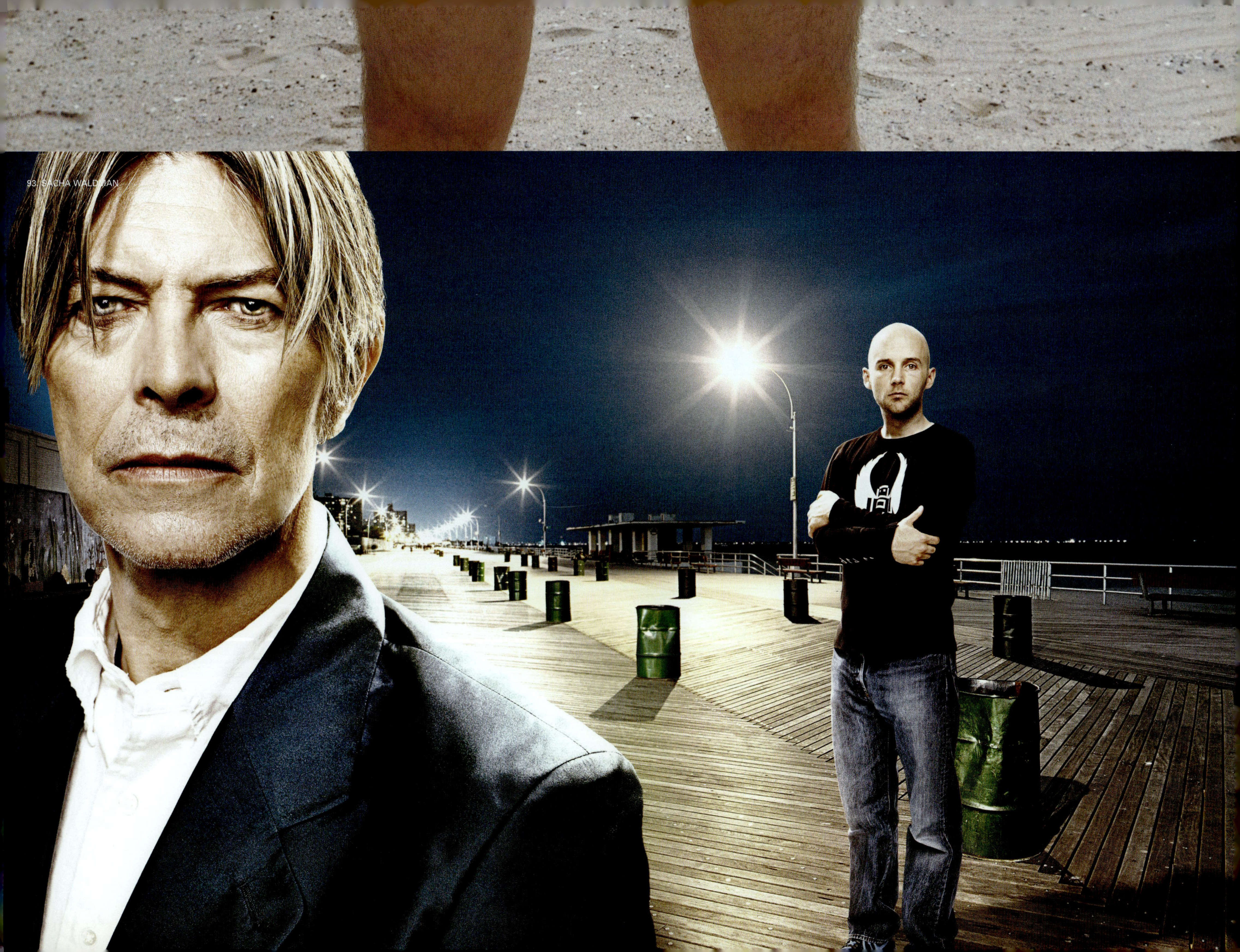

93. SACHA WALDMAN

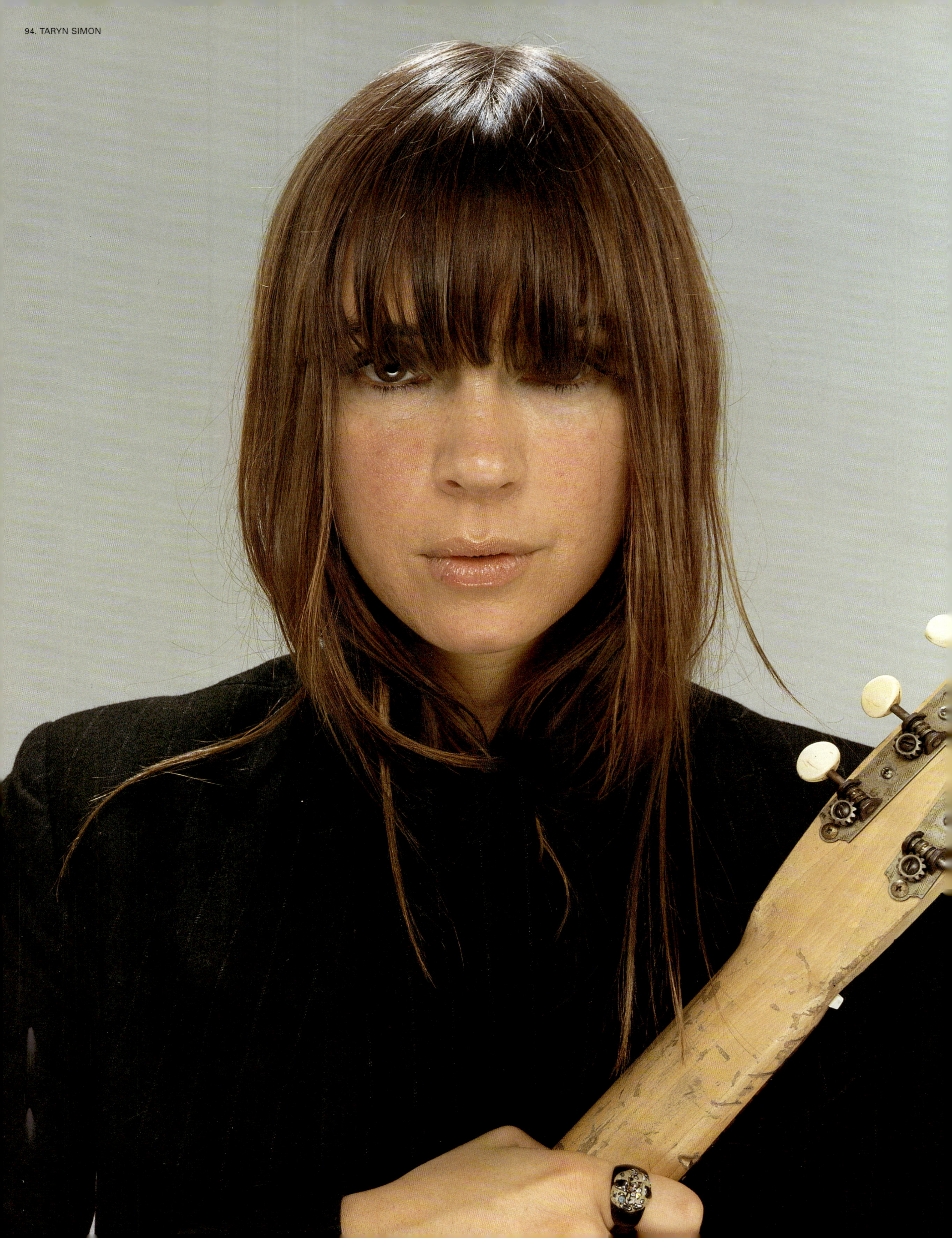

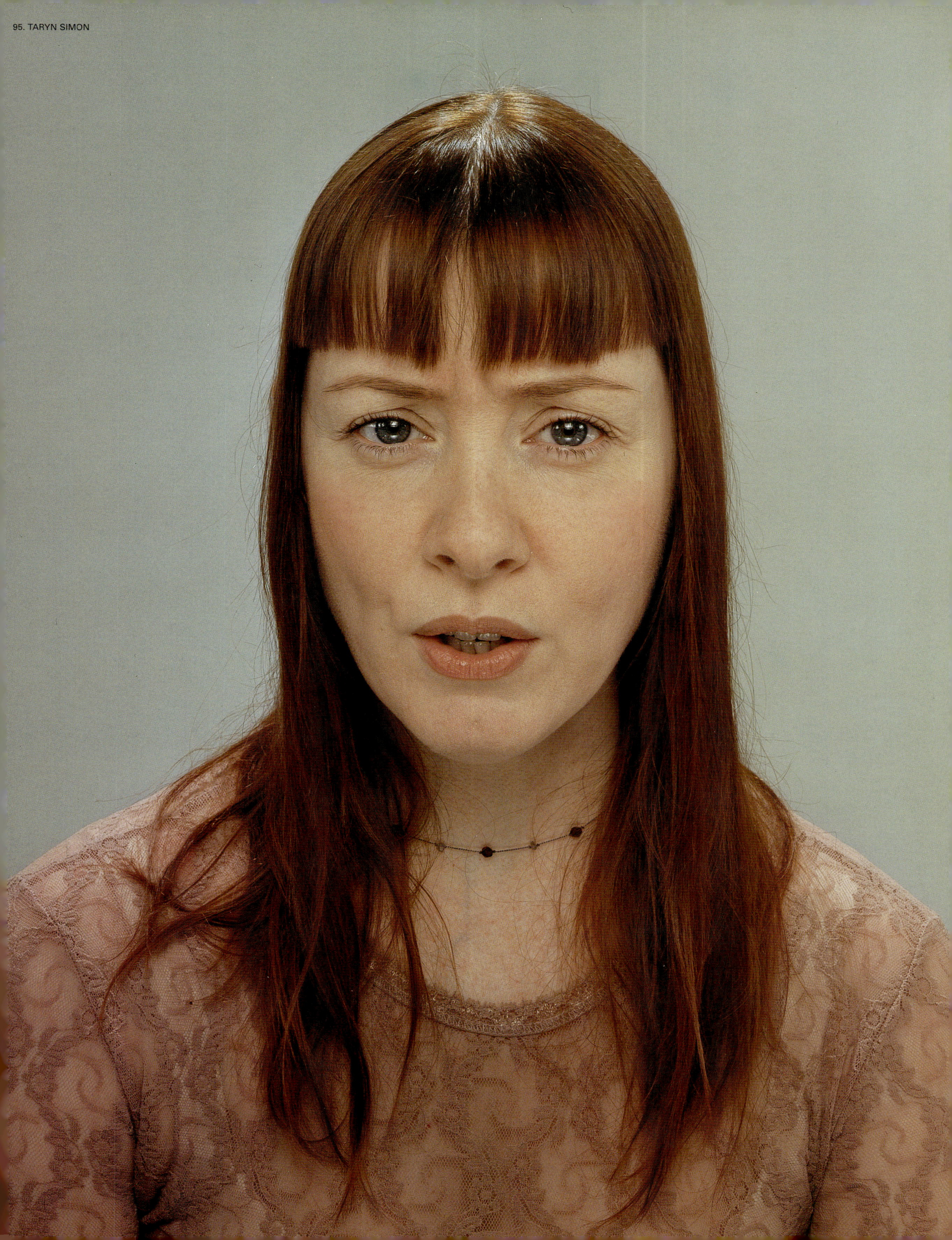

96. TARYN SIMON

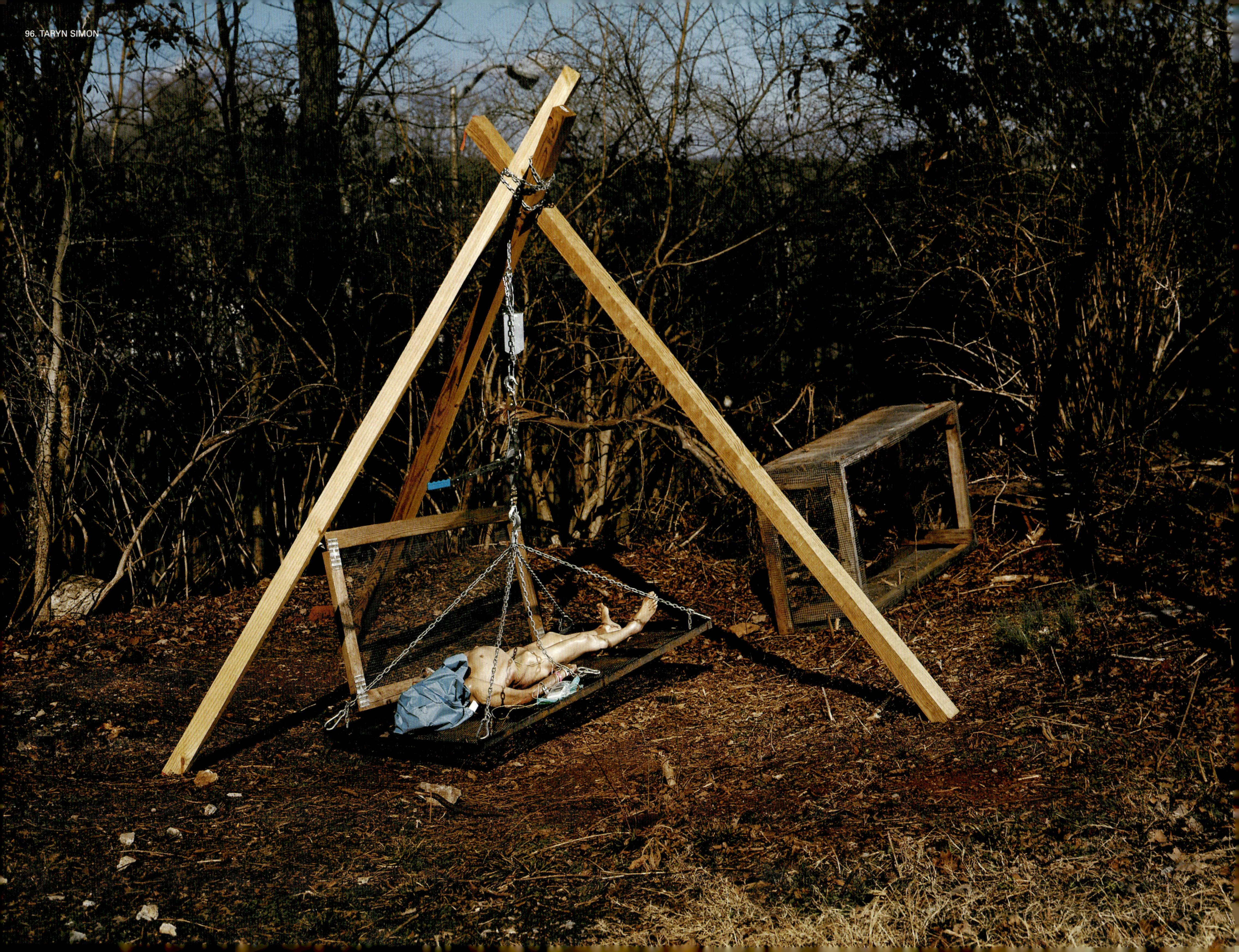

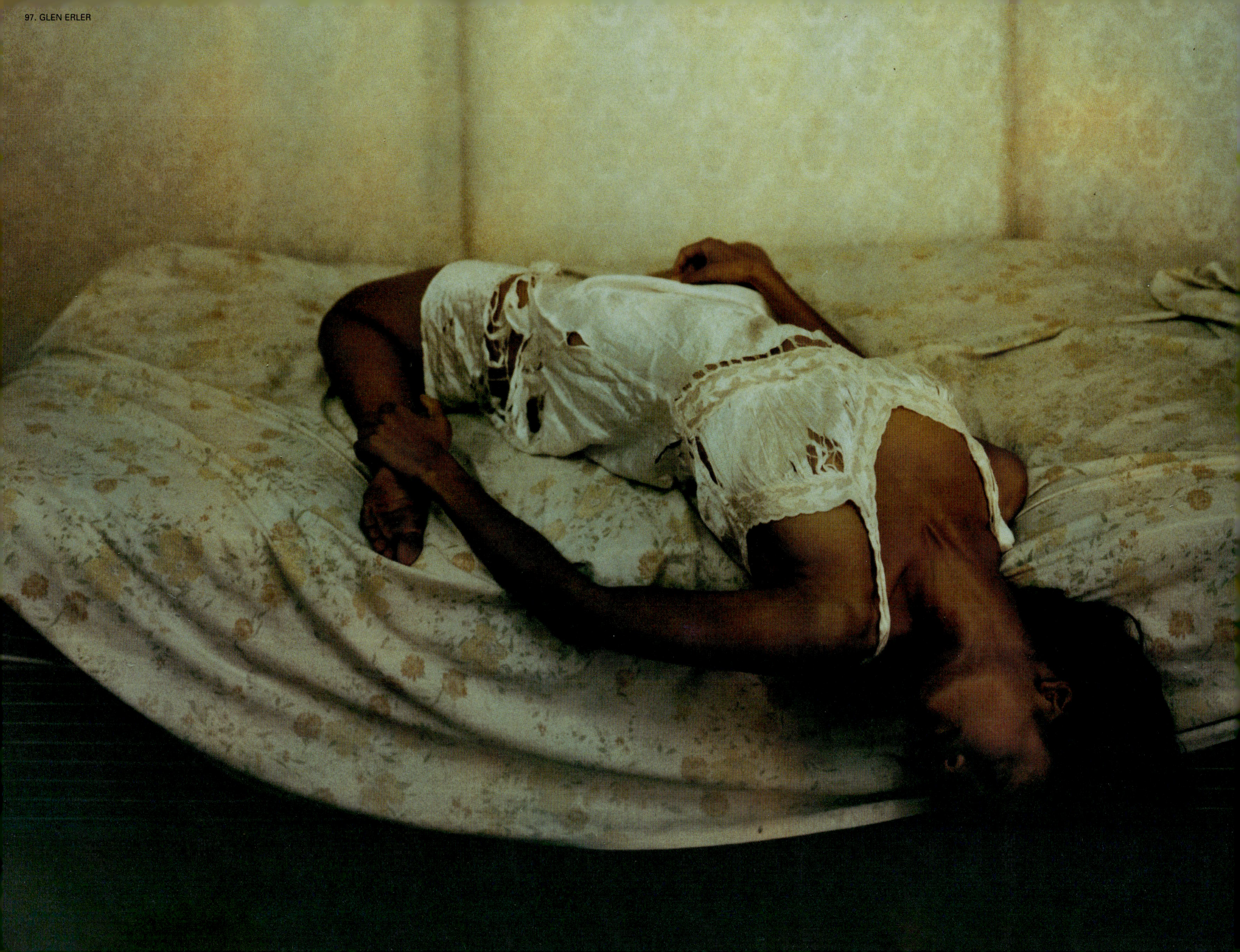

97. GLEN ERLER

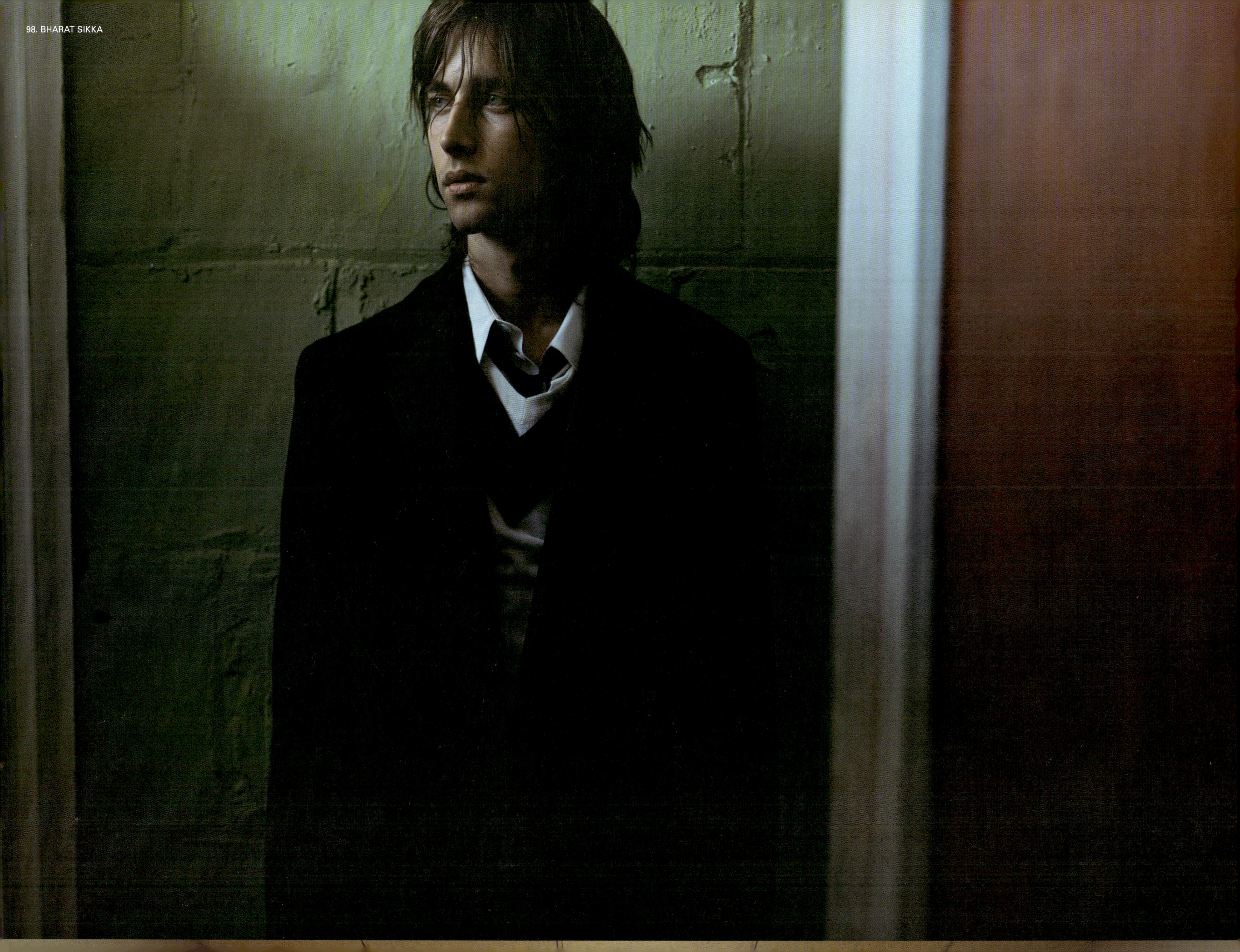
98. BHARAT SIKKA

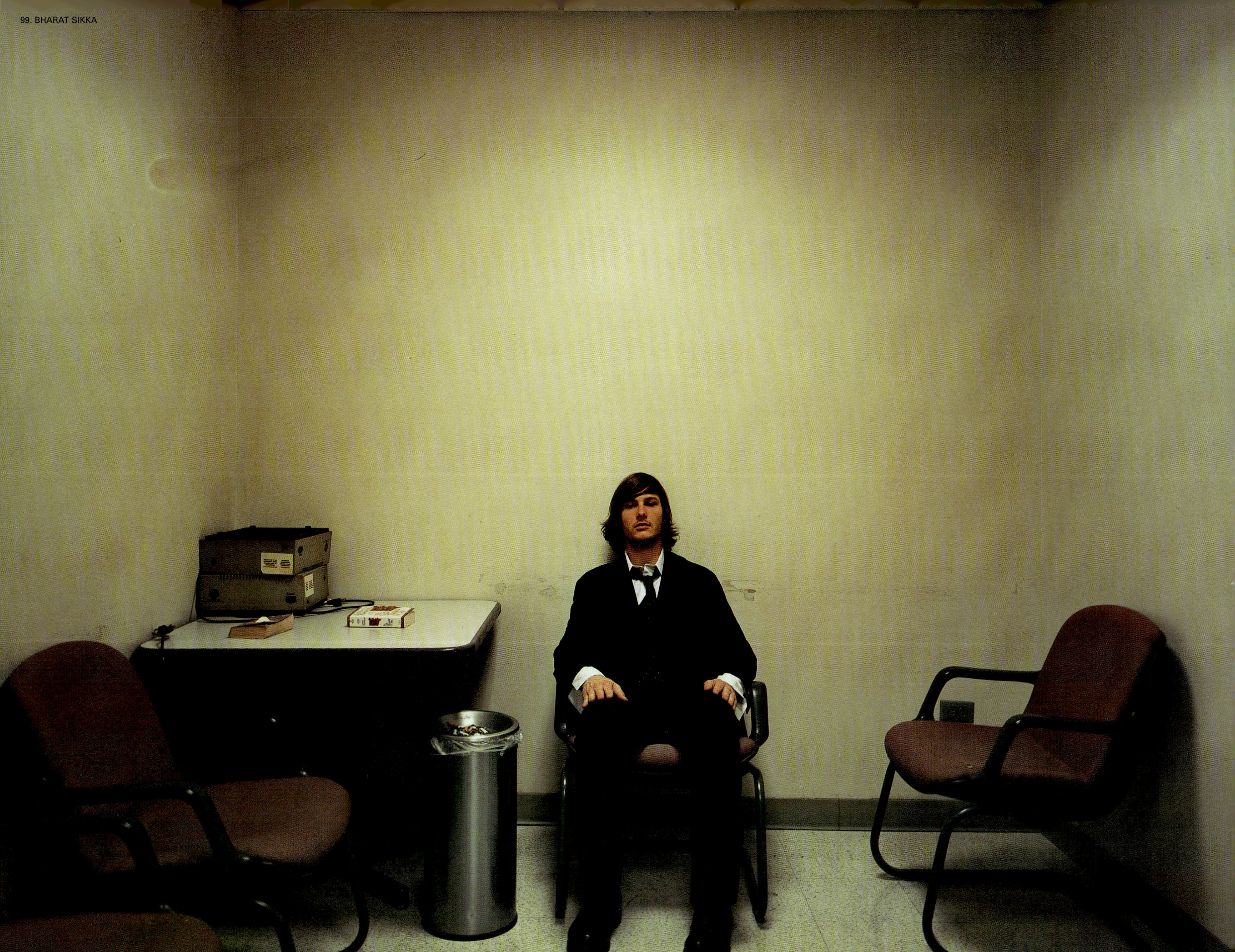

99. BHARAT SIKKA

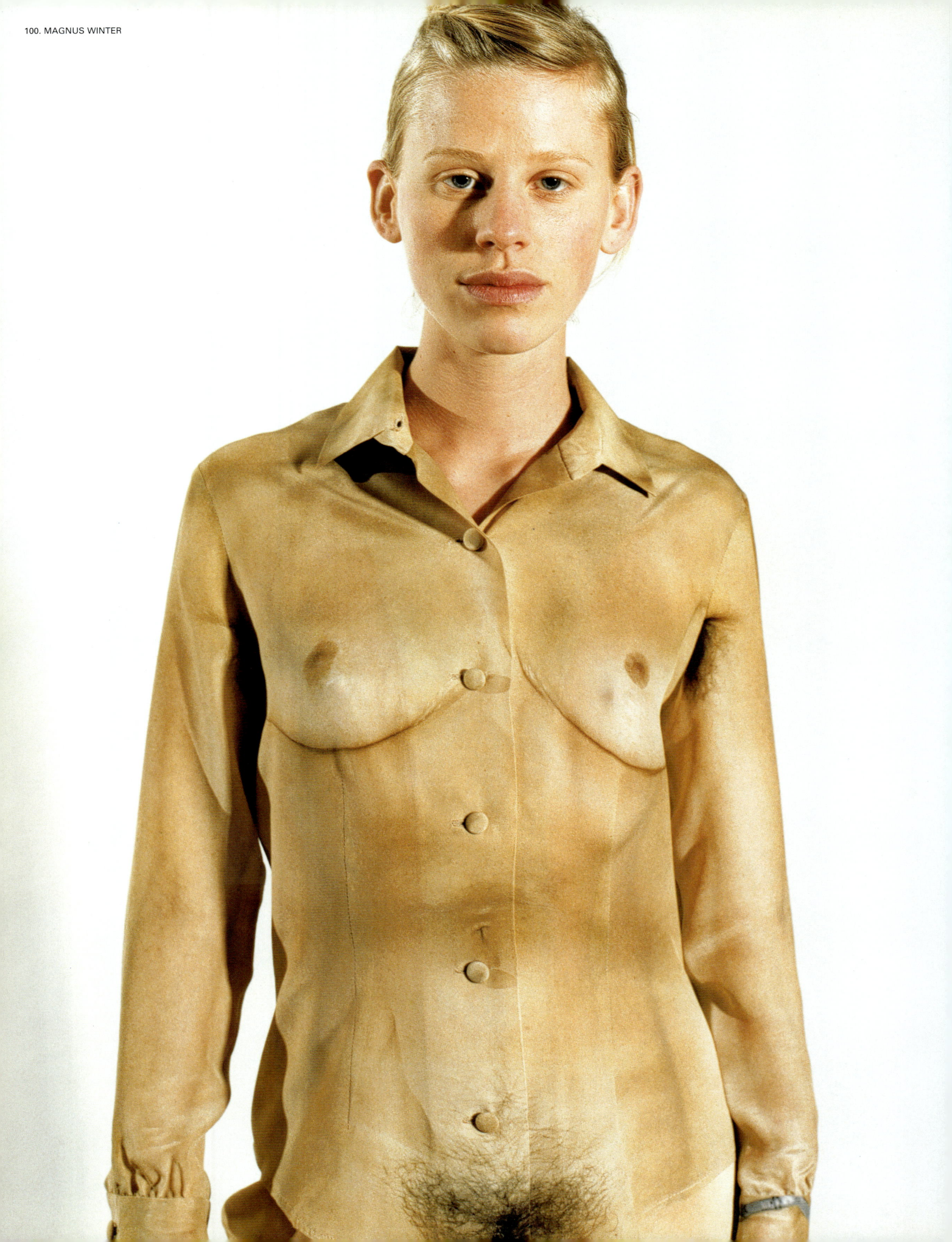

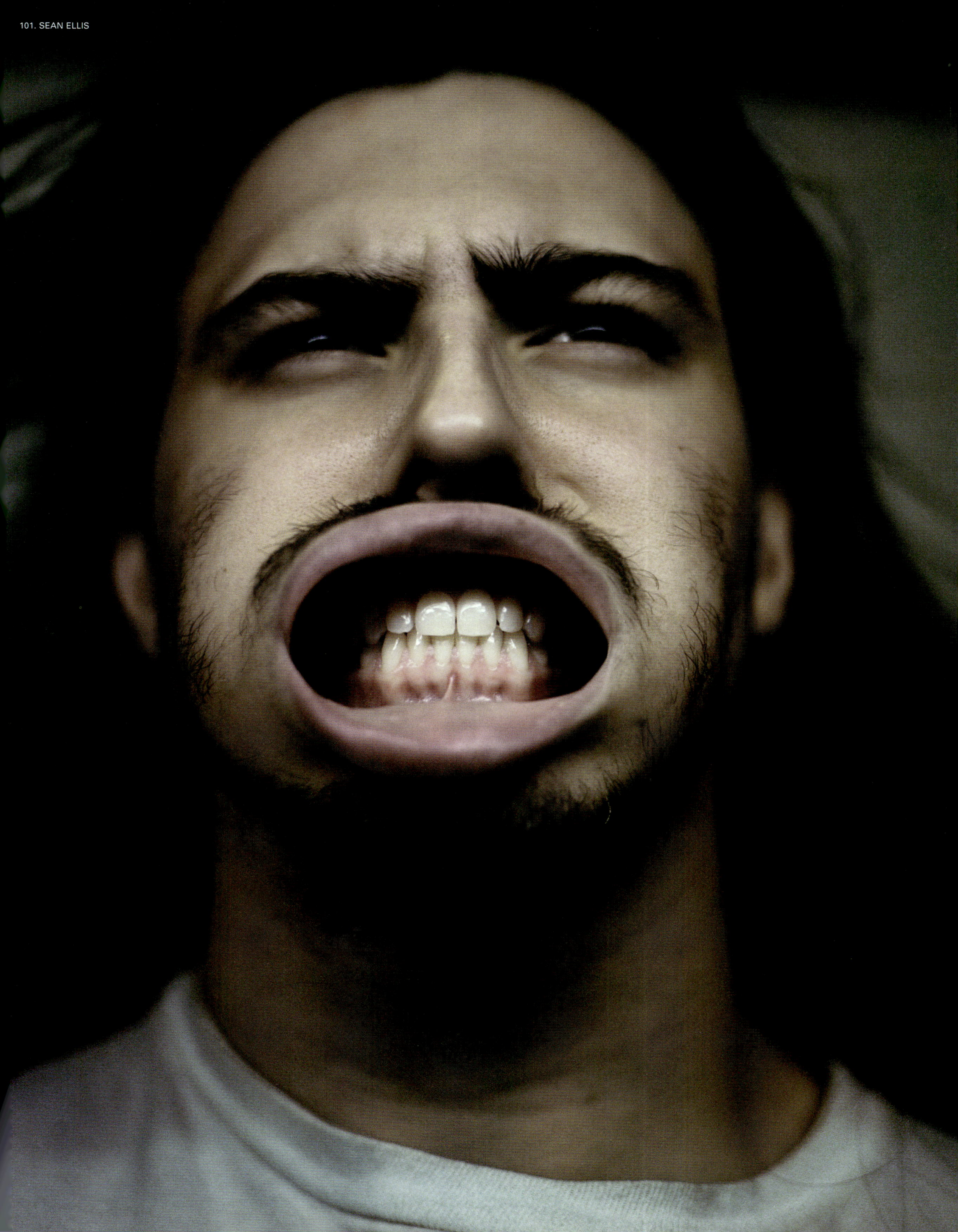

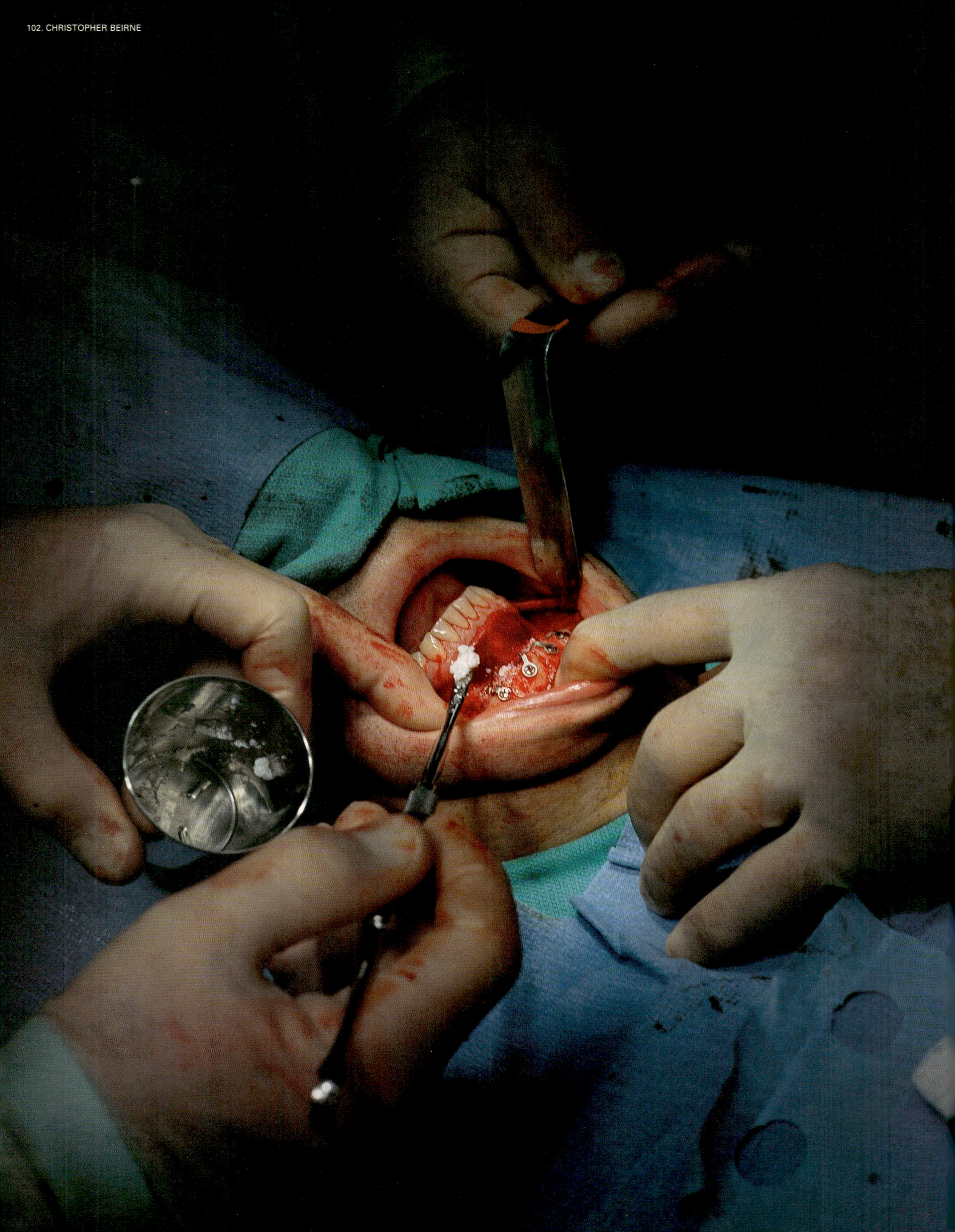

103. CHRISTOPHER BEIRNE

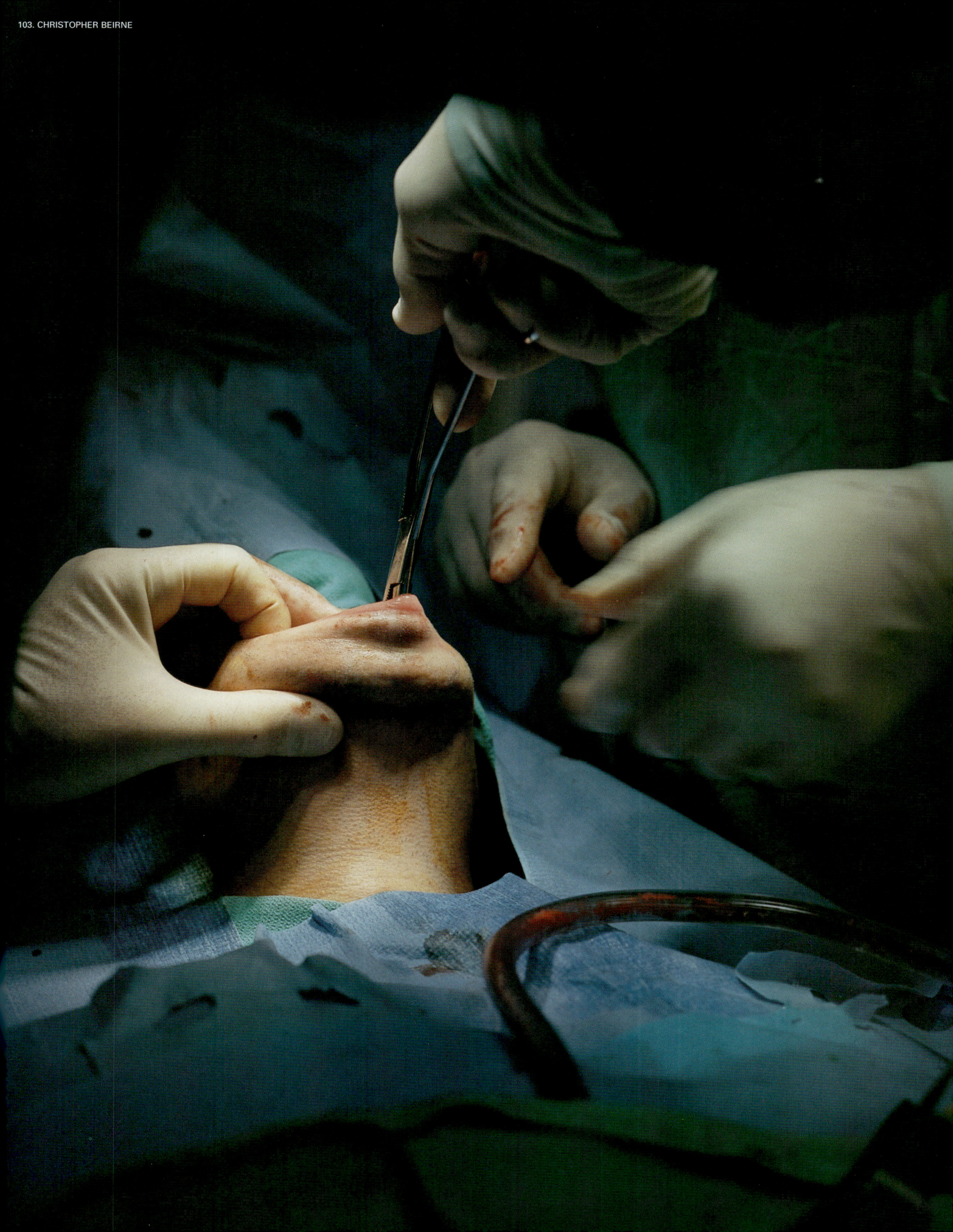

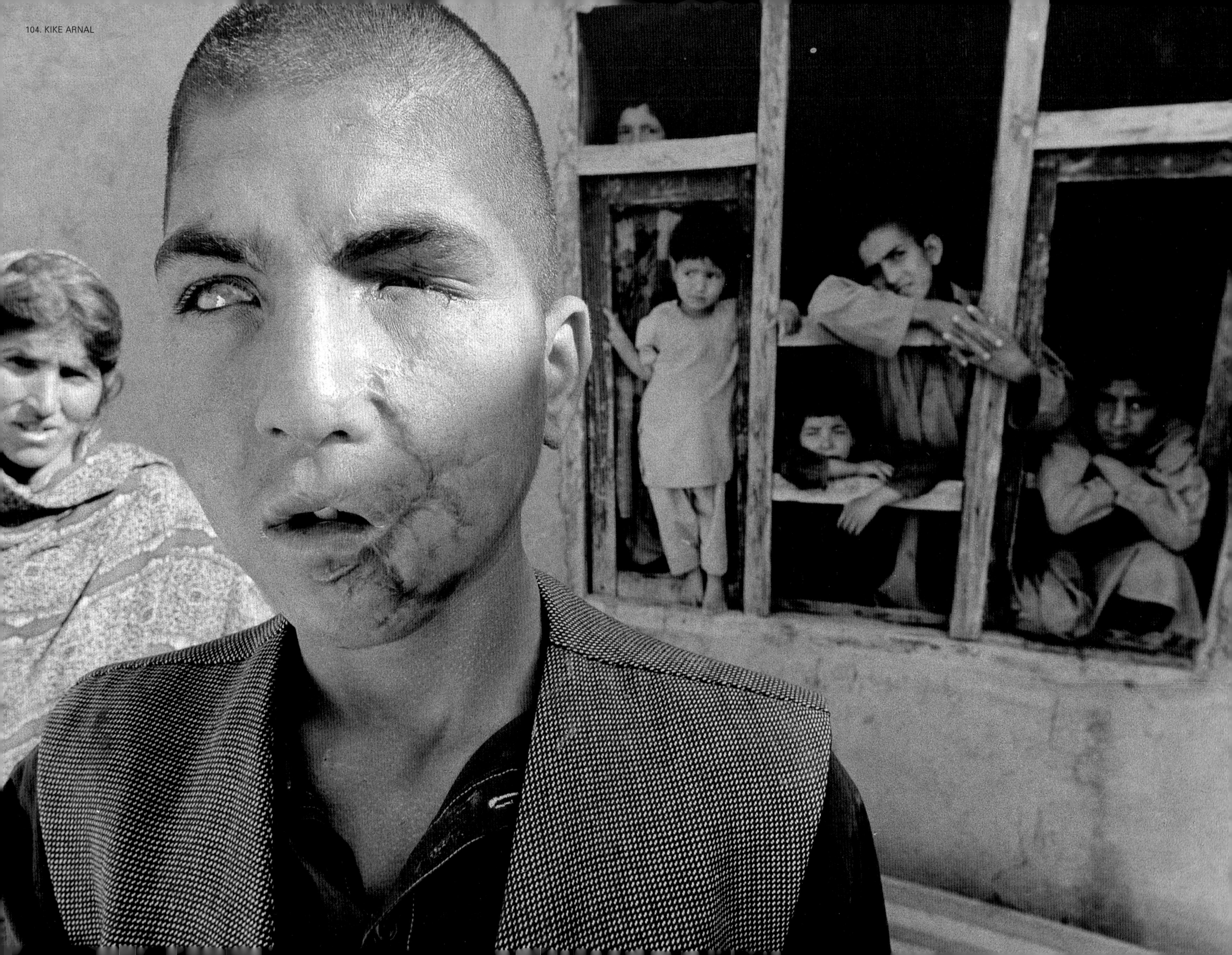

104. KIKE ARNAL

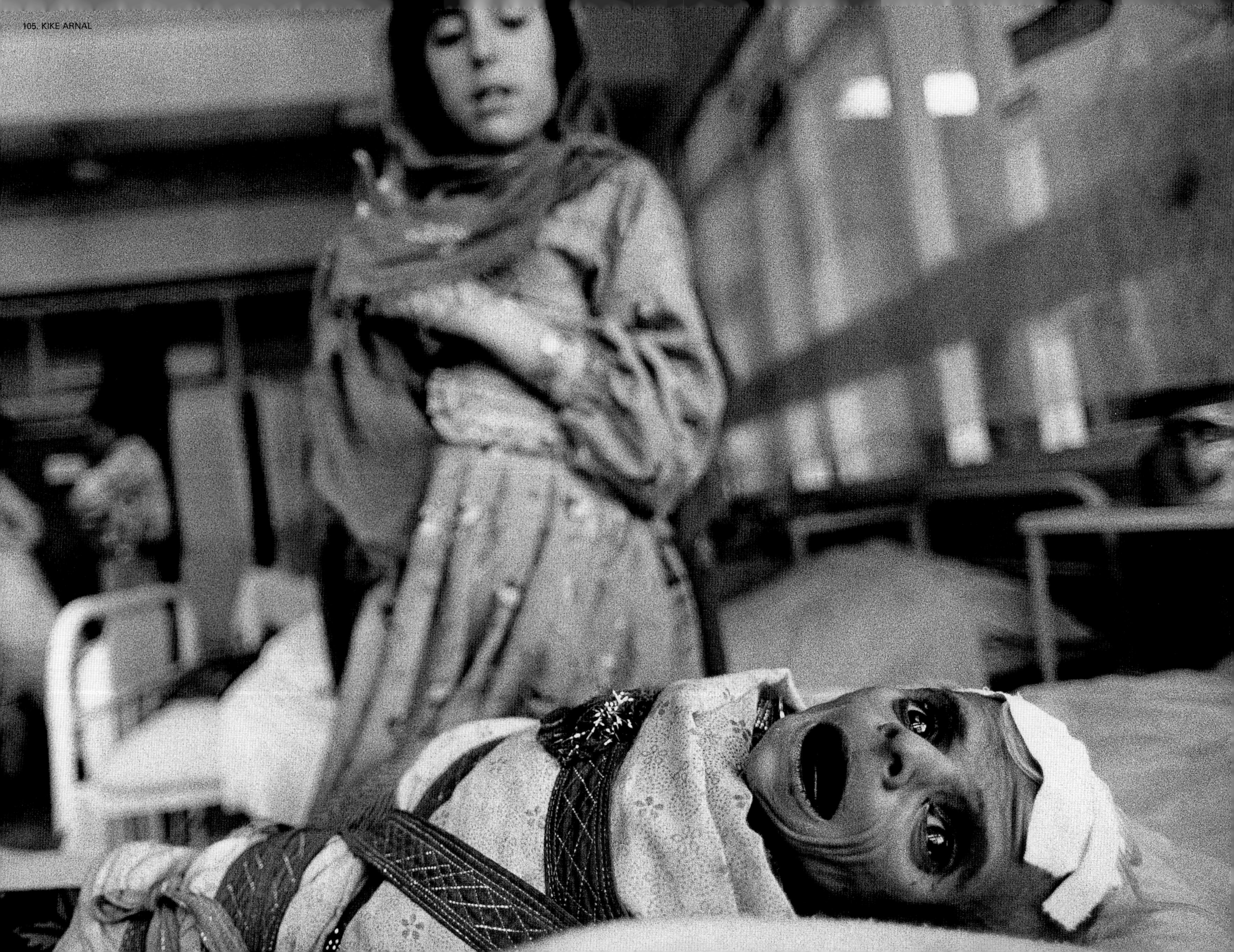

105. KIKE ARNAL

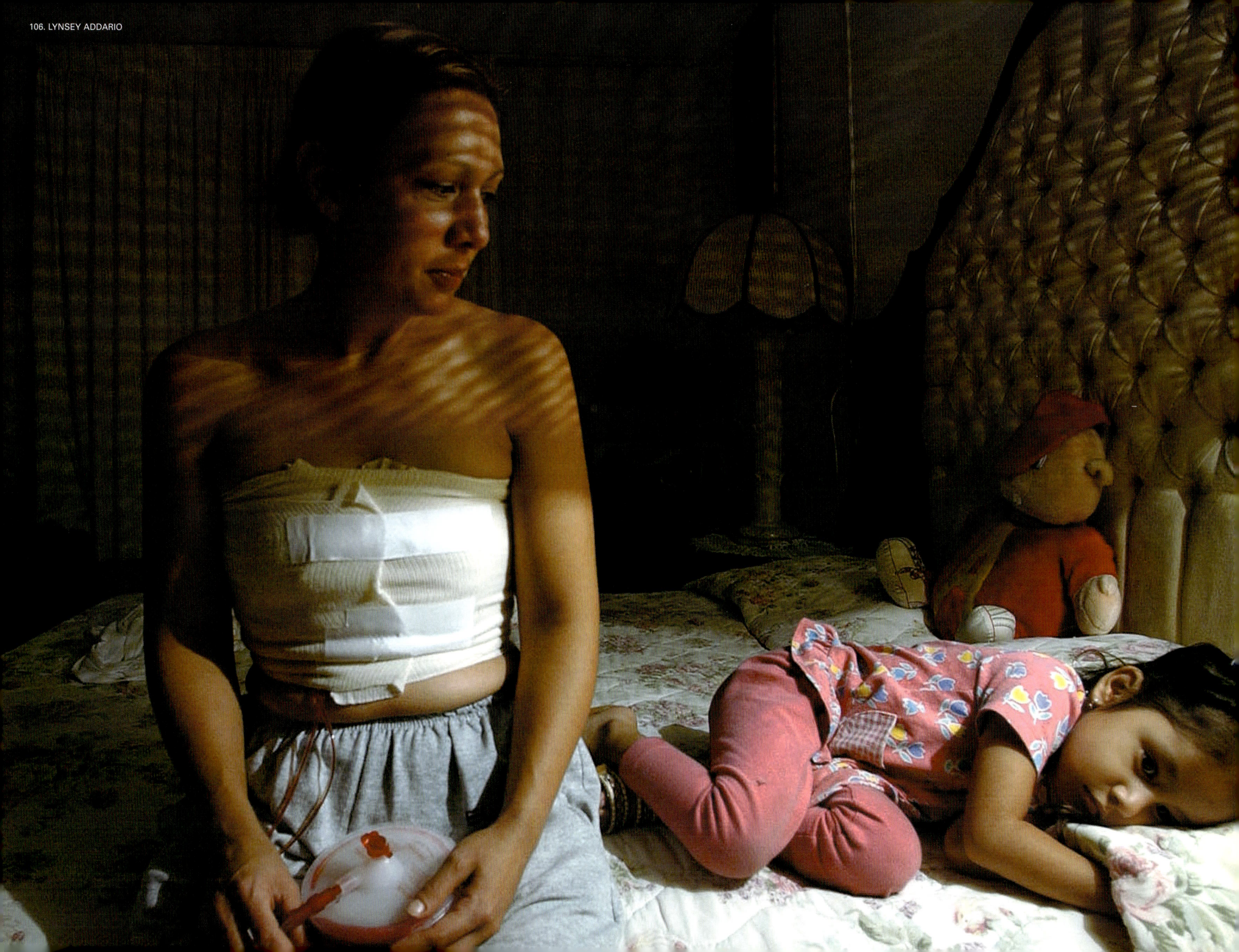

106. LYNSEY ADDARIO

107. LYNSEY ADDARIO

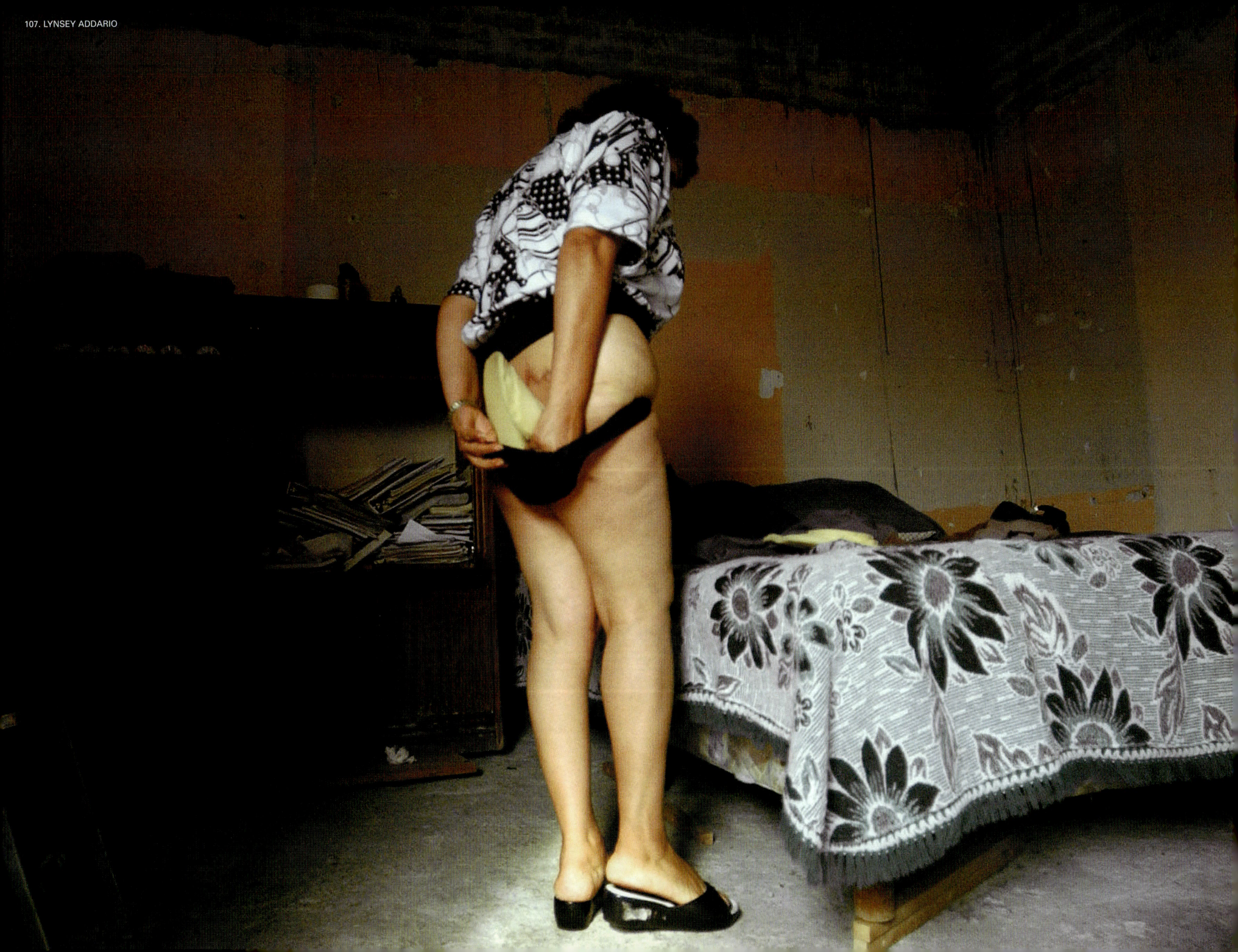

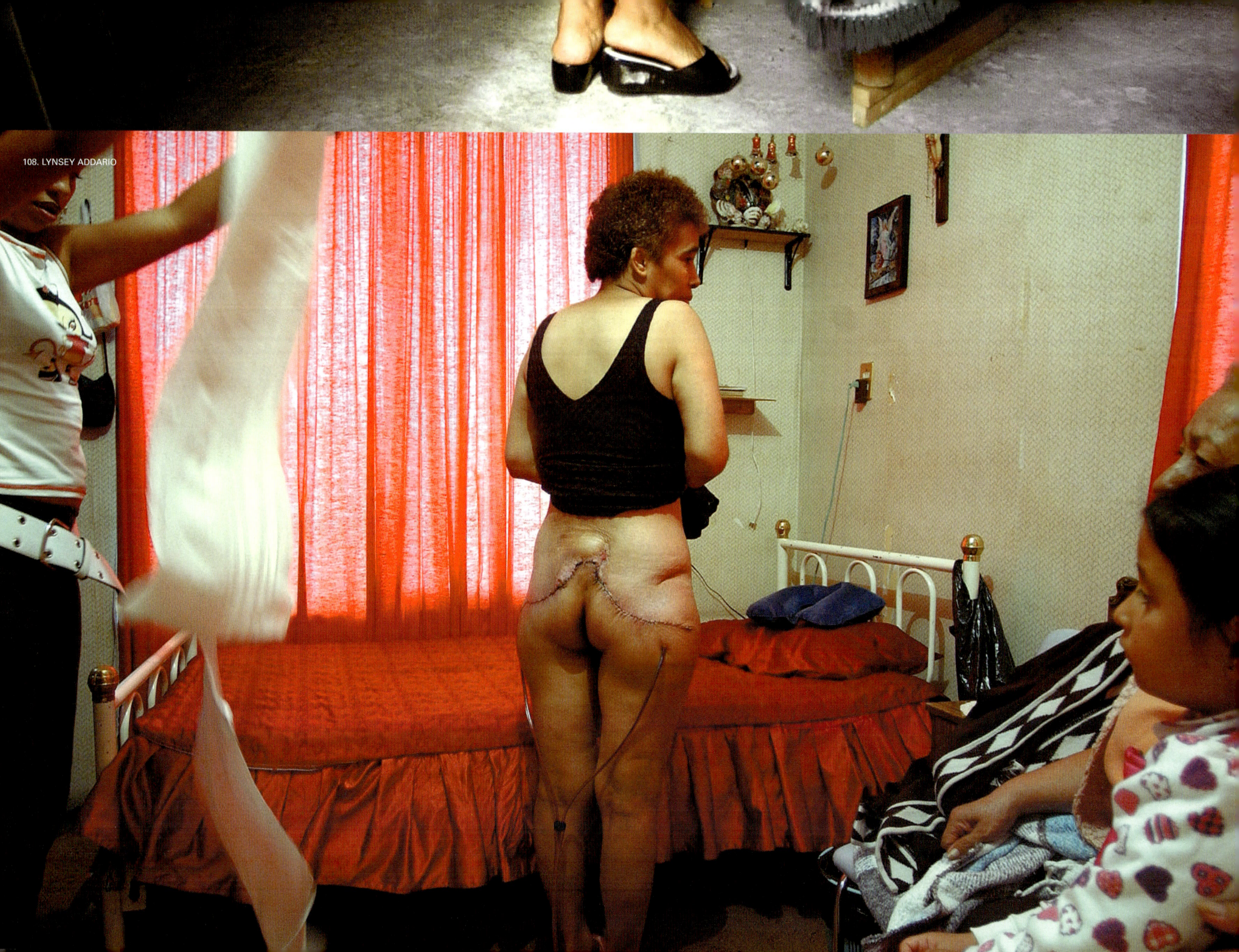

108. LYNSEY ADDARIO

109. LYNSEY ADDARIO

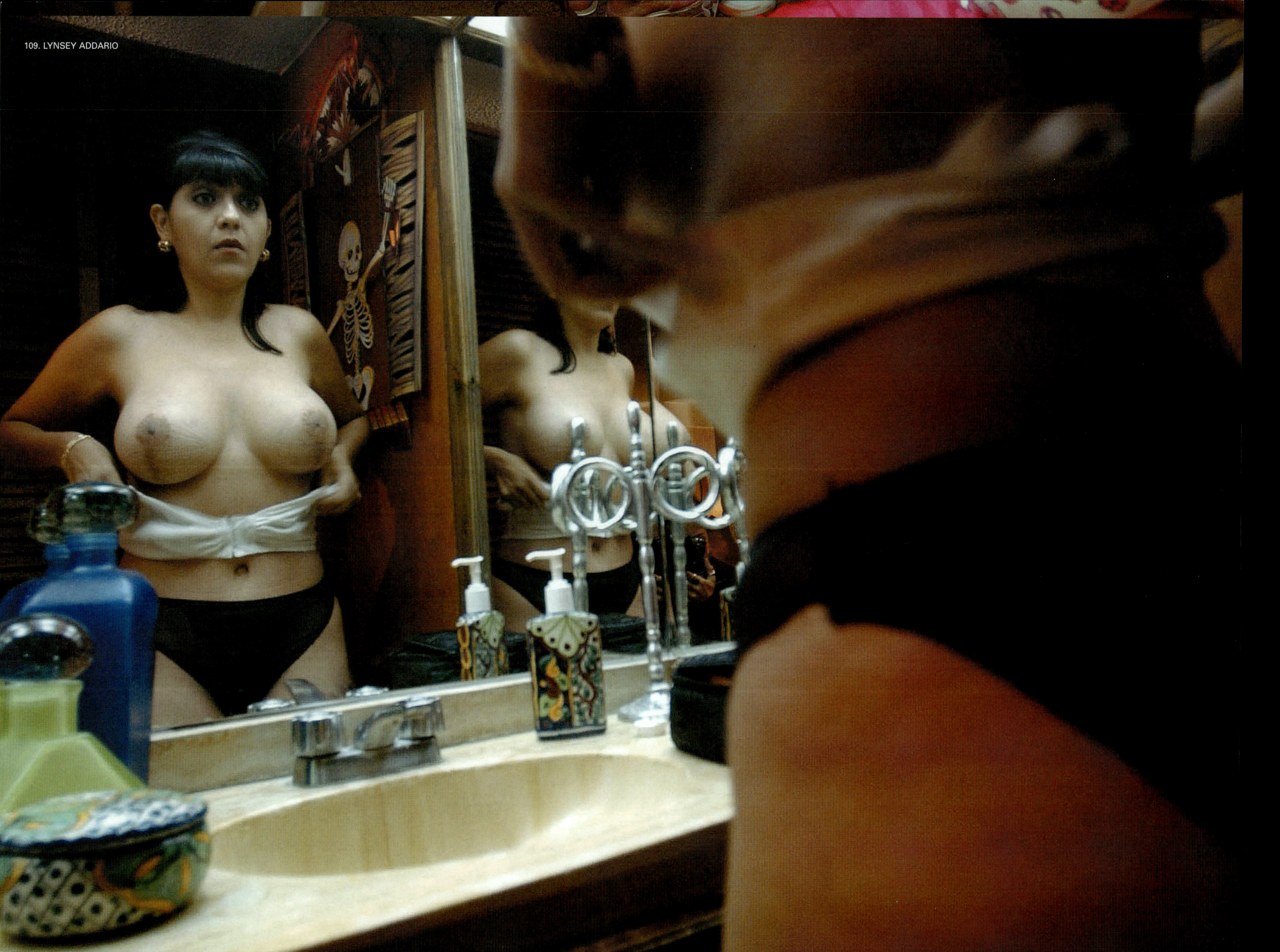

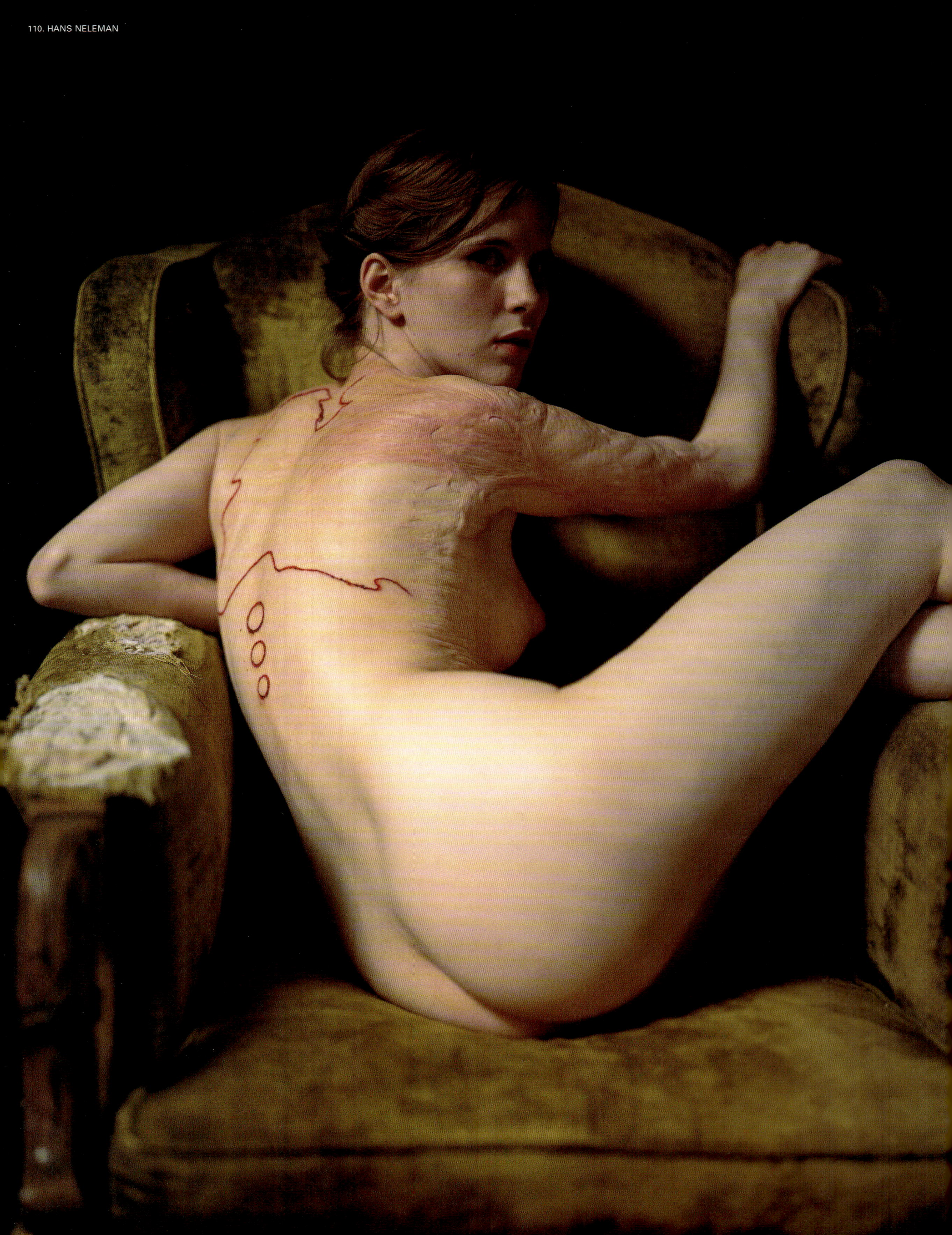

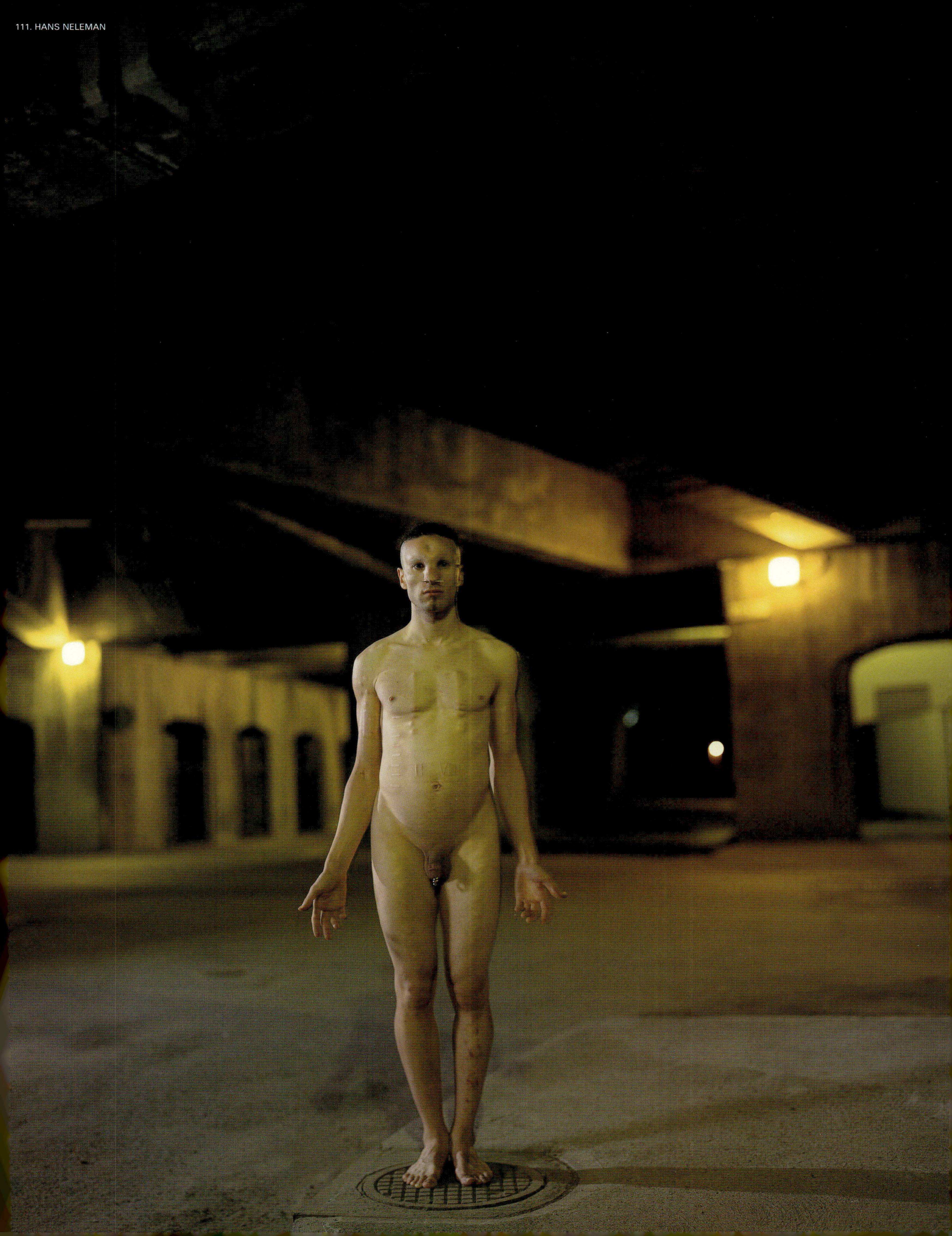

111. HANS NELEMAN

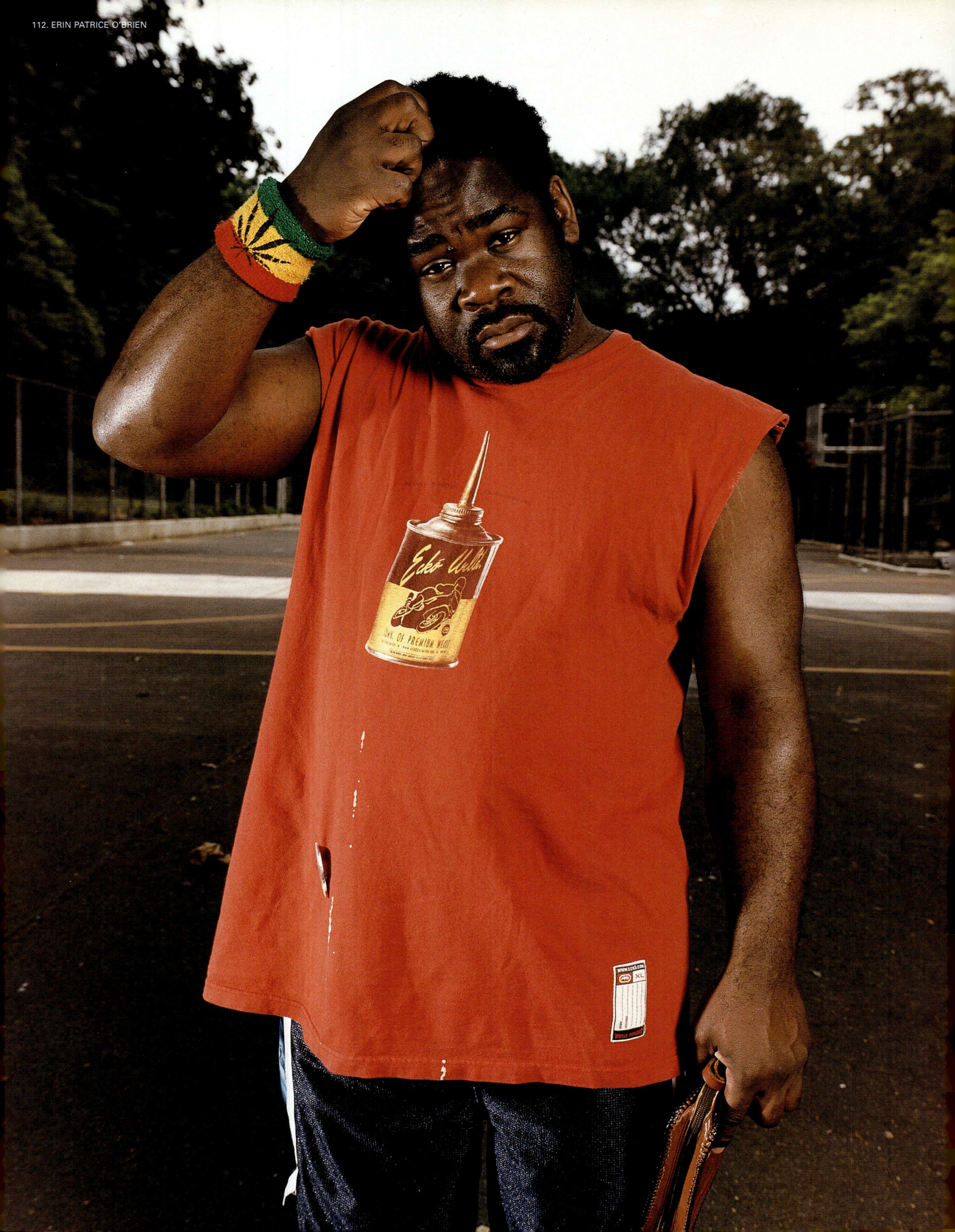

112. ERIN PATRICE O'BRIEN

113. ERIN PATRICE O'BRIEN

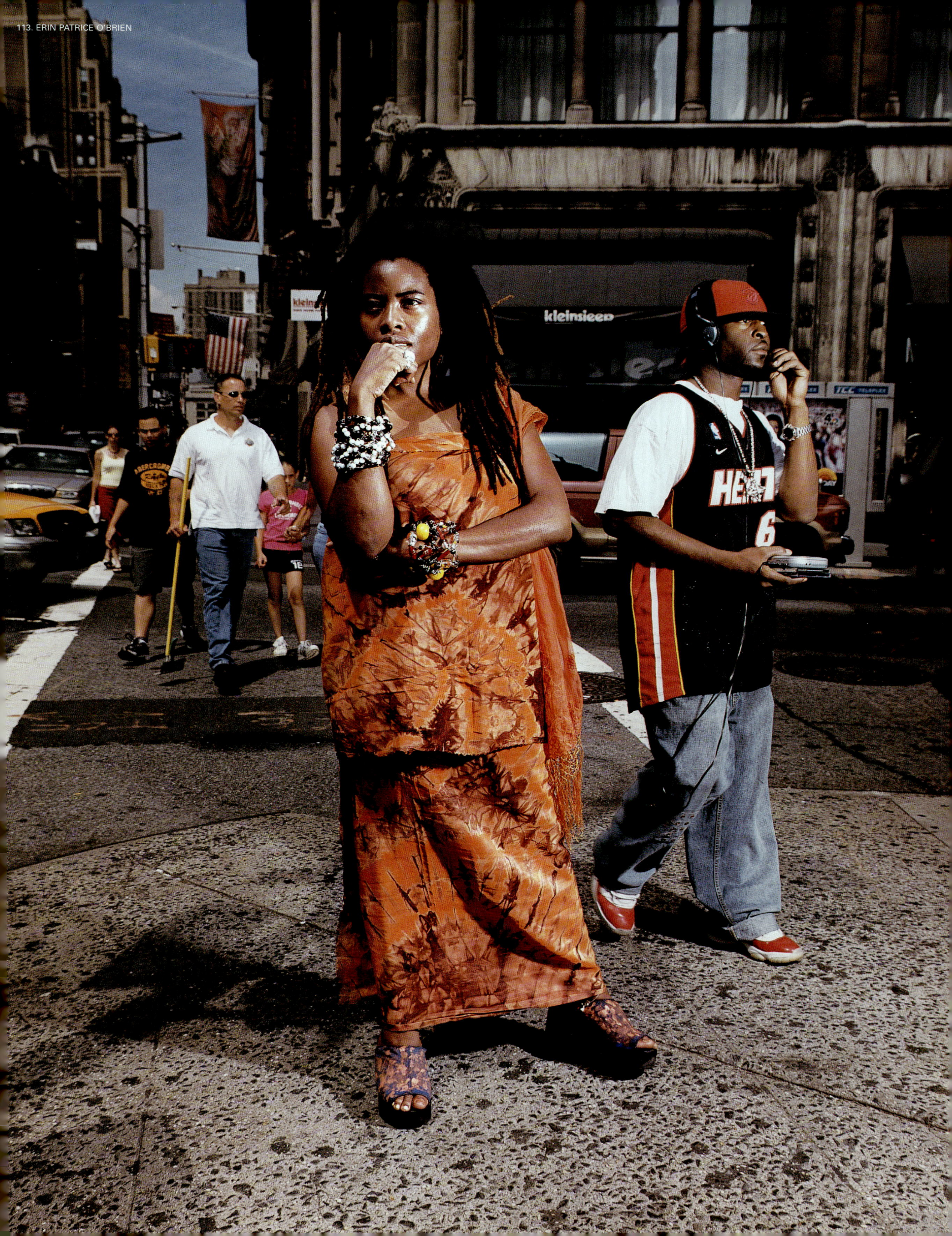

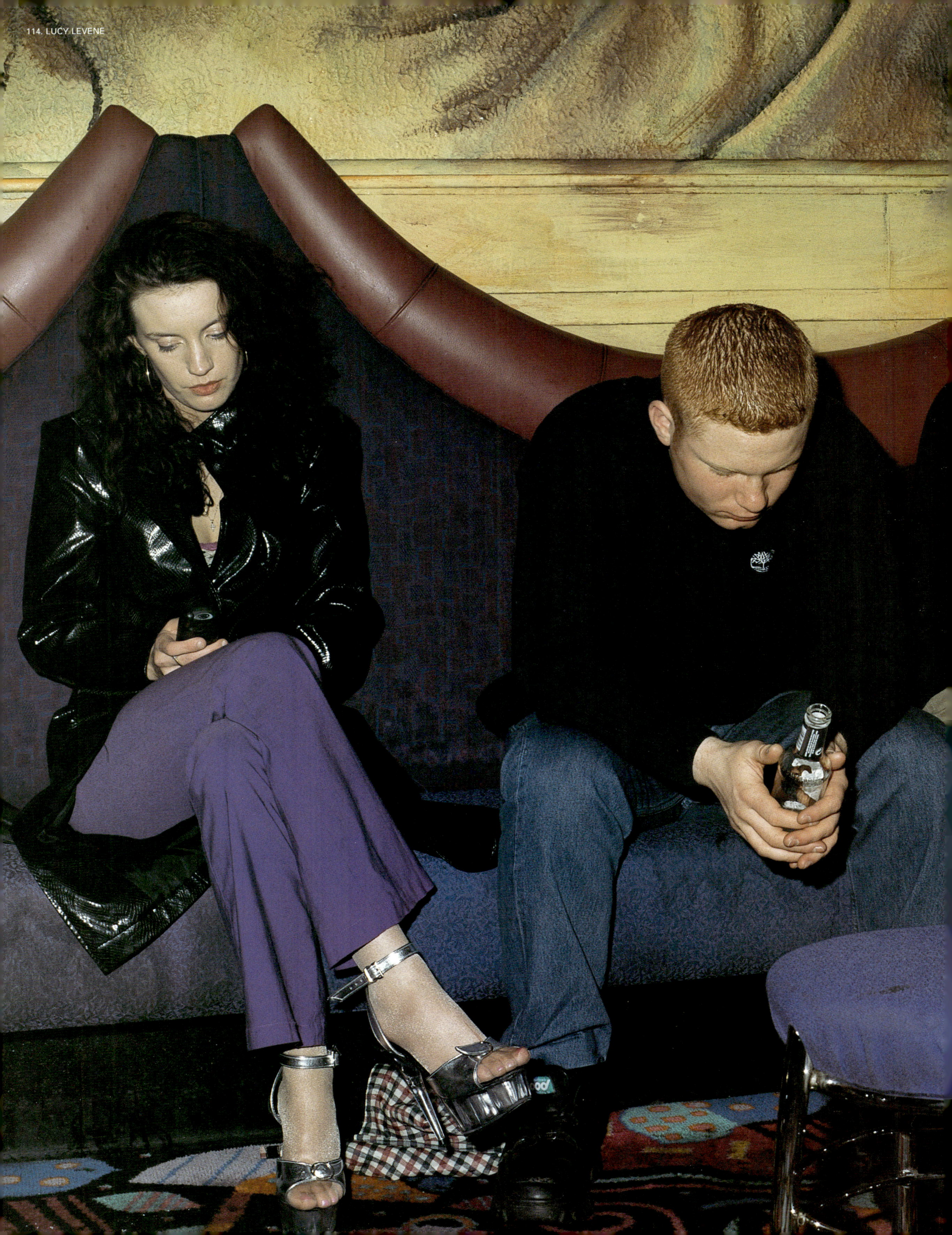

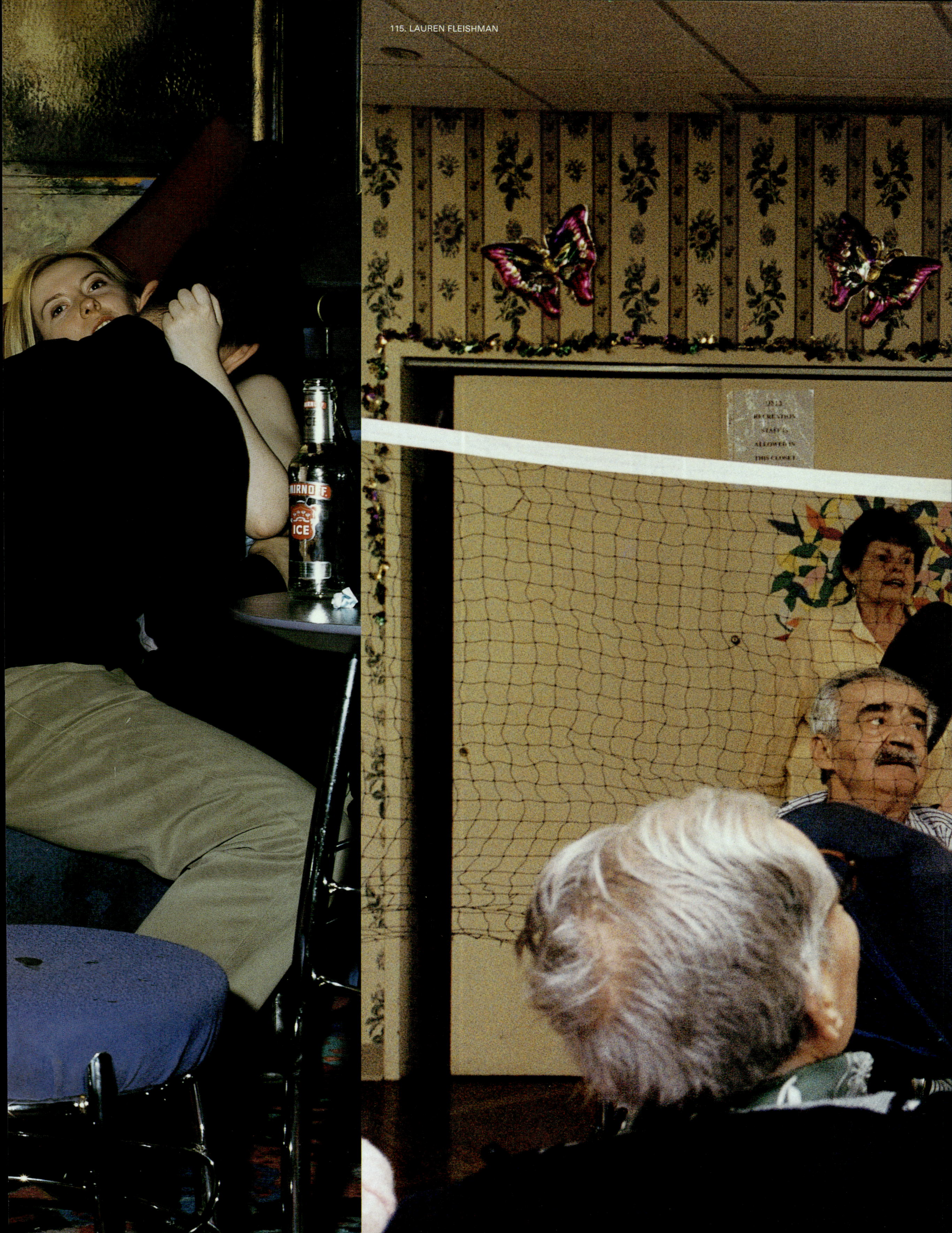
ICE
ALLOWED IN
THIS CLOSET

115. LAUREN FLEISHMAN

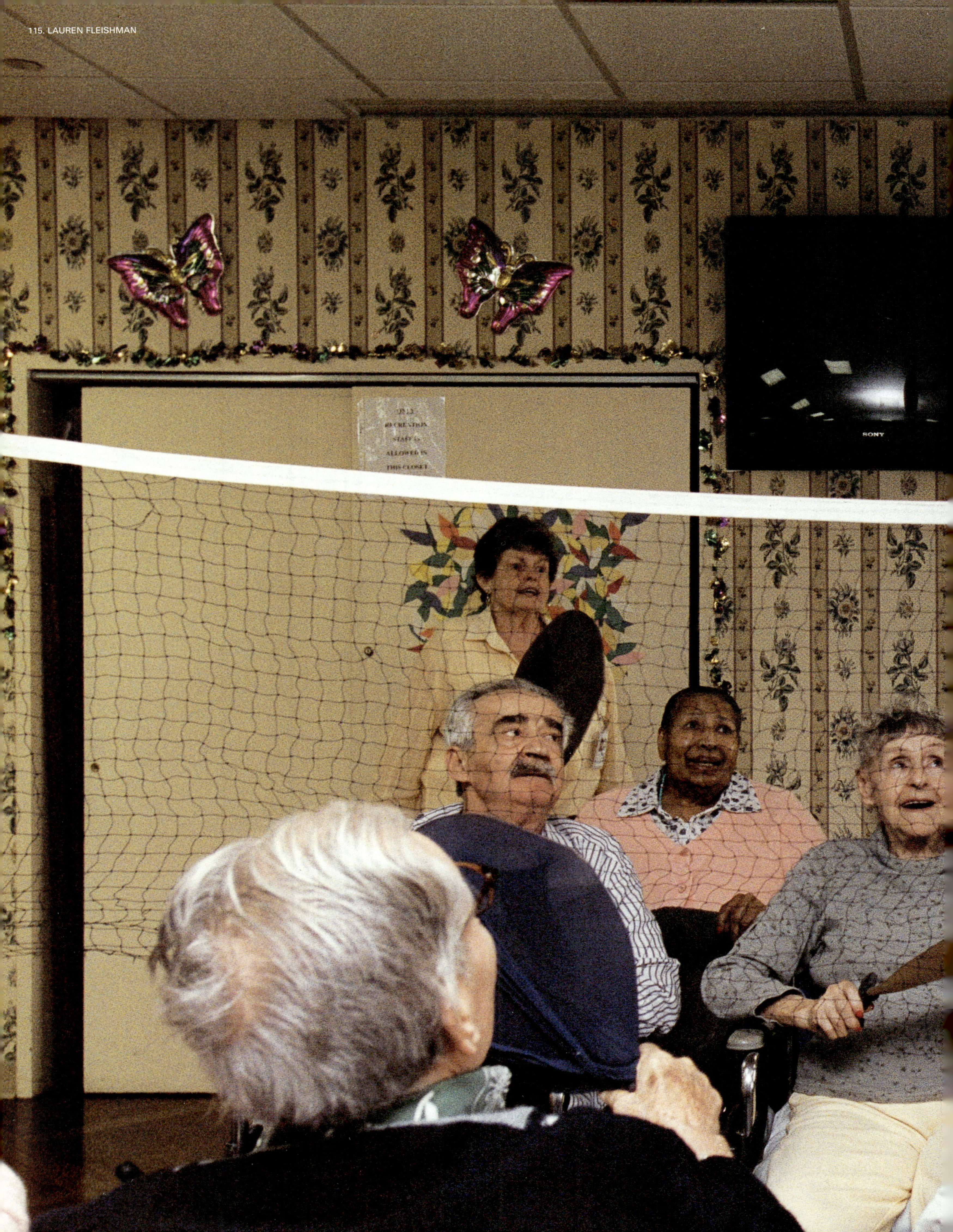

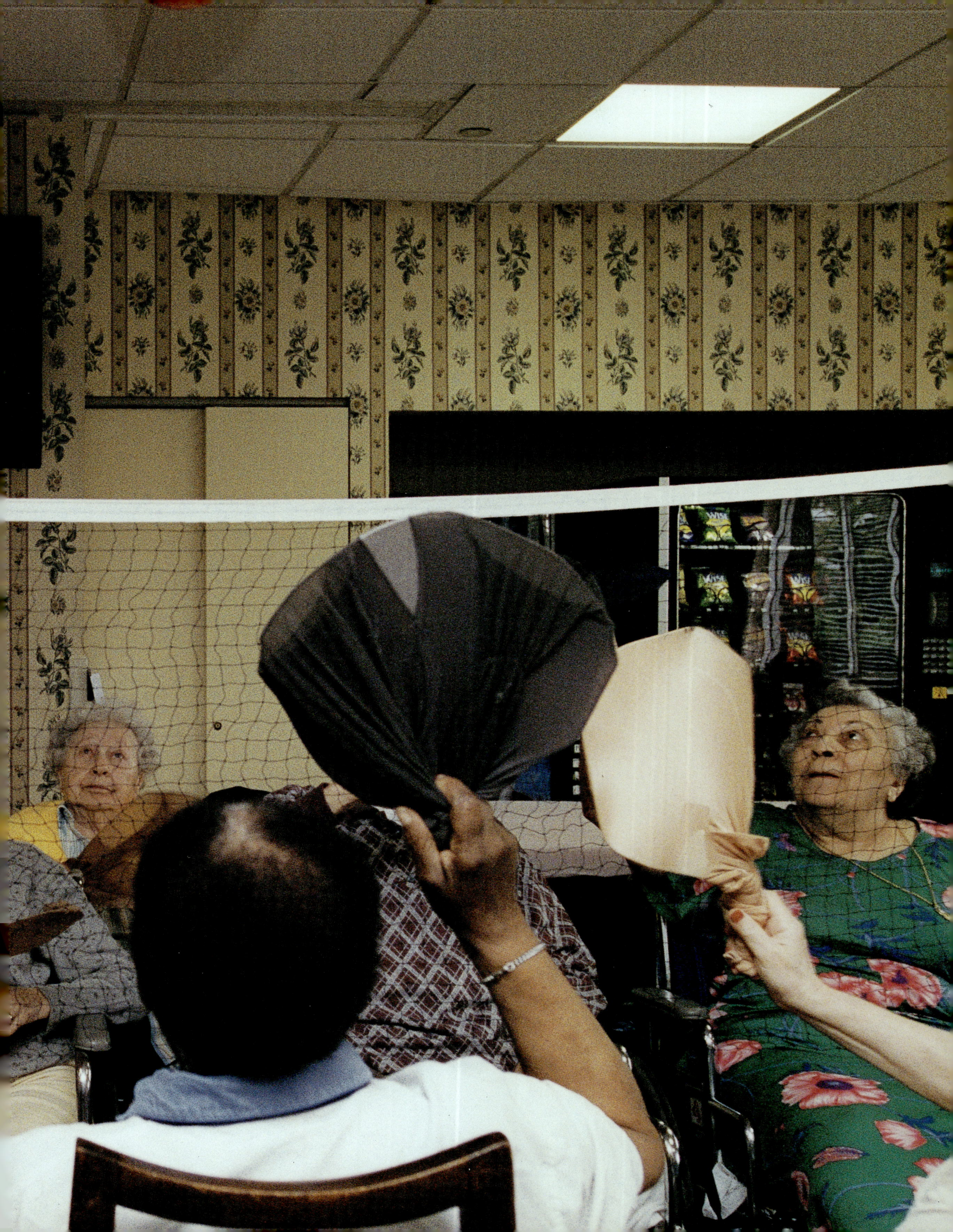
Wise

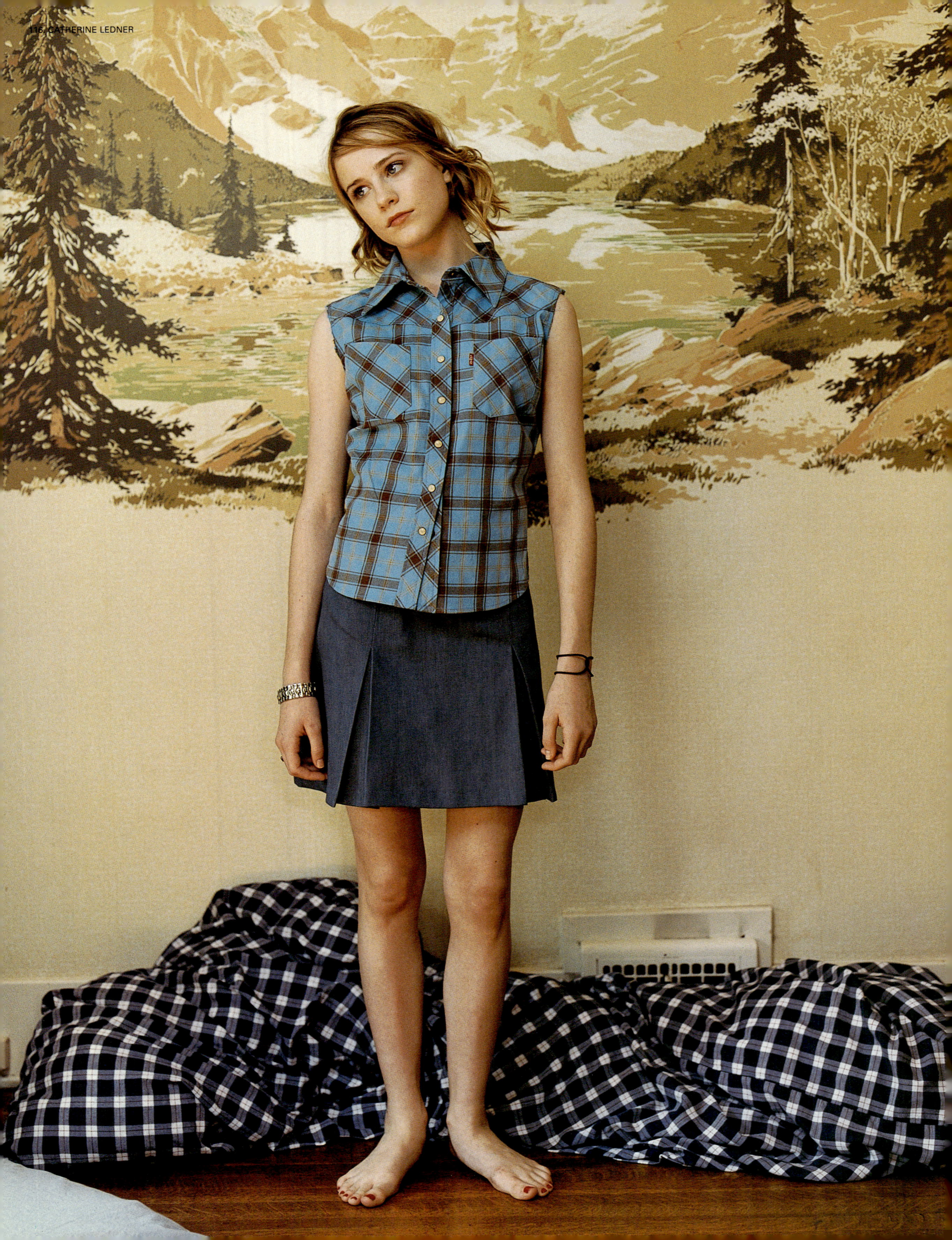

116. CATHERINE LEDNER

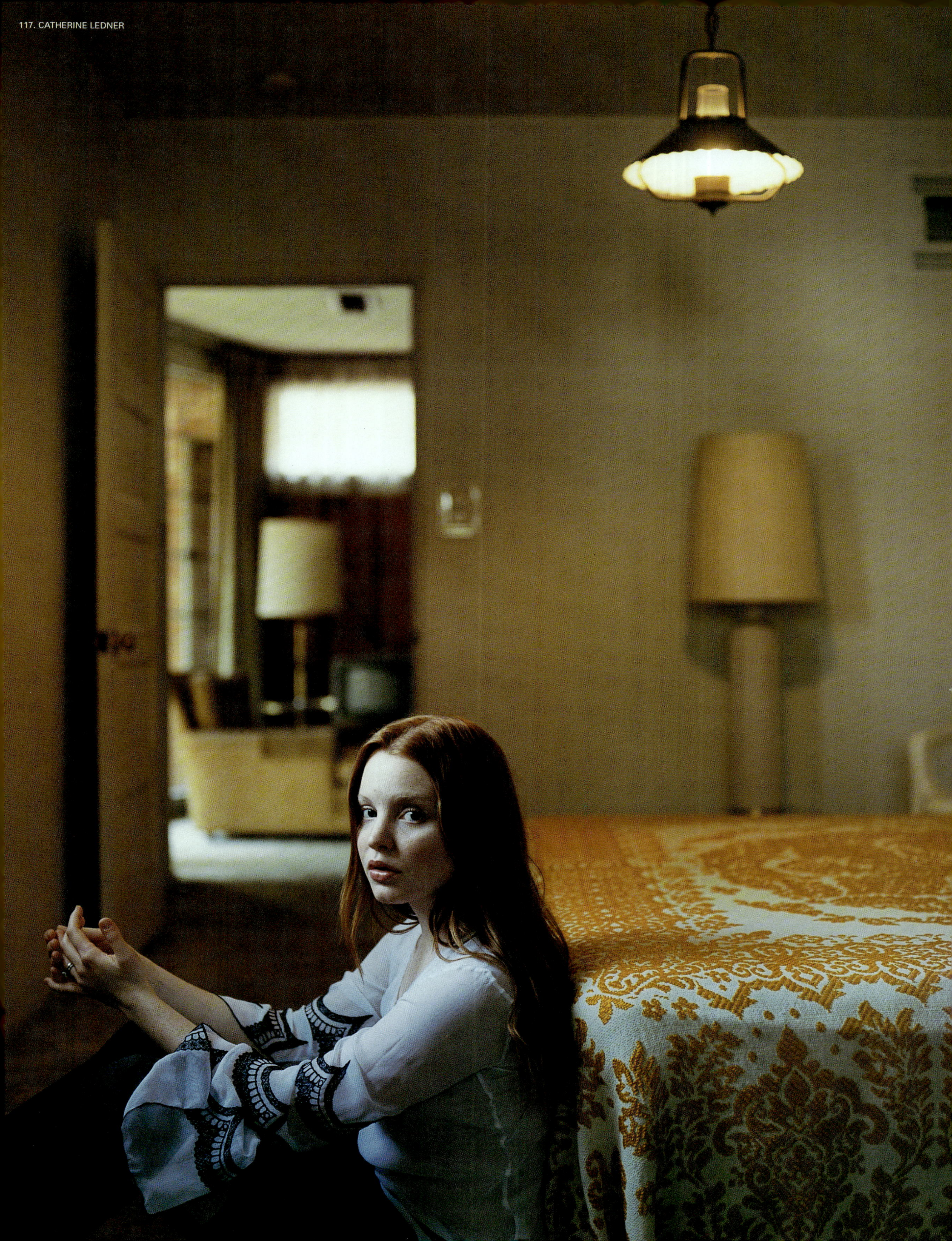

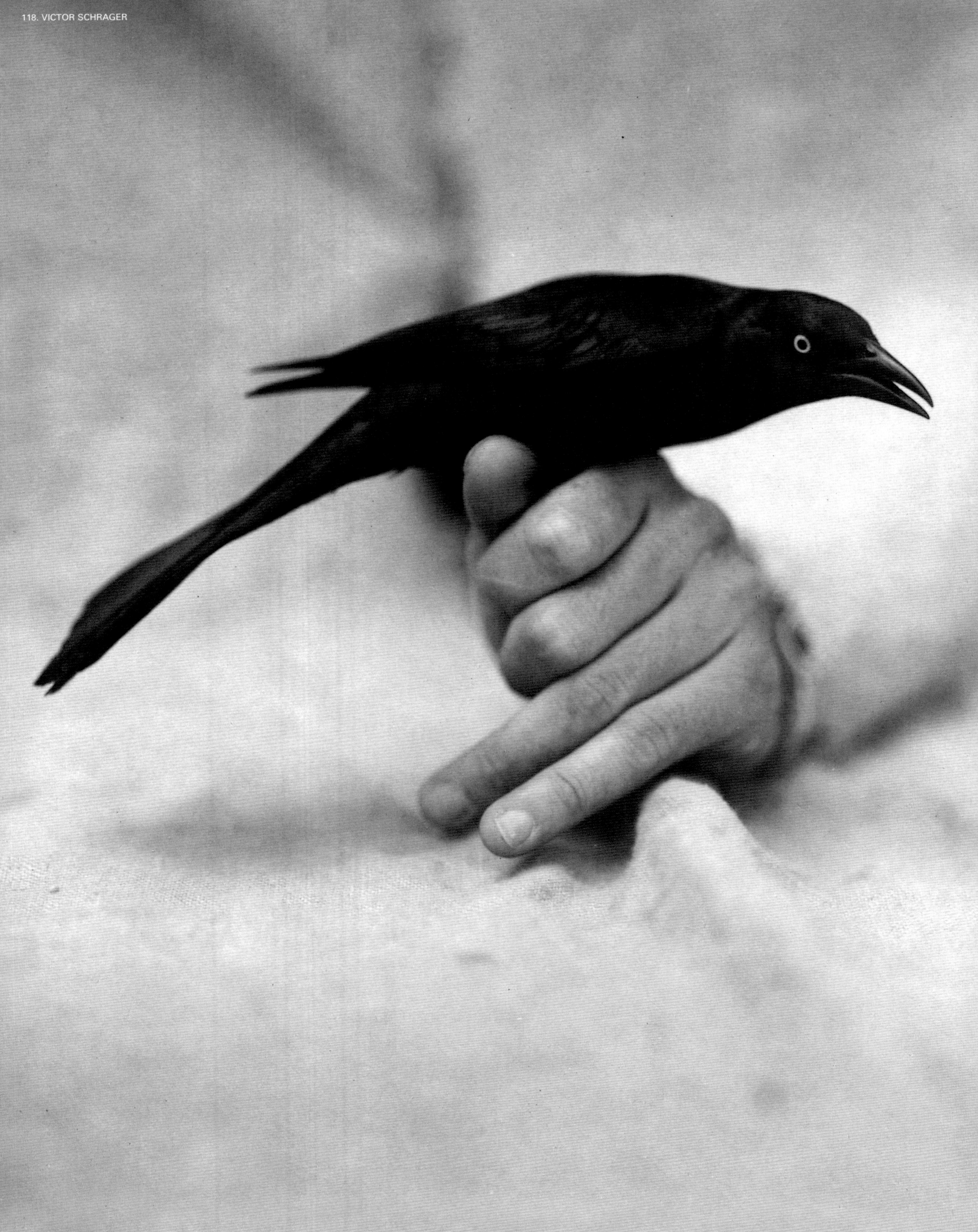

118. VICTOR SCHRAGER

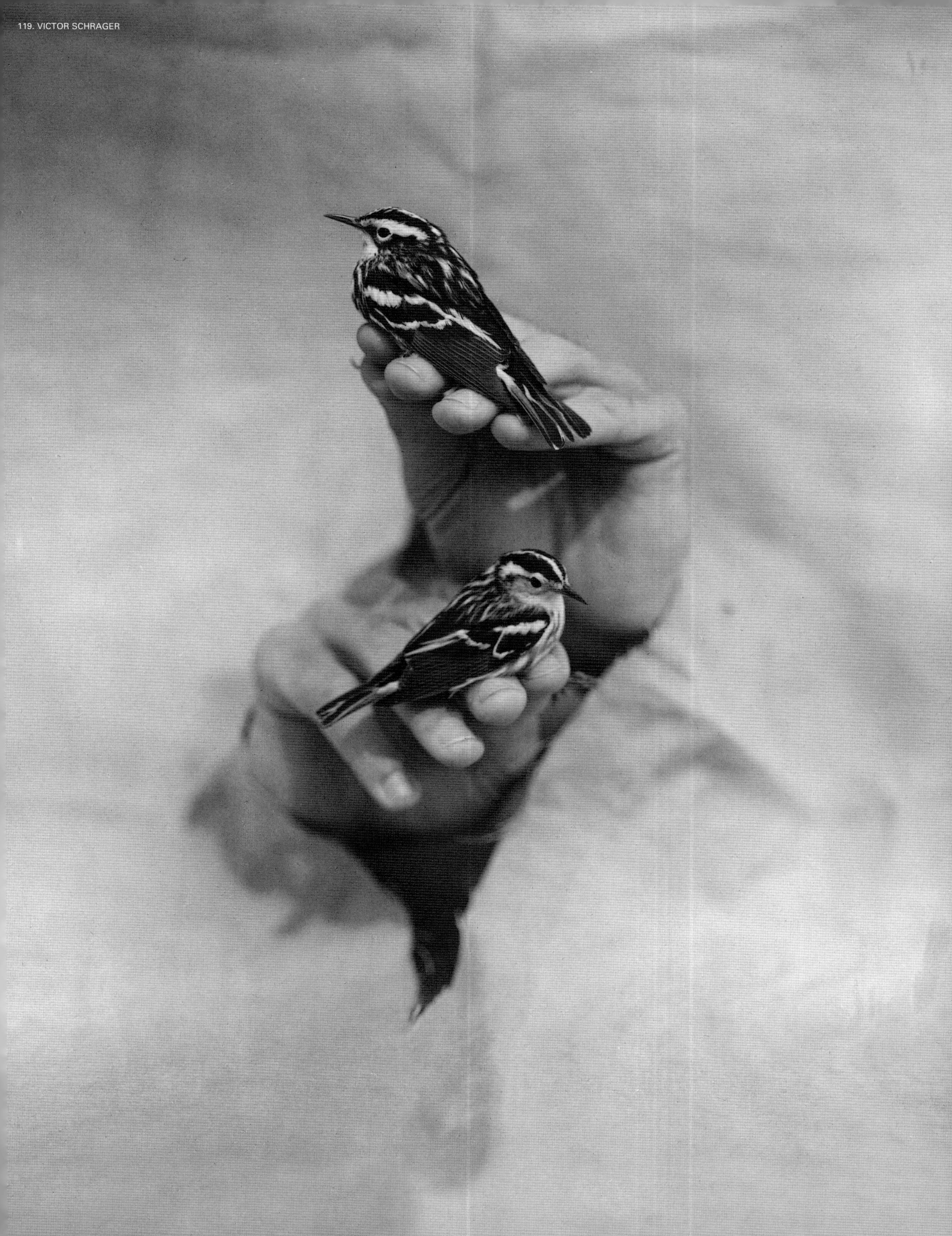

119. VICTOR SCHRAGER

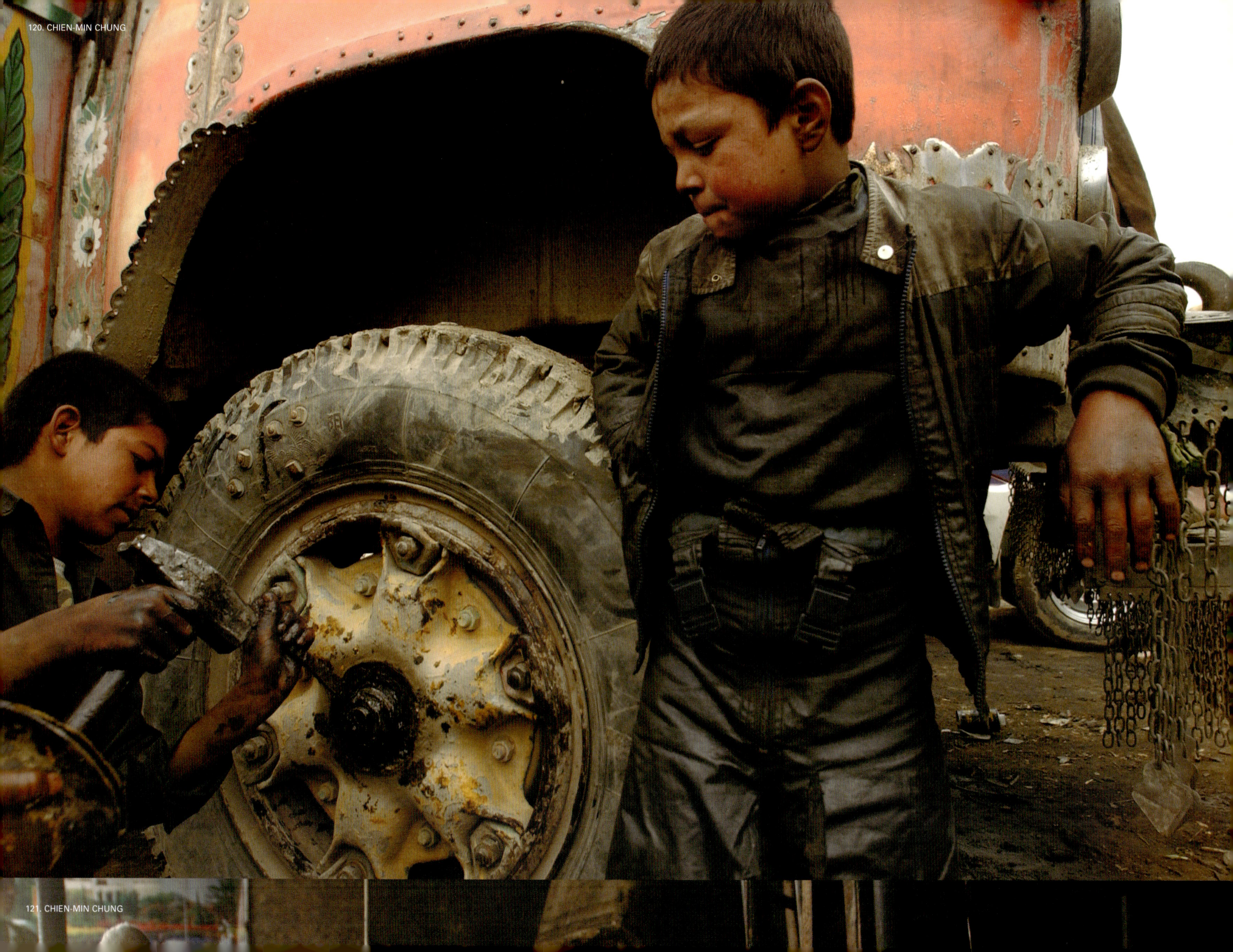

120. CHIEN-MIN CHUNG

121. CHIEN-MIN CHUNG

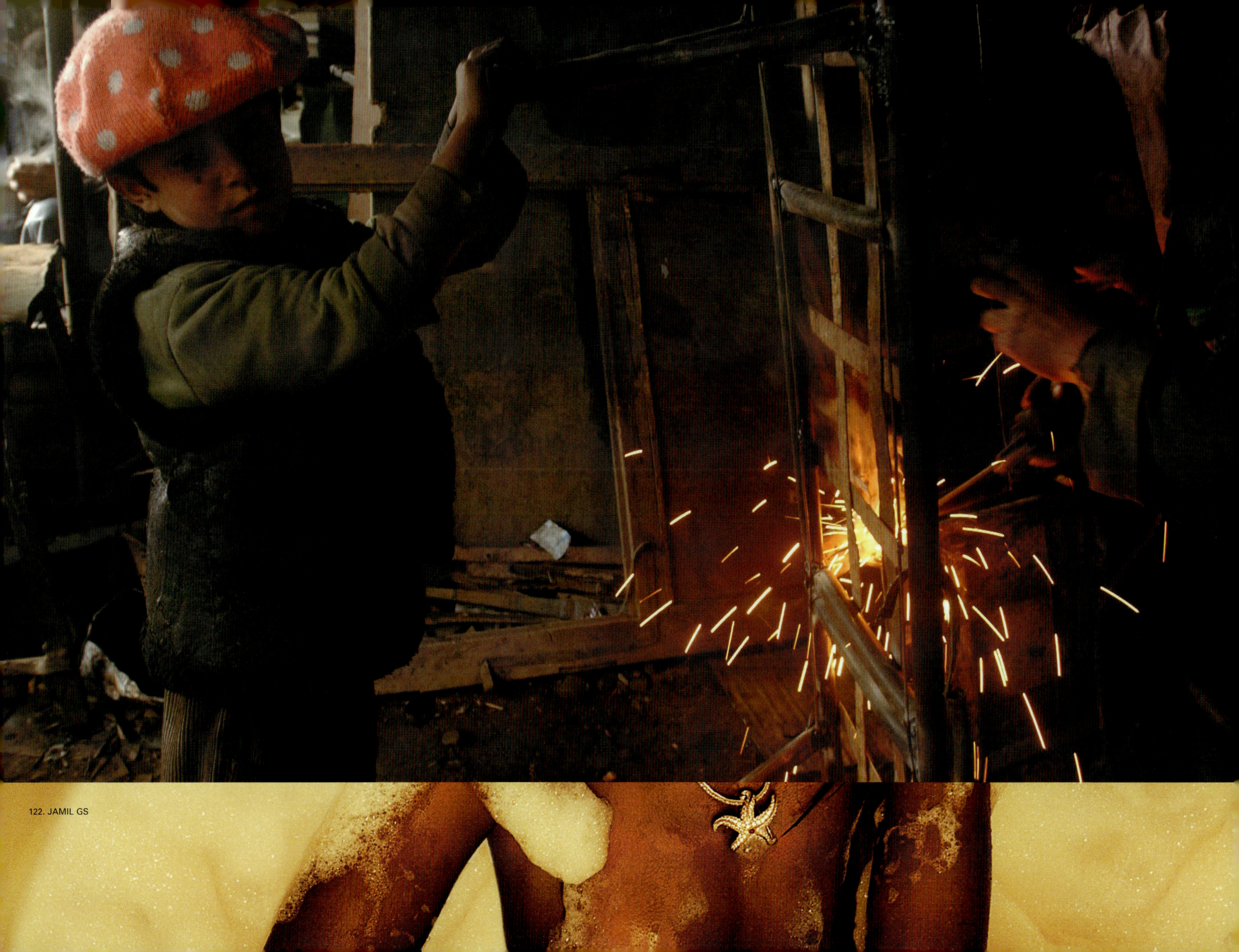

122. JAMIL GS

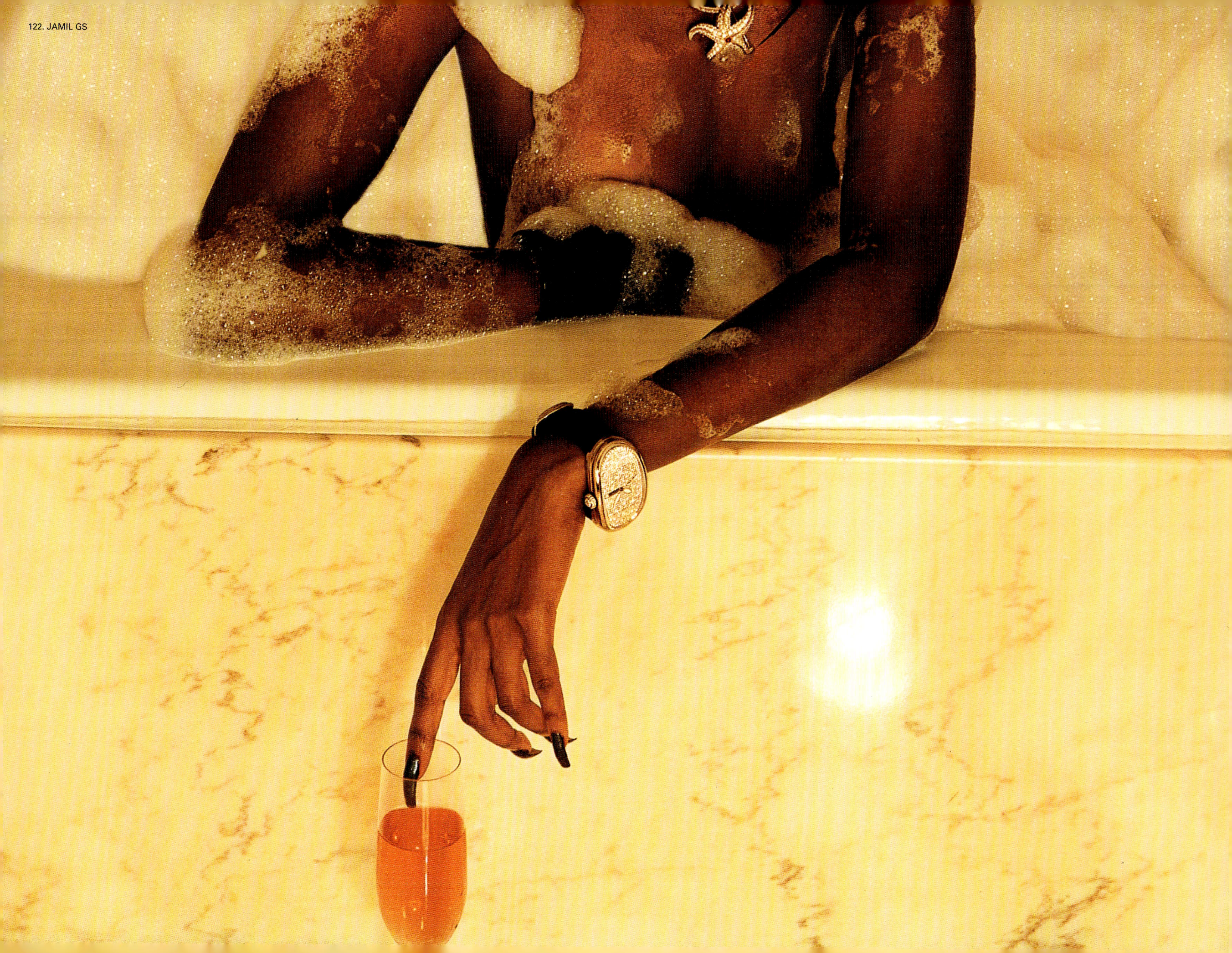

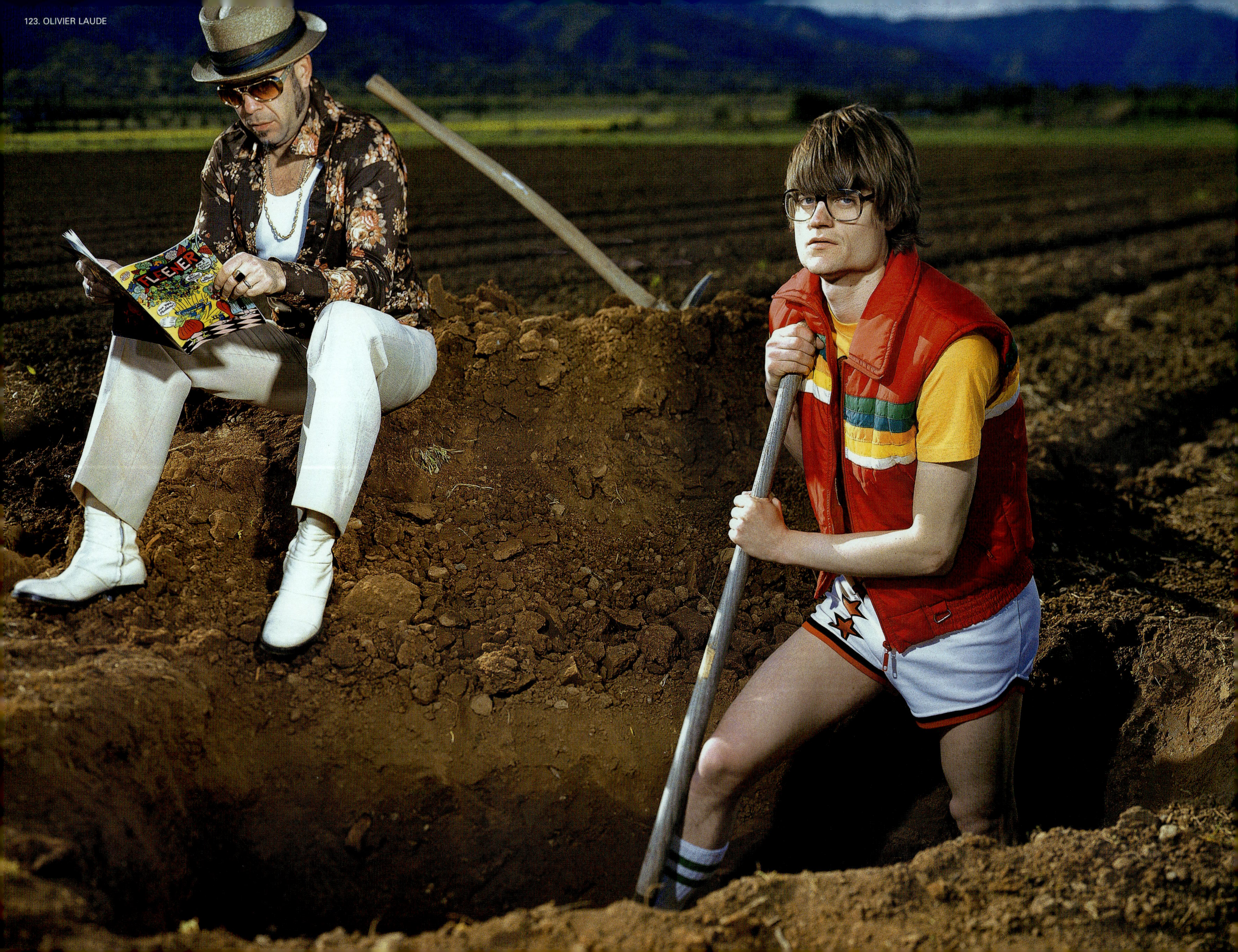

123. OLIVIER LAUDE

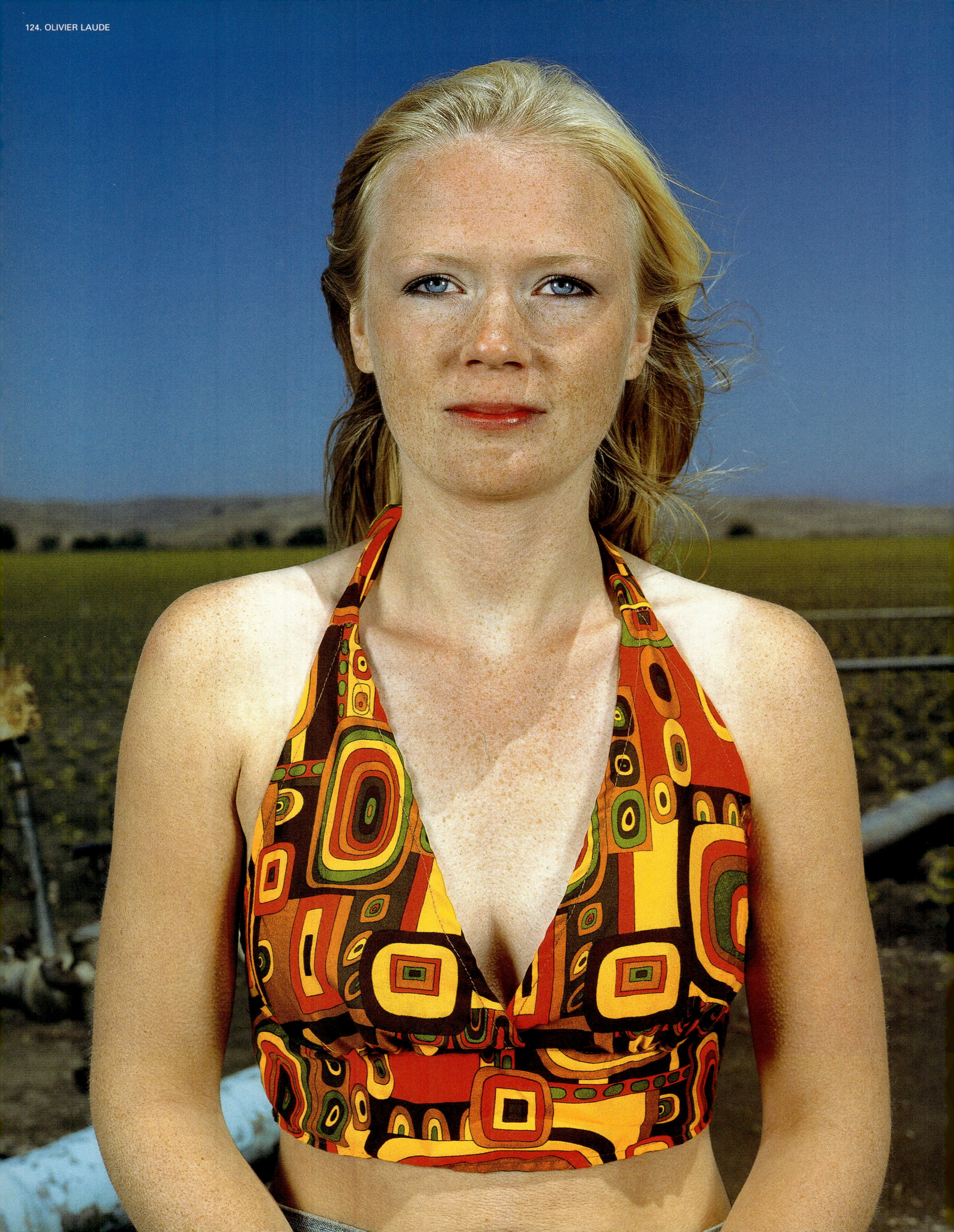

125. CHIEN-CHI CHANG

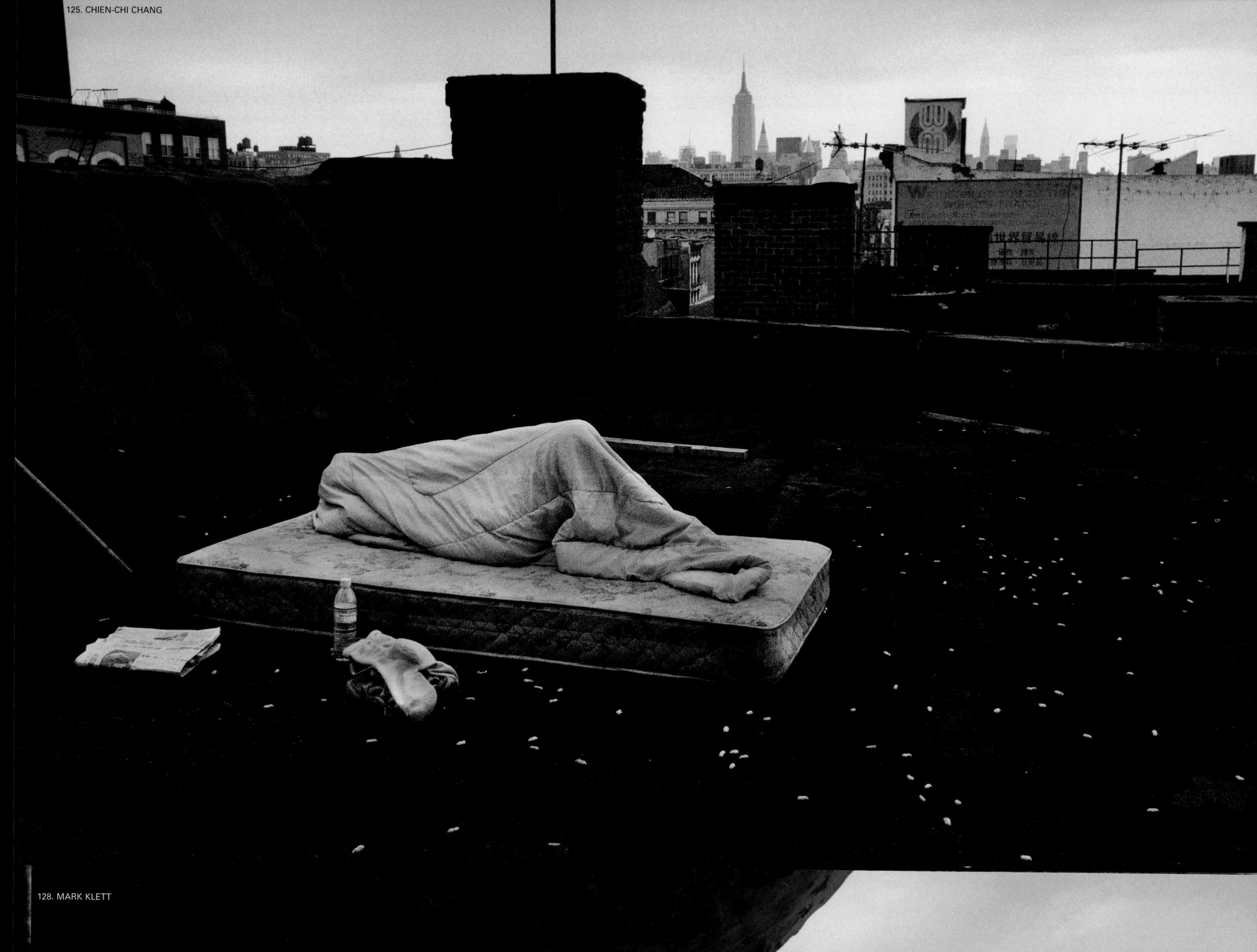

128. MARK KLETT

126. MARK KLETT

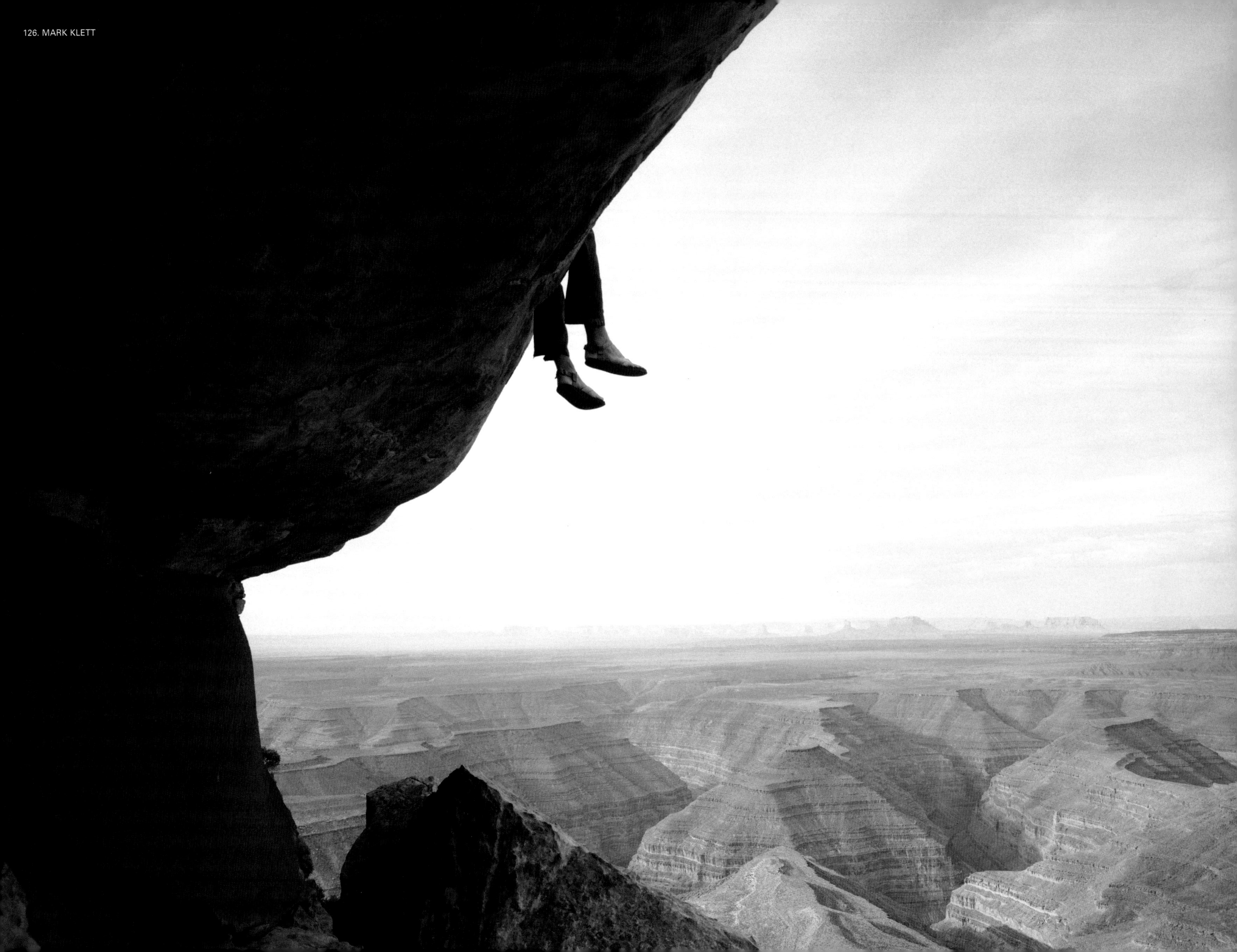

127. MOLLIE LAURIENZO

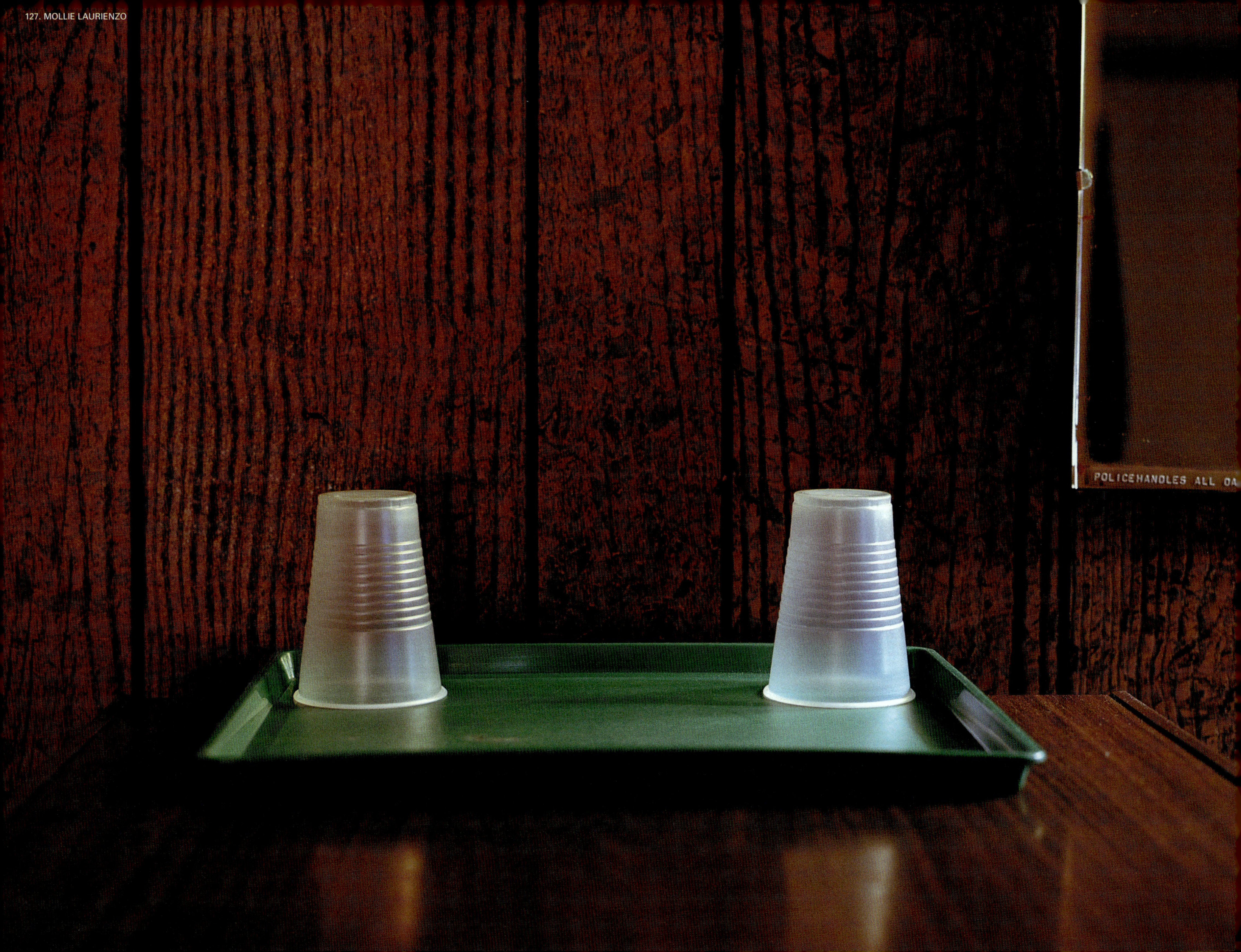

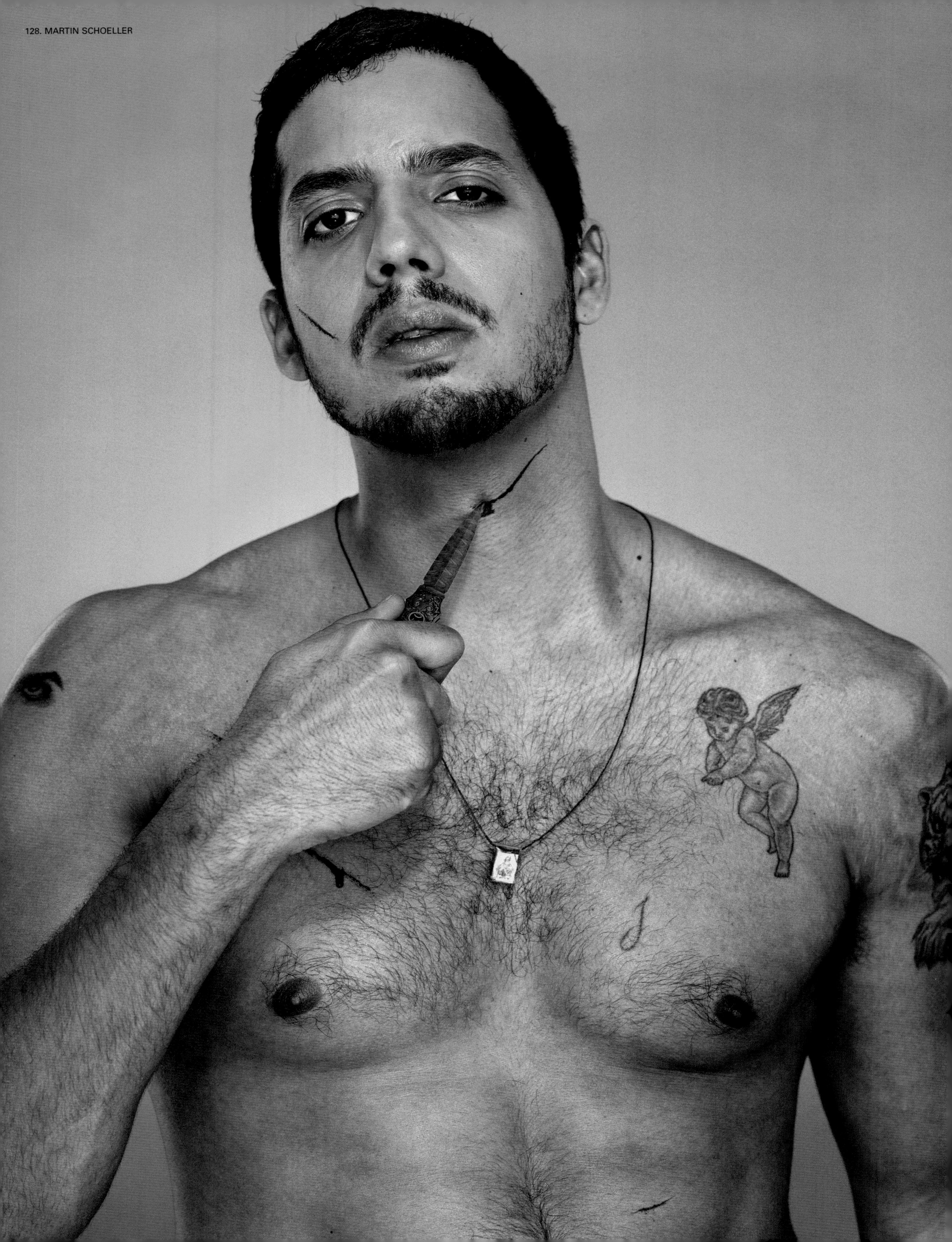

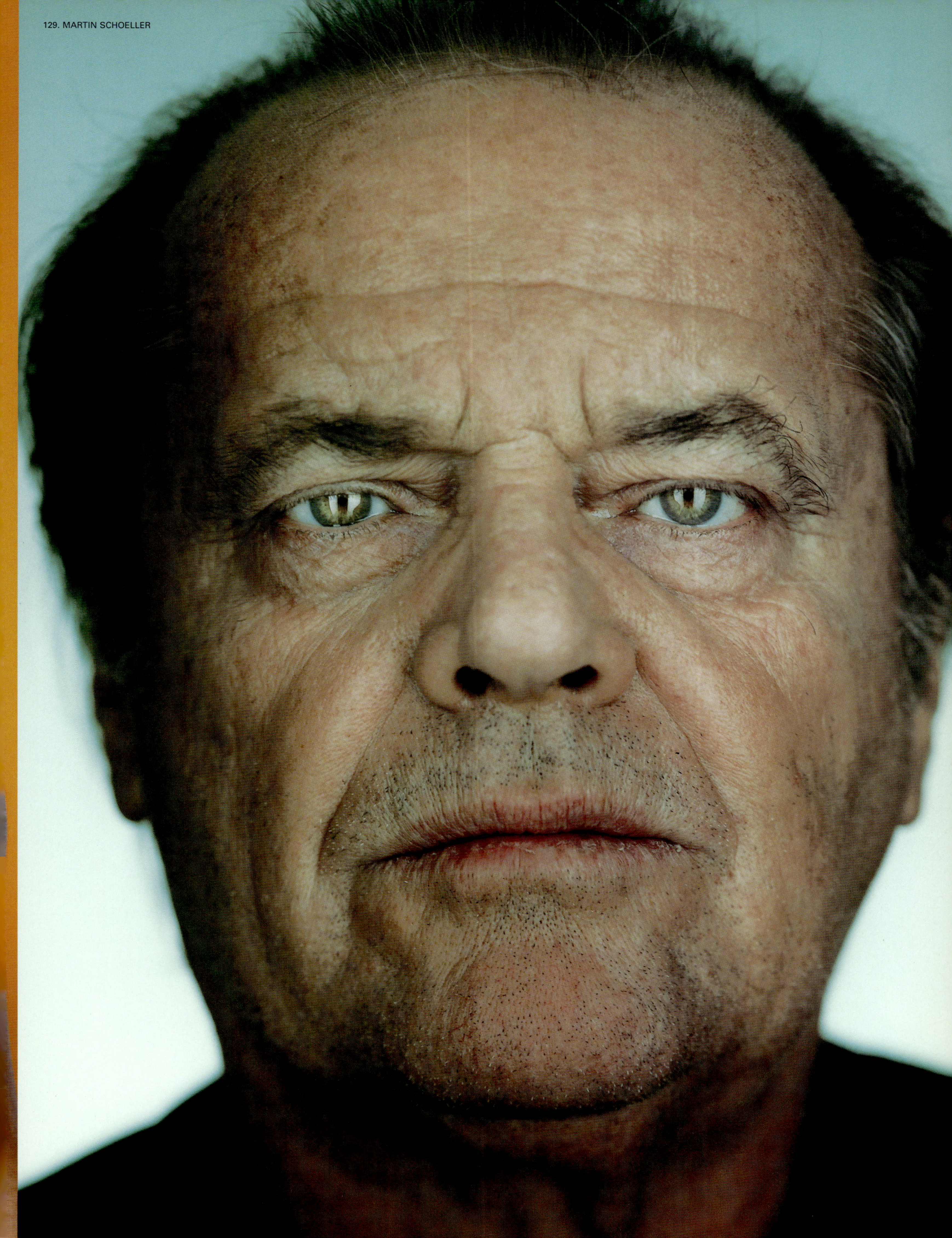

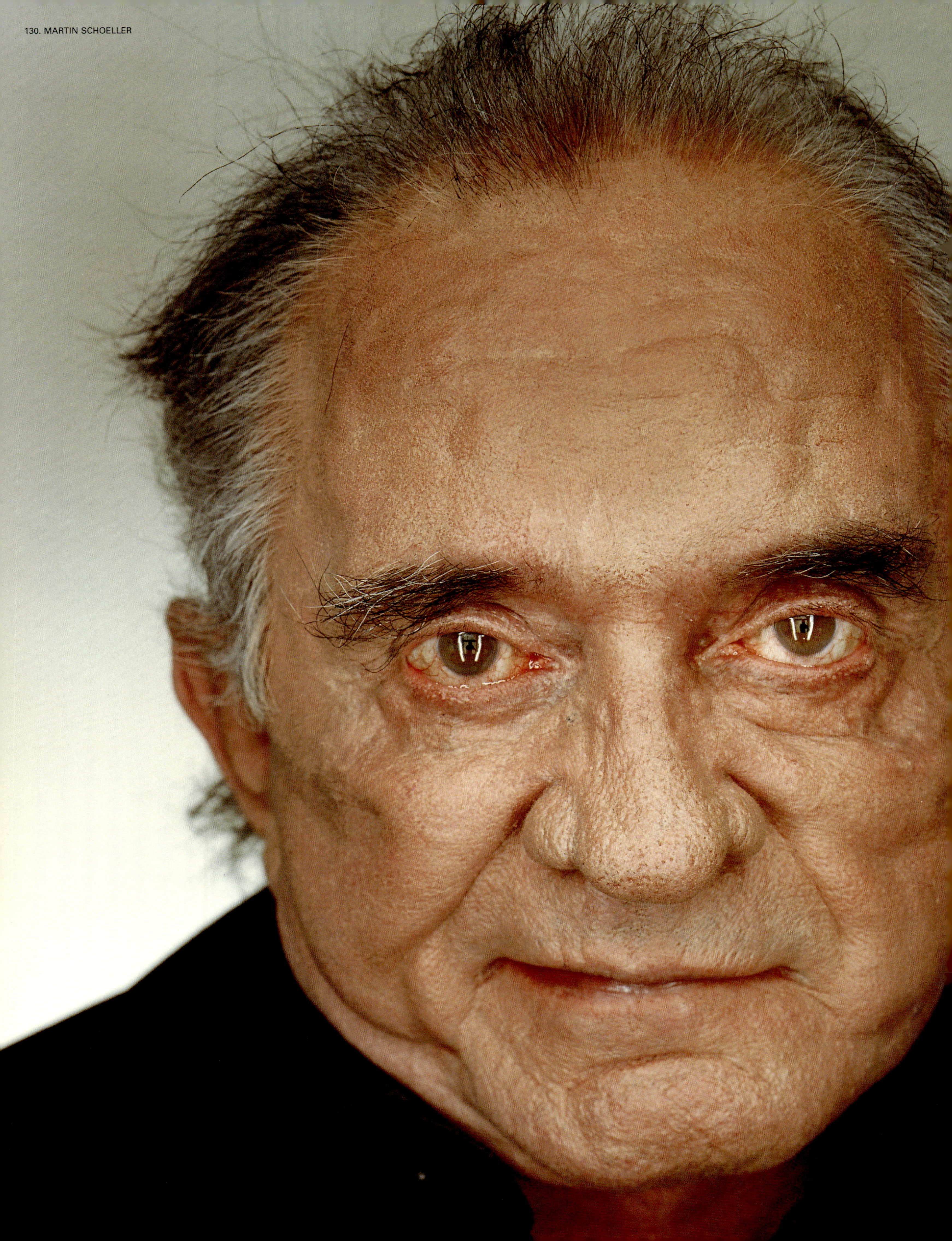

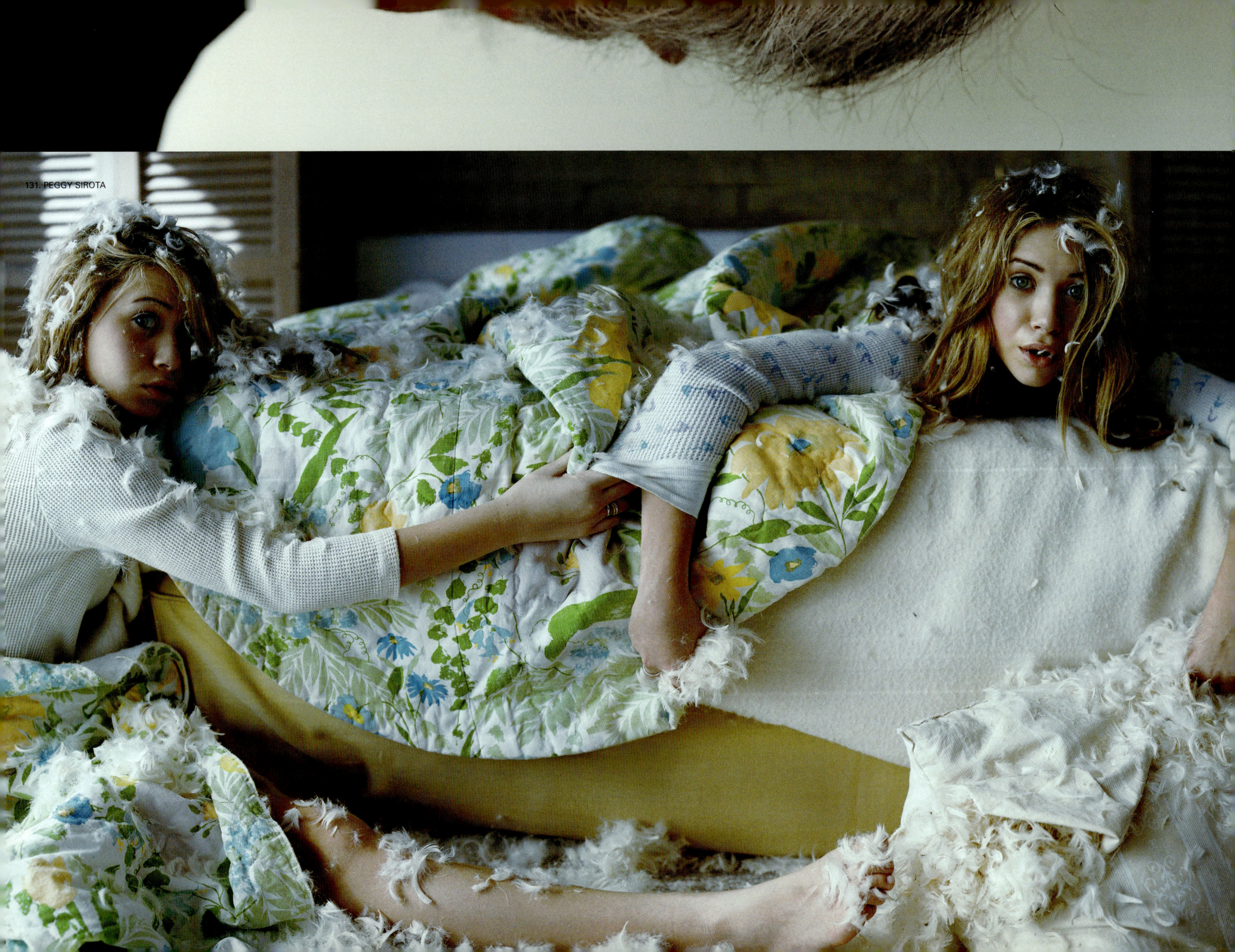

131. PEGGY SIROTA

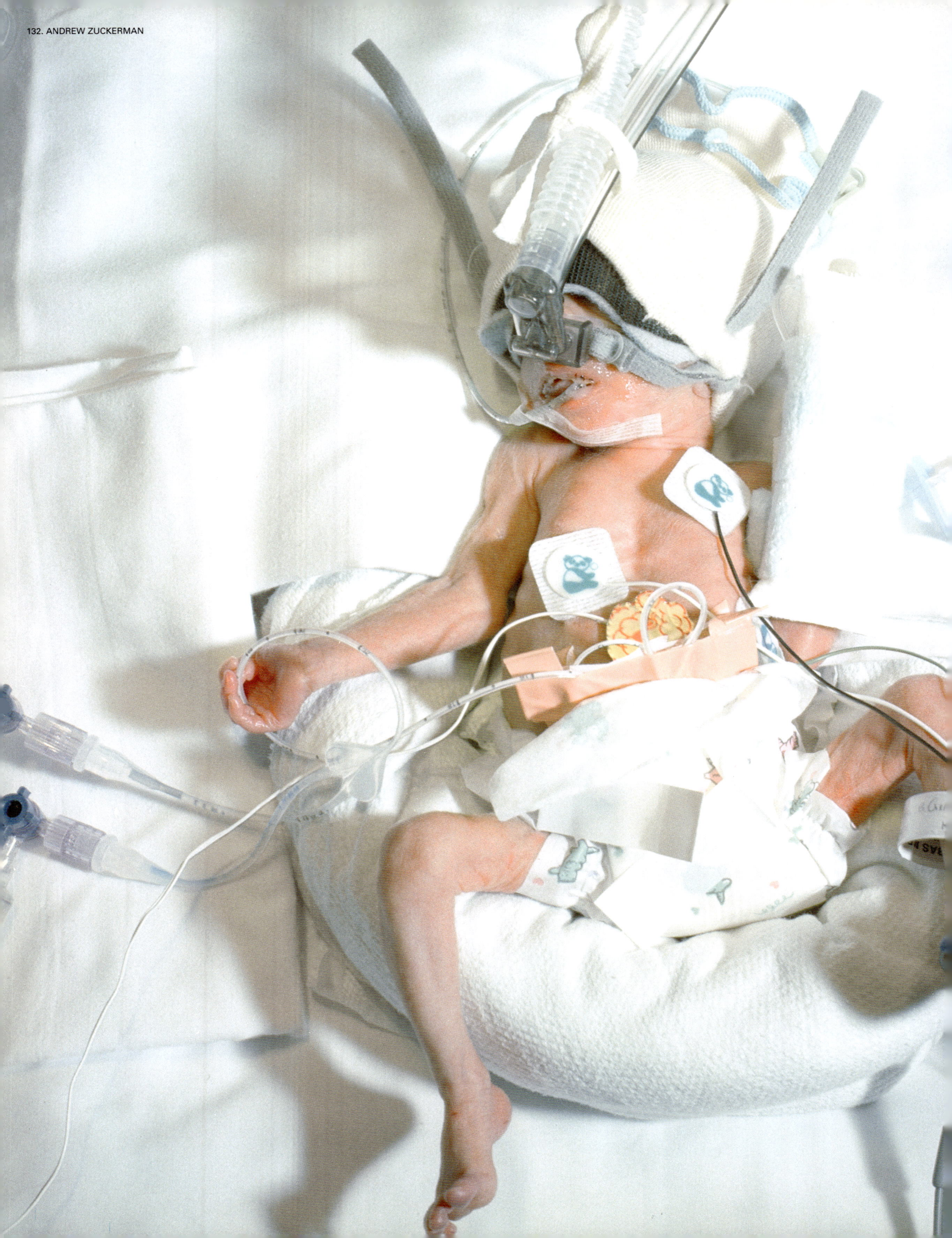

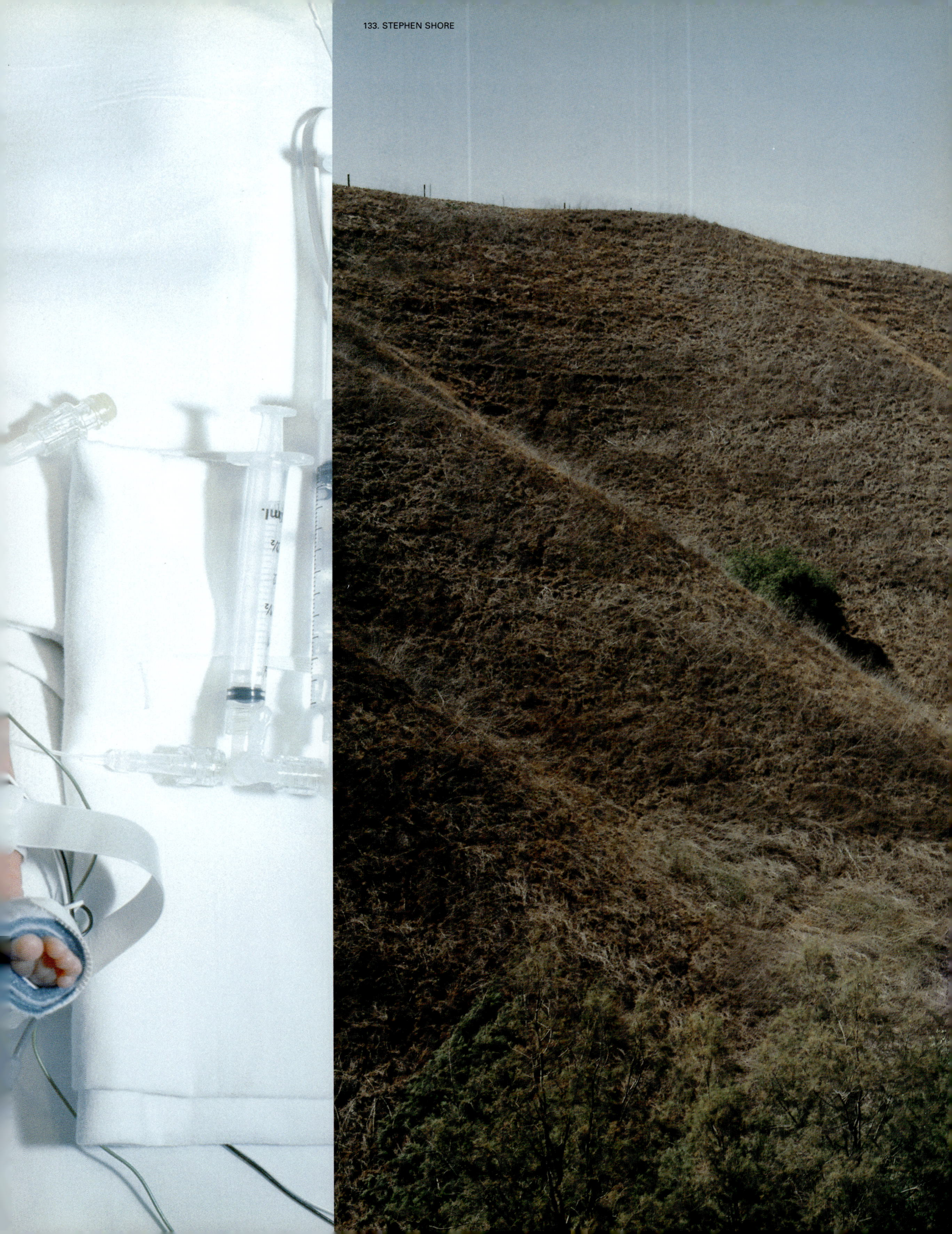

133. STEPHEN SHORE

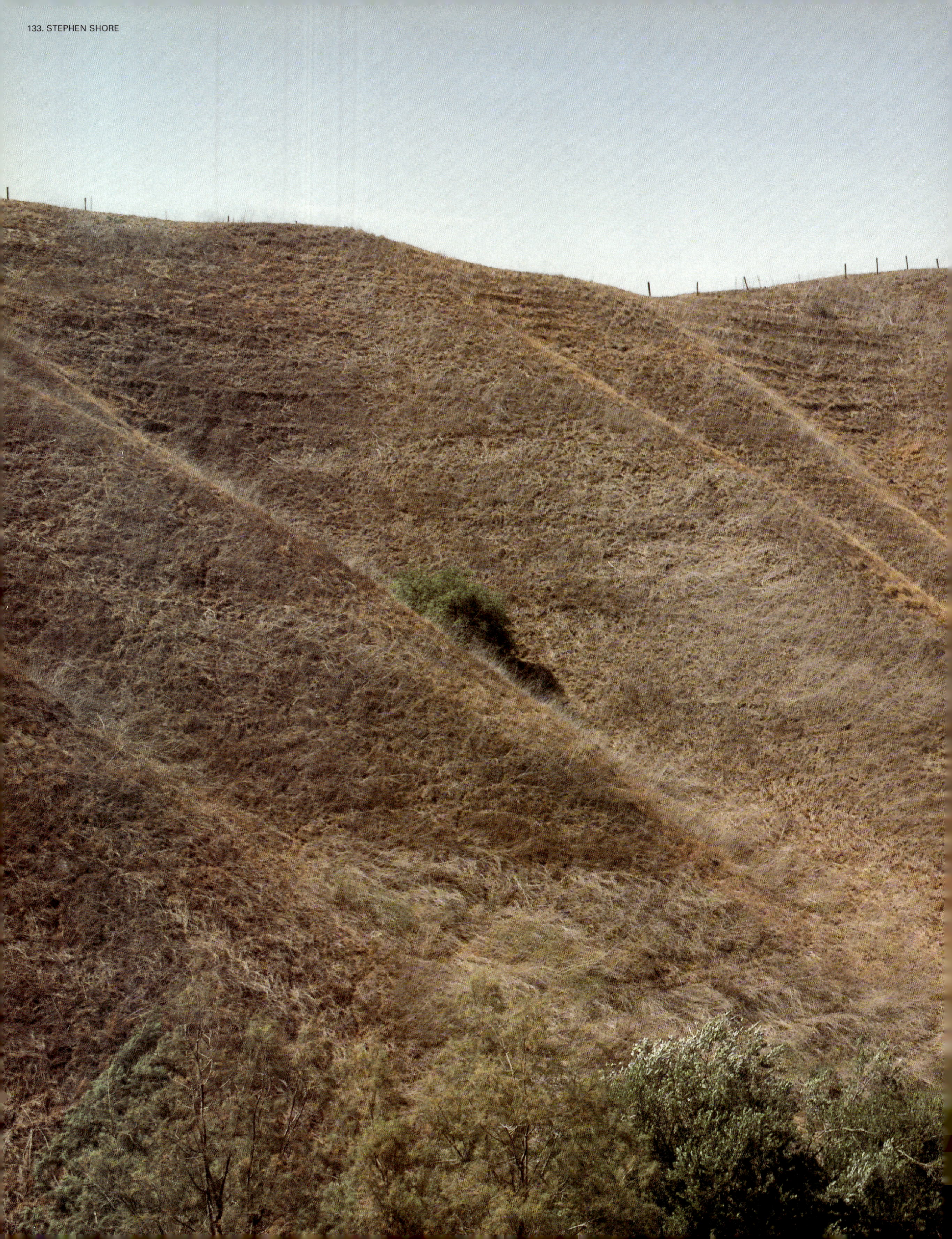

133. STEPHEN SHORE

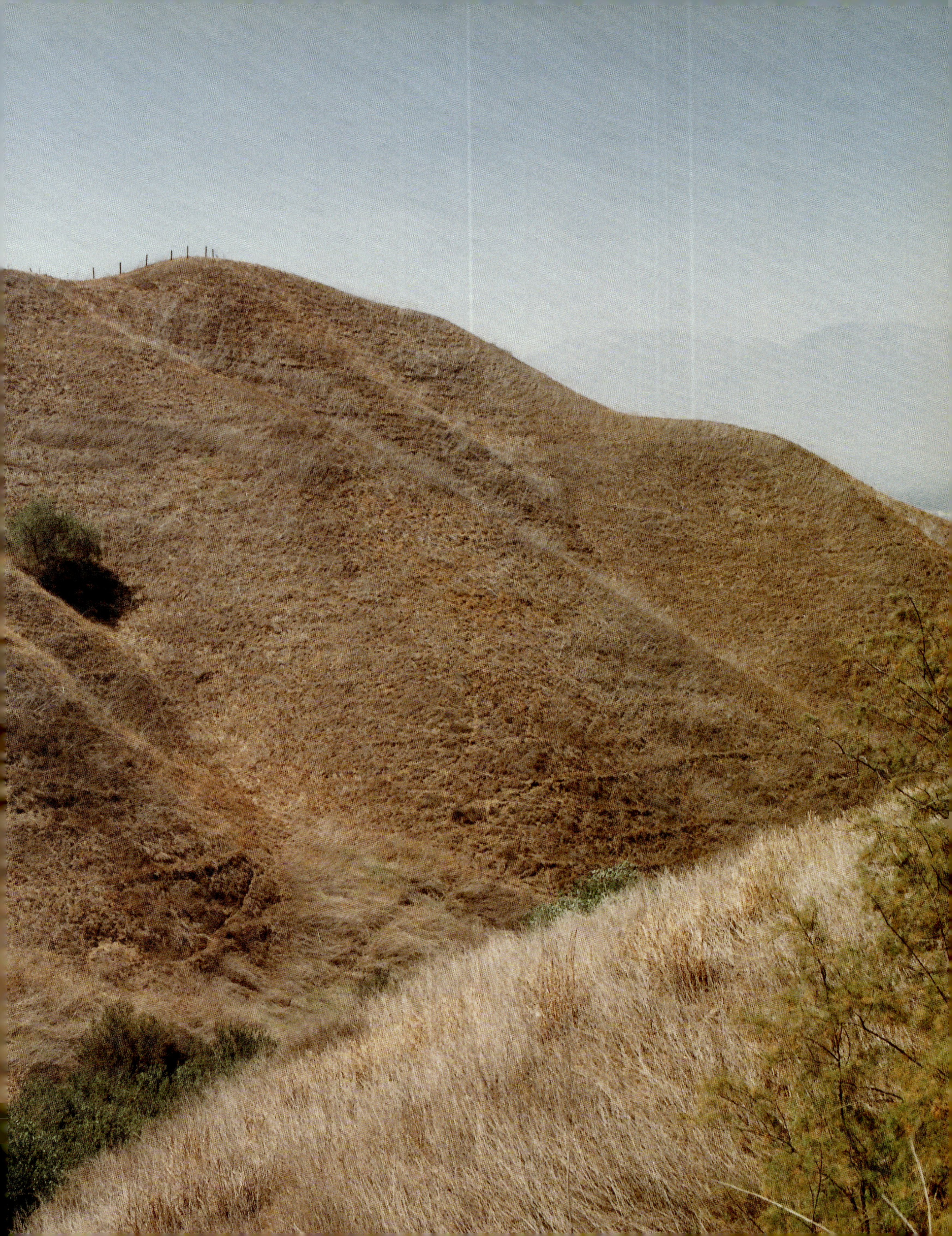

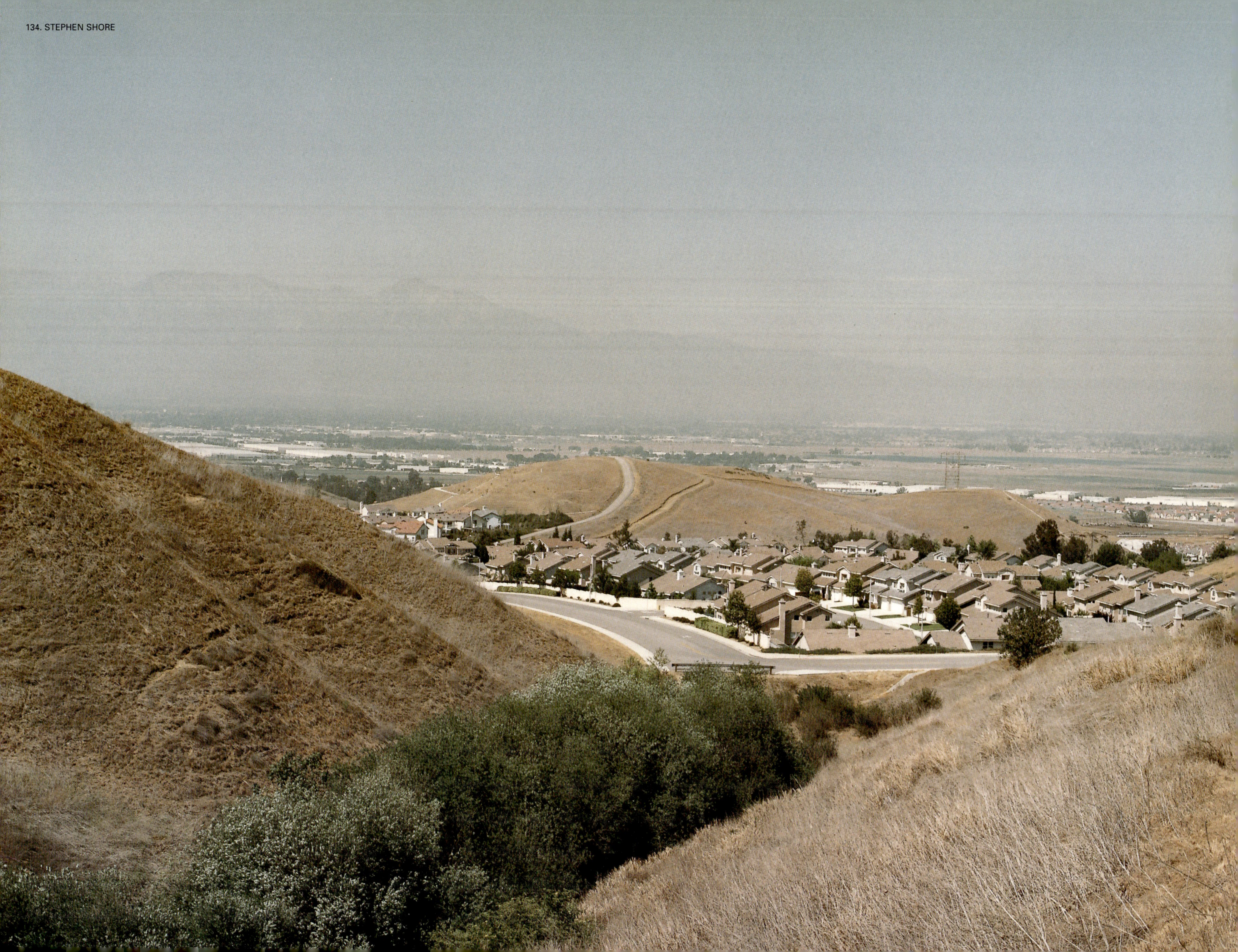
134. STEPHEN SHORE

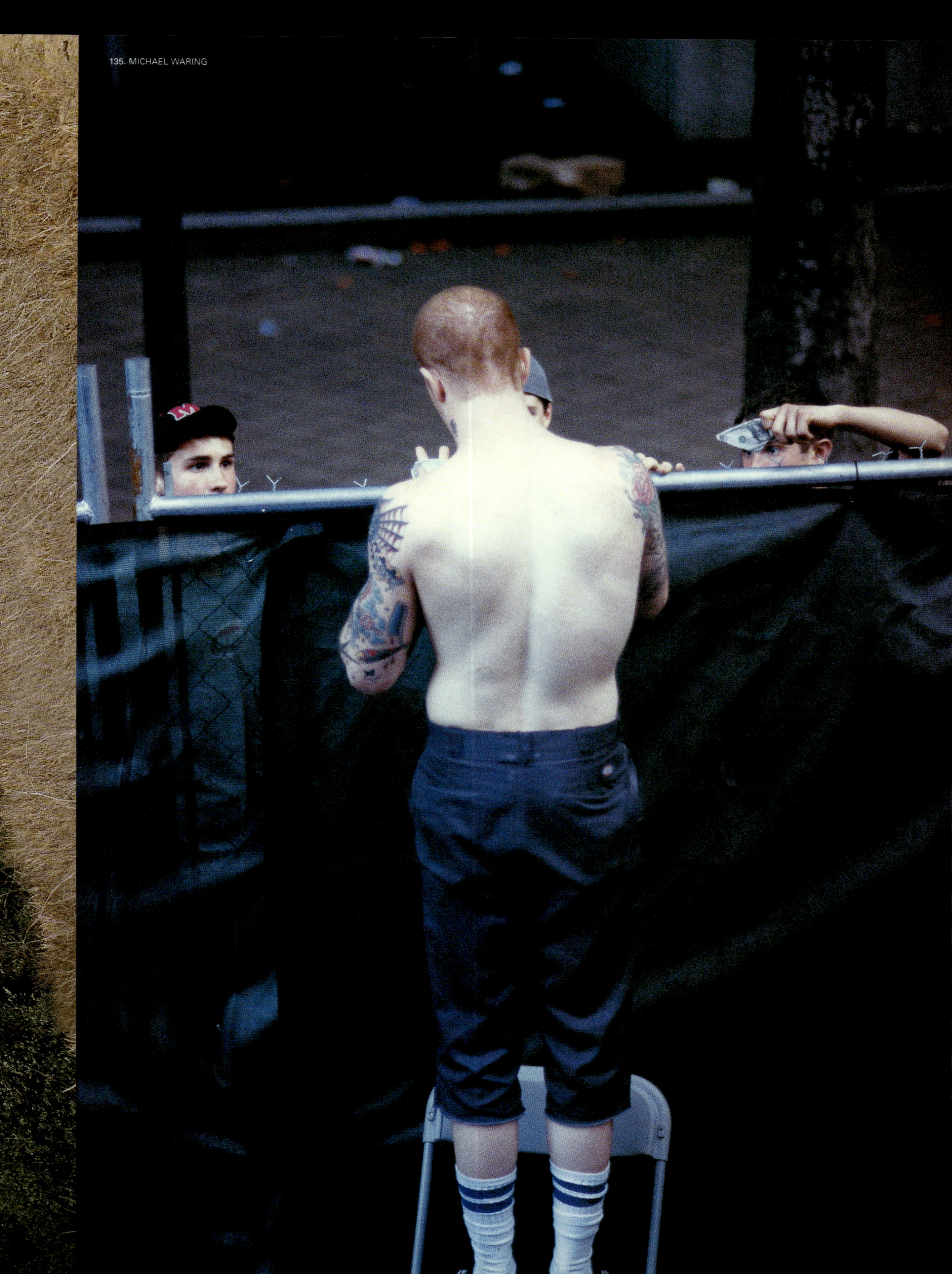

135. MICHAEL WARING

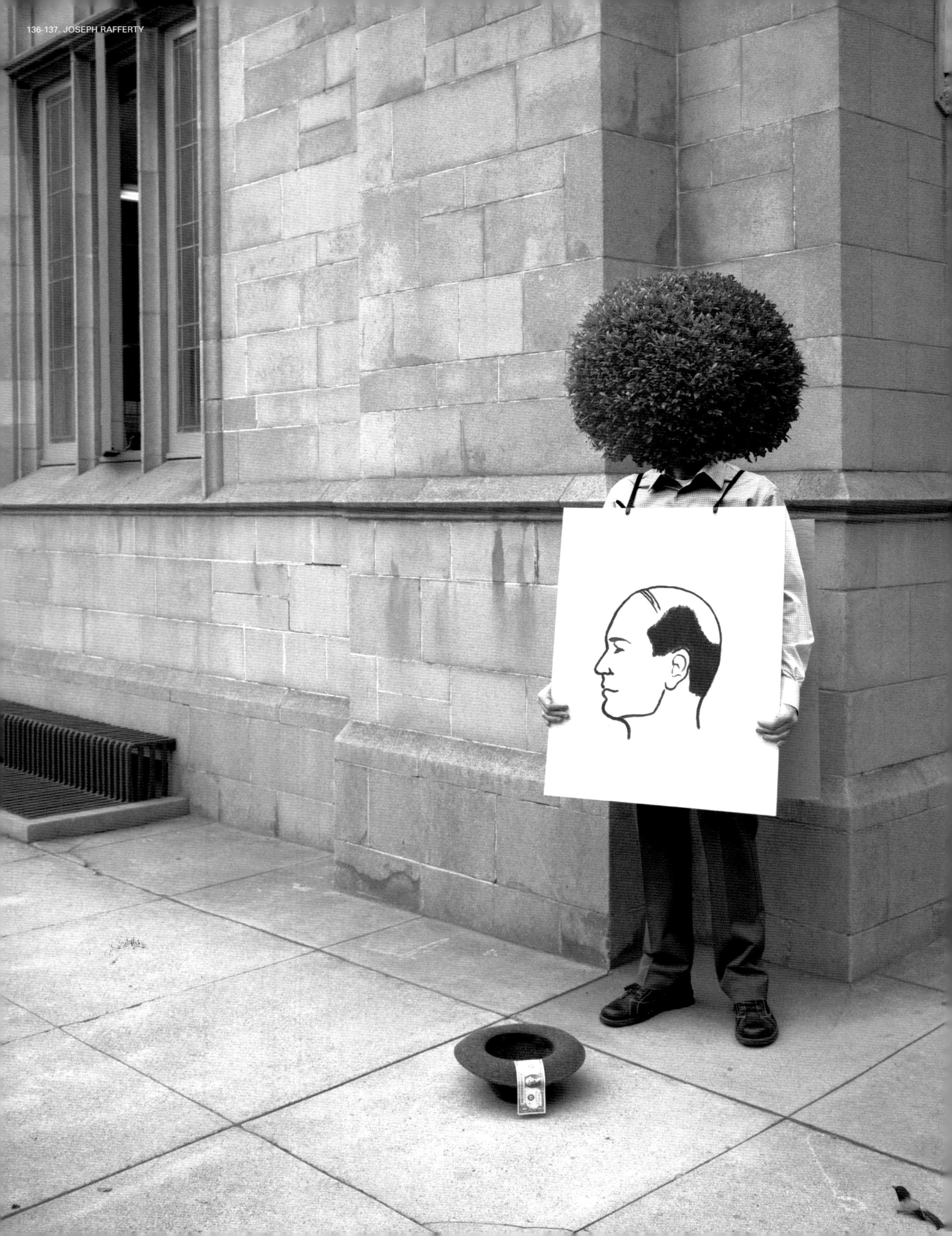

136-137. JOSEPH RAFFERTY

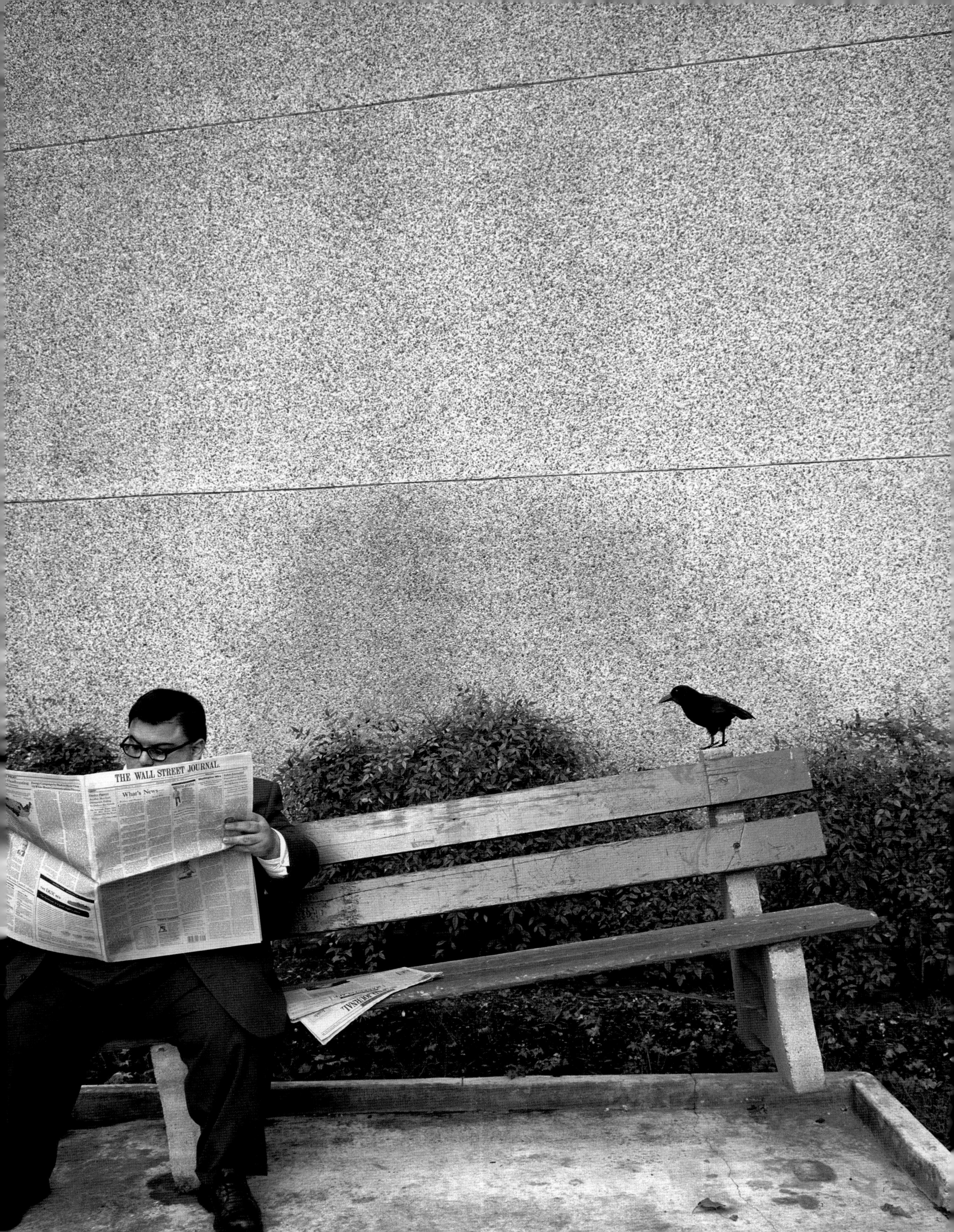
THE WALL STREET JOURNAL.
What's News

138. JOSEPH RAFFERTY

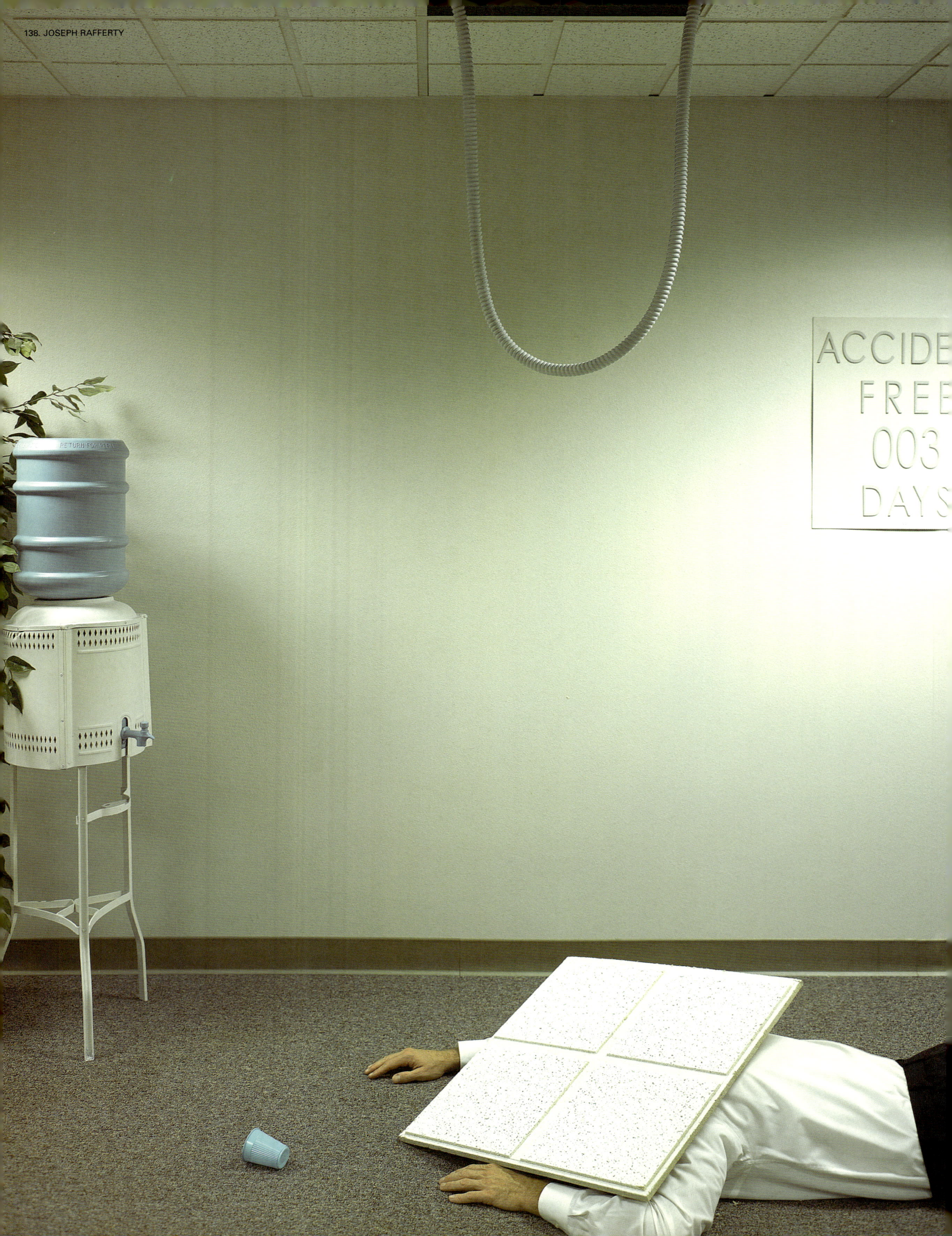

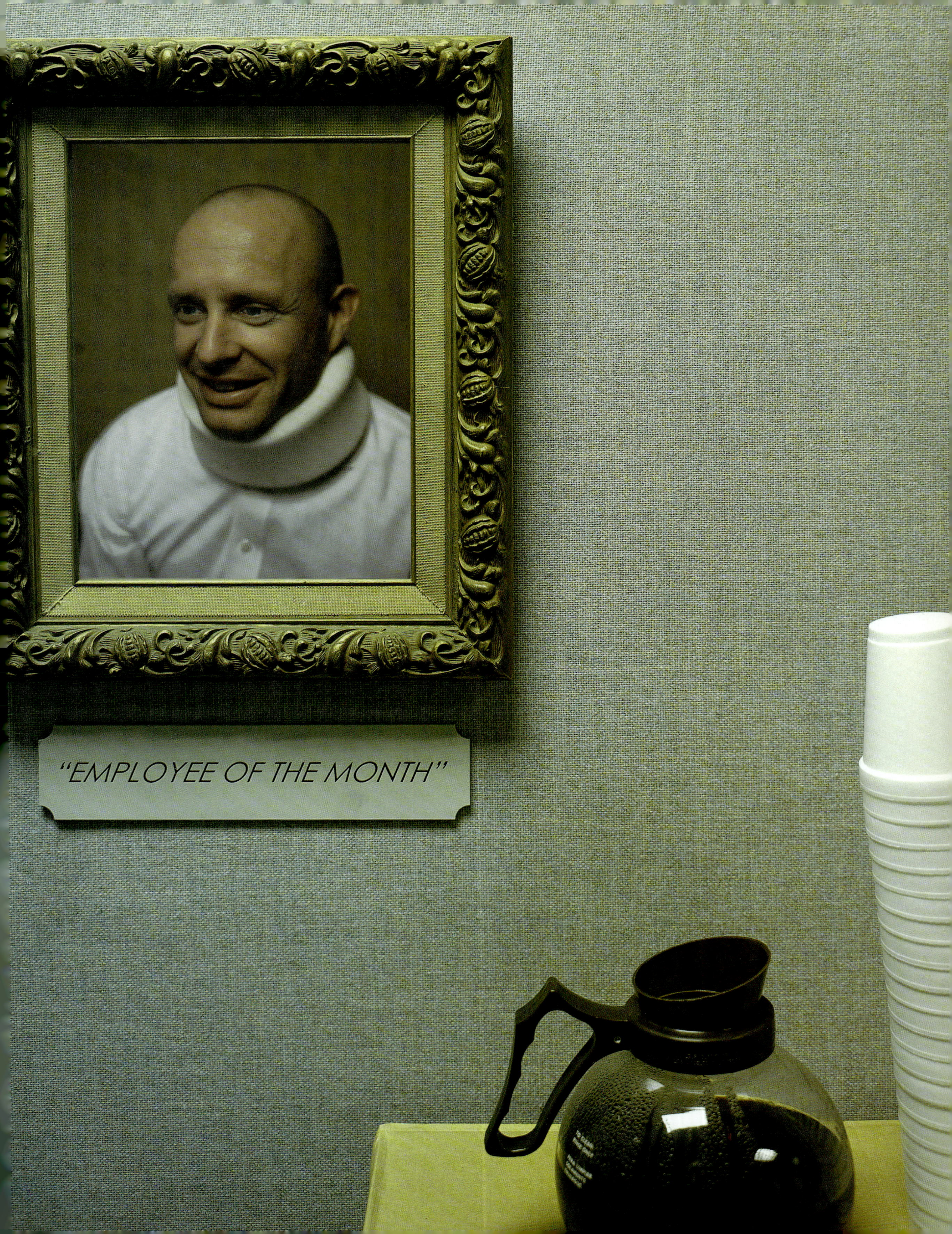
"EMPLOYEE OF THE MONTH"

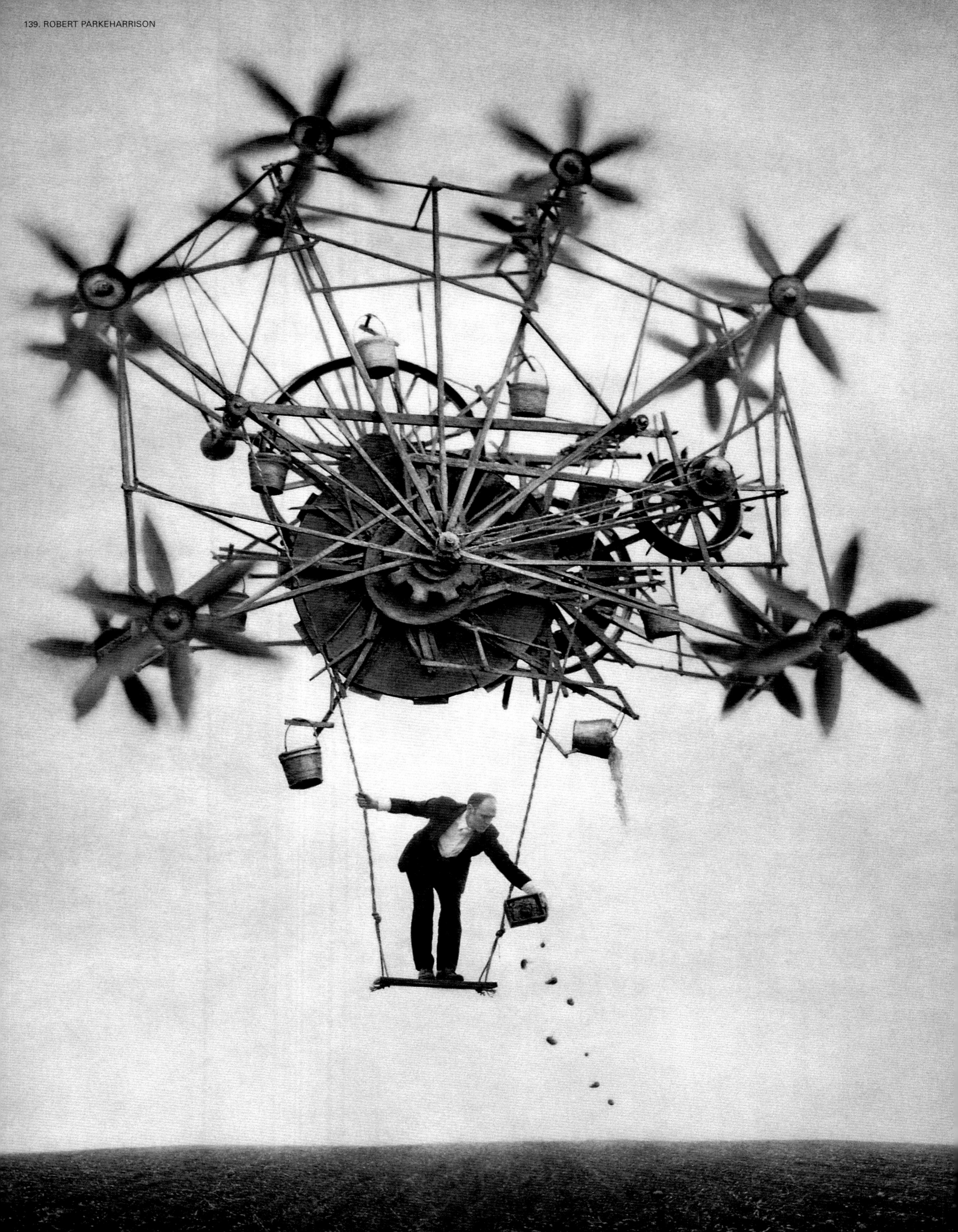

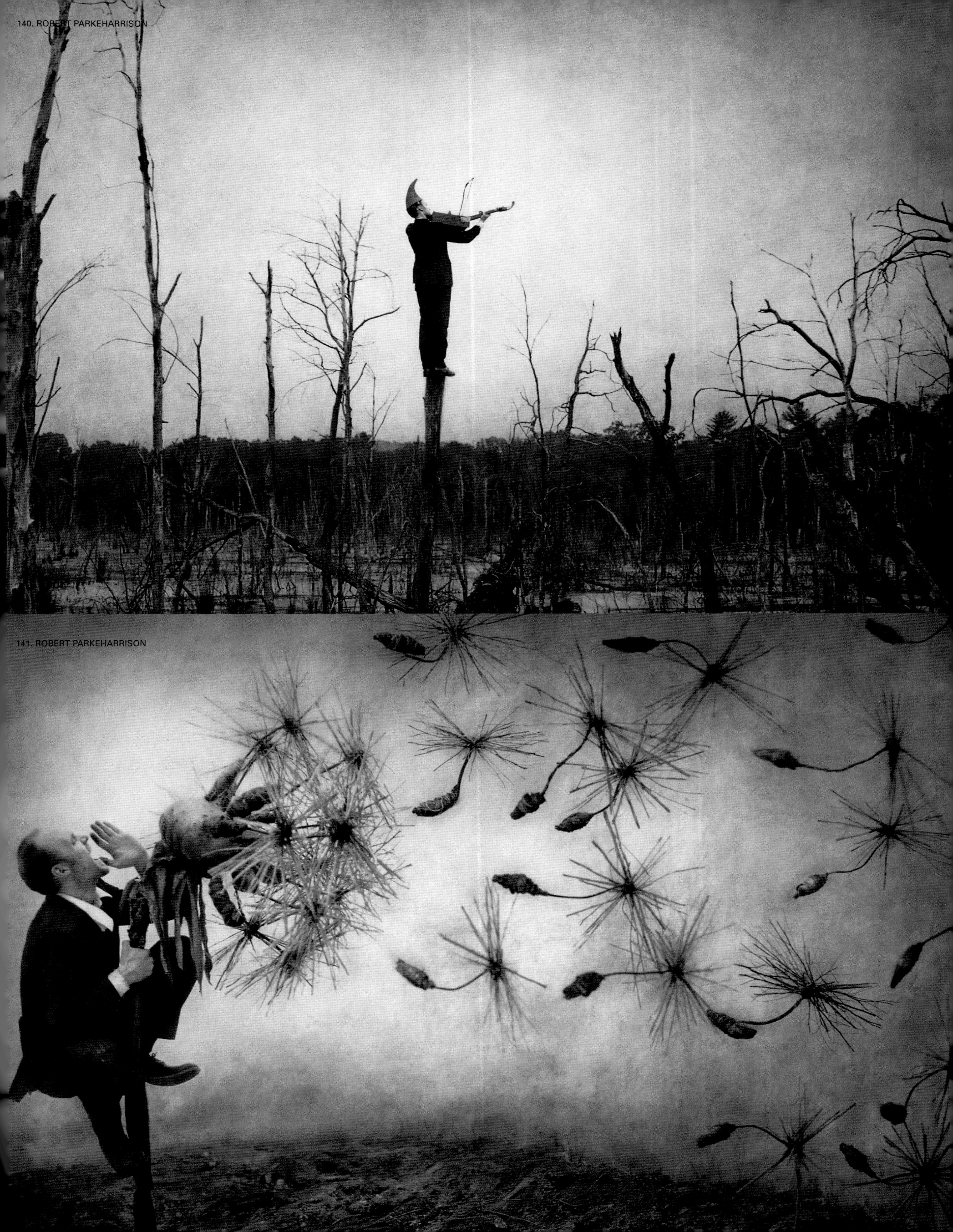

140. ROBERT PARKEHARRISON

141. ROBERT PARKEHARRISON

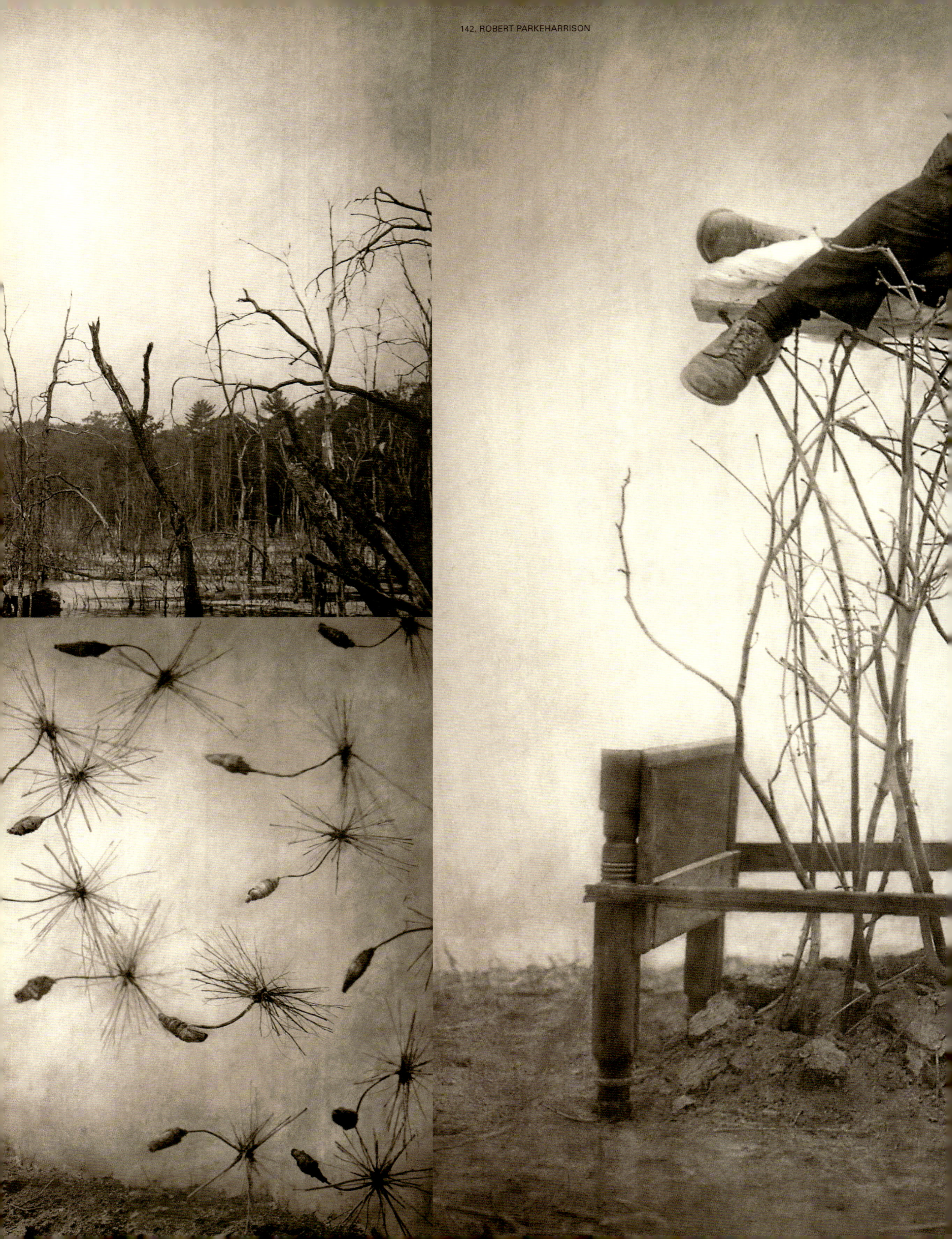

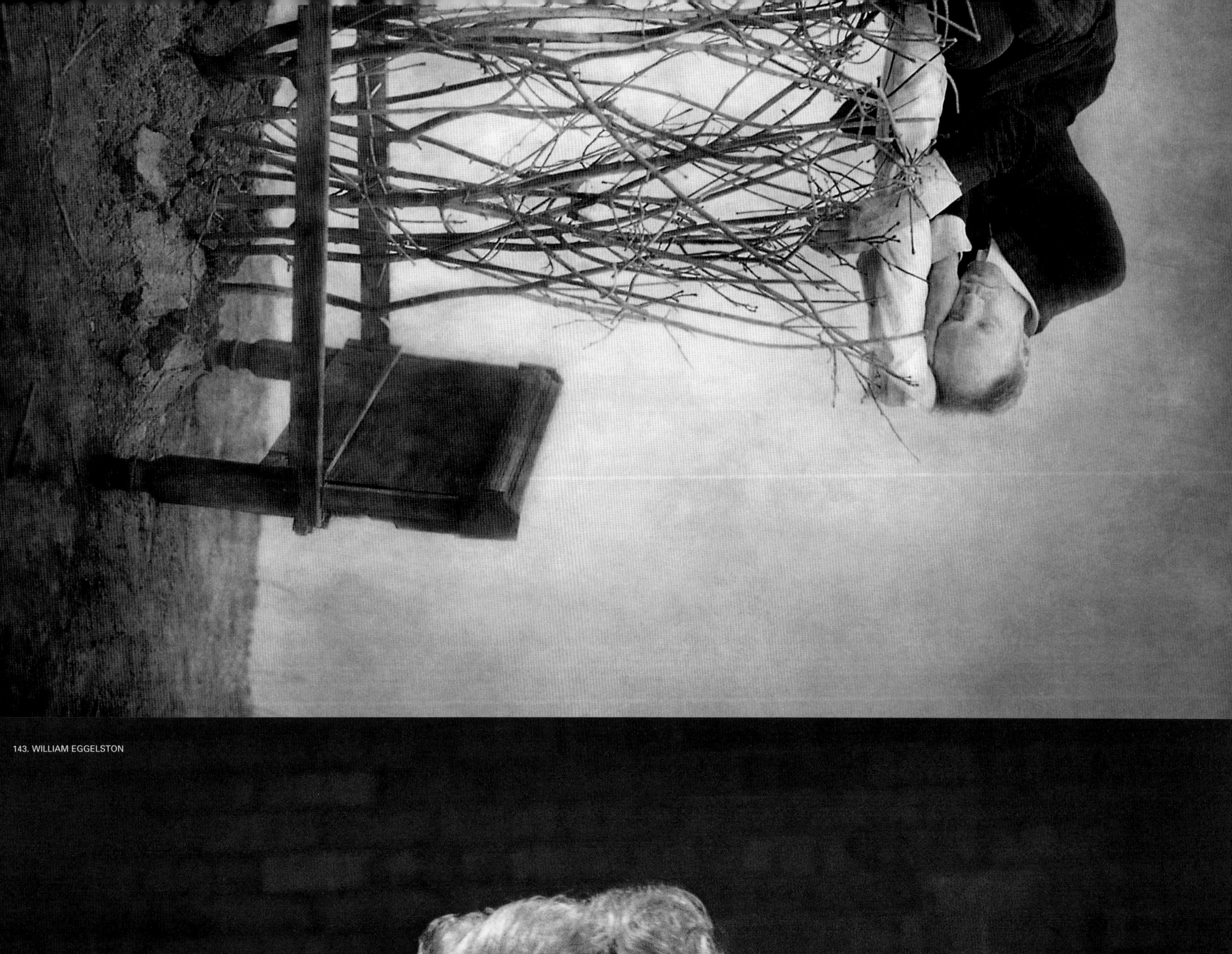

143. WILLIAM EGGELSTON

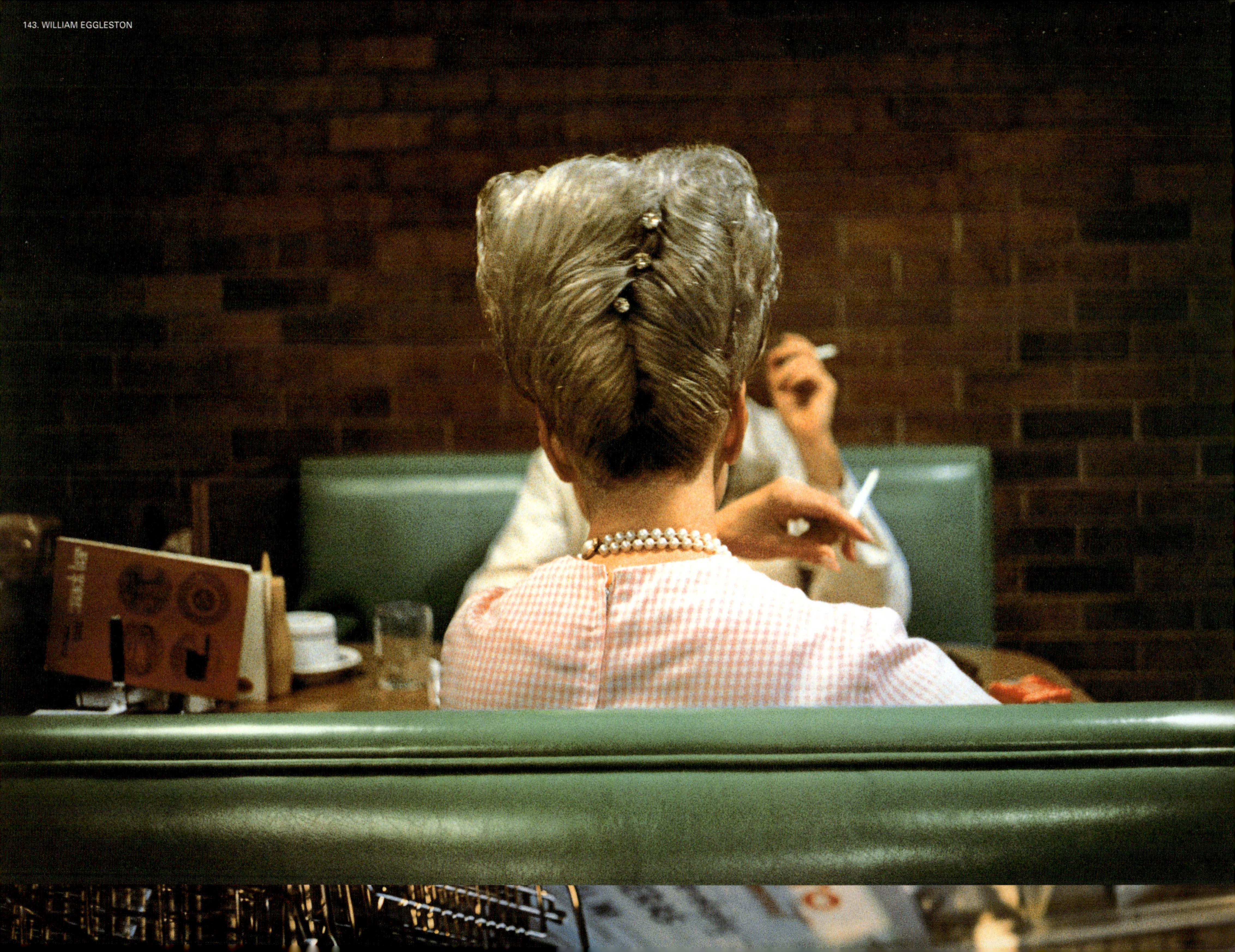

143. WILLIAM EGGLESTON

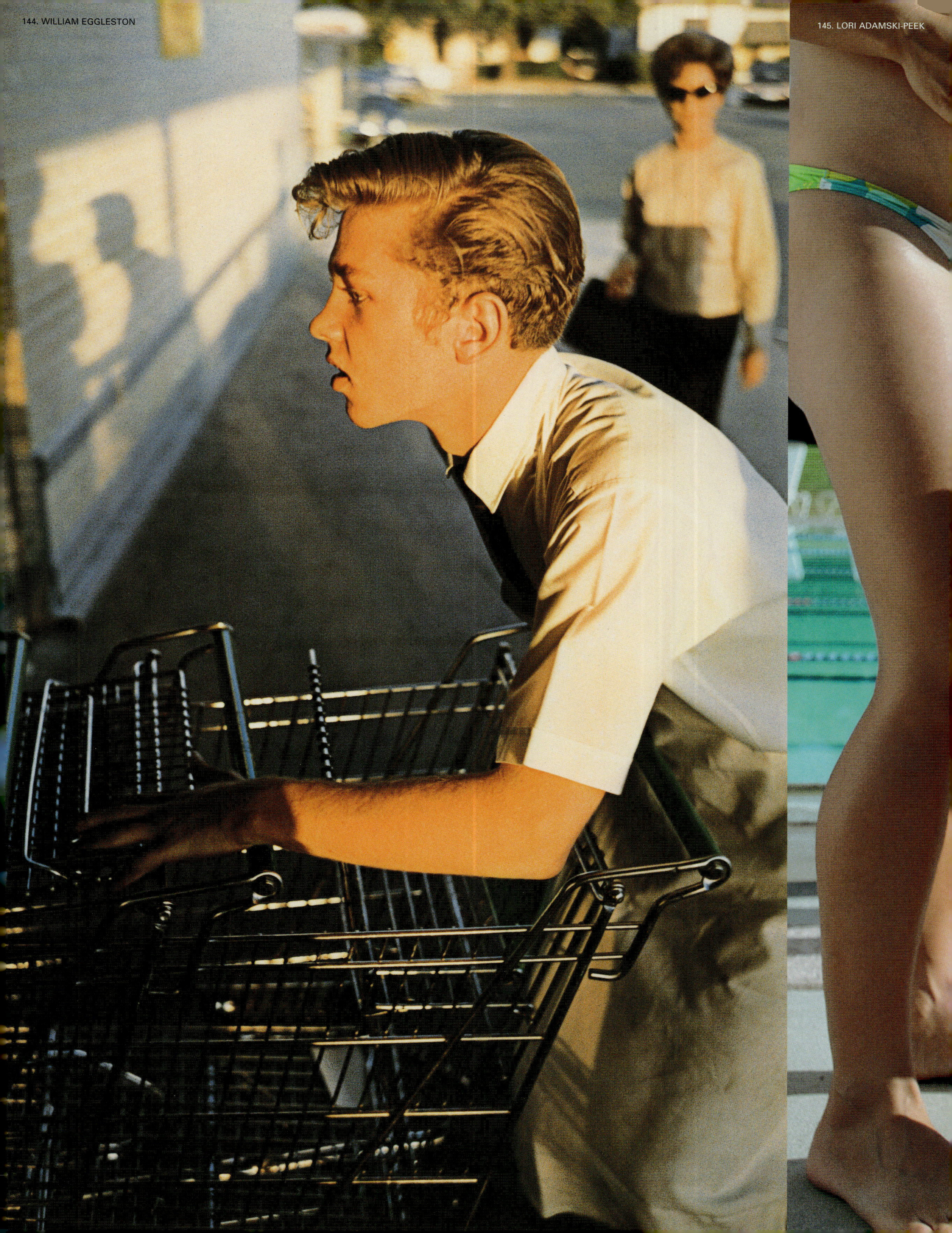

144. WILLIAM EGGLESTON

145. LORI ADAMSKI-PEEK

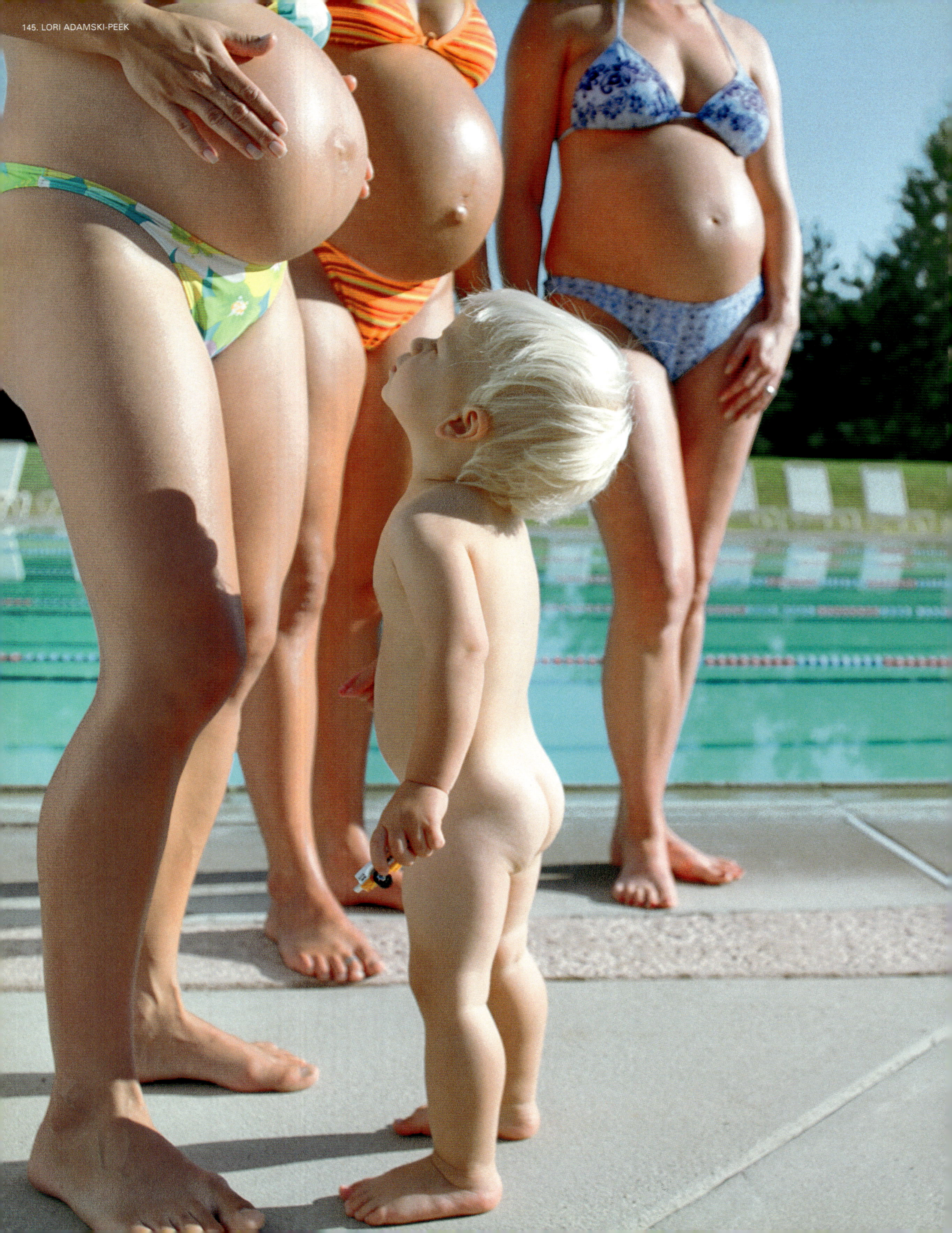
145. LORI ADAMSKI-PEEK

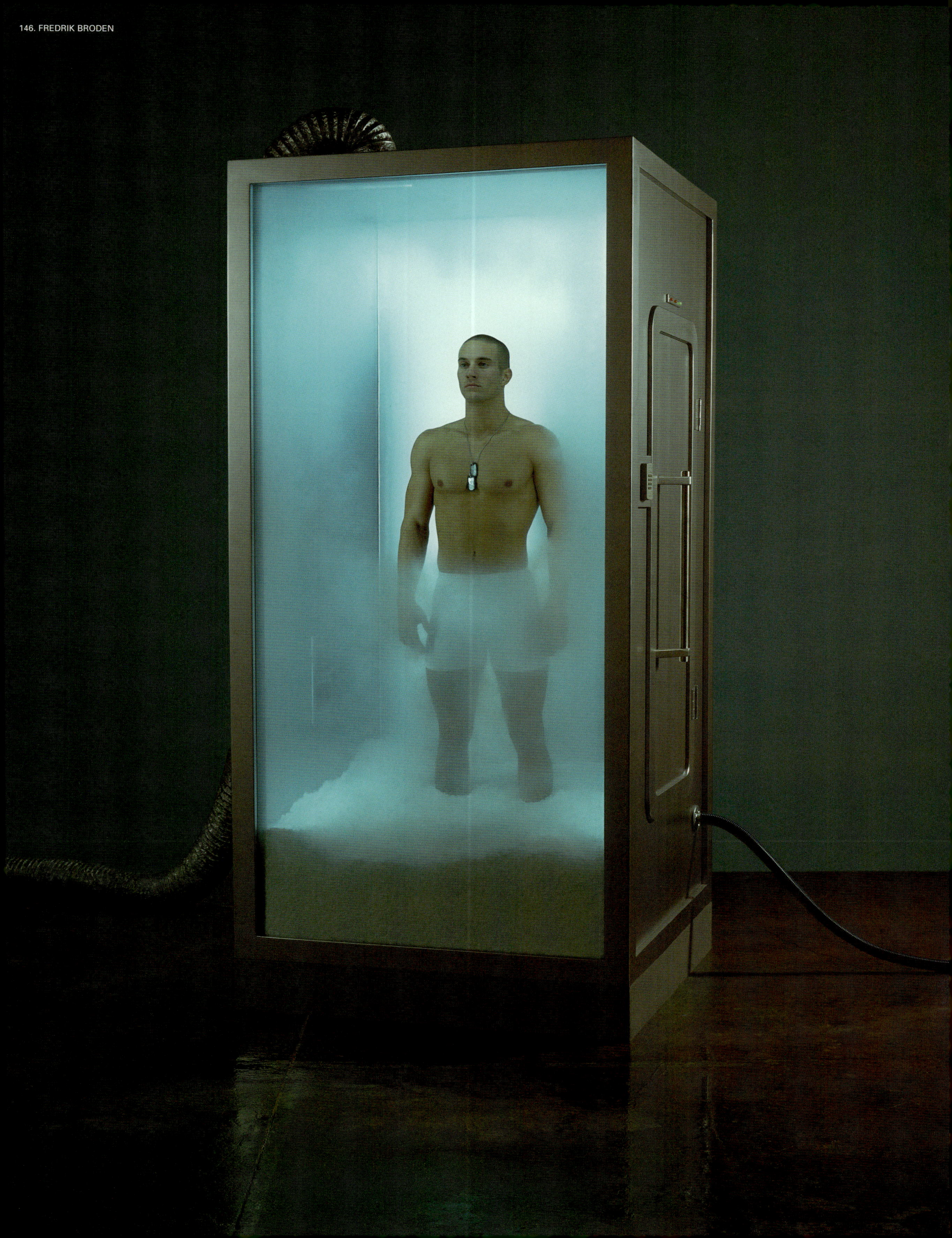

147. FREDRIK BRODEN

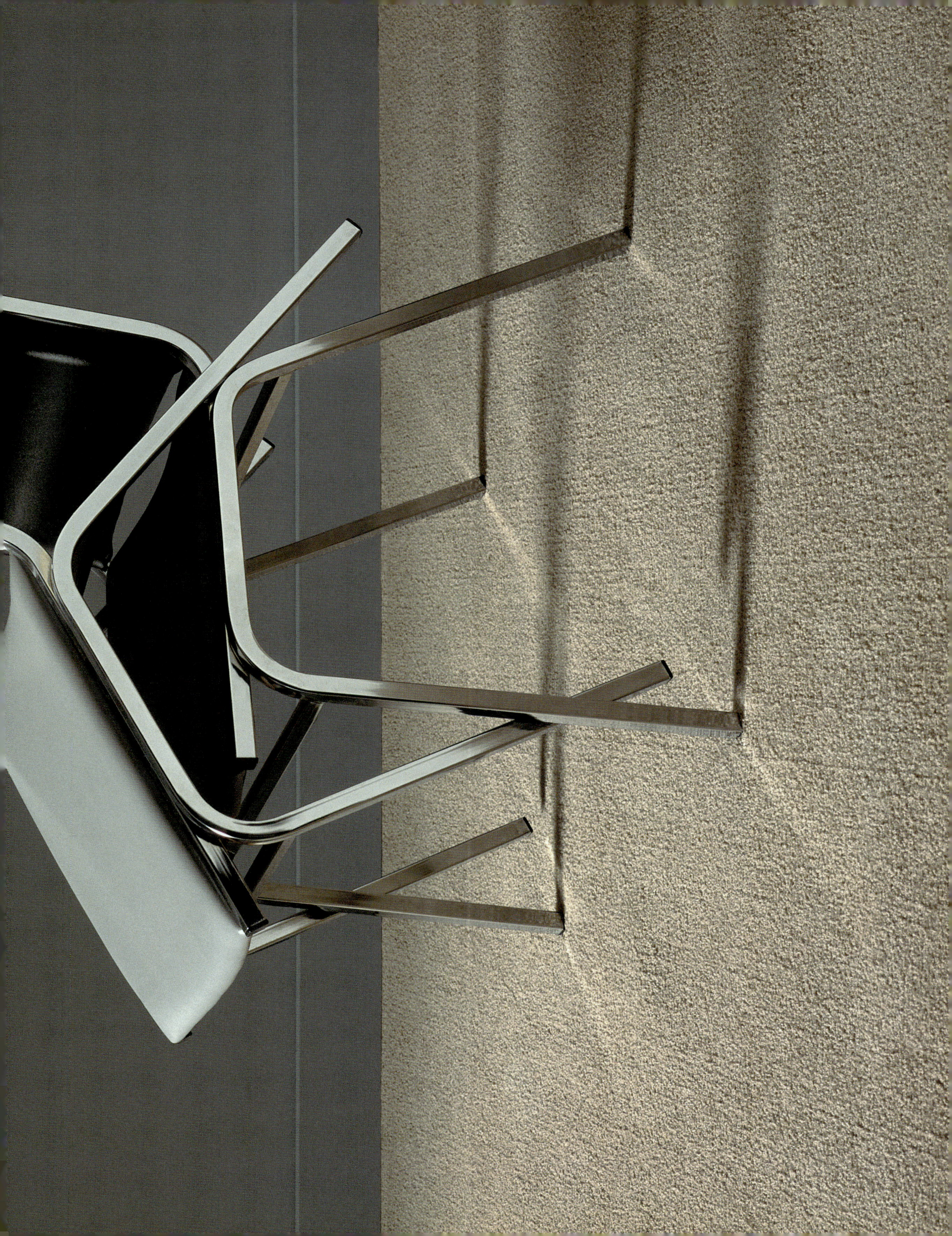

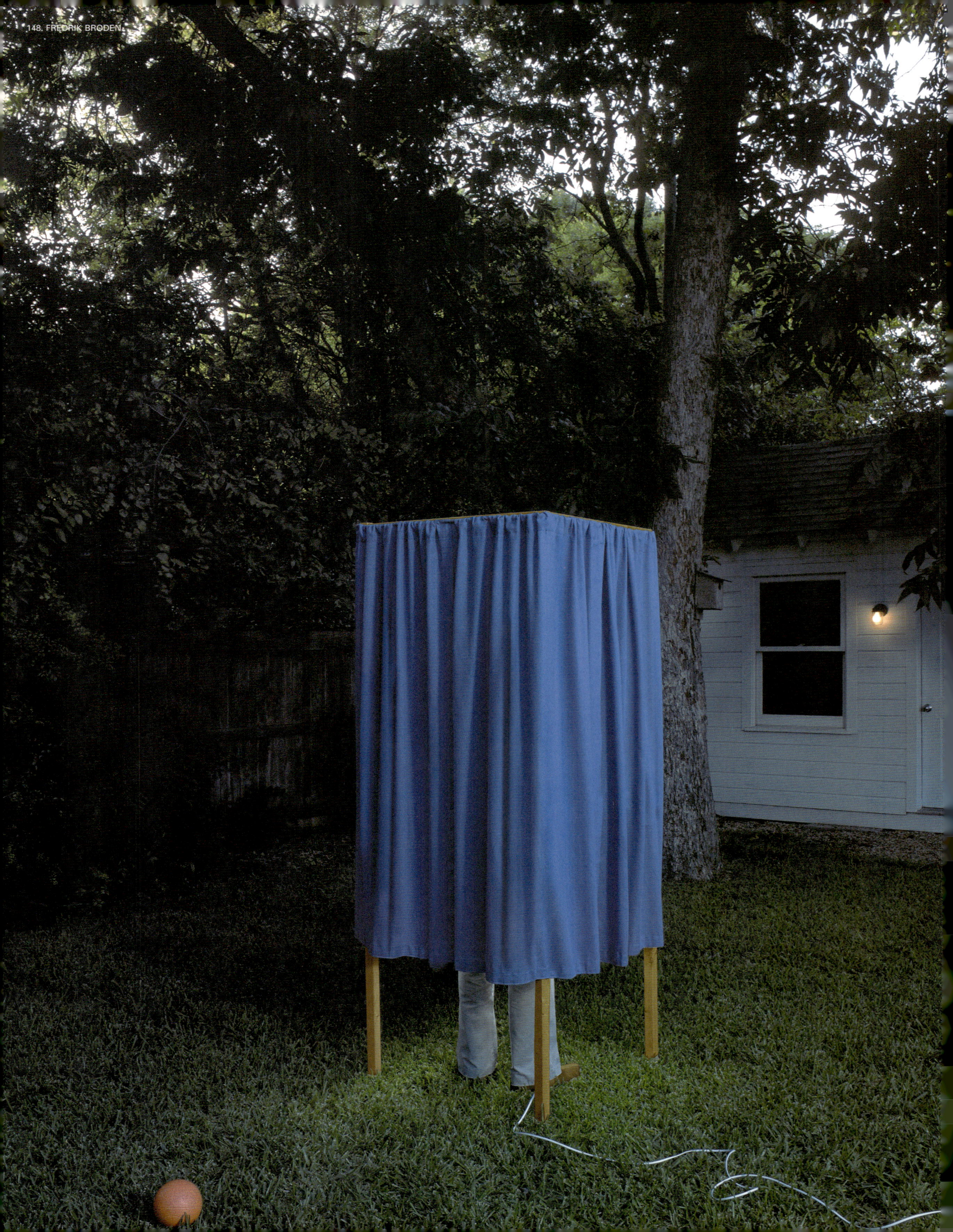

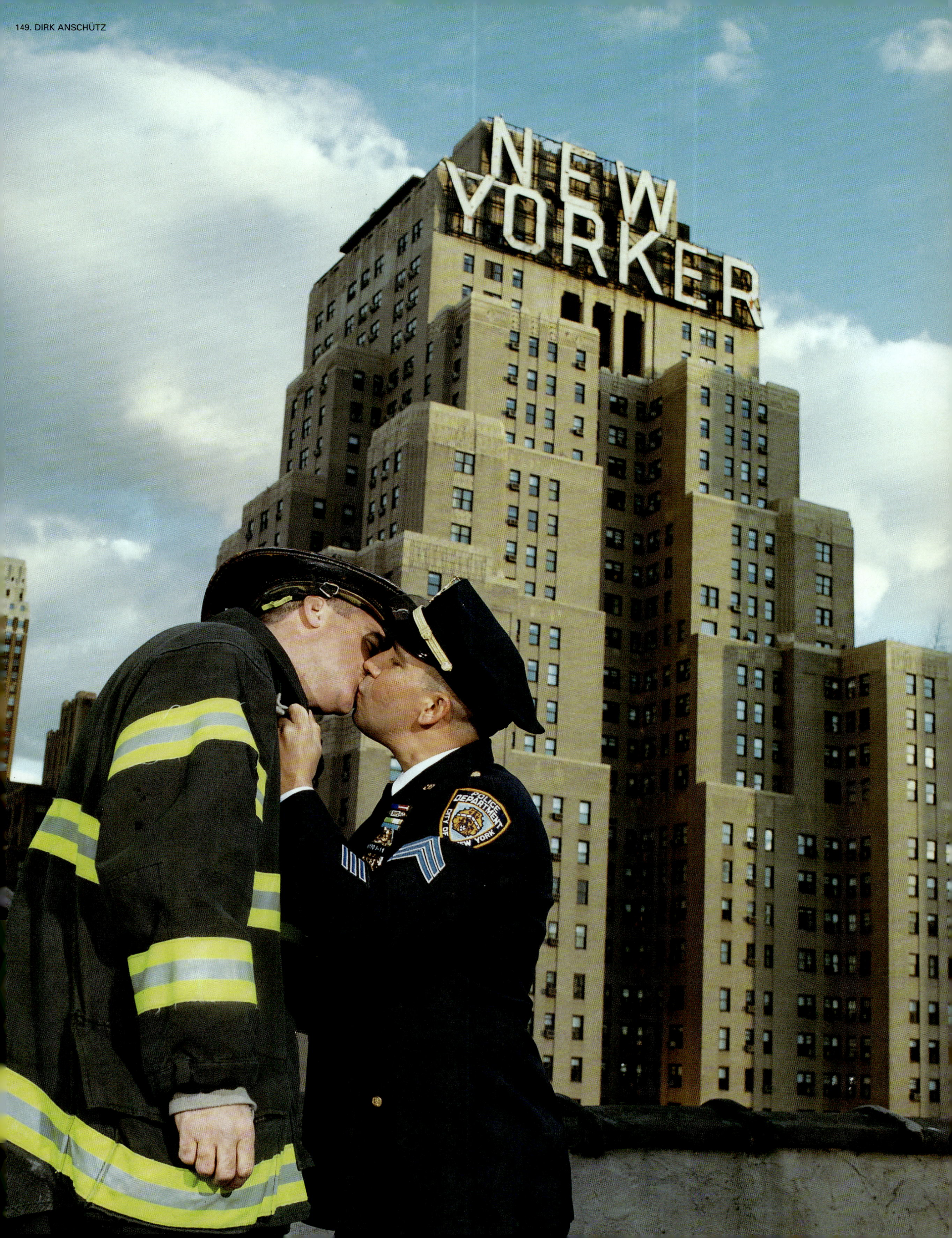

149. DIRK ANSCHÜTZ

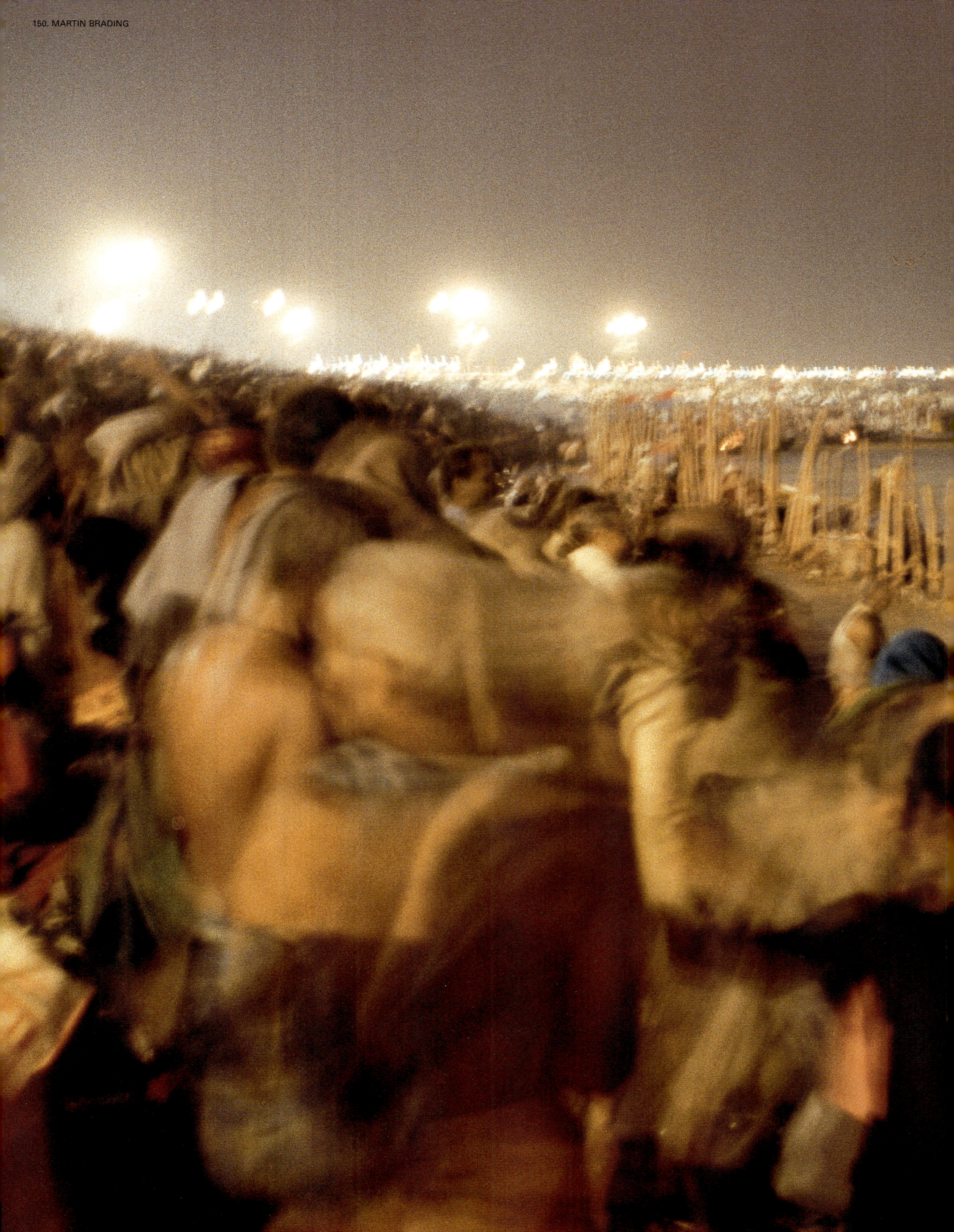

150. MARTIN BRADING

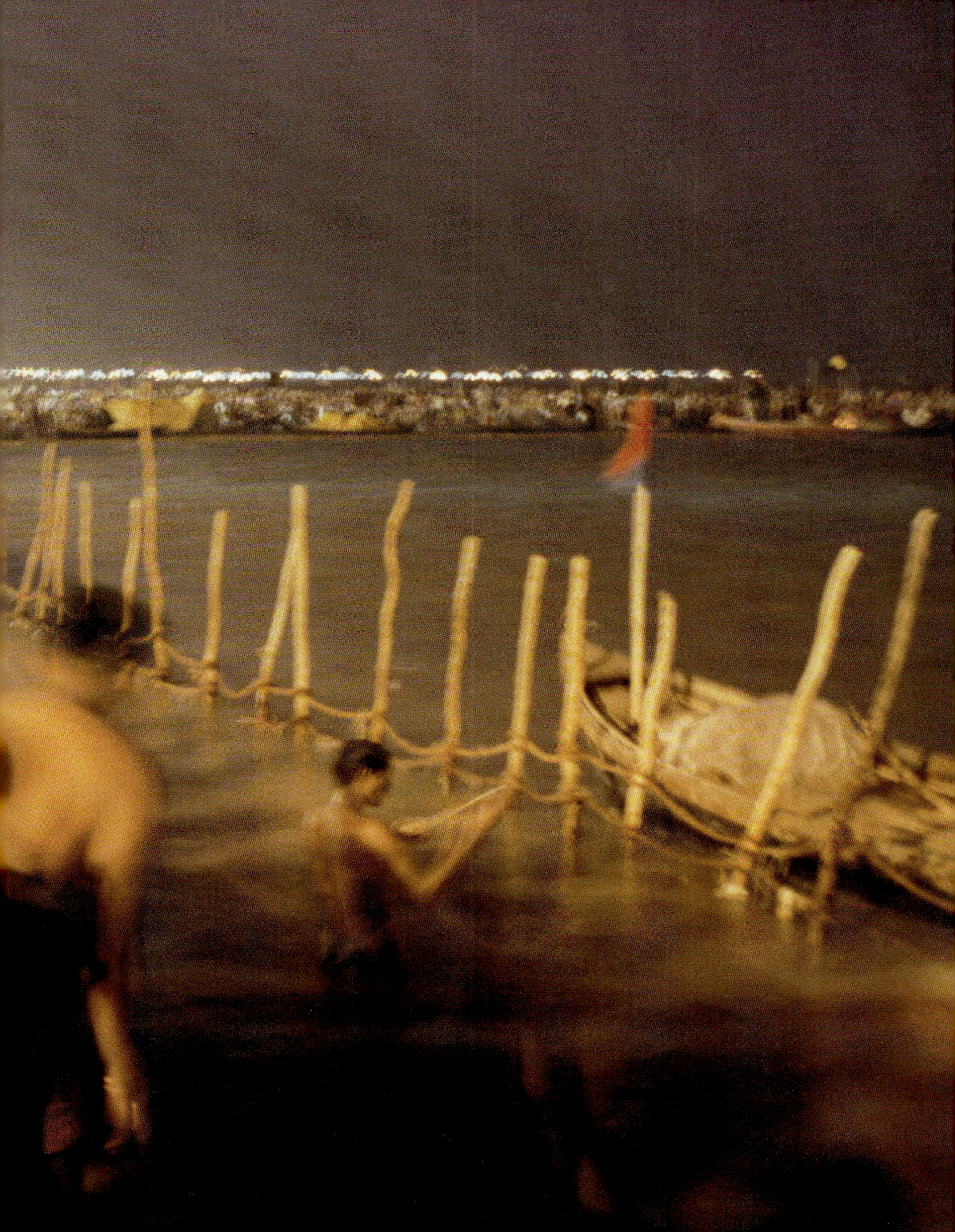

151. MARTIN BRADING

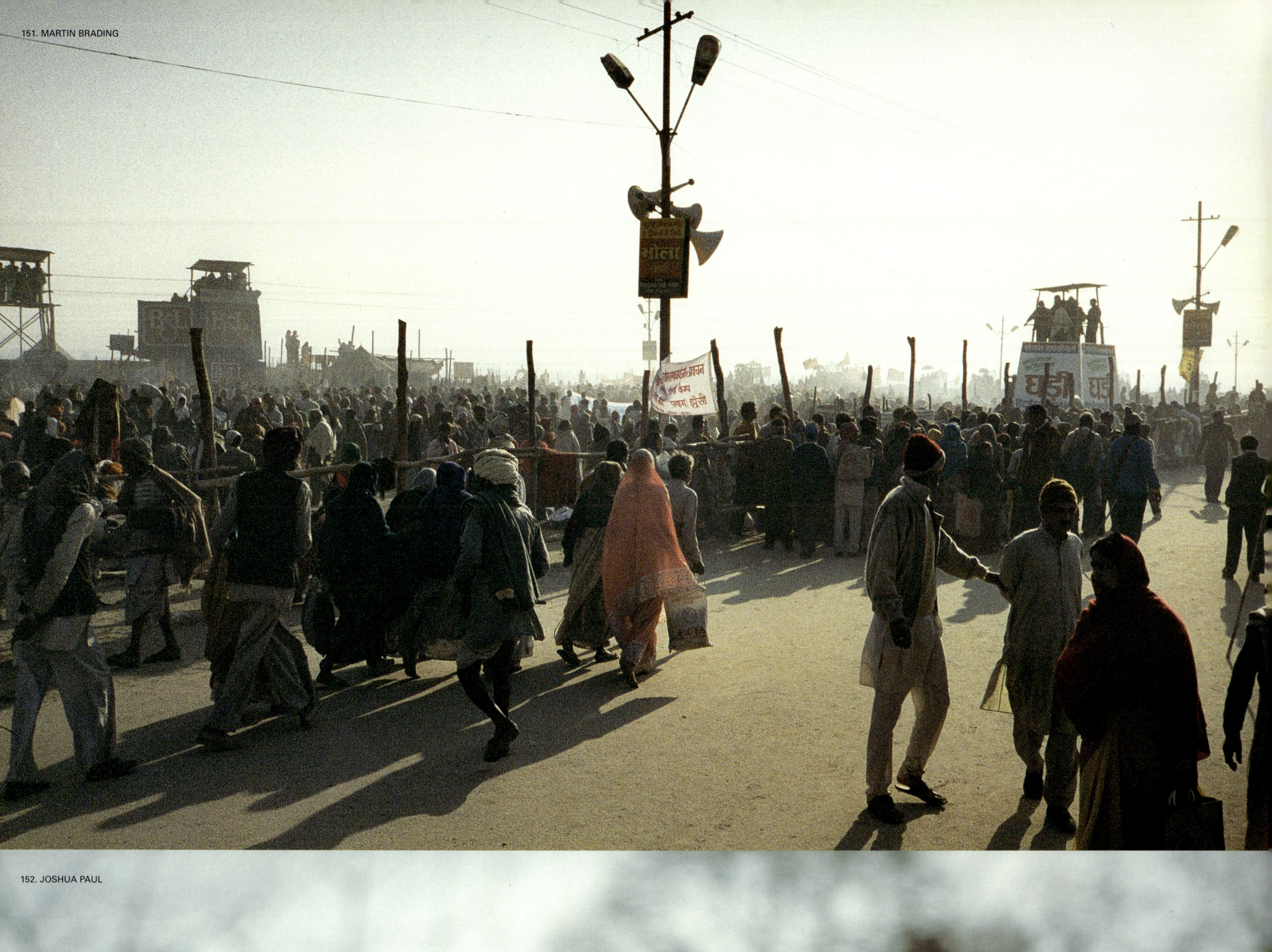

152. JOSHUA PAUL

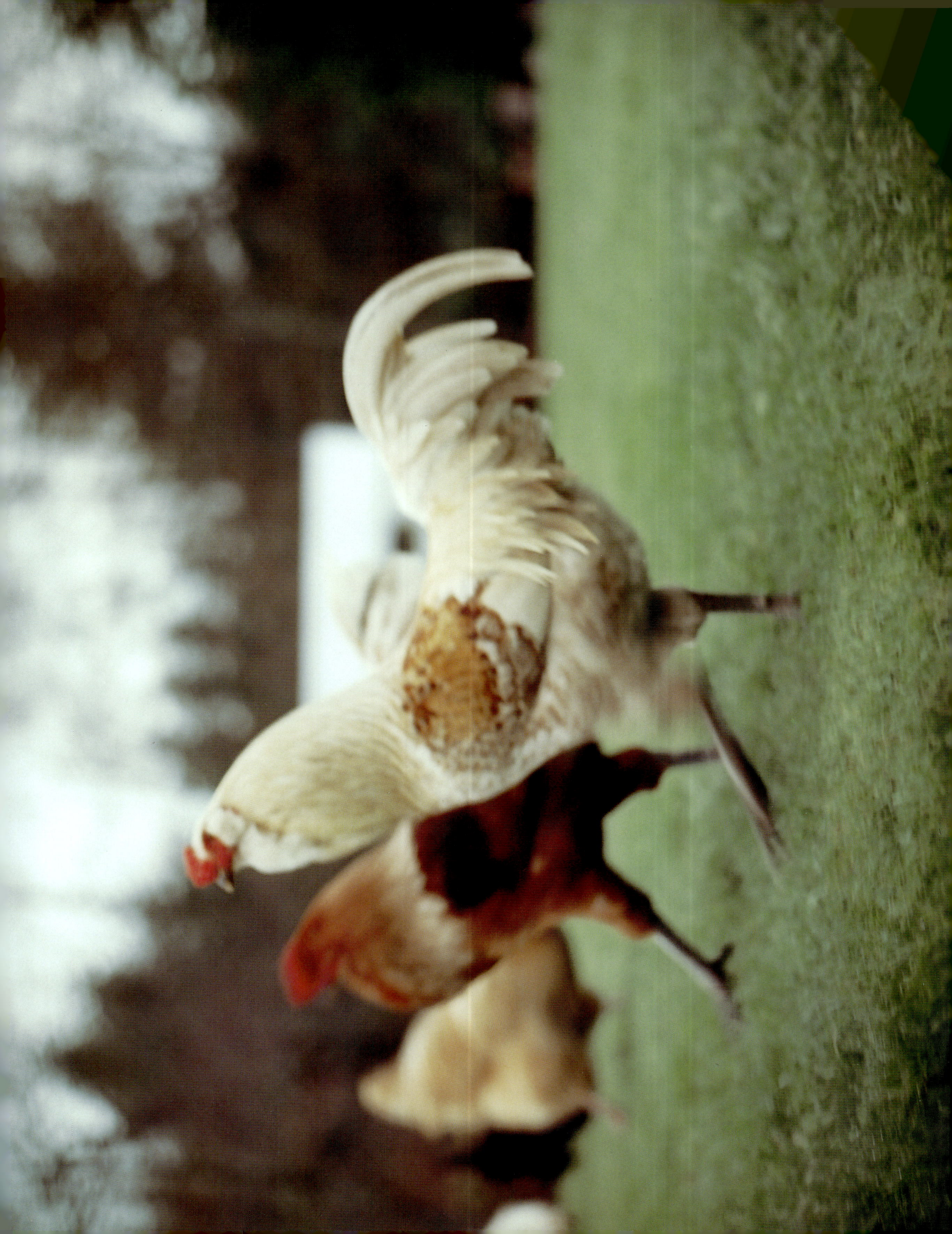

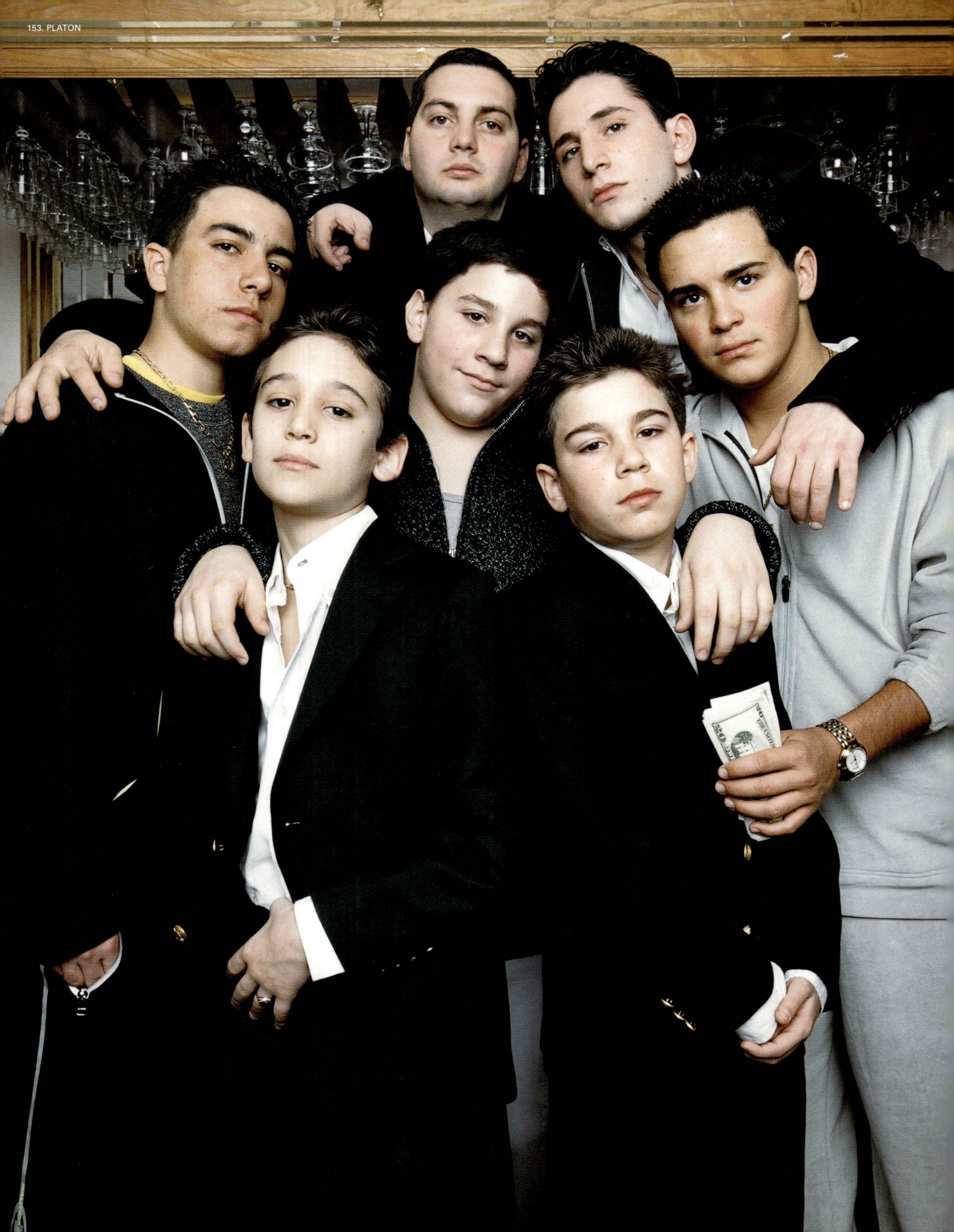

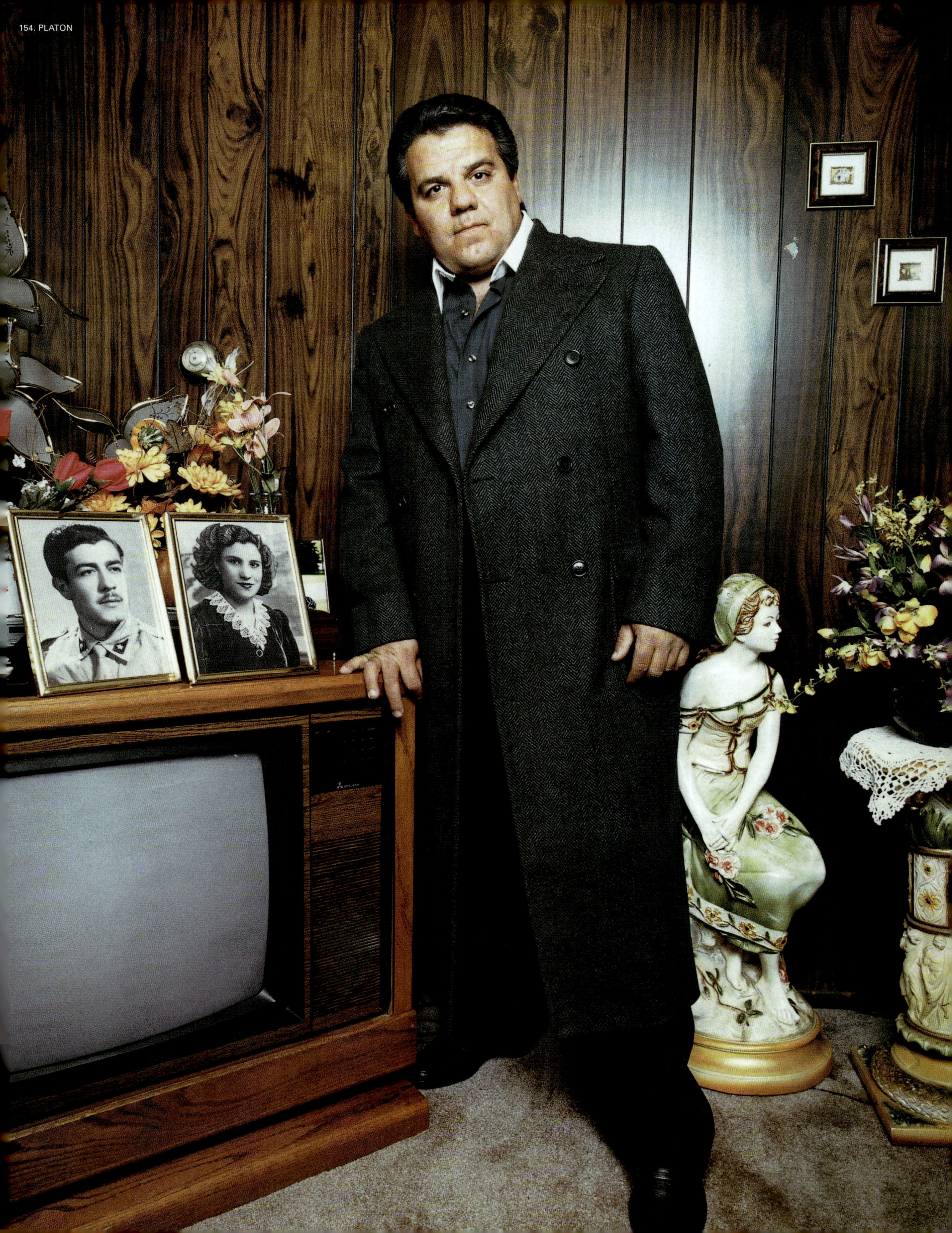

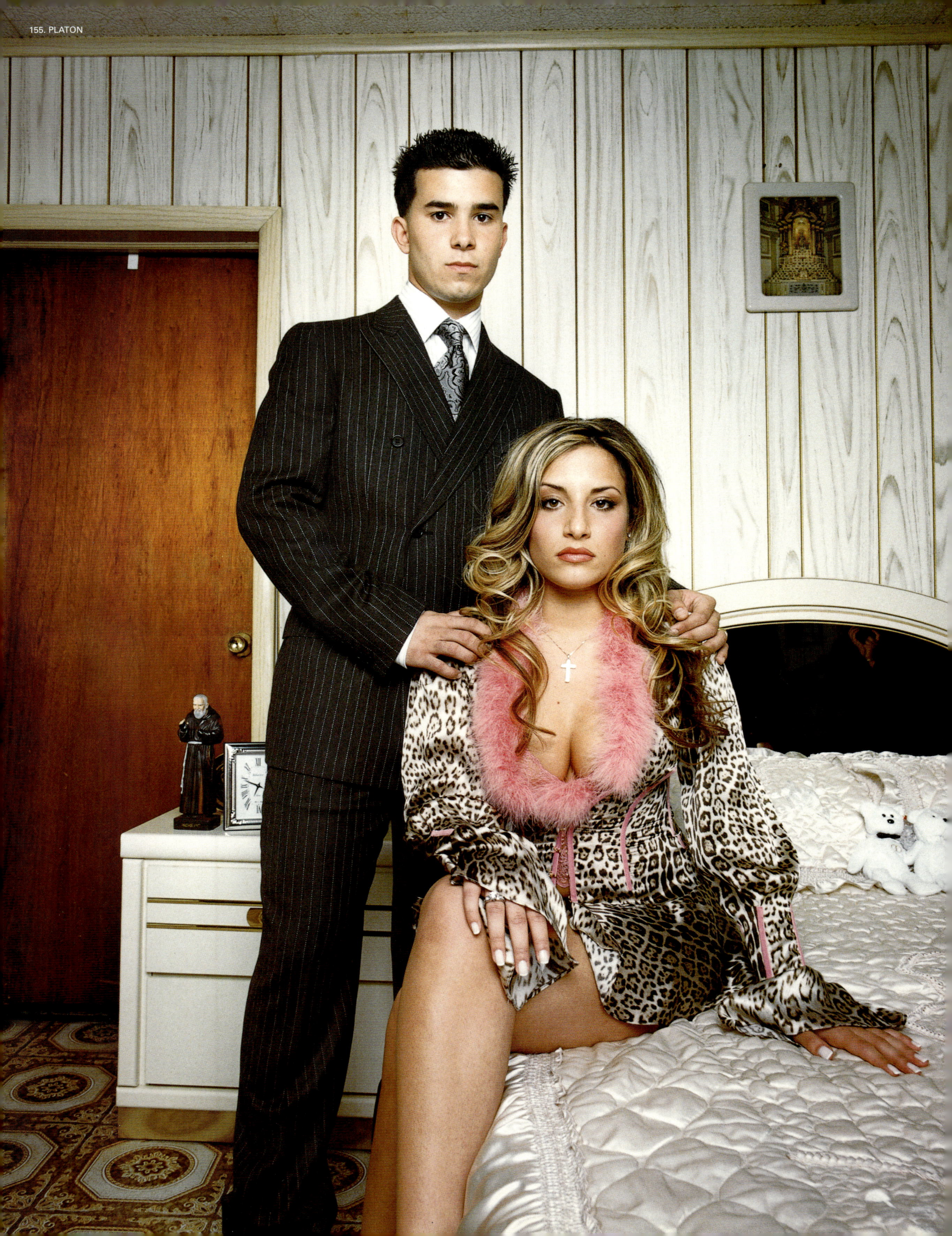

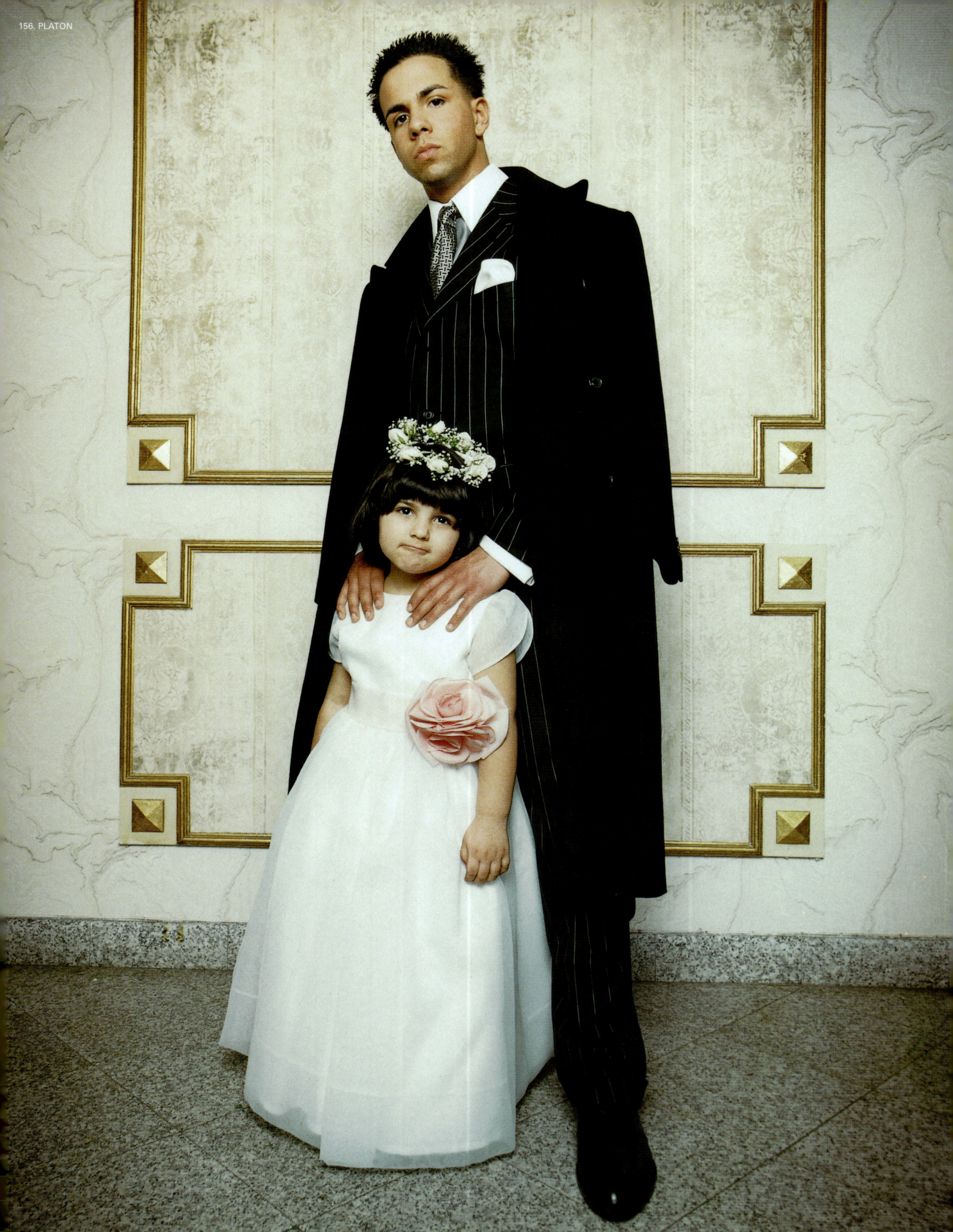

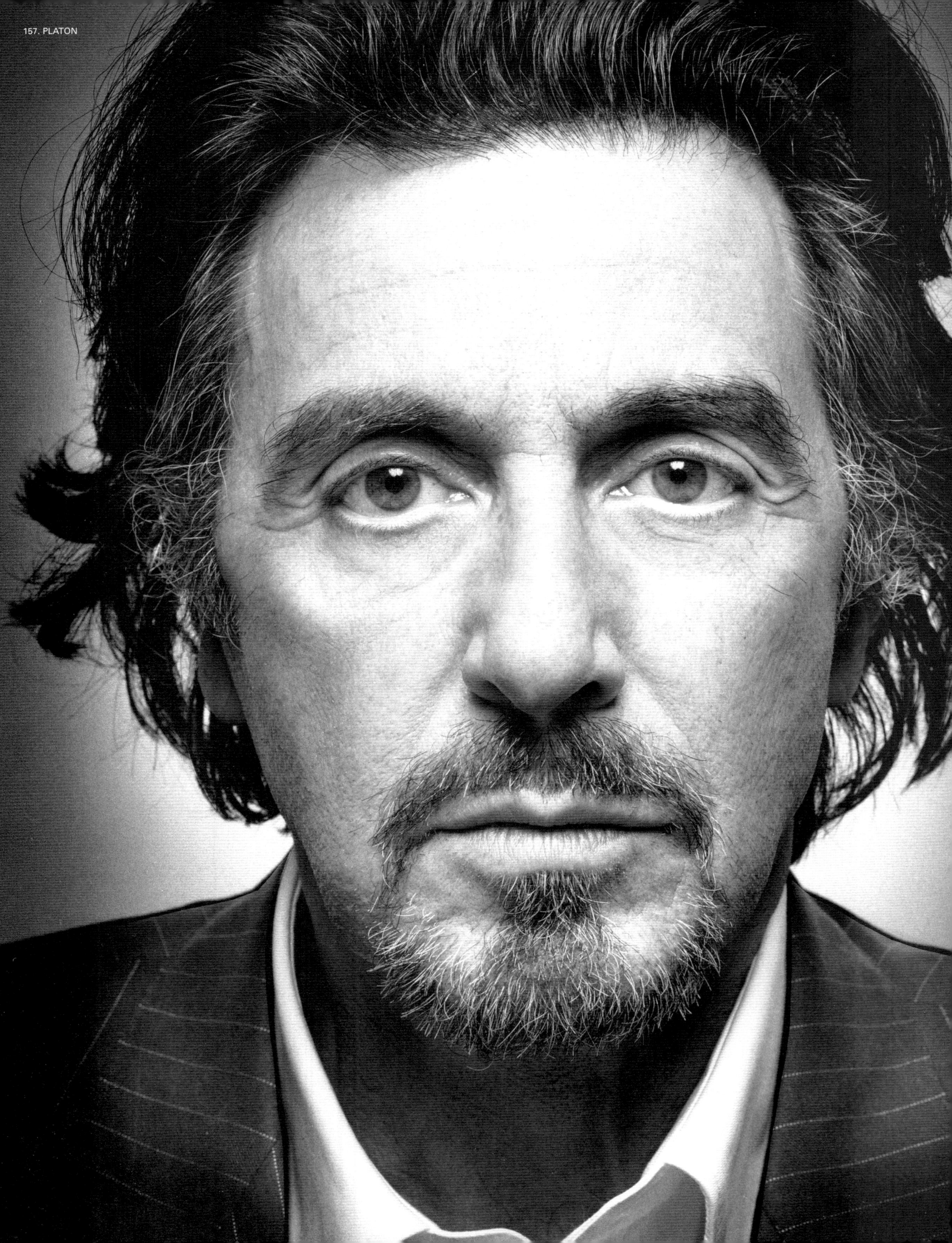

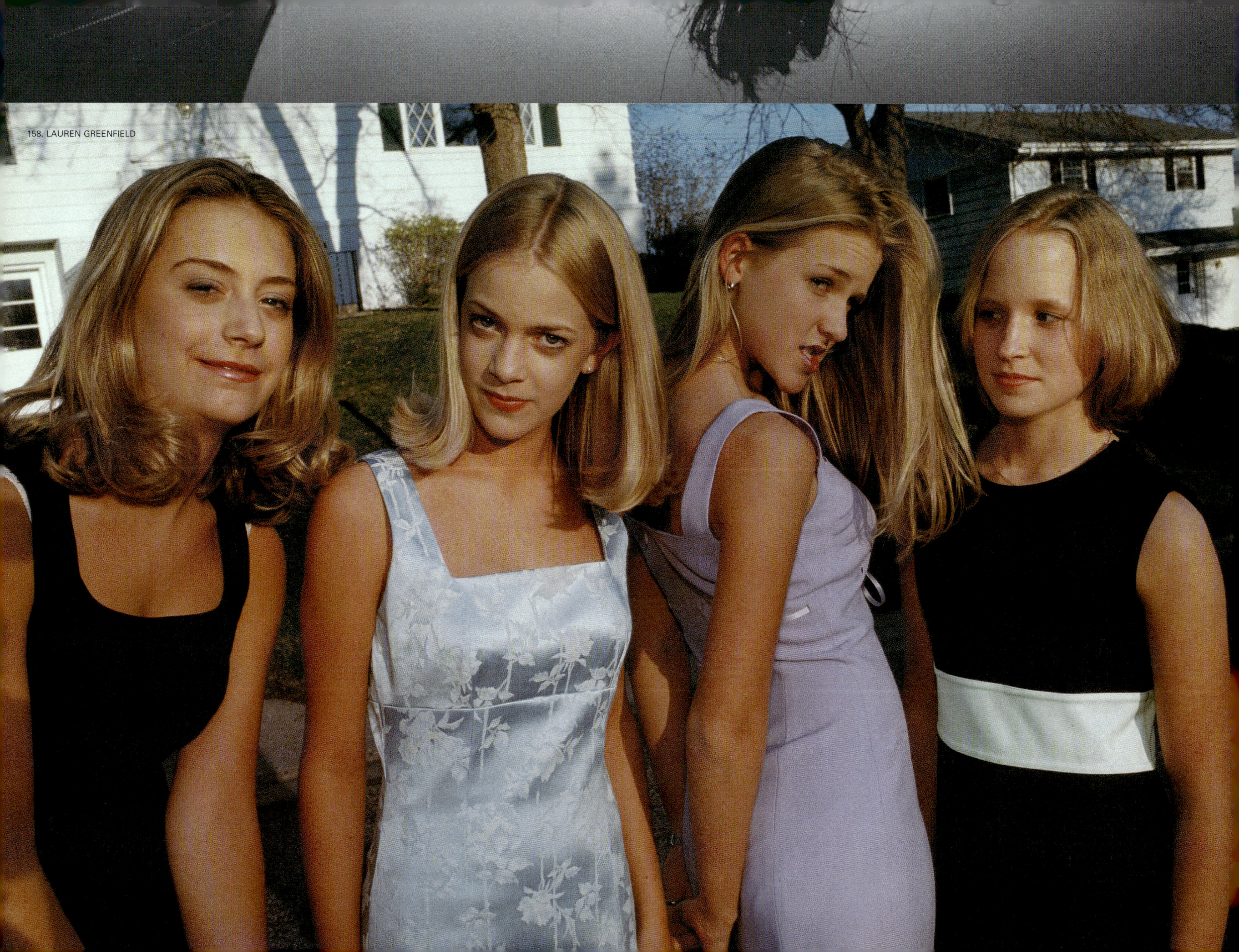

158. LAUREN GREENFIELD

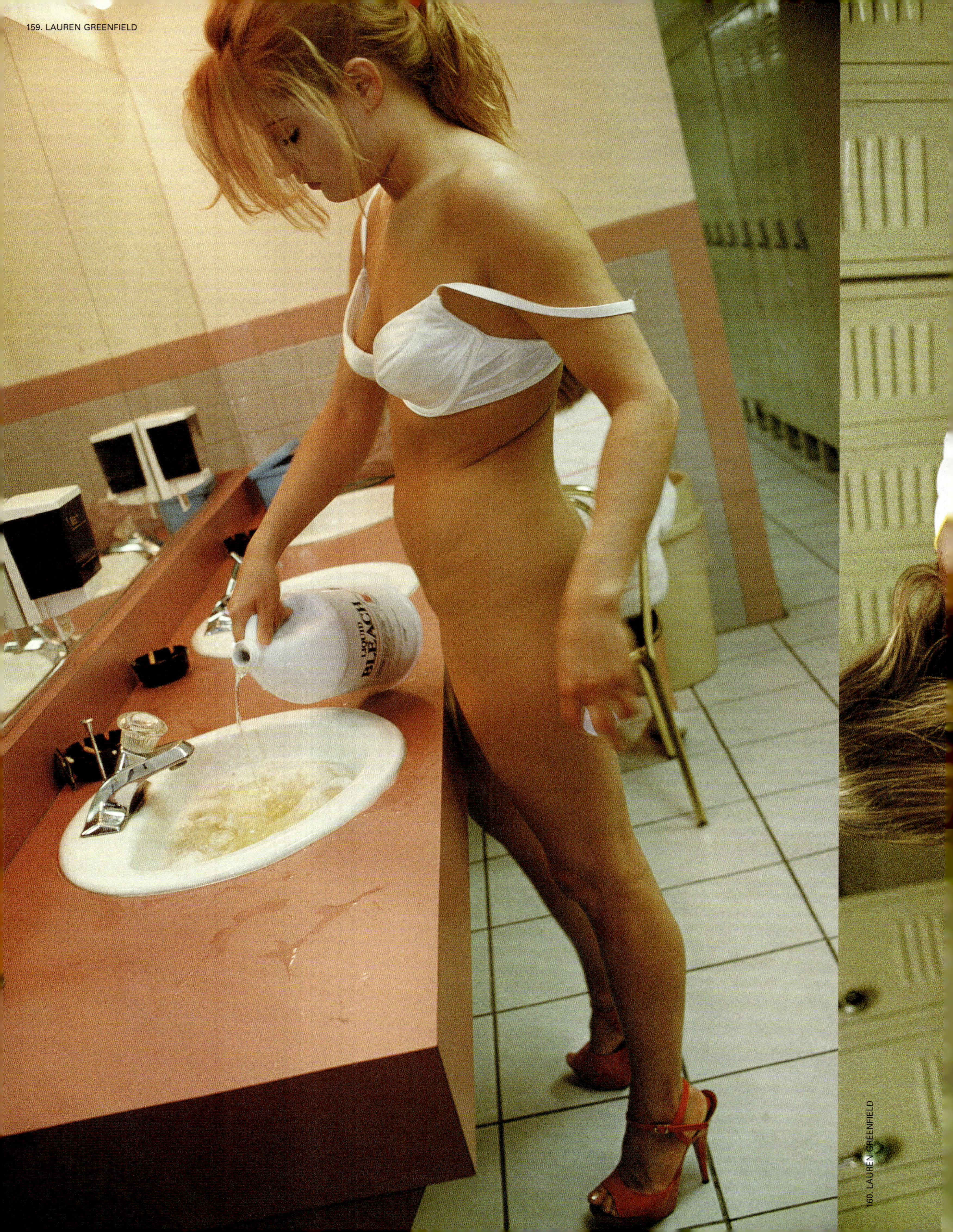

159. LAUREN GREENFIELD

160. LAUREN GREENFIELD

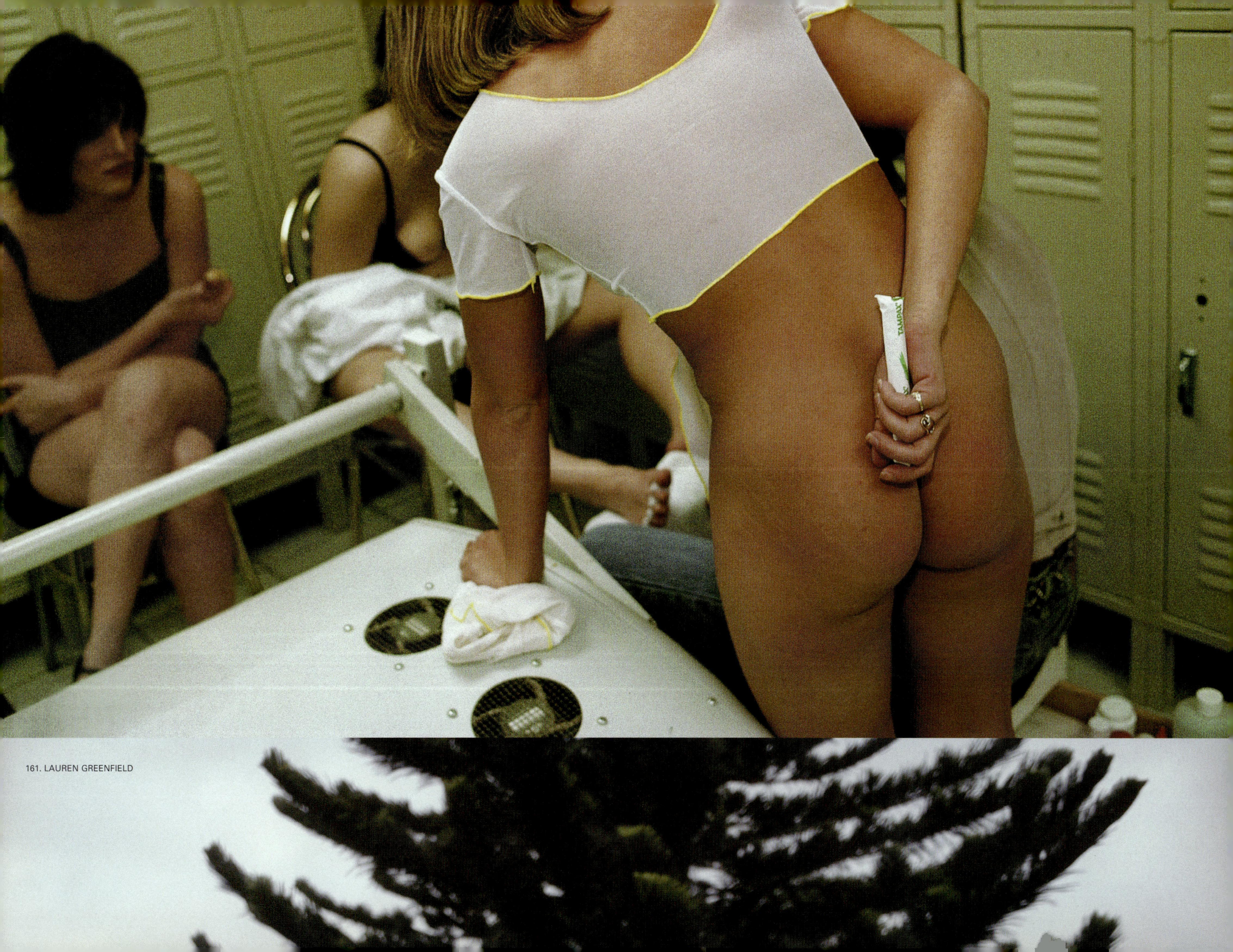

161. LAUREN GREENFIELD

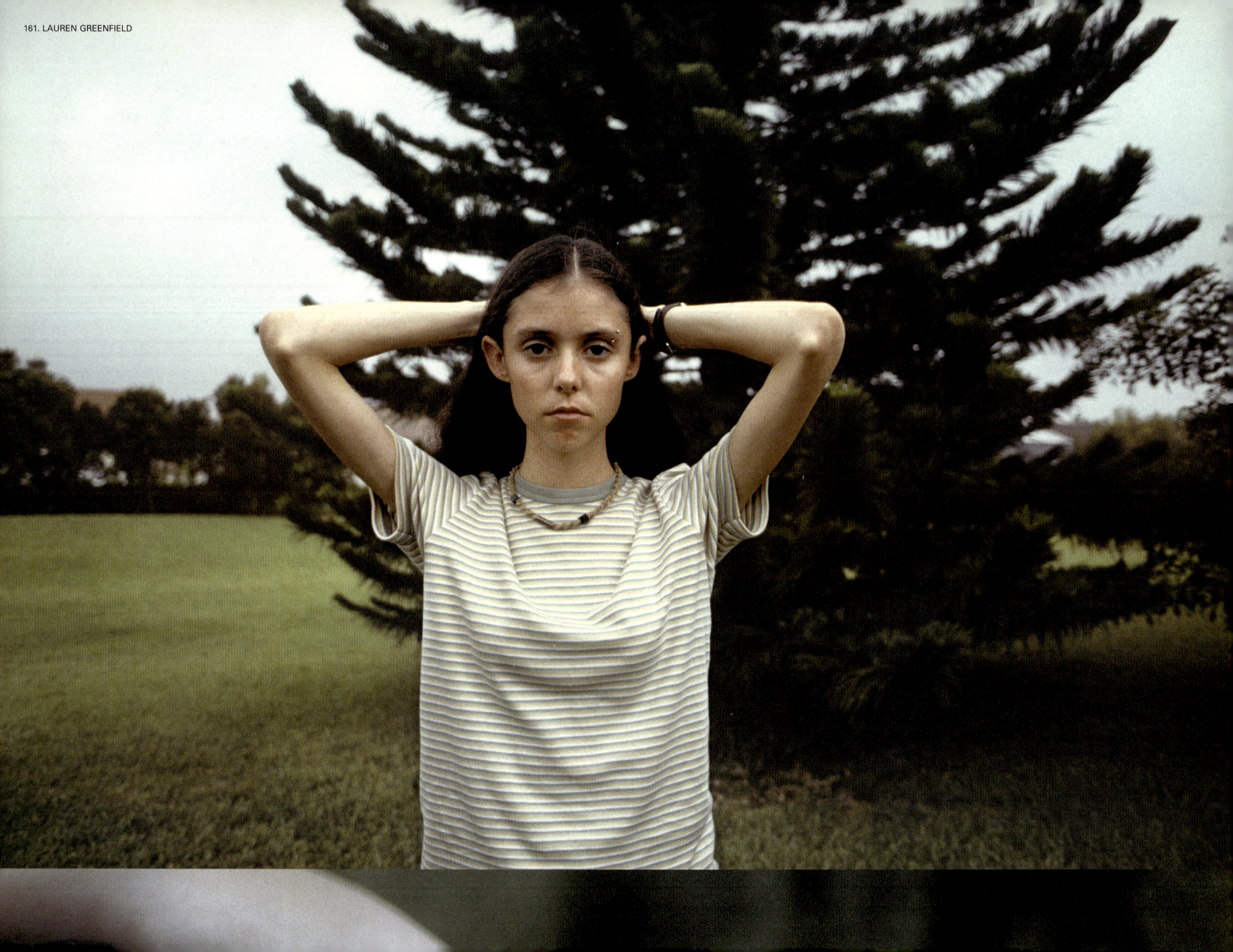

161. LAUREN GREENFIELD

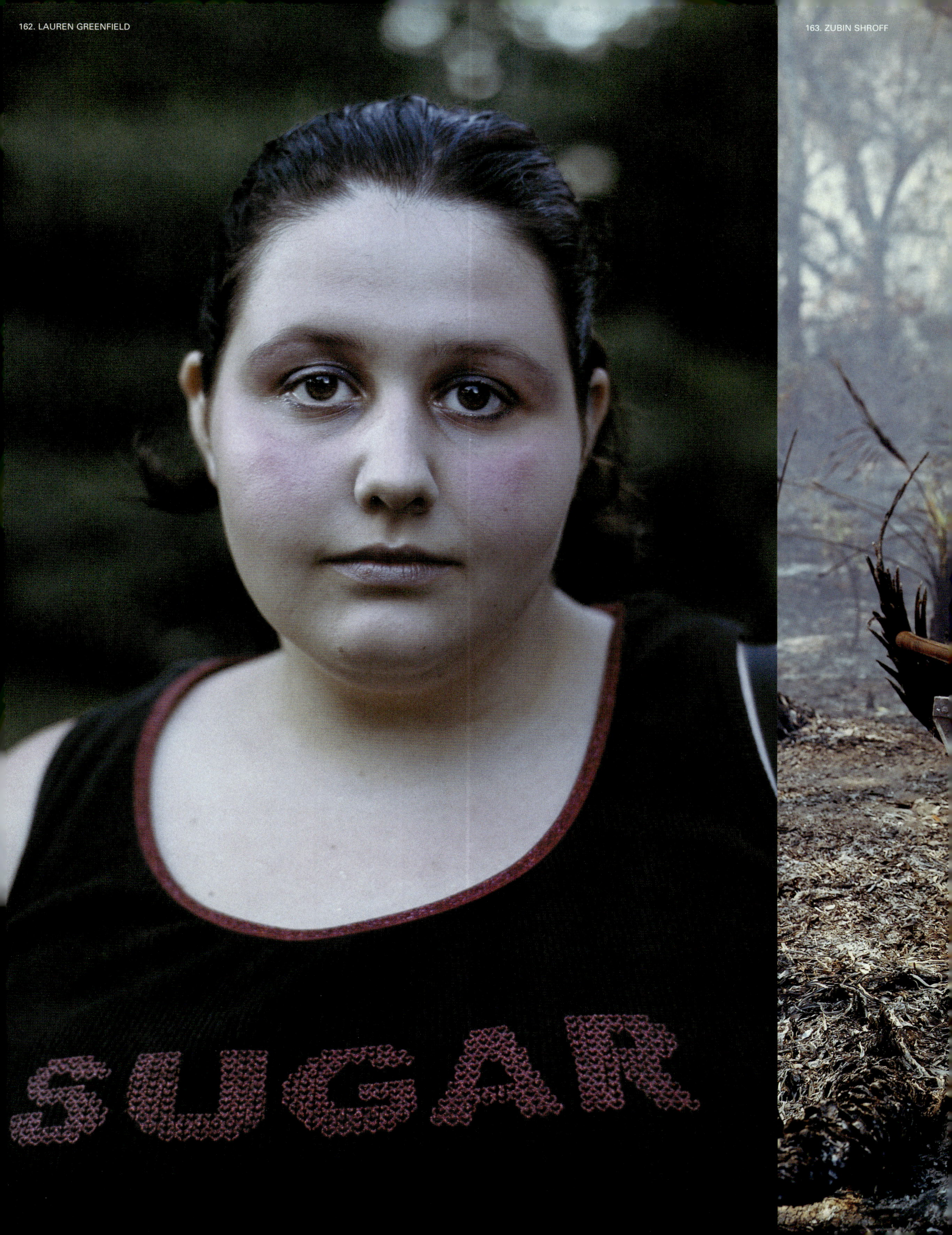
SUGAR

163. ZUBIN SHROFF

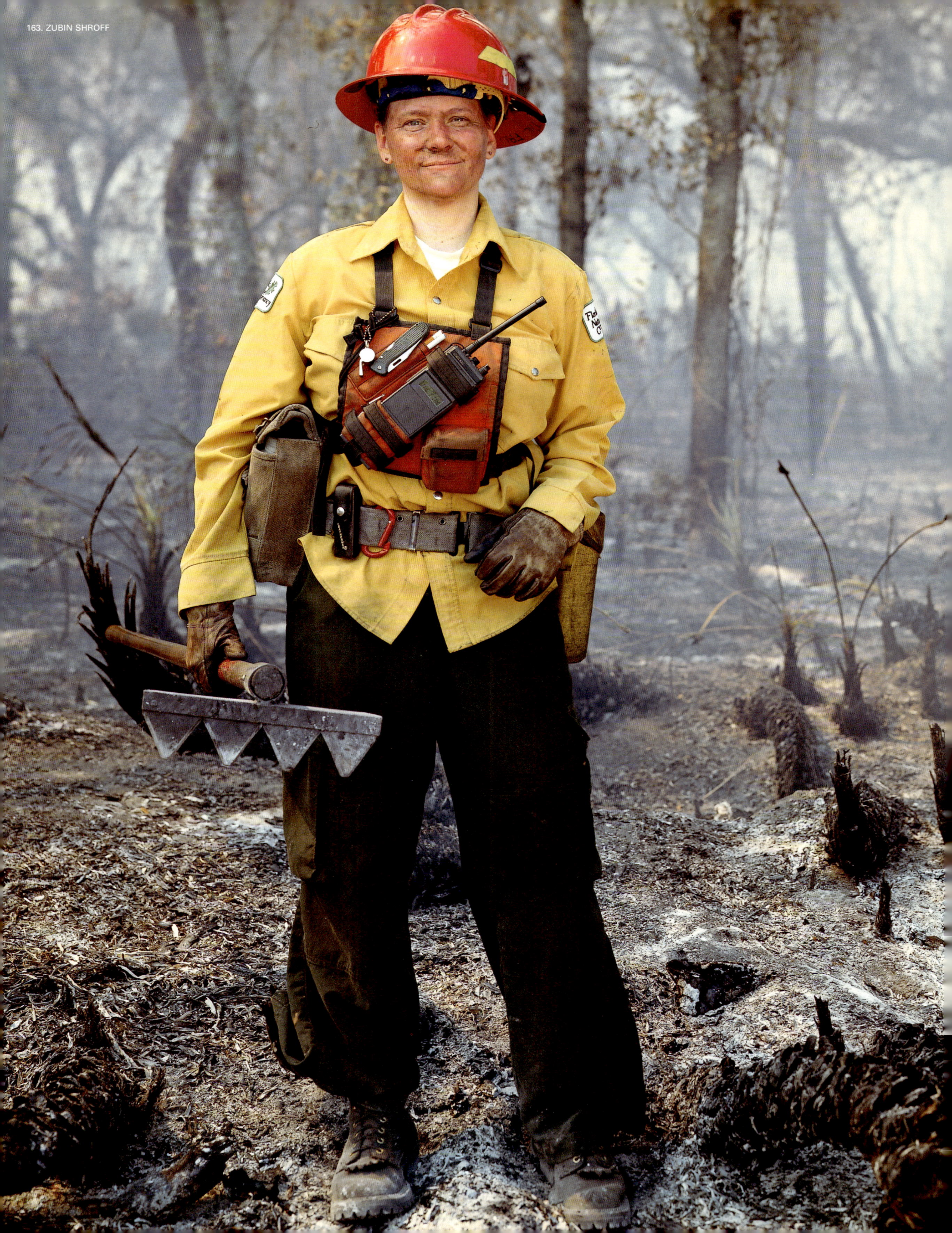

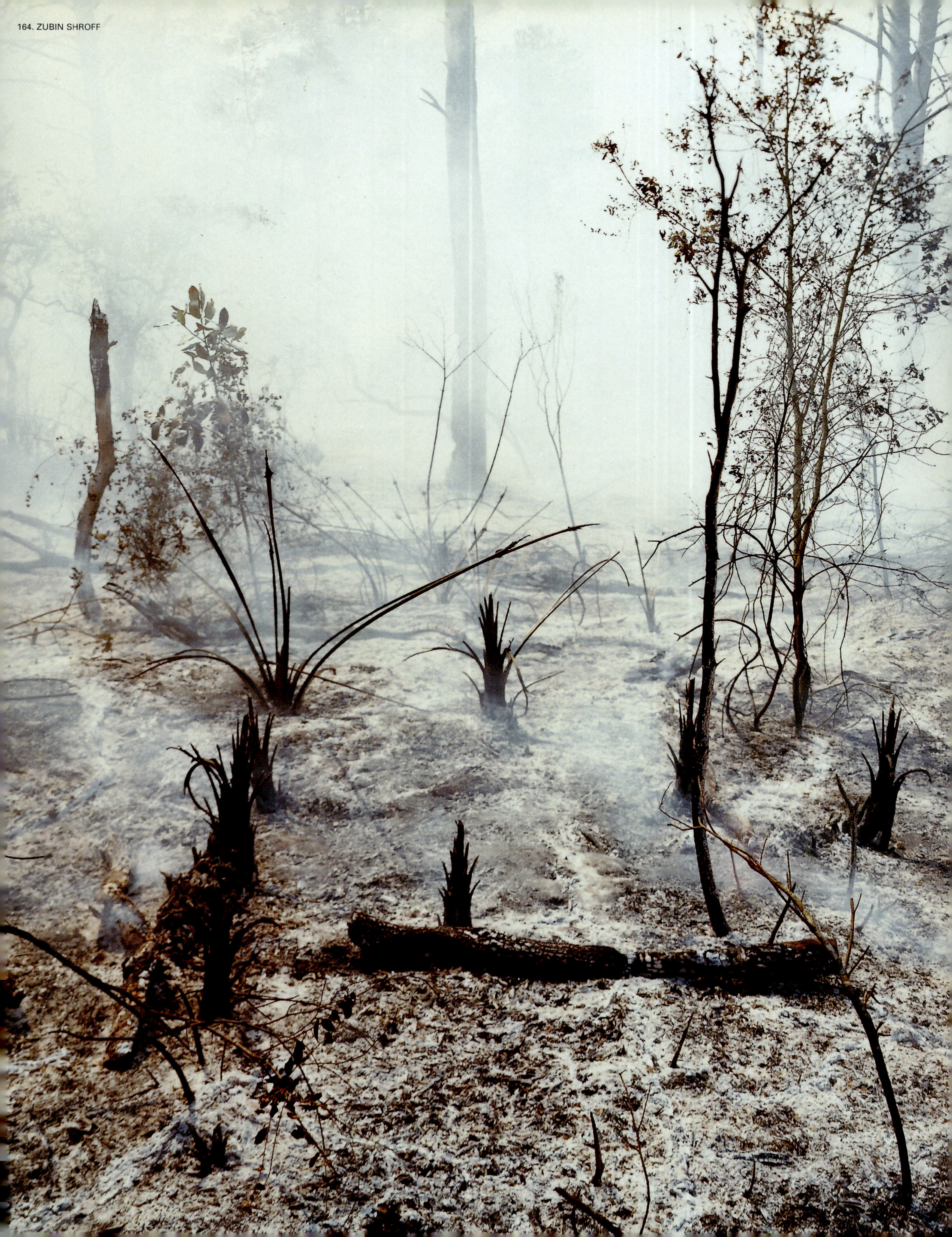

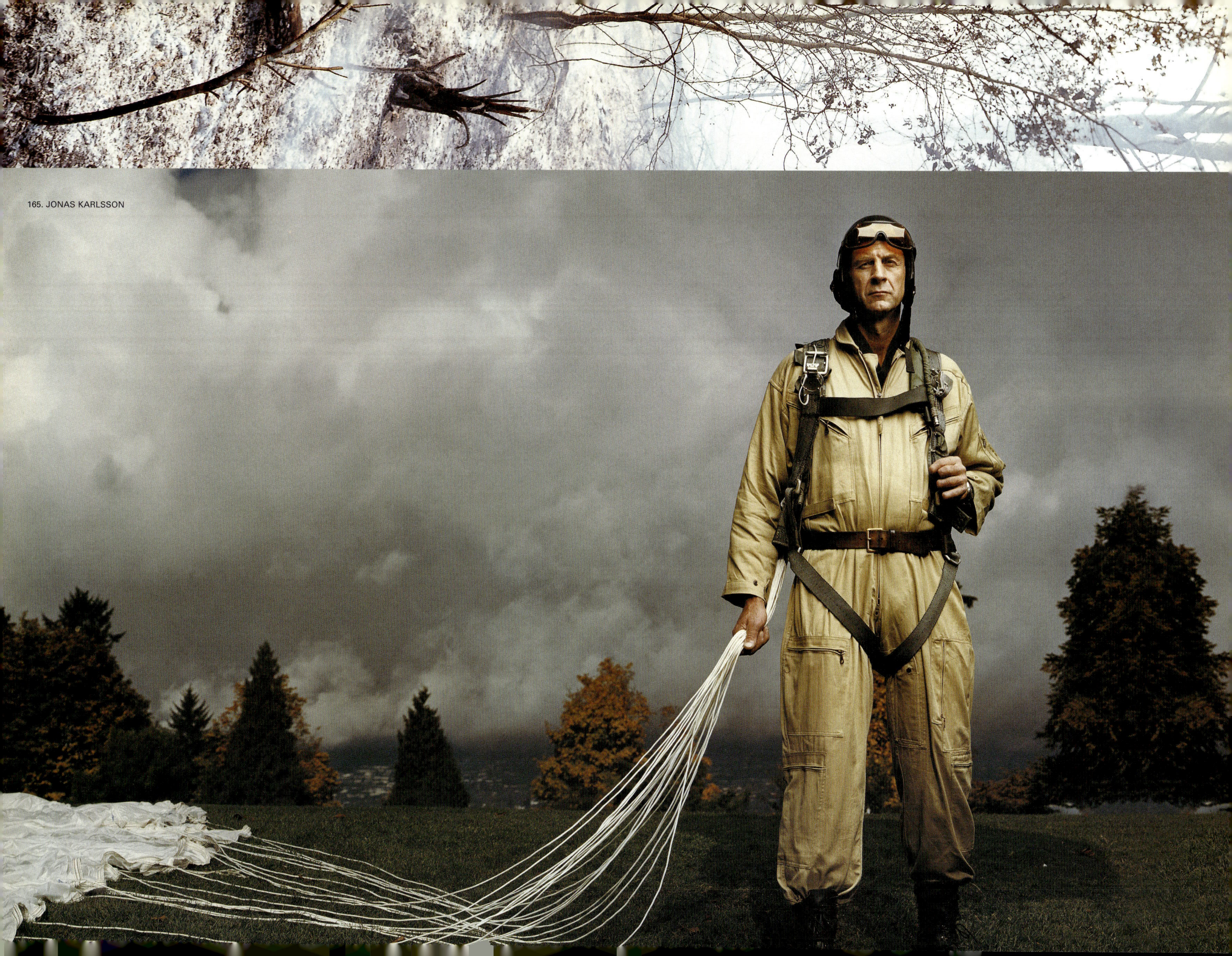

165. JONAS KARLSSON

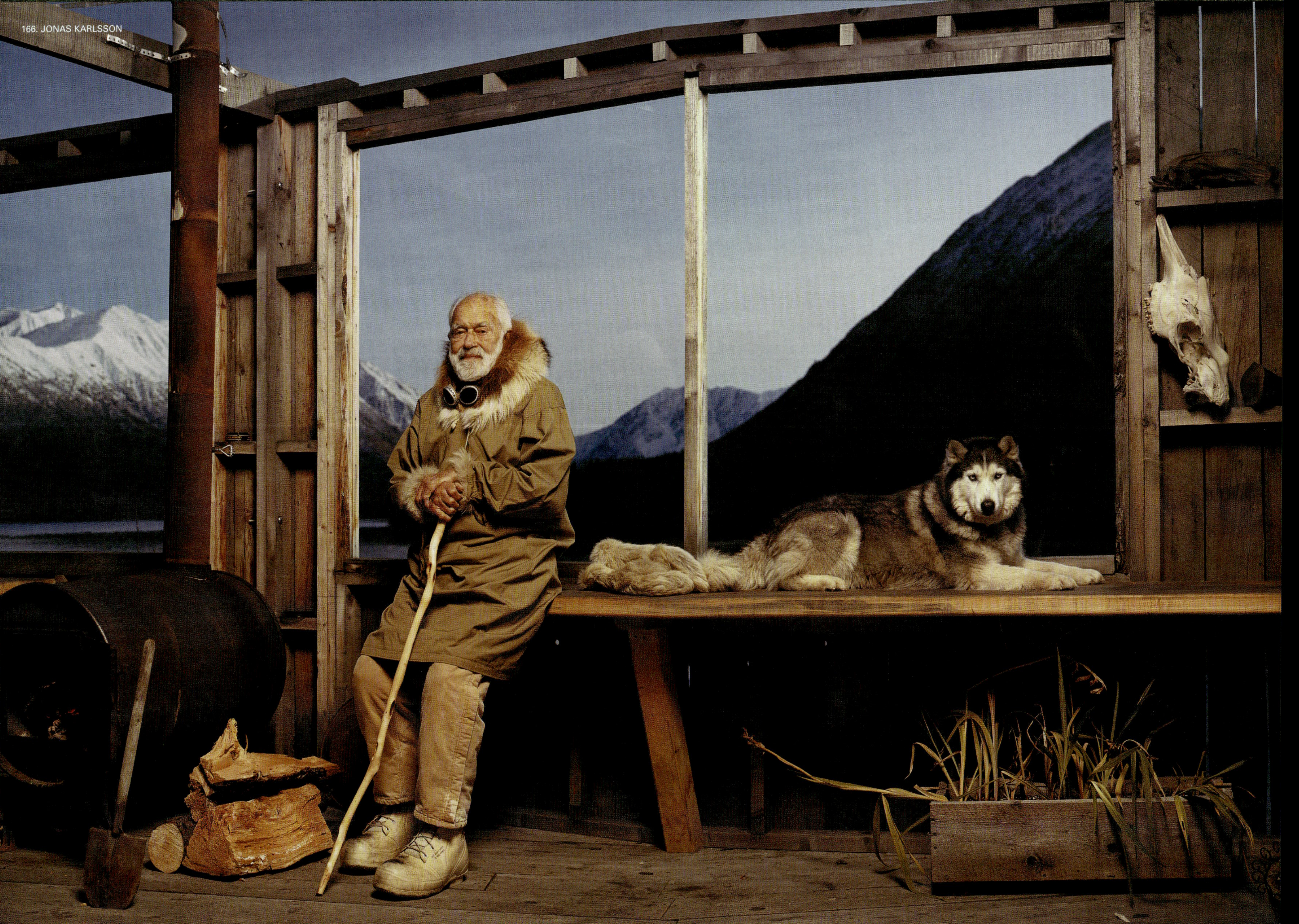

166. JONAS KARLSSON

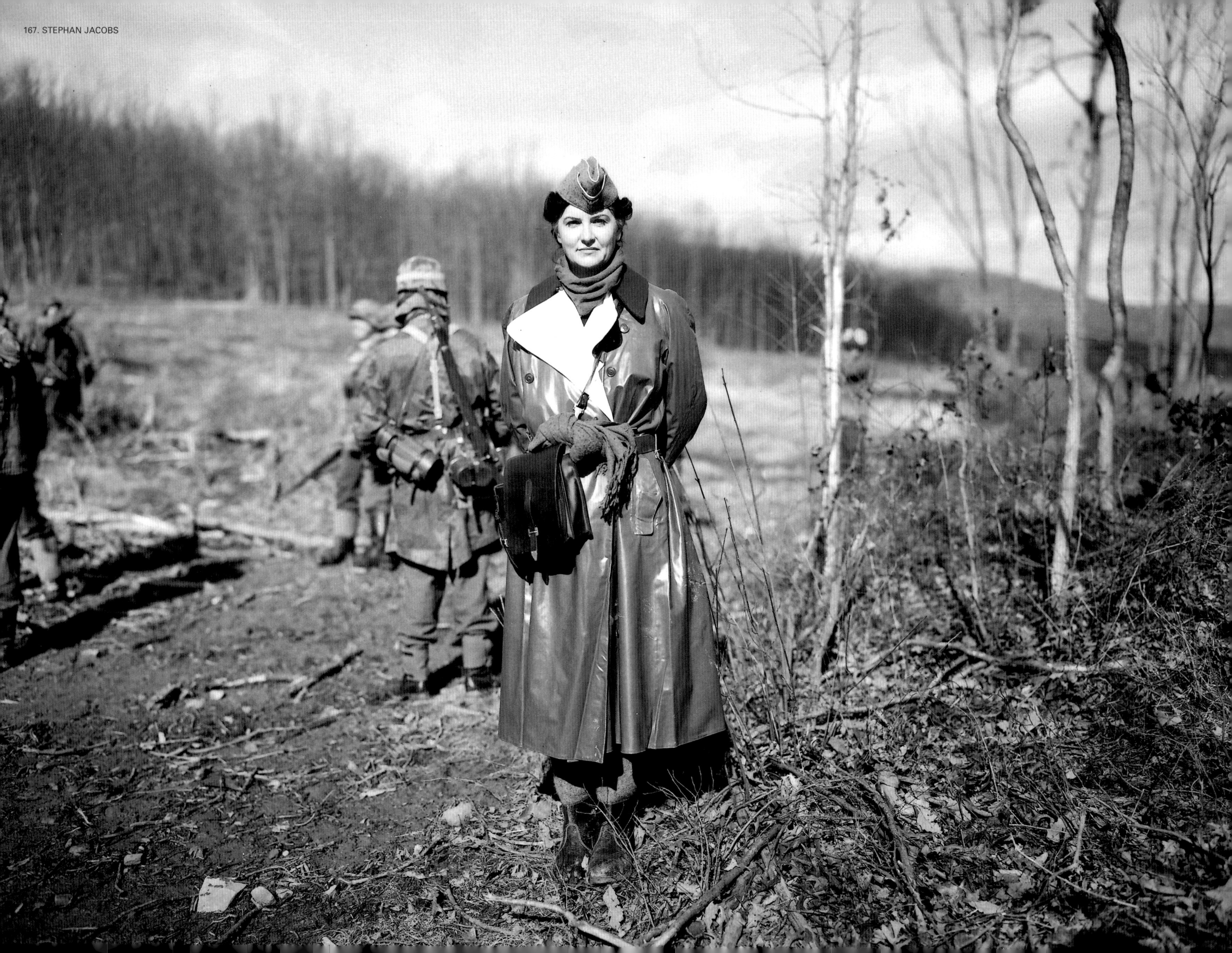

167. STEPHAN JACOBS

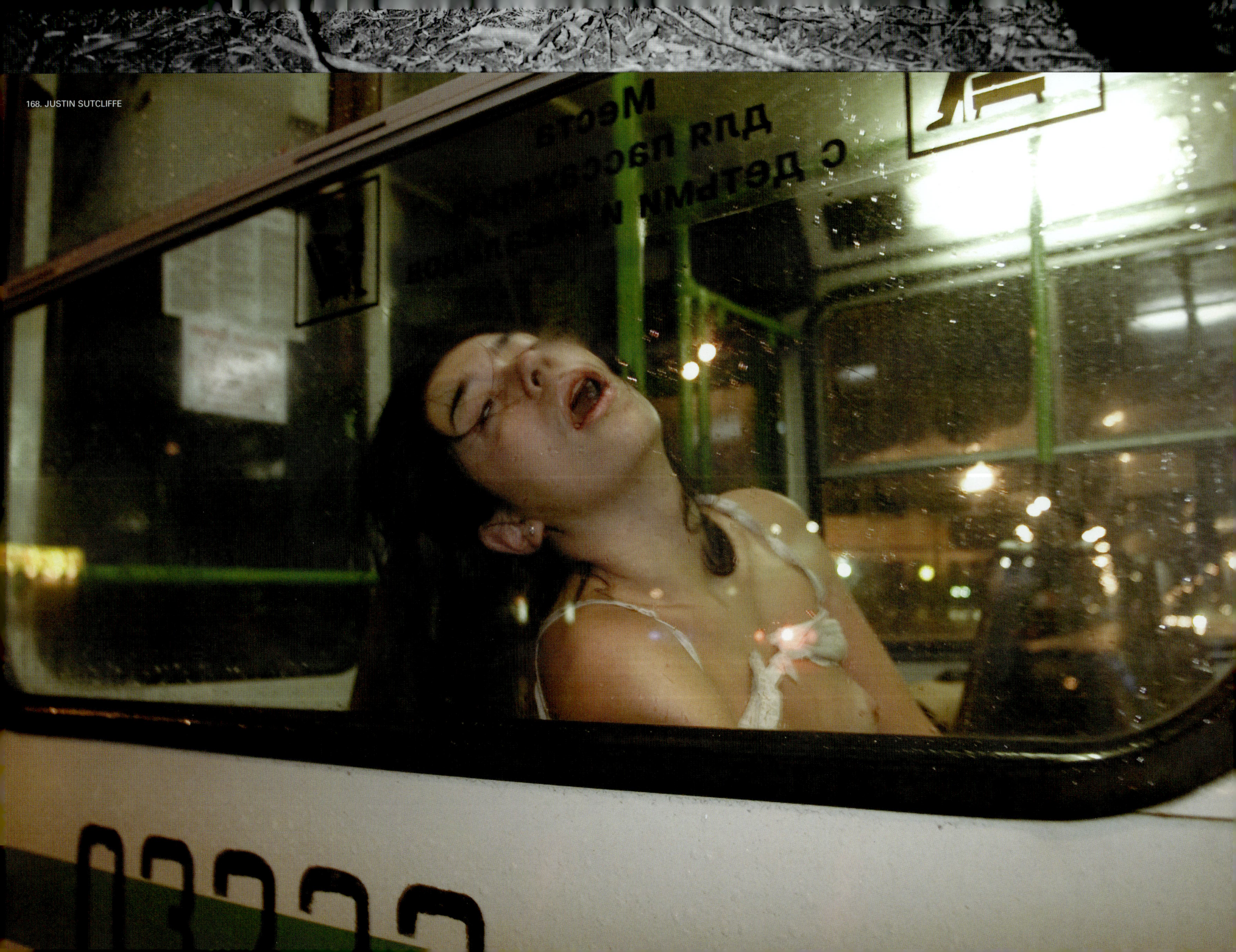

168. JUSTIN SUTCLIFFE

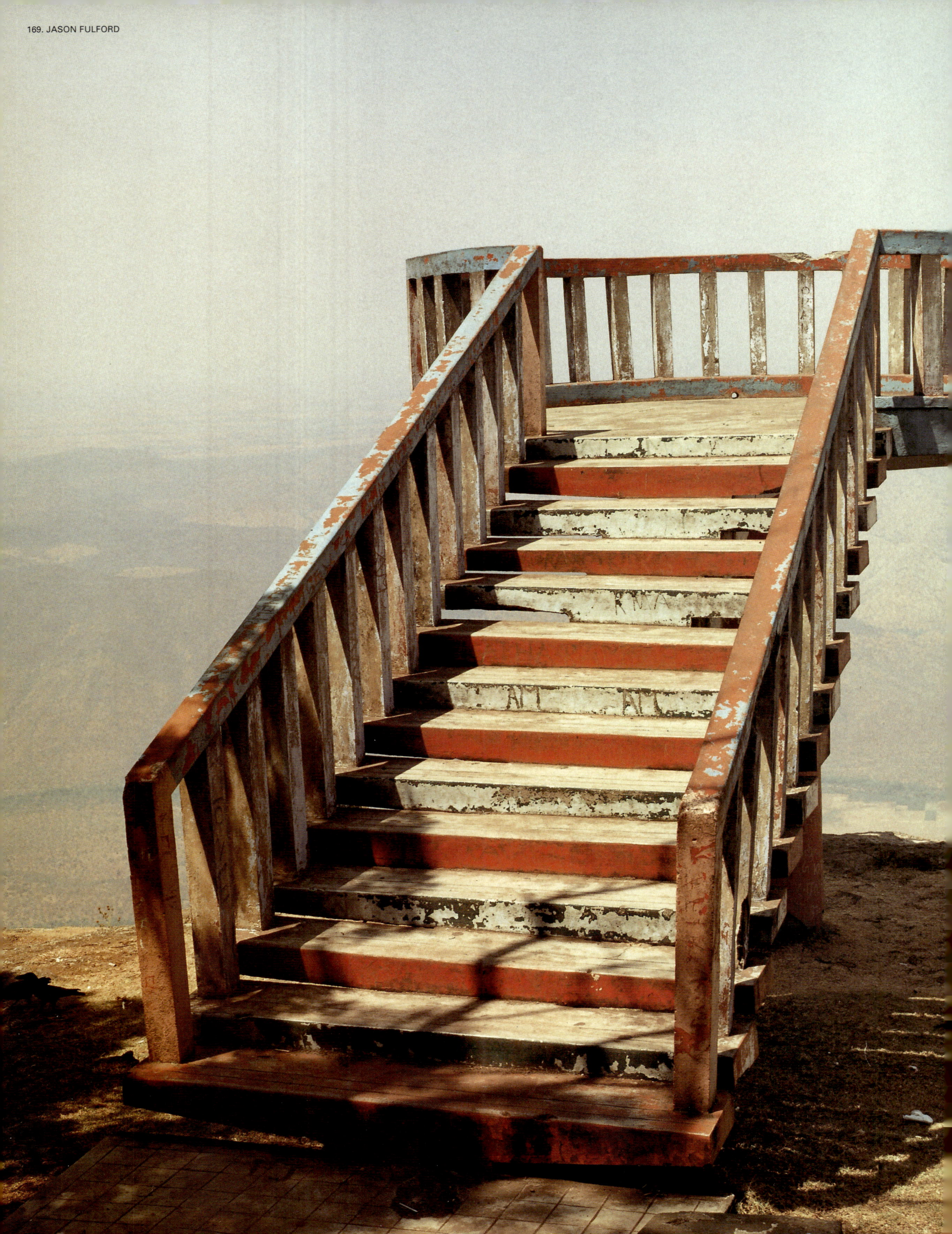

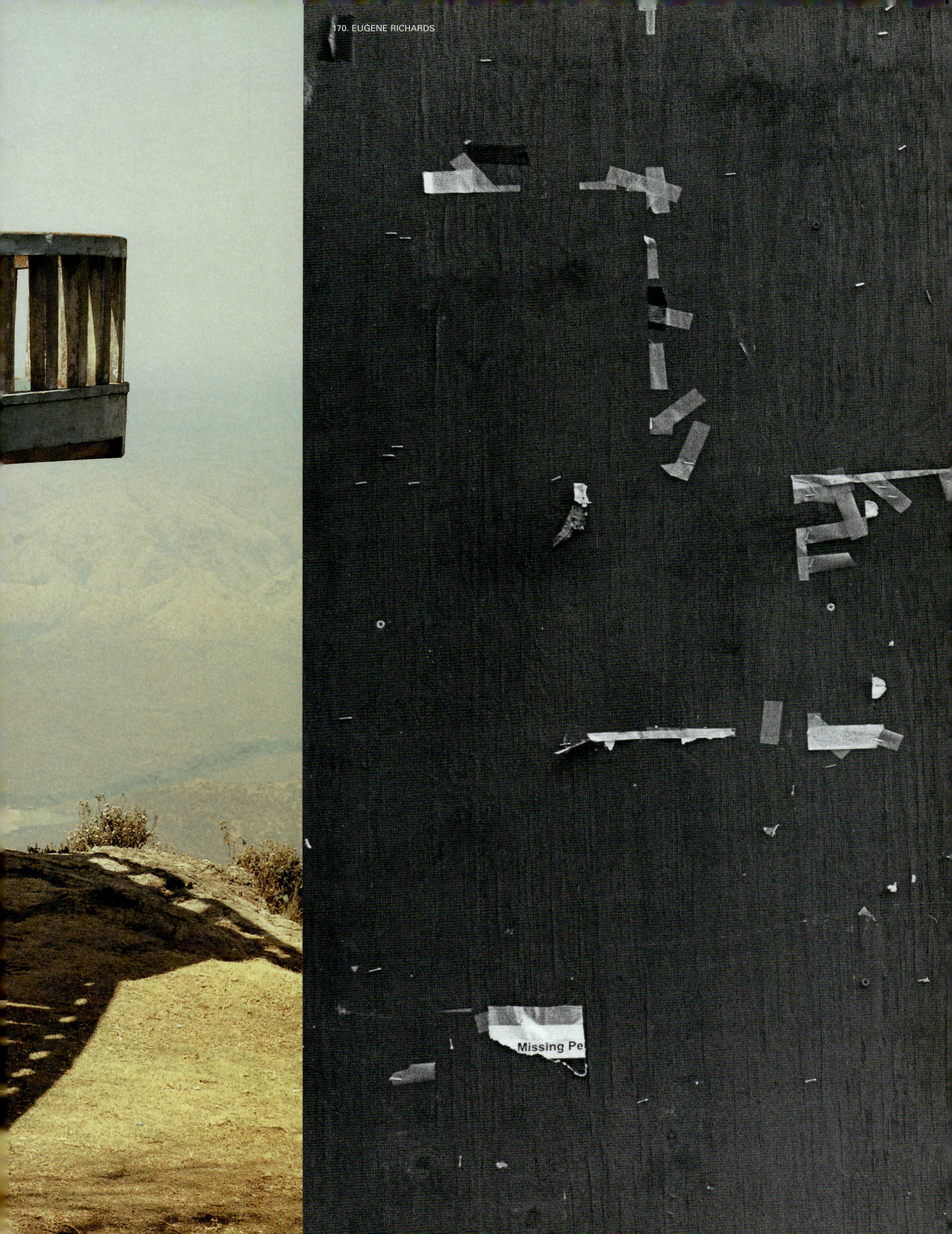

170. EUGENE RICHARDS

170. EUGENE RICHARDS

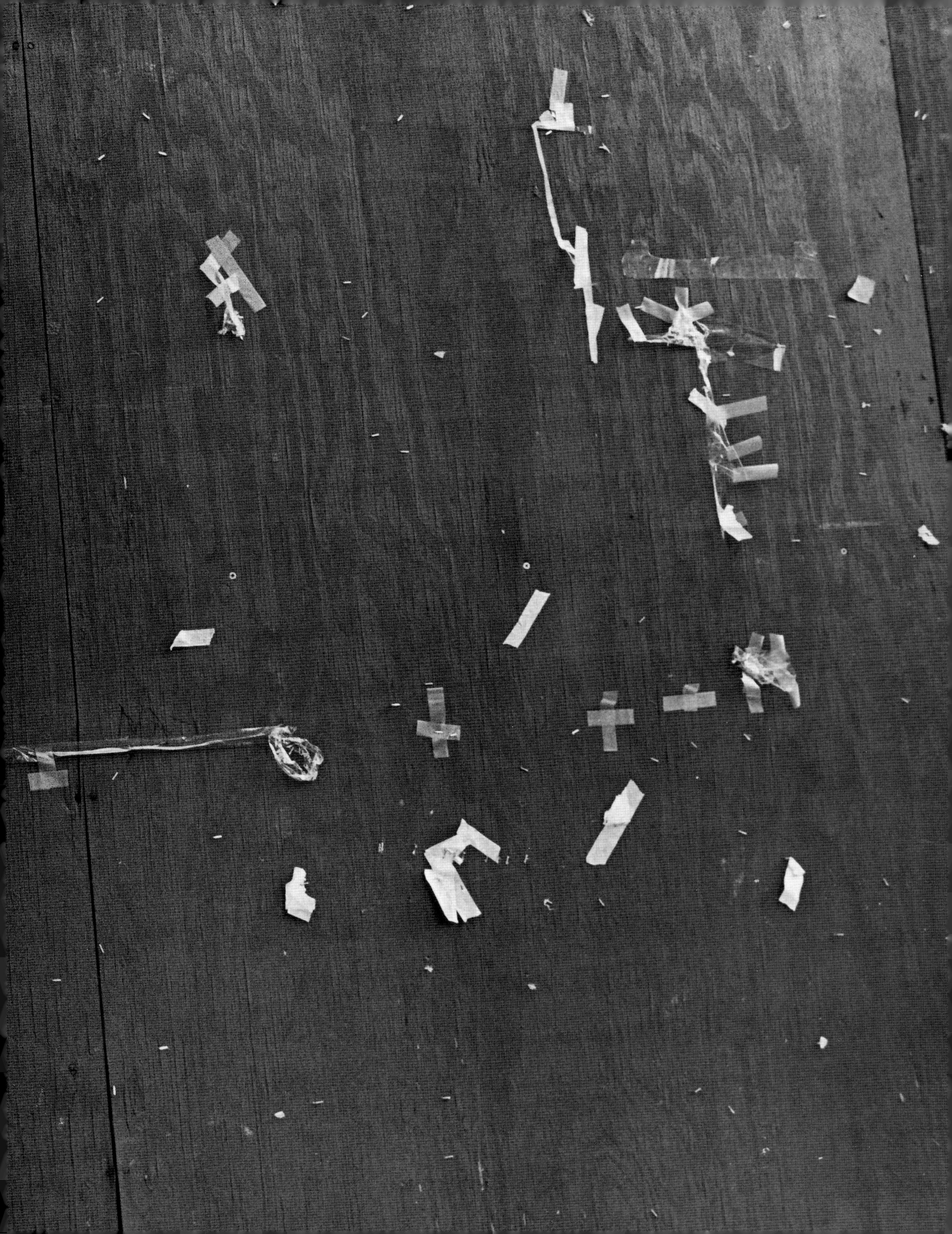

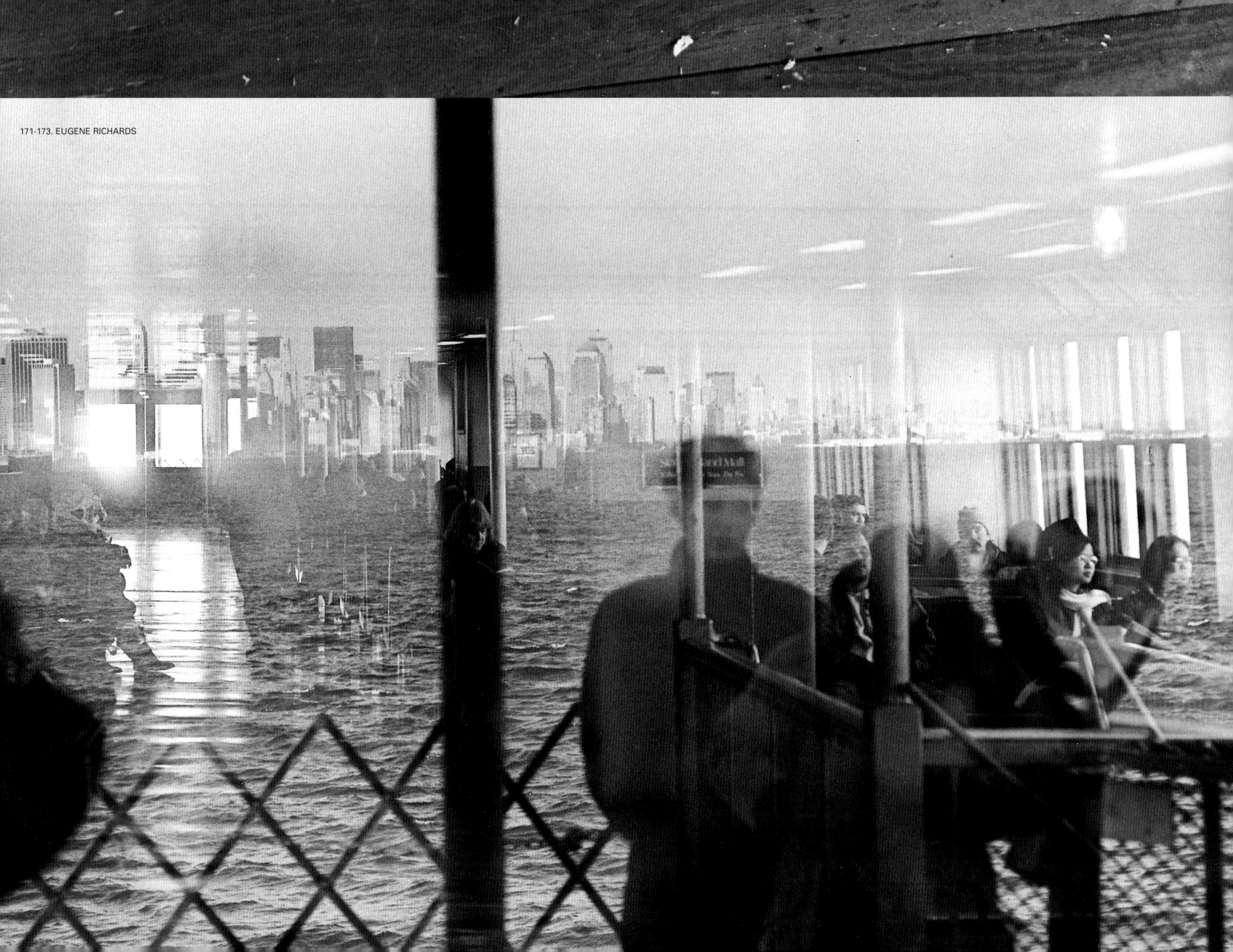

171-173. EUGENE RICHARDS

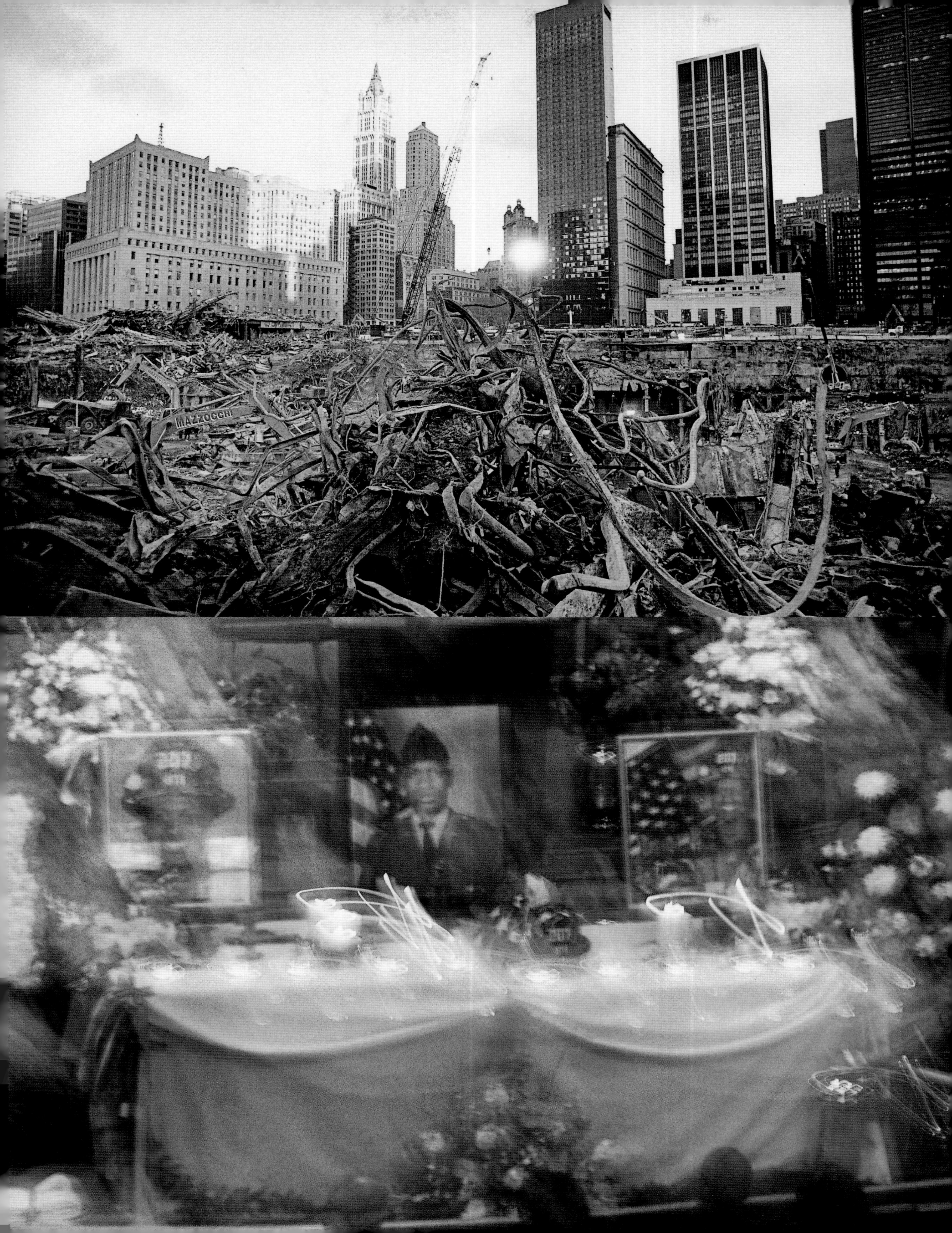
MAZZOCCHI

174-177. LYLE OWERKO

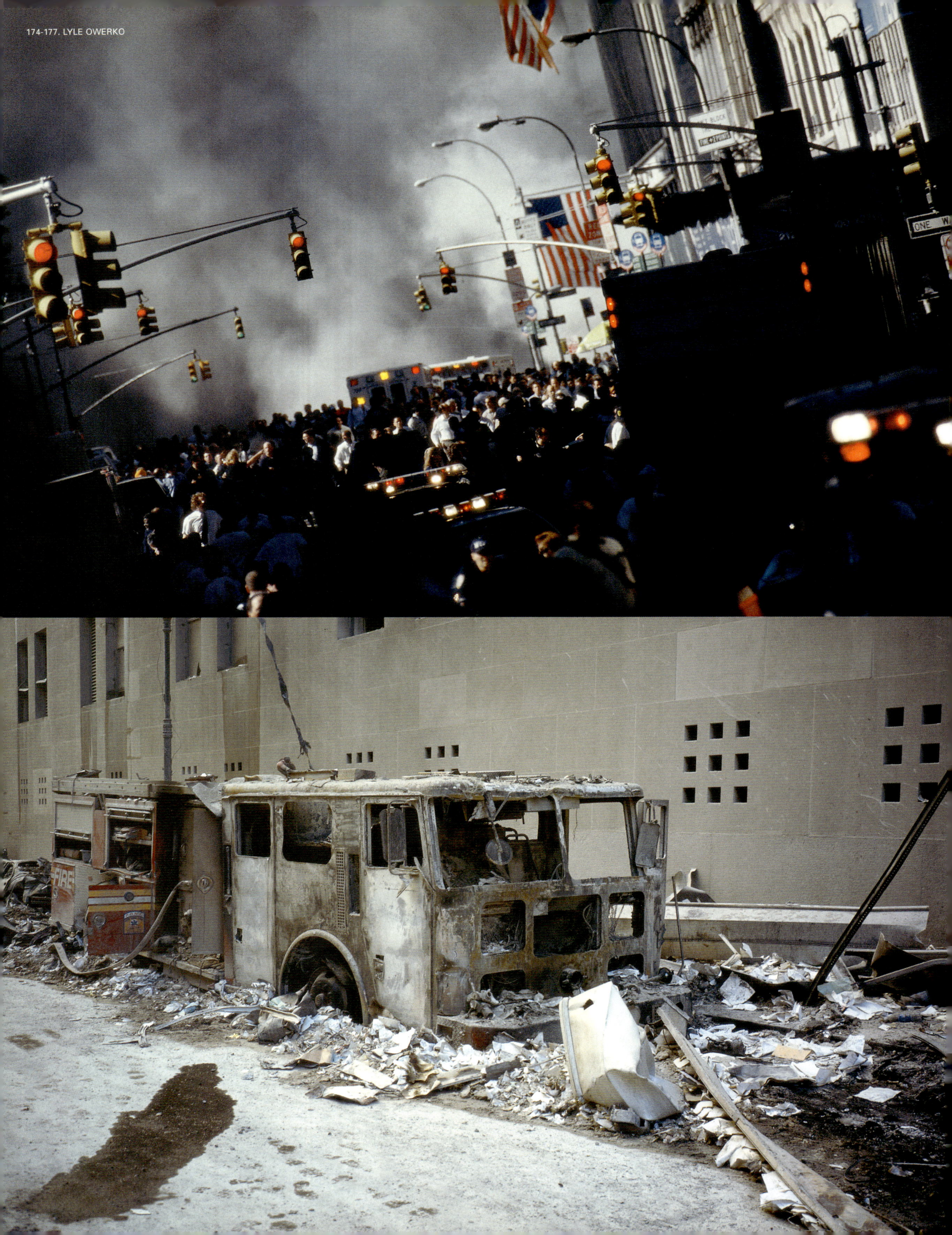

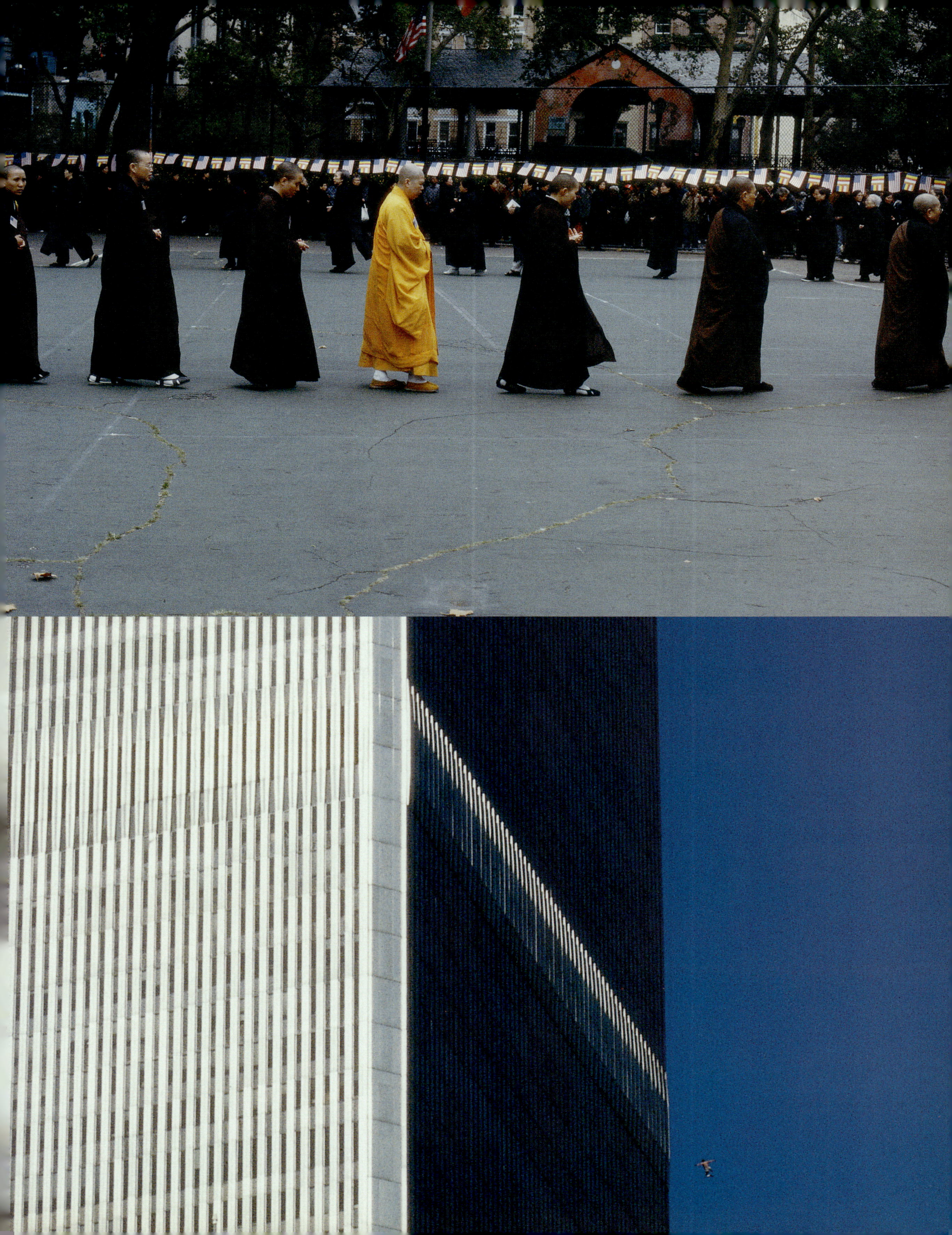

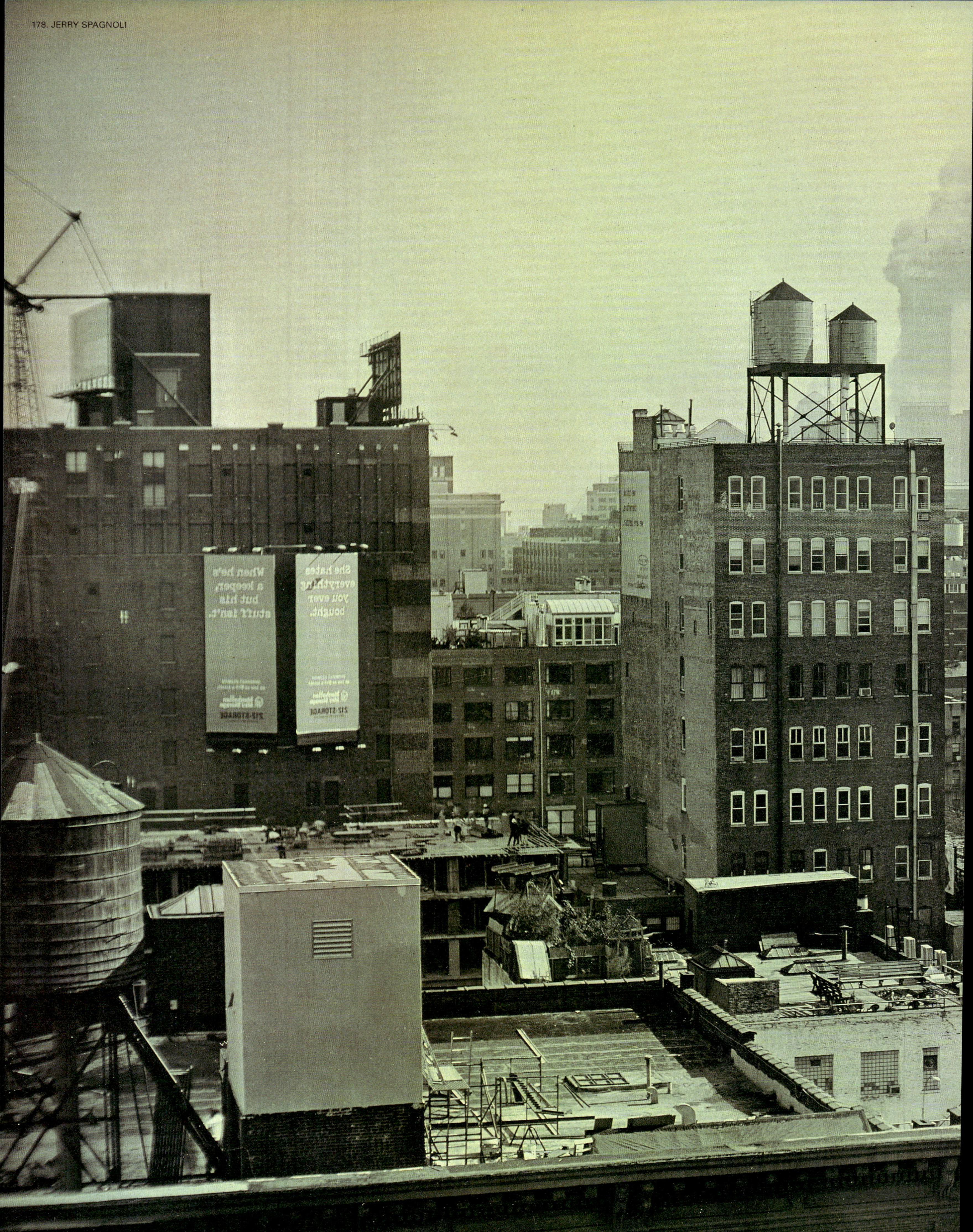
When he's
a keeper,
but his
stuff isn't.
212-STORAGE
She hates
everything
you ever
bought.
212-STORAGE

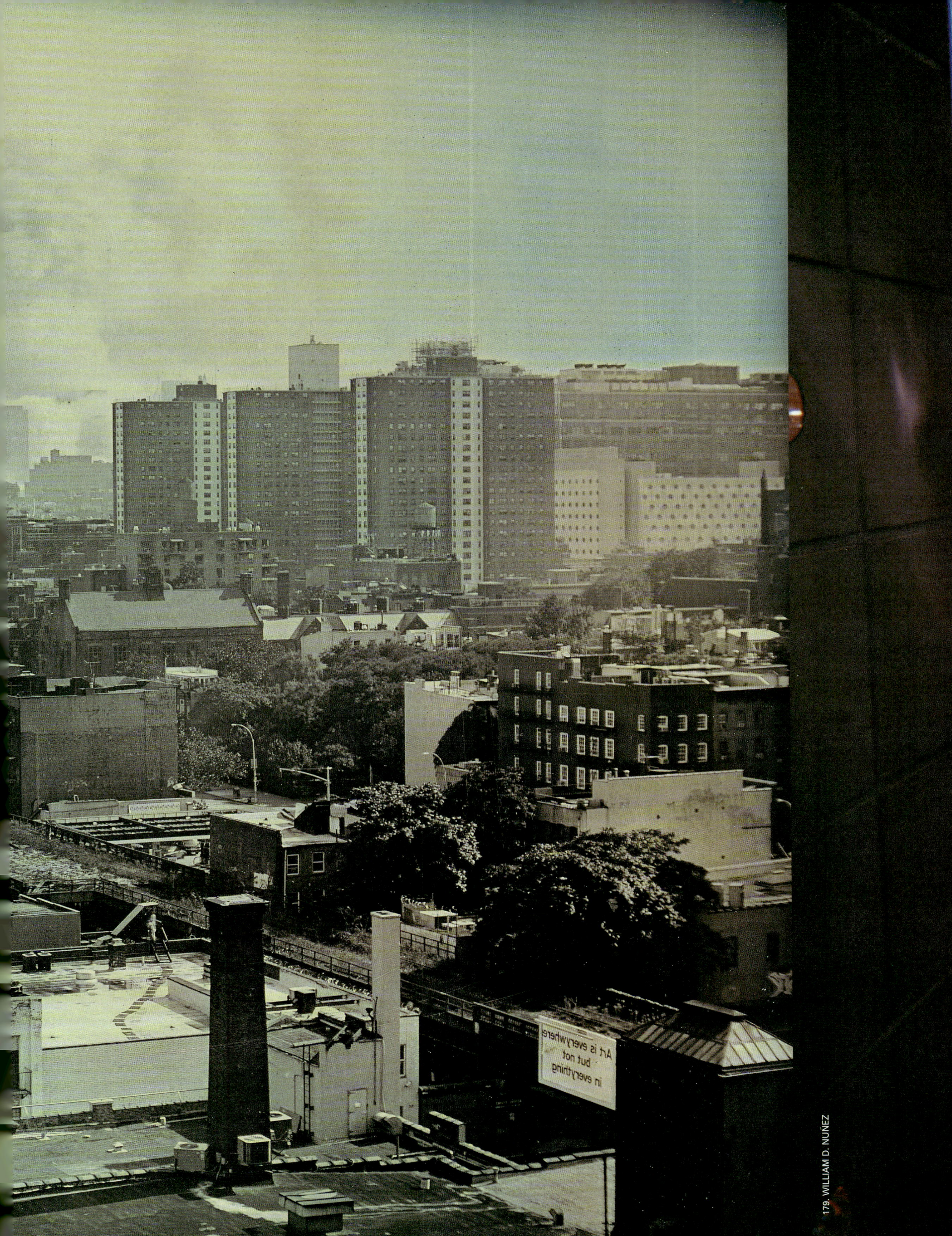

179. WILLIAM D. NUÑEZ

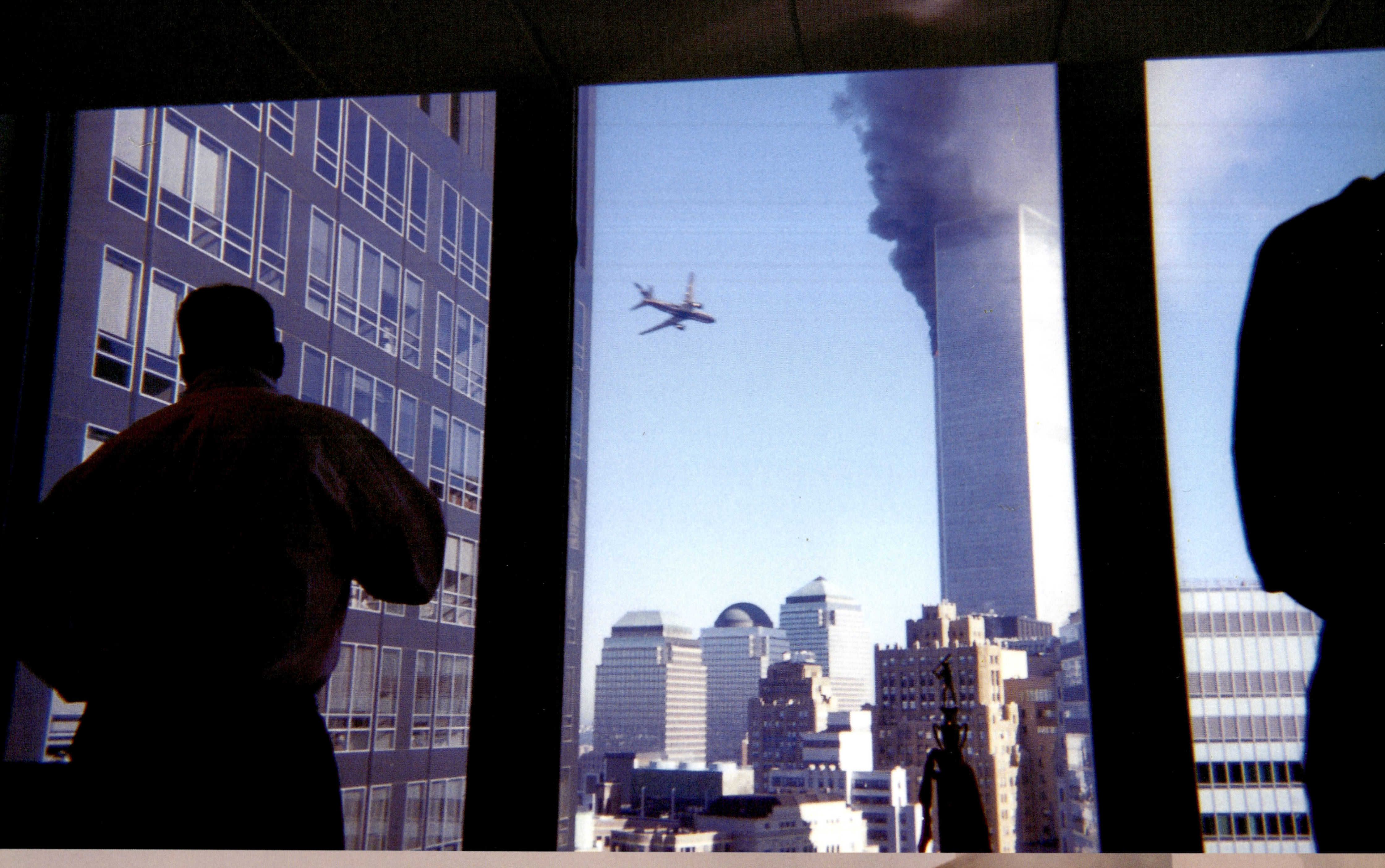

180. ANDREA BOOHER

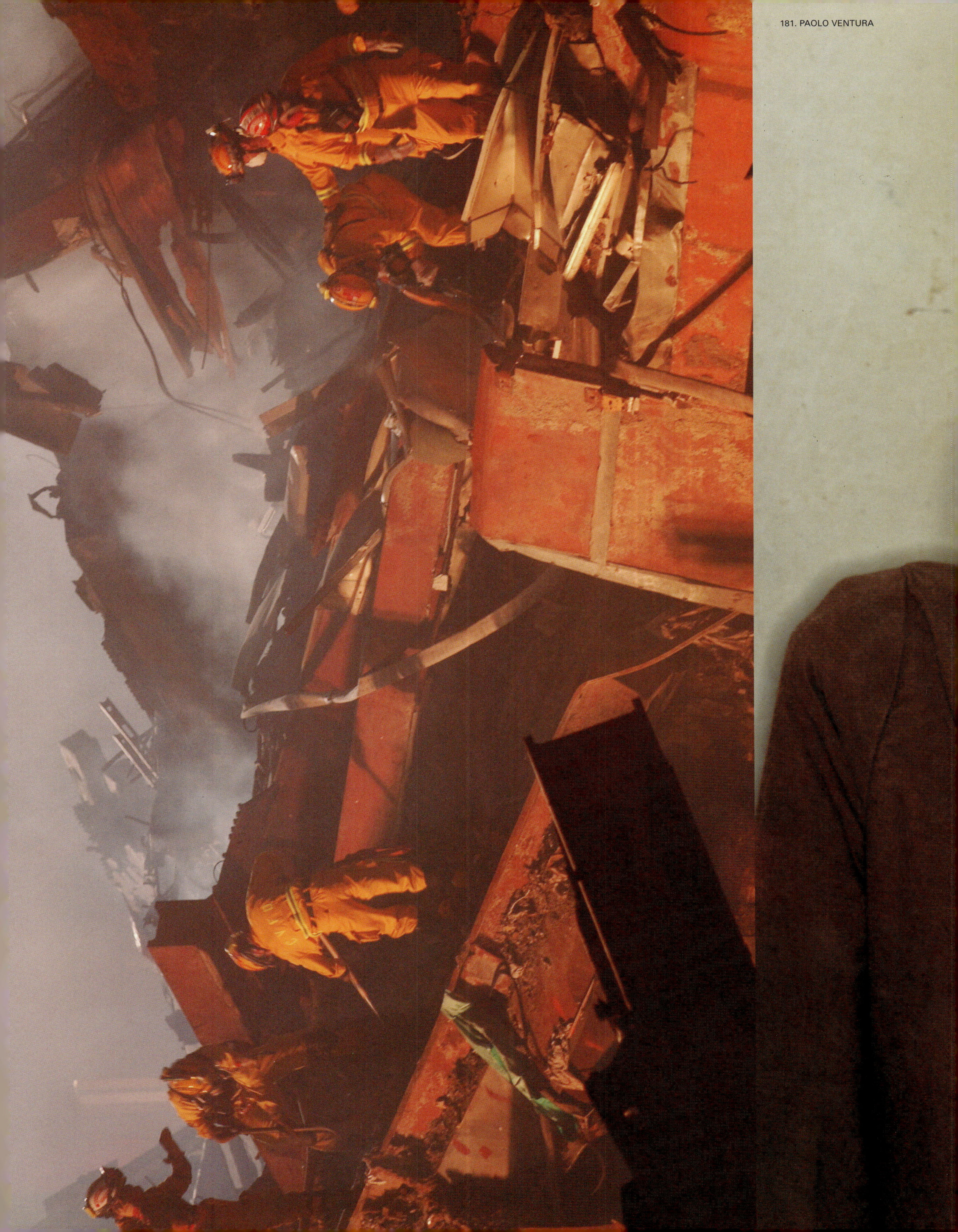

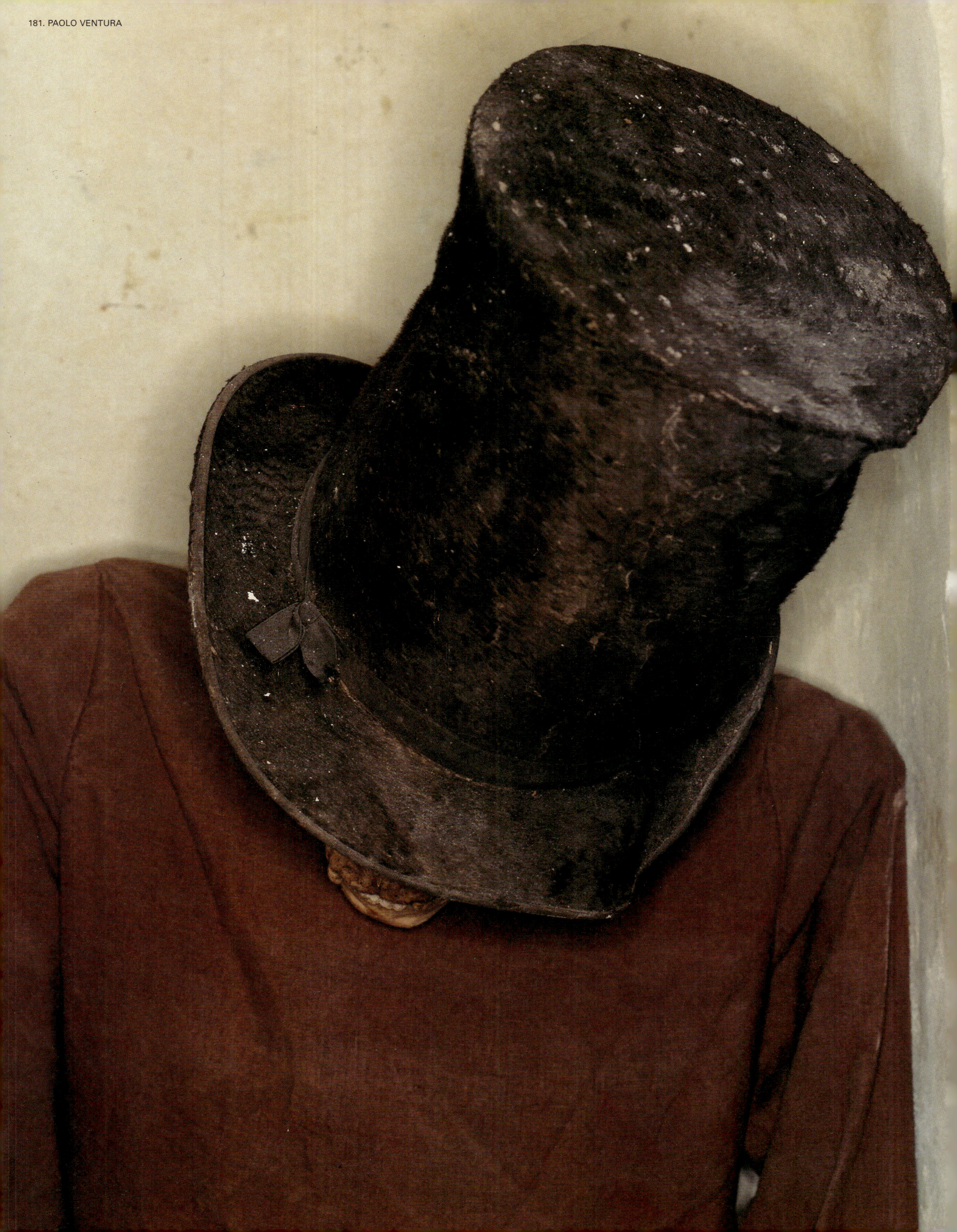

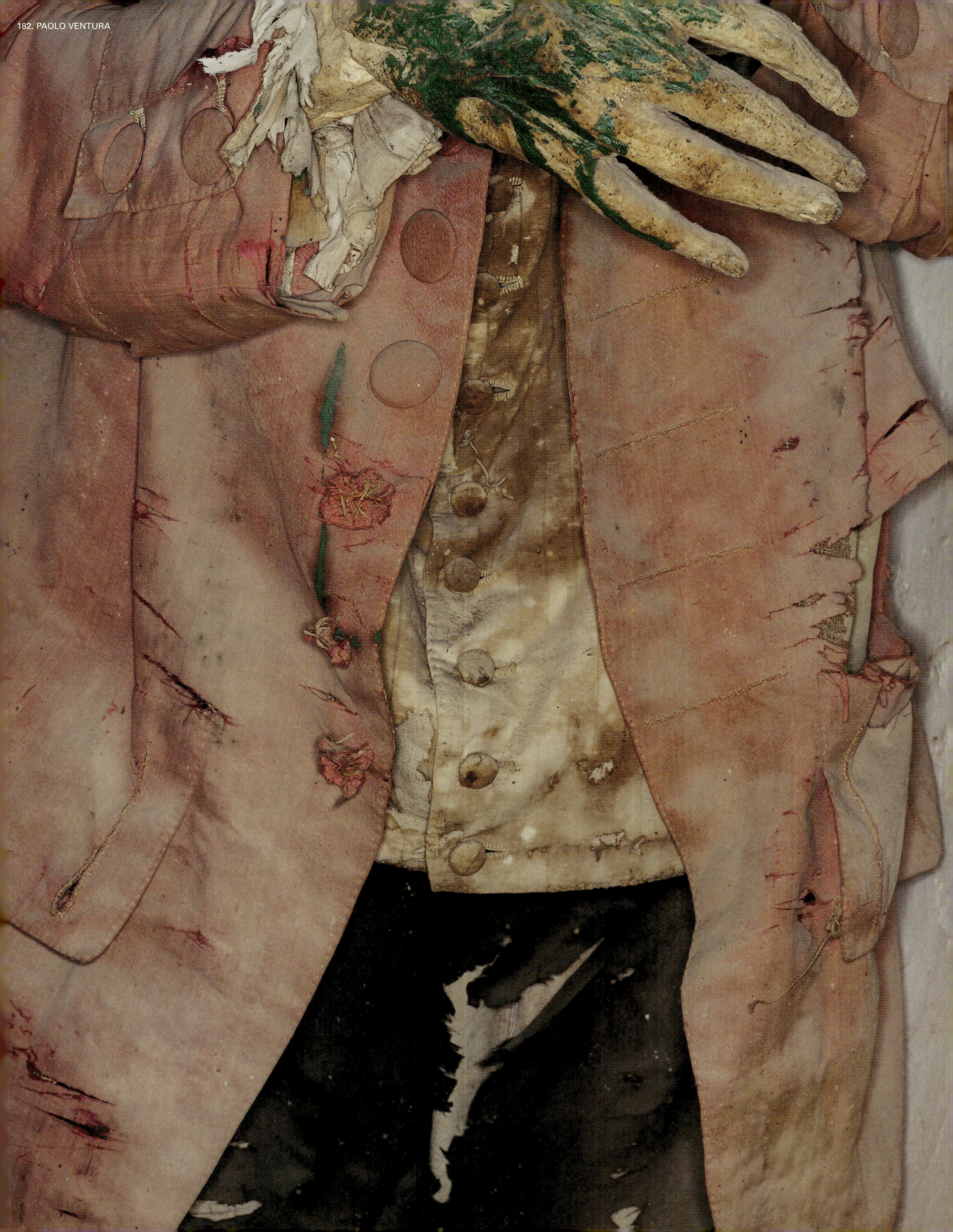

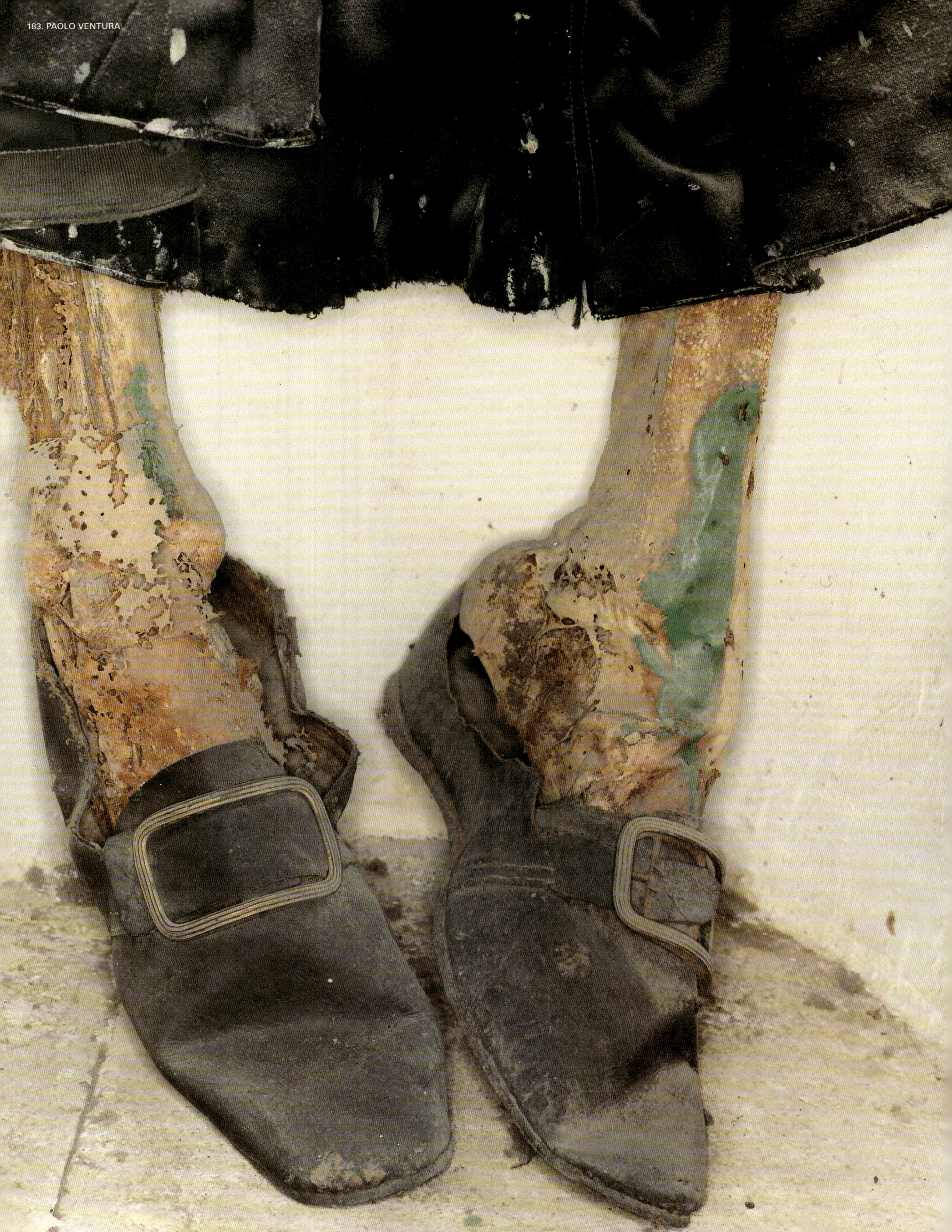

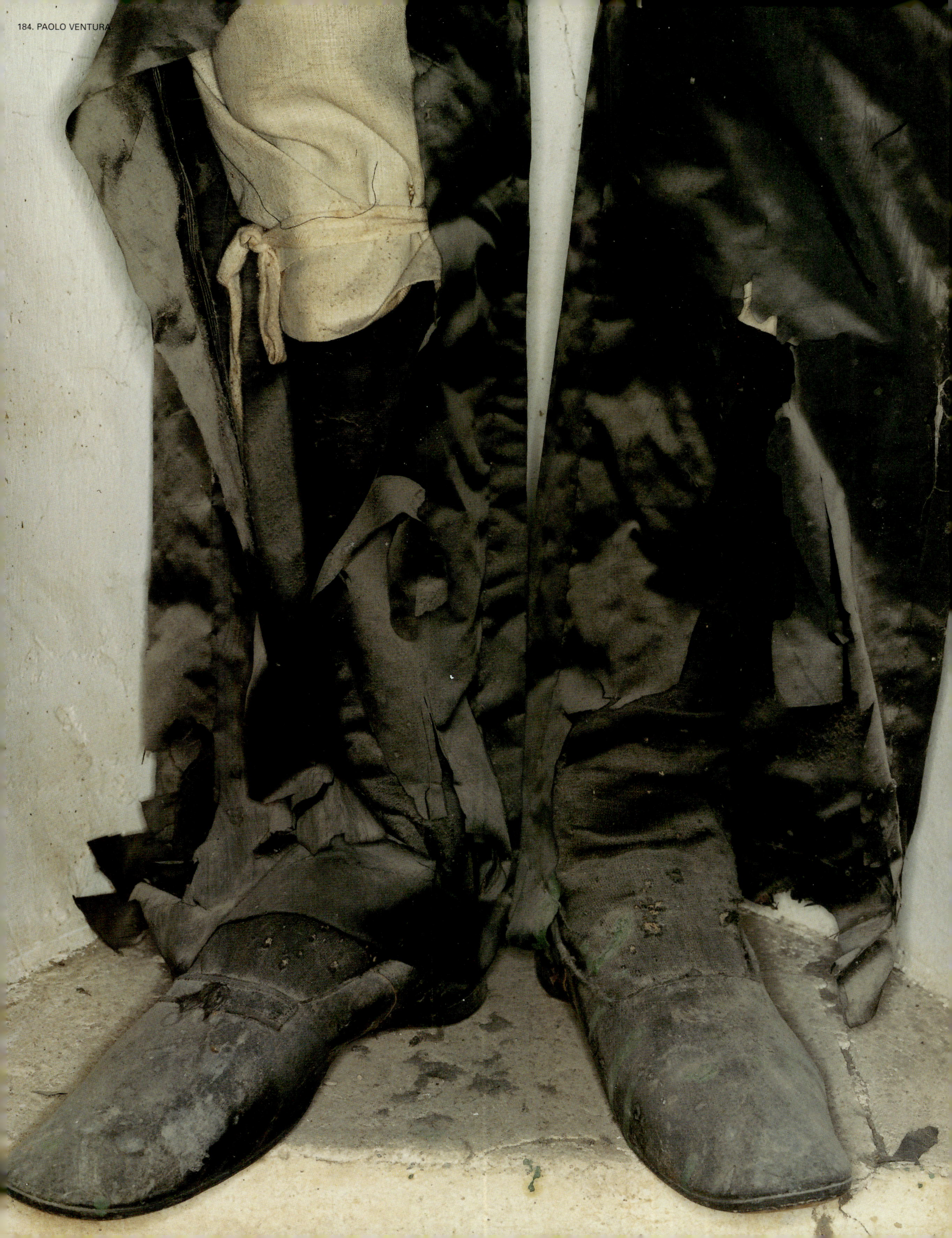

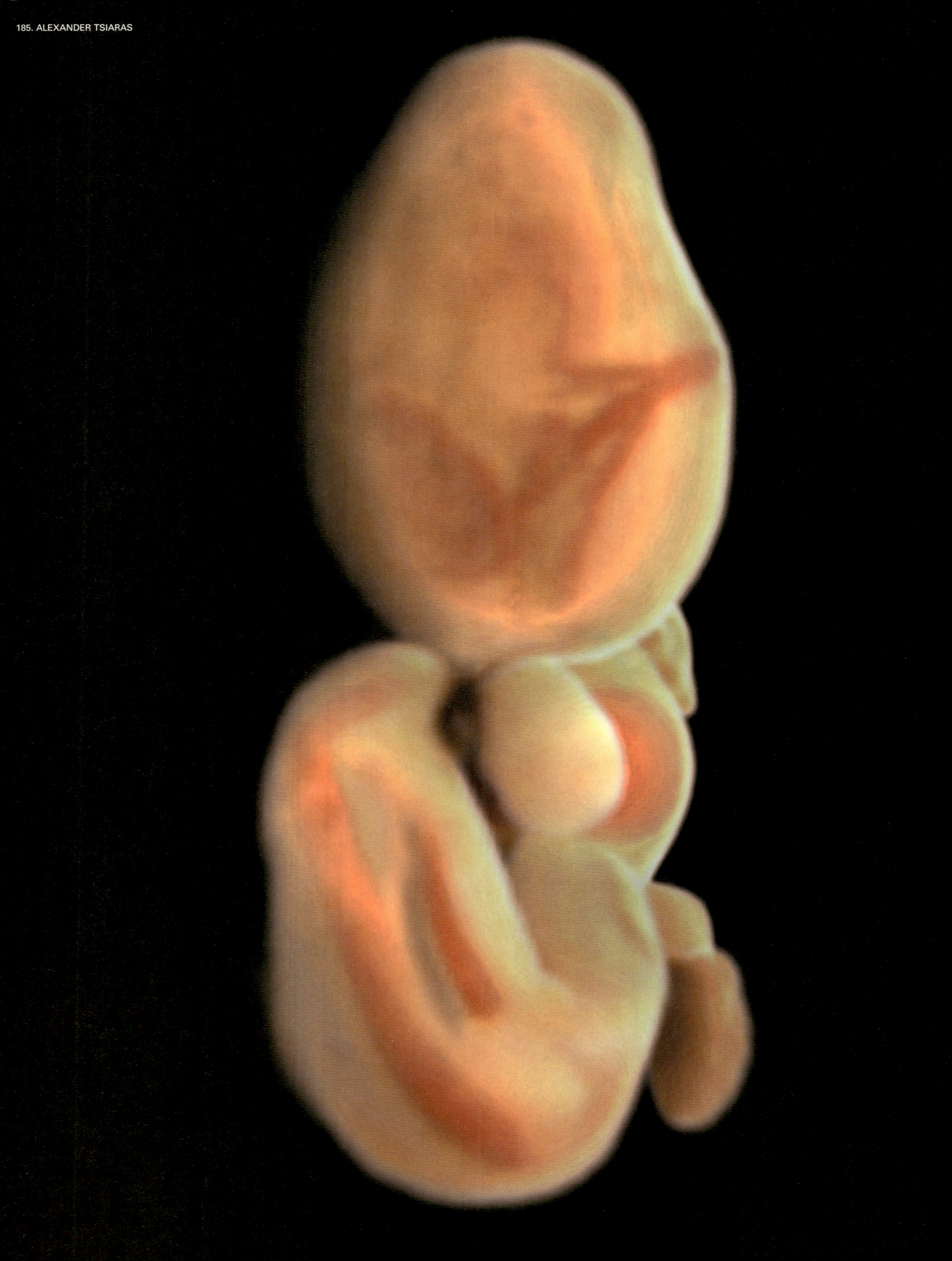

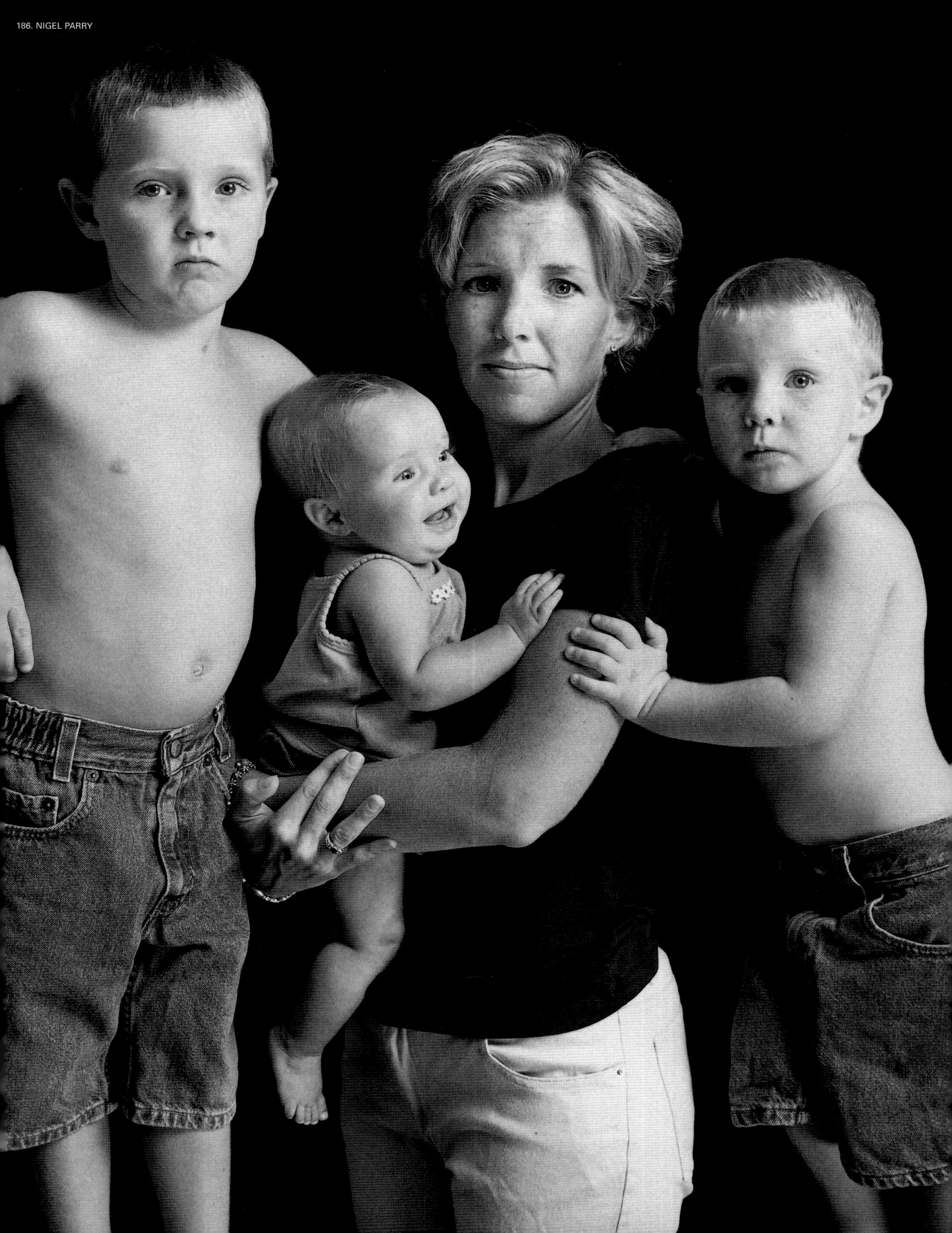

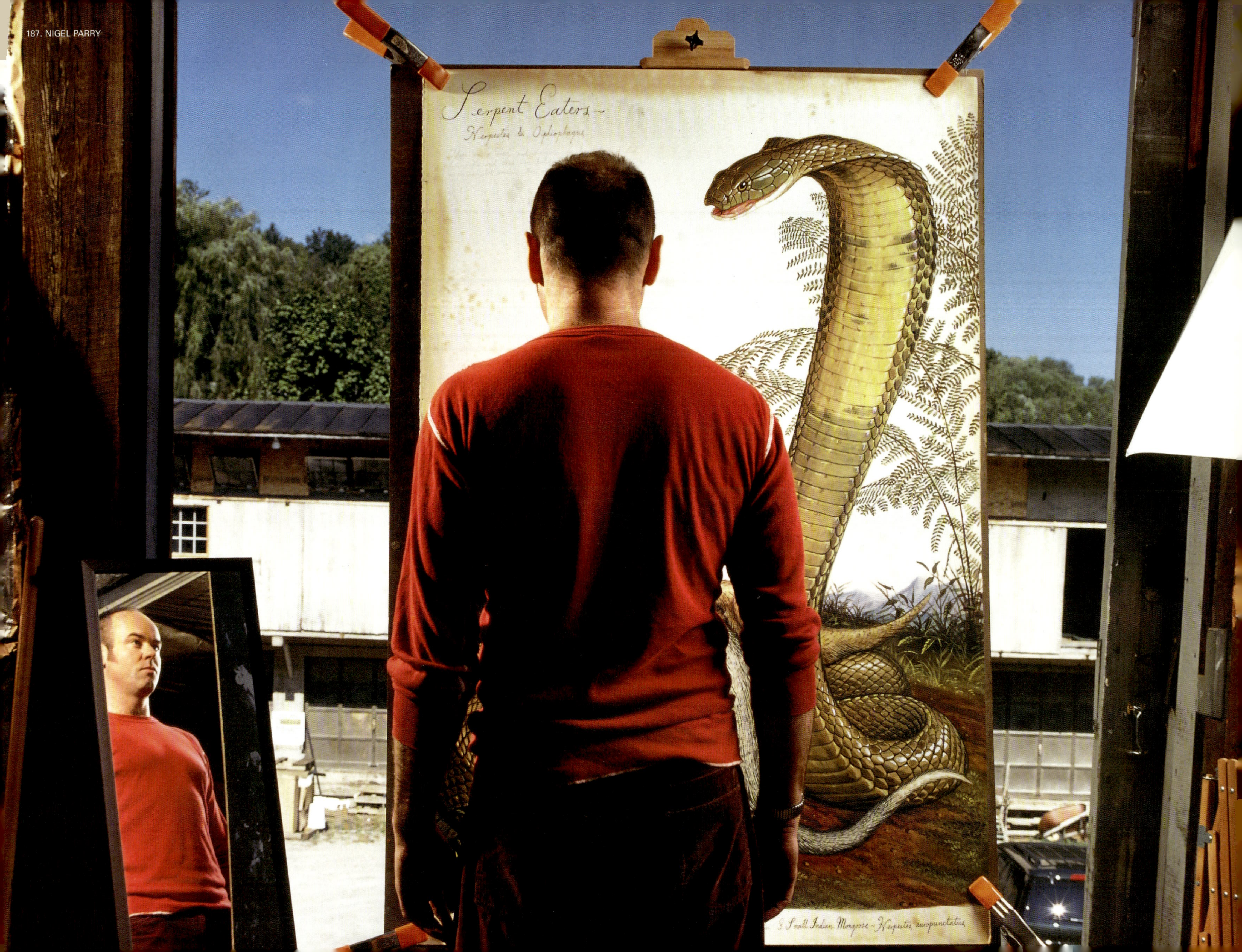

187. NIGEL PARRY

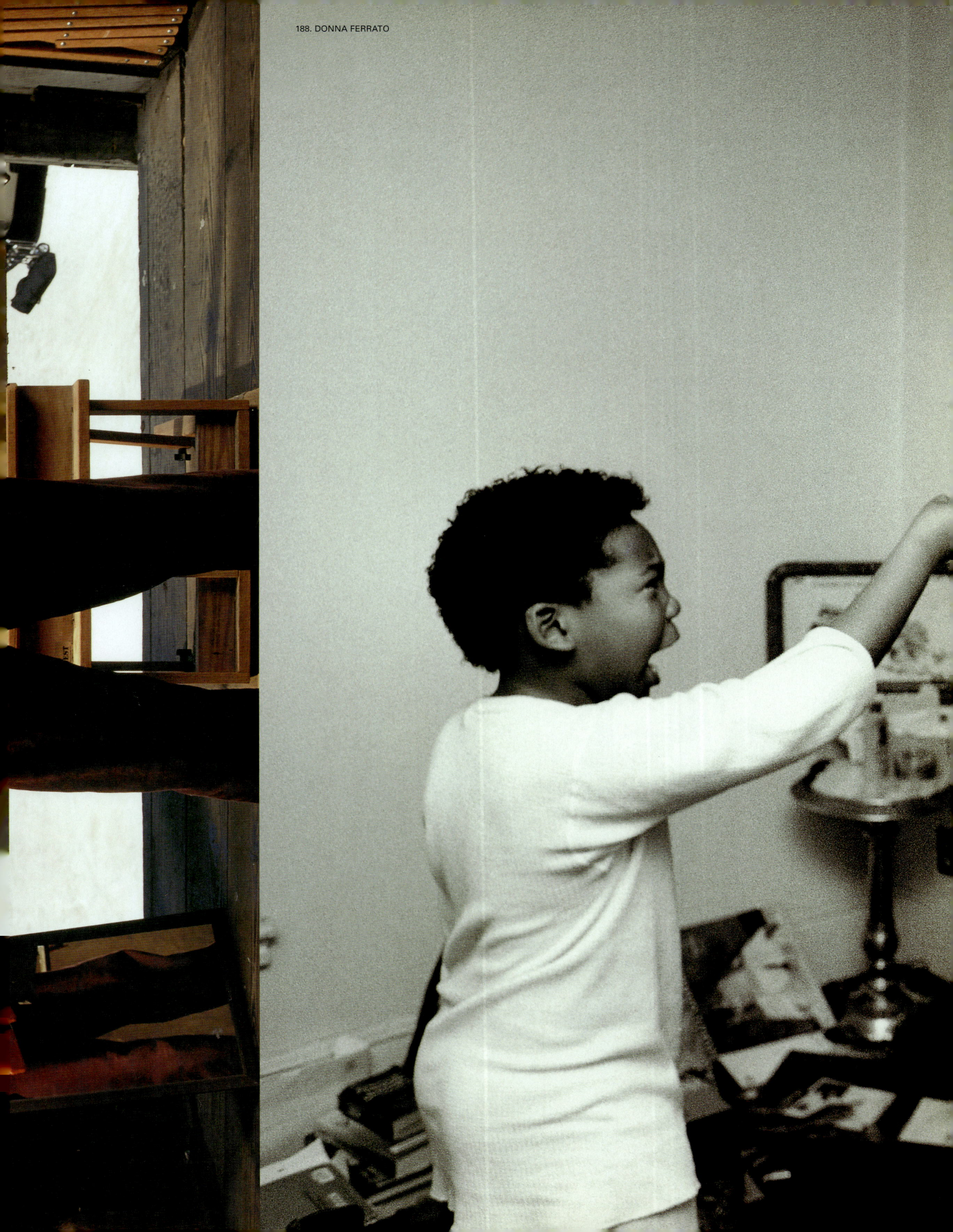

188. DONNA FERRATO

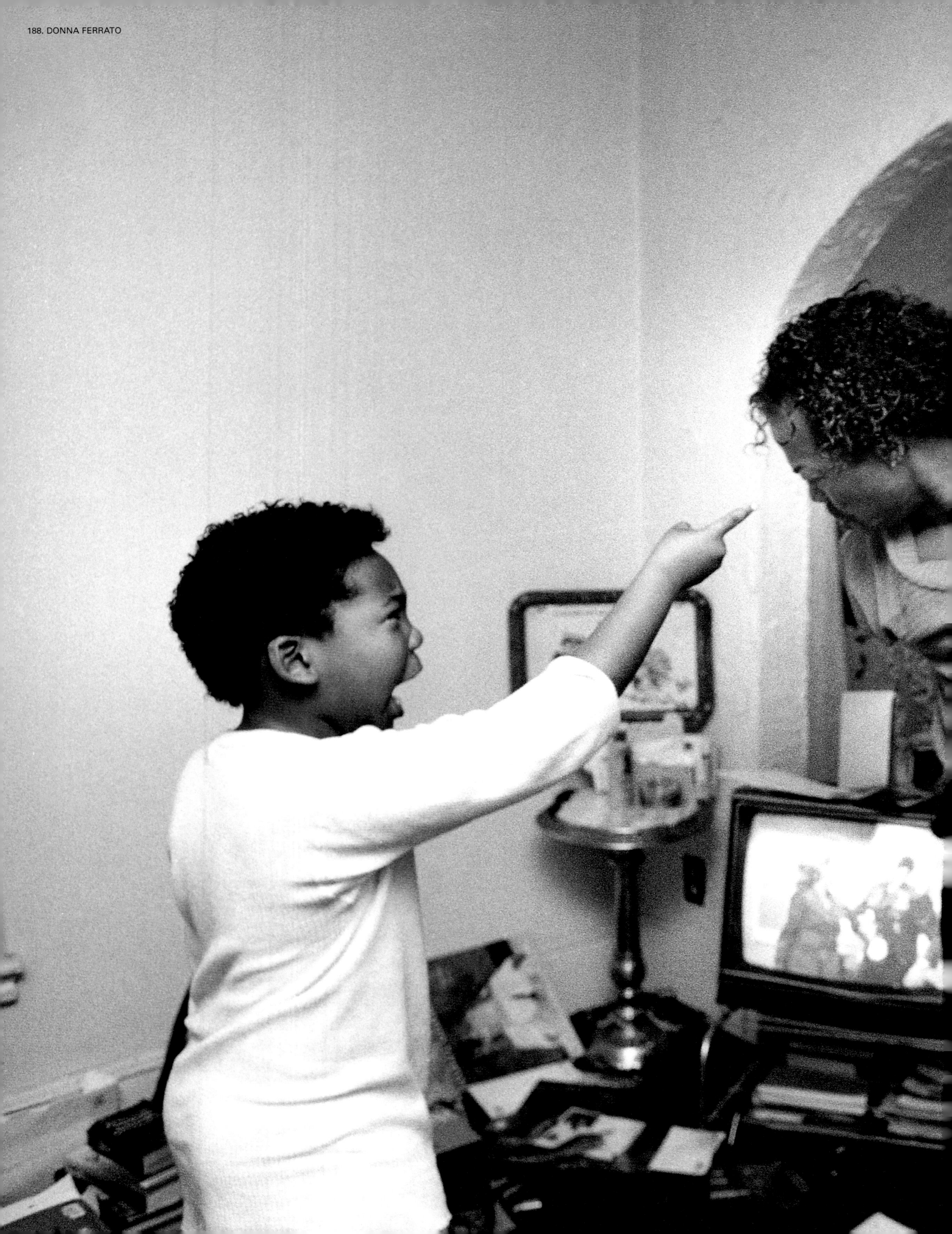

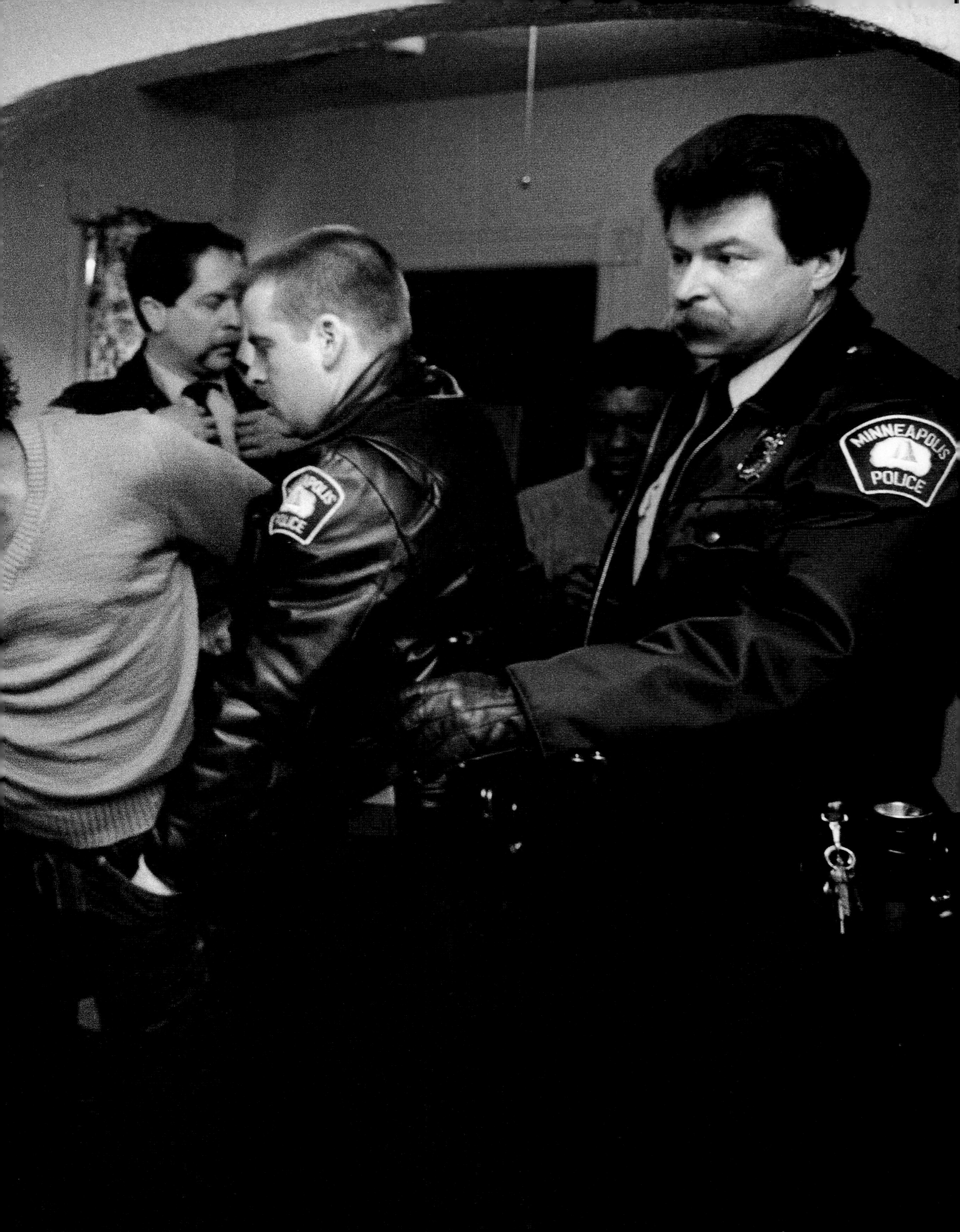
MINNEAPOLIS
POLICE

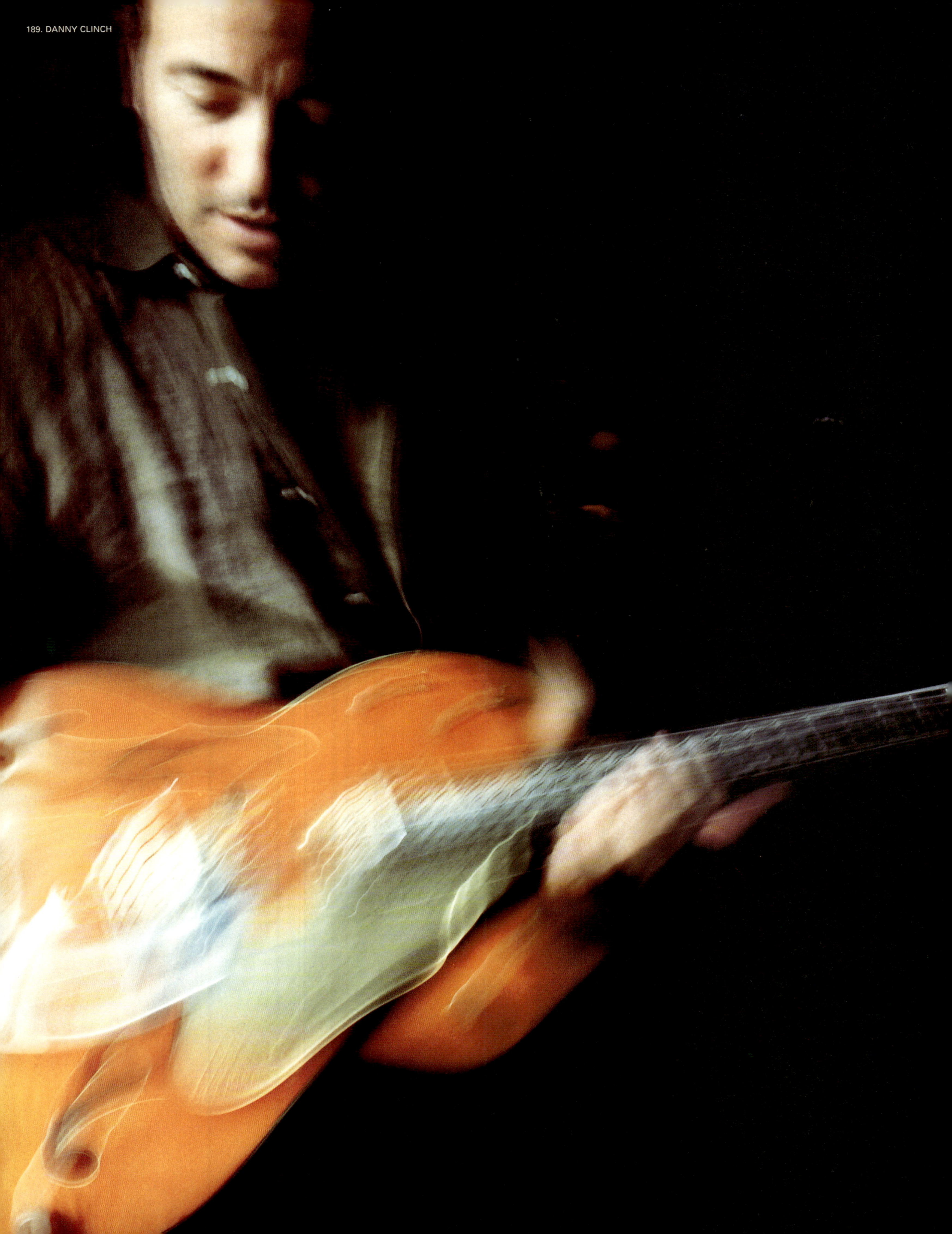

189. DANNY CLINCH

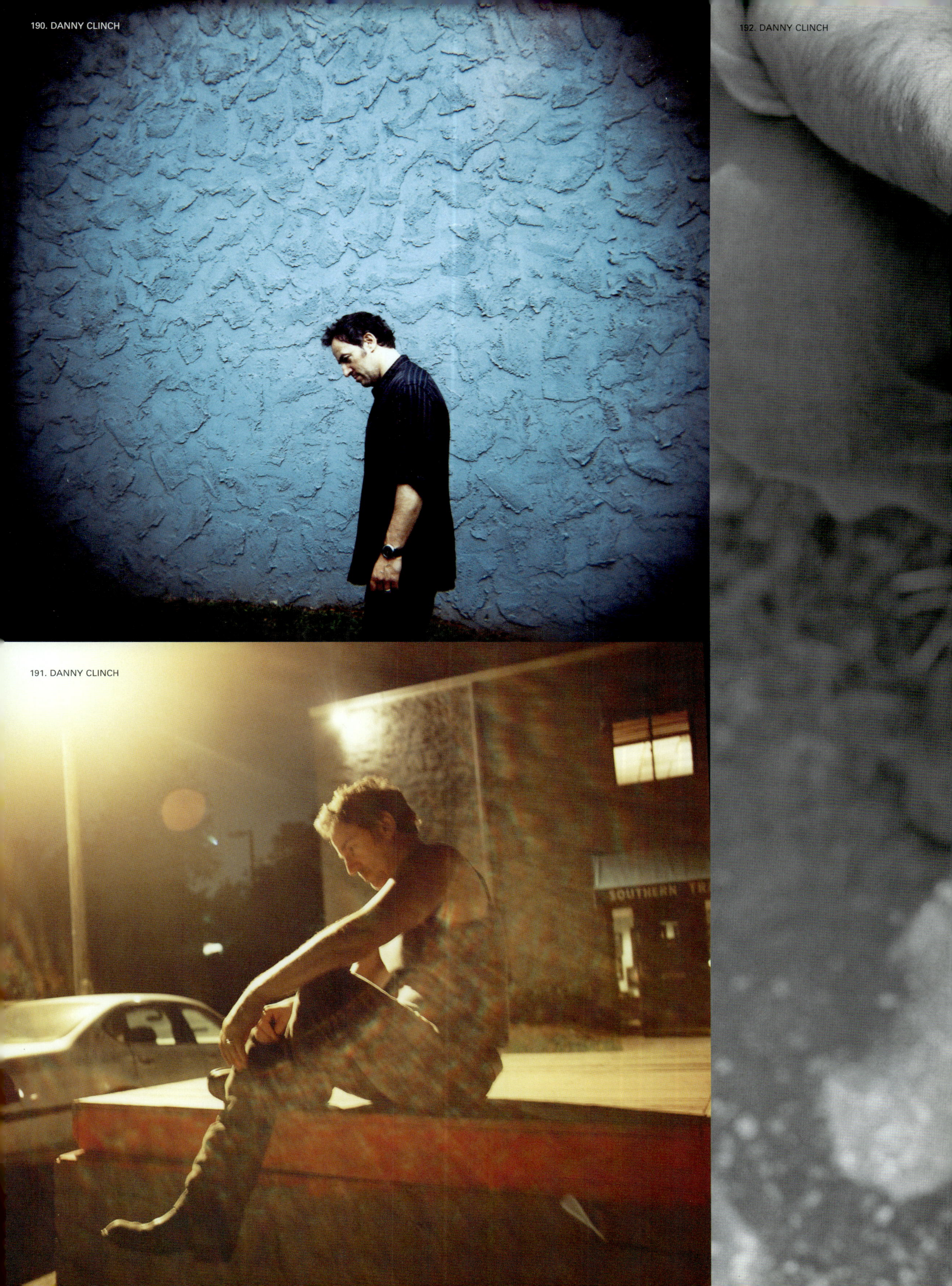

190. DANNY CLINCH

191. DANNY CLINCH

192. DANNY CLINCH

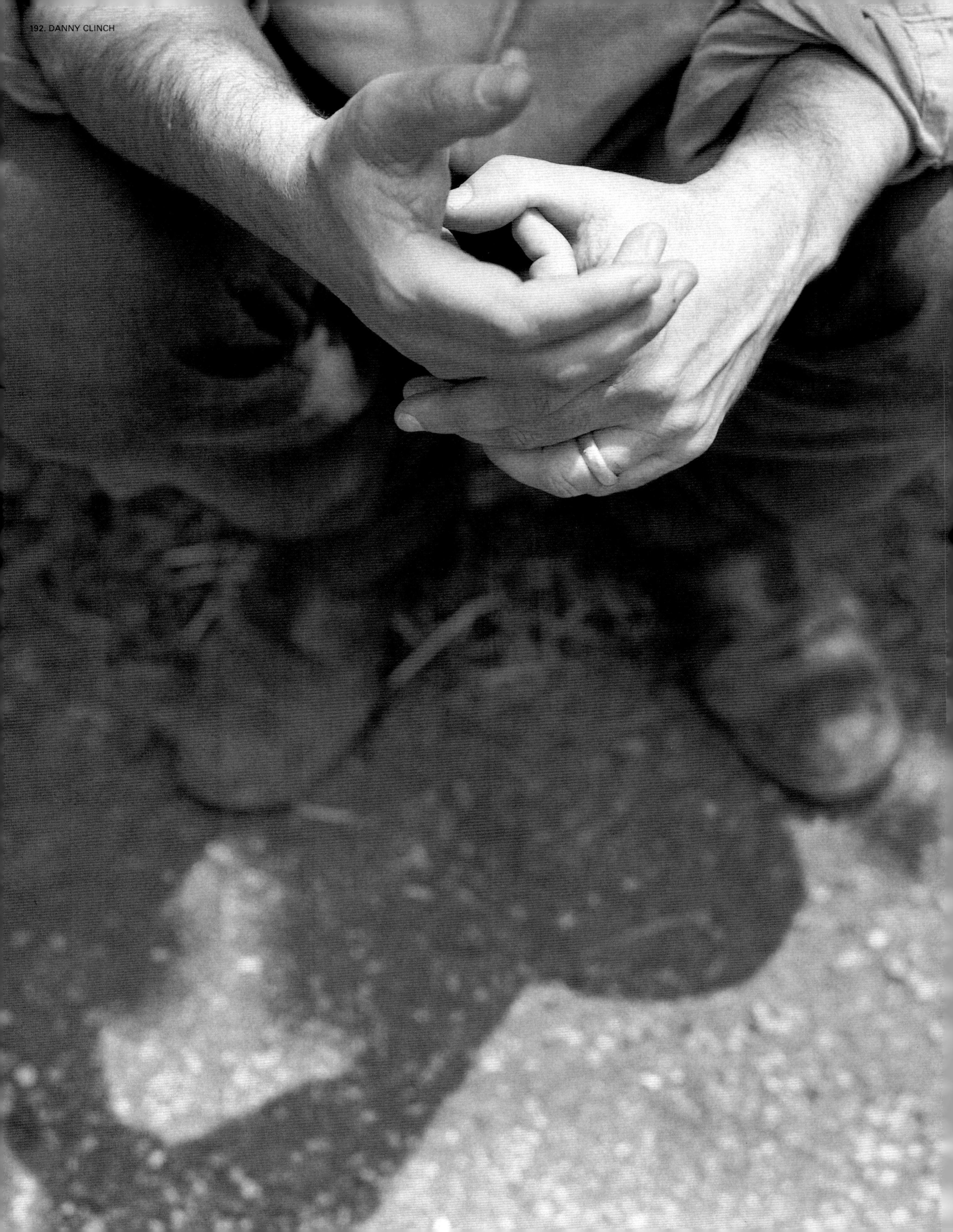

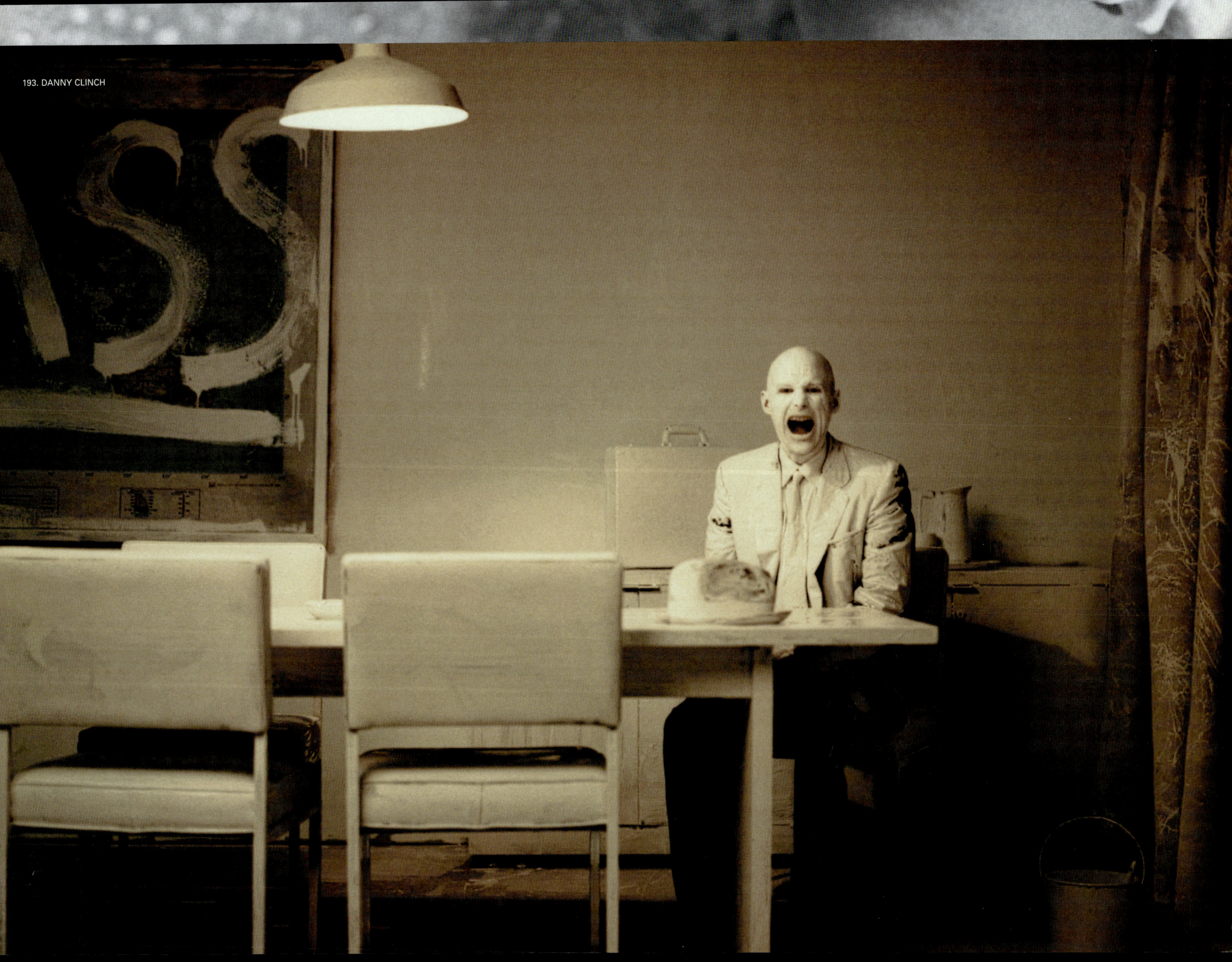

193. DANNY CLINCH

194. DANNY CLINCH

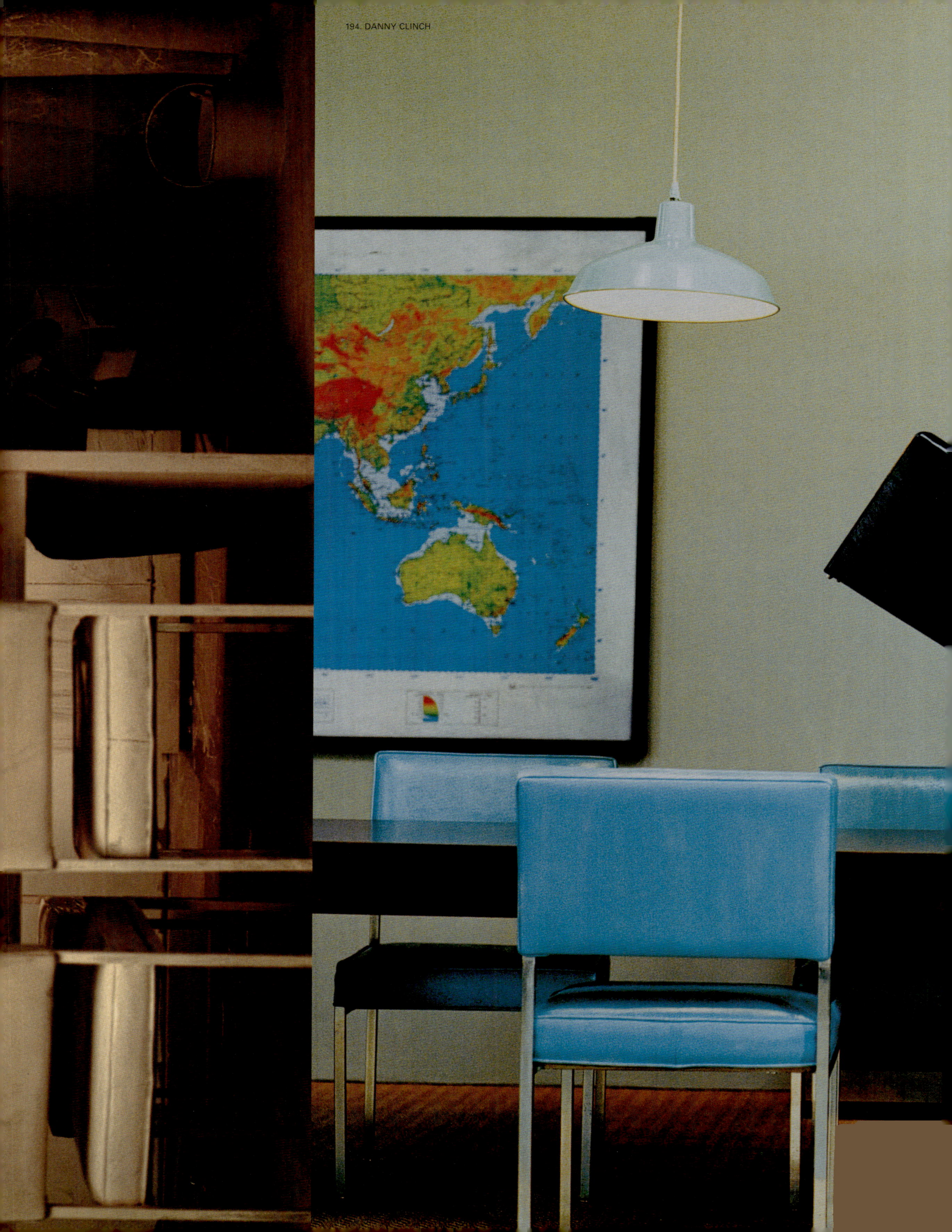

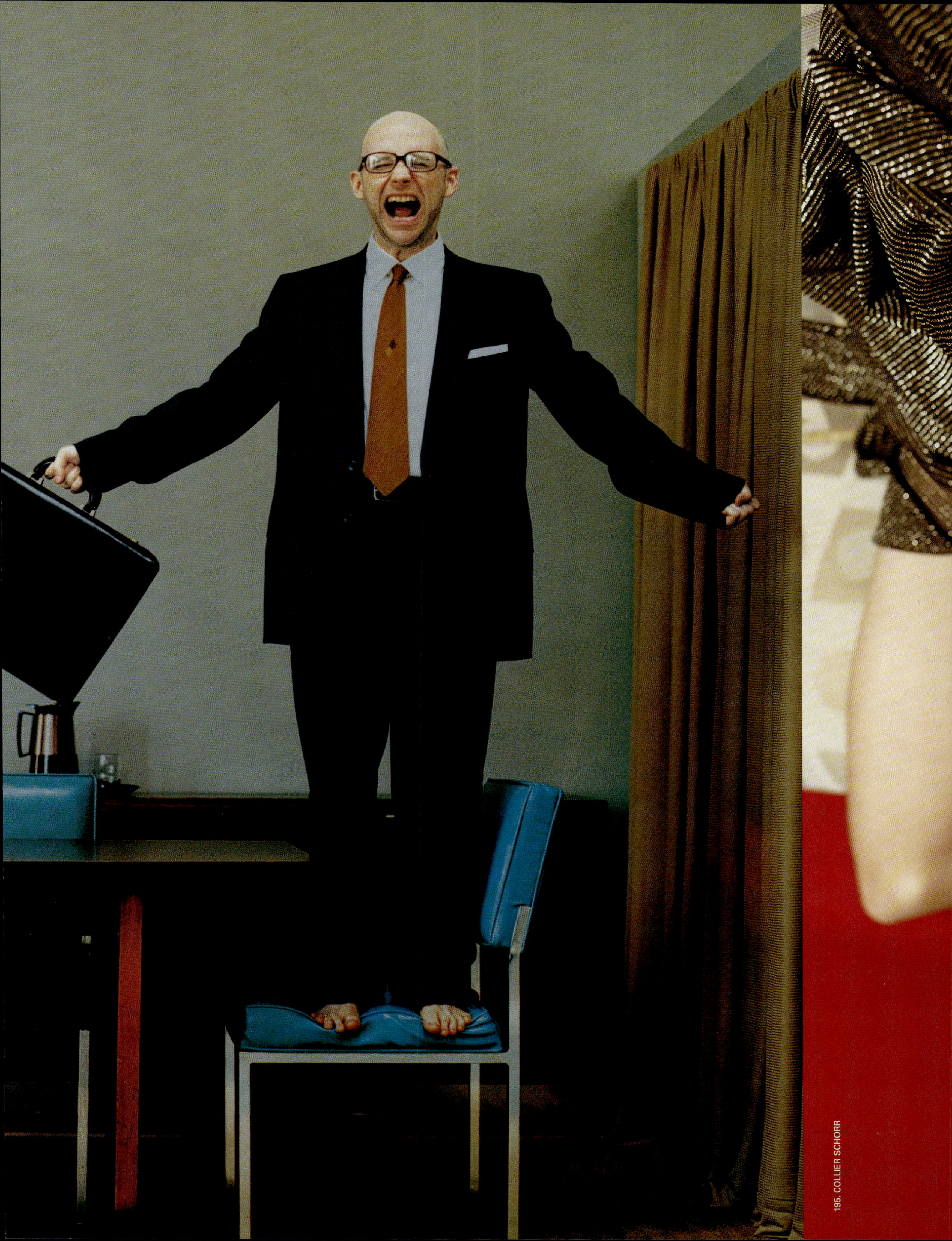

195. COLLIER SCHORR

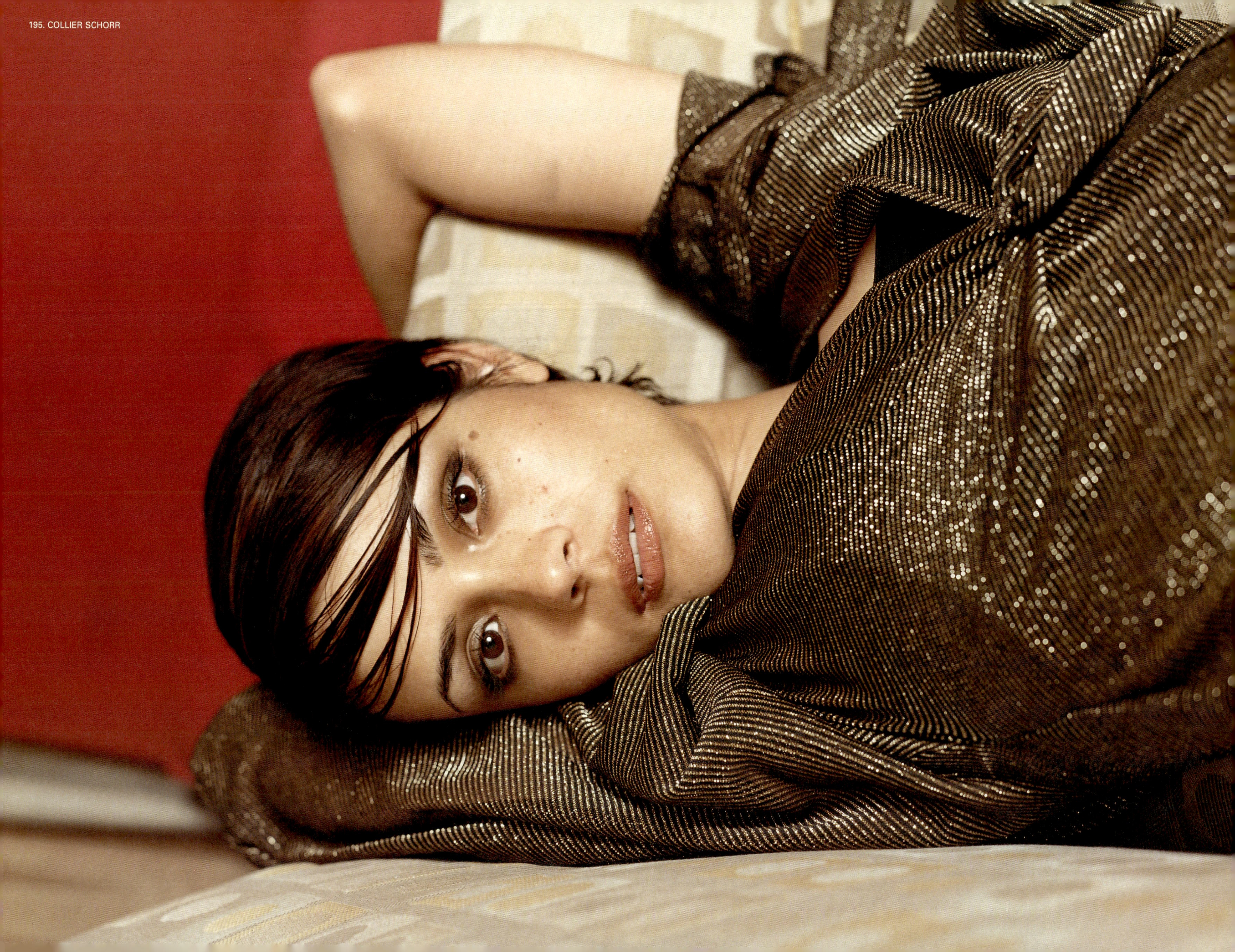

195. COLLIER SCHORR

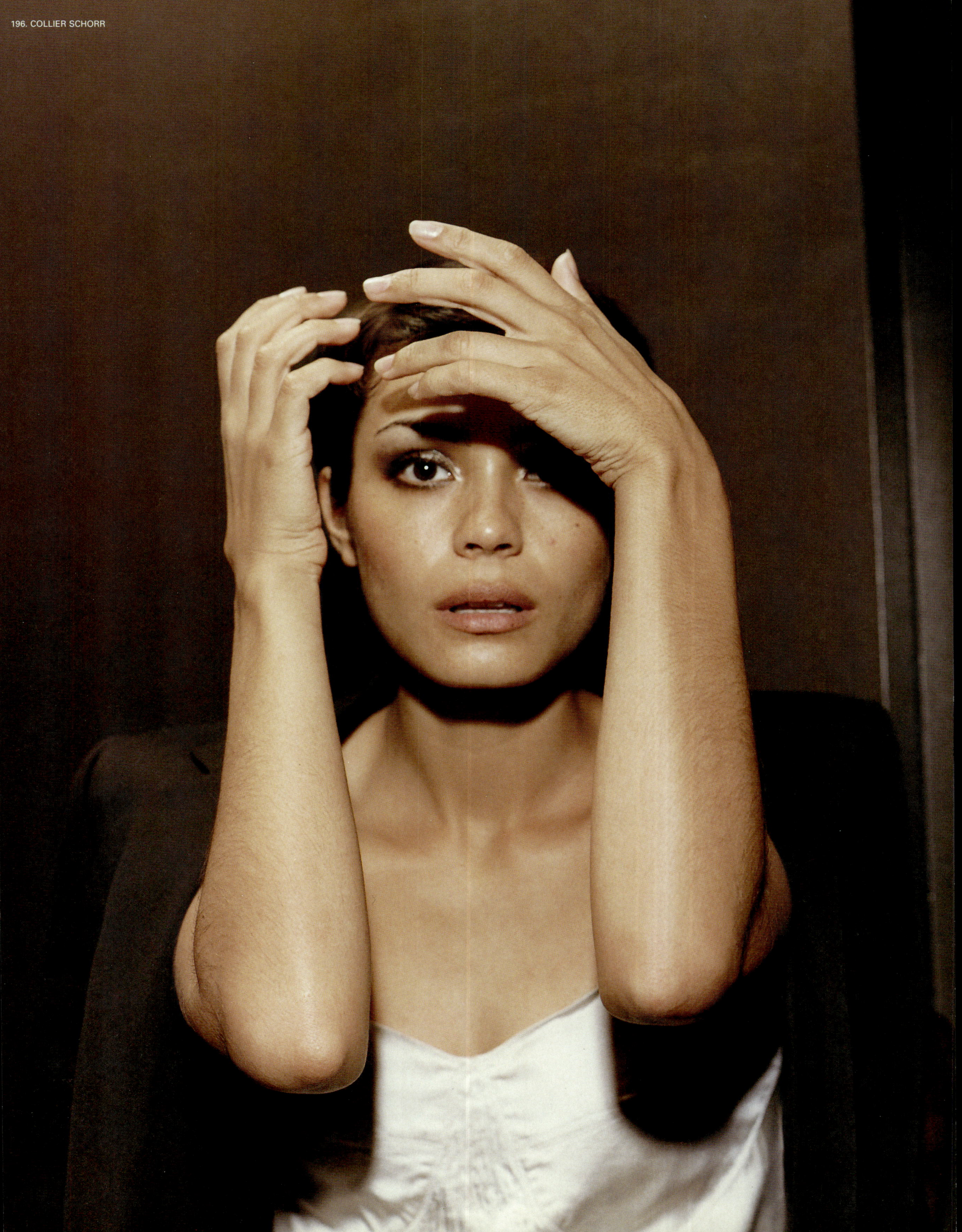

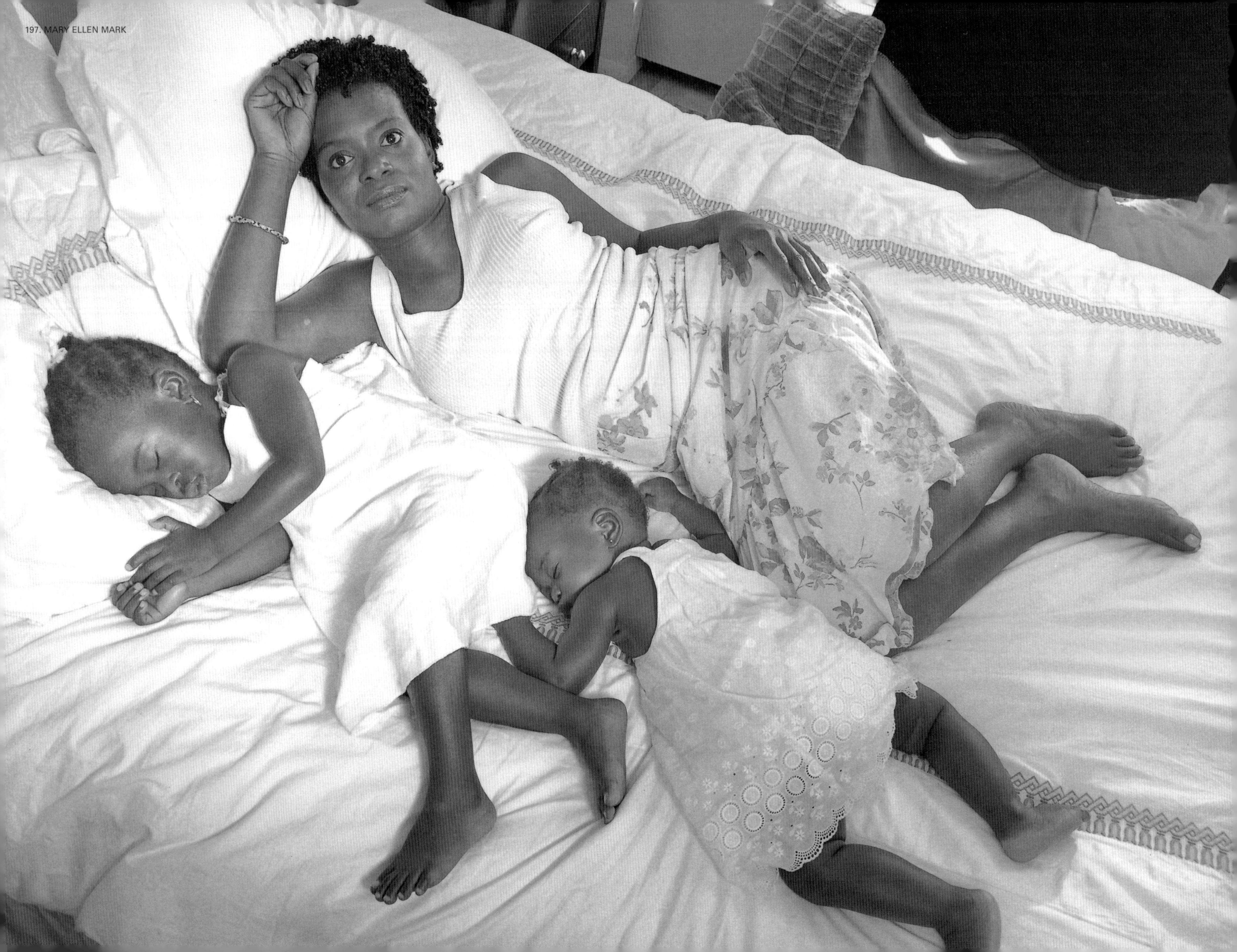

197. MARY ELLEN MARK

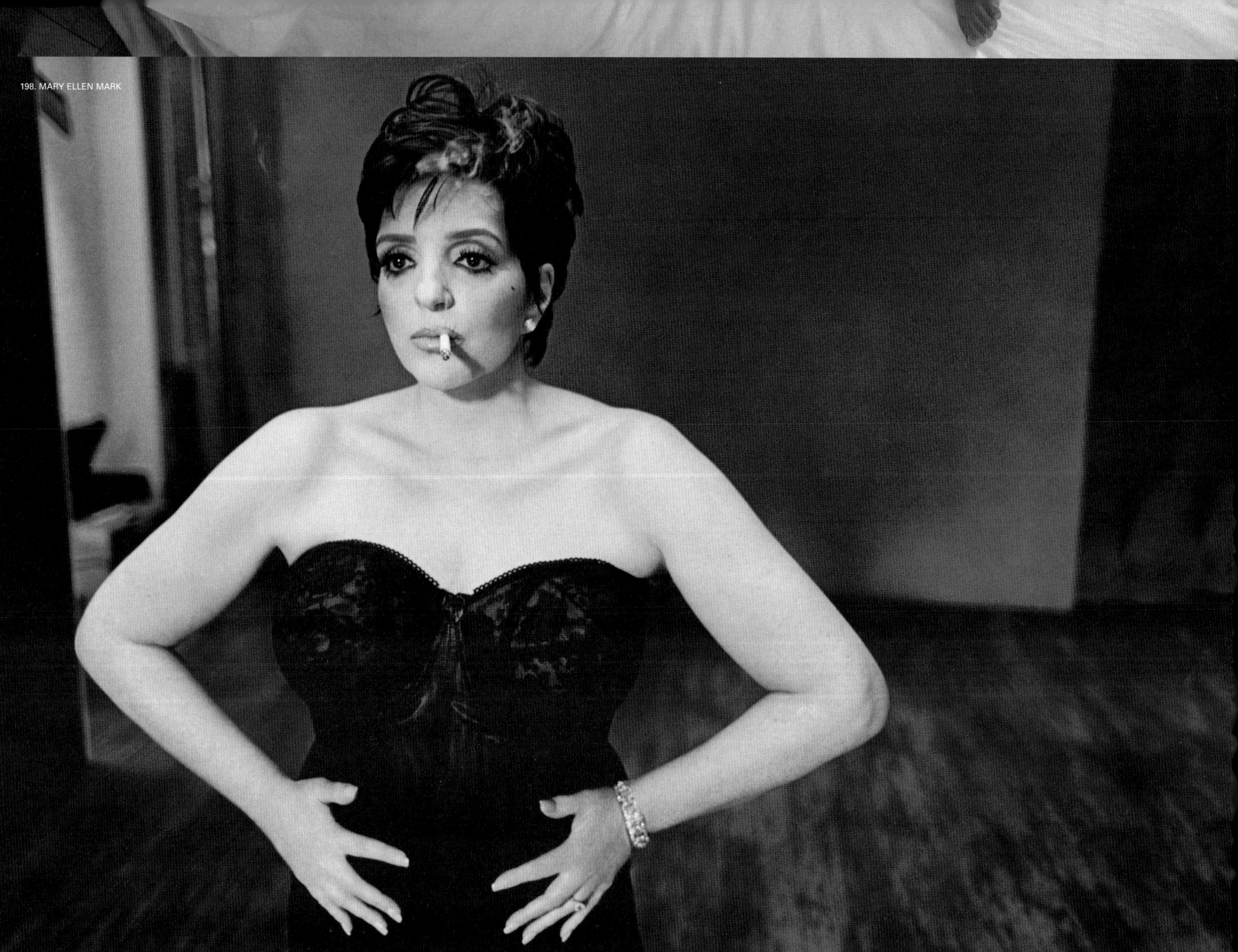

198. MARY ELLEN MARK

199. ROBERT MAXWELL

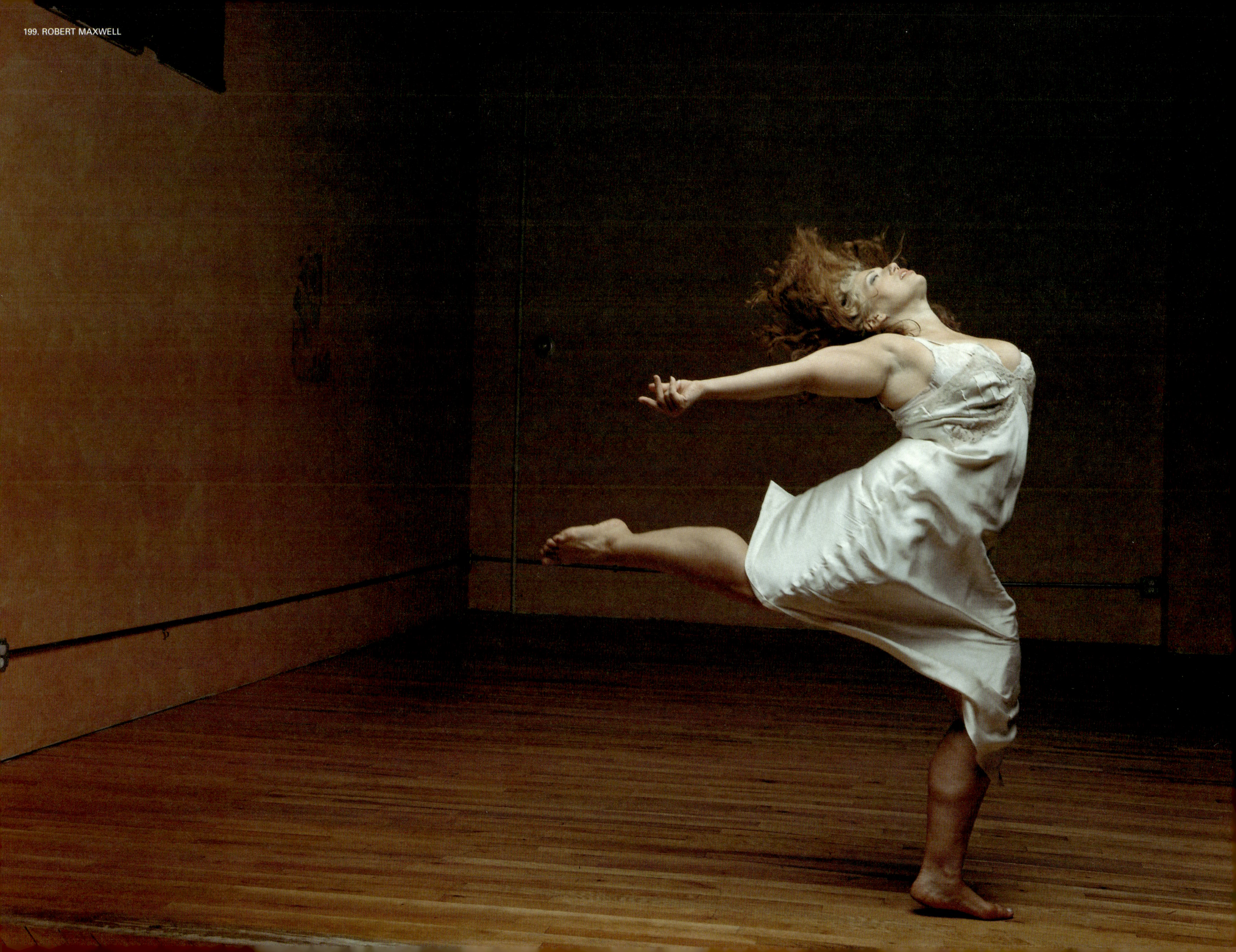

200. ROBERT MAXWELL

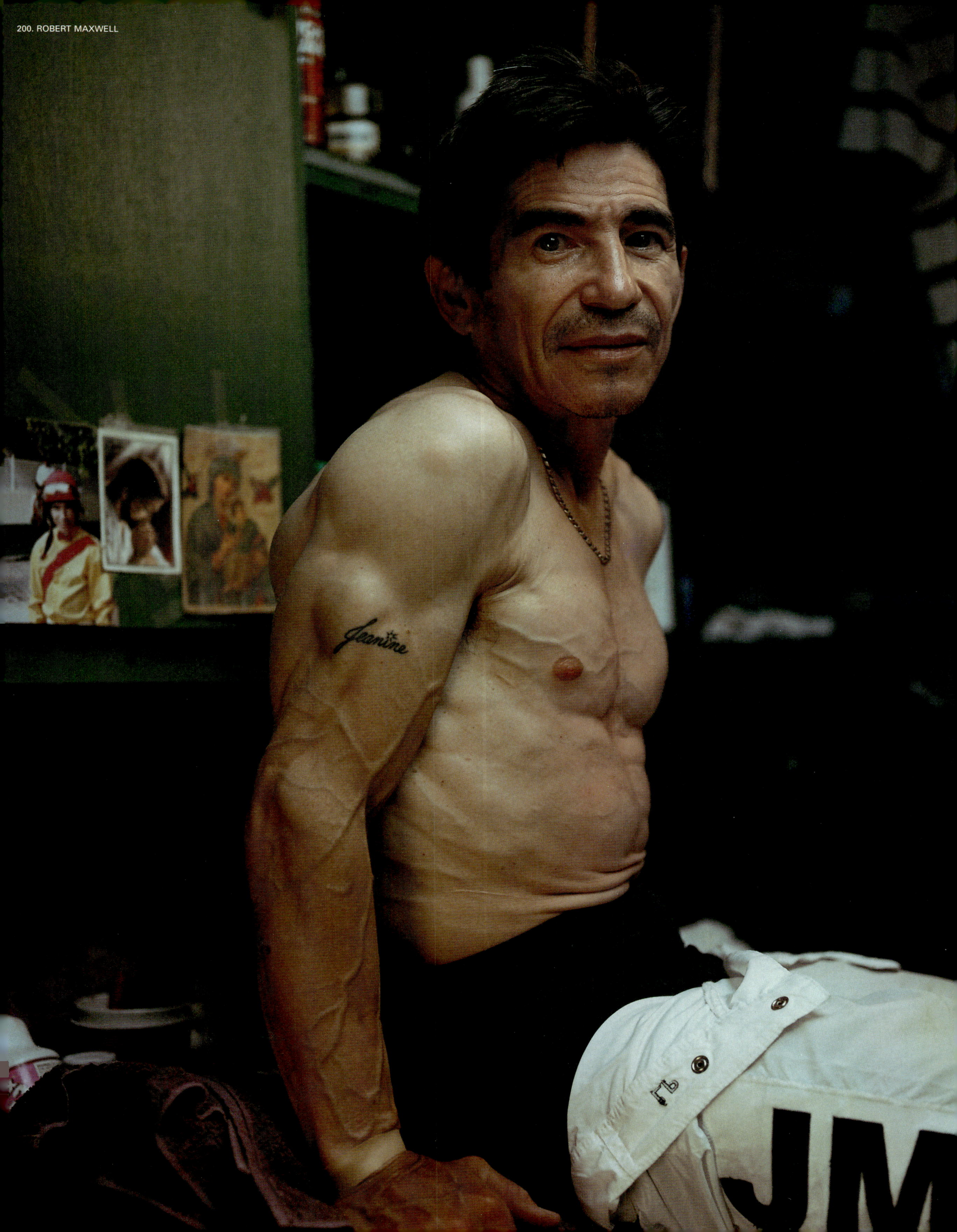

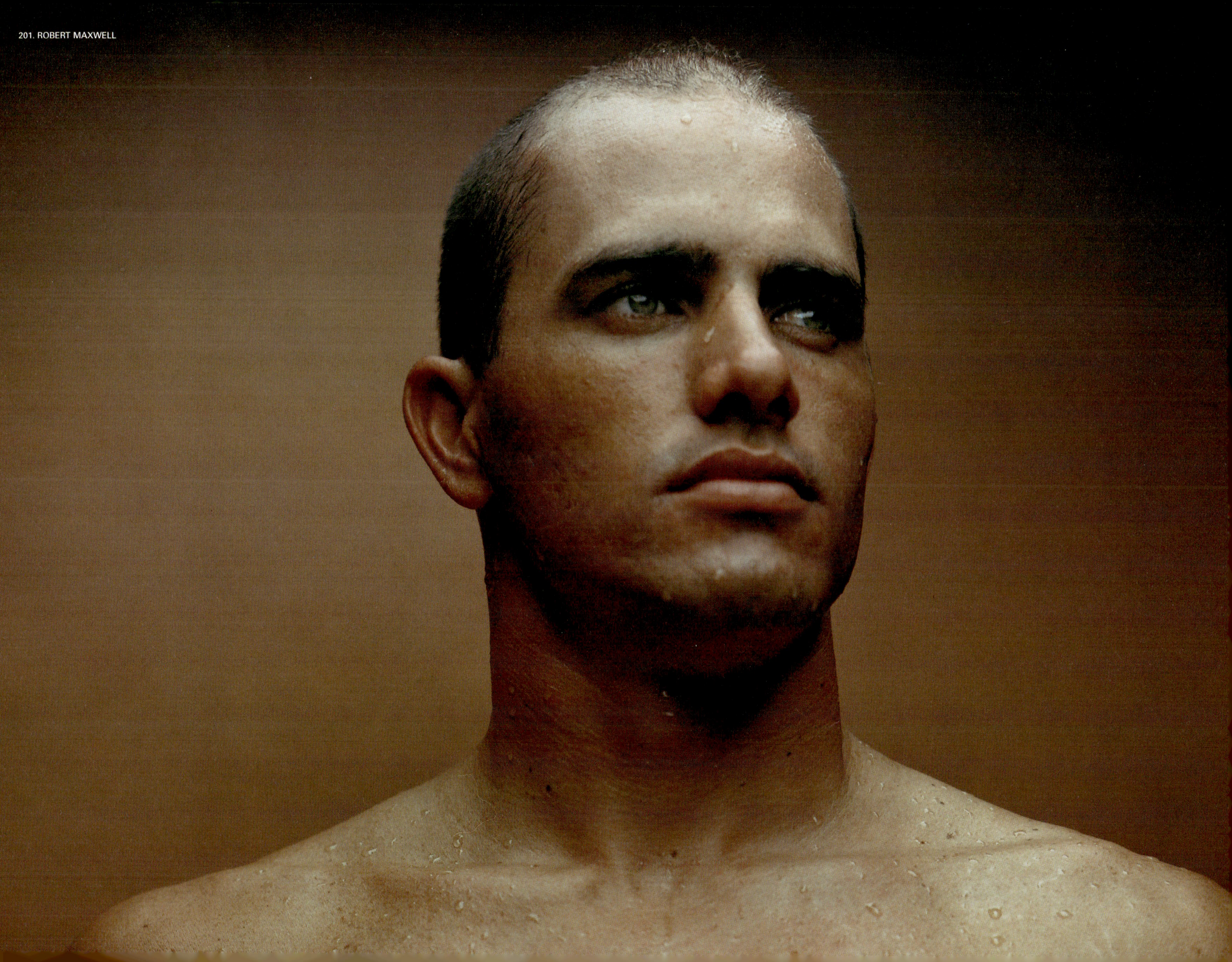

201. ROBERT MAXWELL

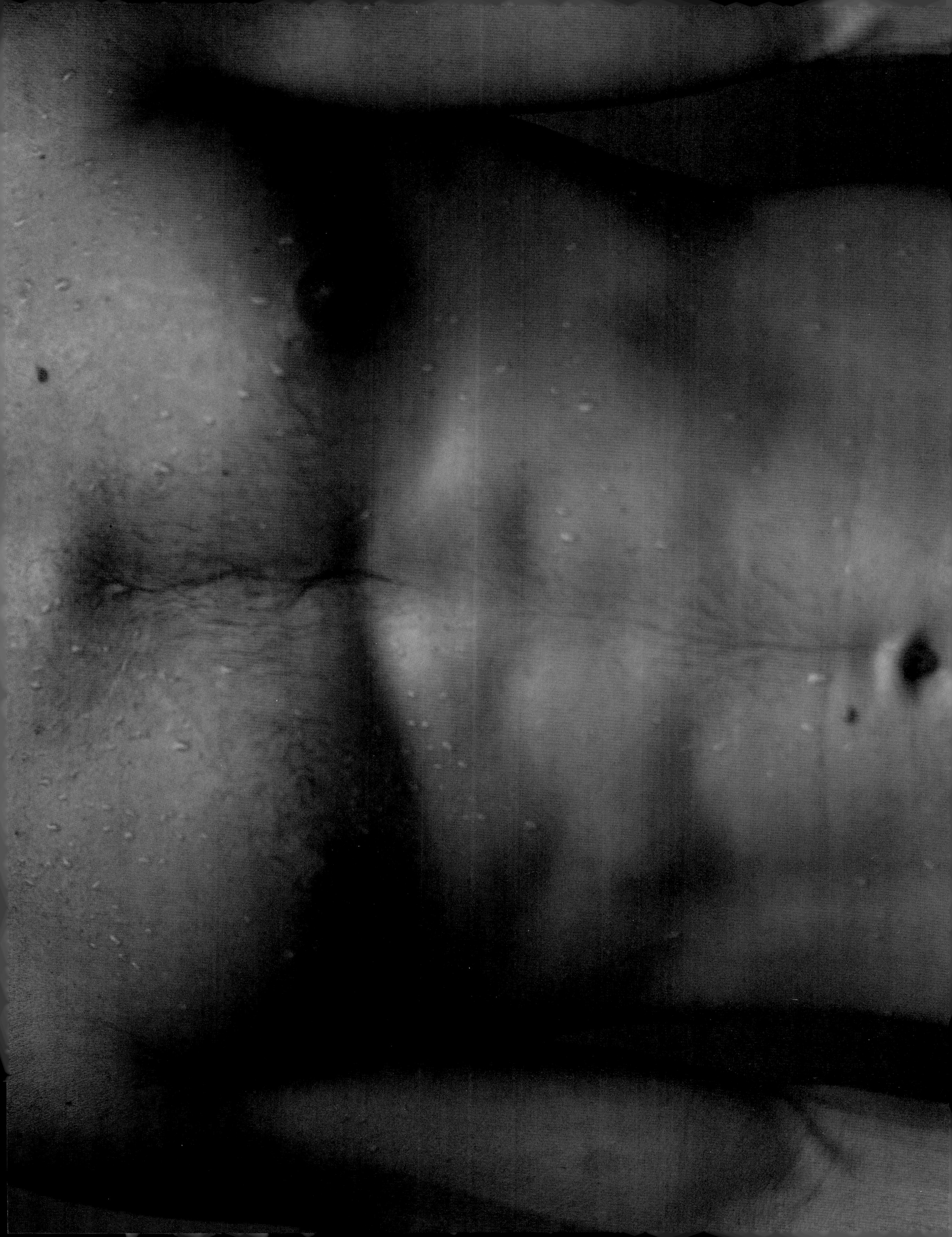

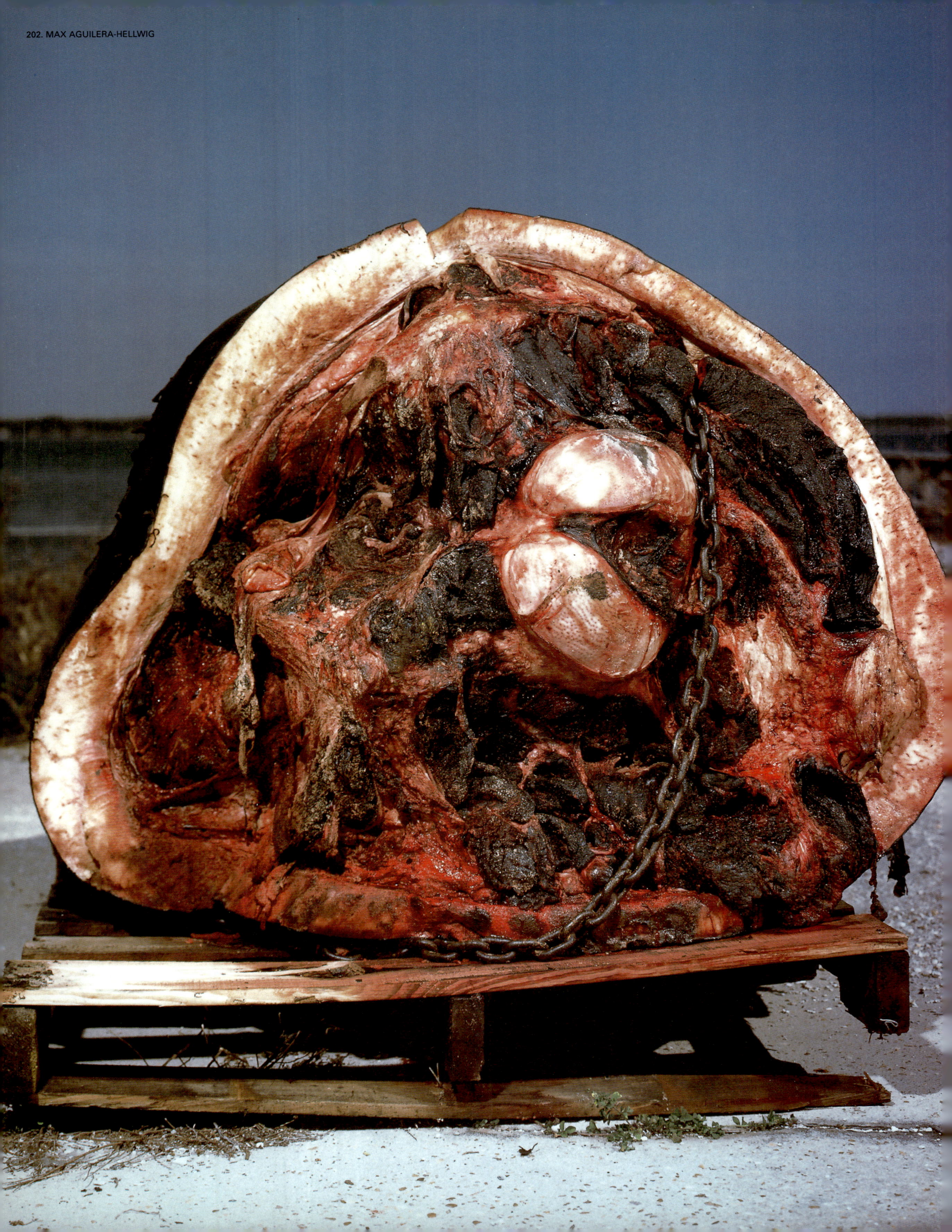

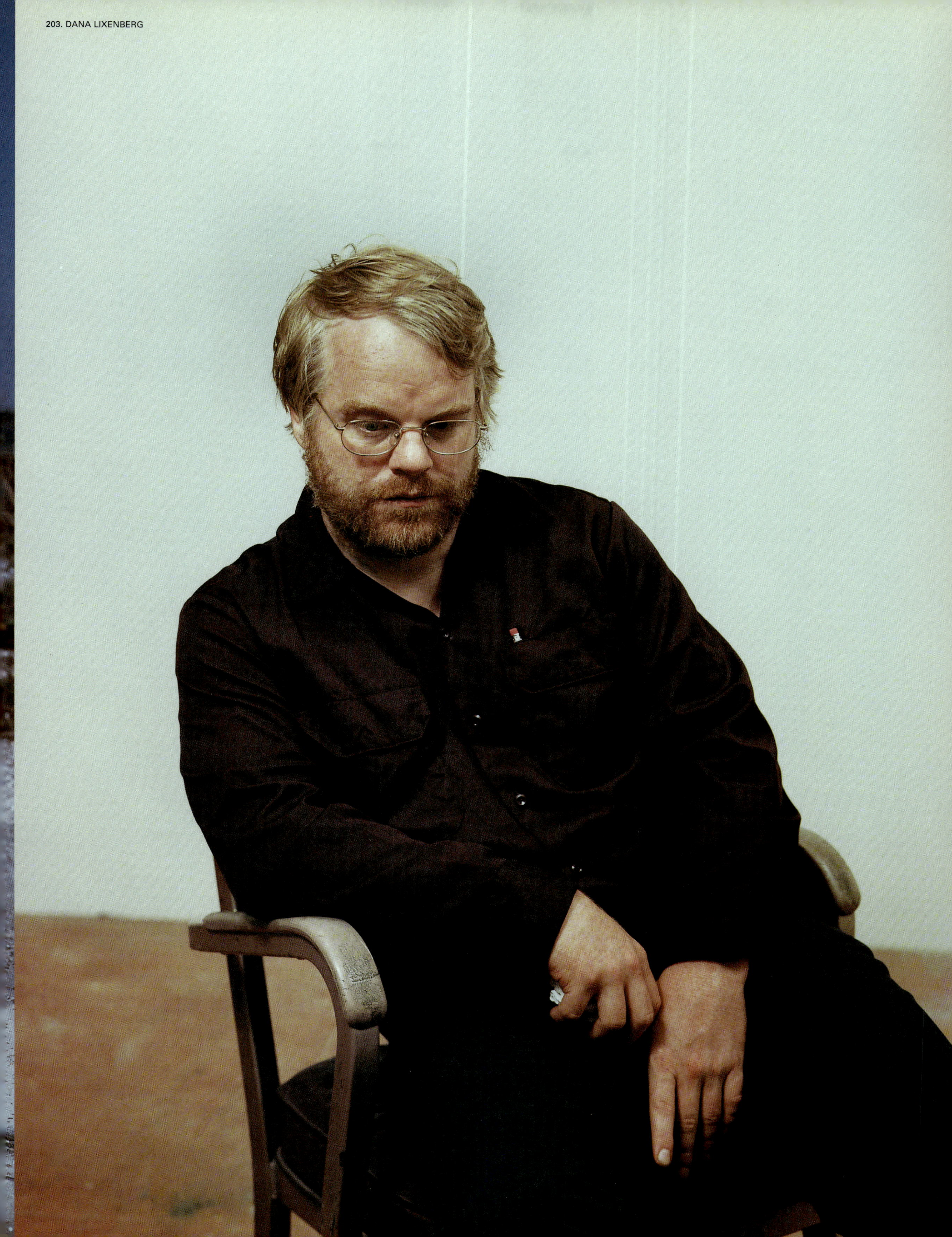

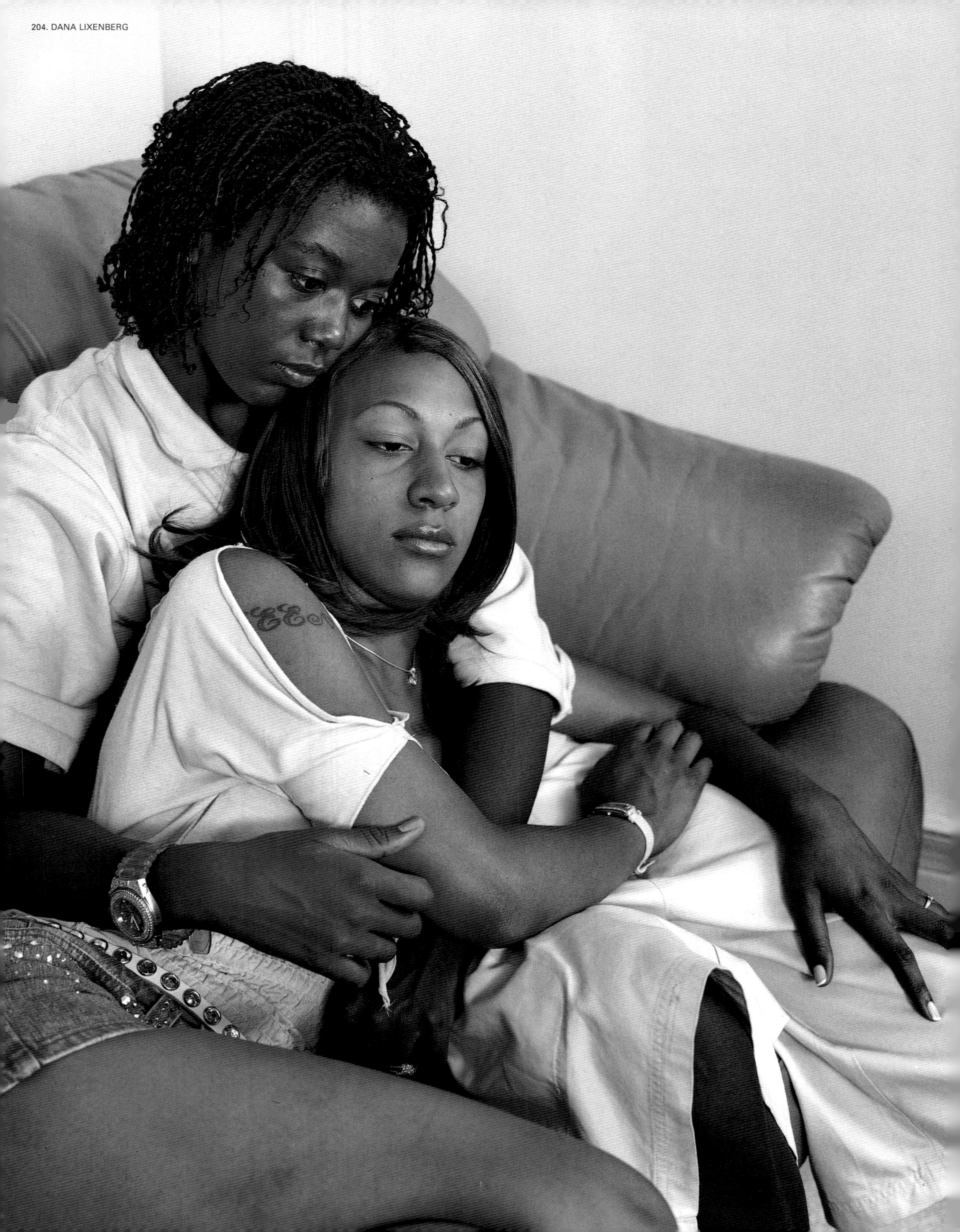

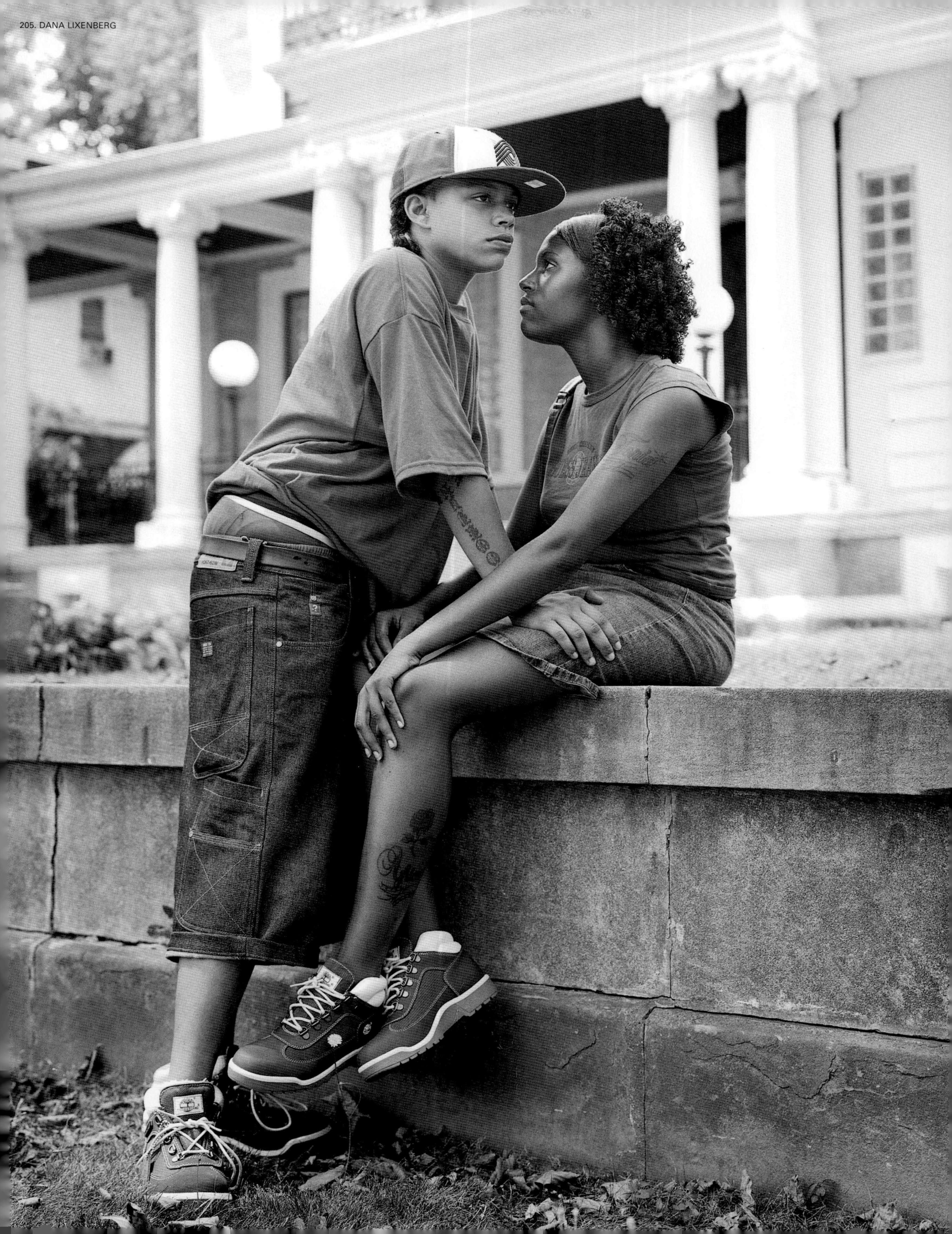

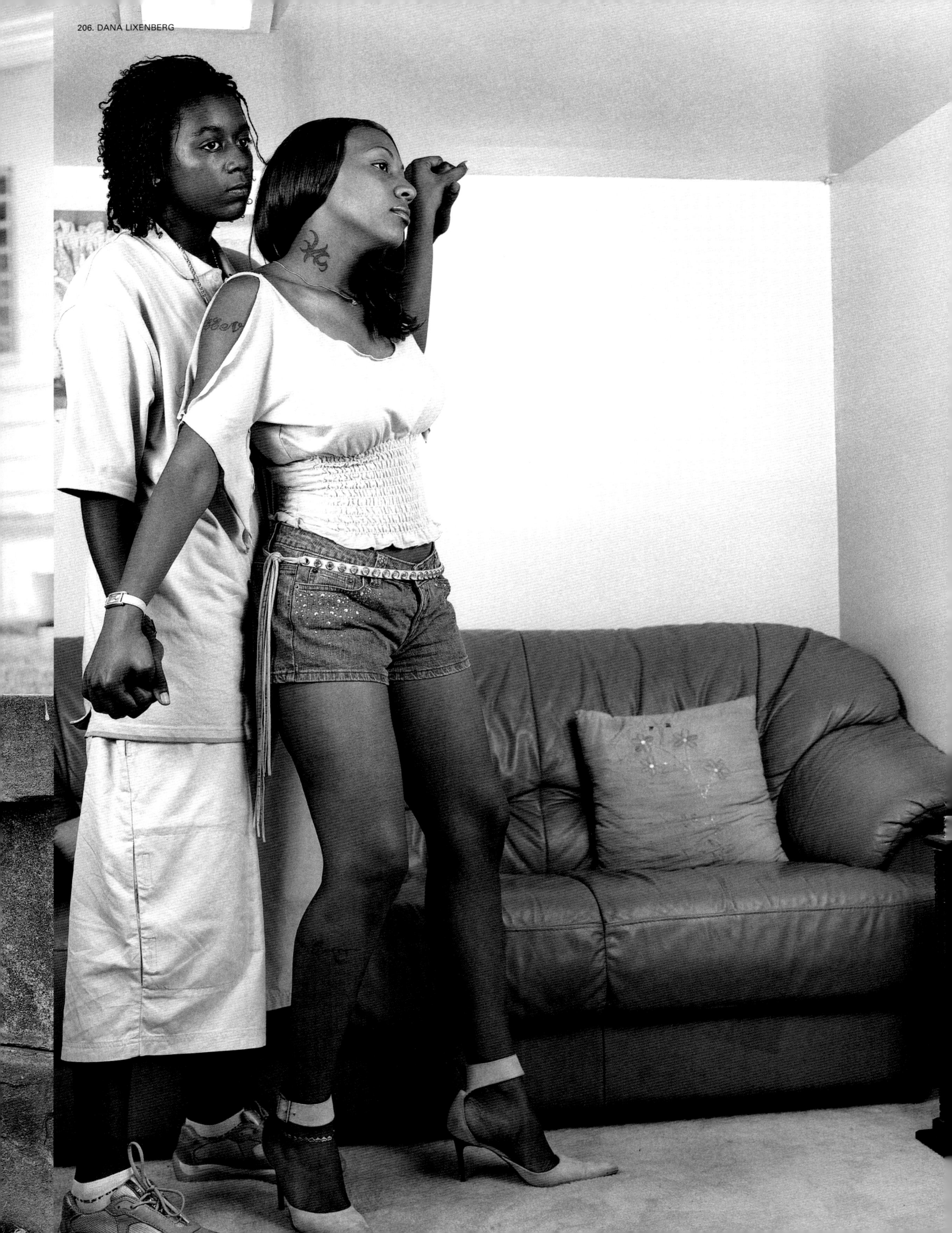

207. DANA LIXENBERG

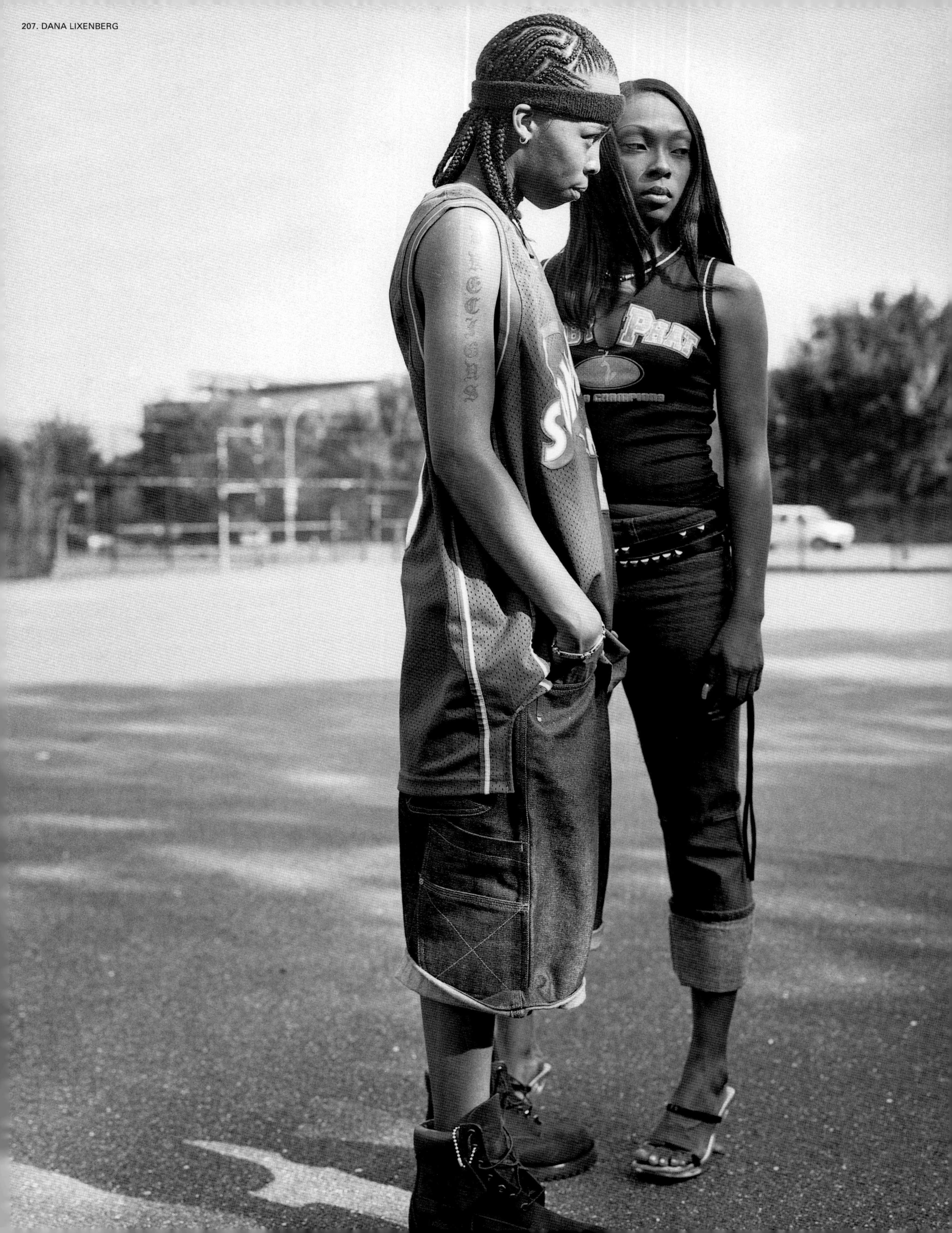

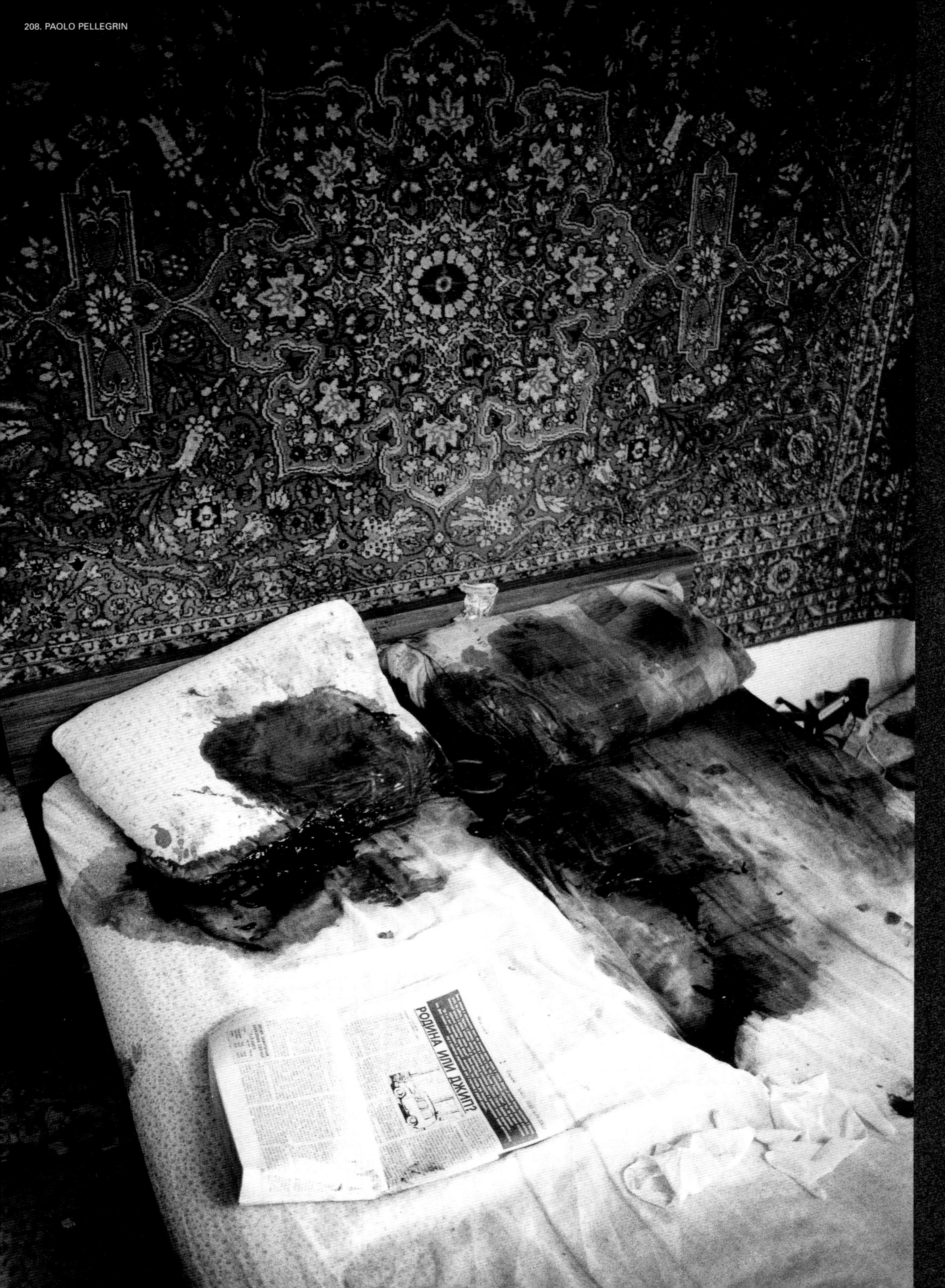
РОДИНА ИЛИ ДЖИП?

209. PAOLO PELLEGRIN

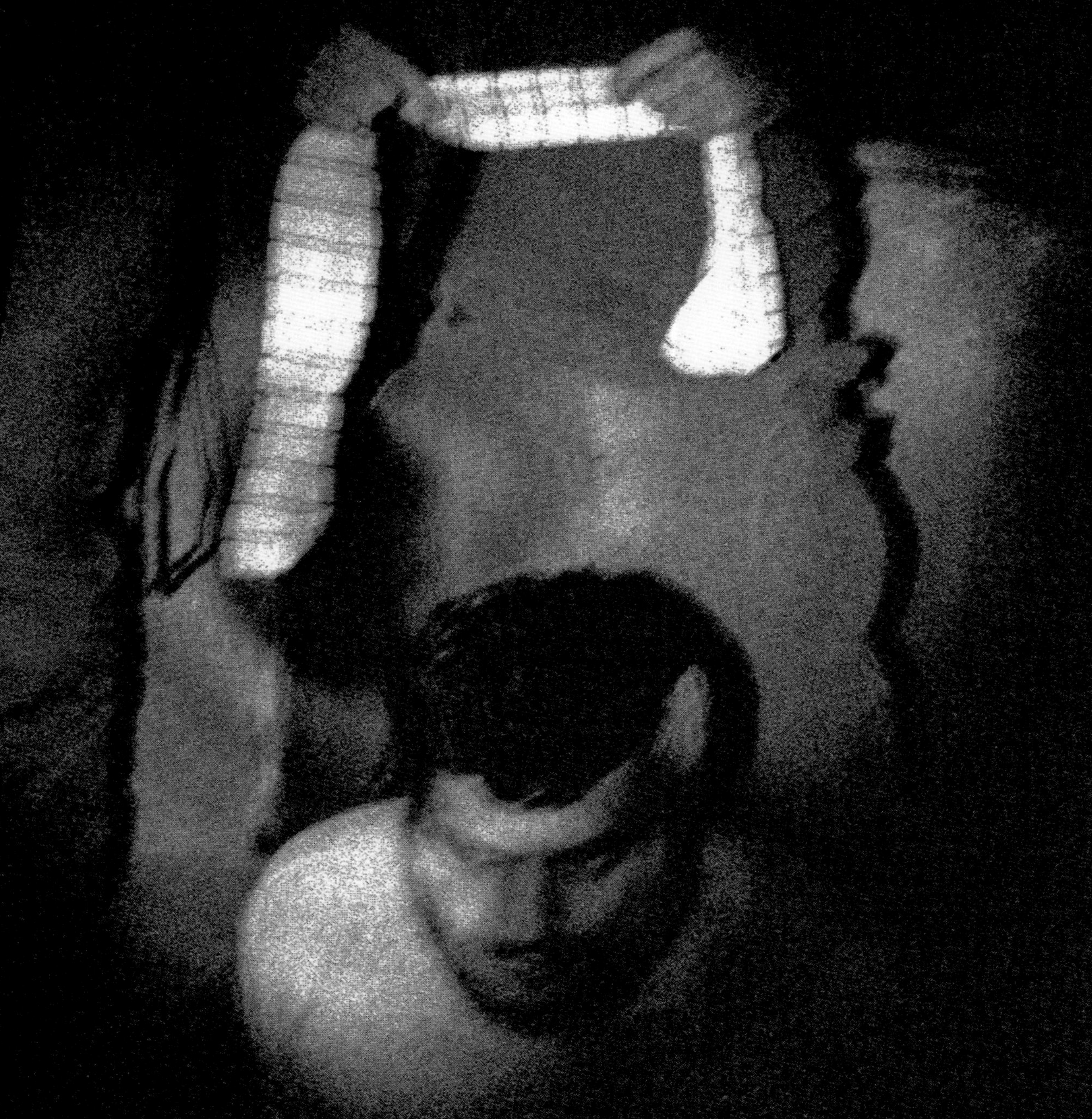

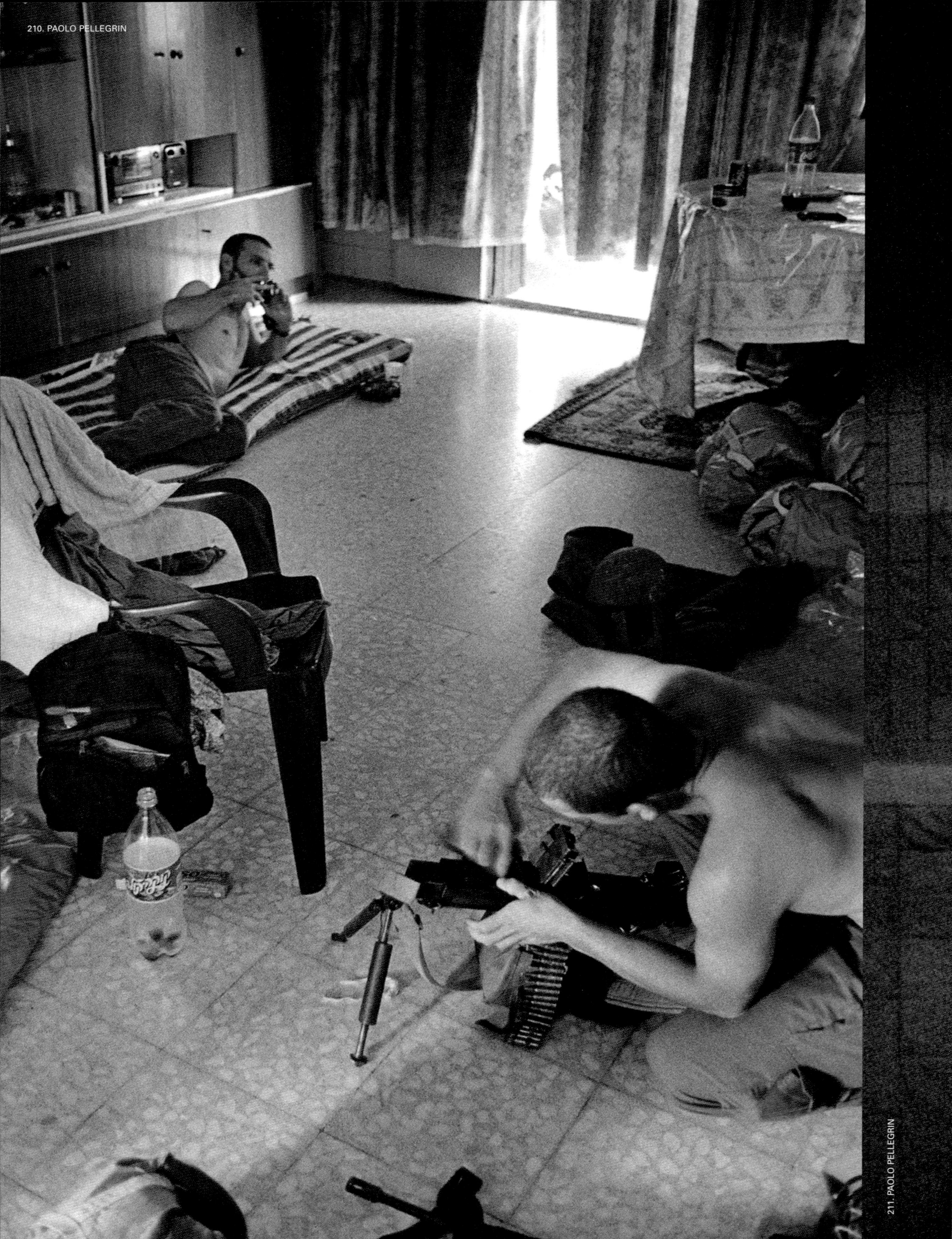

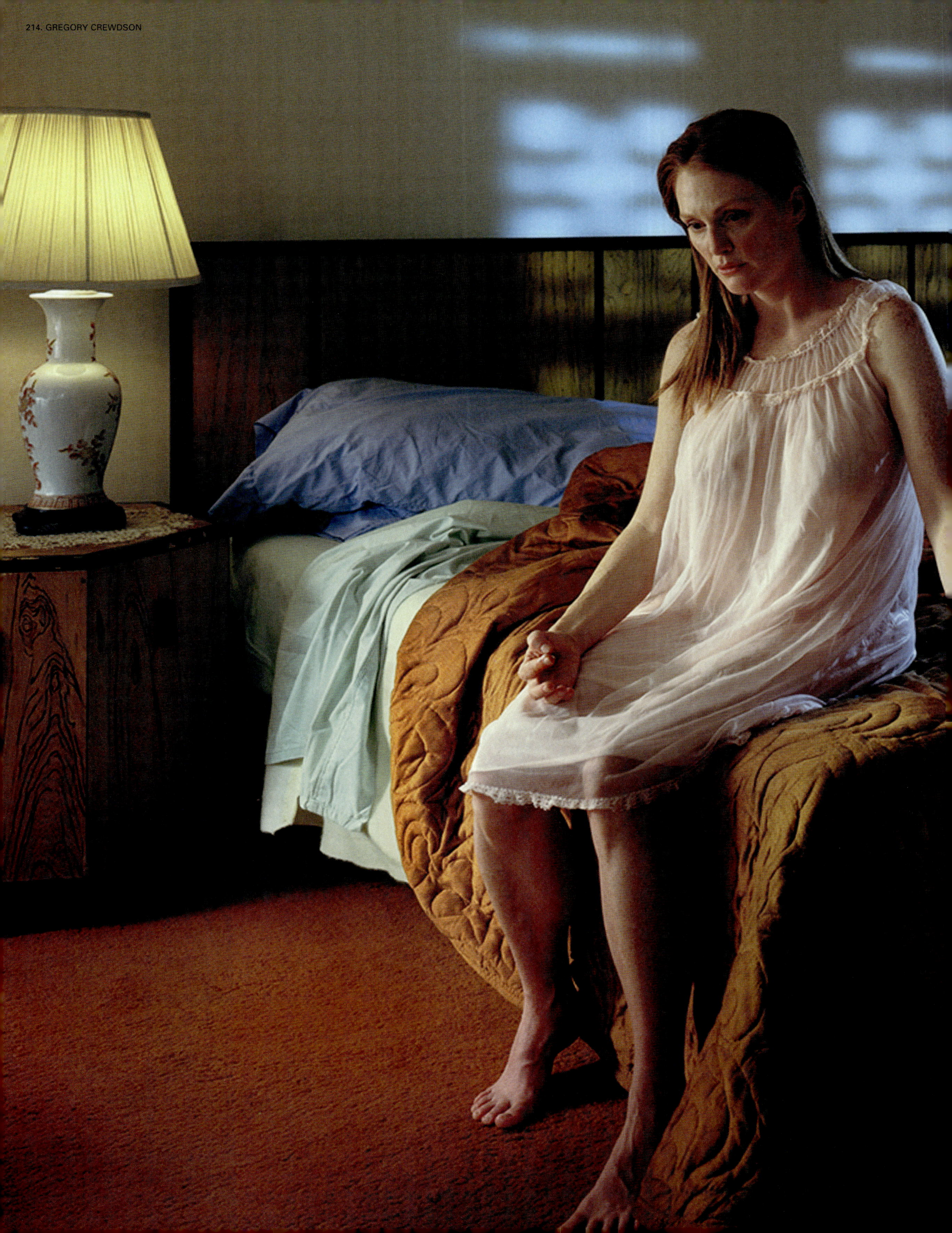

213. GREGORY CREWDSON

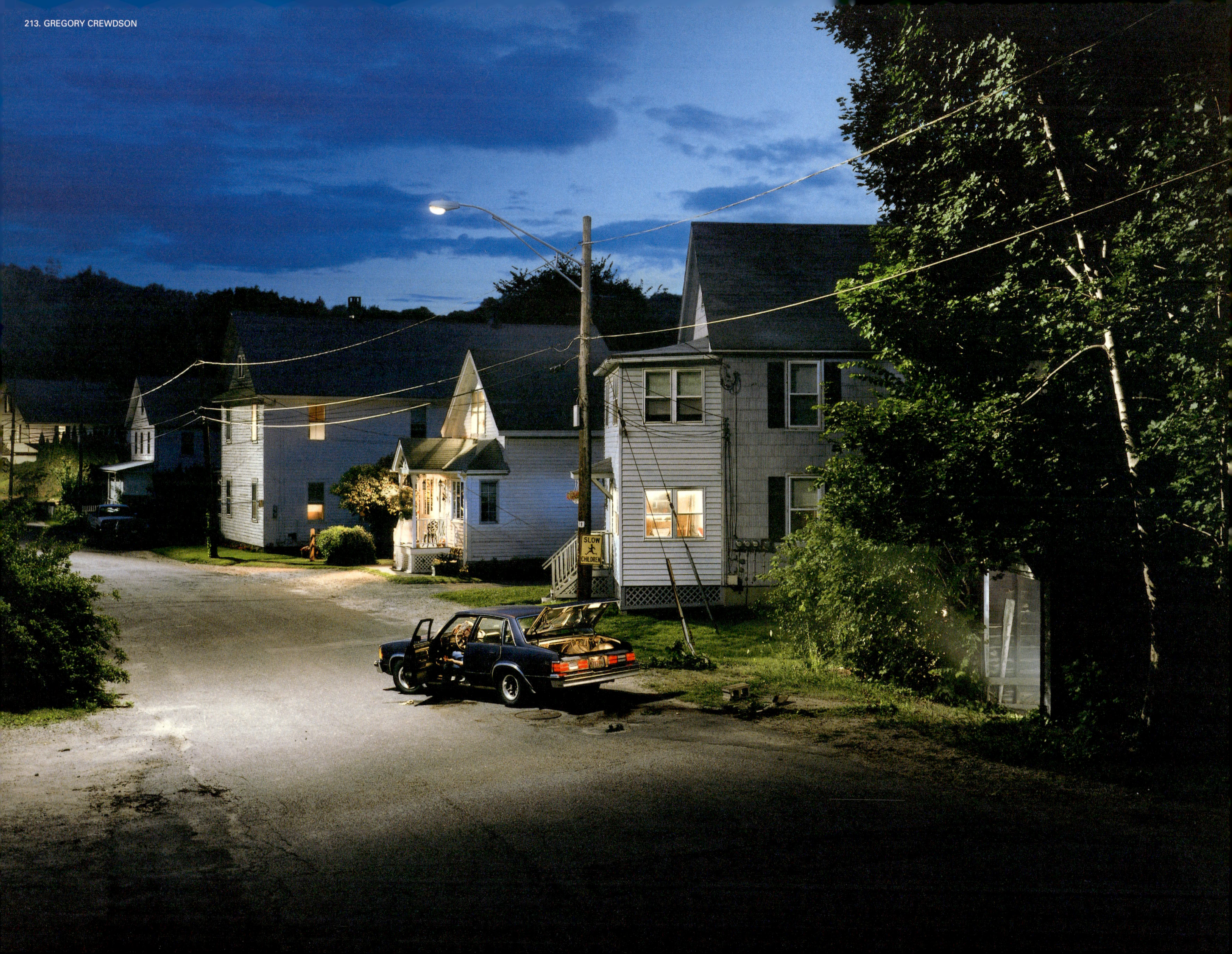

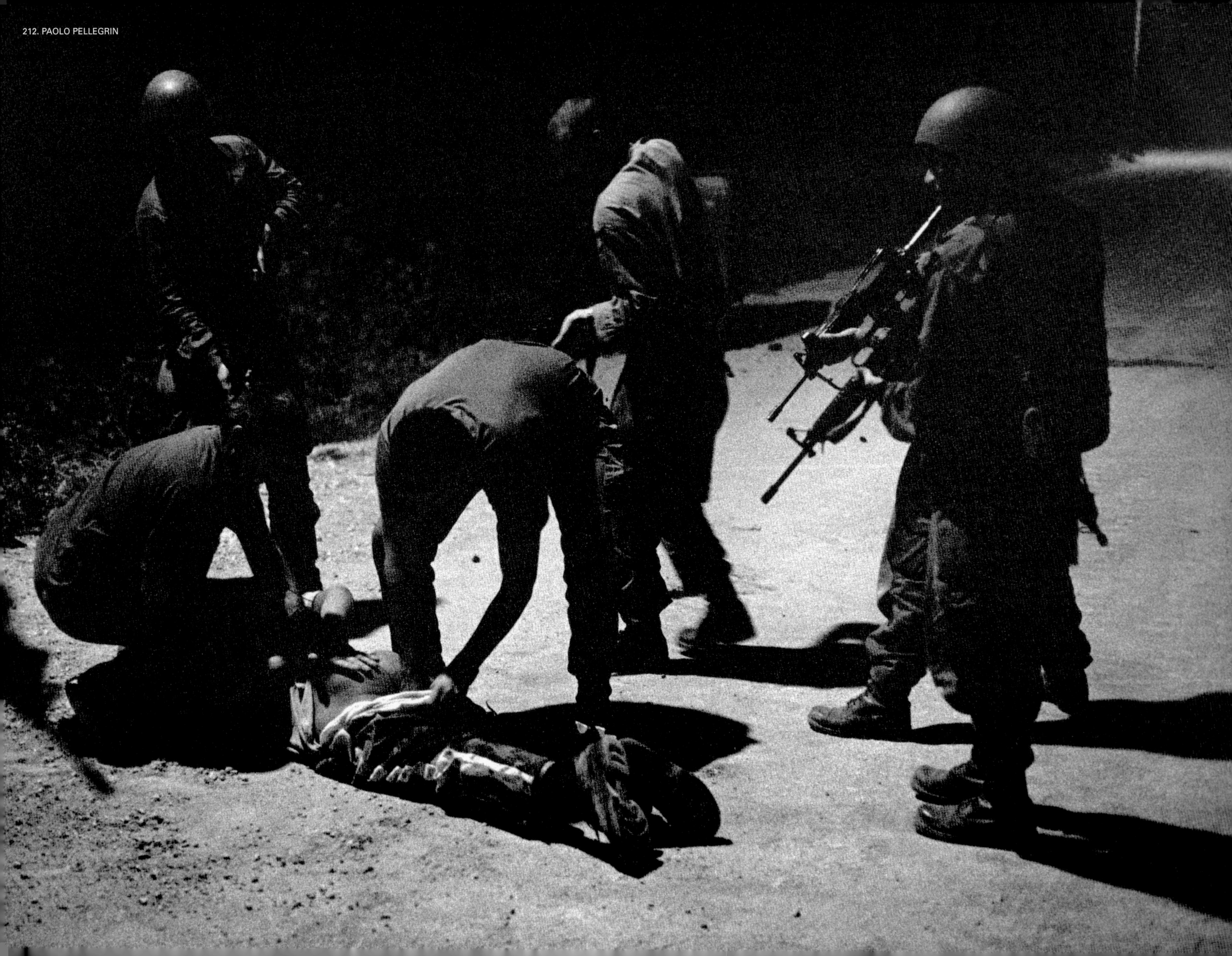

212. PAOLO PELLEGRIN

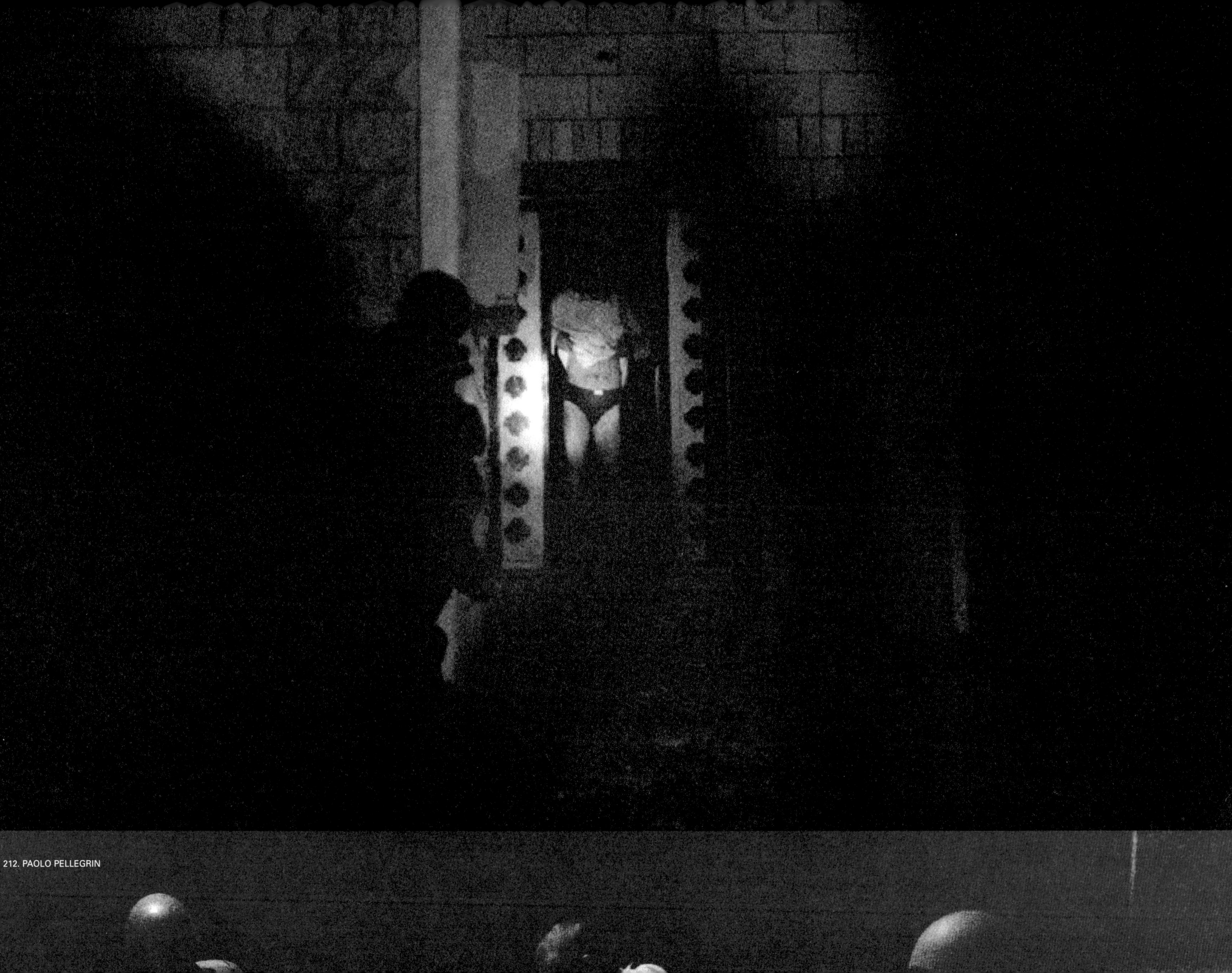

212. PAOLO PELLEGRIN

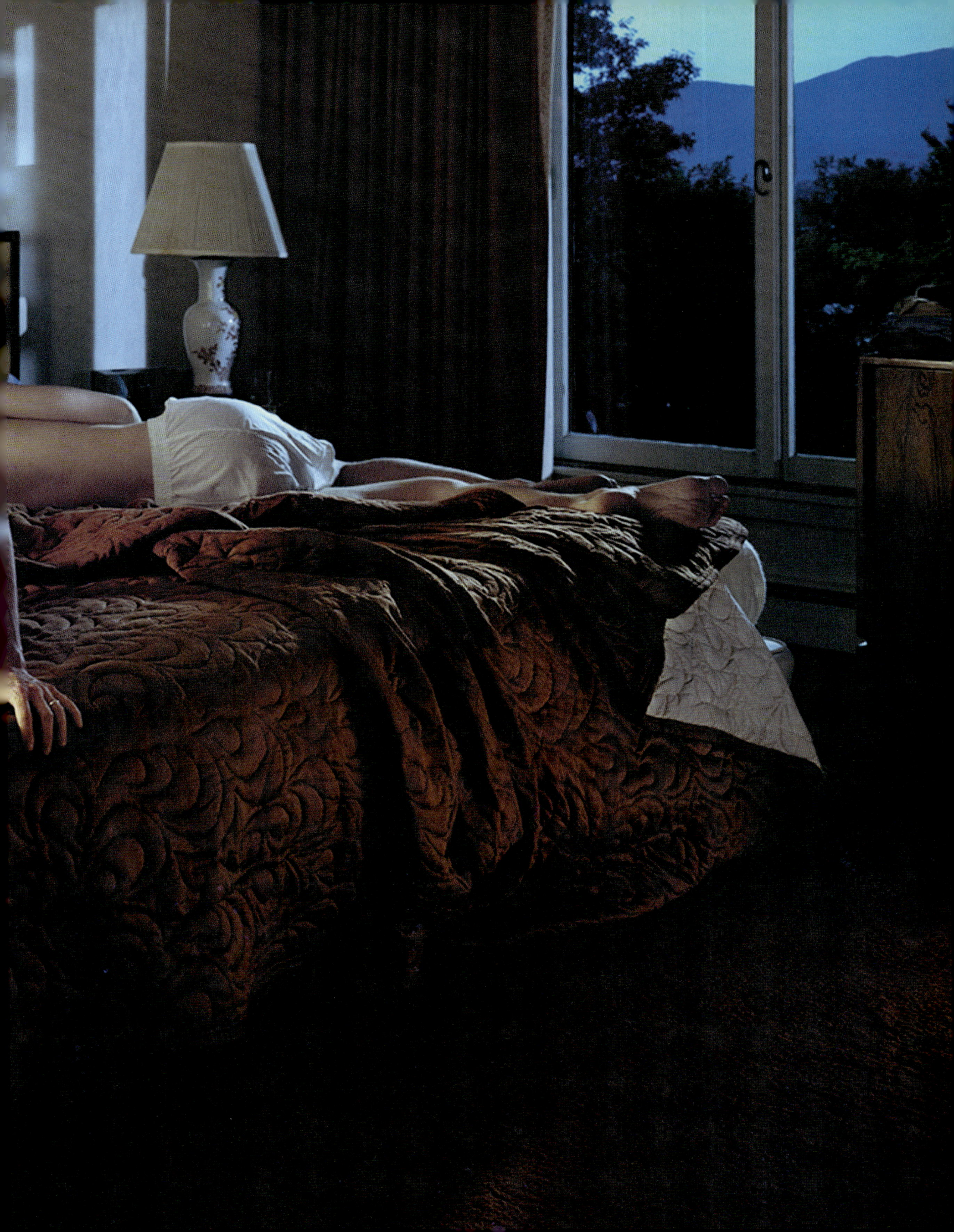

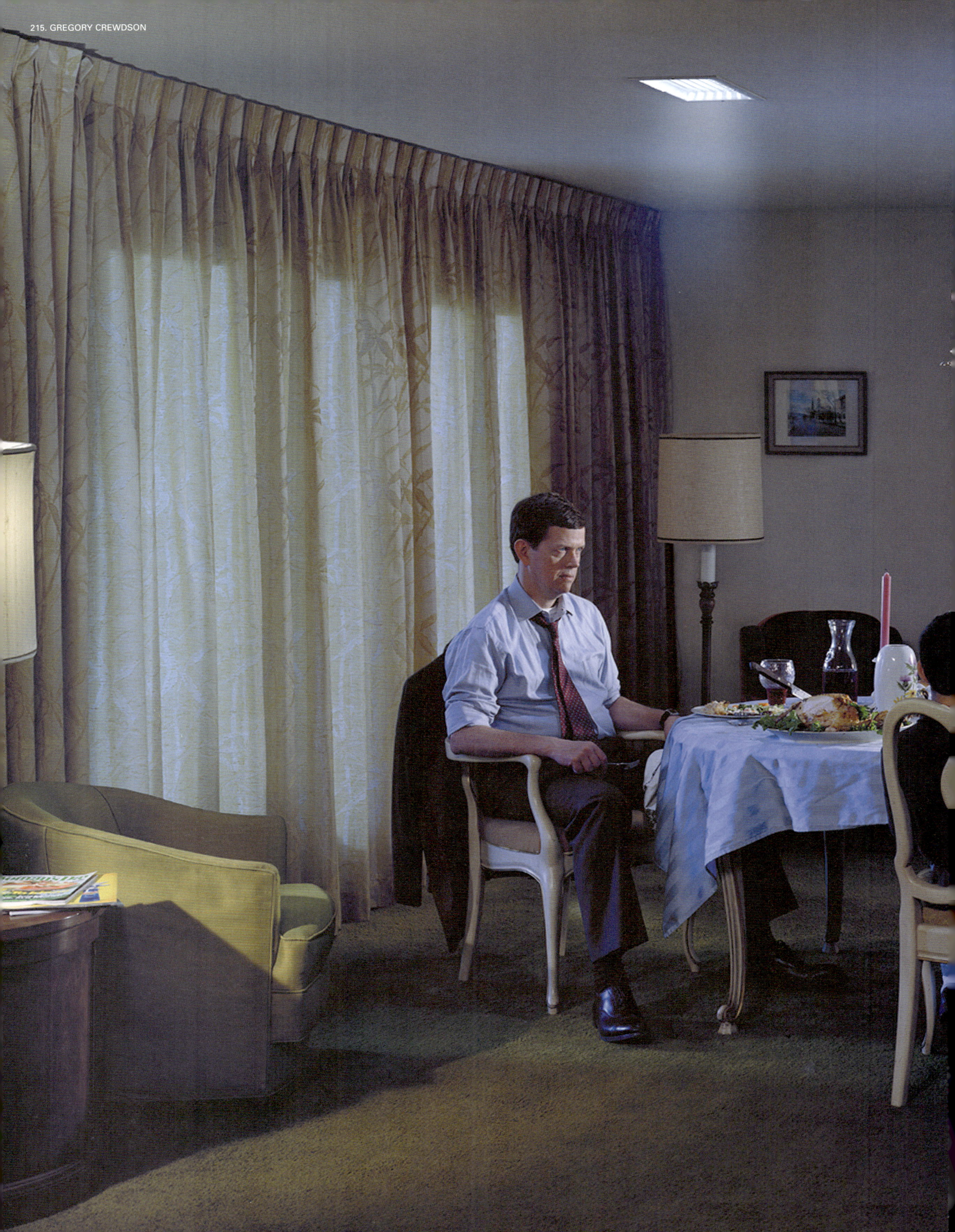
215. GREGORY CREWDSON

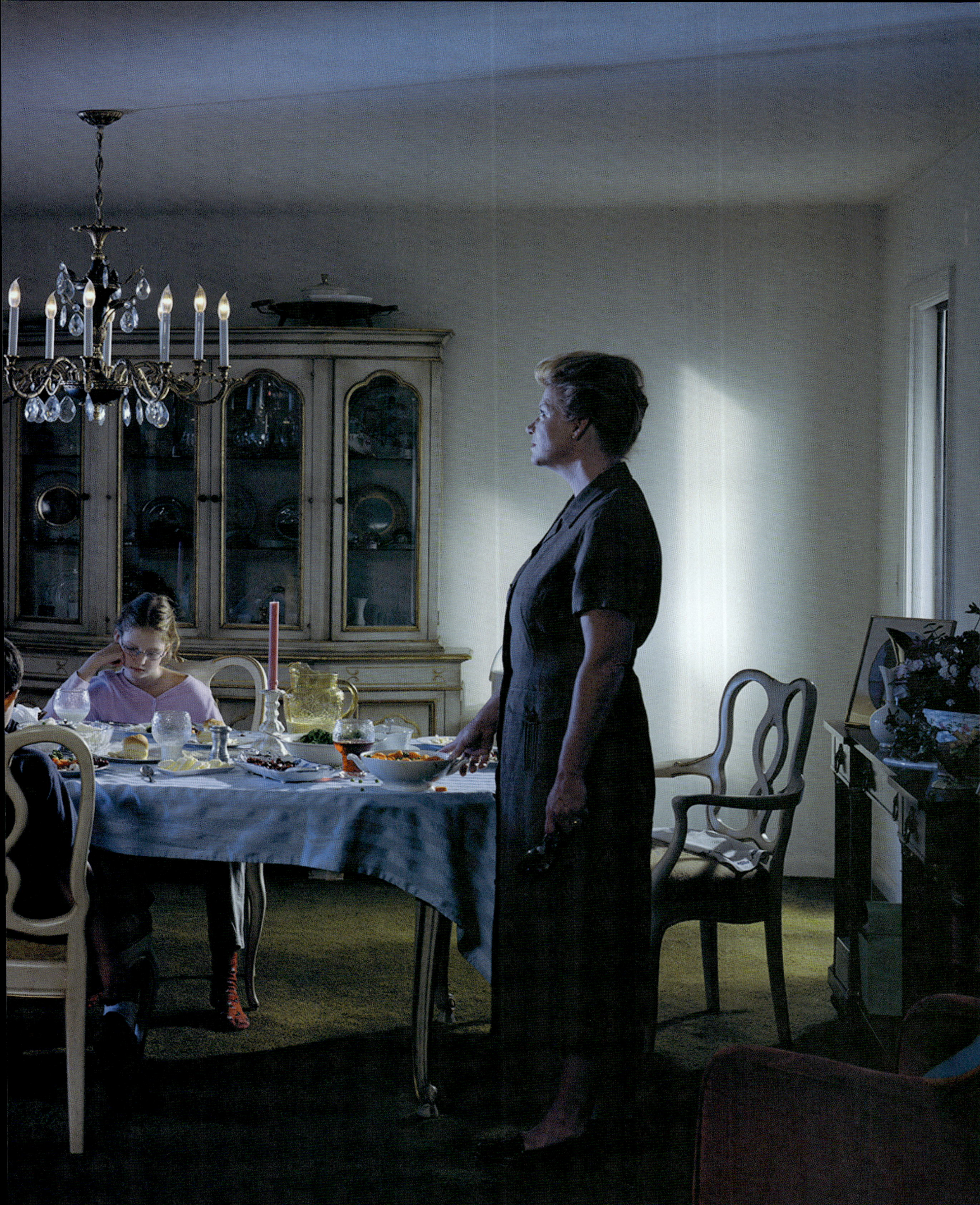

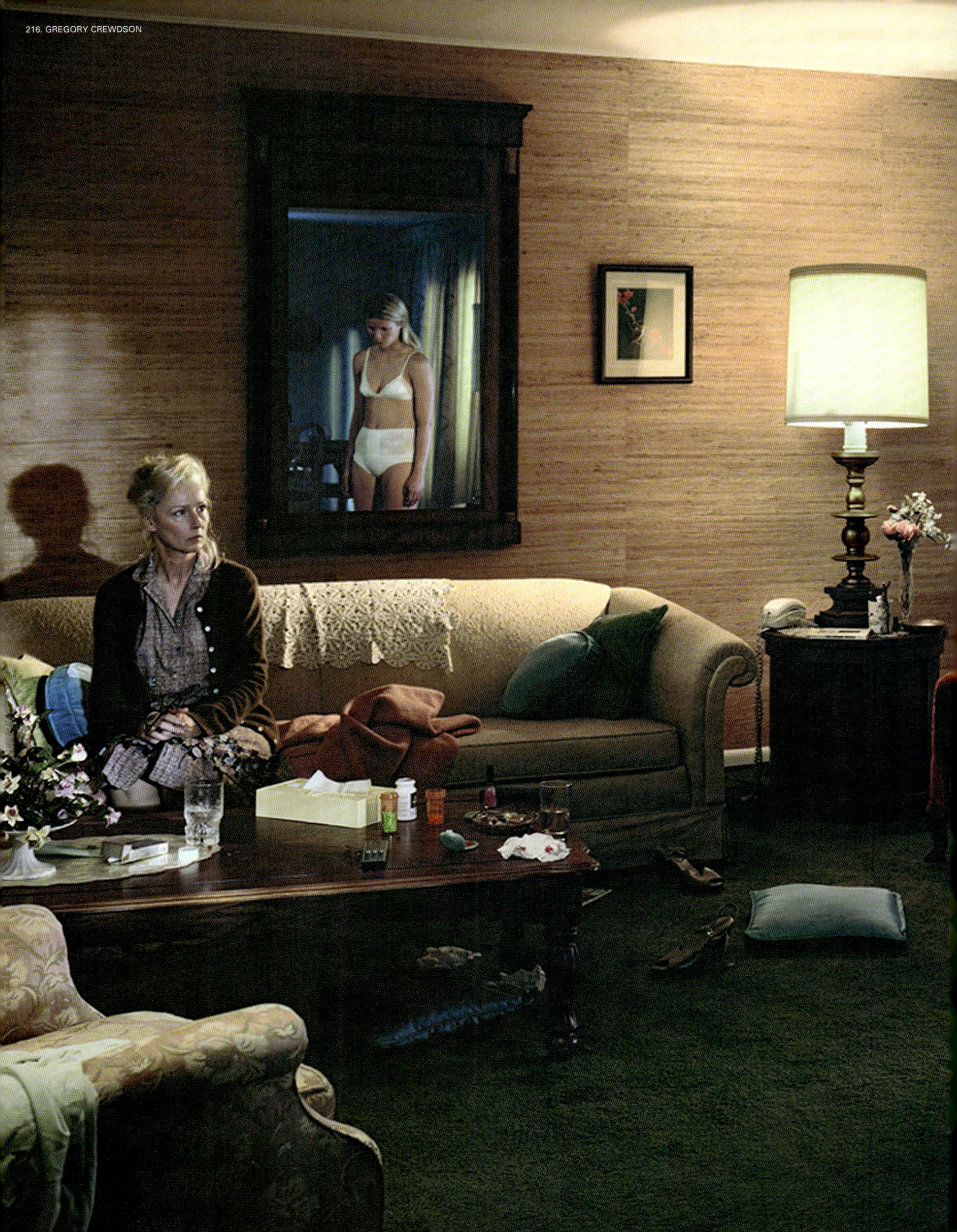

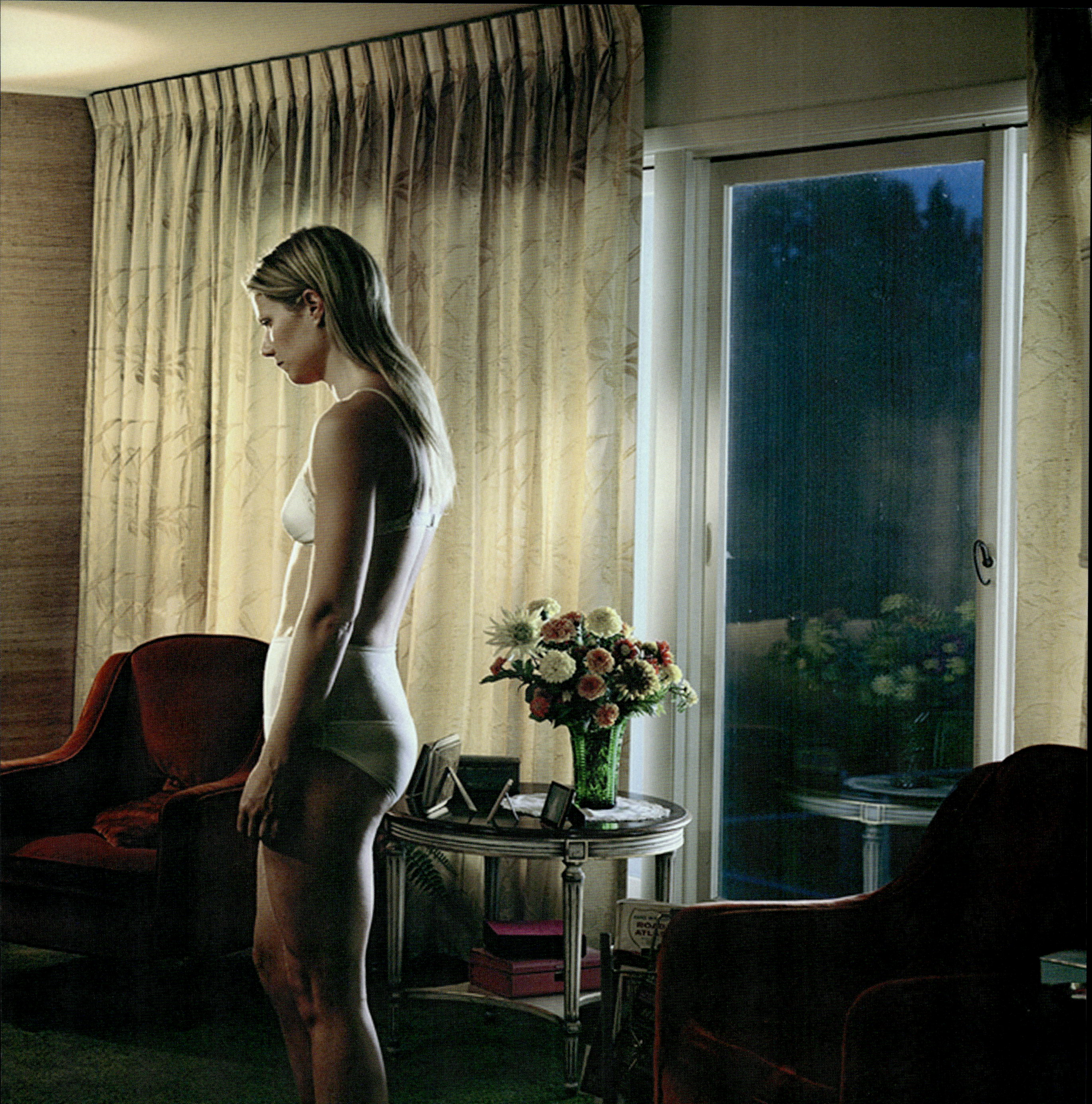

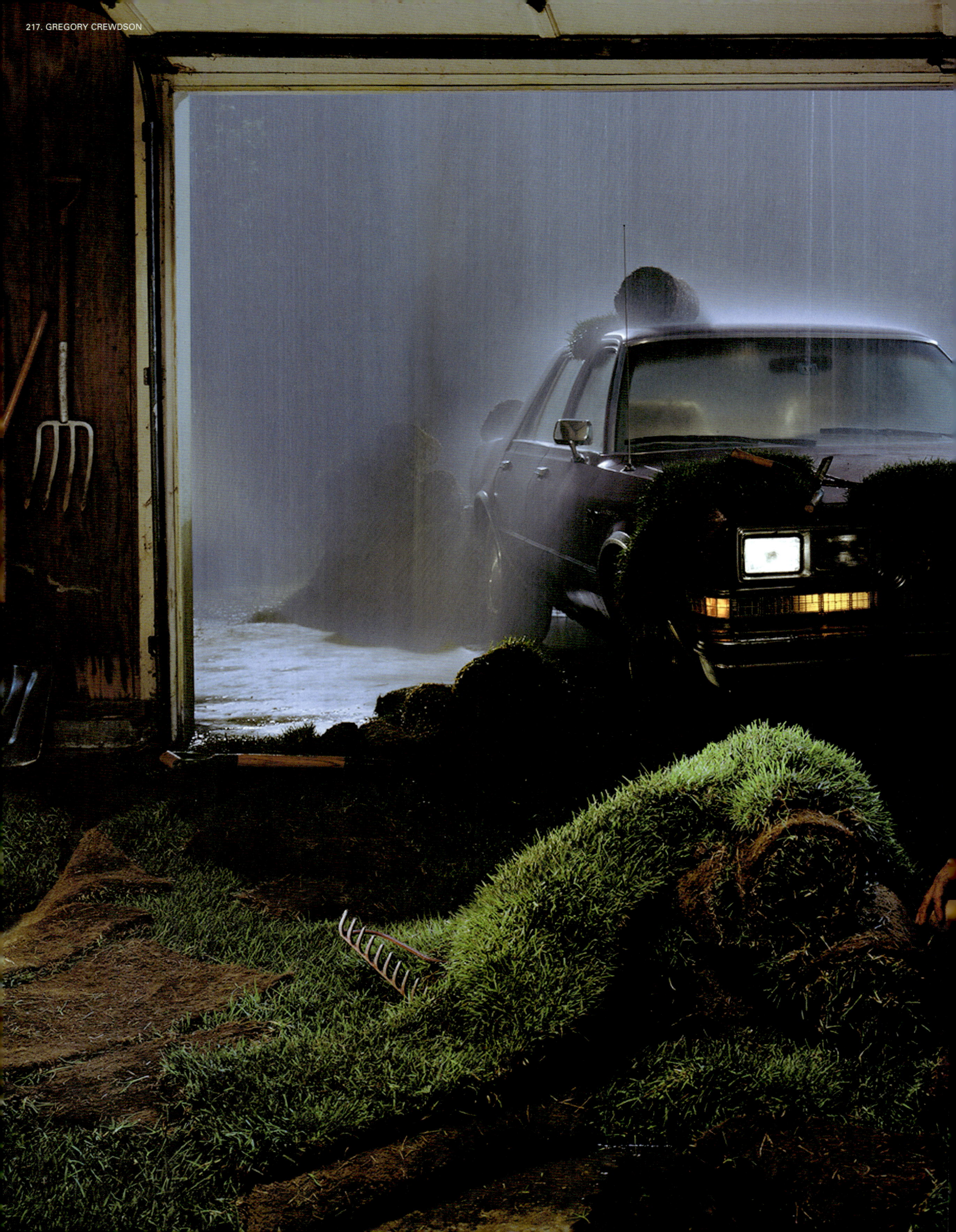

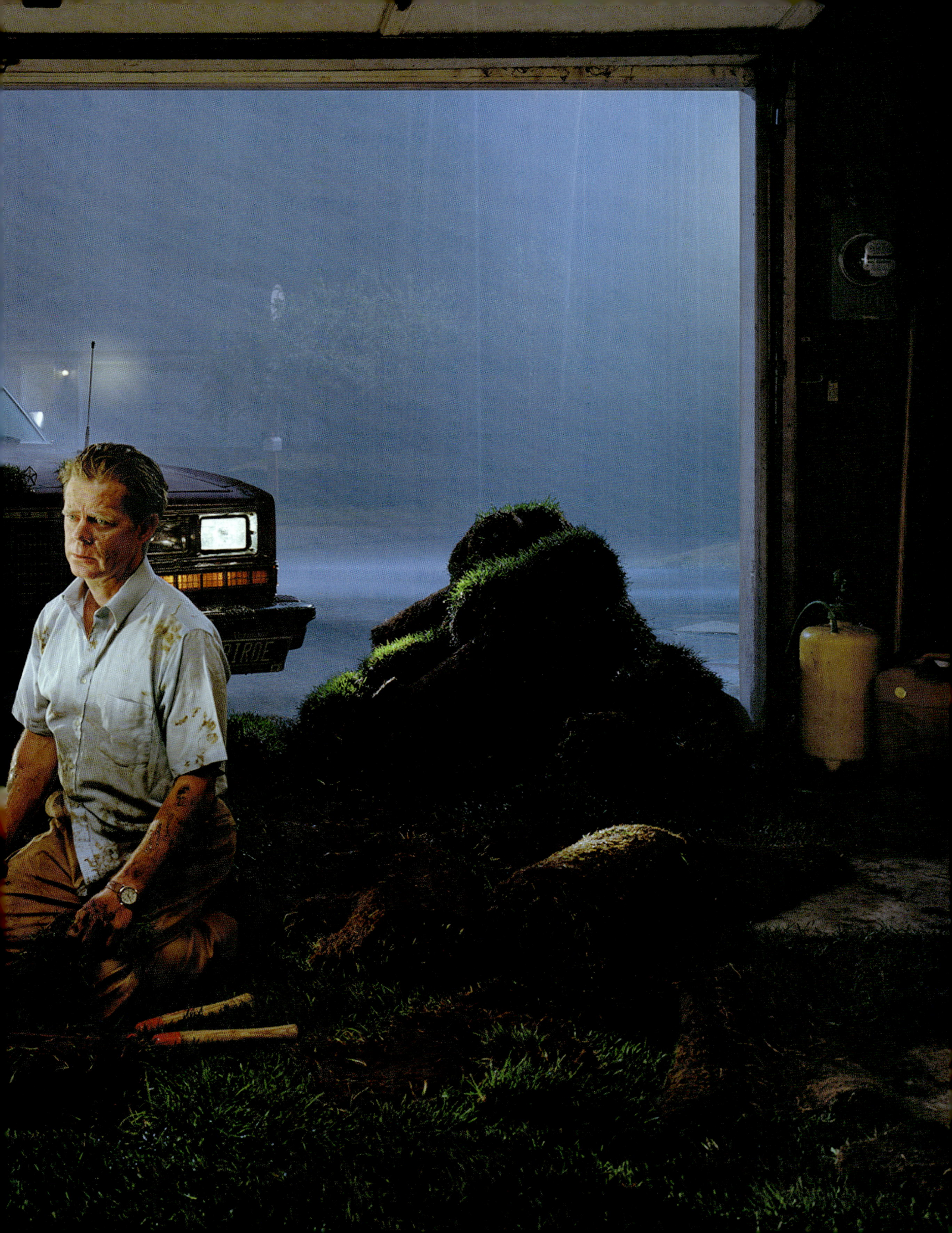

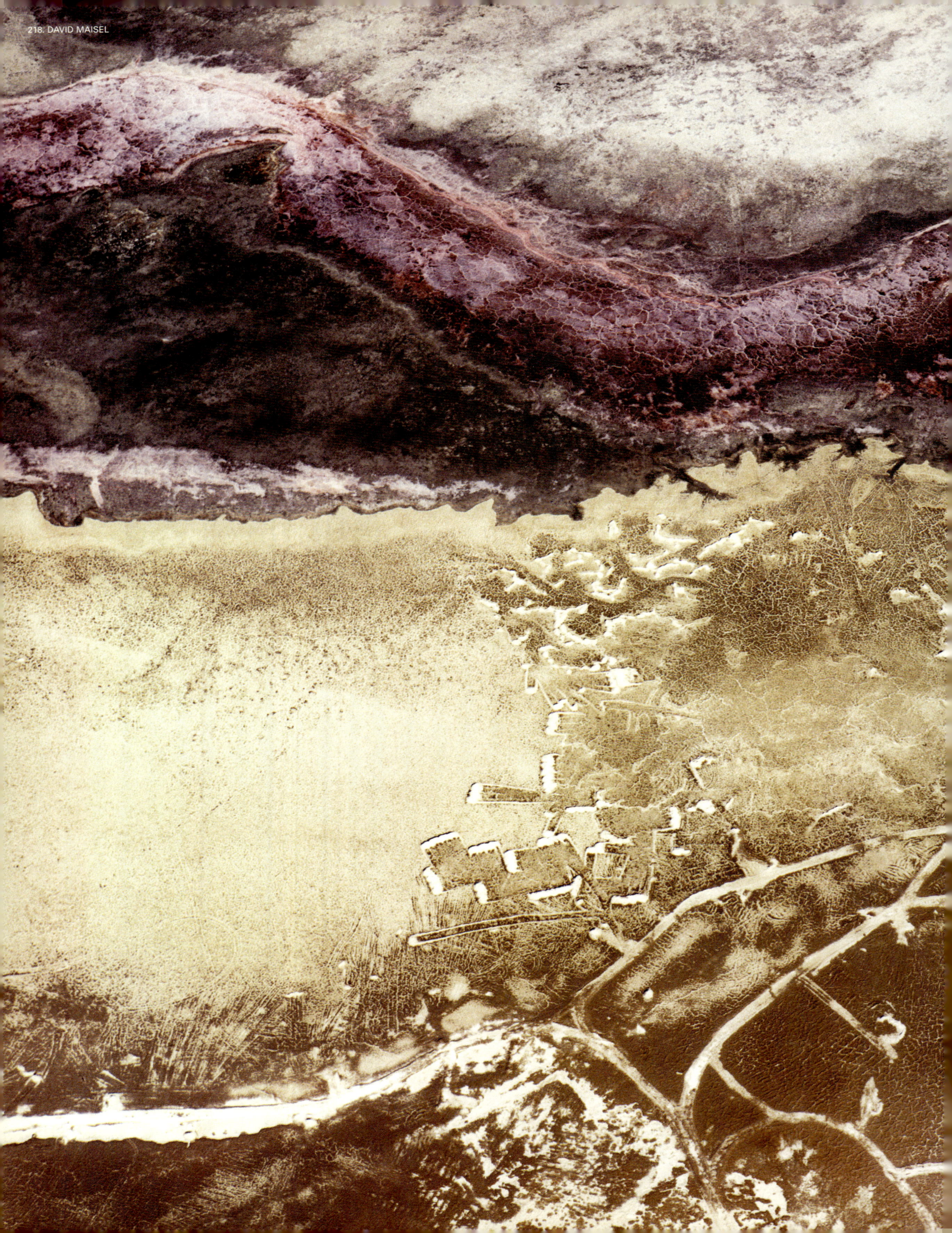

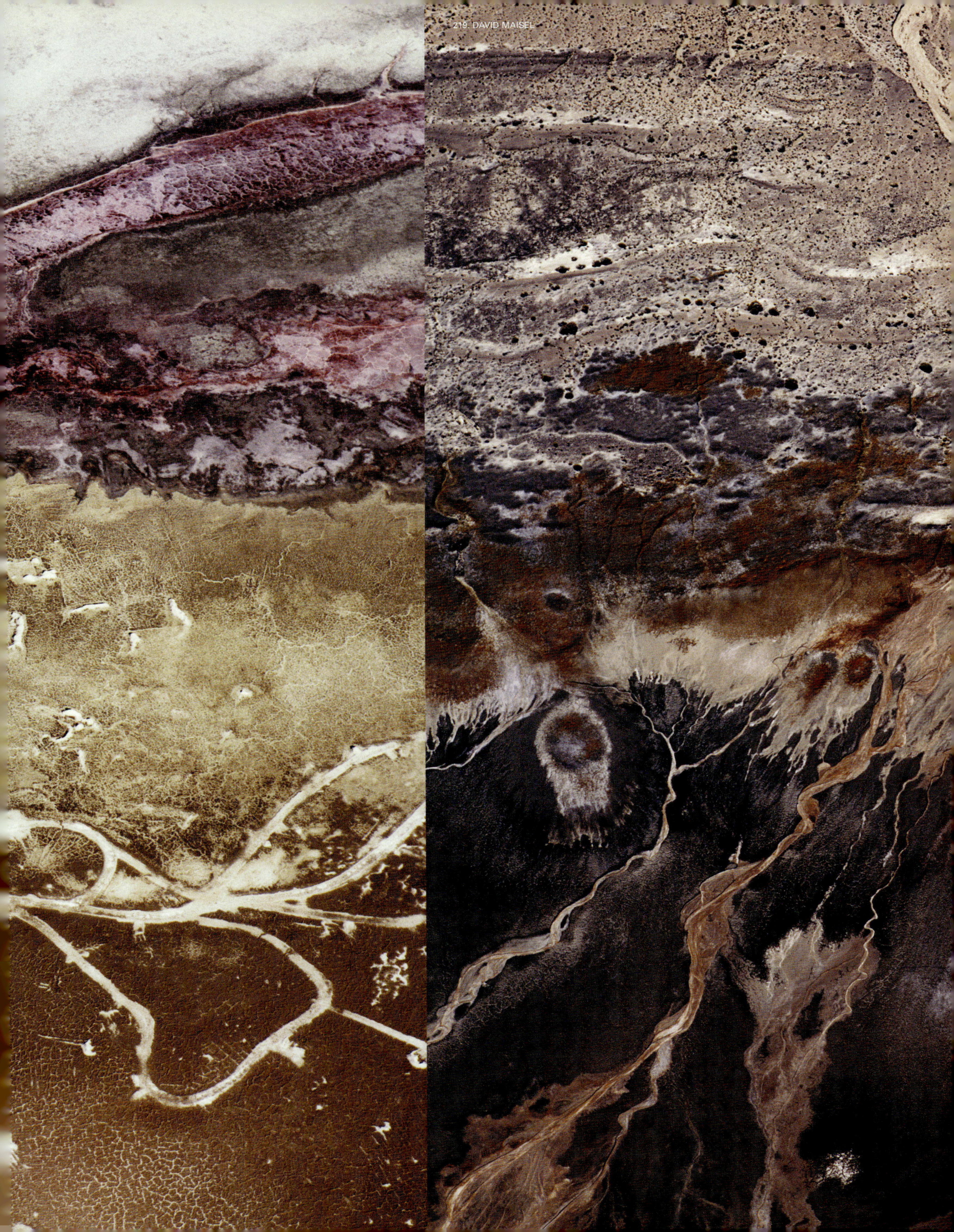

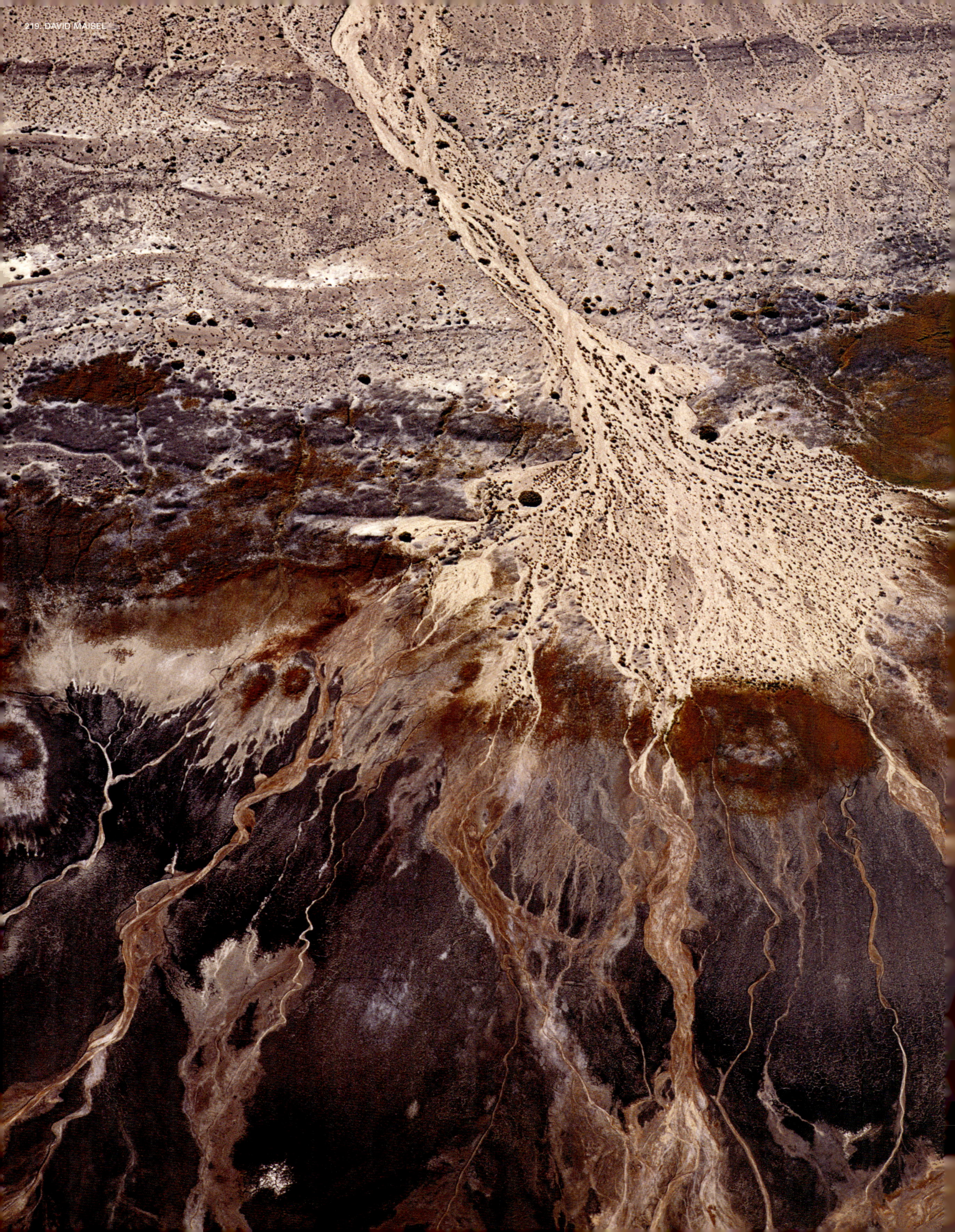

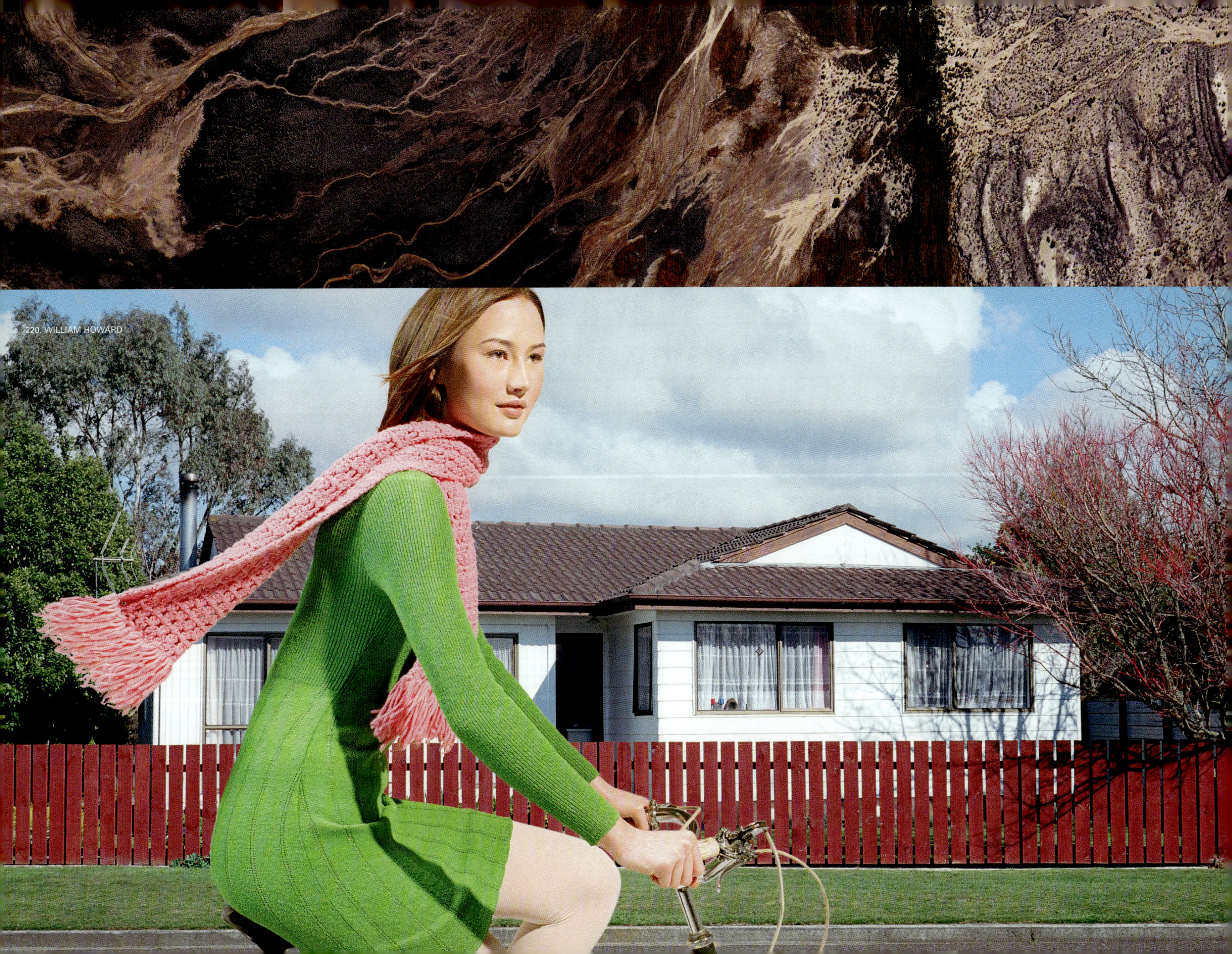

220 WILLIAM HOWARD

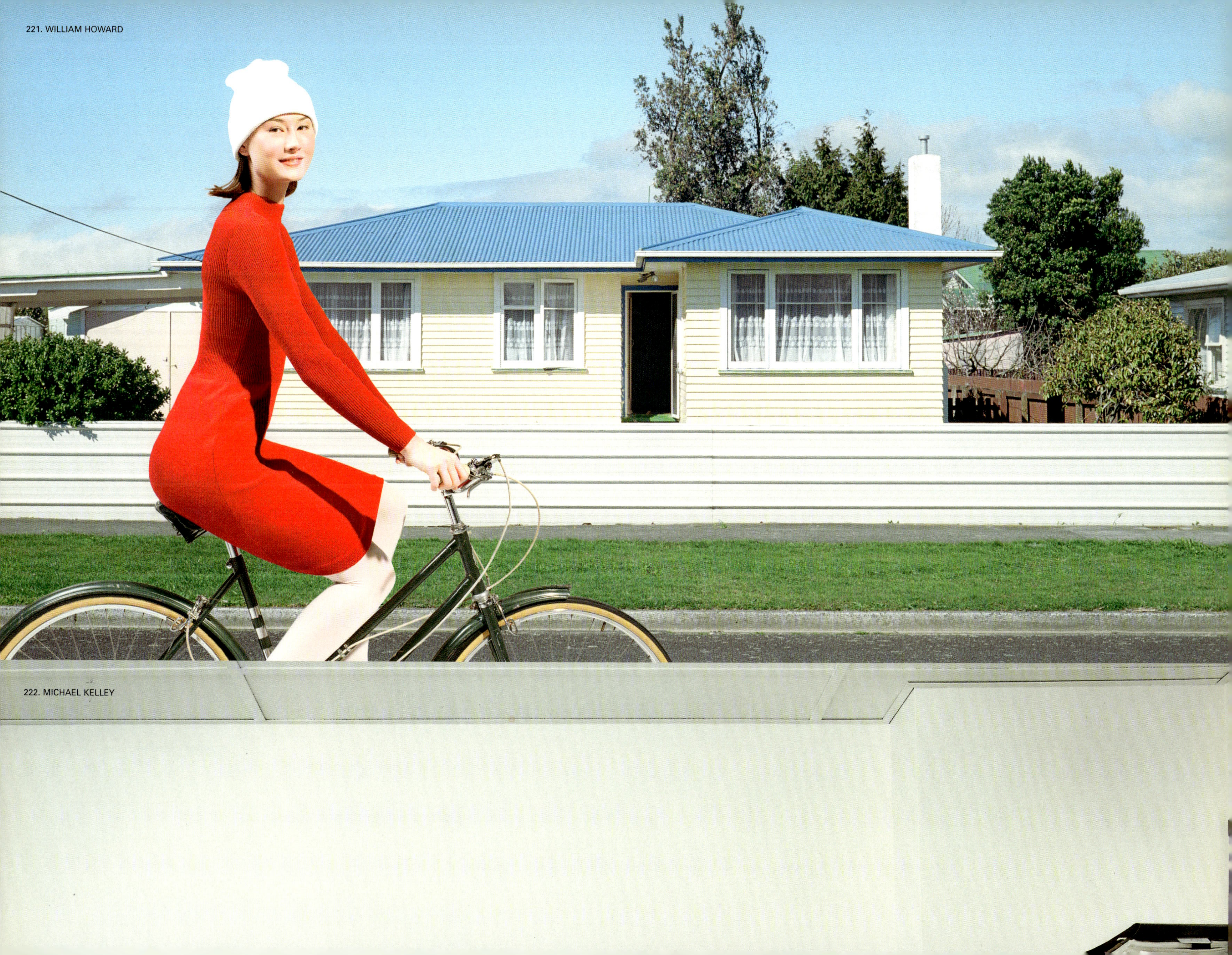
221. WILLIAM HOWARD

222. MICHAEL KELLEY

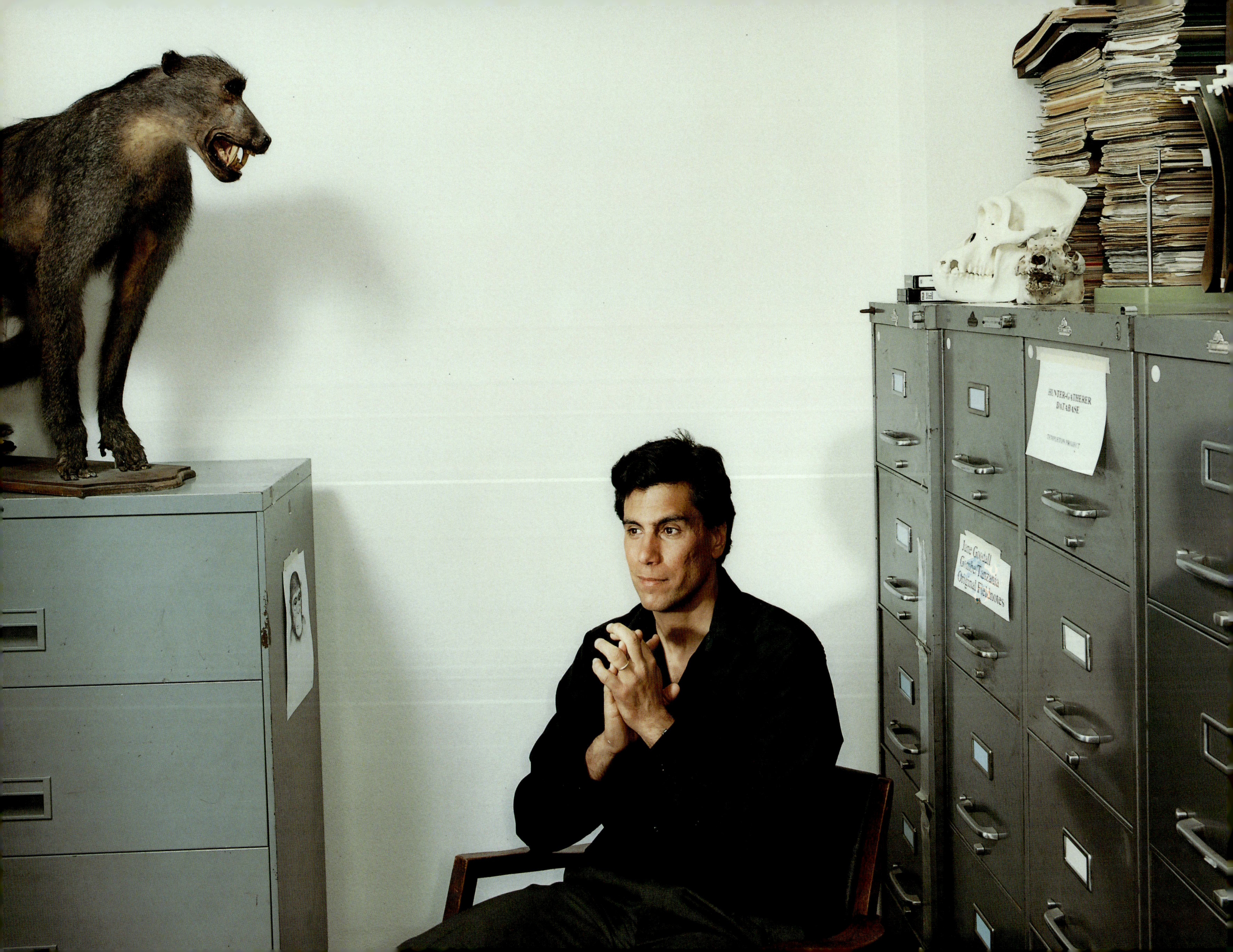
HUNTER-GATHERER
DATABASE

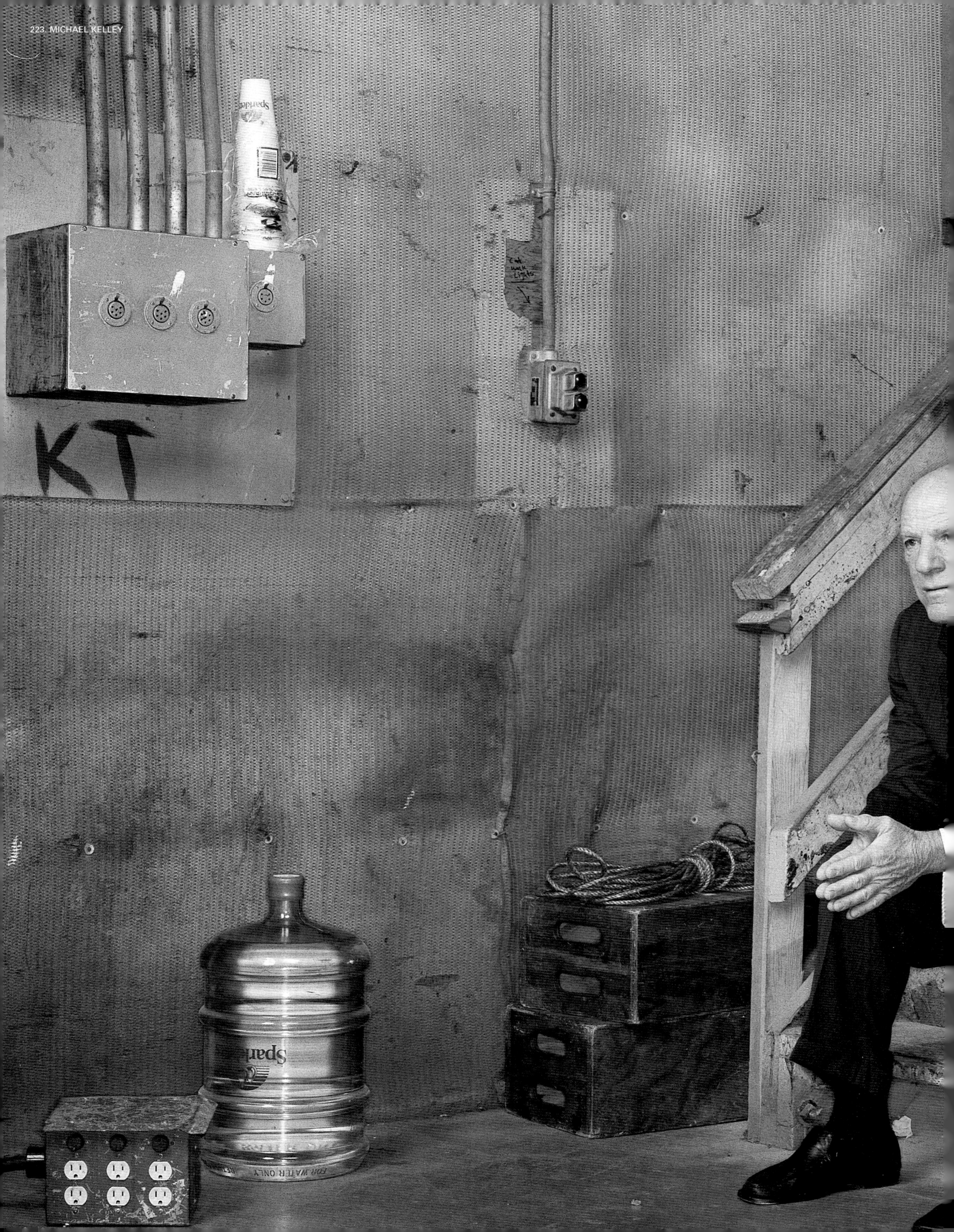

223. MICHAEL KELLEY

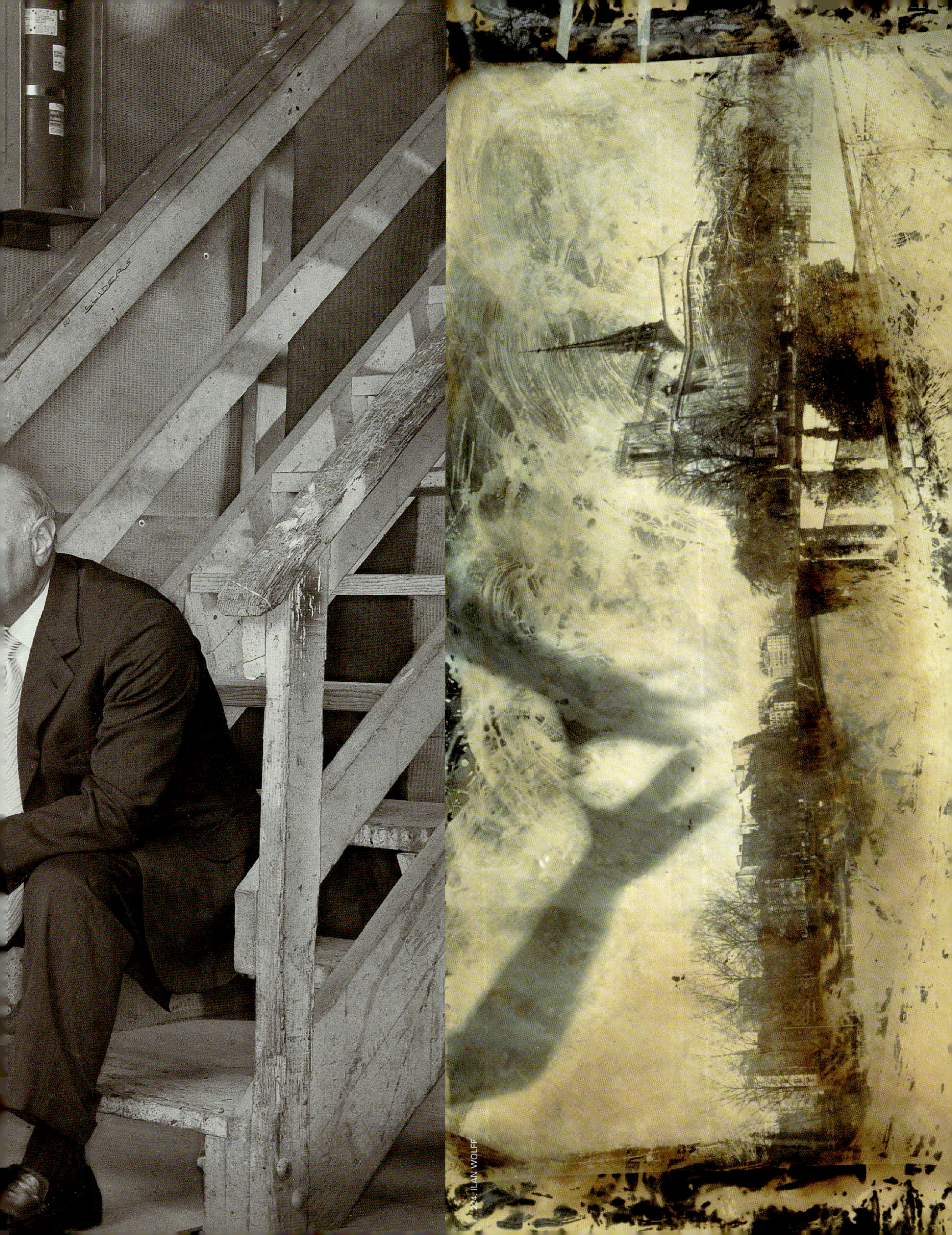

224. ILAN WOLFF

225. ANTONIN KRATOCHVIL

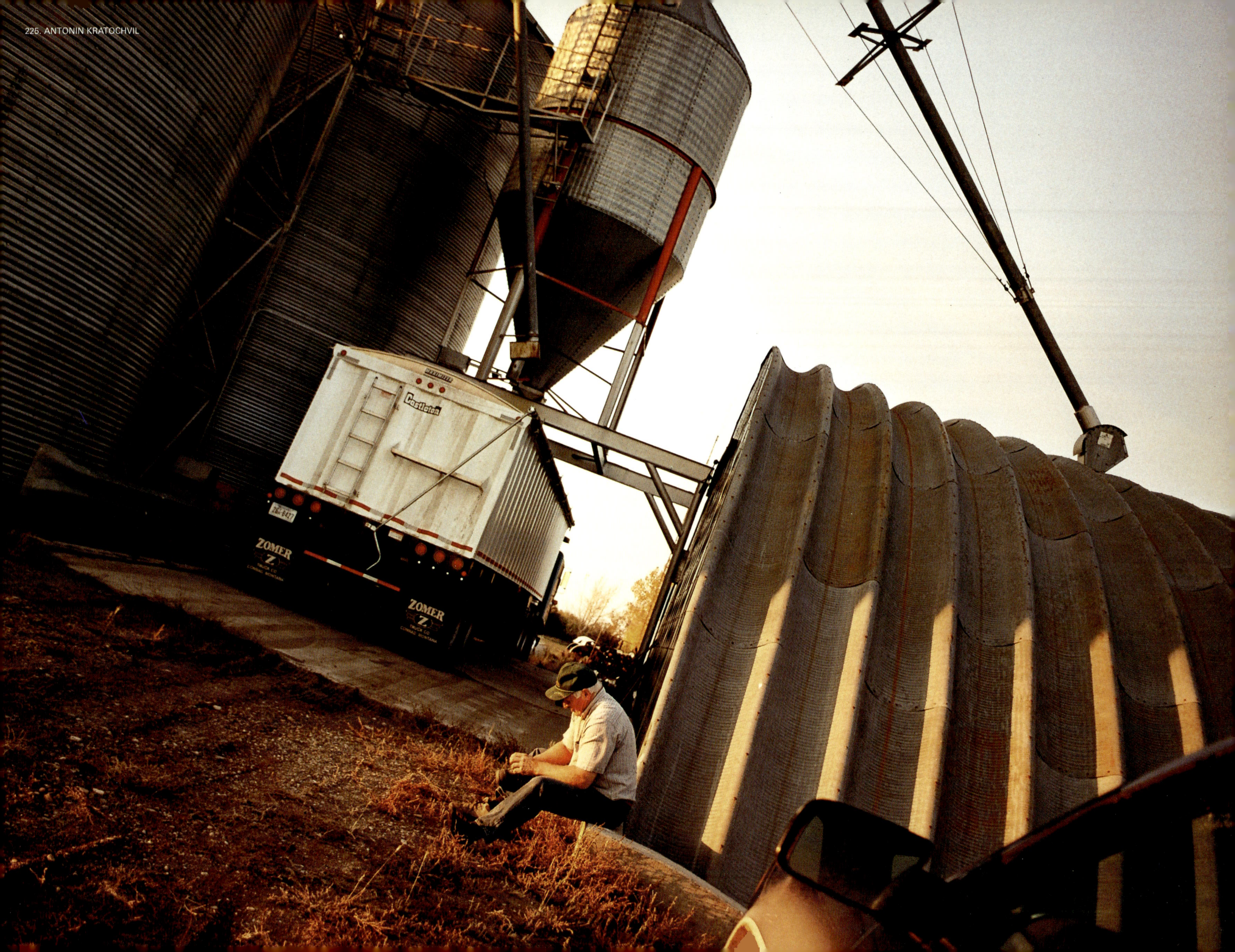

226. ANTONIN KRATOCHVIL

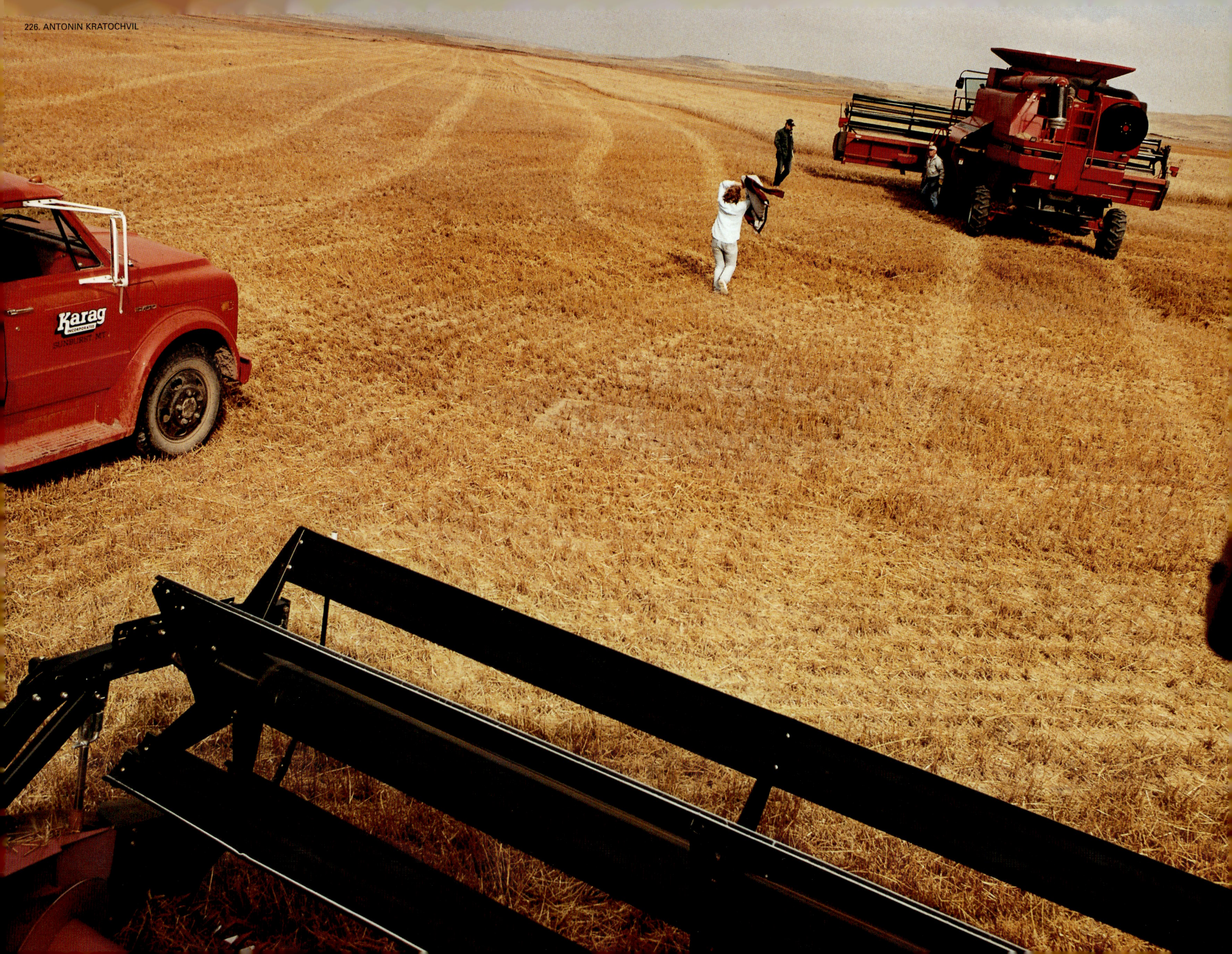

227. ANTONIN KRATOCHVIL

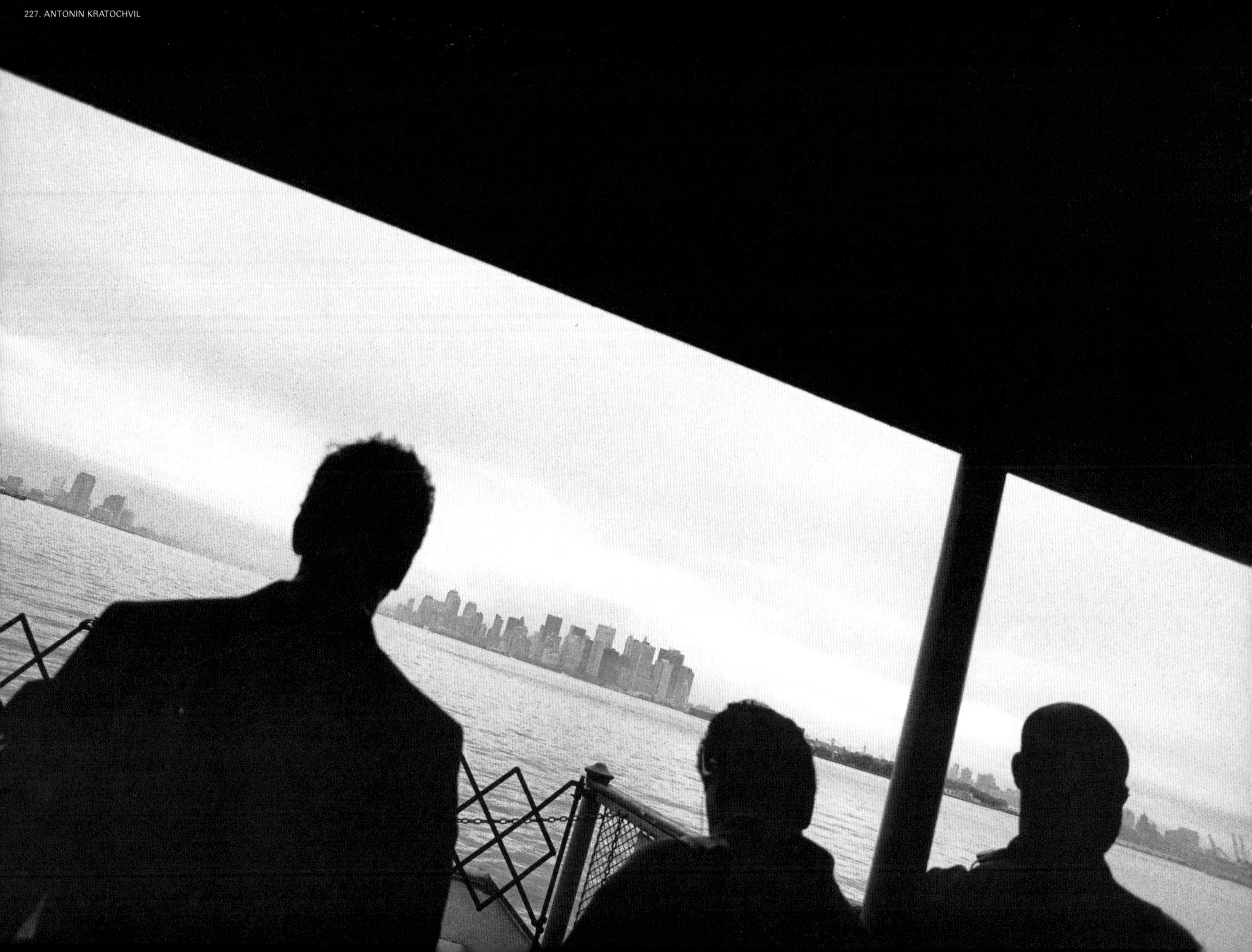

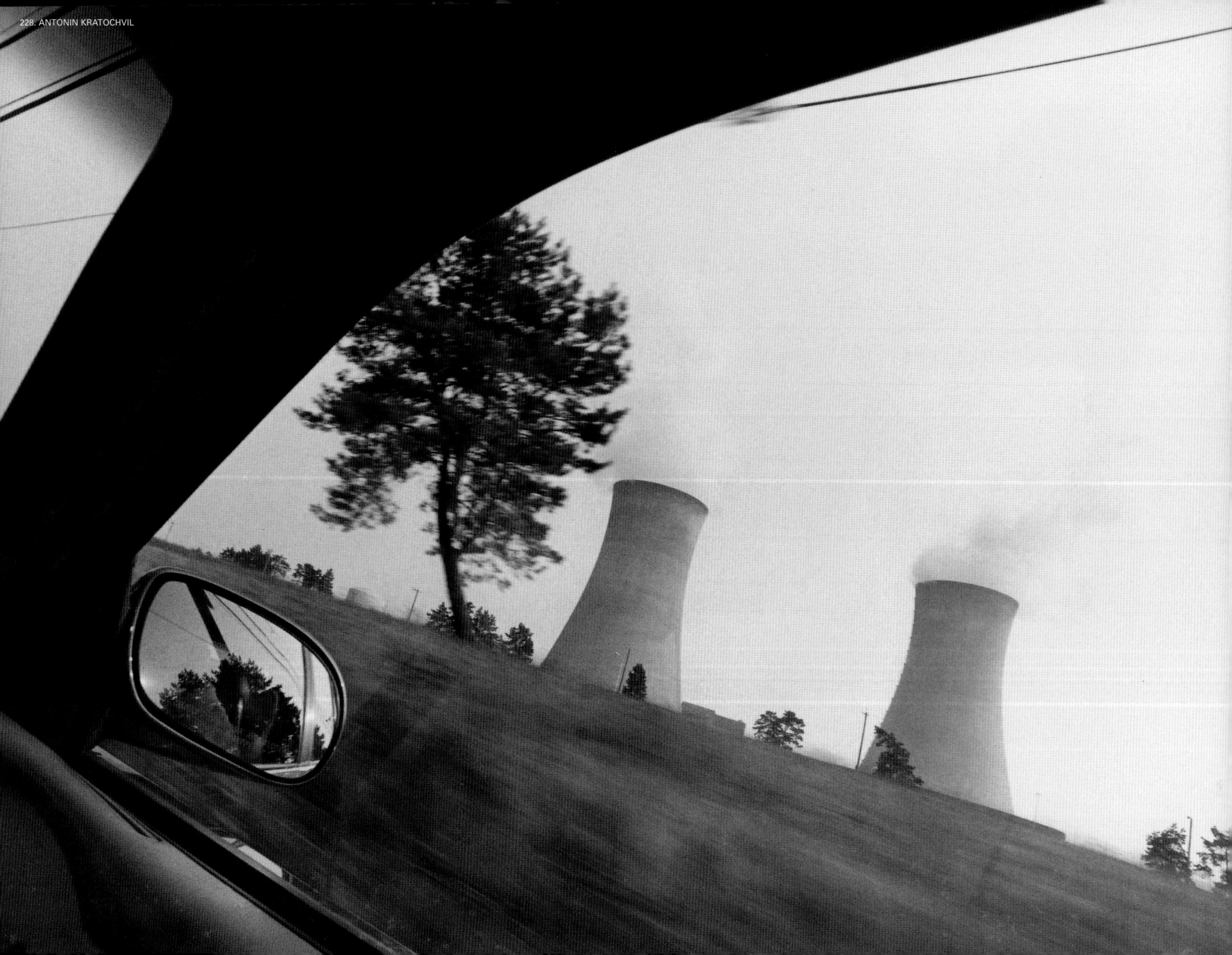

228. ANTONIN KRATOCHVIL

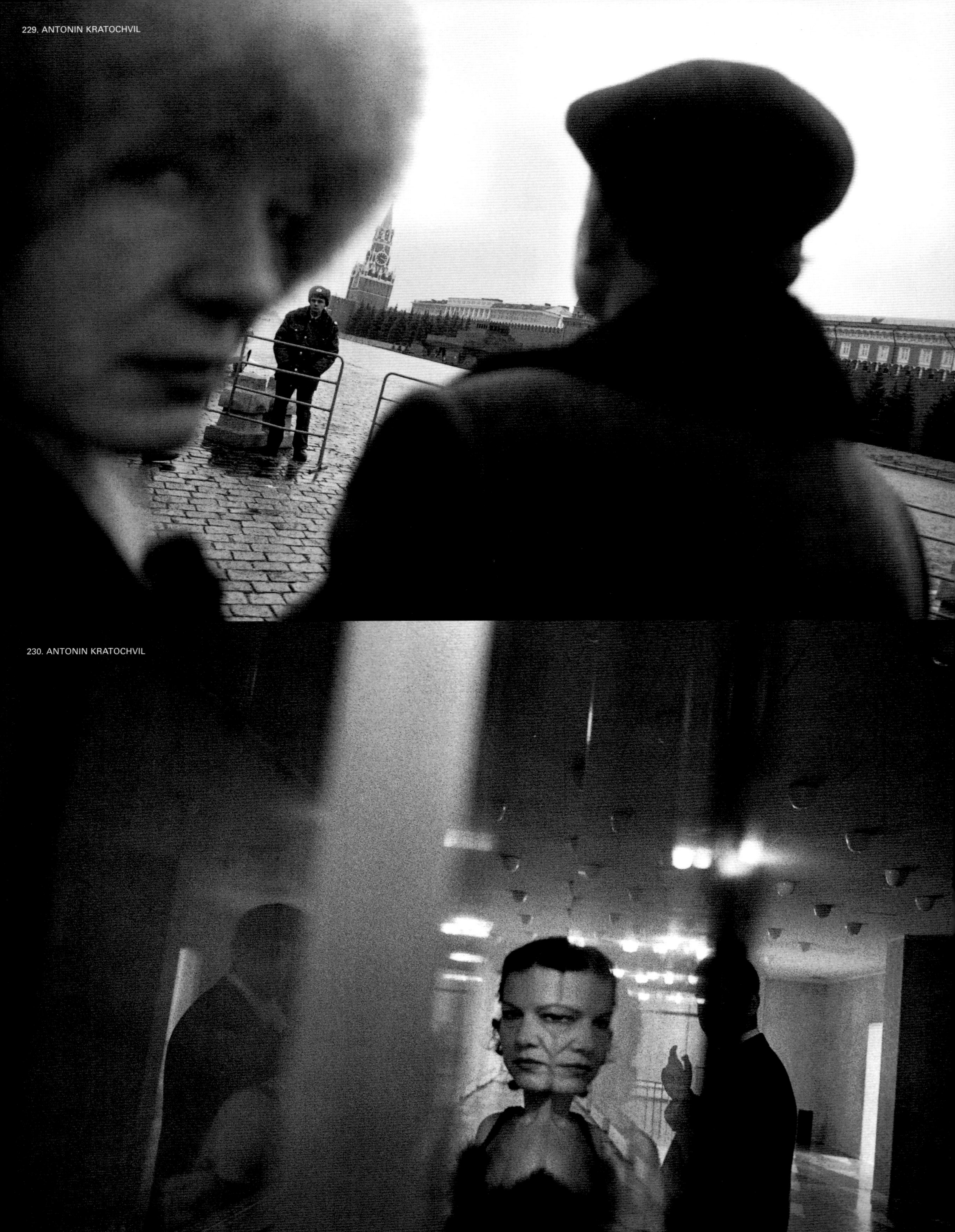

229. ANTONIN KRATOCHVIL

230. ANTONIN KRATOCHVIL

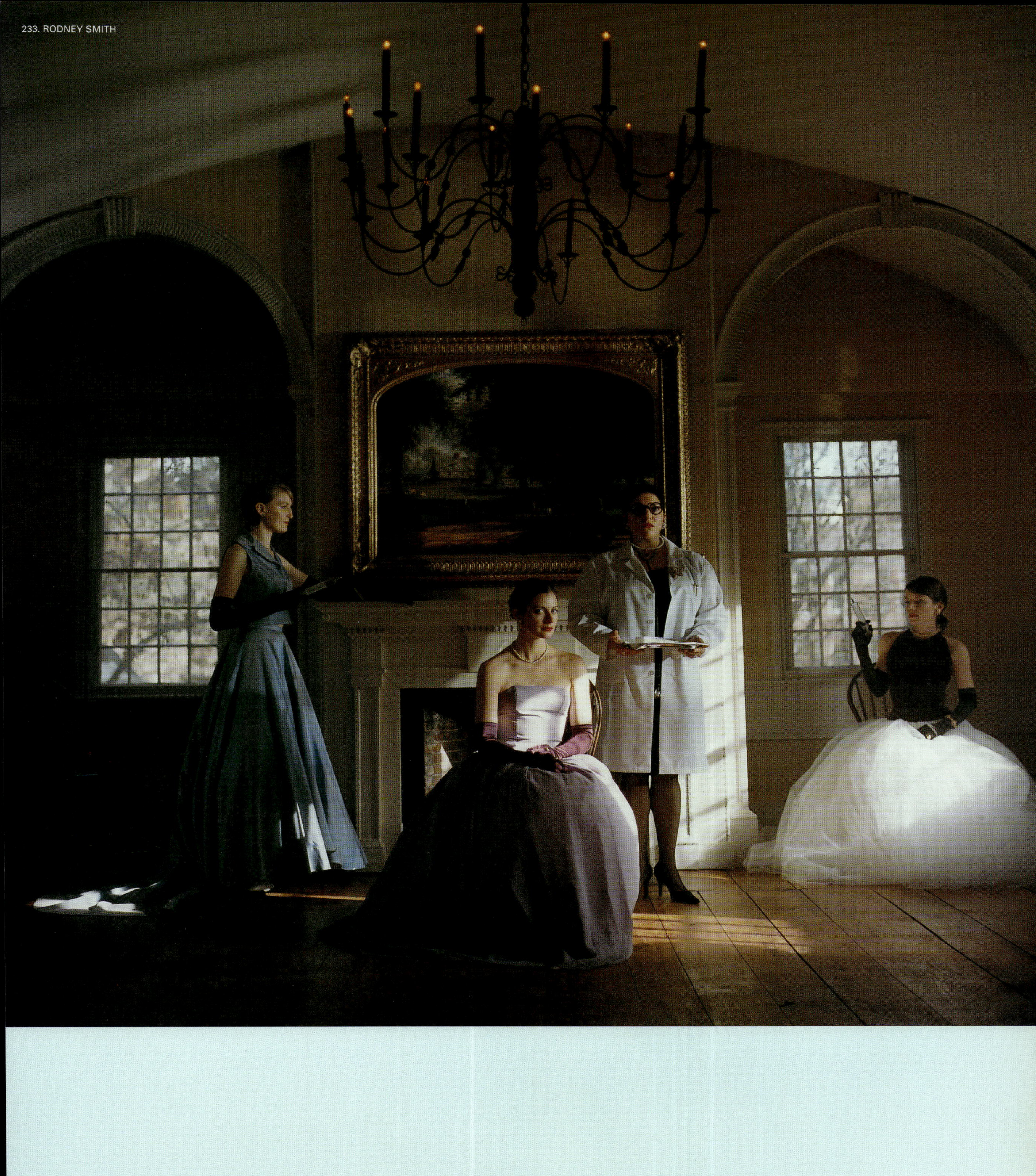
233. RODNEY SMITH

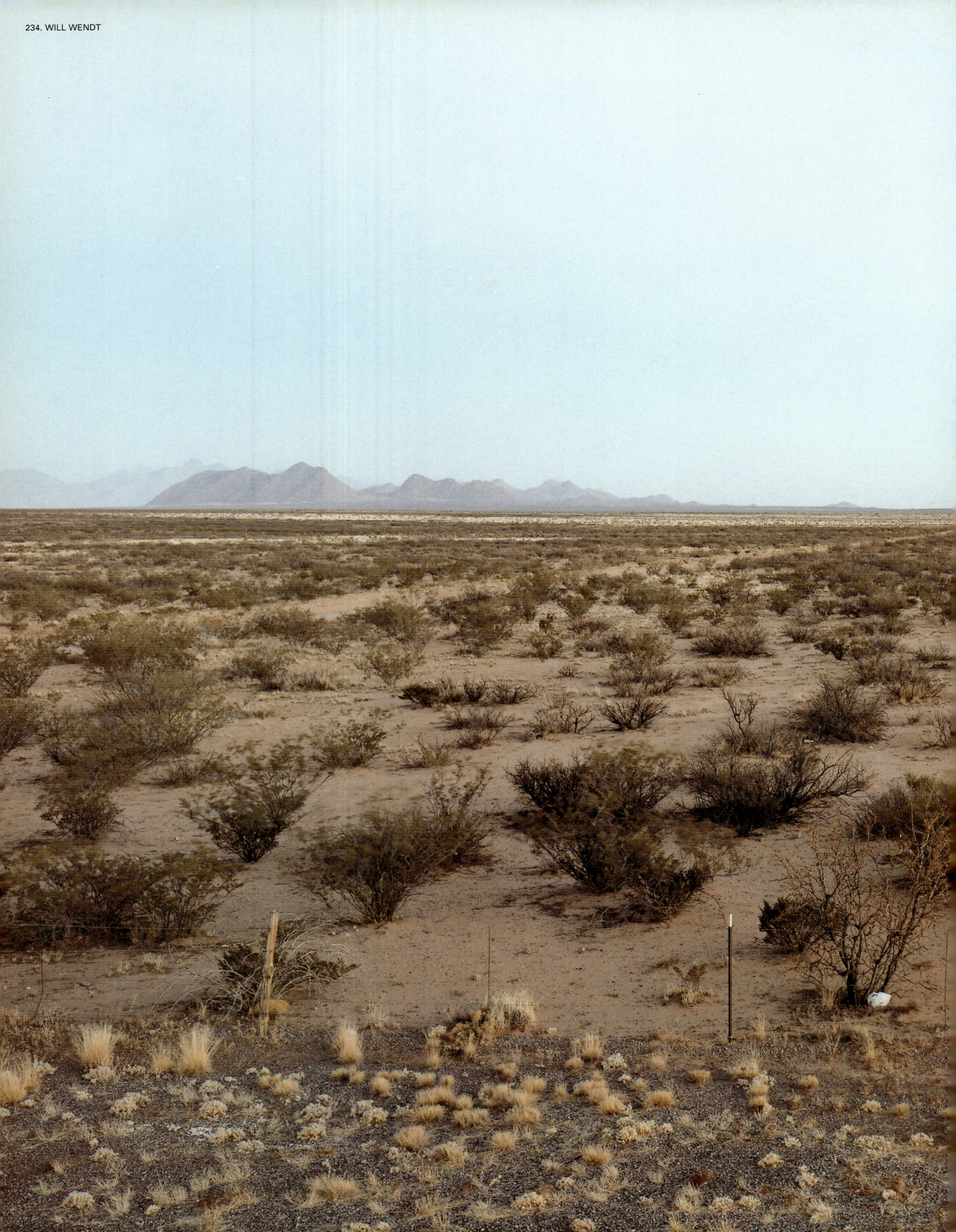

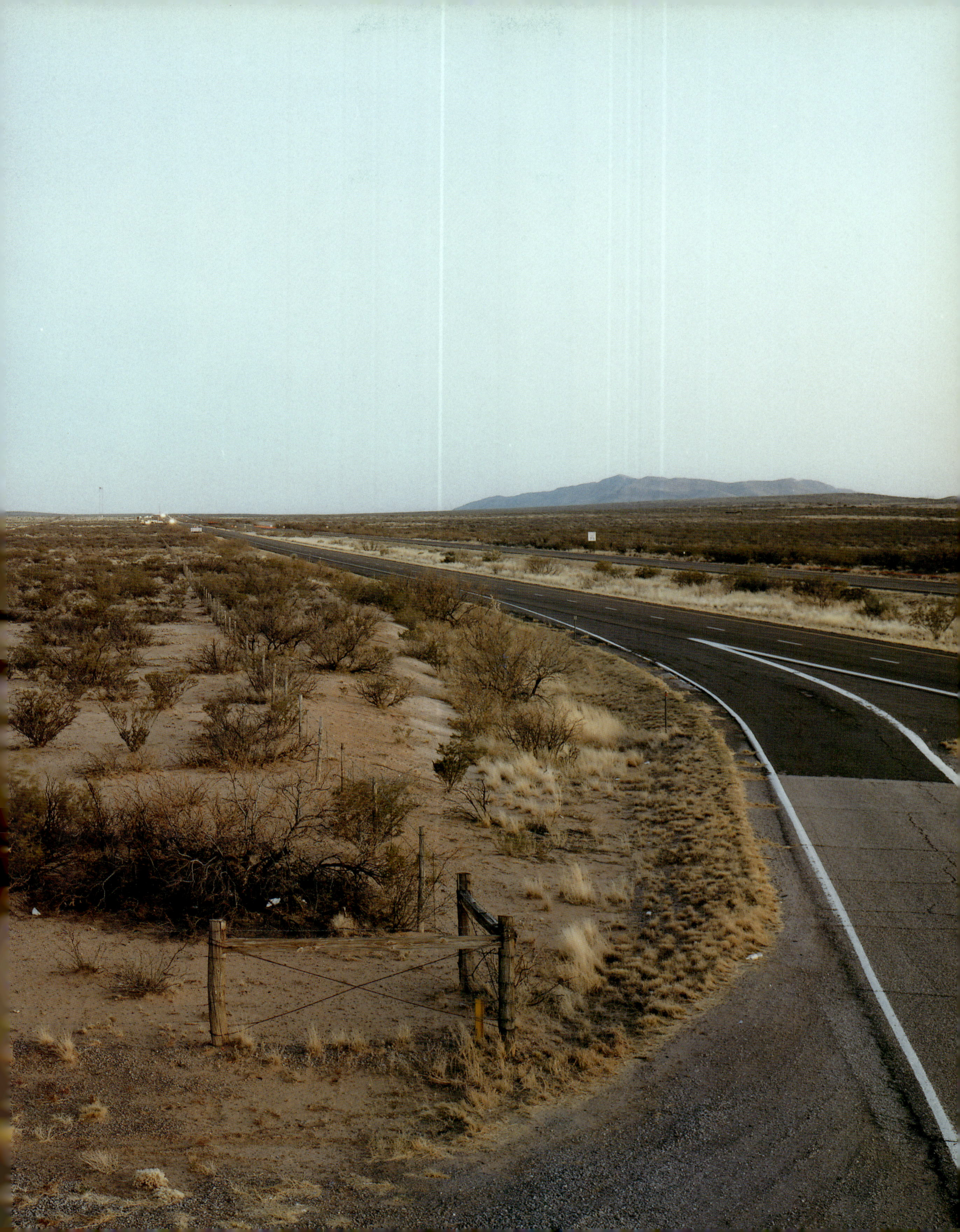

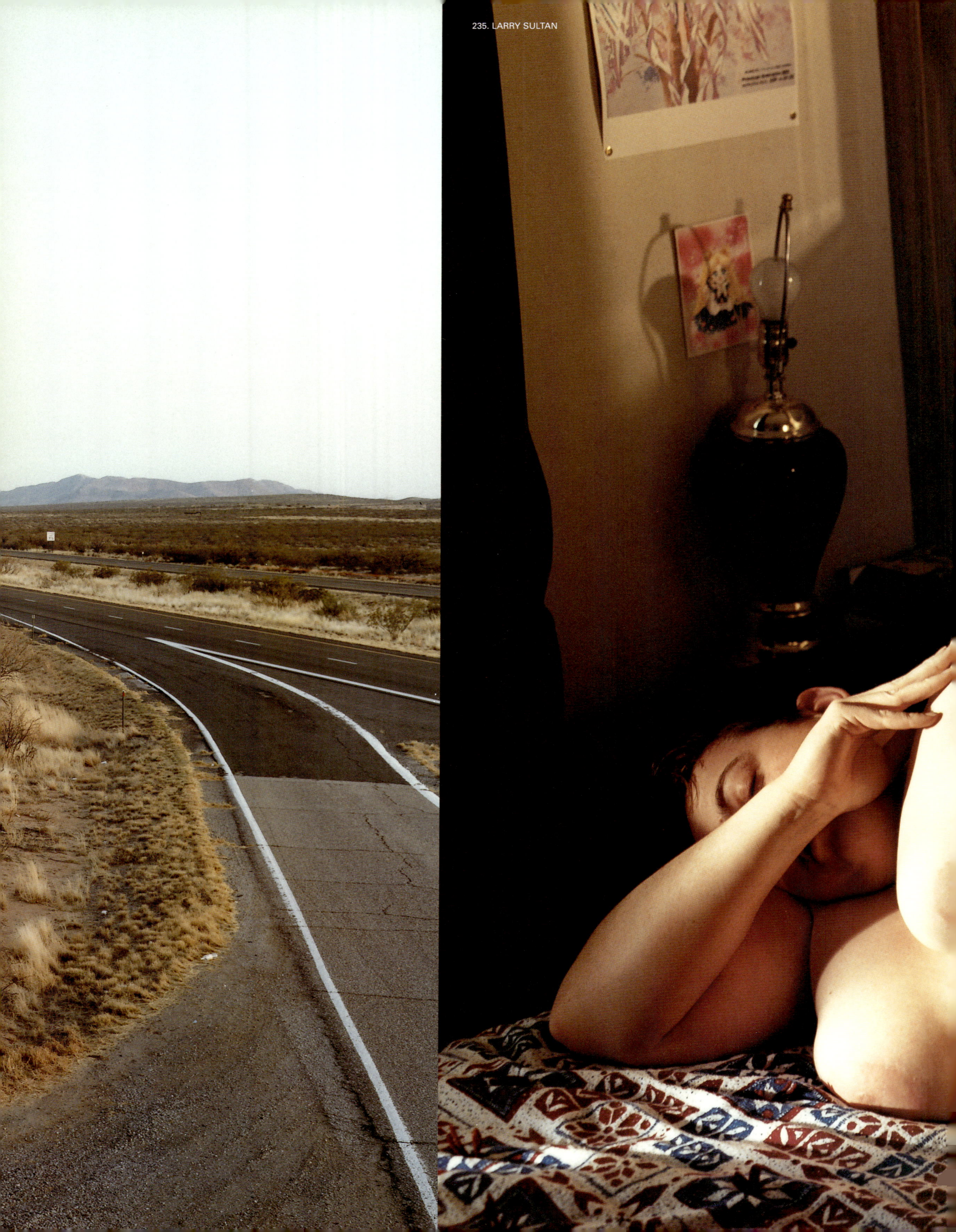

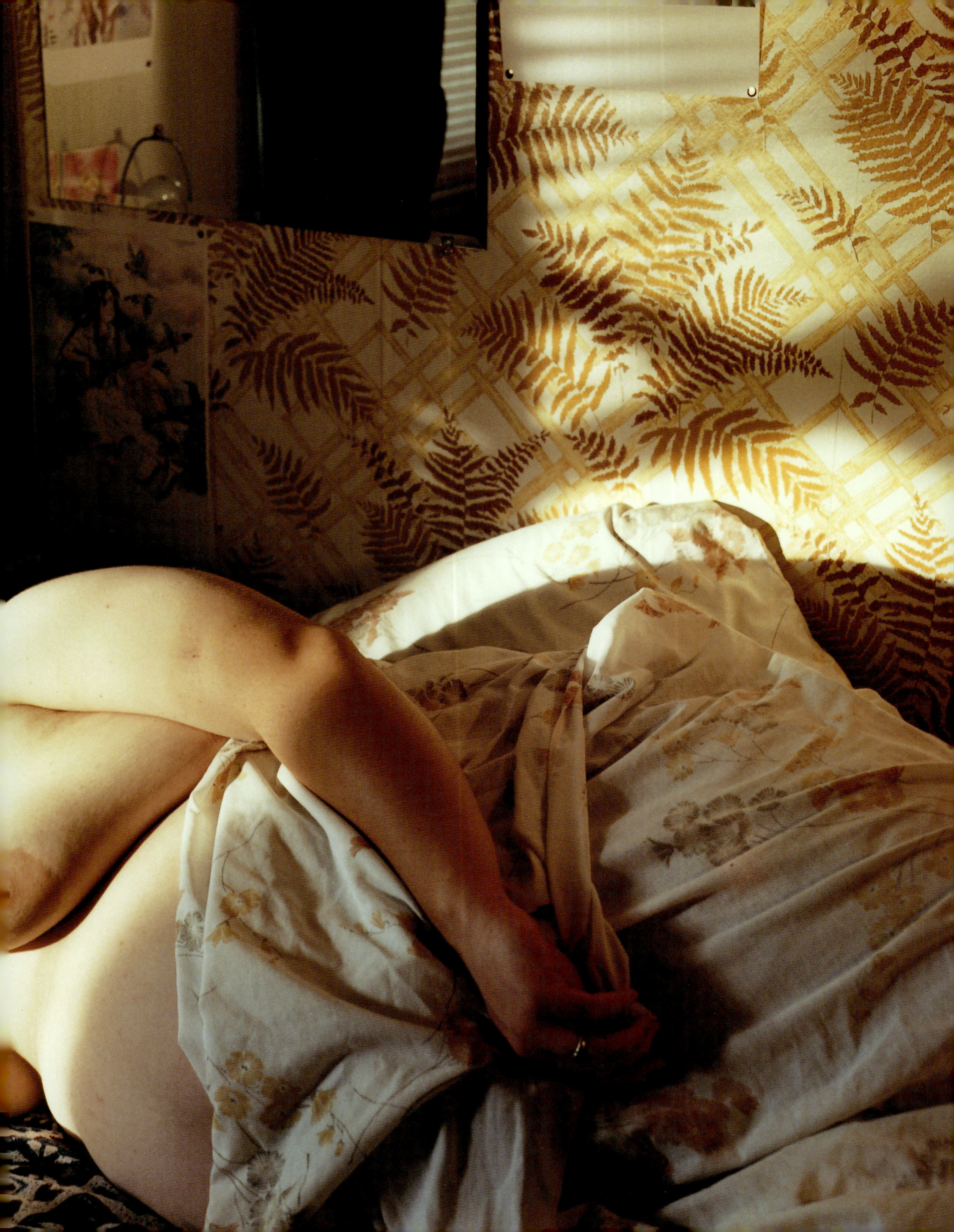

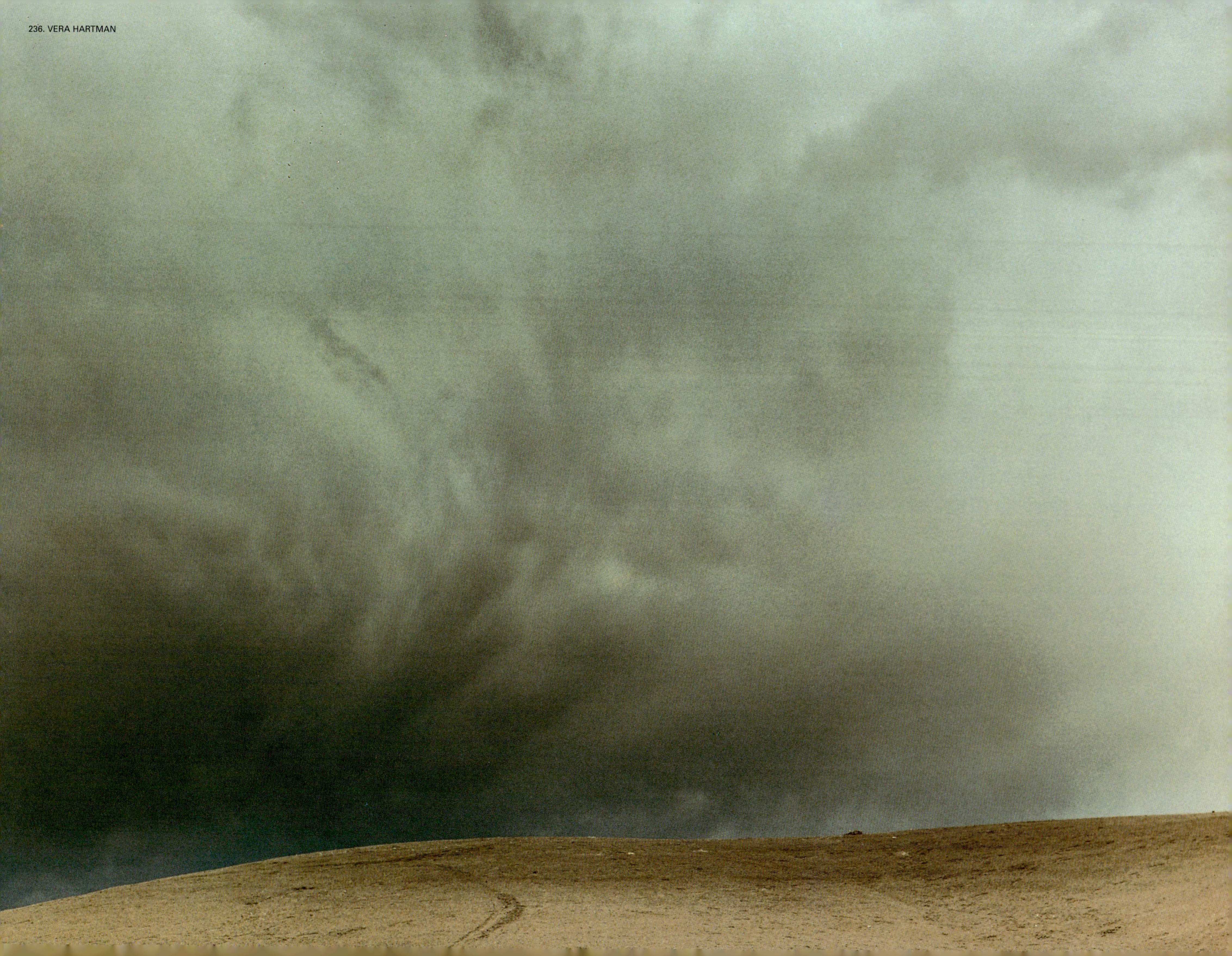

236. VERA HARTMAN

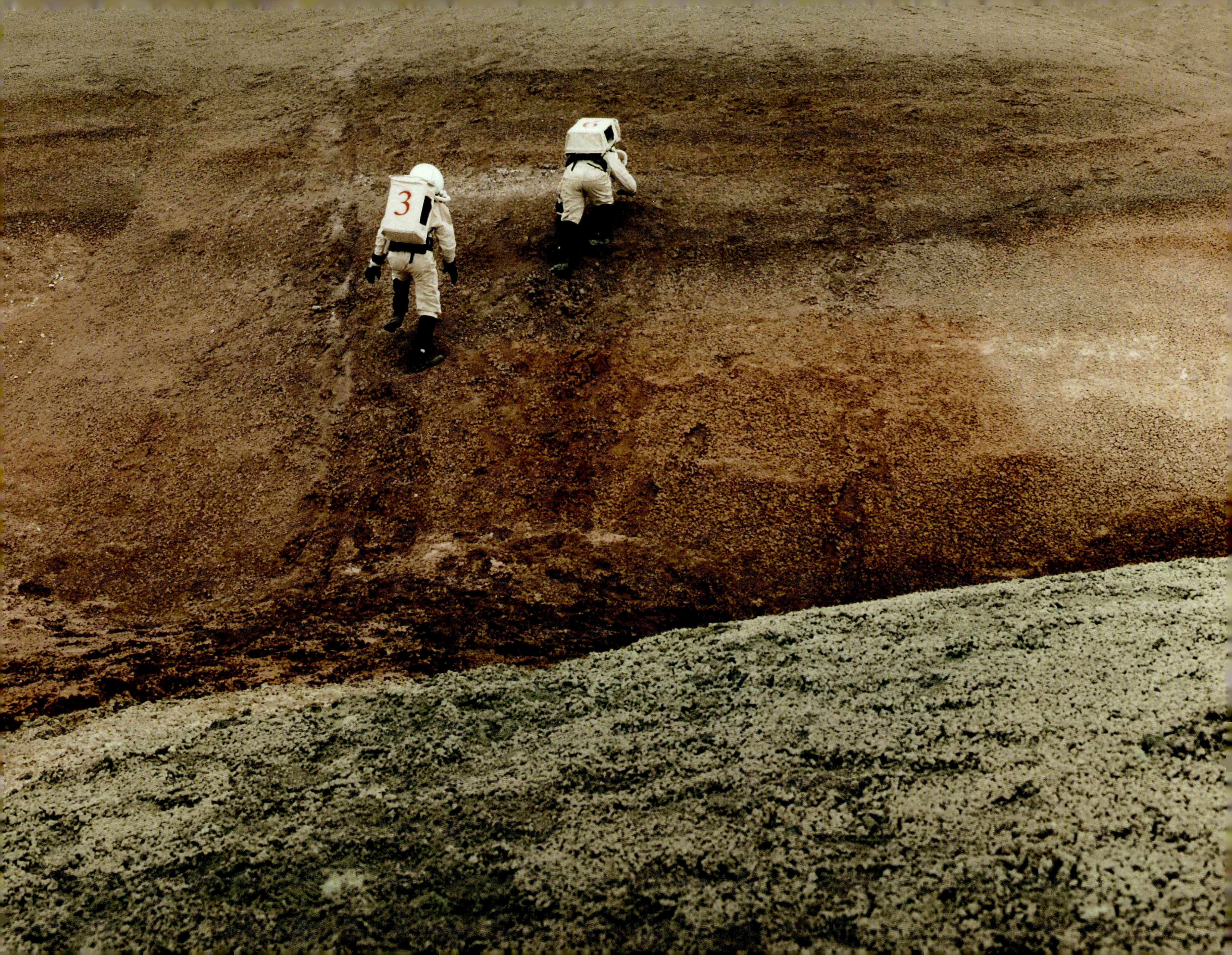
3

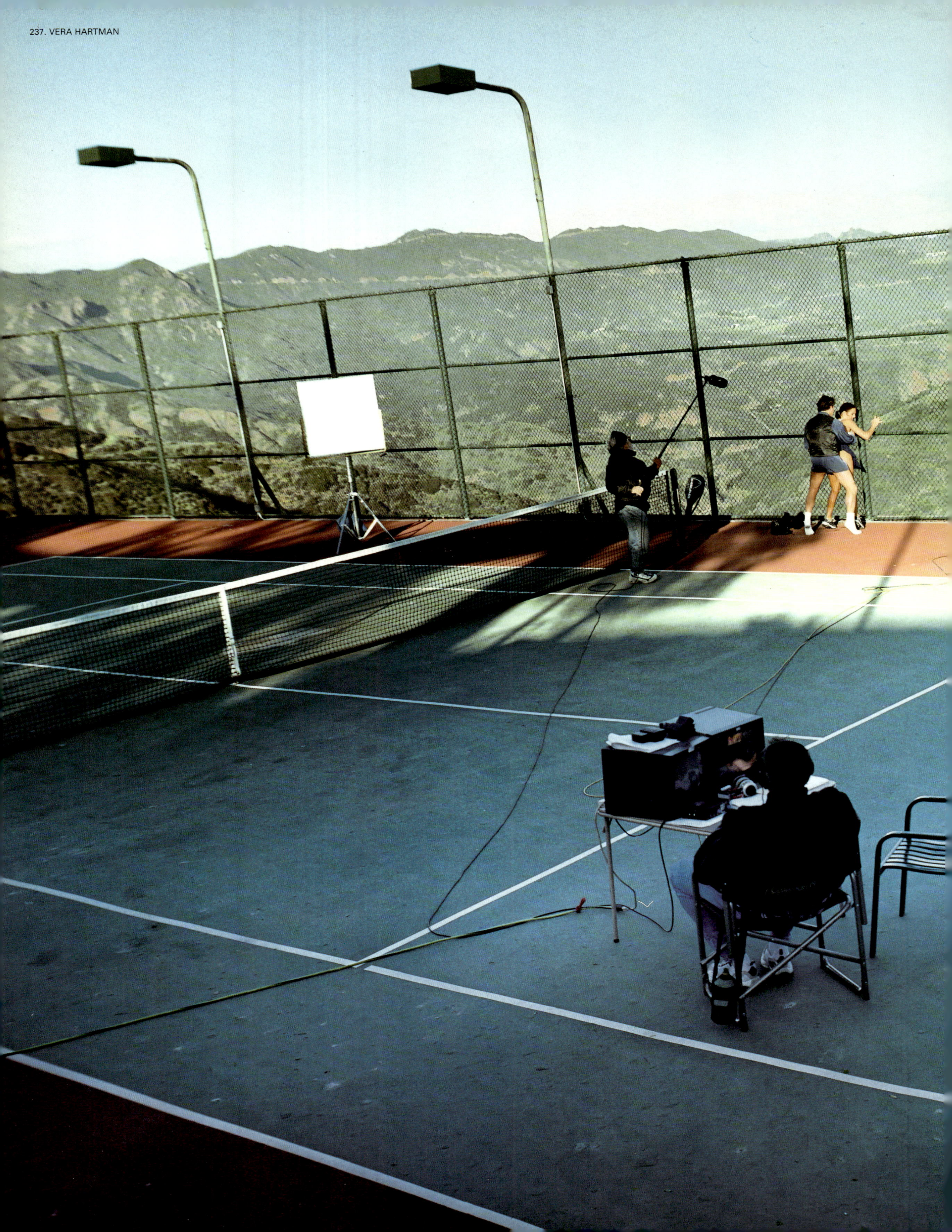

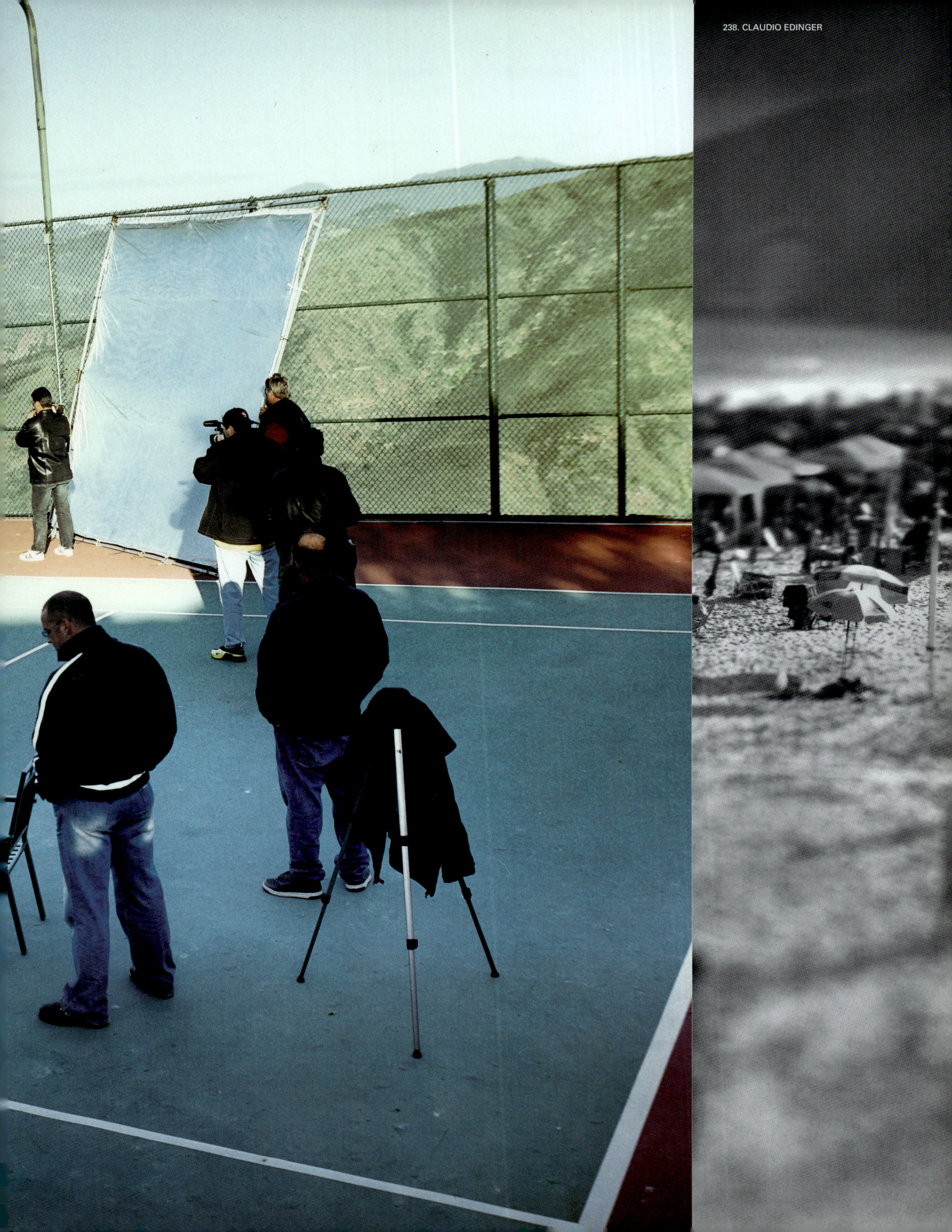

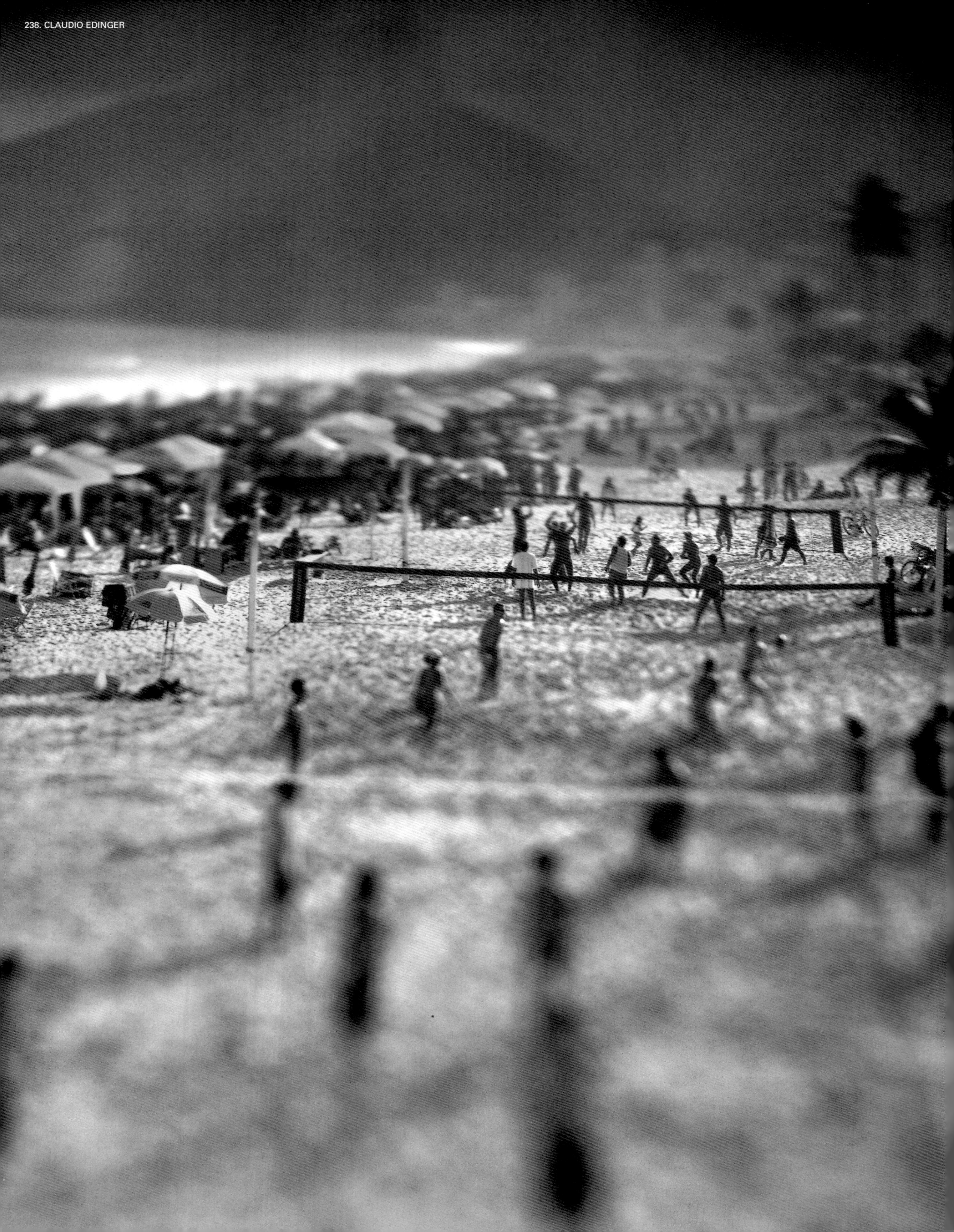

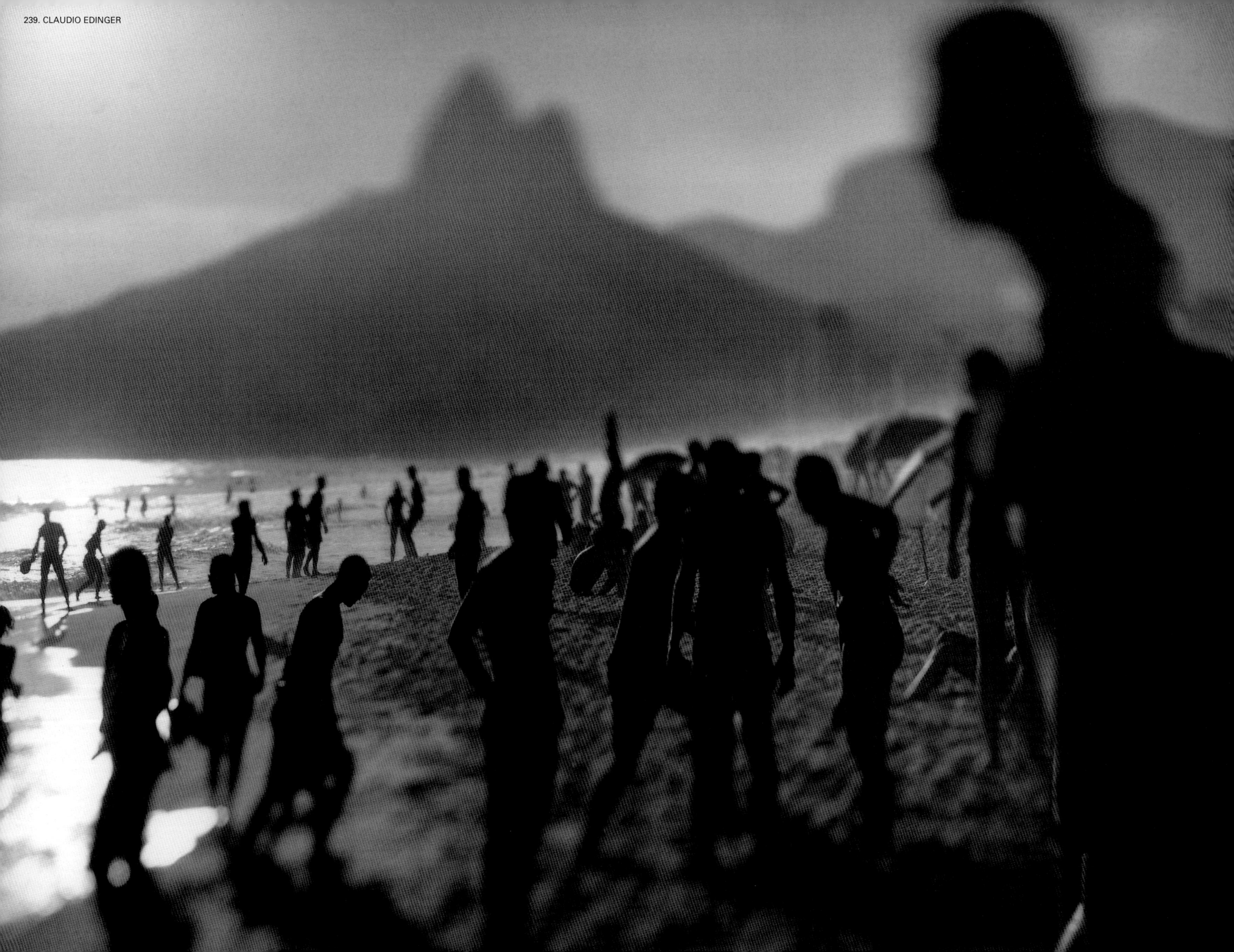

239. CLAUDIO EDINGER

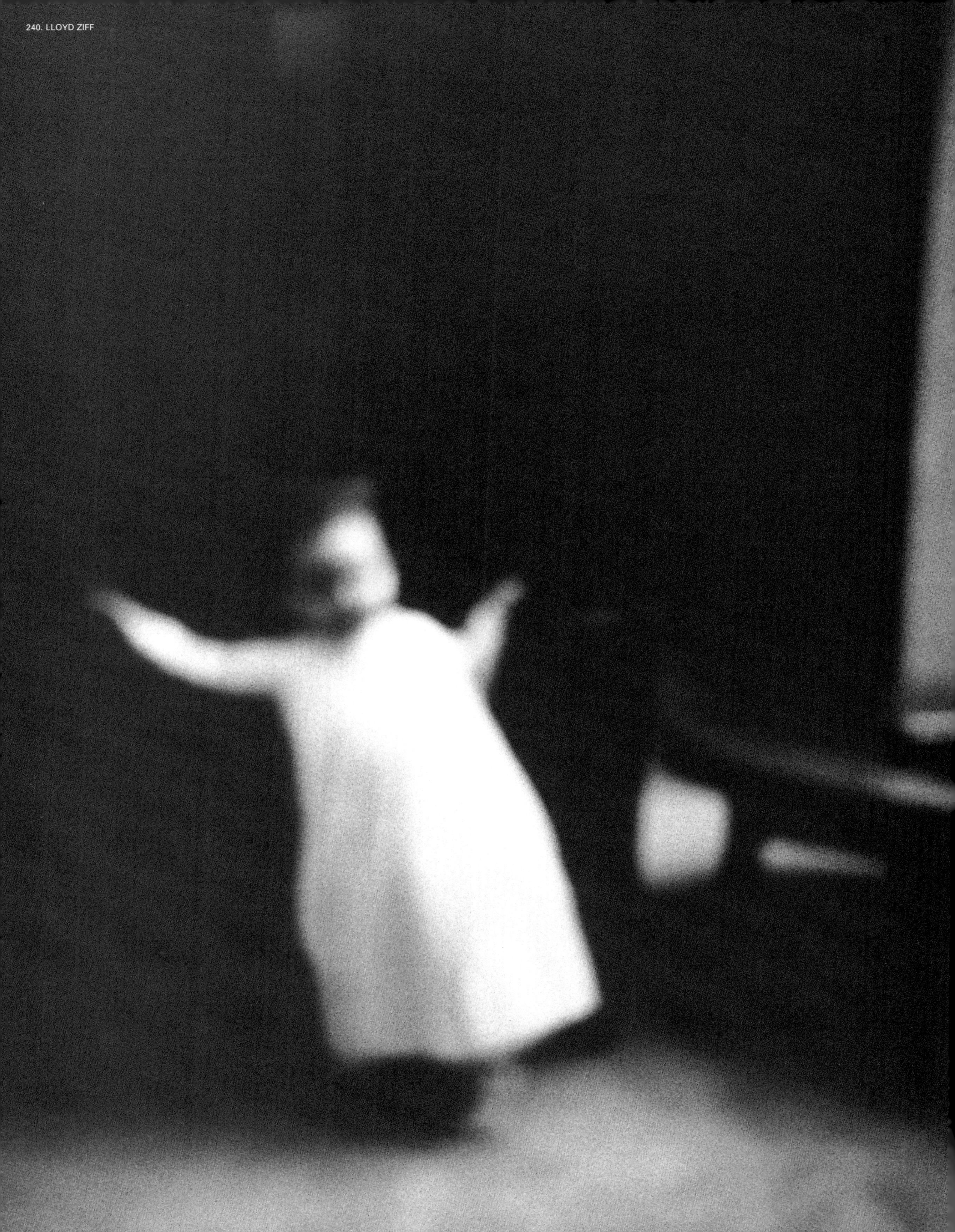

240. LLOYD ZIFF

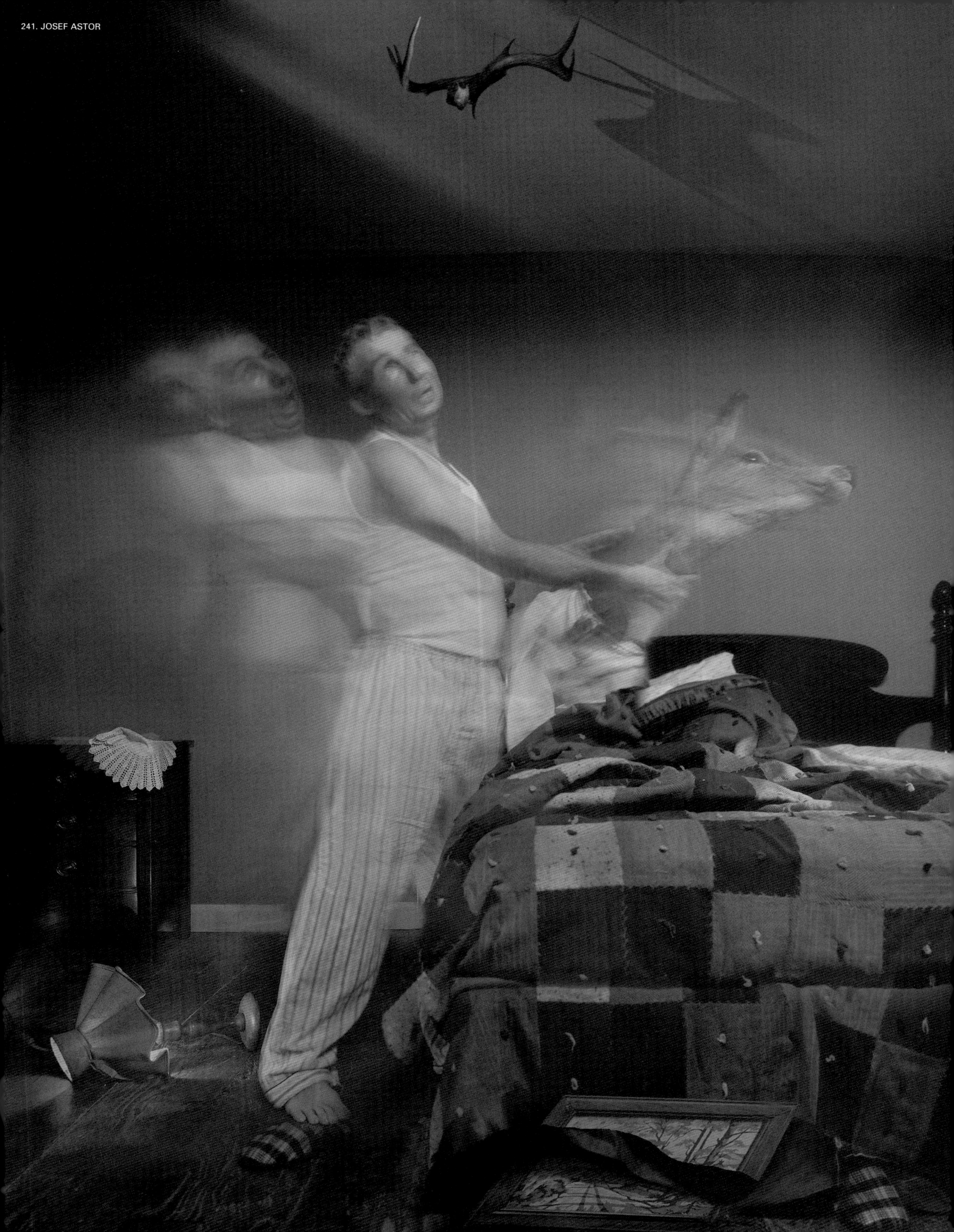
241. JOSEF ASTOR

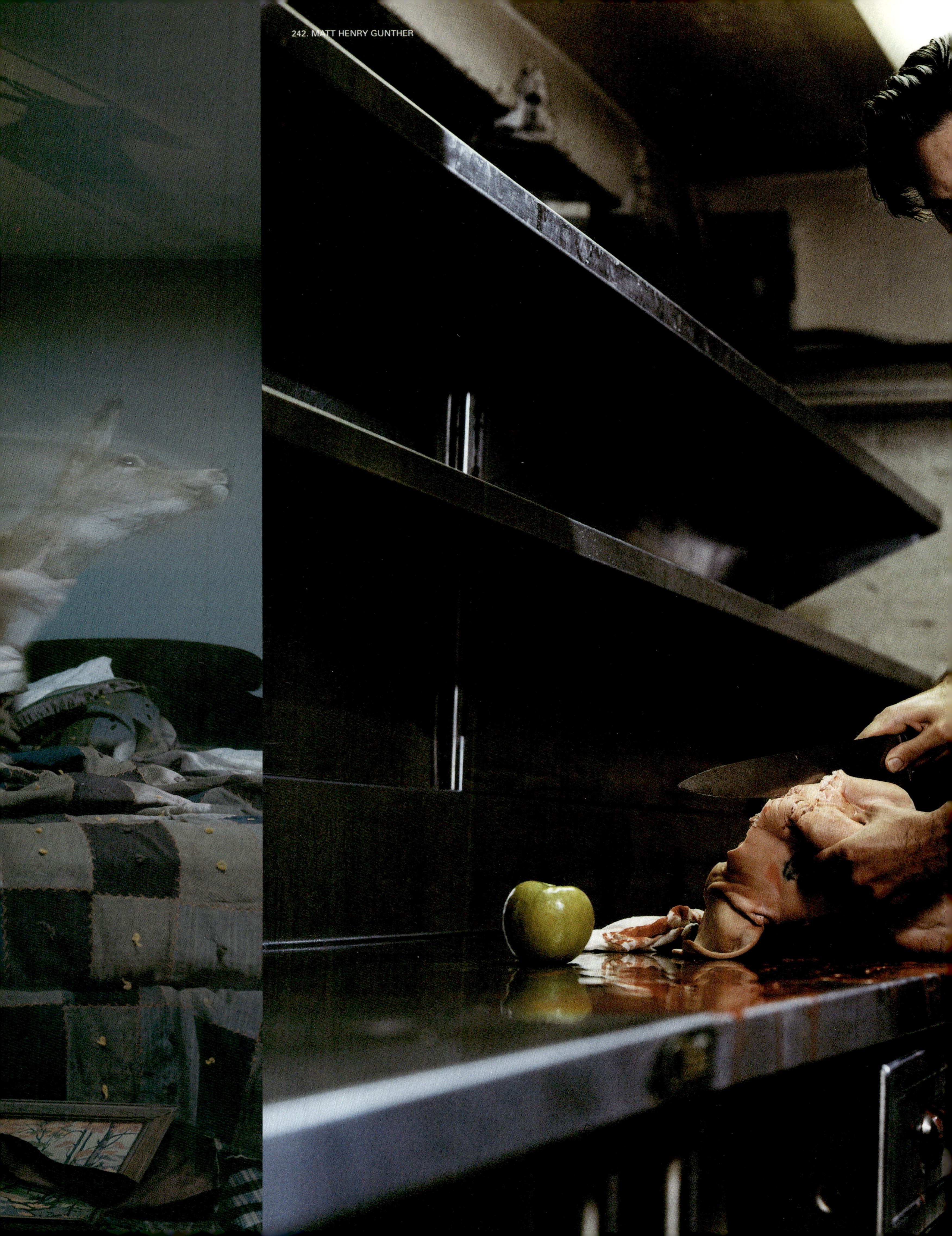

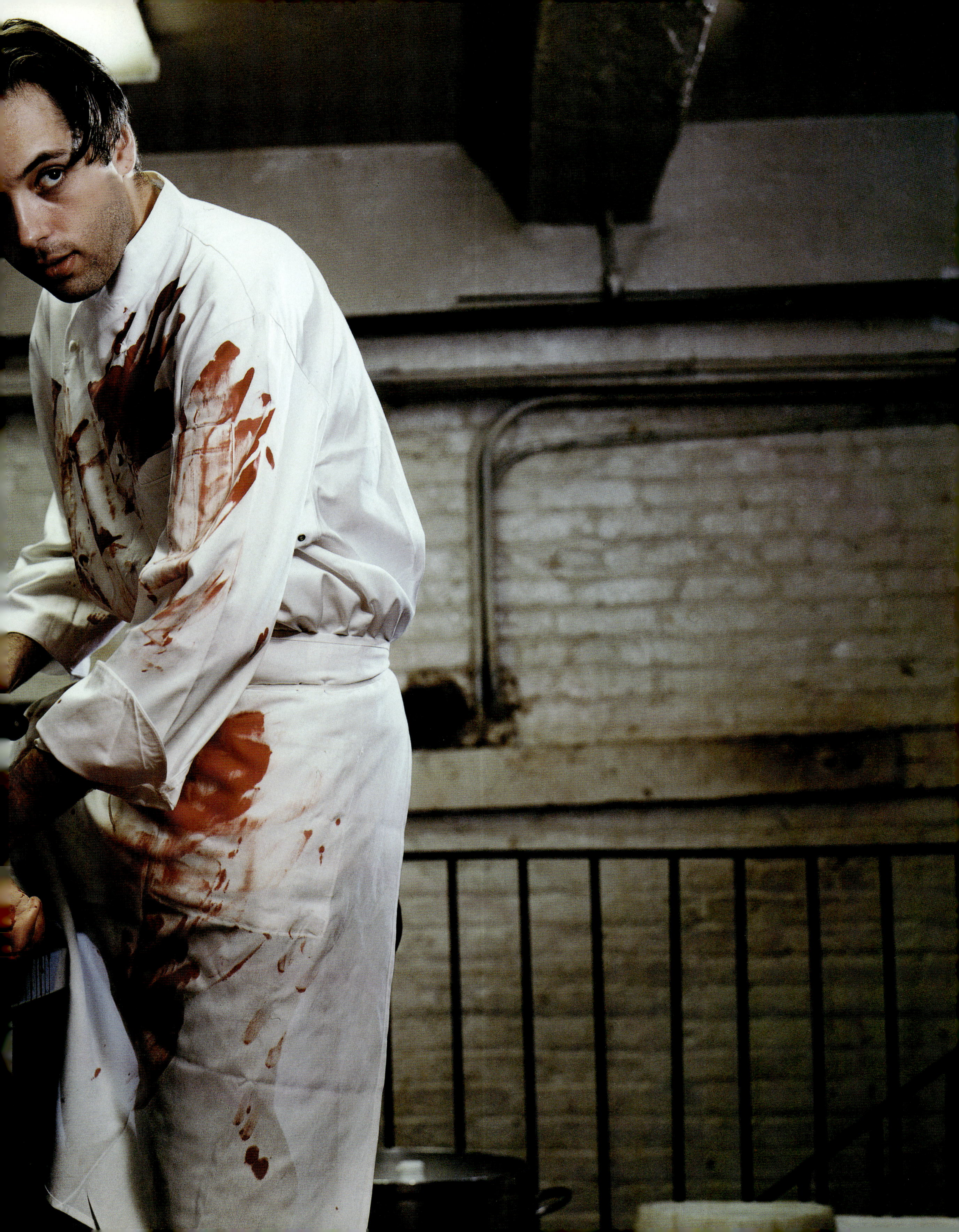

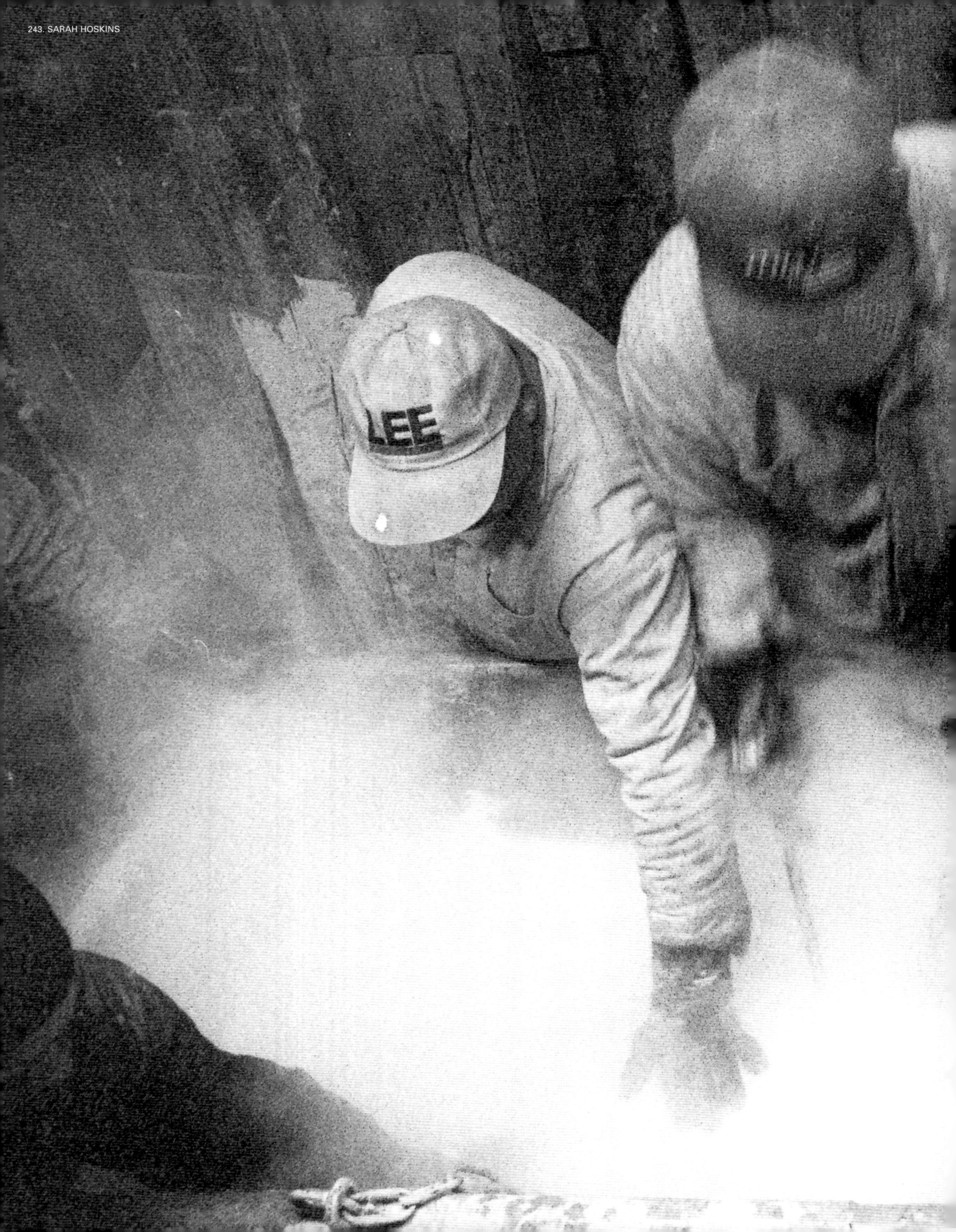

243. SARAH HOSKINS

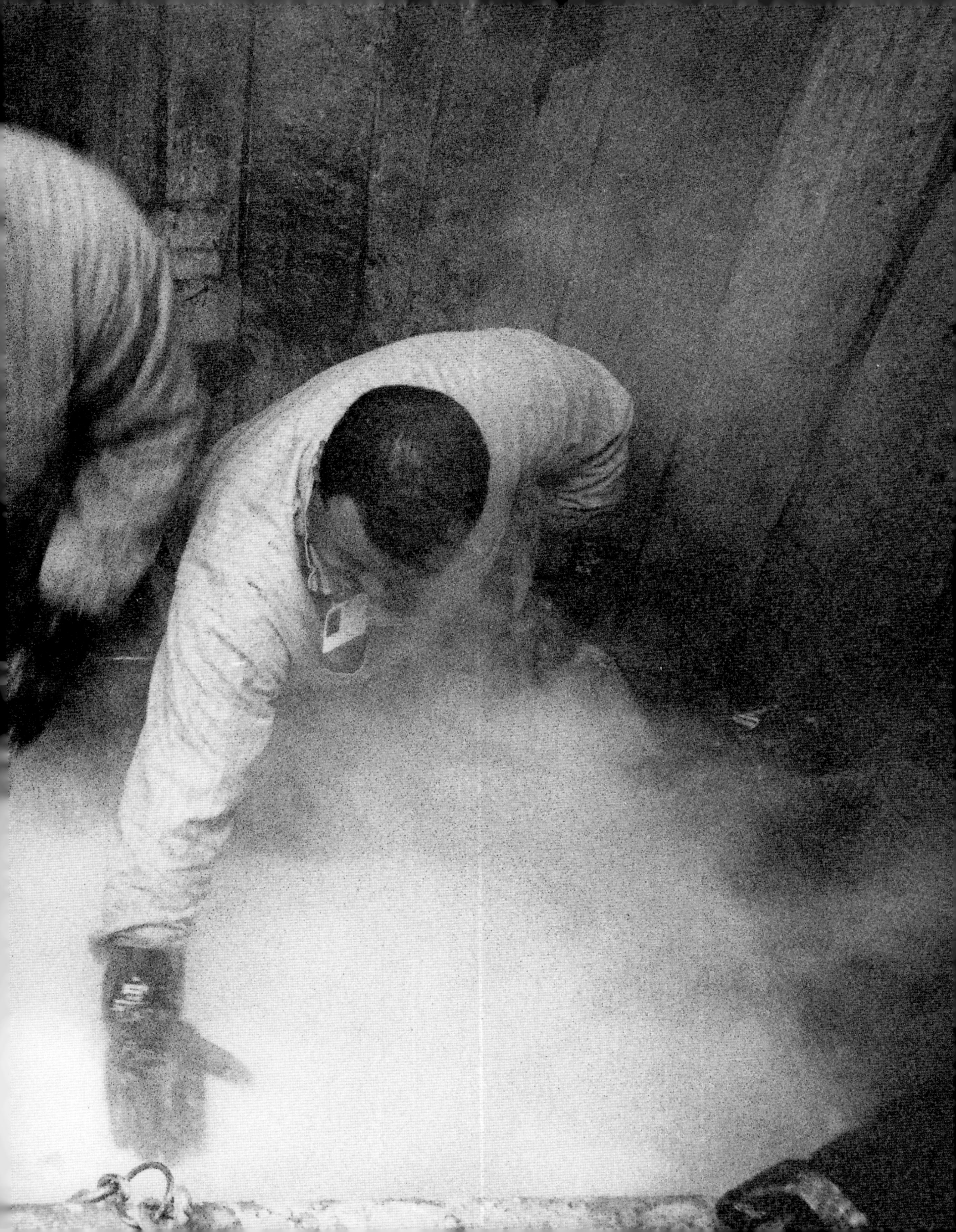

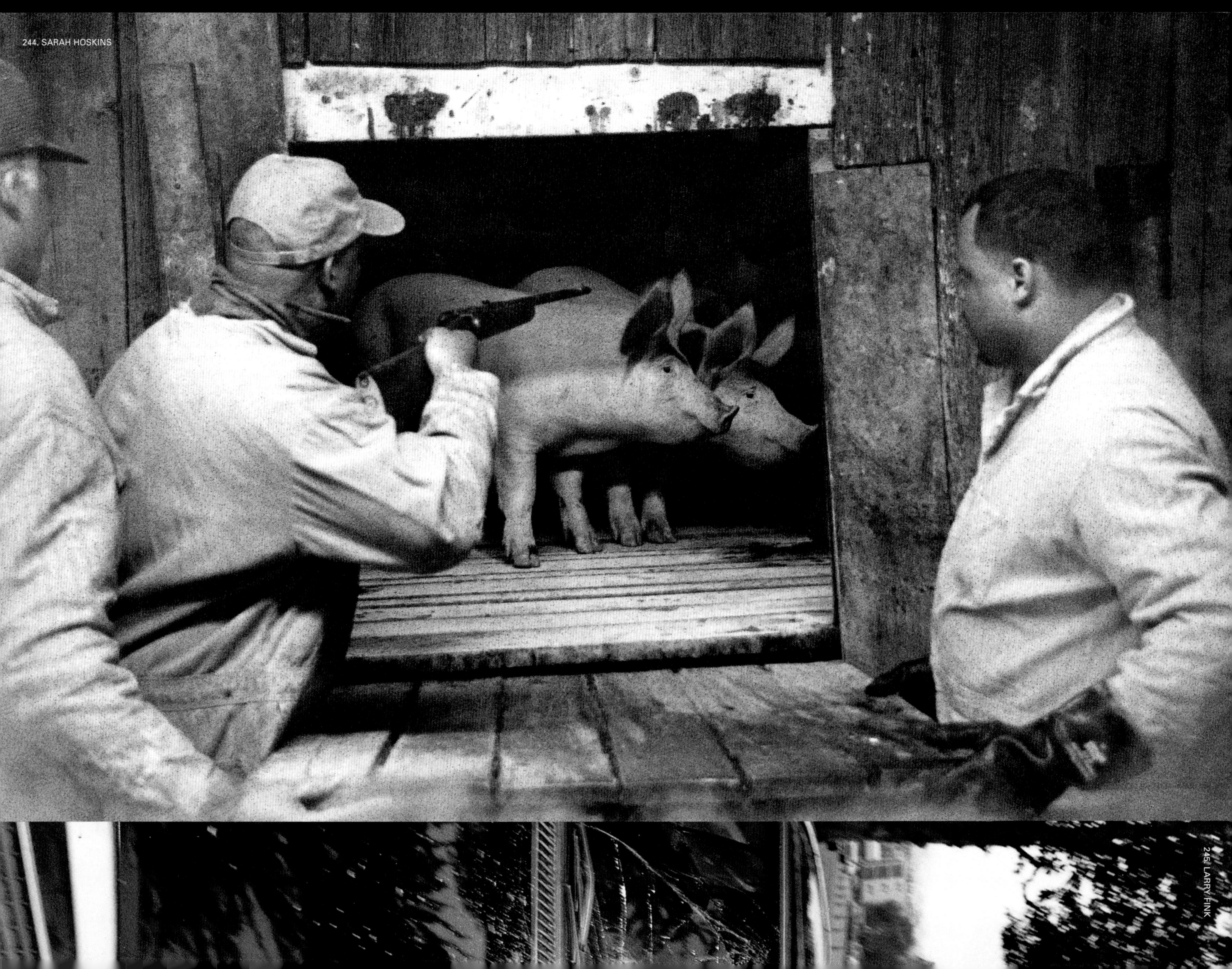

244. SARAH HOSKINS

245. LARRY FINK

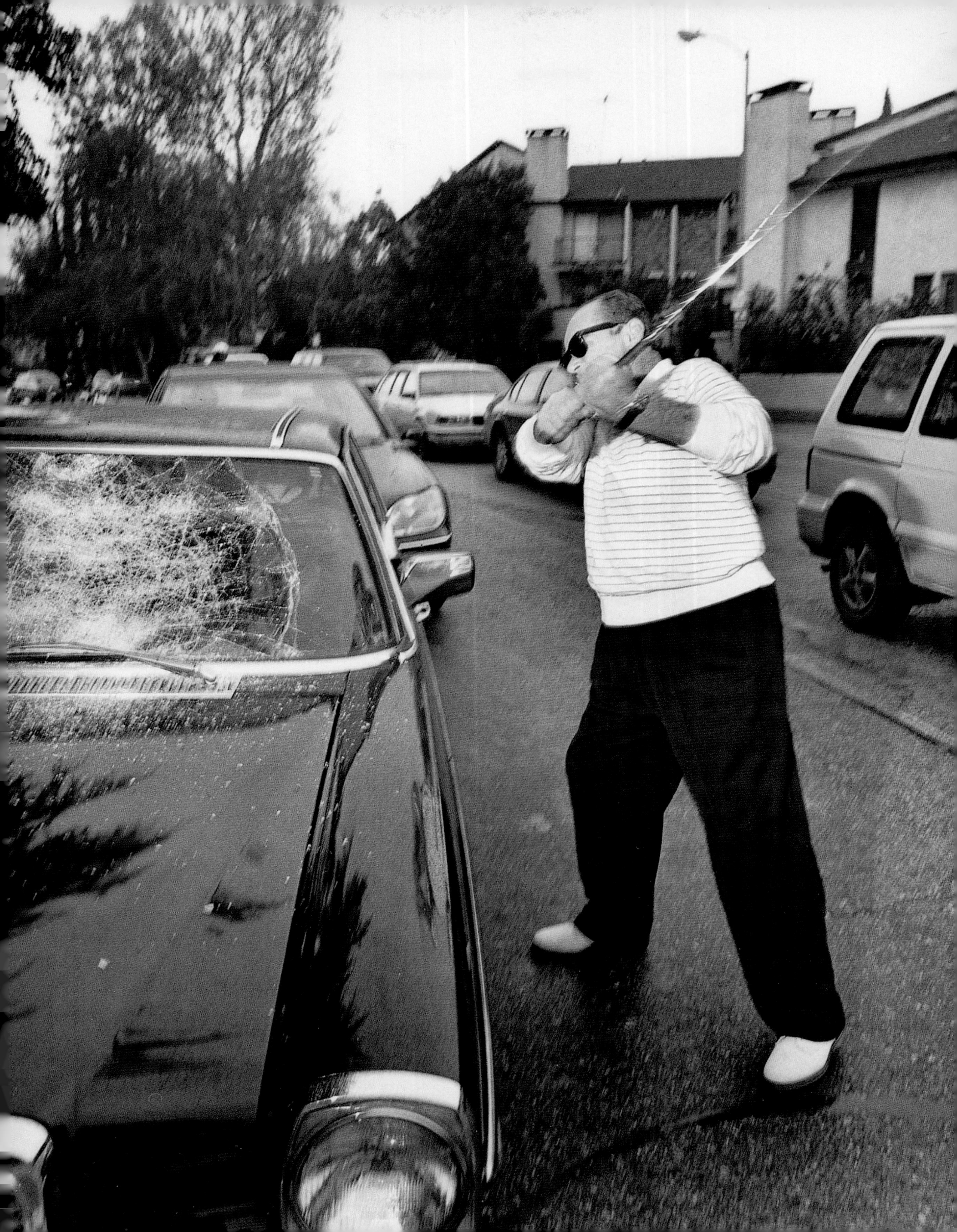

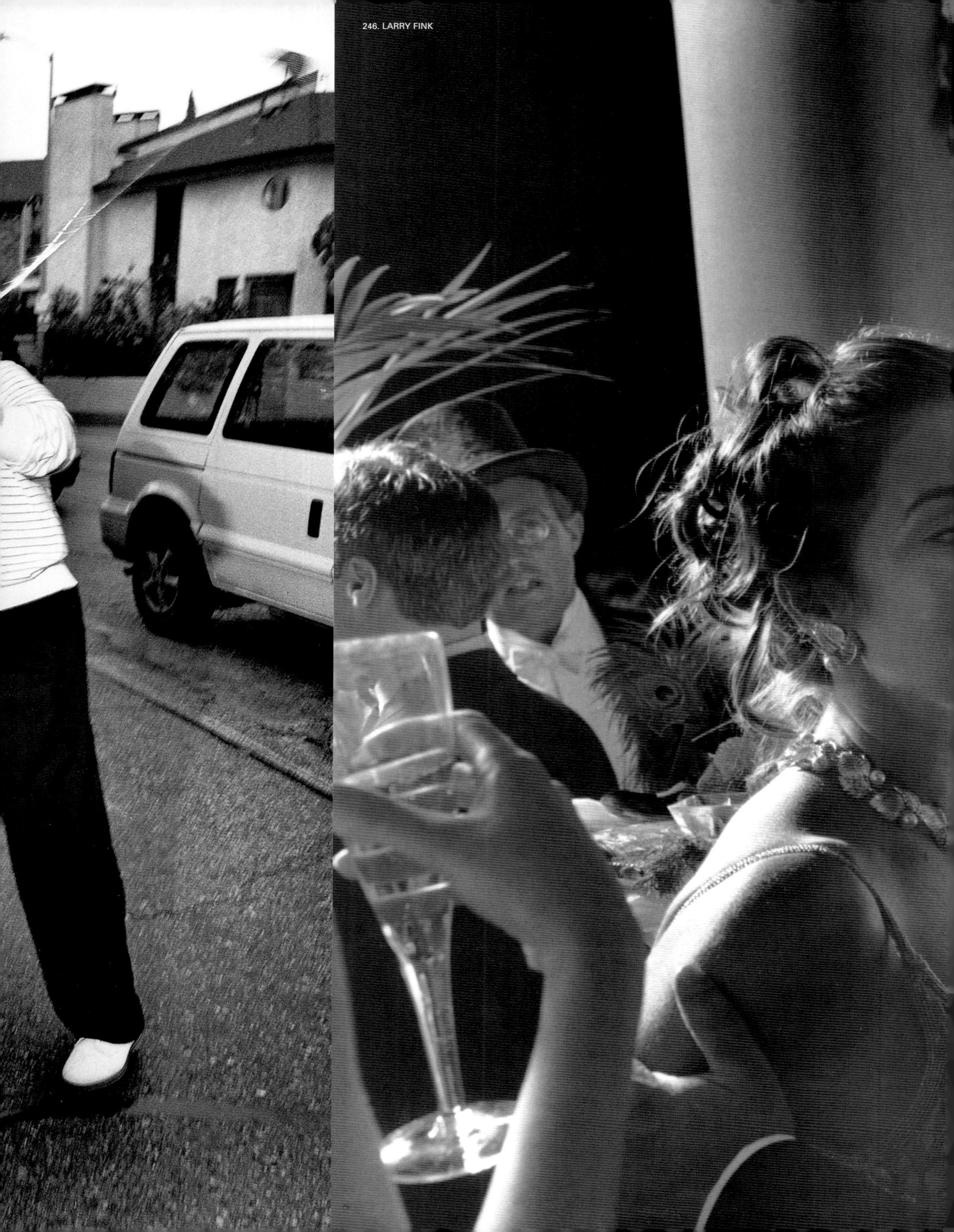

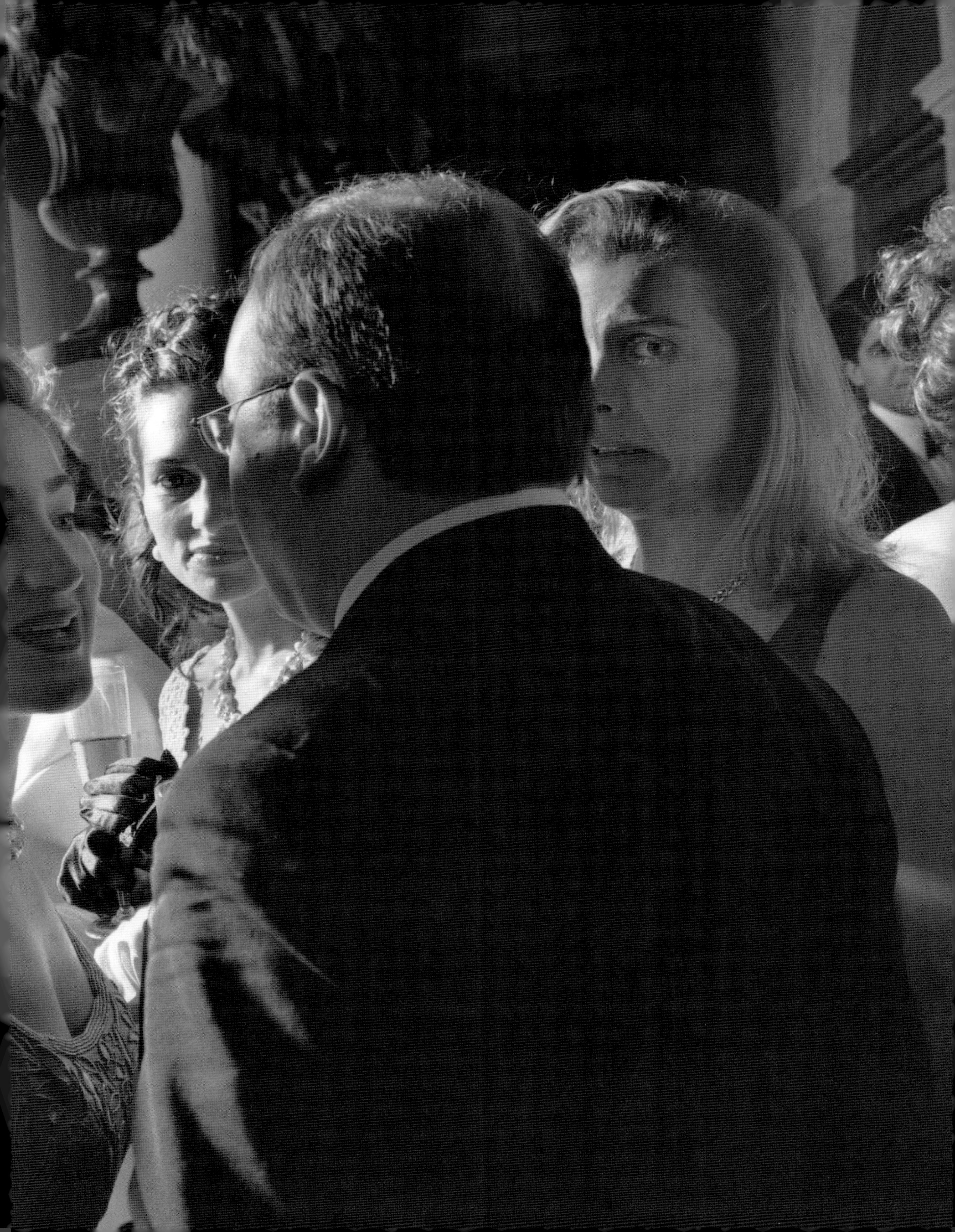

247. LARRY FINK

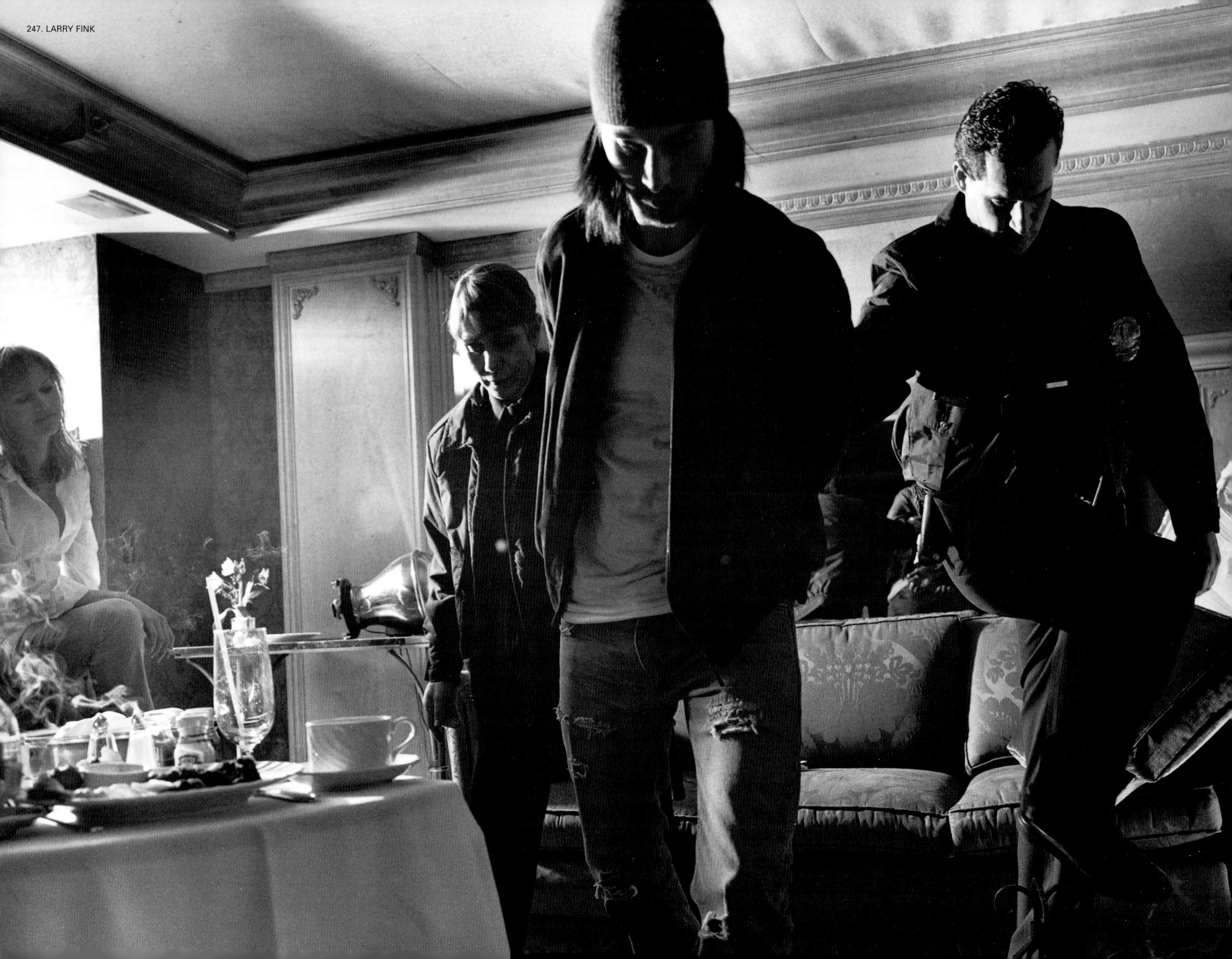

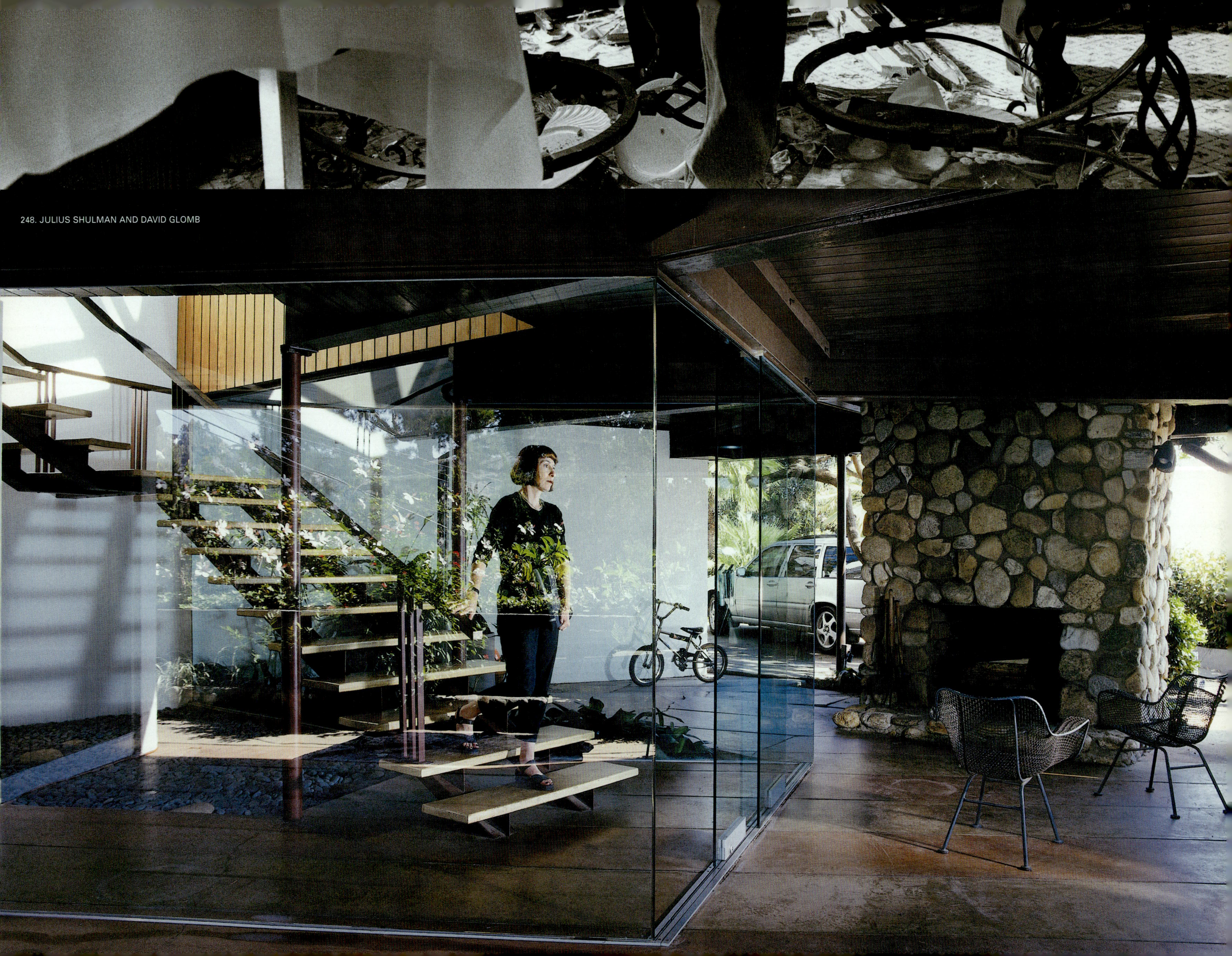

248. JULIUS SHULMAN AND DAVID GLOMB

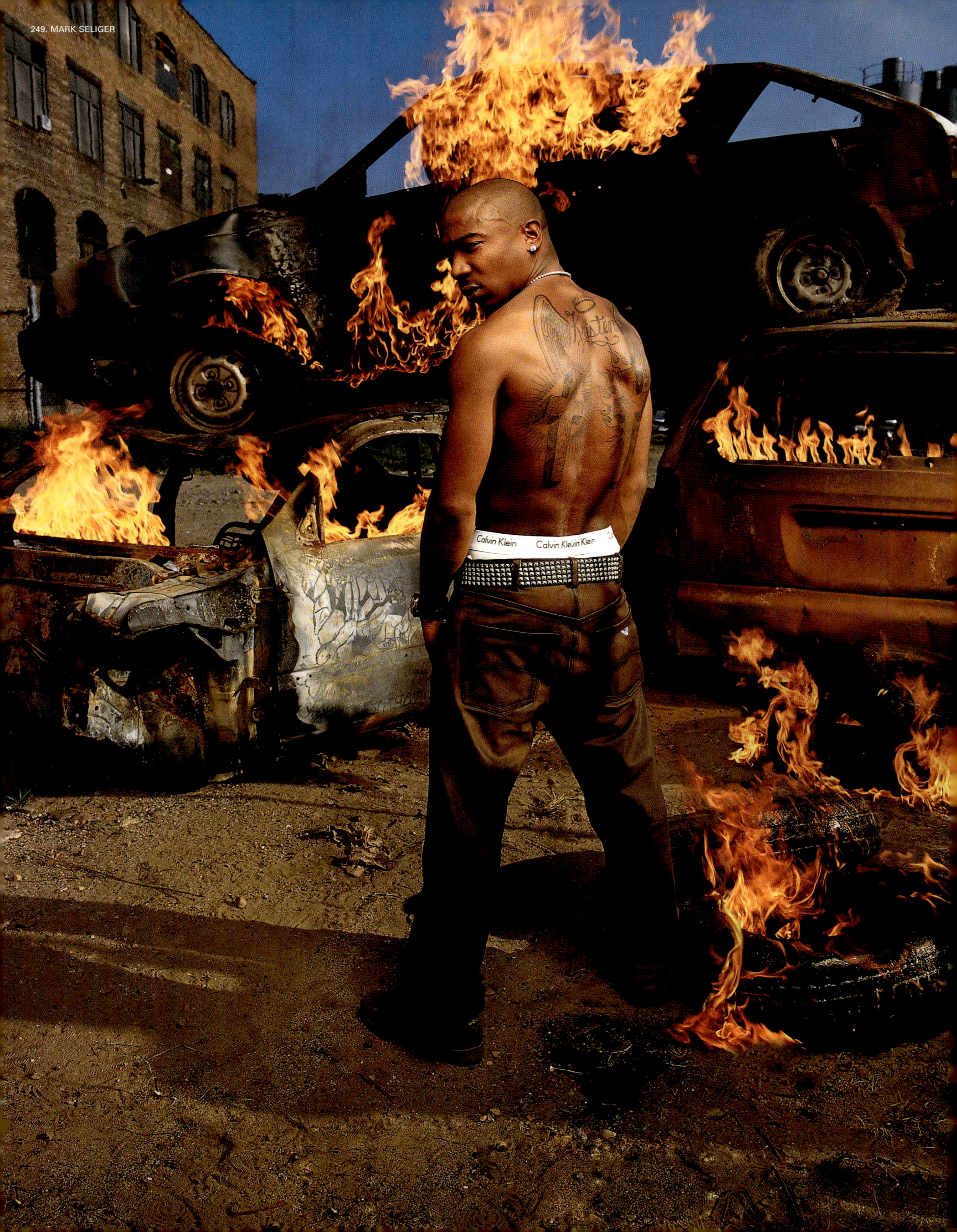

249. MARK SELIGER

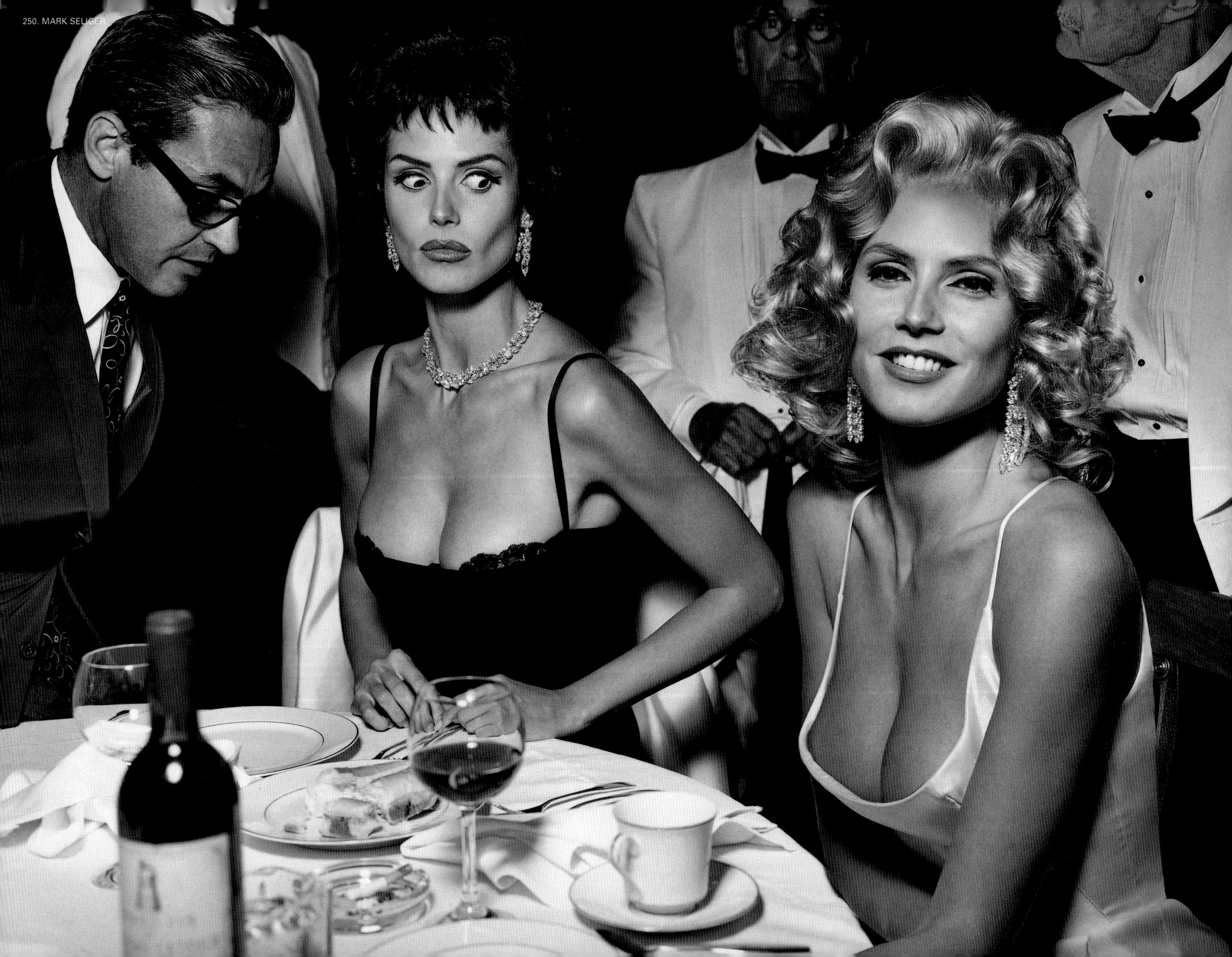

250. MARK SELIGER

251. JOHN MIDGLEY

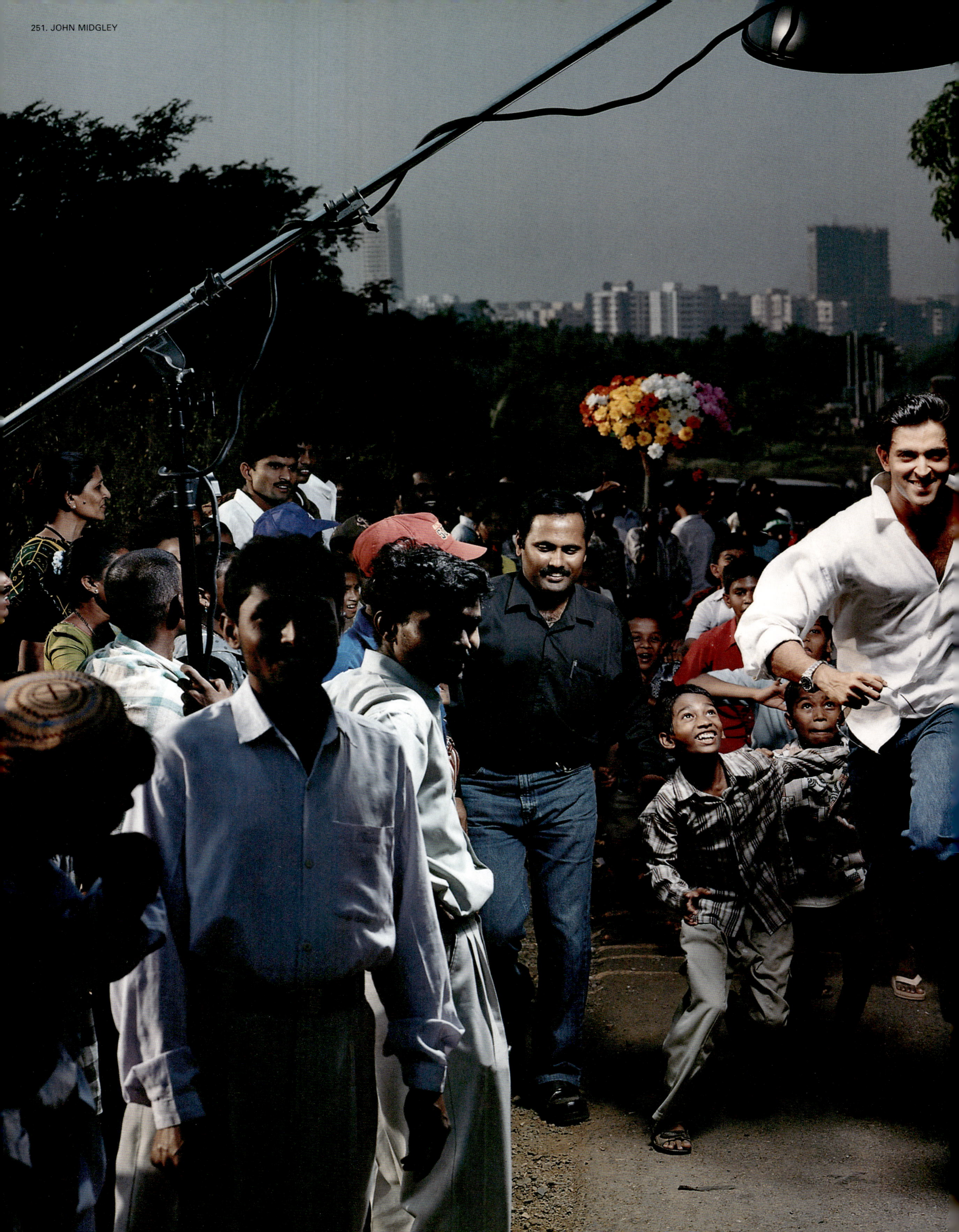

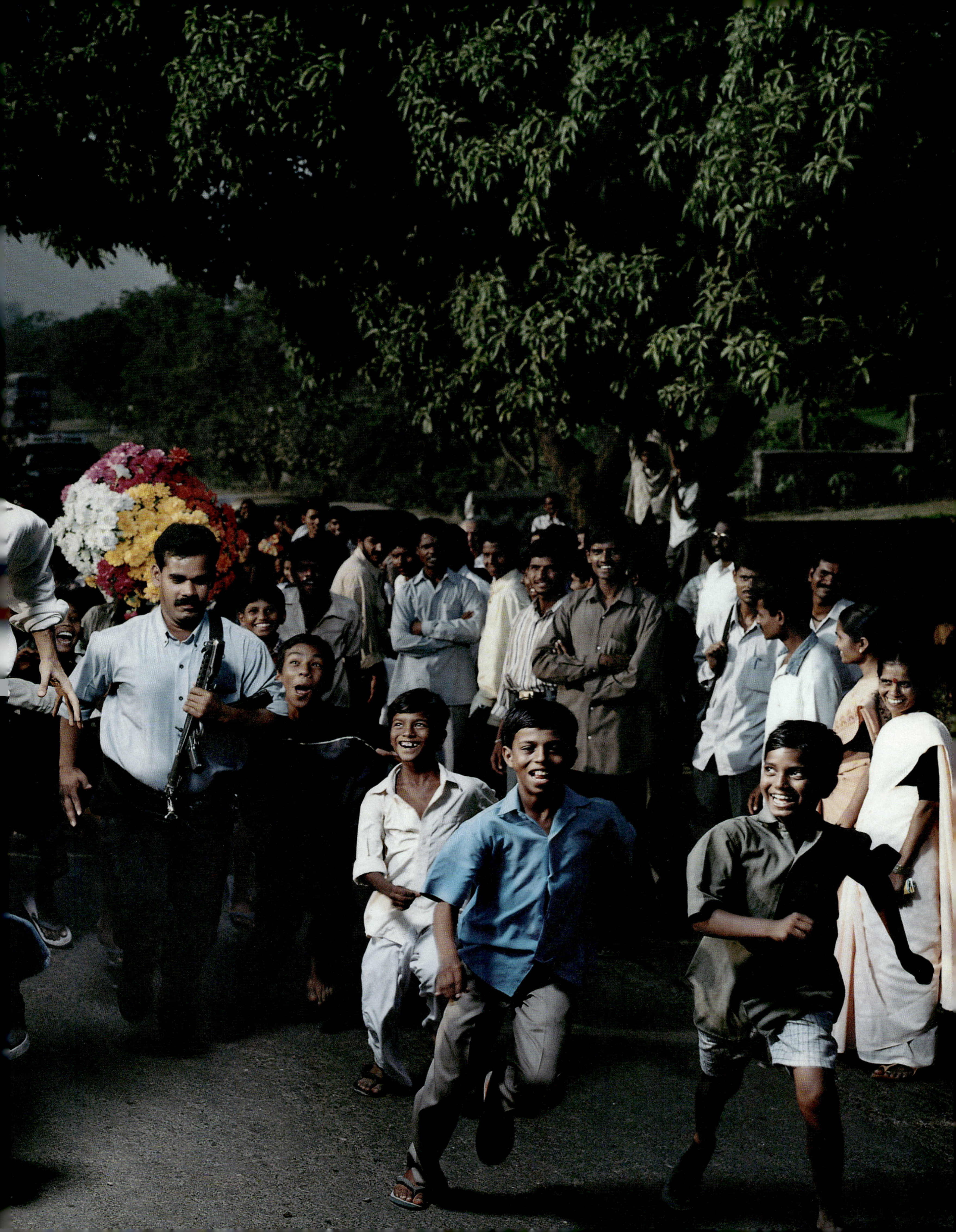

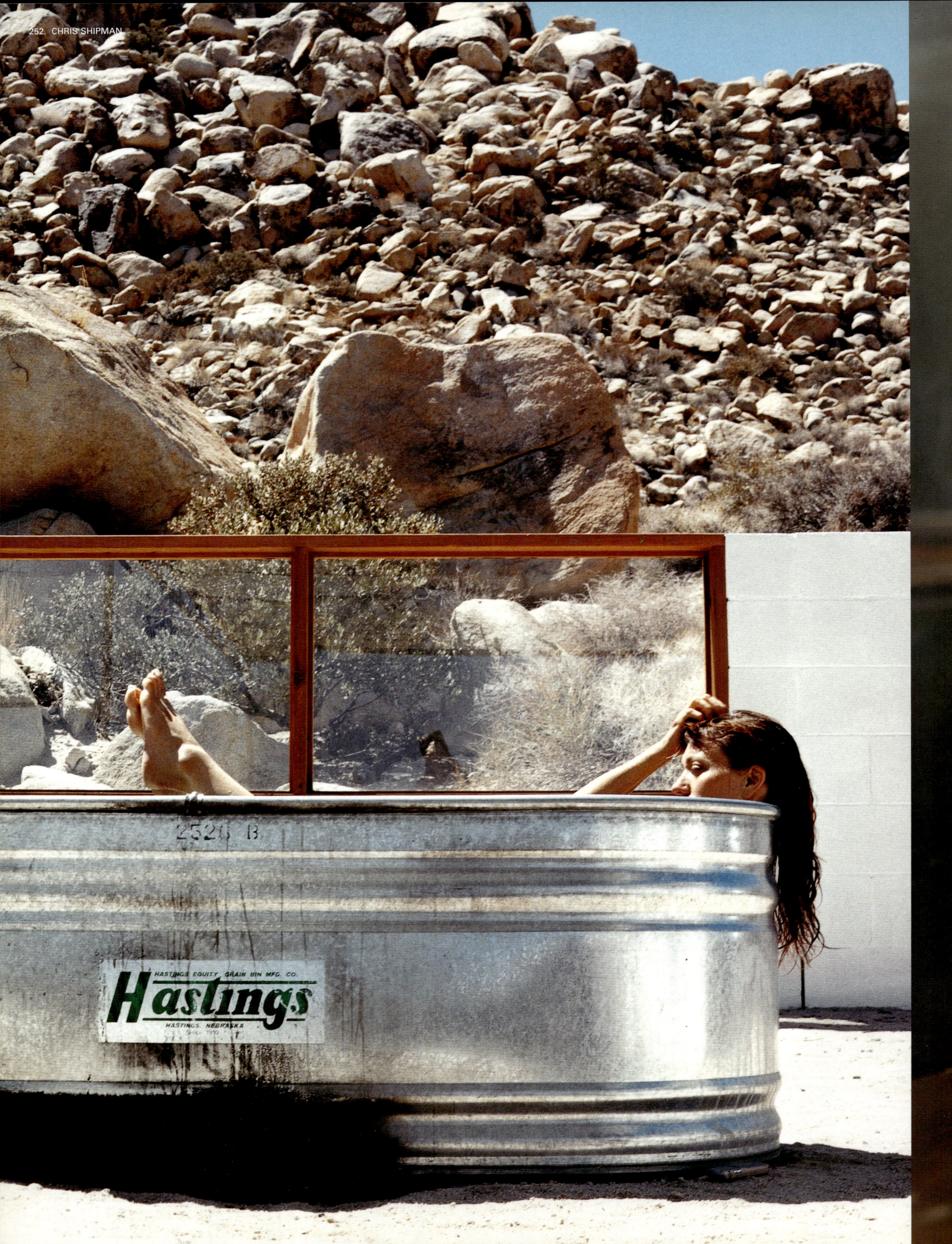
2526 B
HASTINGS EQUITY GRAIN BIN MFG. CO.
Hastings
HASTINGS, NEBRASKA

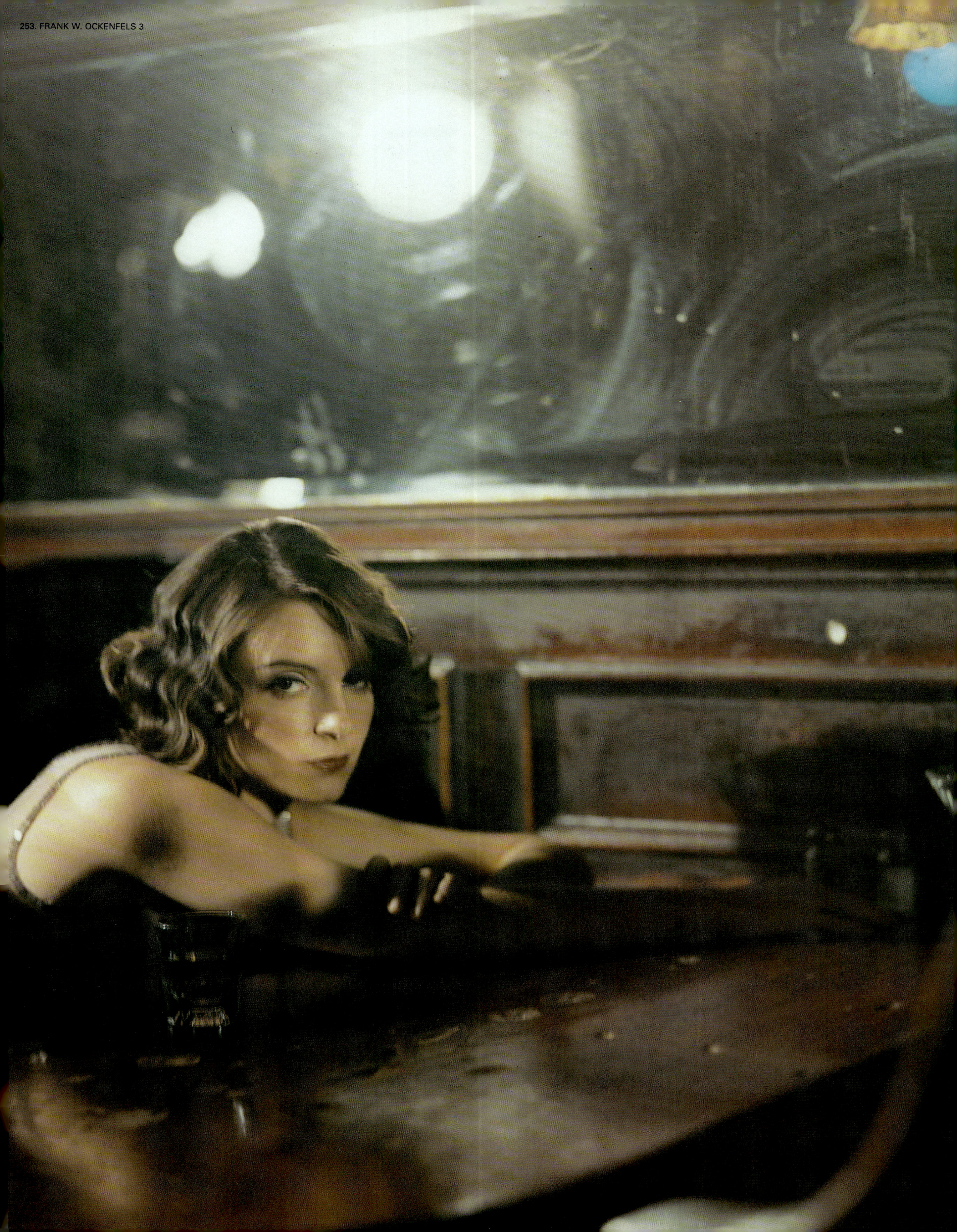

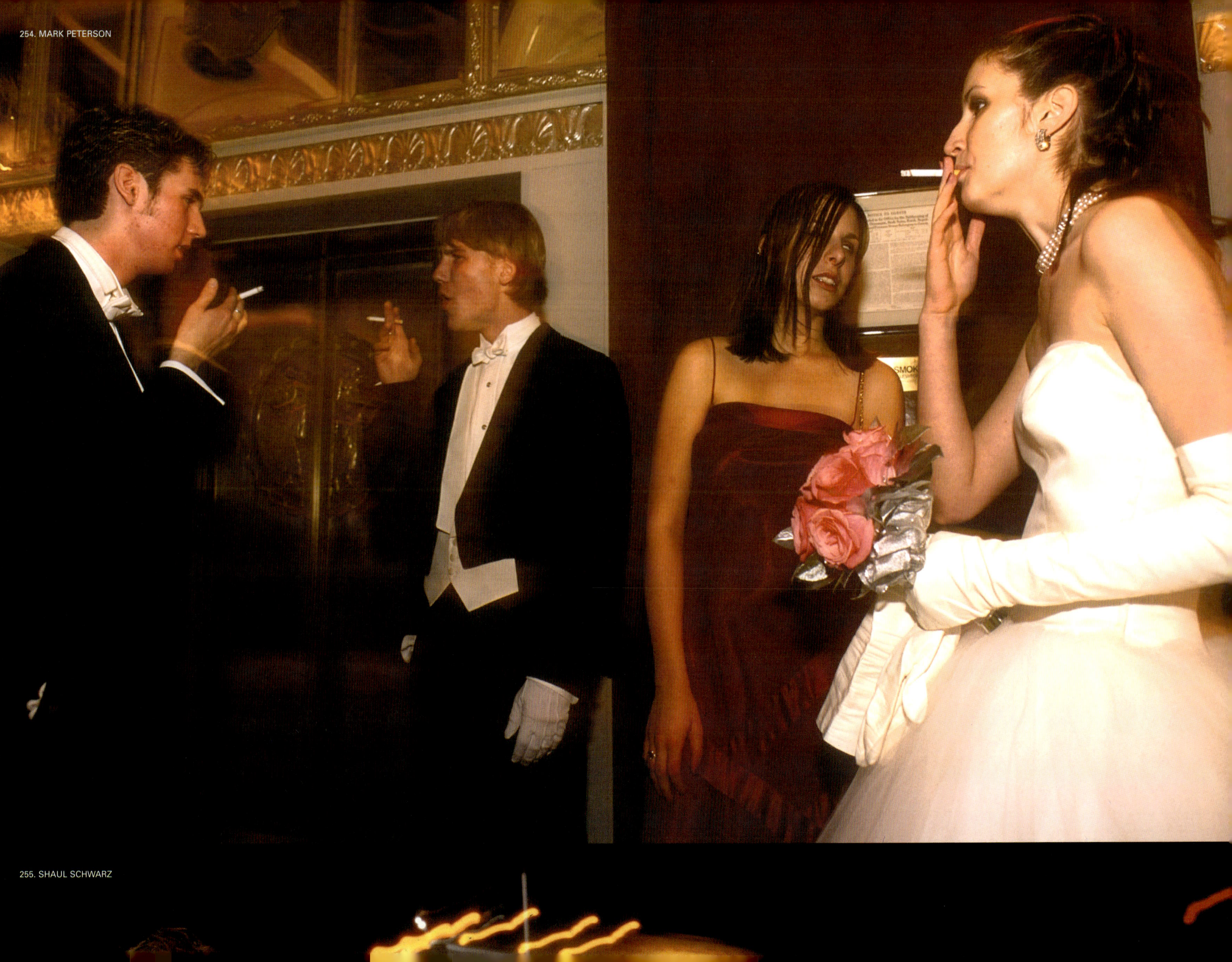

254. MARK PETERSON

255. SHAUL SCHWARZ

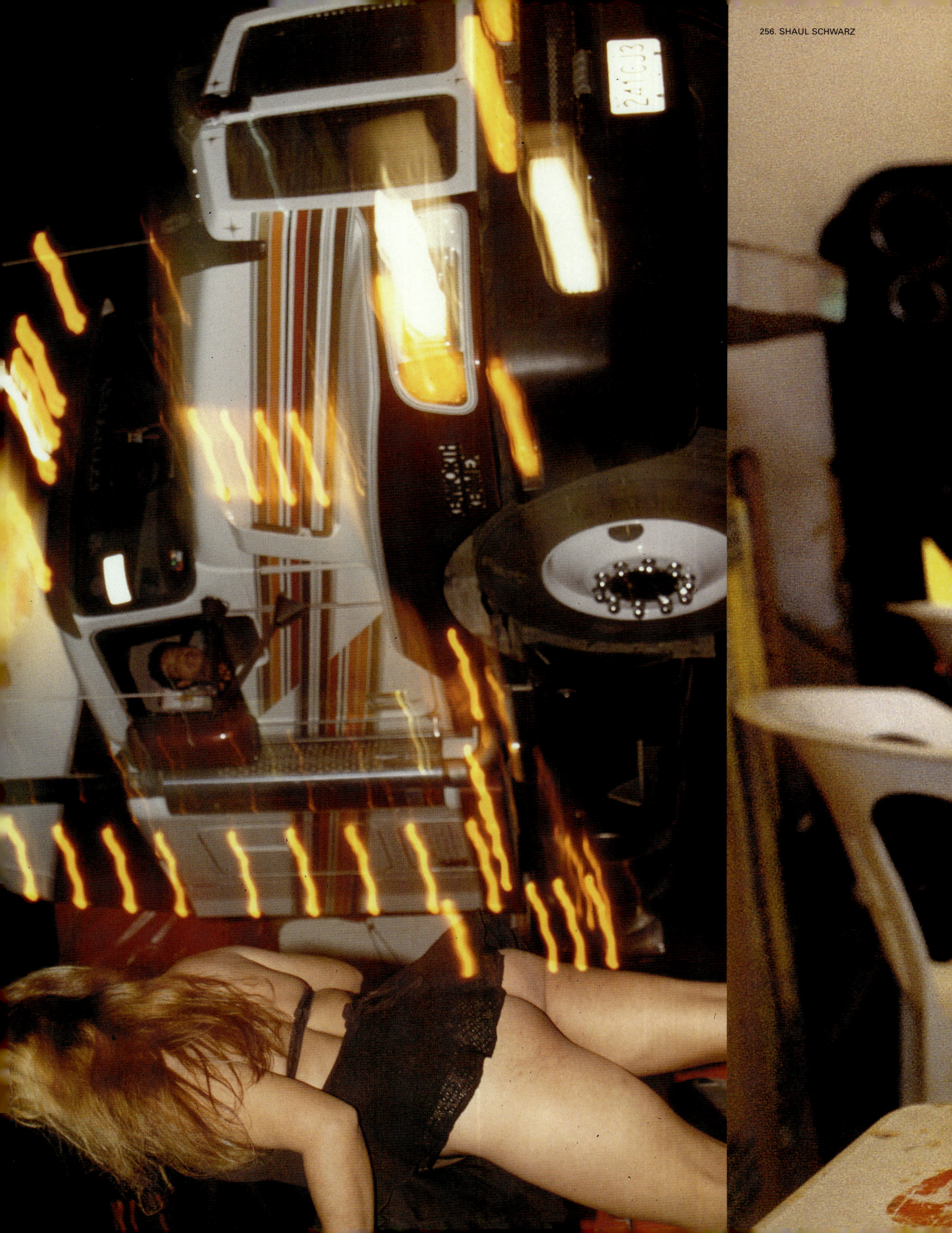

256. SHAUL SCHWARZ

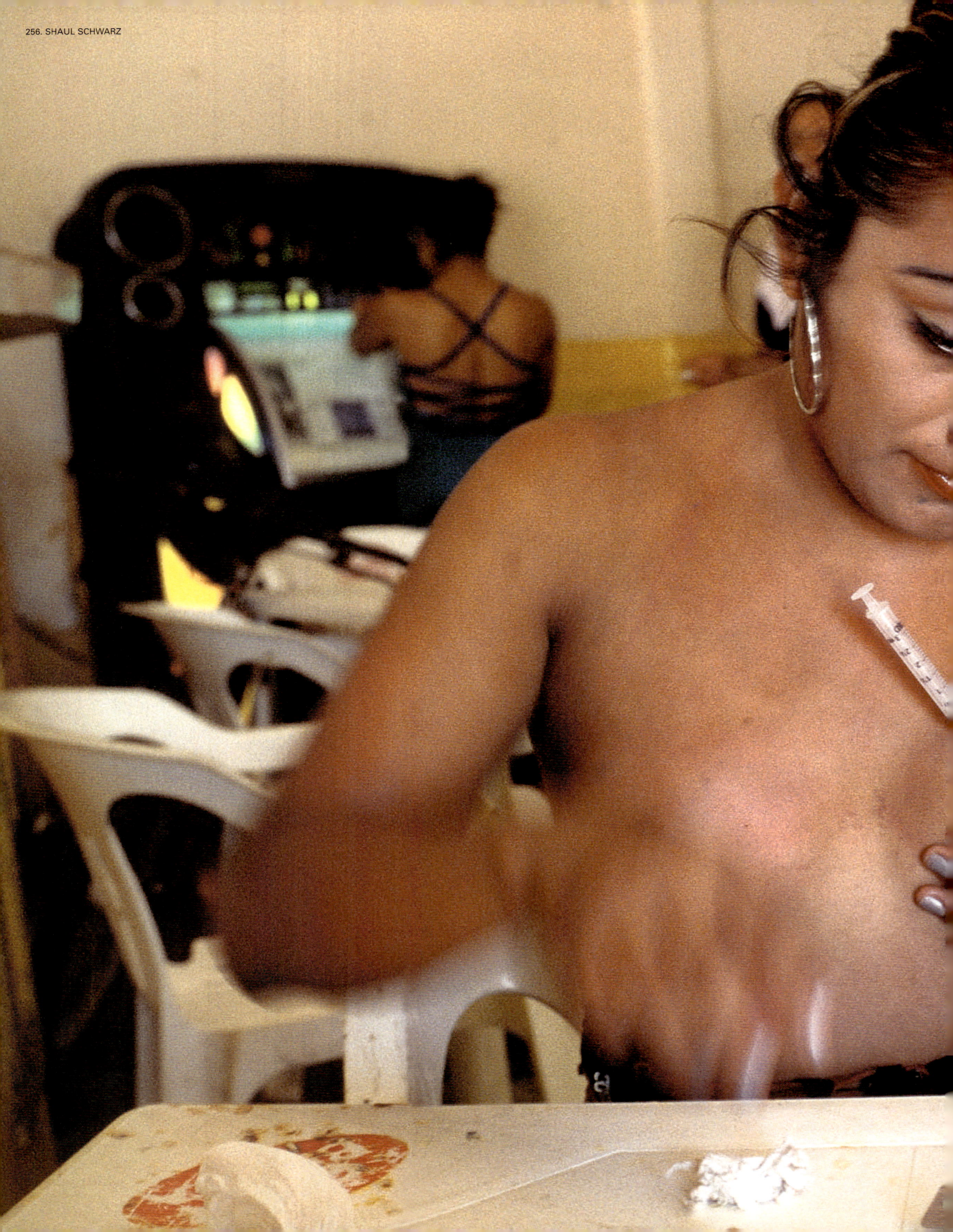

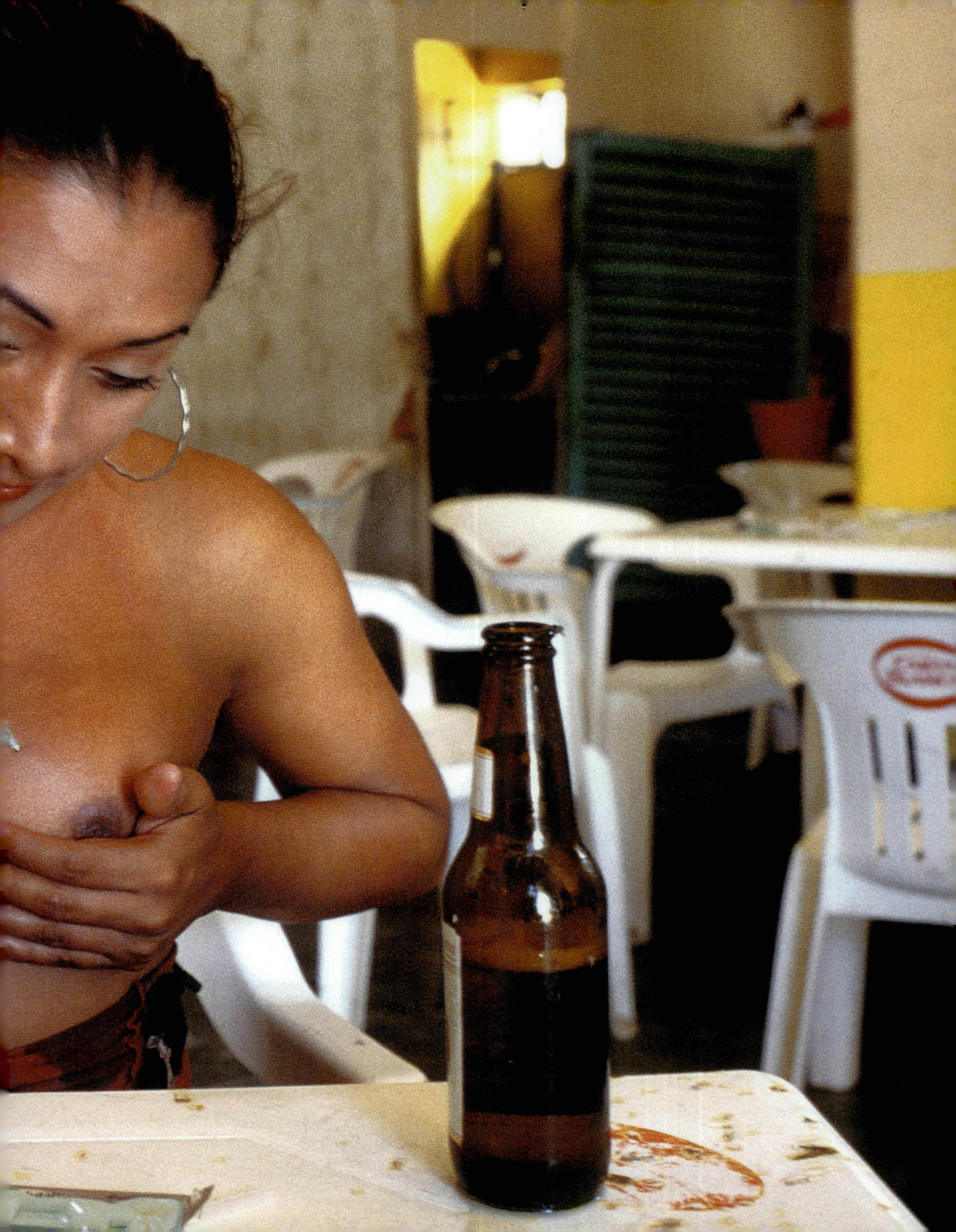

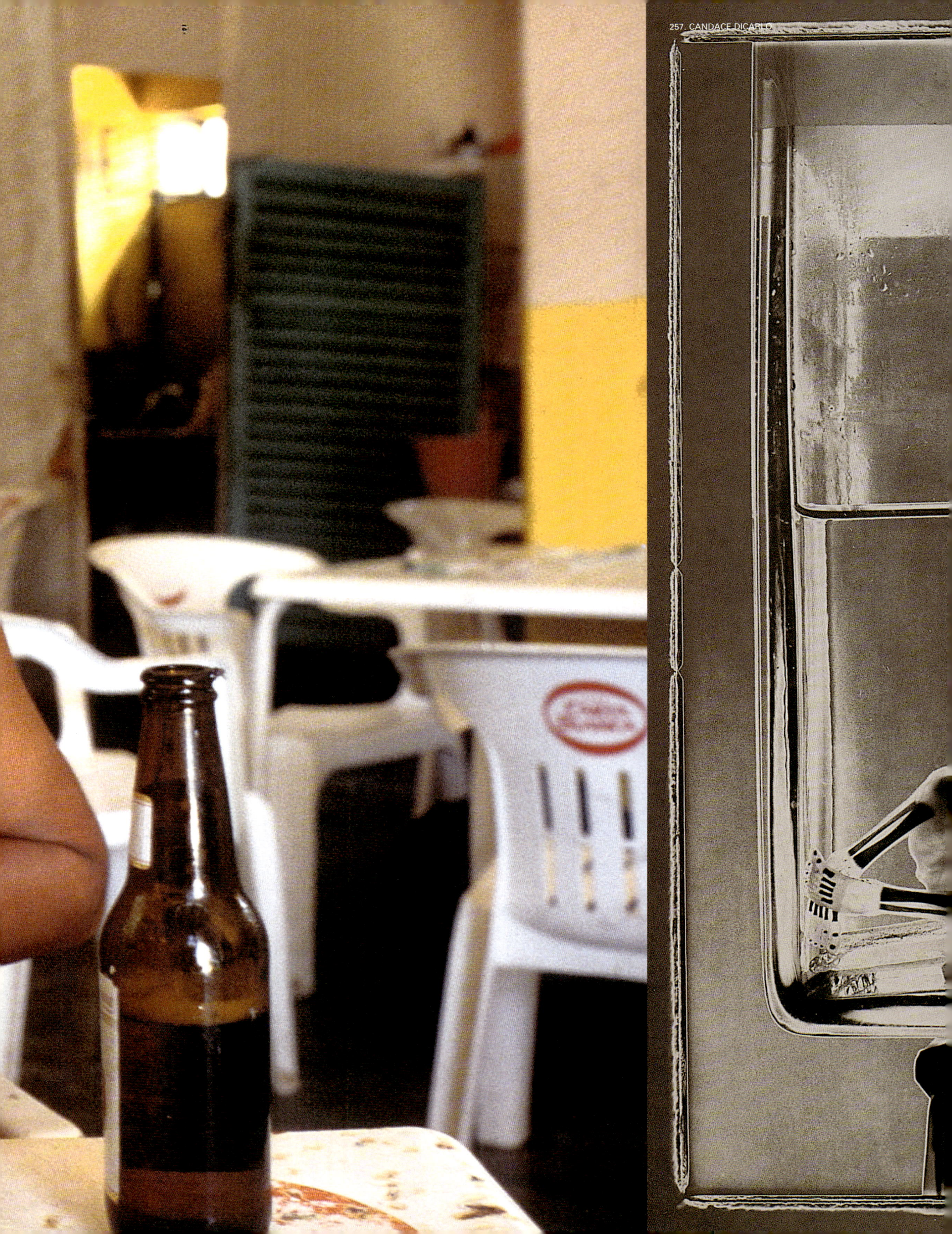

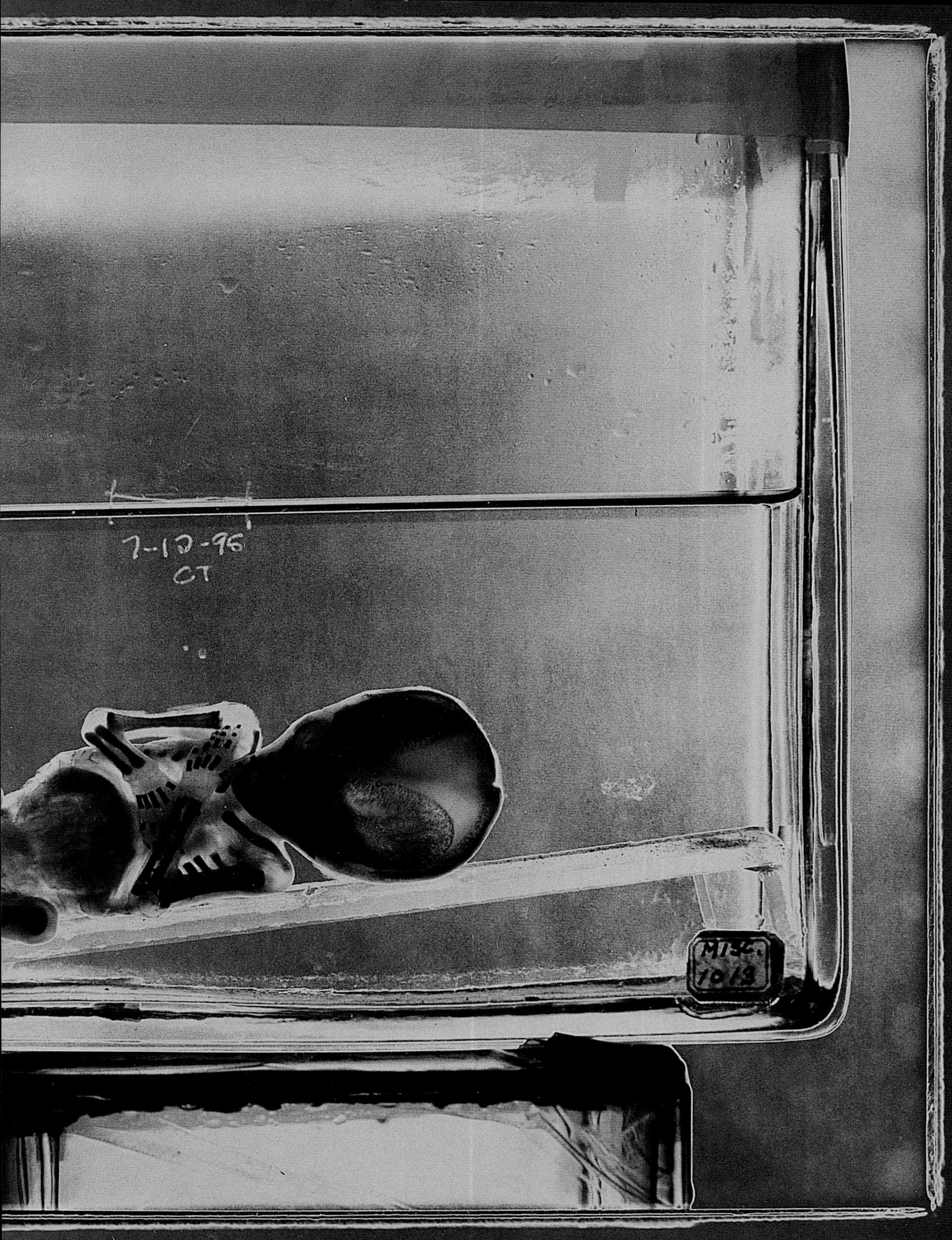
7-12-95
CT
MISC.
1019

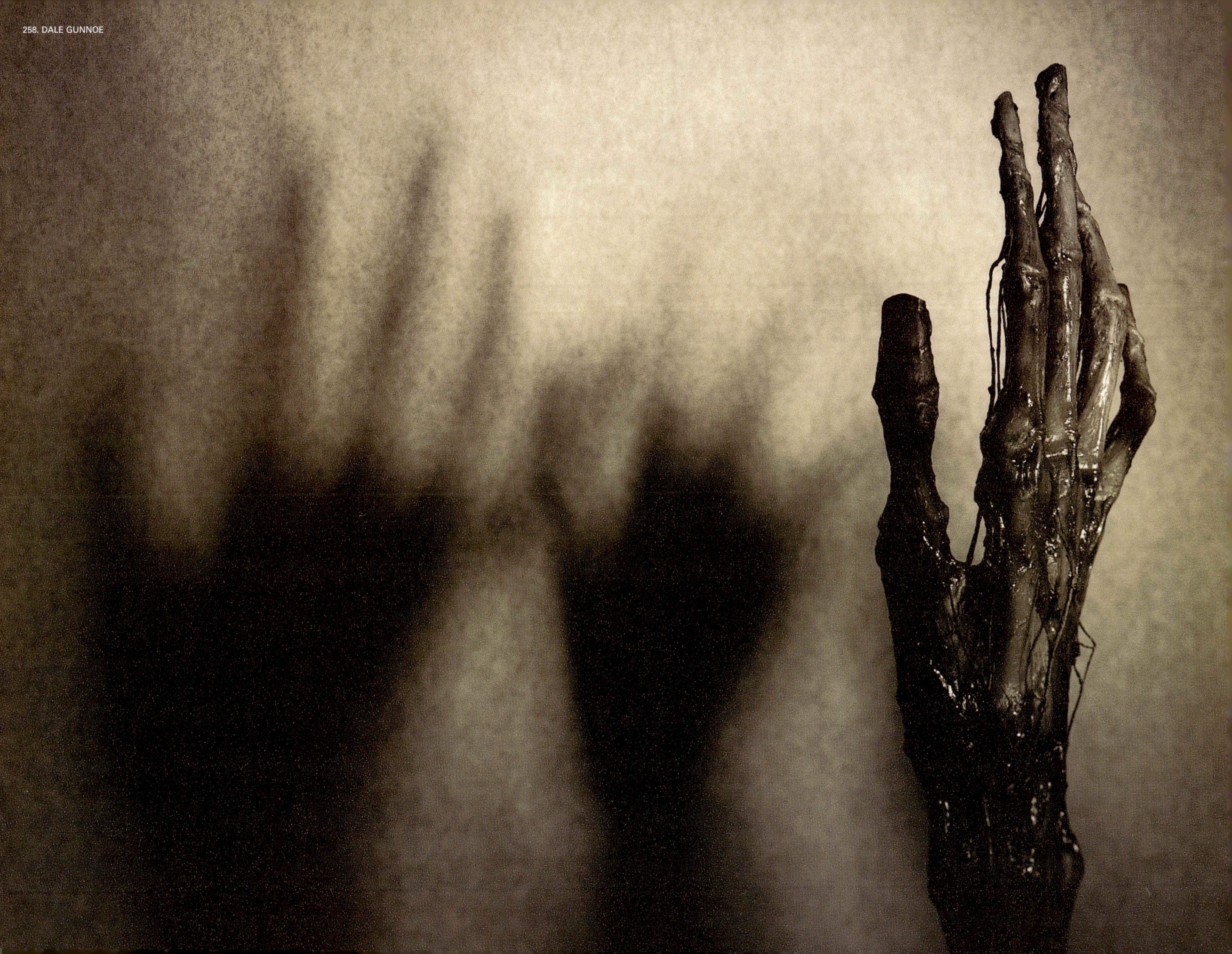

258. DALE GUNNOE

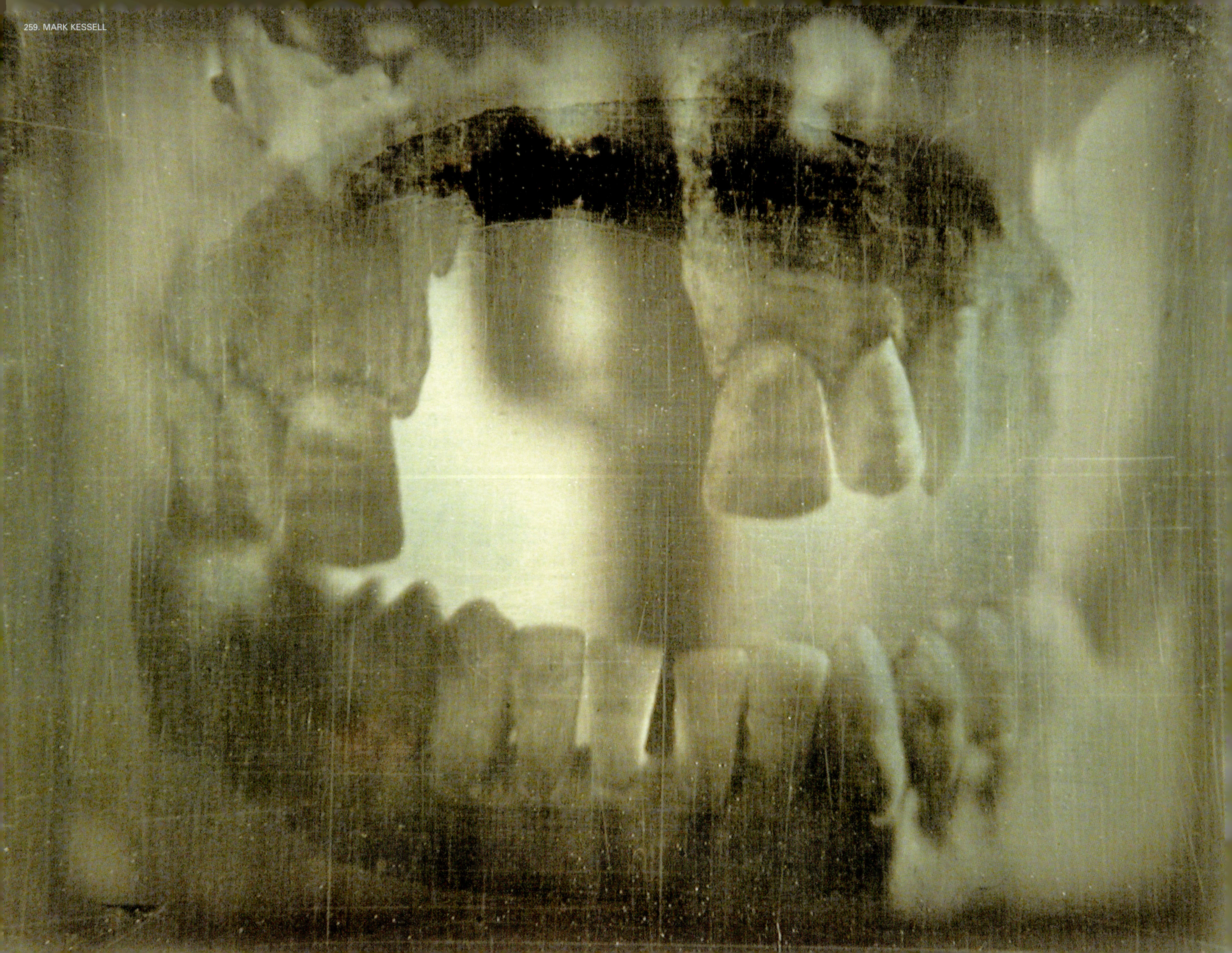

259. MARK KESSELL

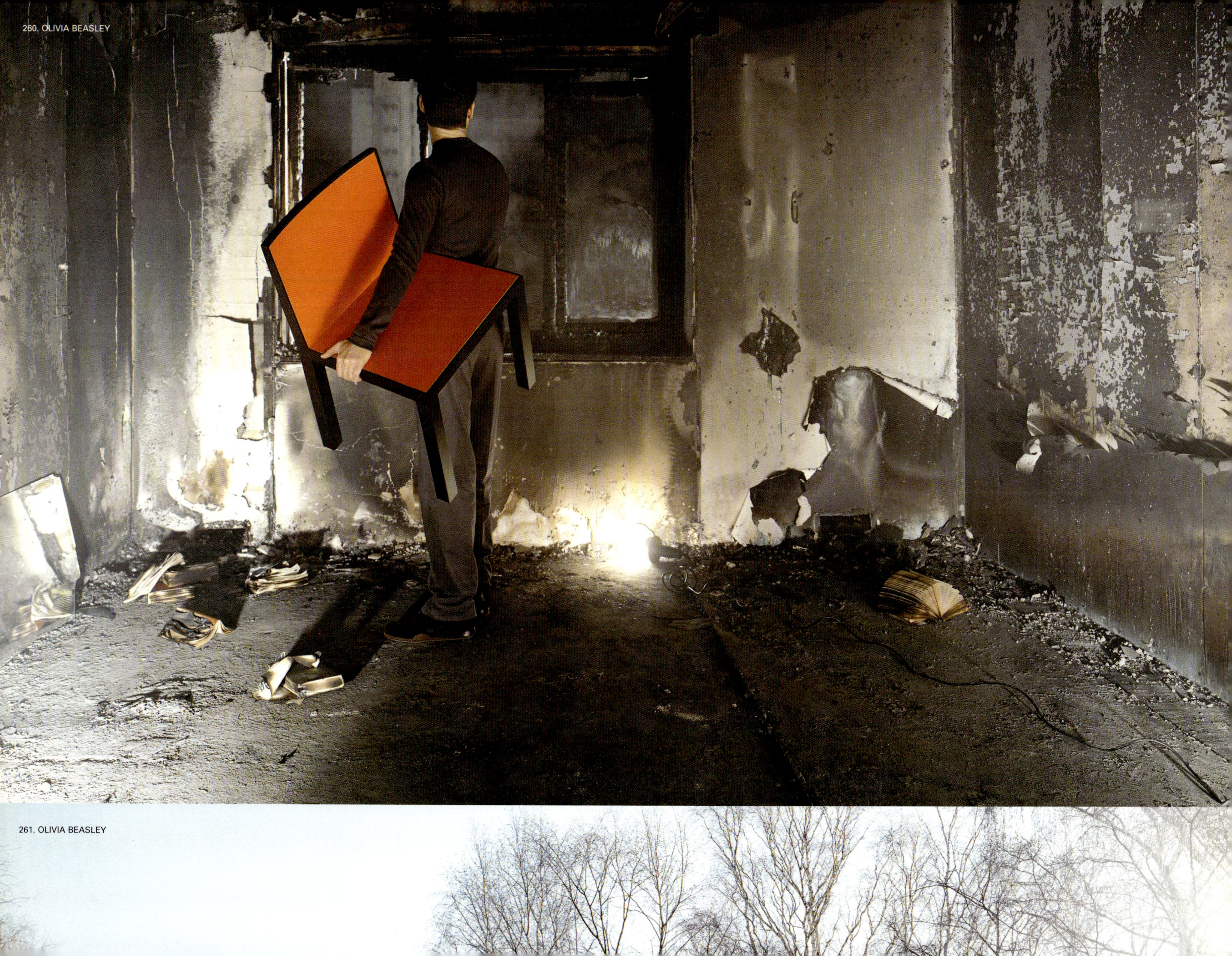

260. OLIVIA BEASLEY

261. OLIVIA BEASLEY

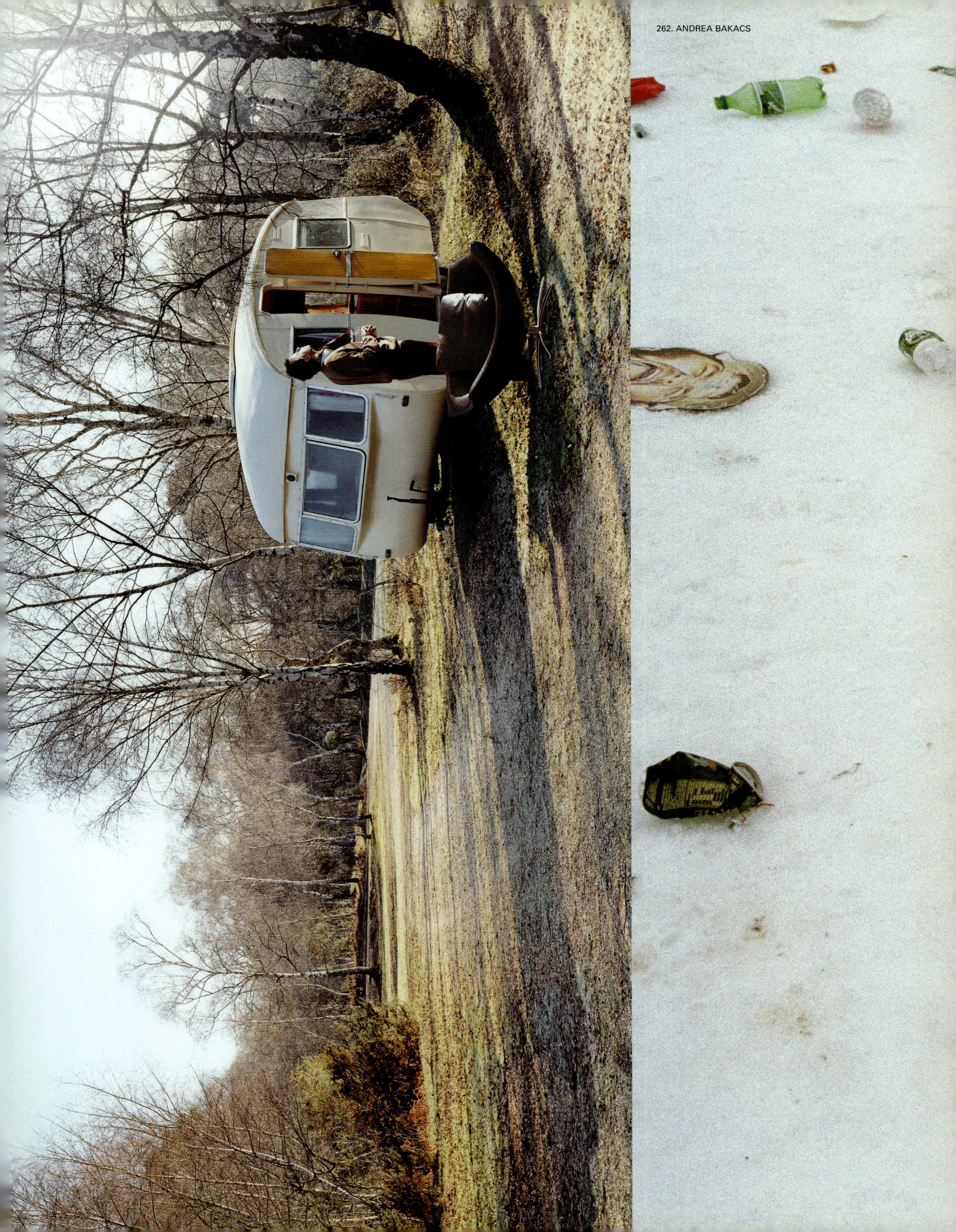

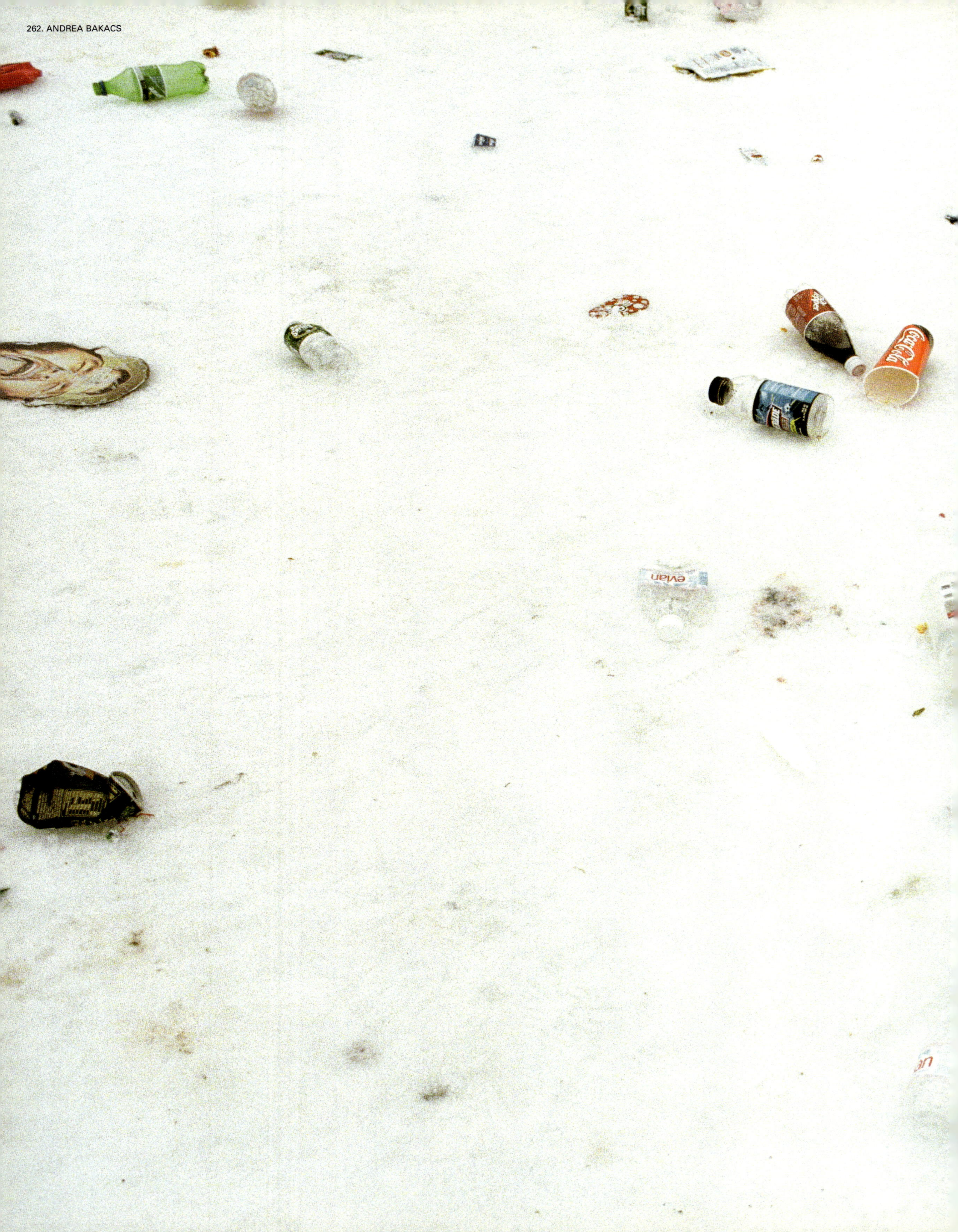
Coca-Cola
evian

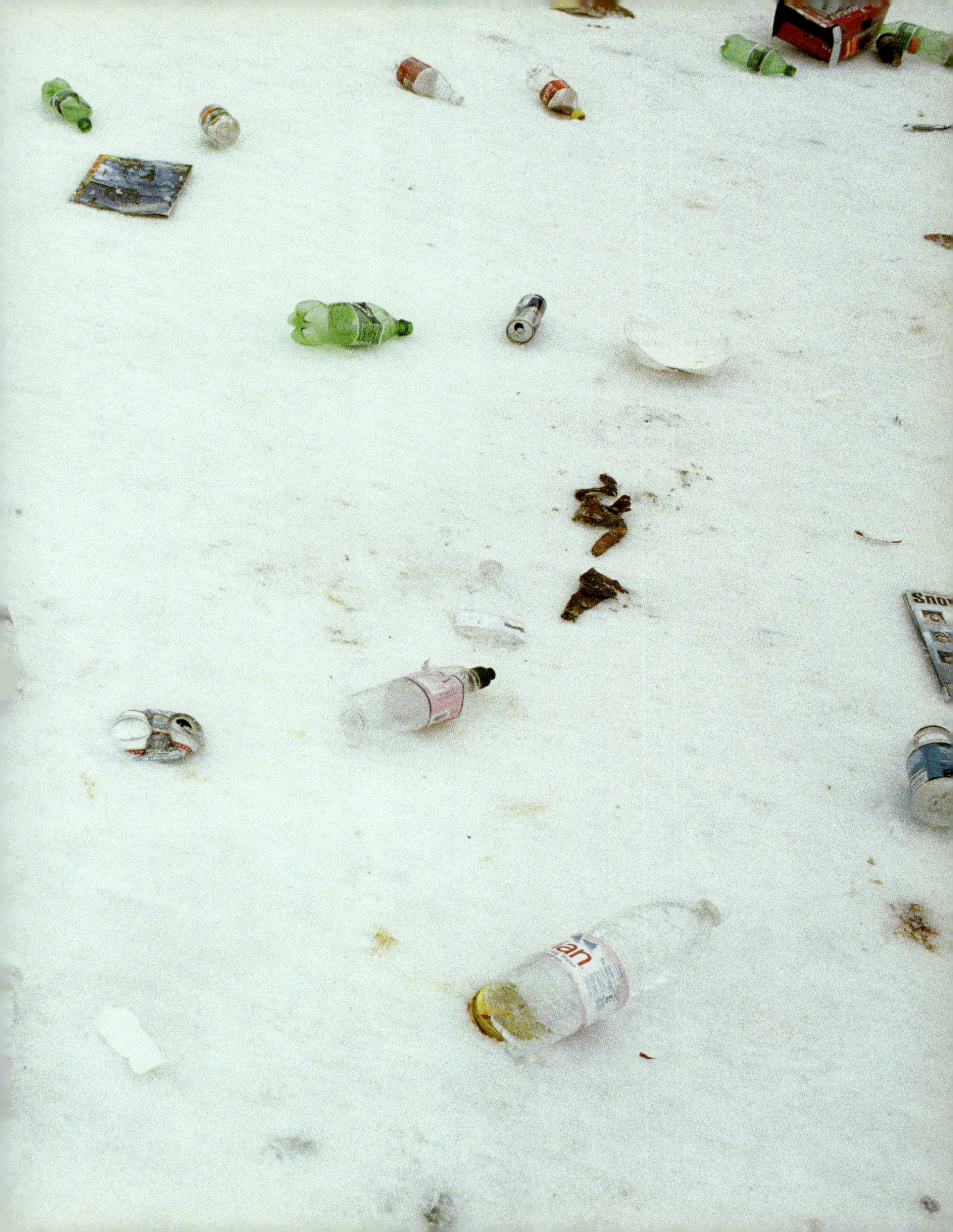

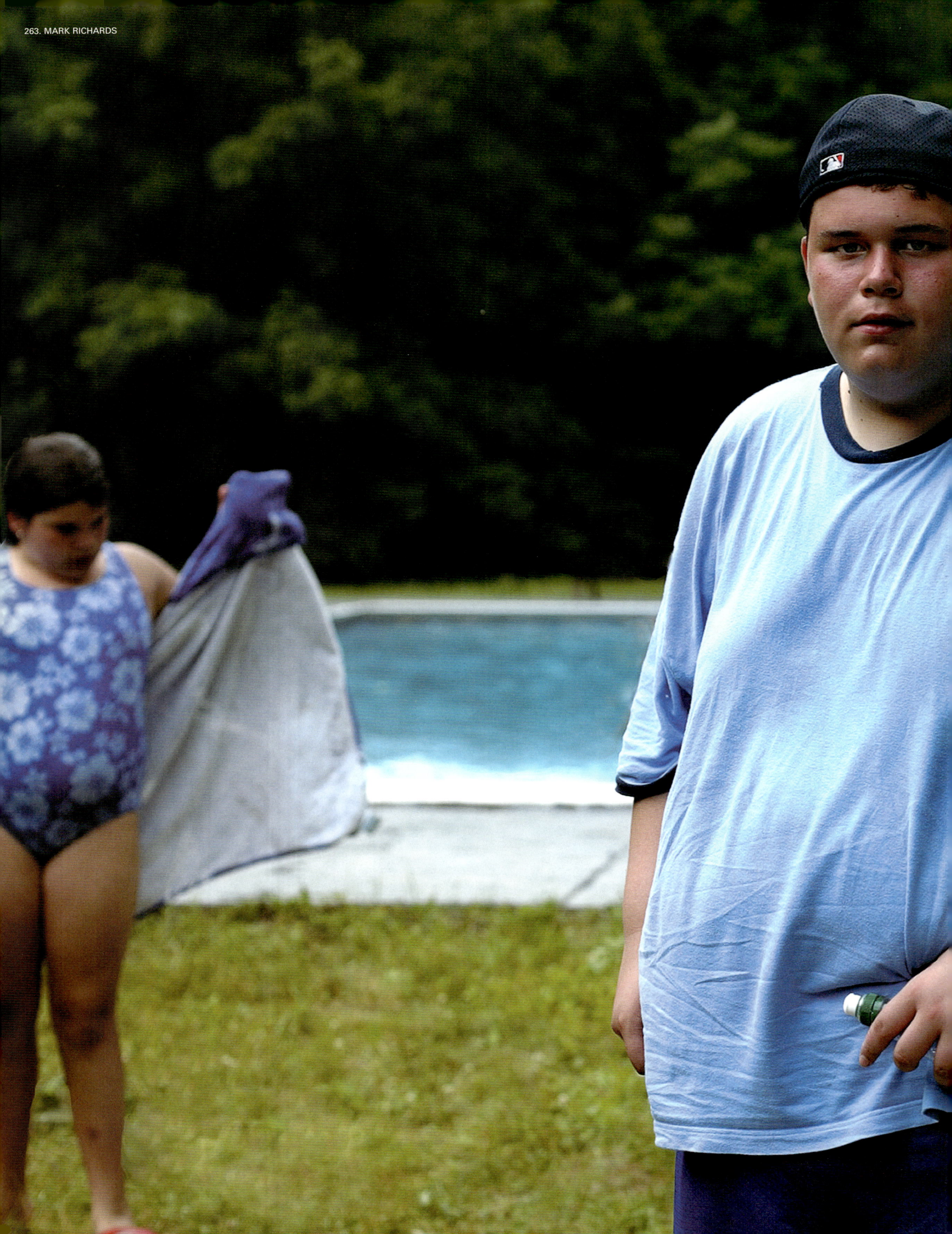

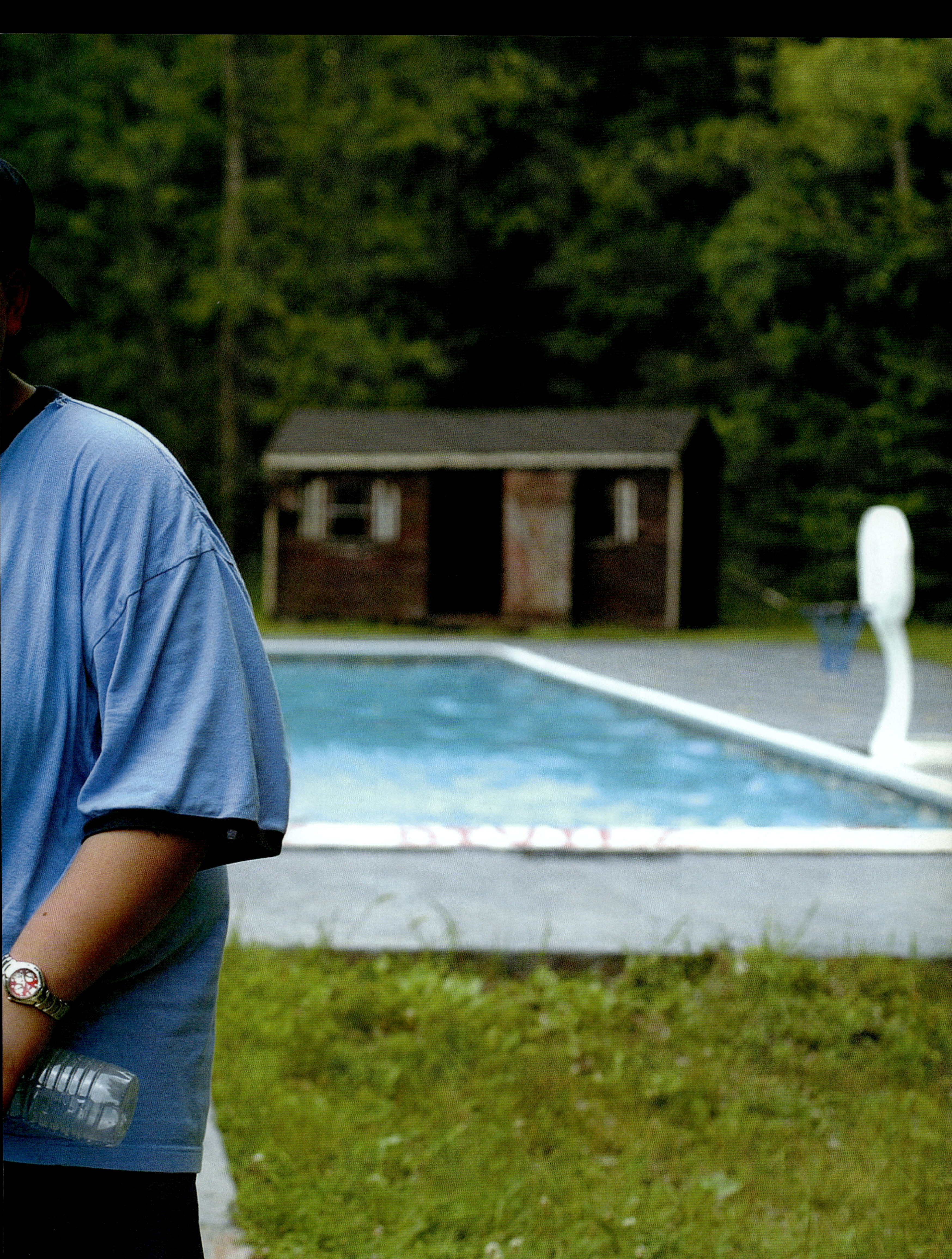

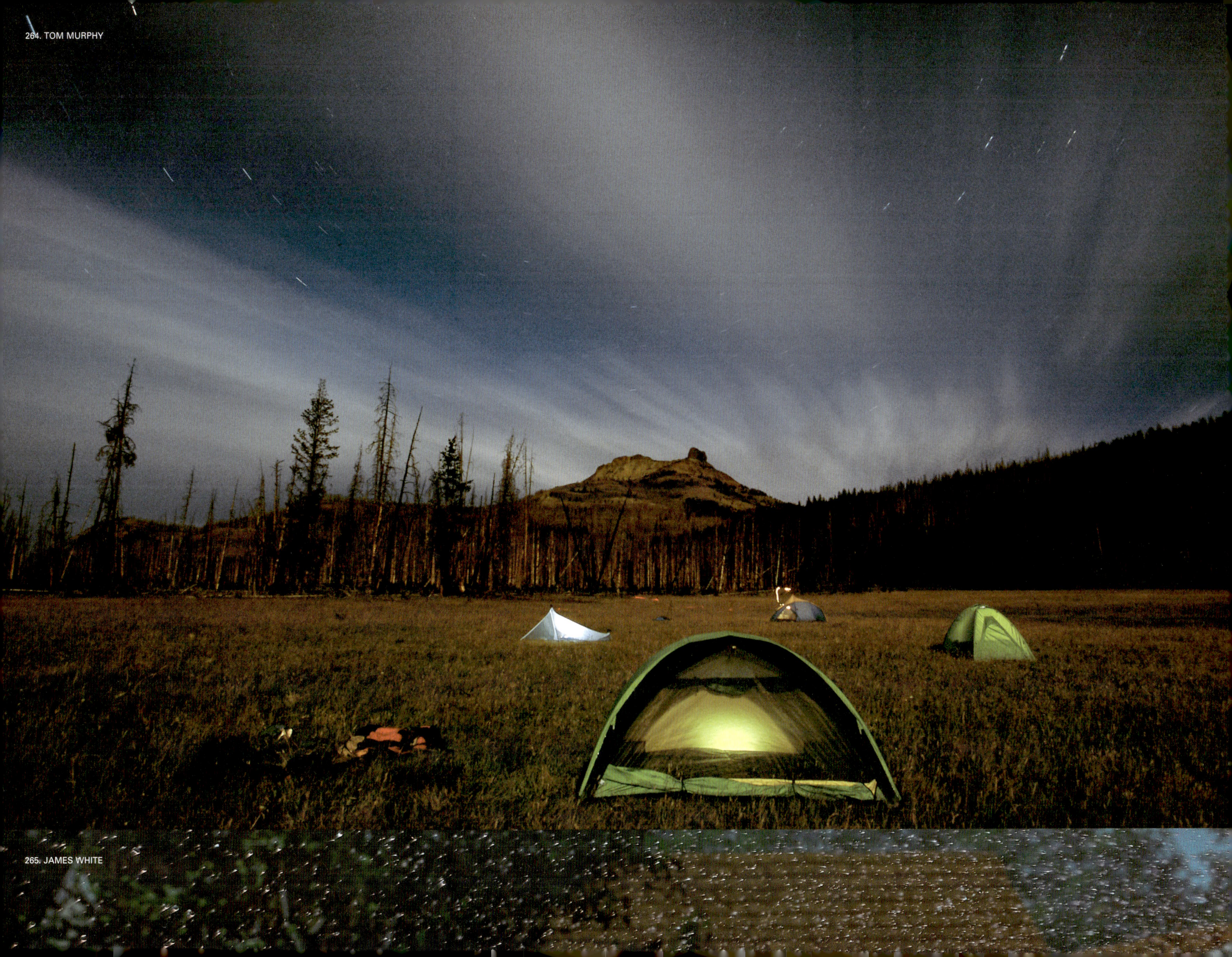

264. TOM MURPHY

265. JAMES WHITE

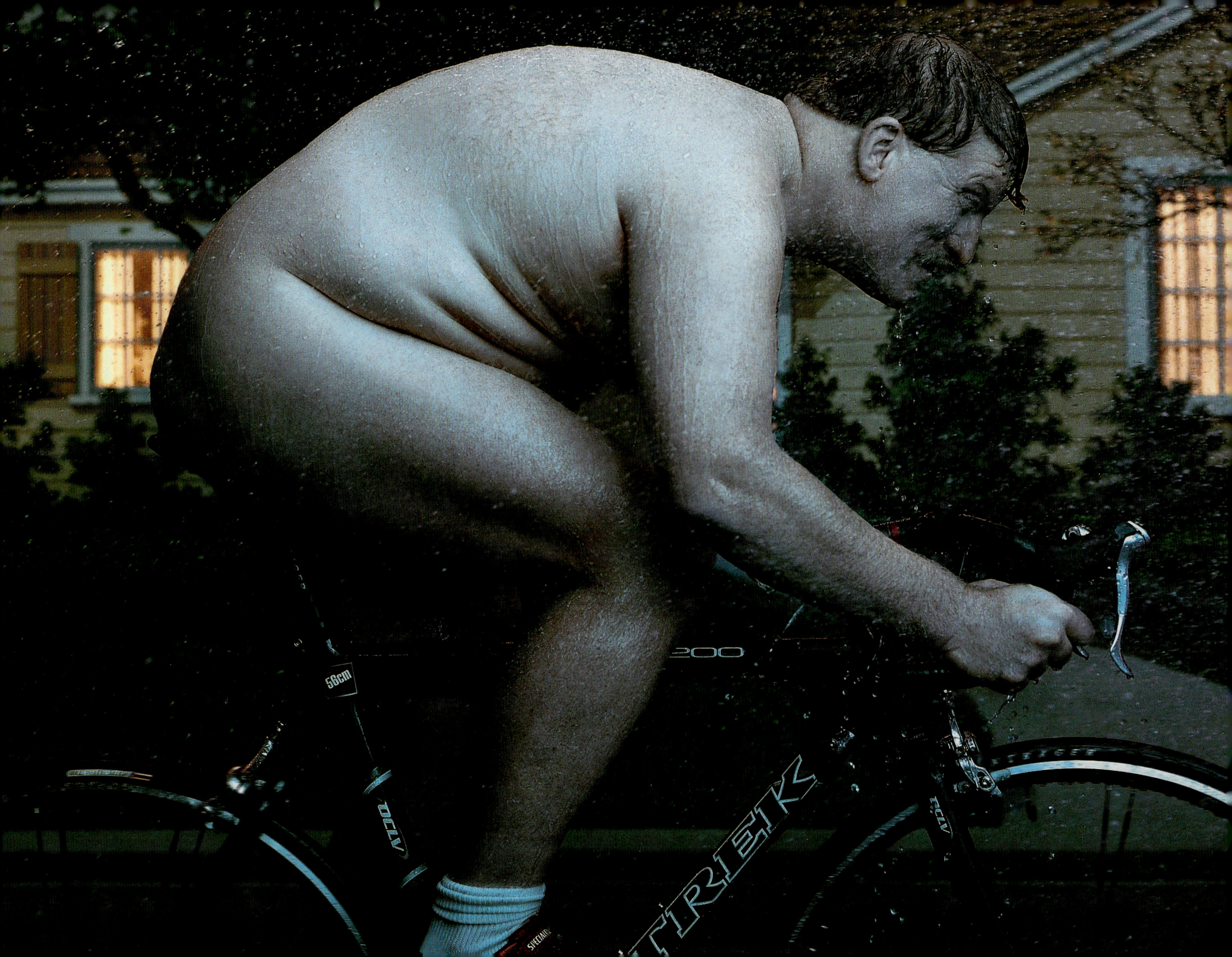
TREK
OCLV
OCLV
56cm

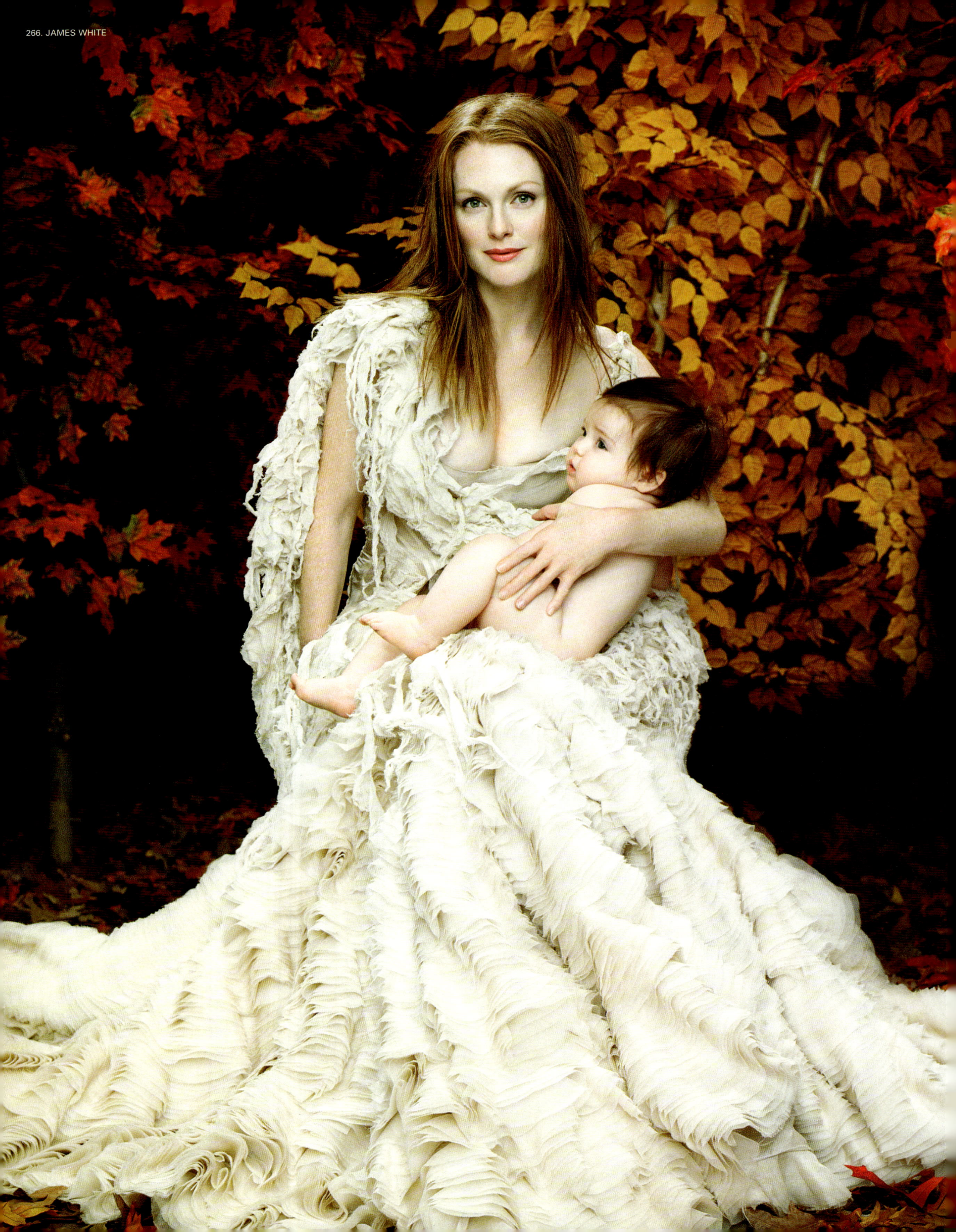

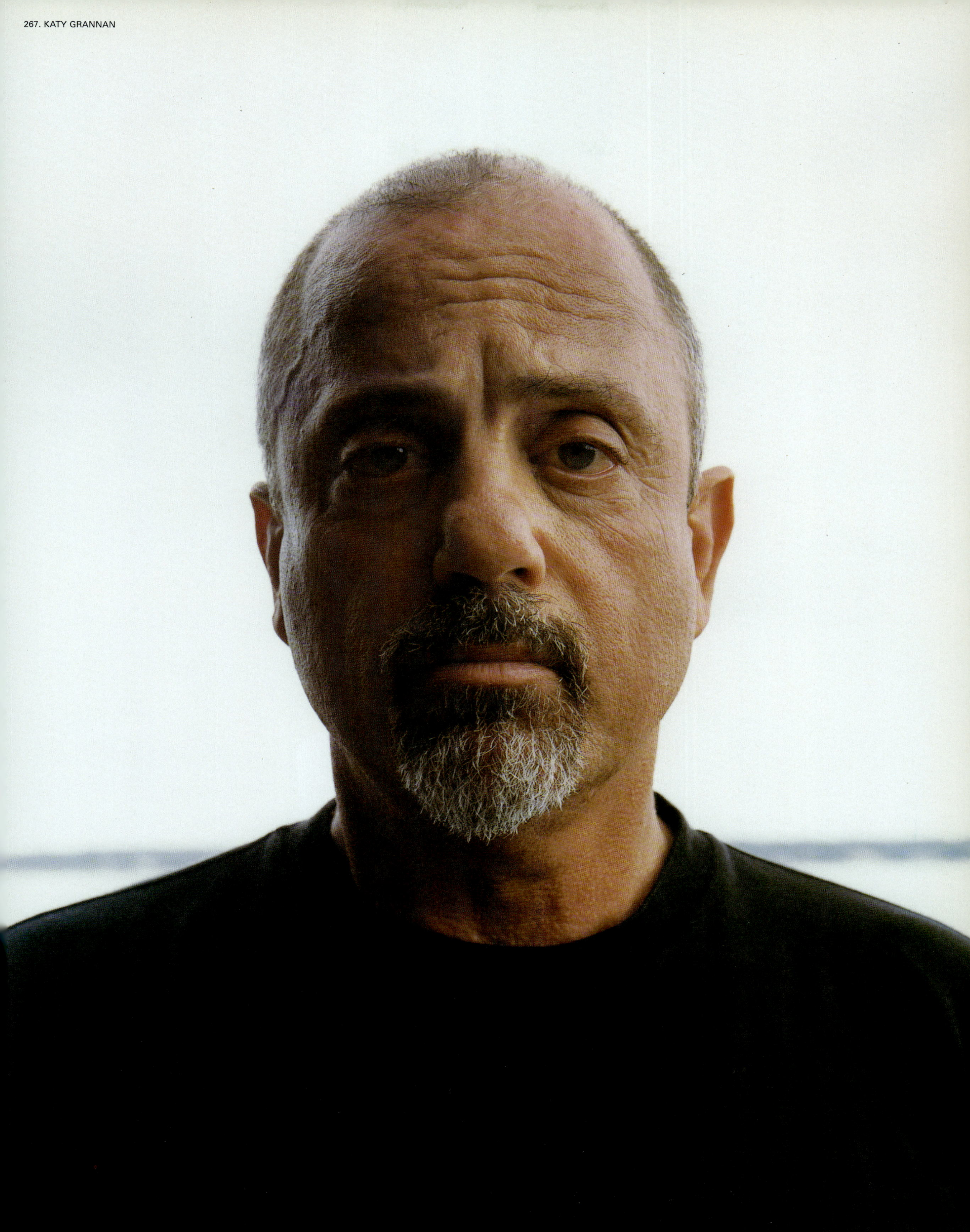

268. KATY GRANNAN

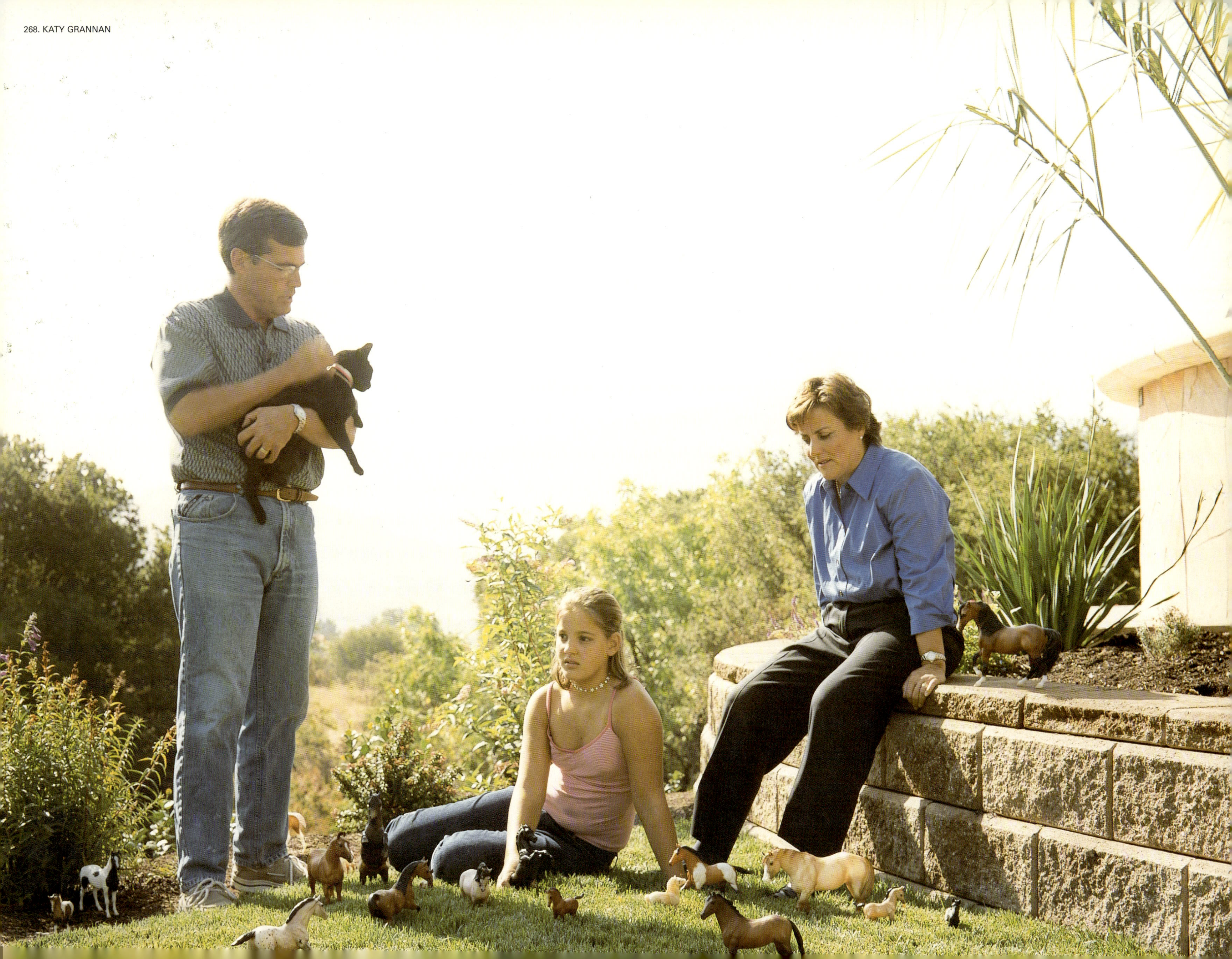

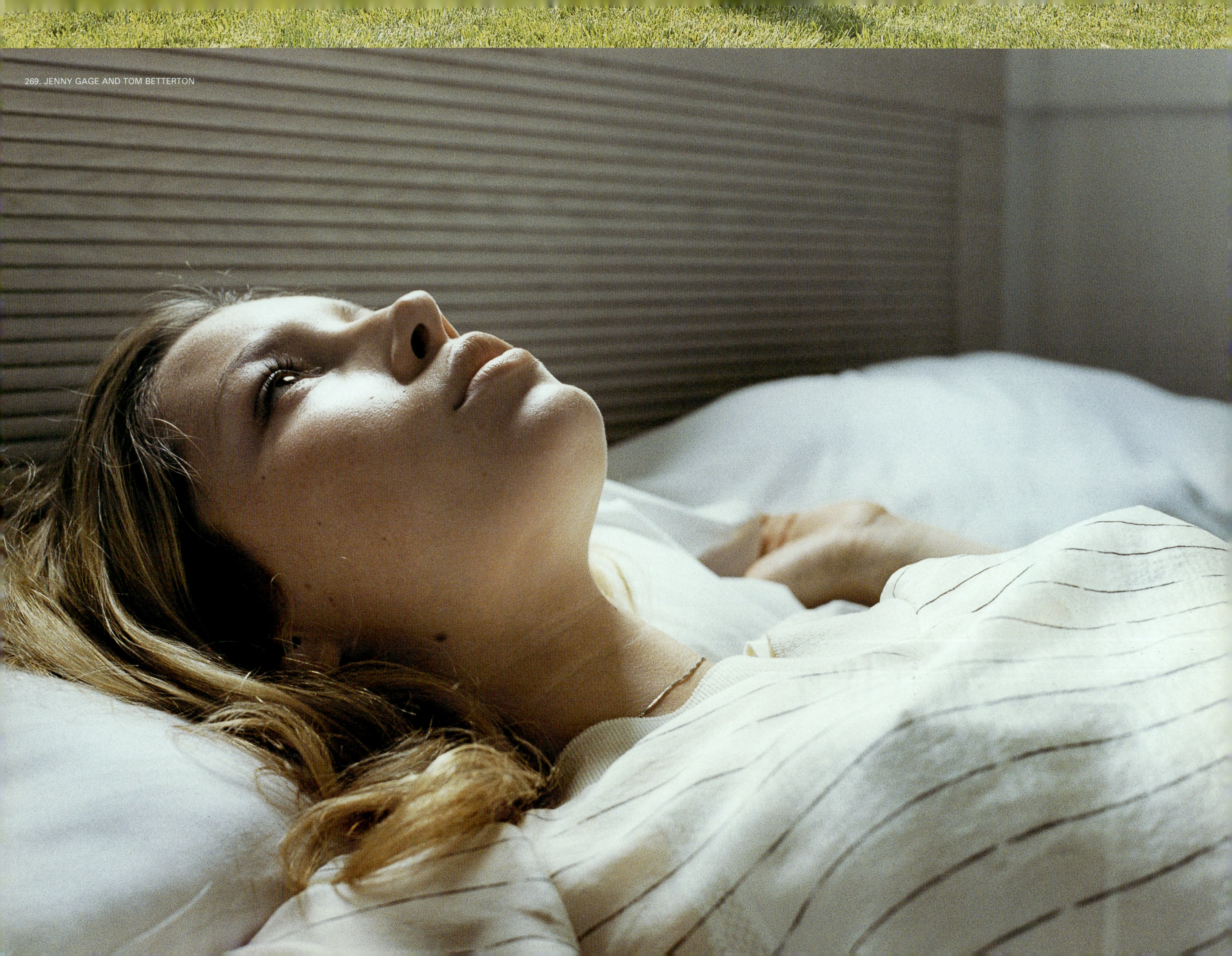

269. JENNY GAGE AND TOM BETTERTON

270. DAVID STRICK

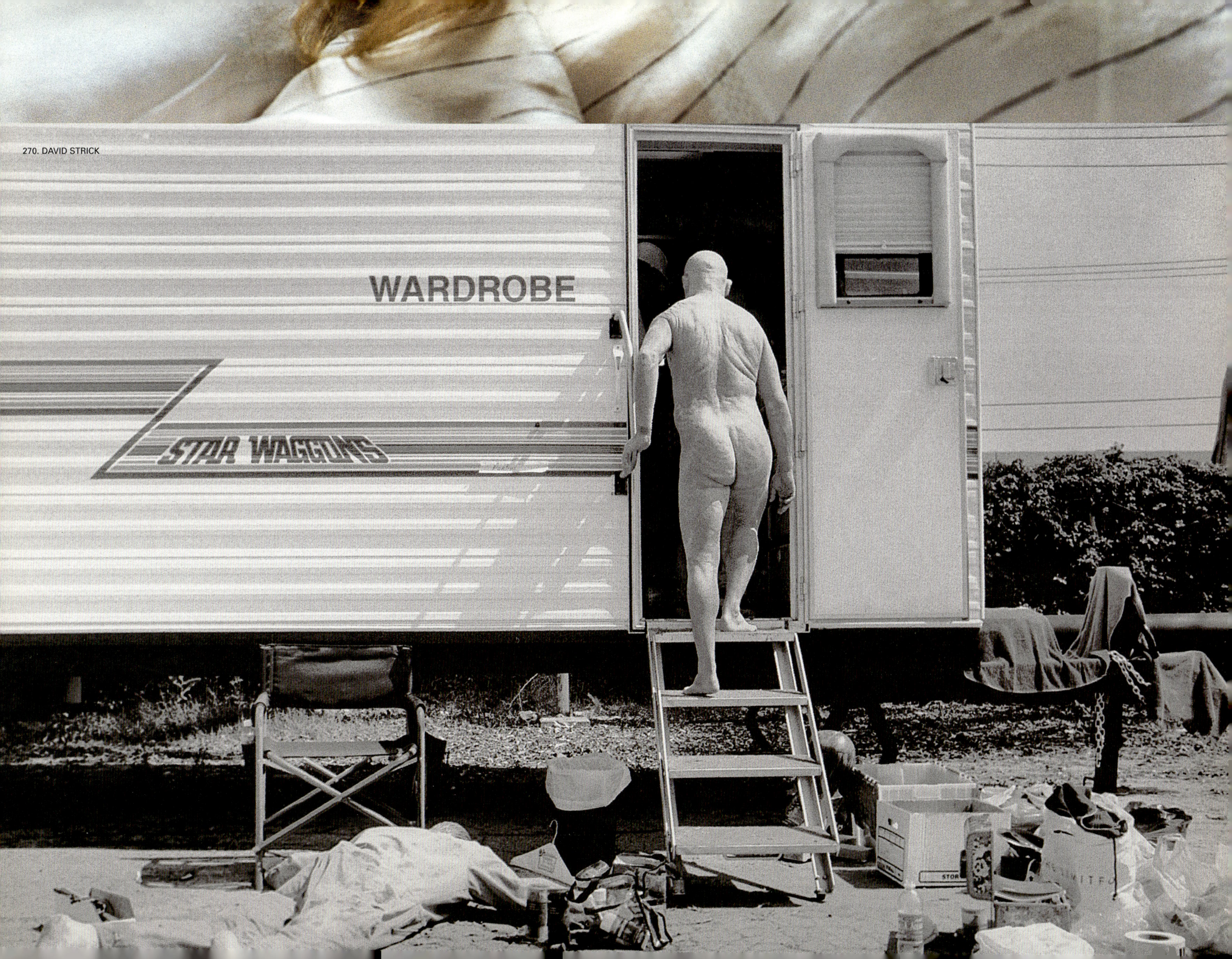

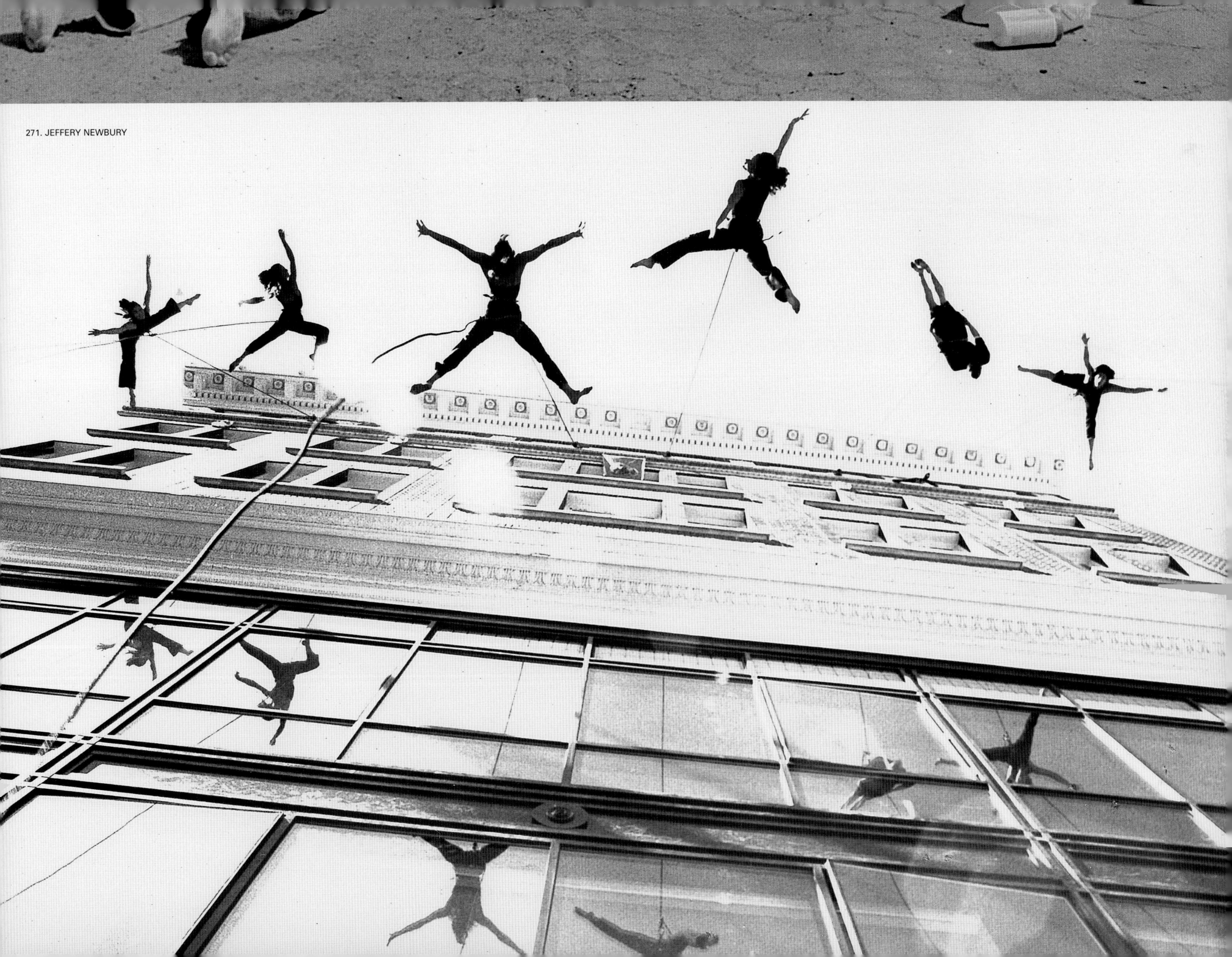

271. JEFFERY NEWBURY

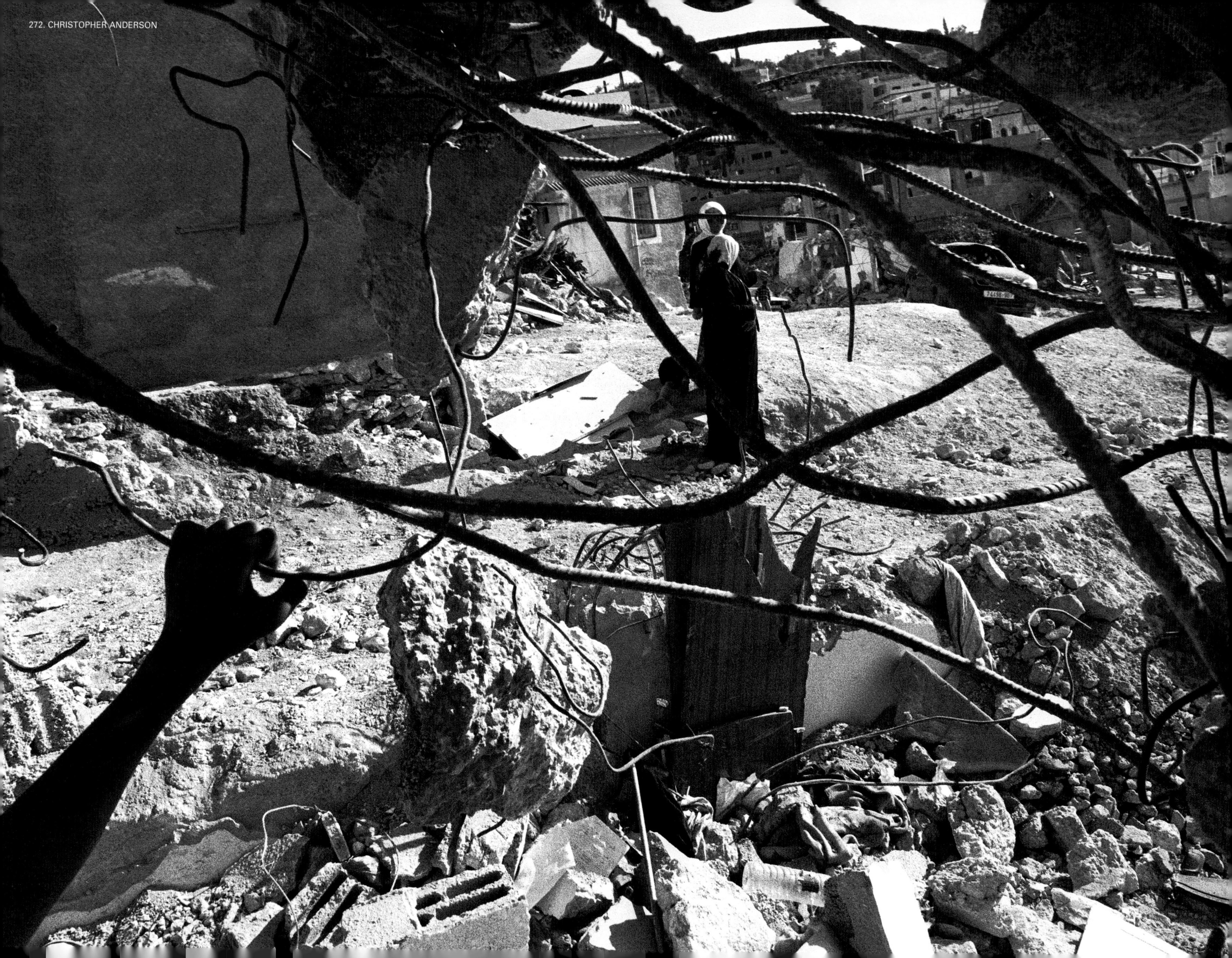

272. CHRISTOPHER ANDERSON

273. CHRISTOPHER ANDERSON

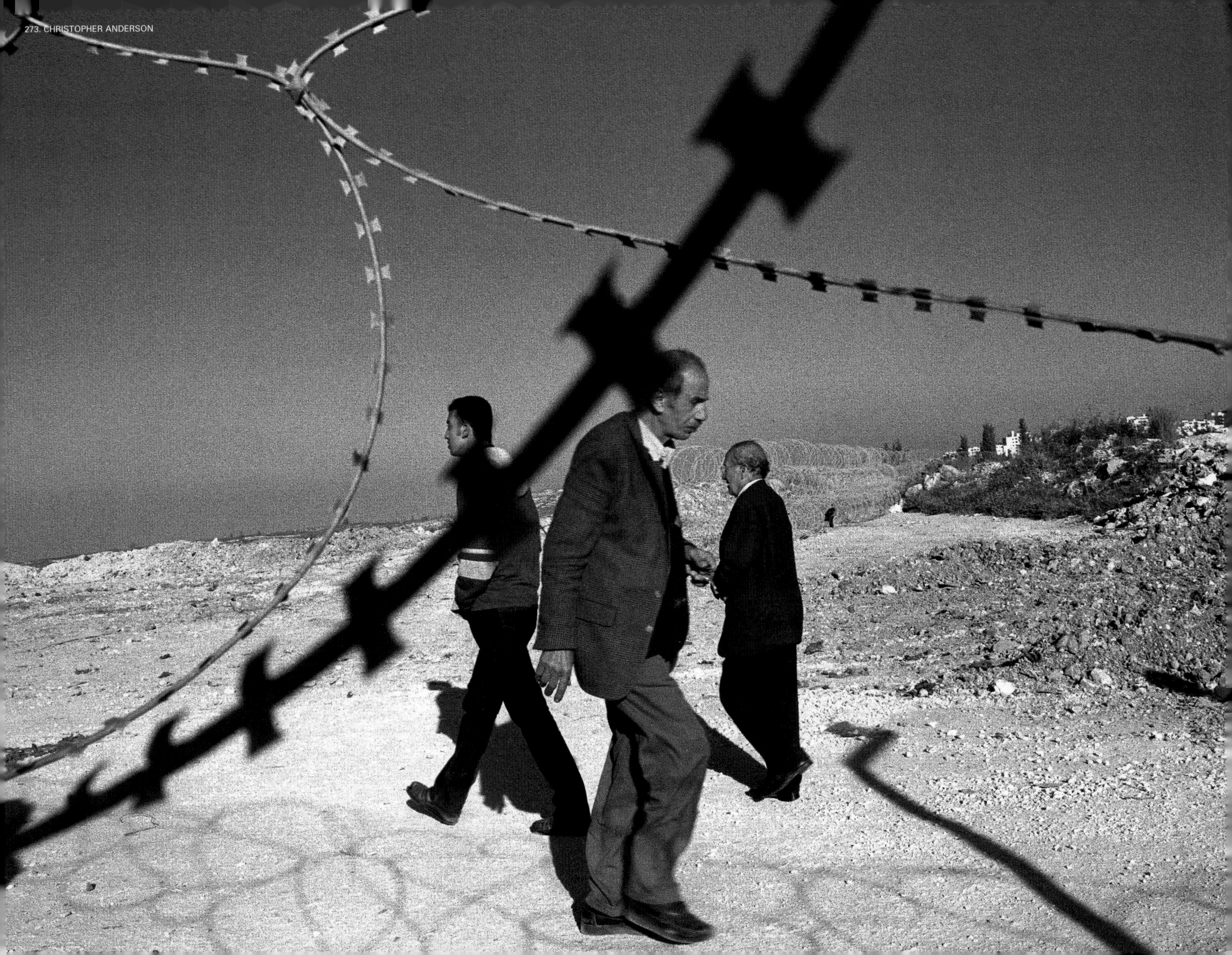

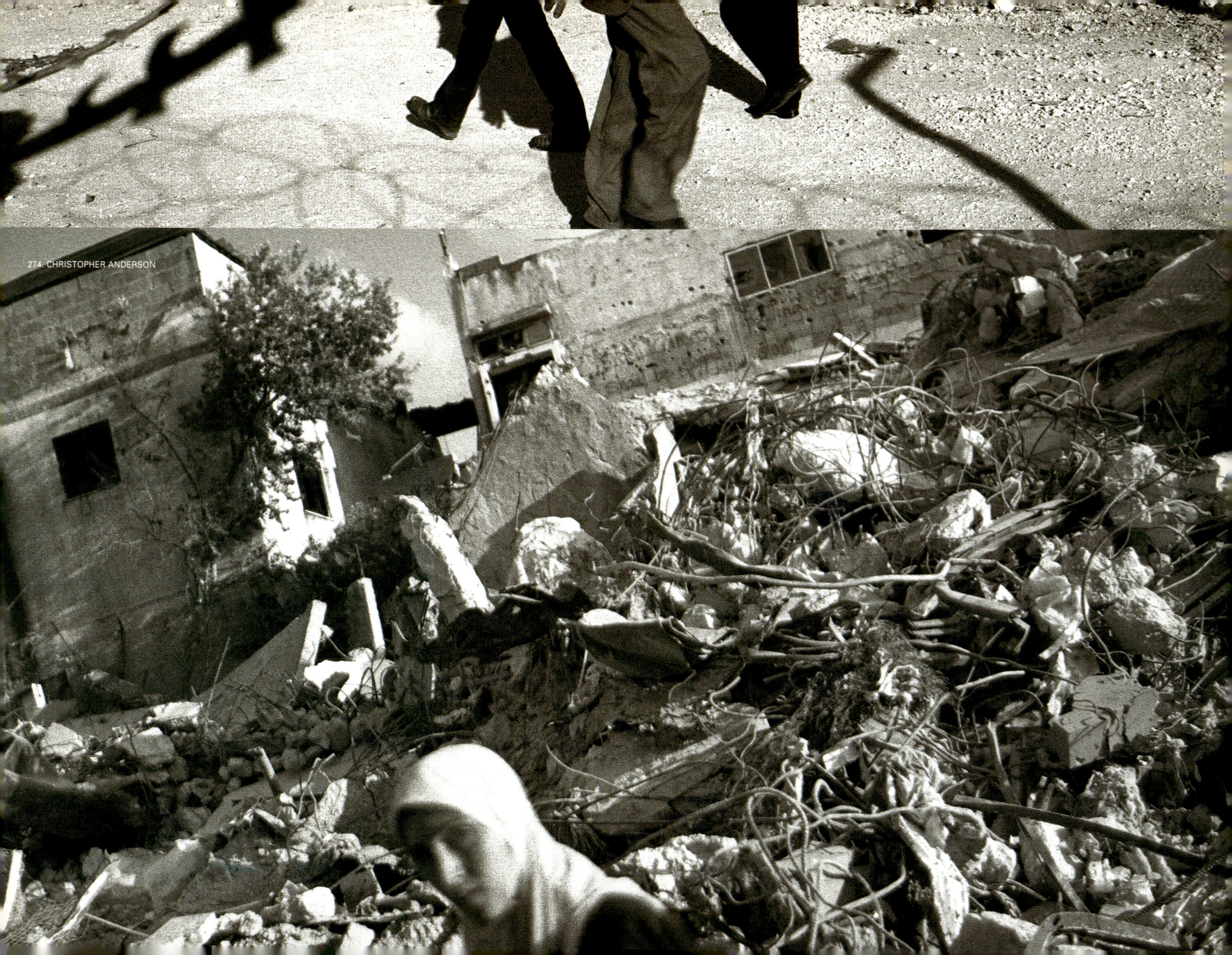

274. CHRISTOPHER ANDERSON

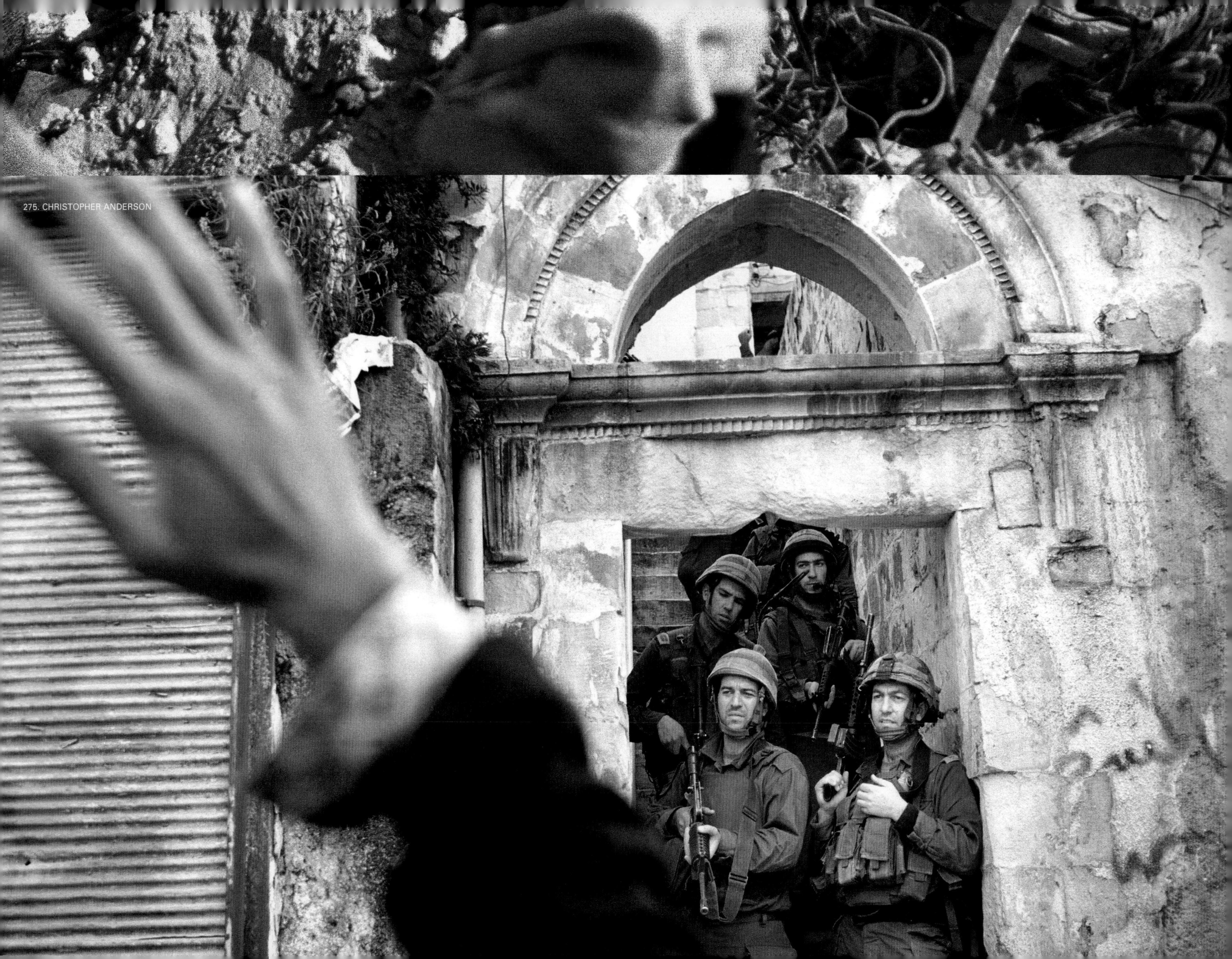

275. CHRISTOPHER ANDERSON

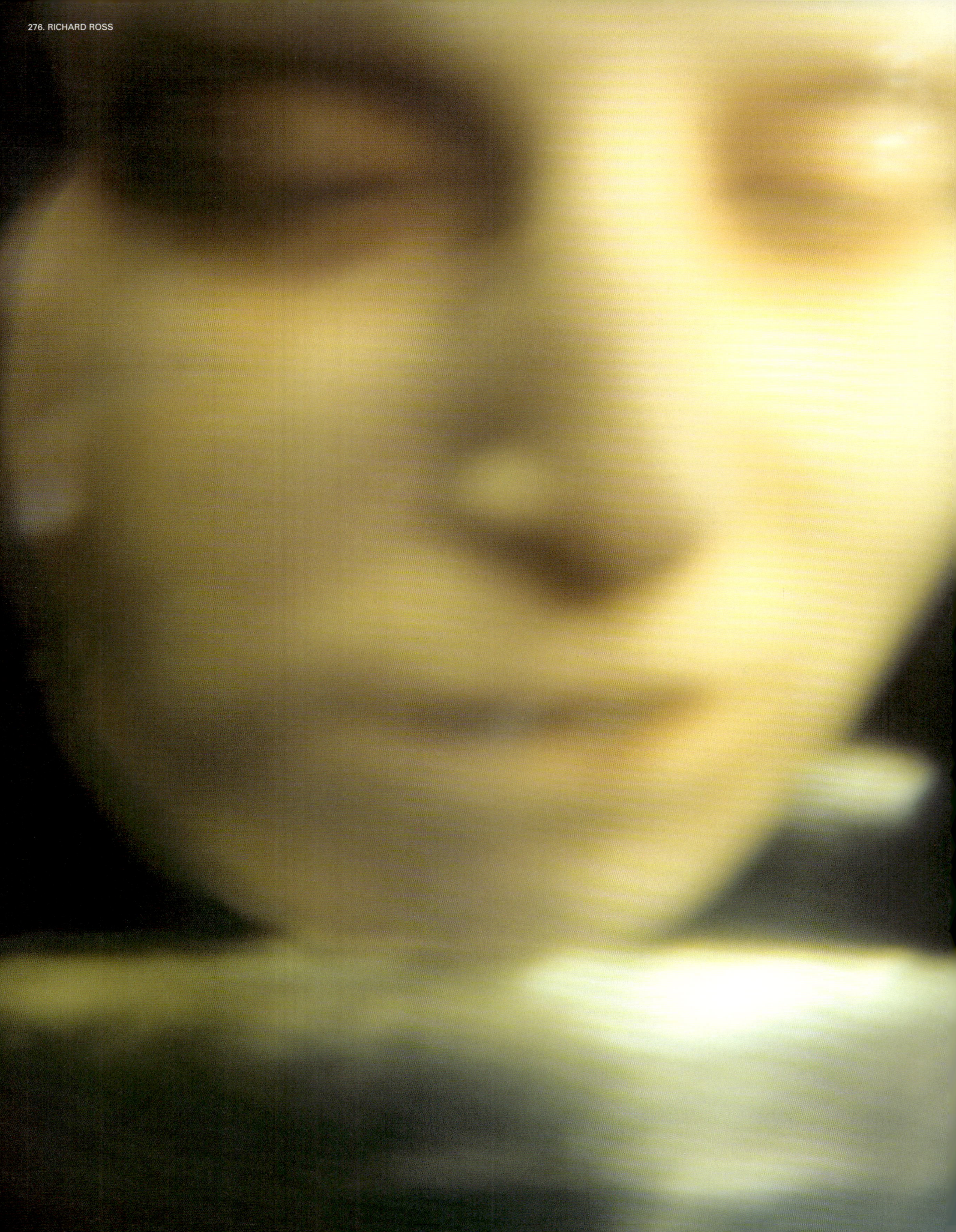

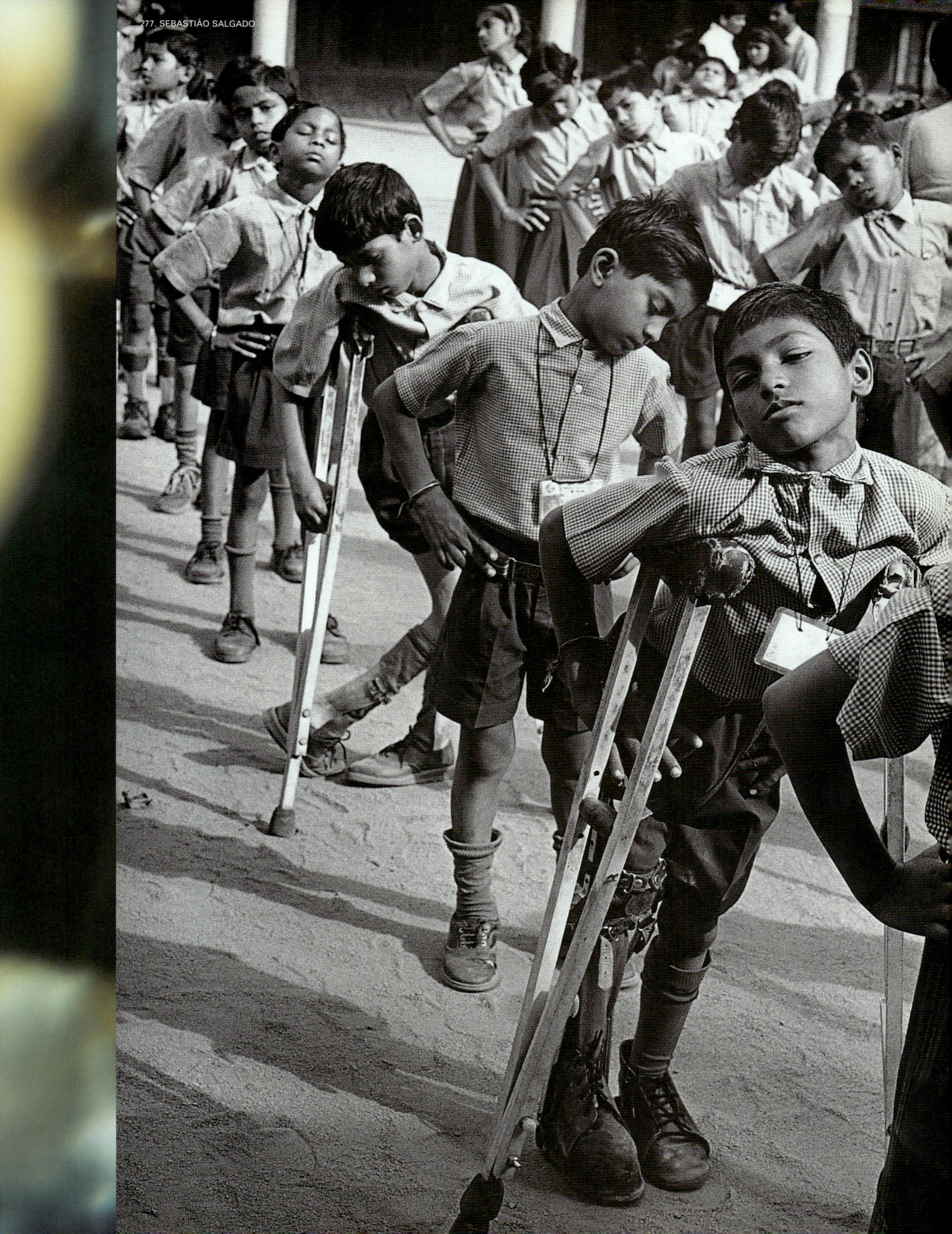

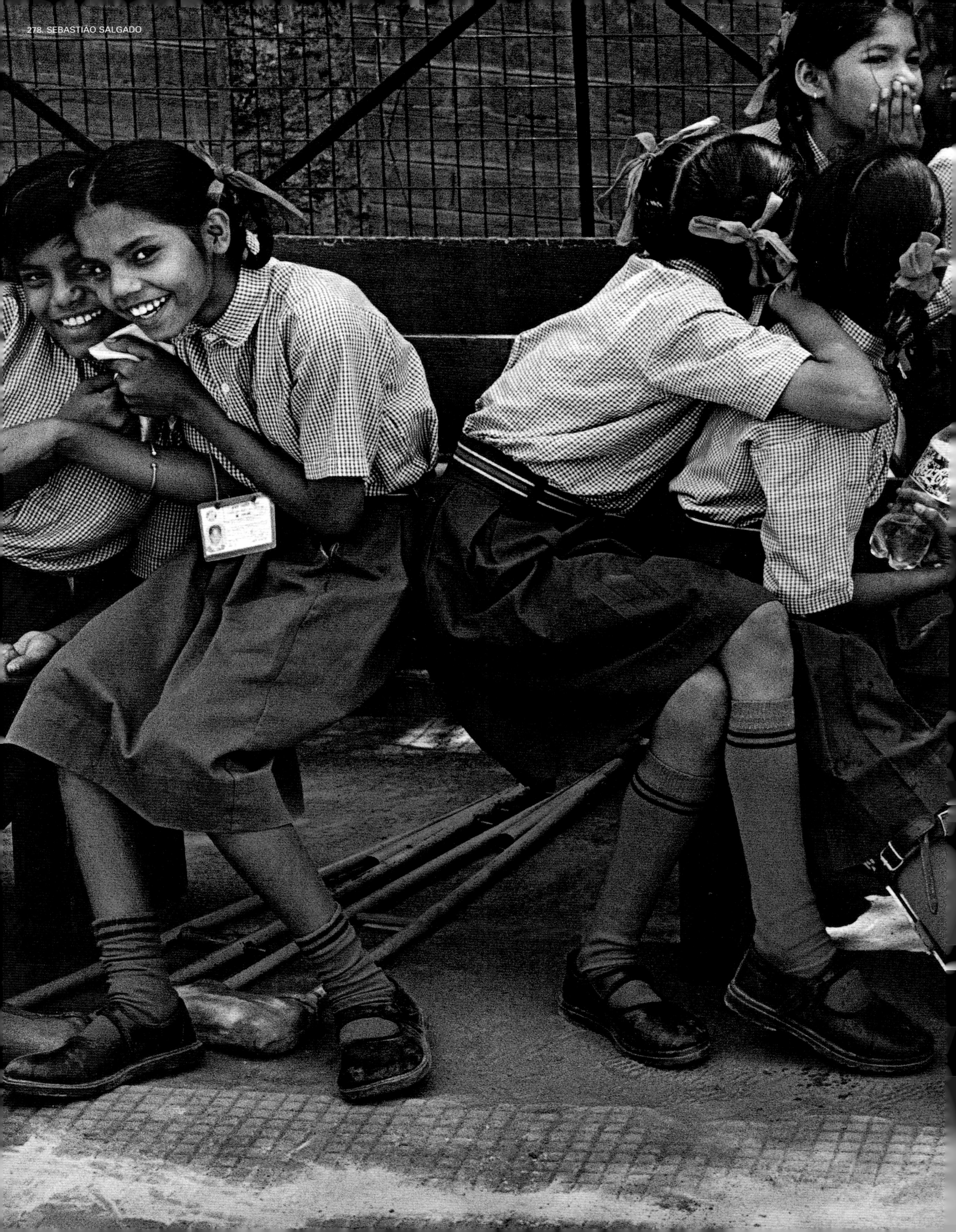

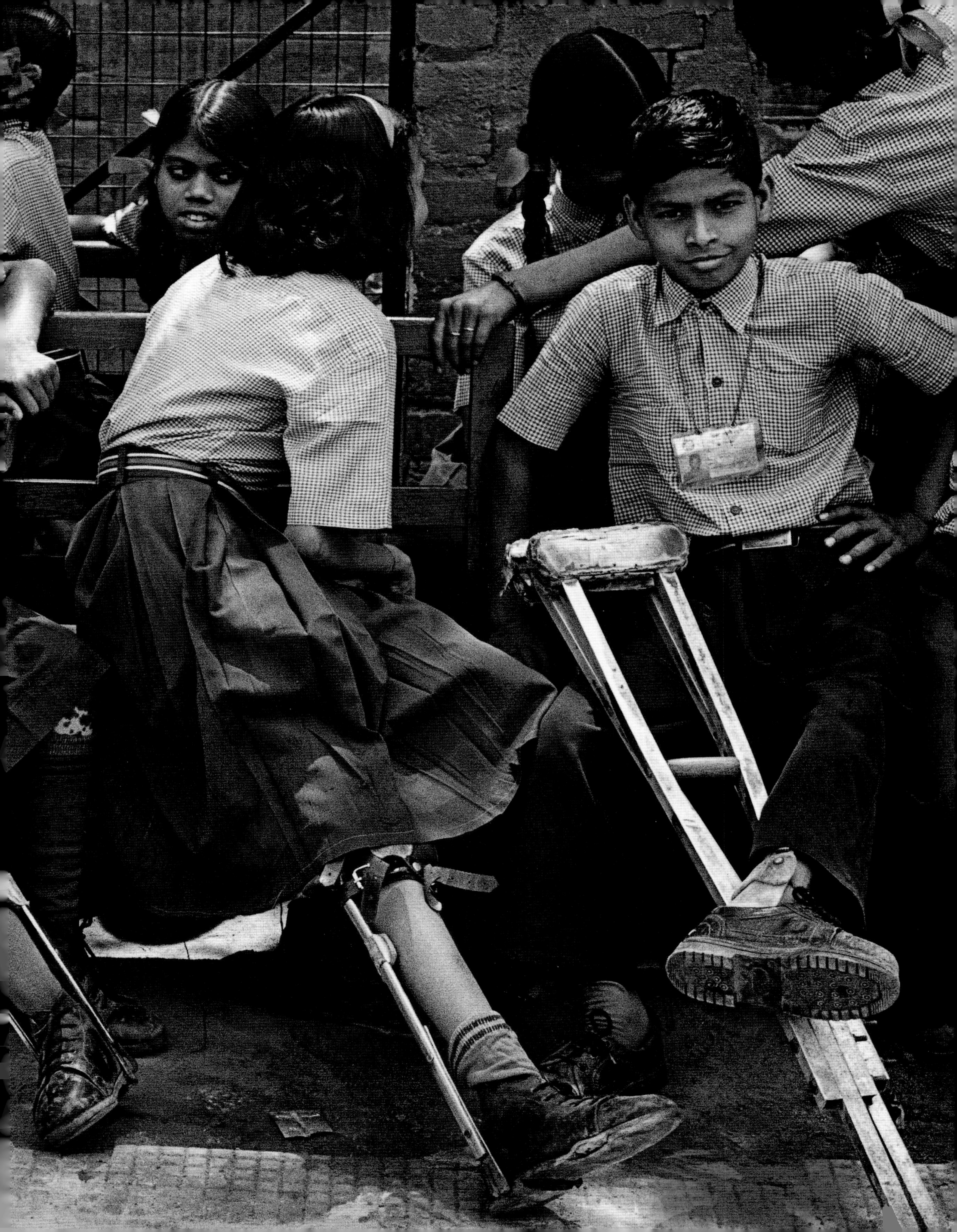

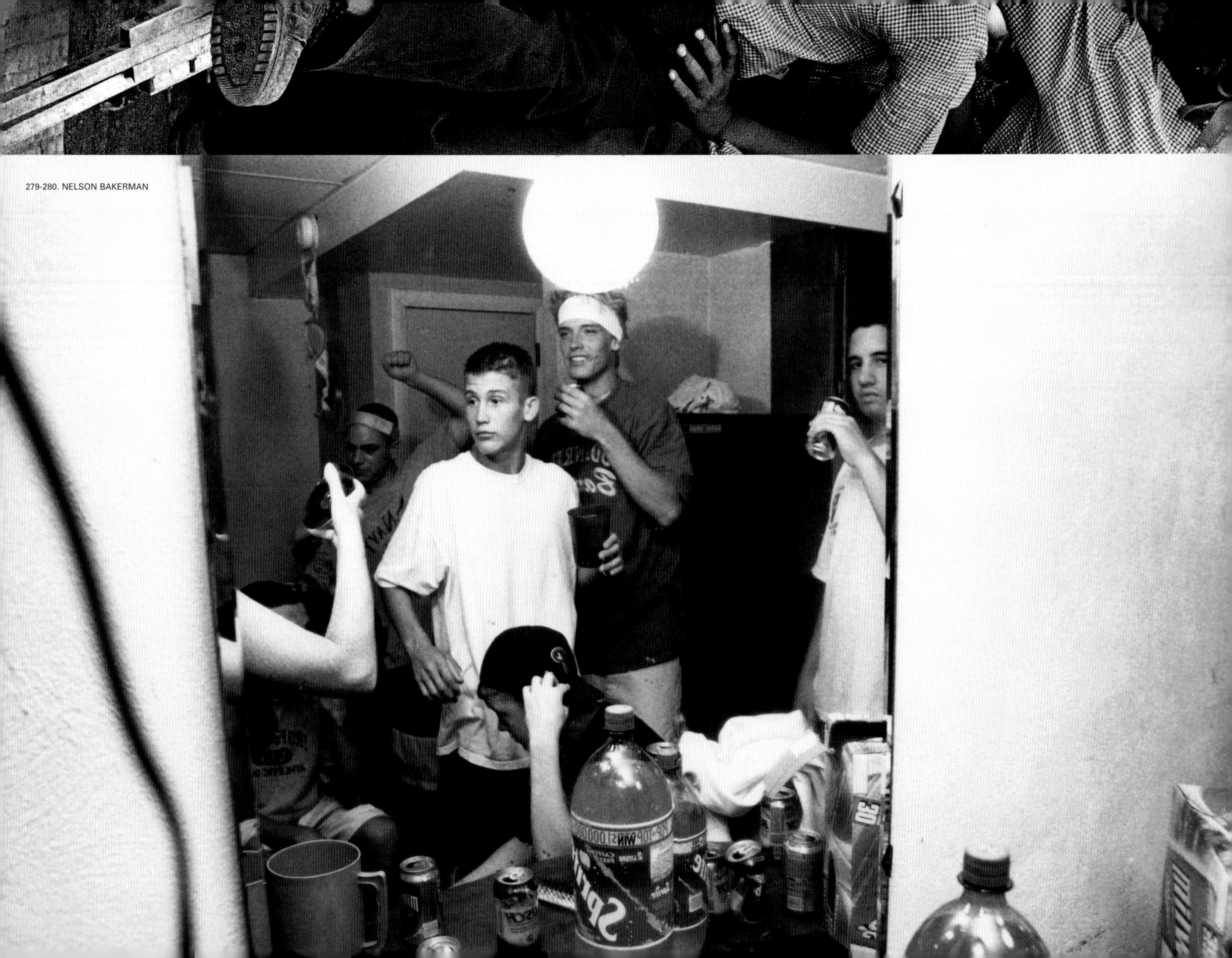

279-280. NELSON BAKERMAN

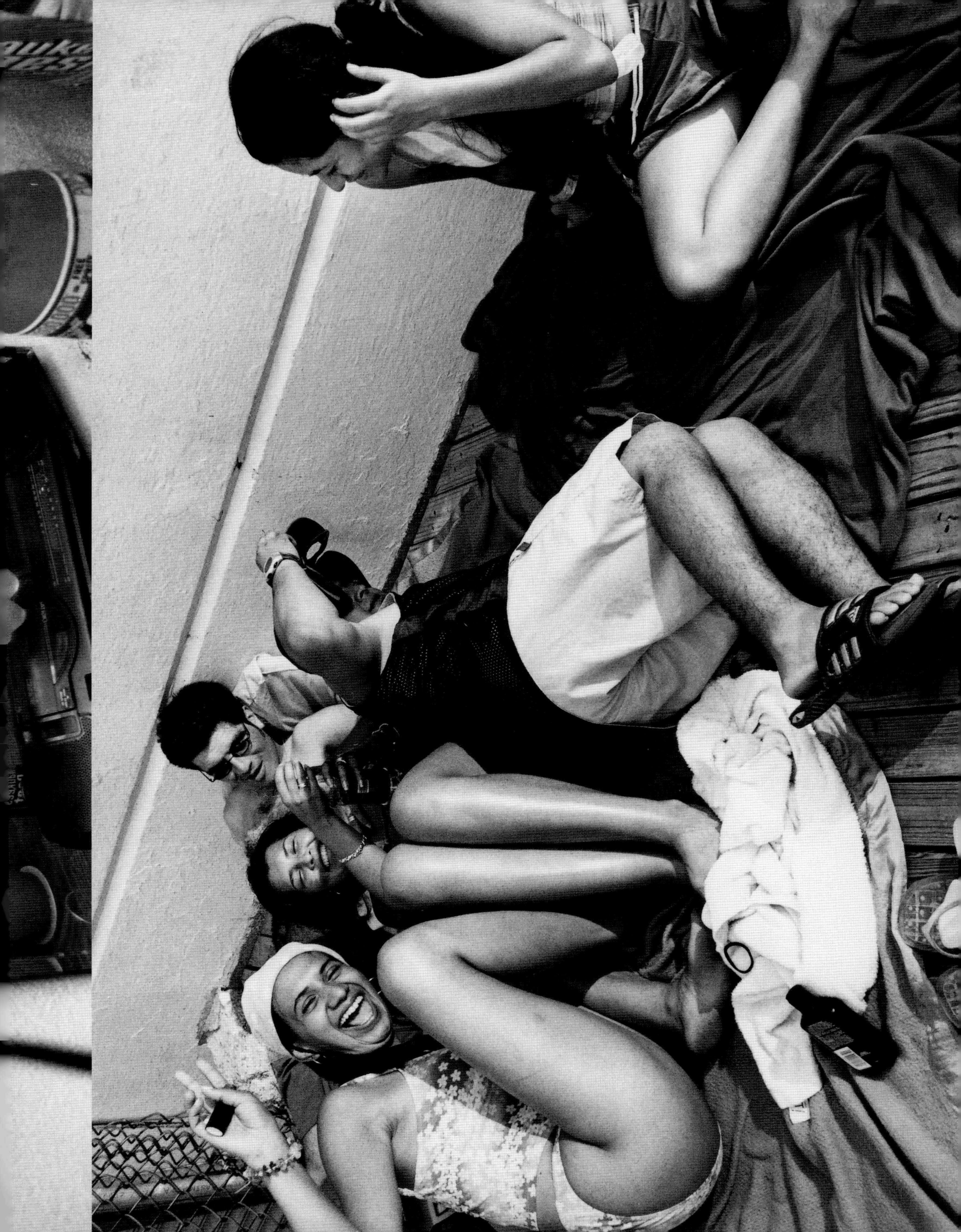

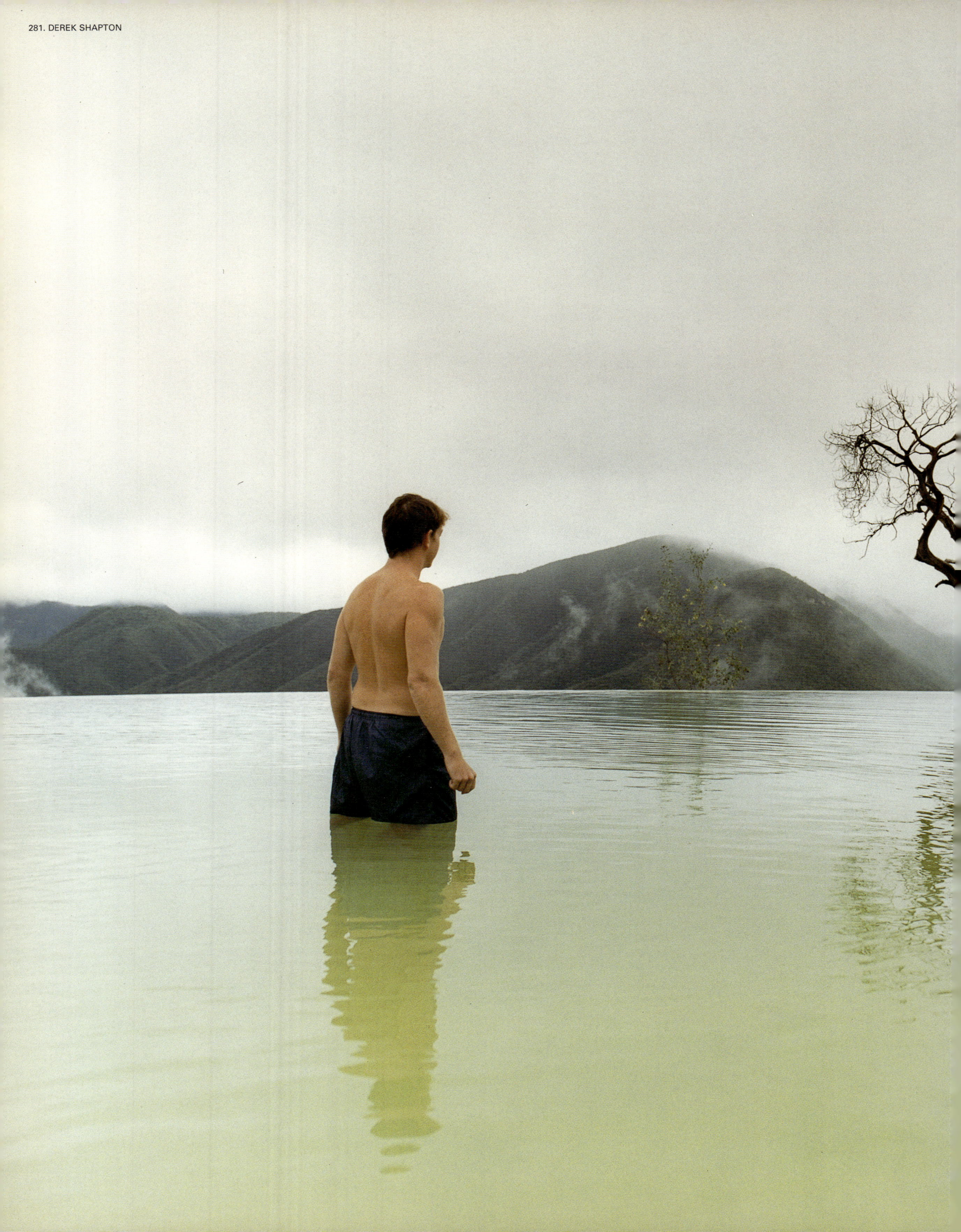

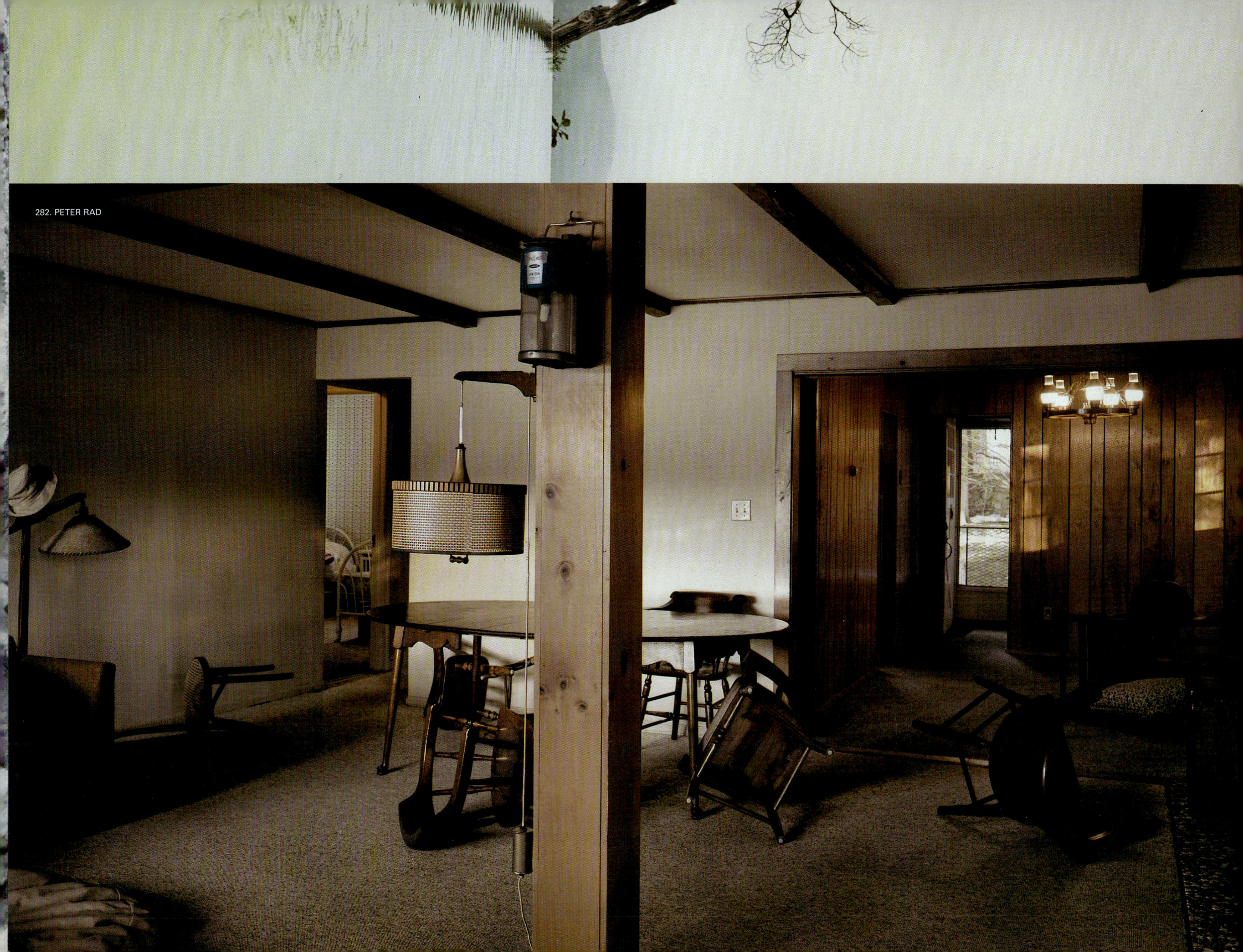

282. PETER RAD

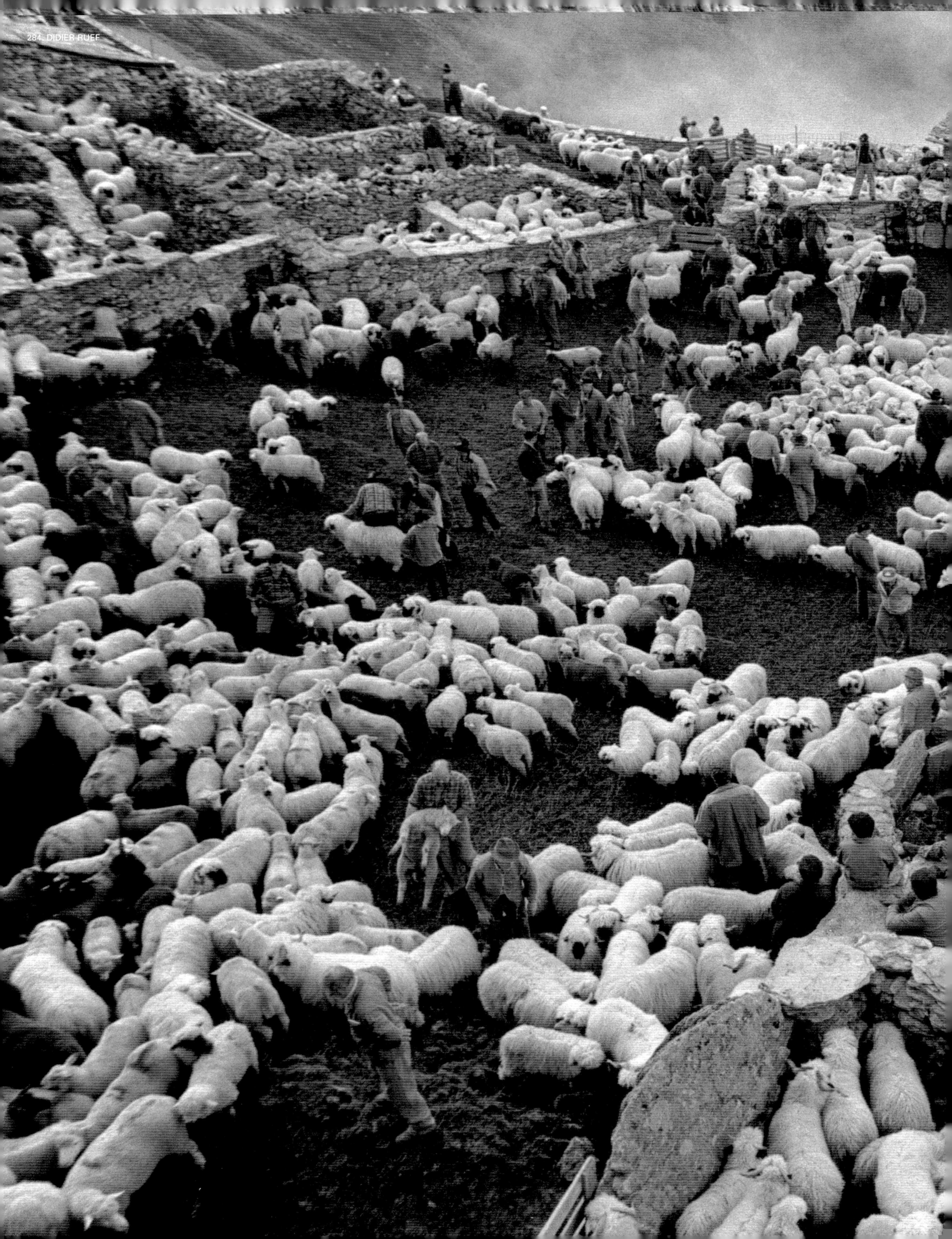

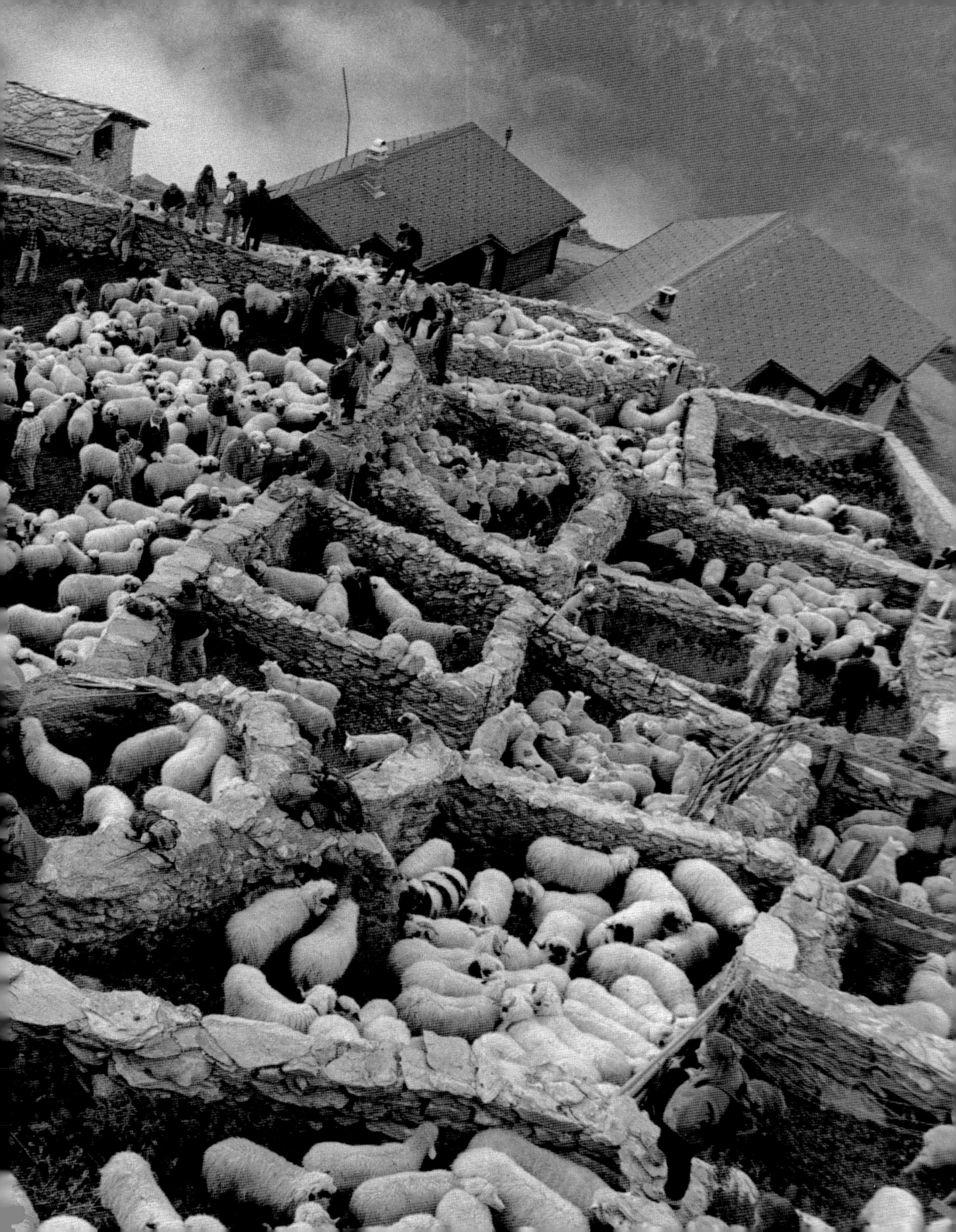

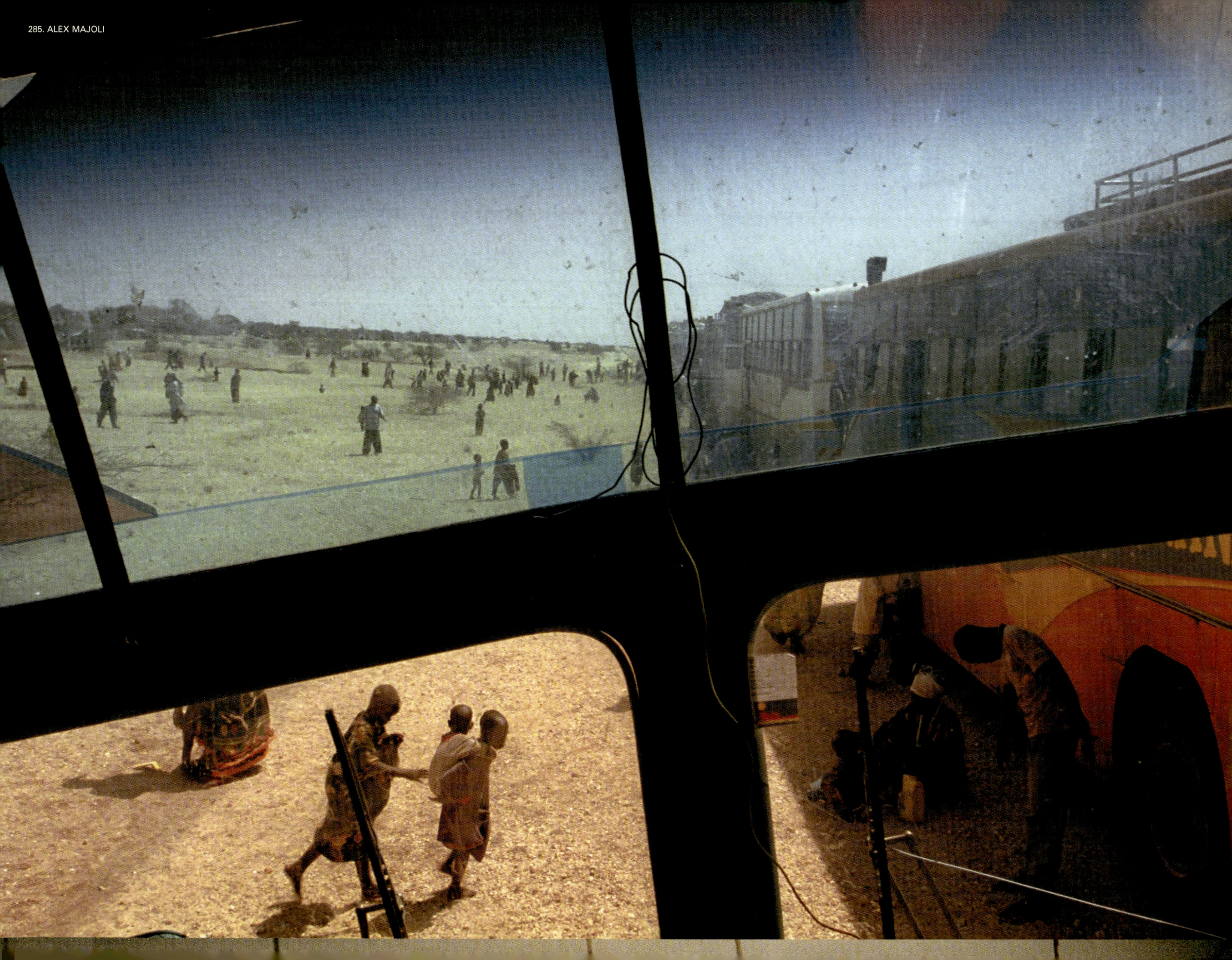

285. ALEX MAJOLI

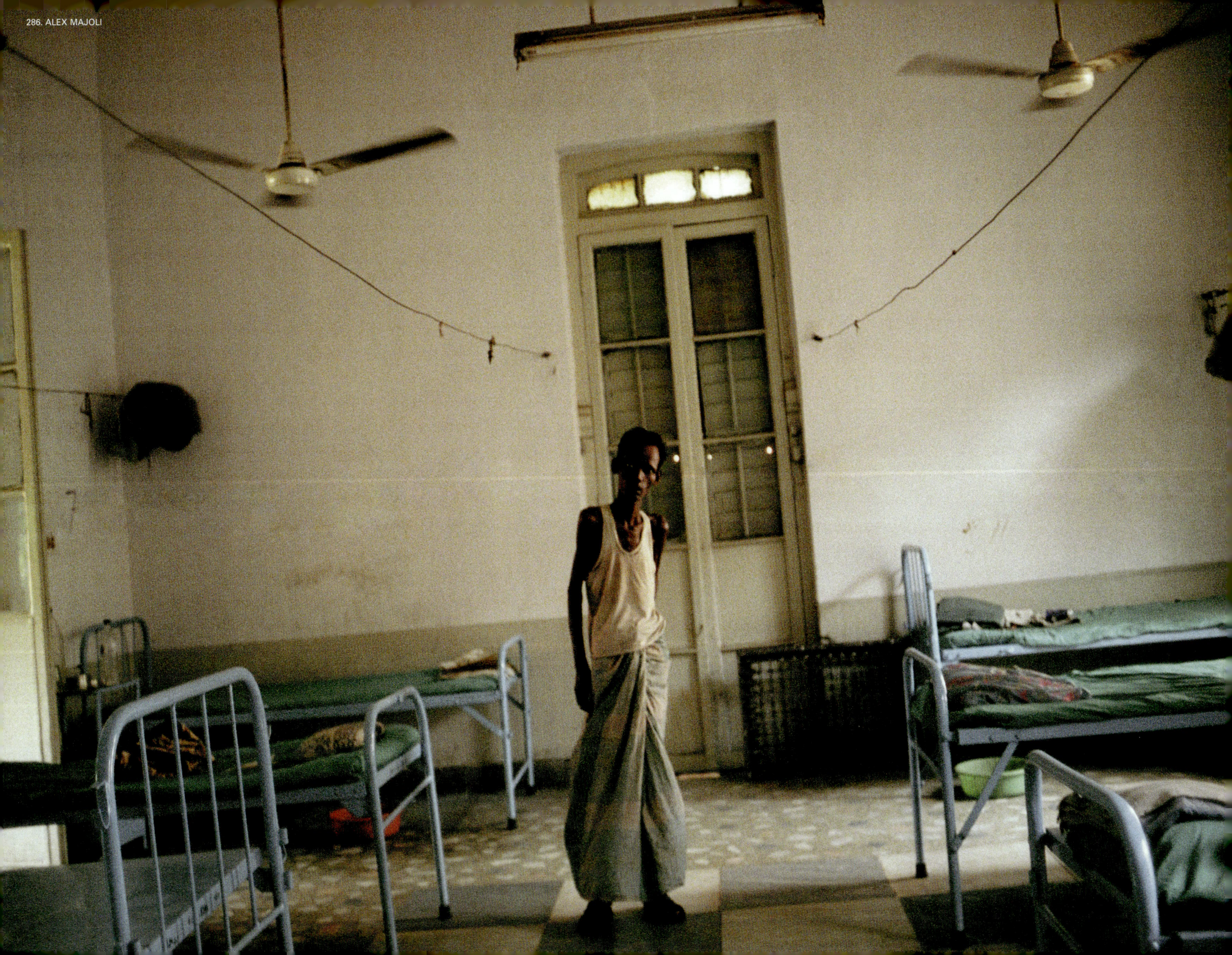

286. ALEX MAJOLI

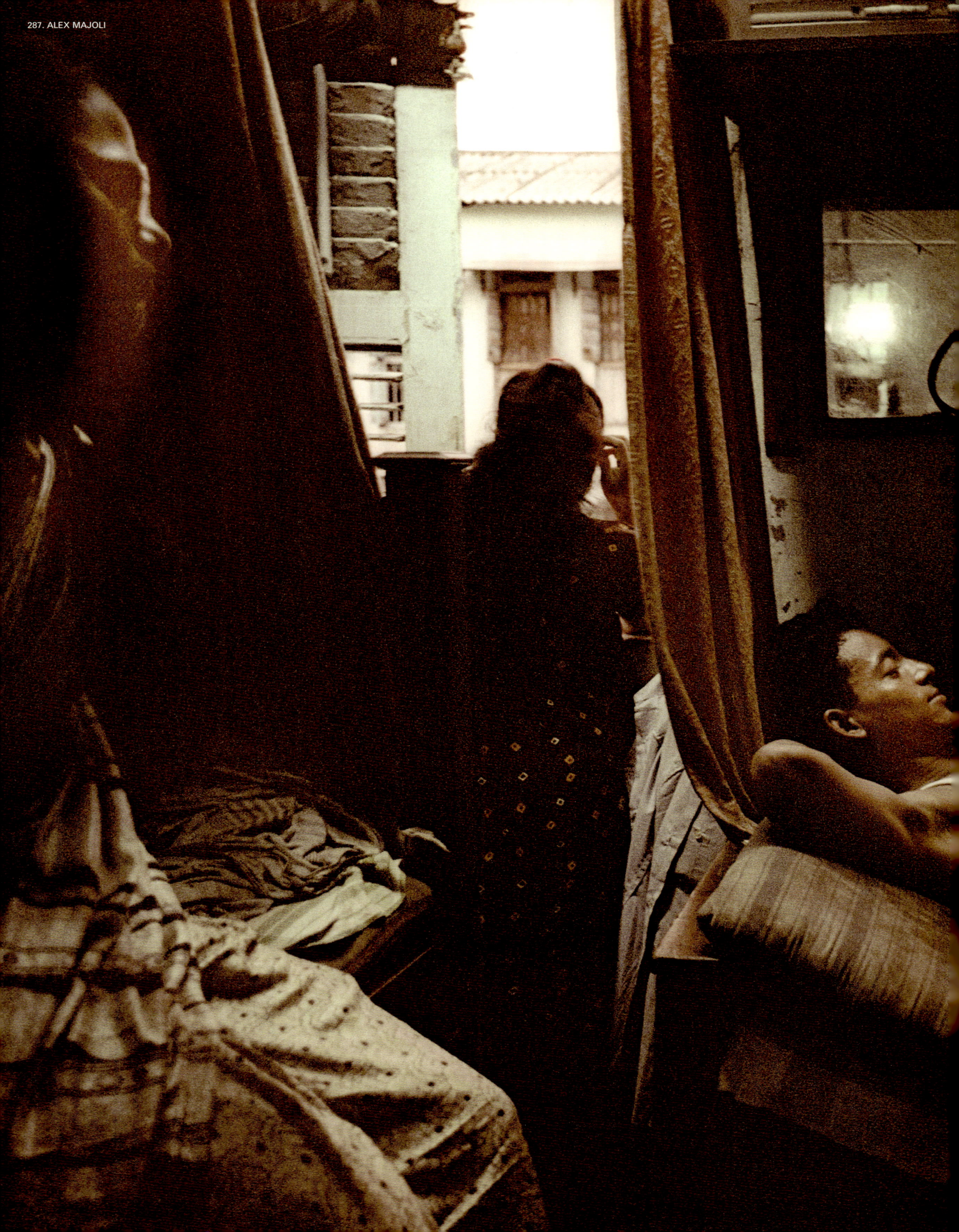

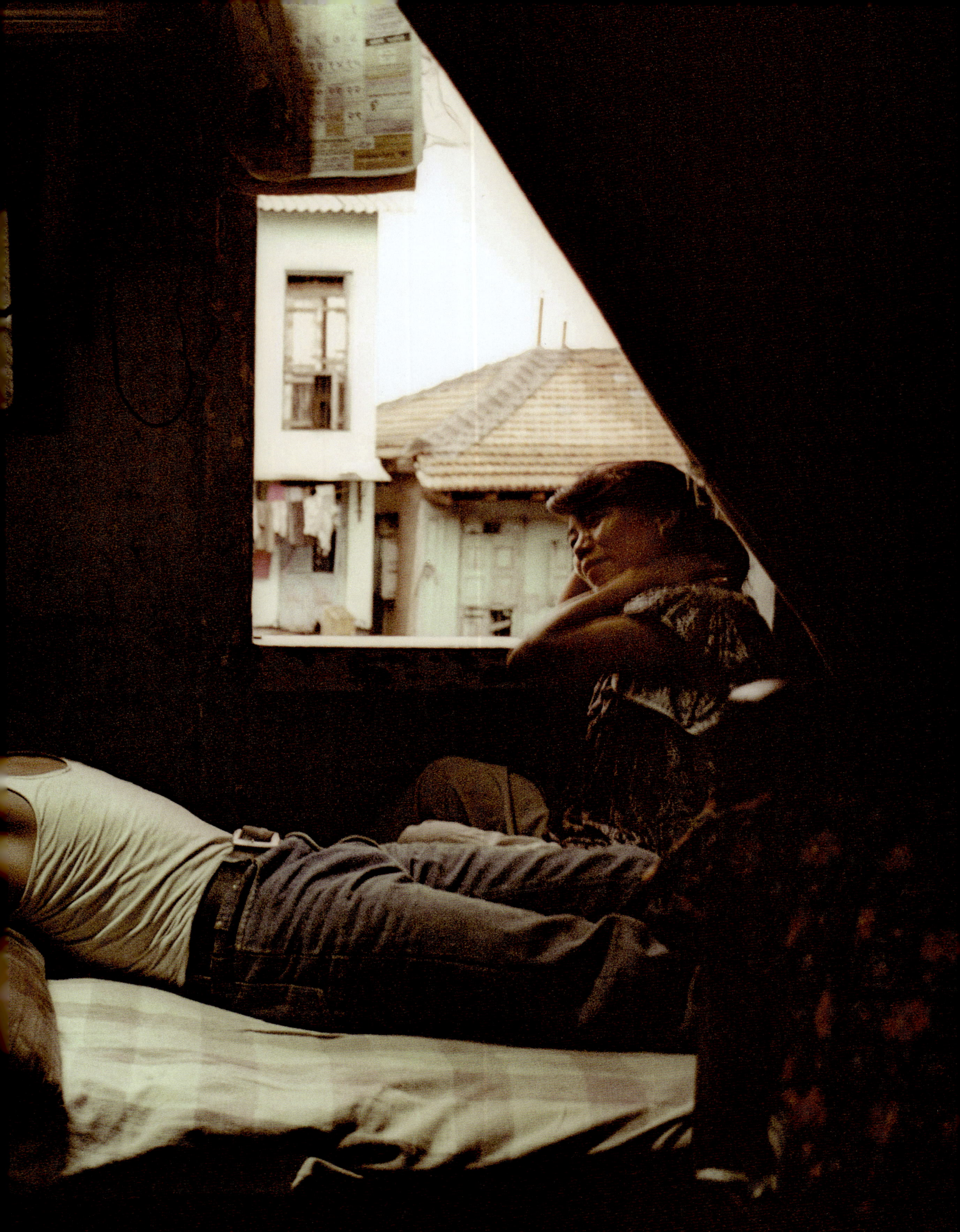

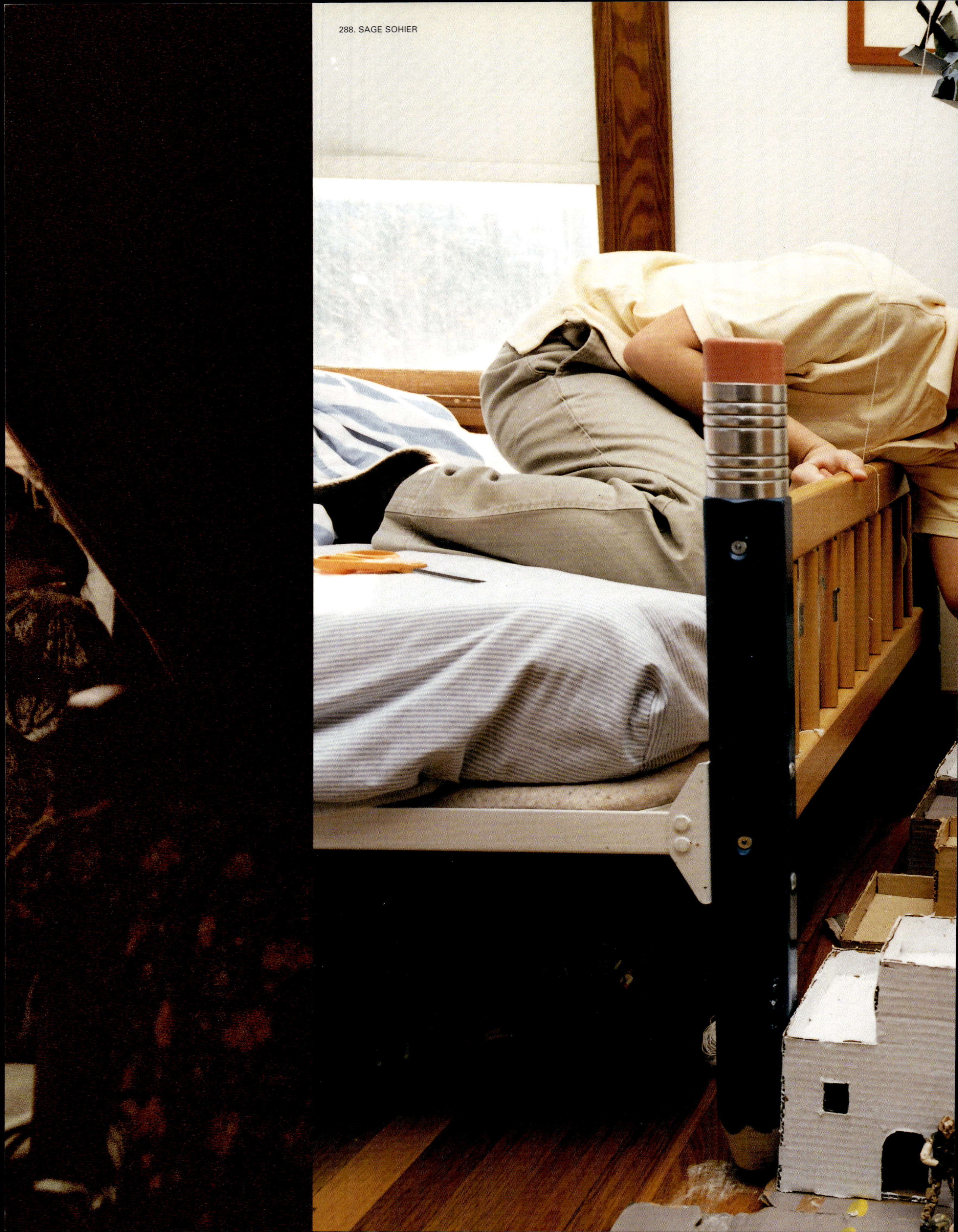

288. SAGE SOHIER

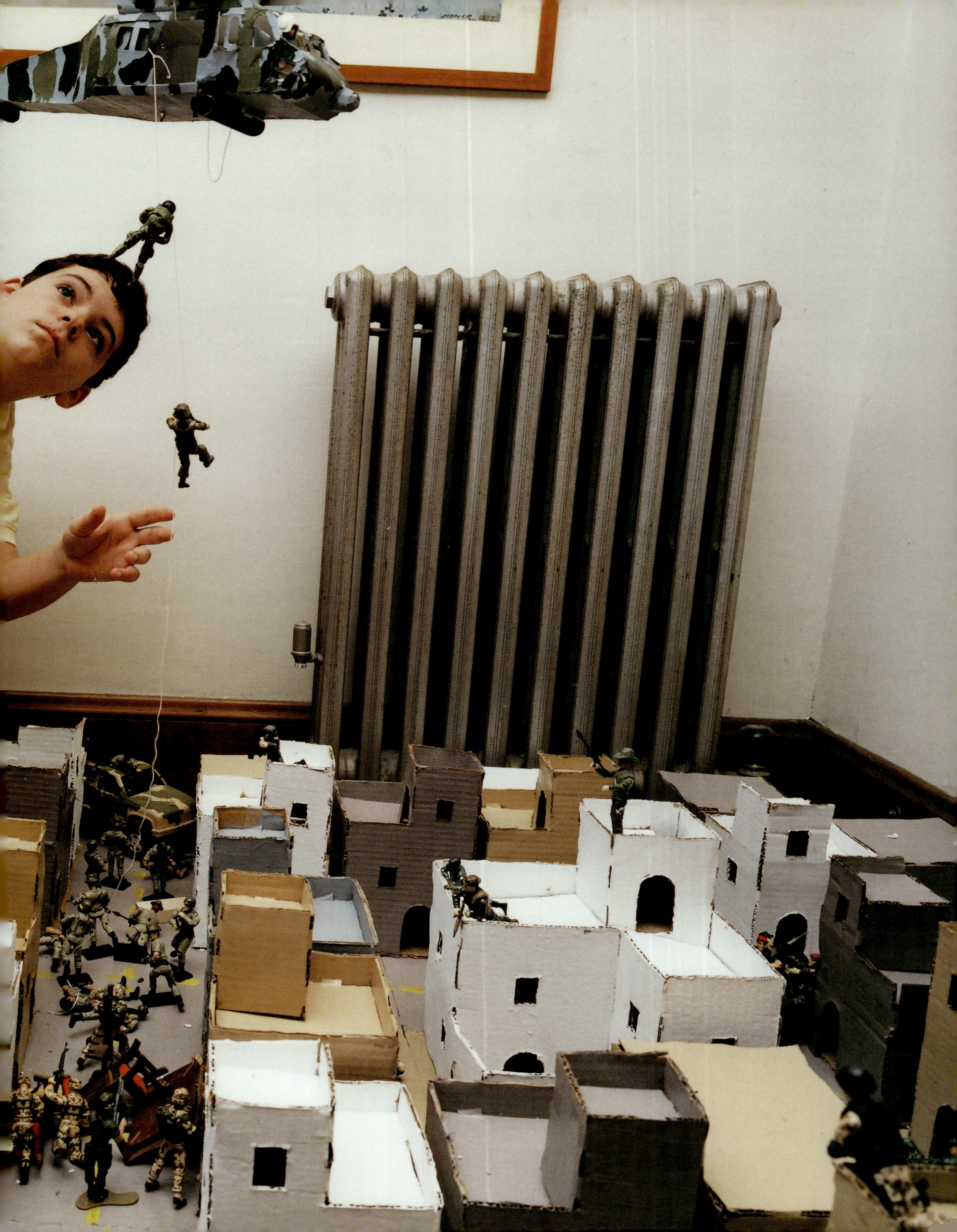

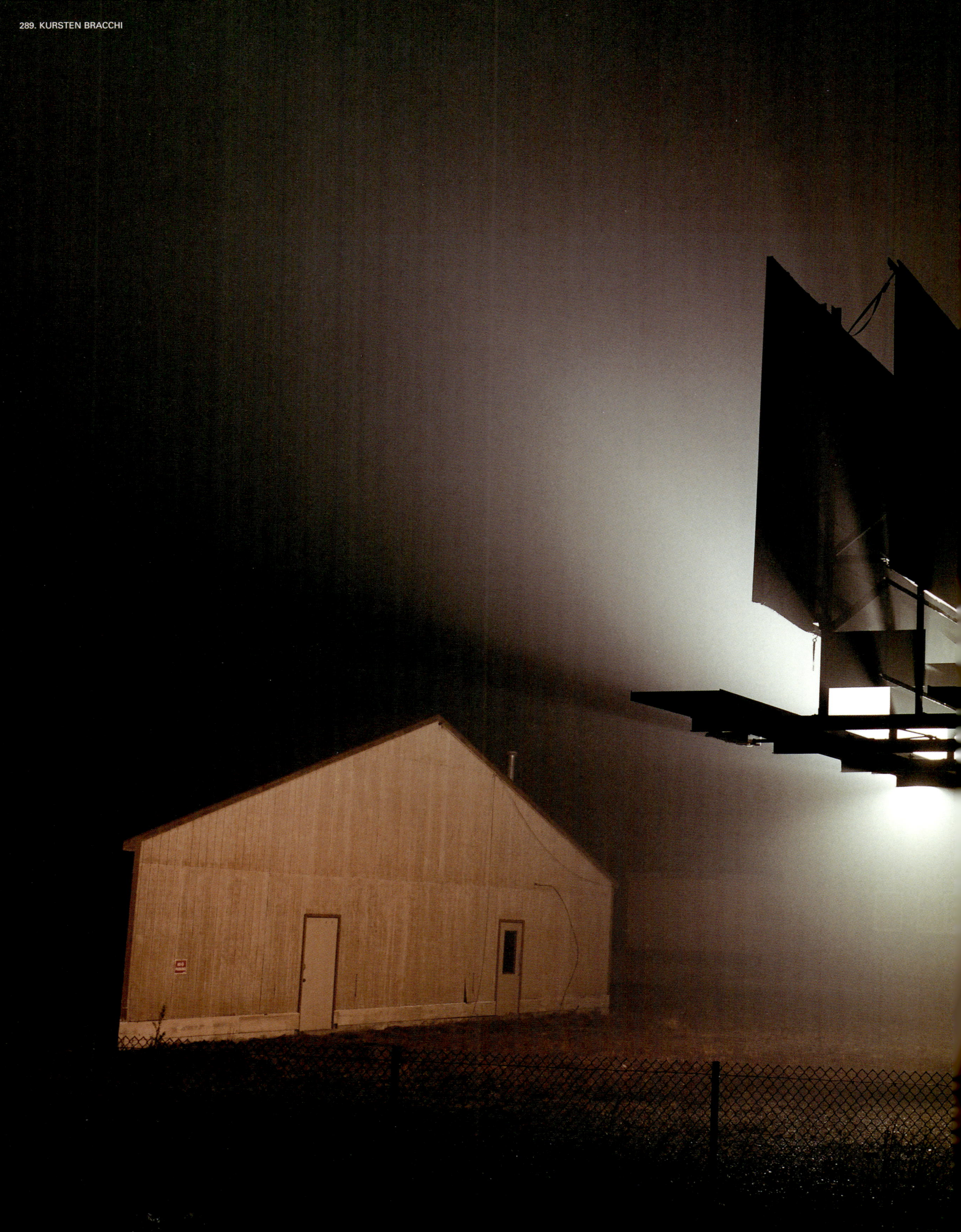

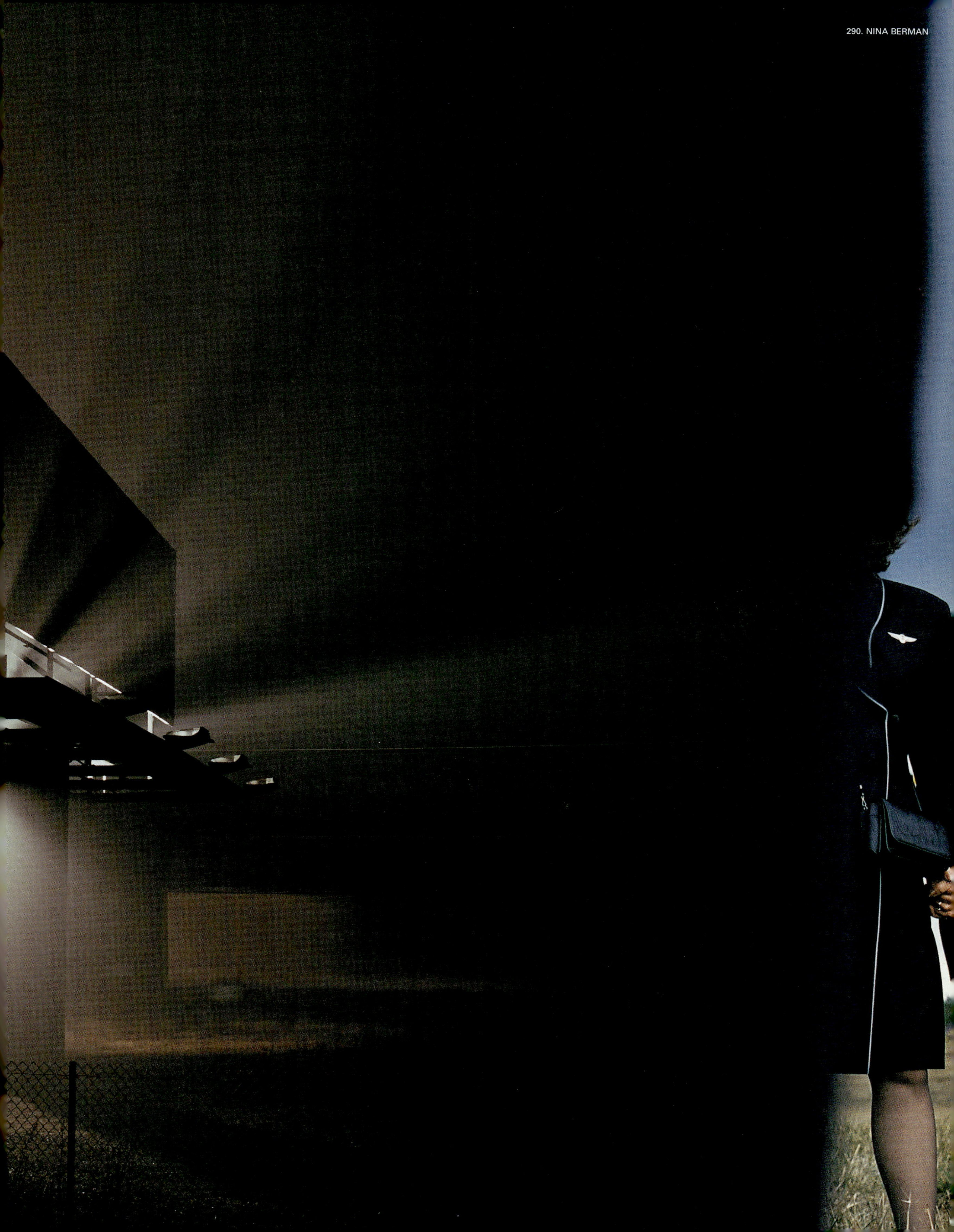

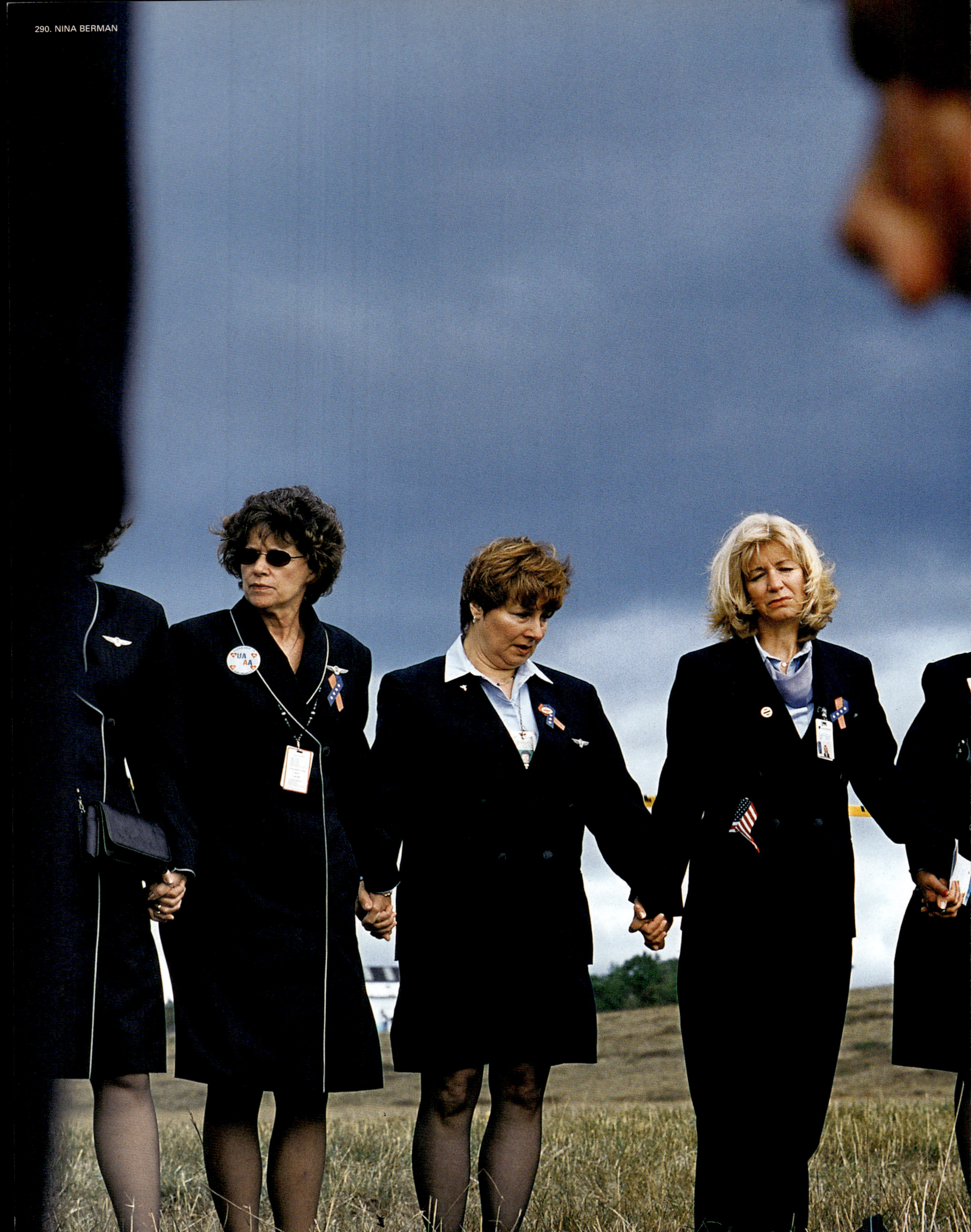
UA
AA

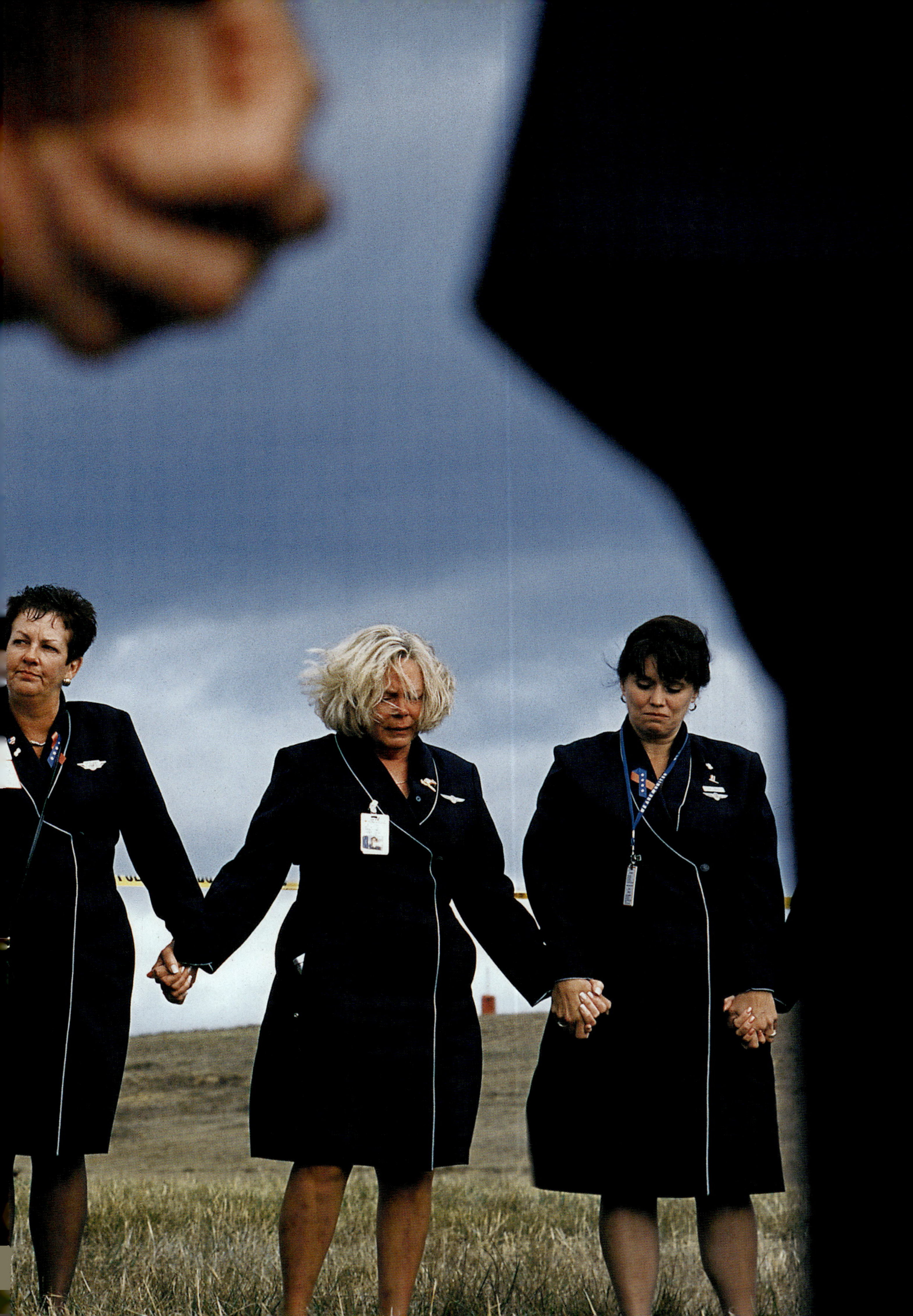

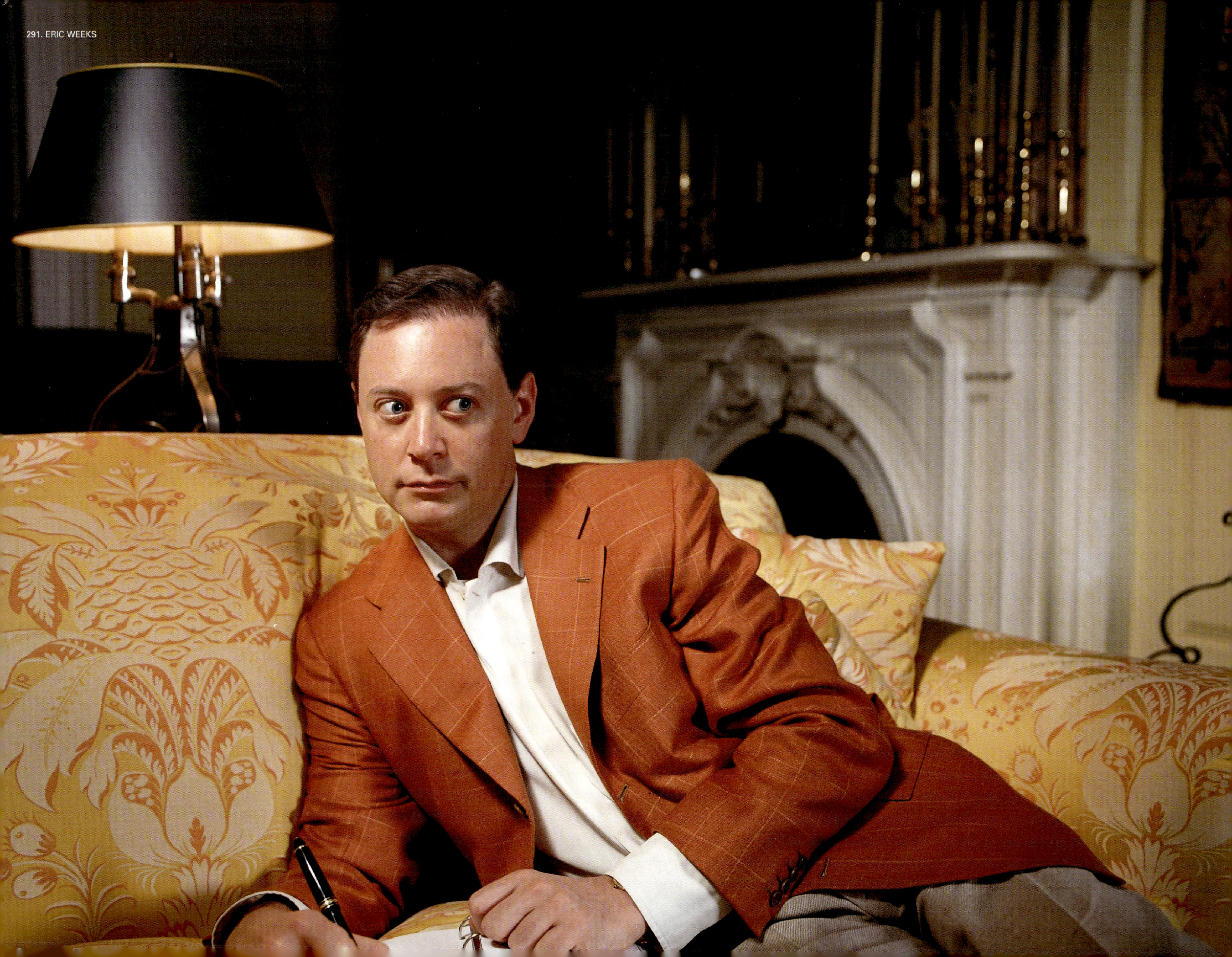

291. ERIC WEEKS

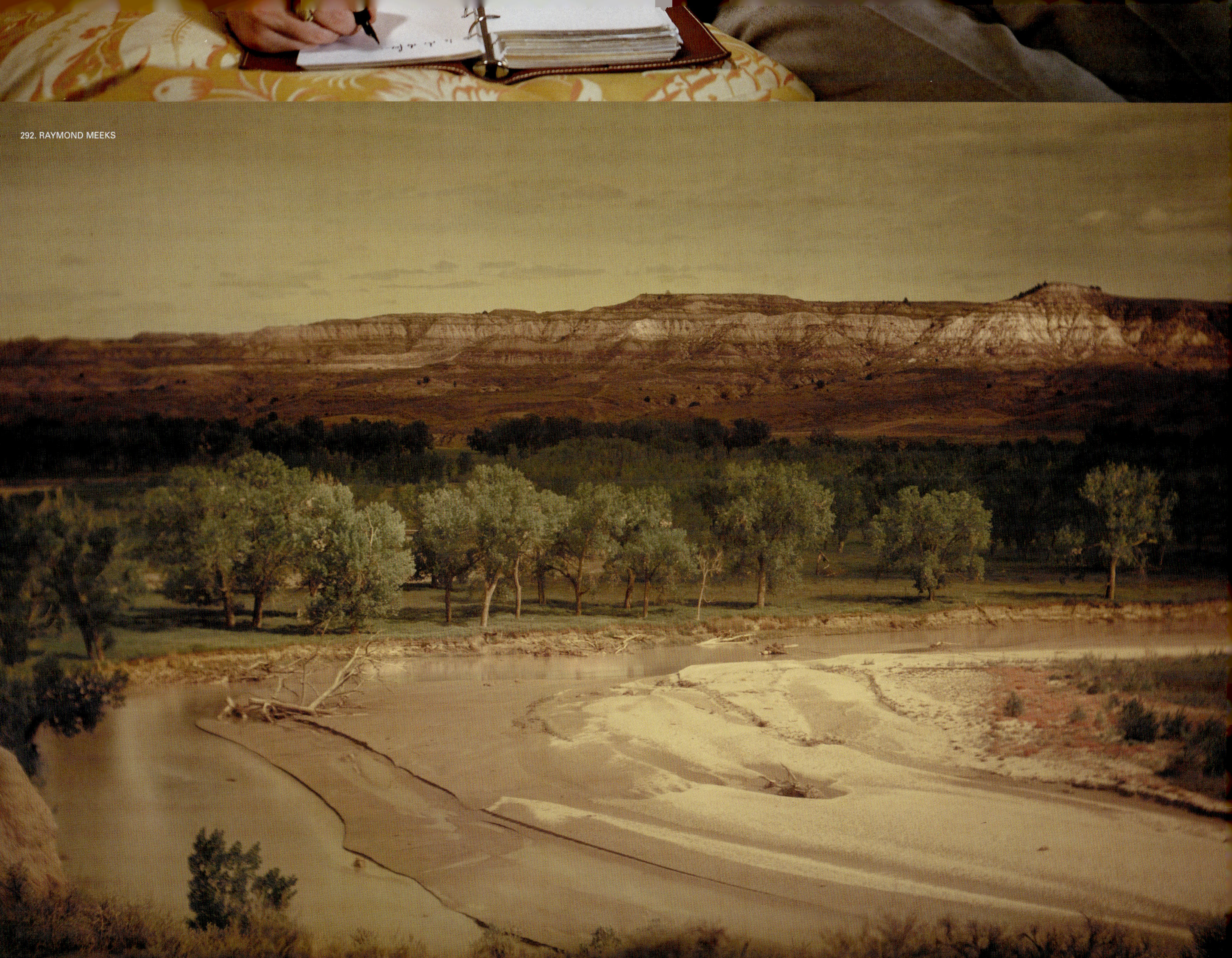

292. RAYMOND MEEKS

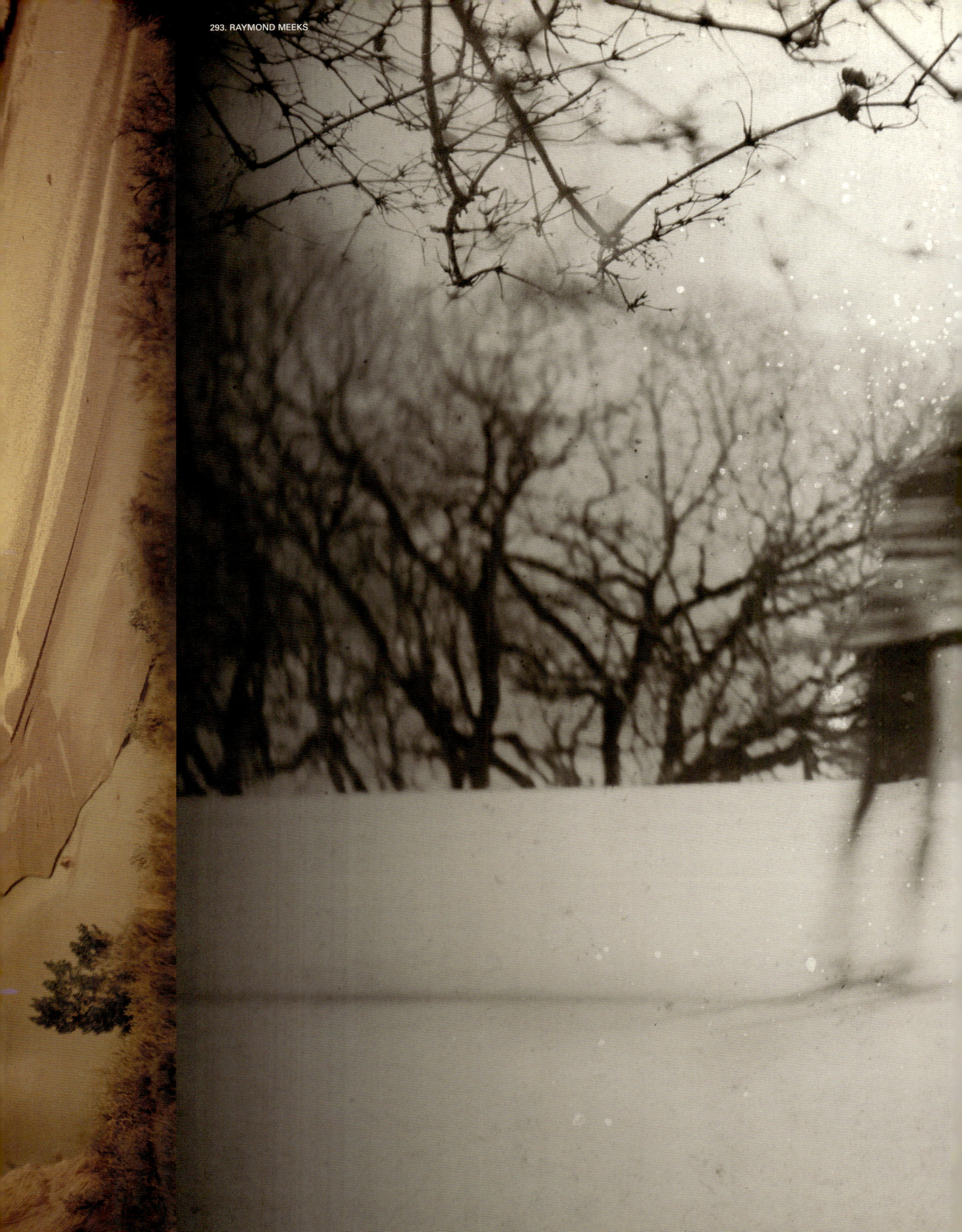

293. RAYMOND MEEKS

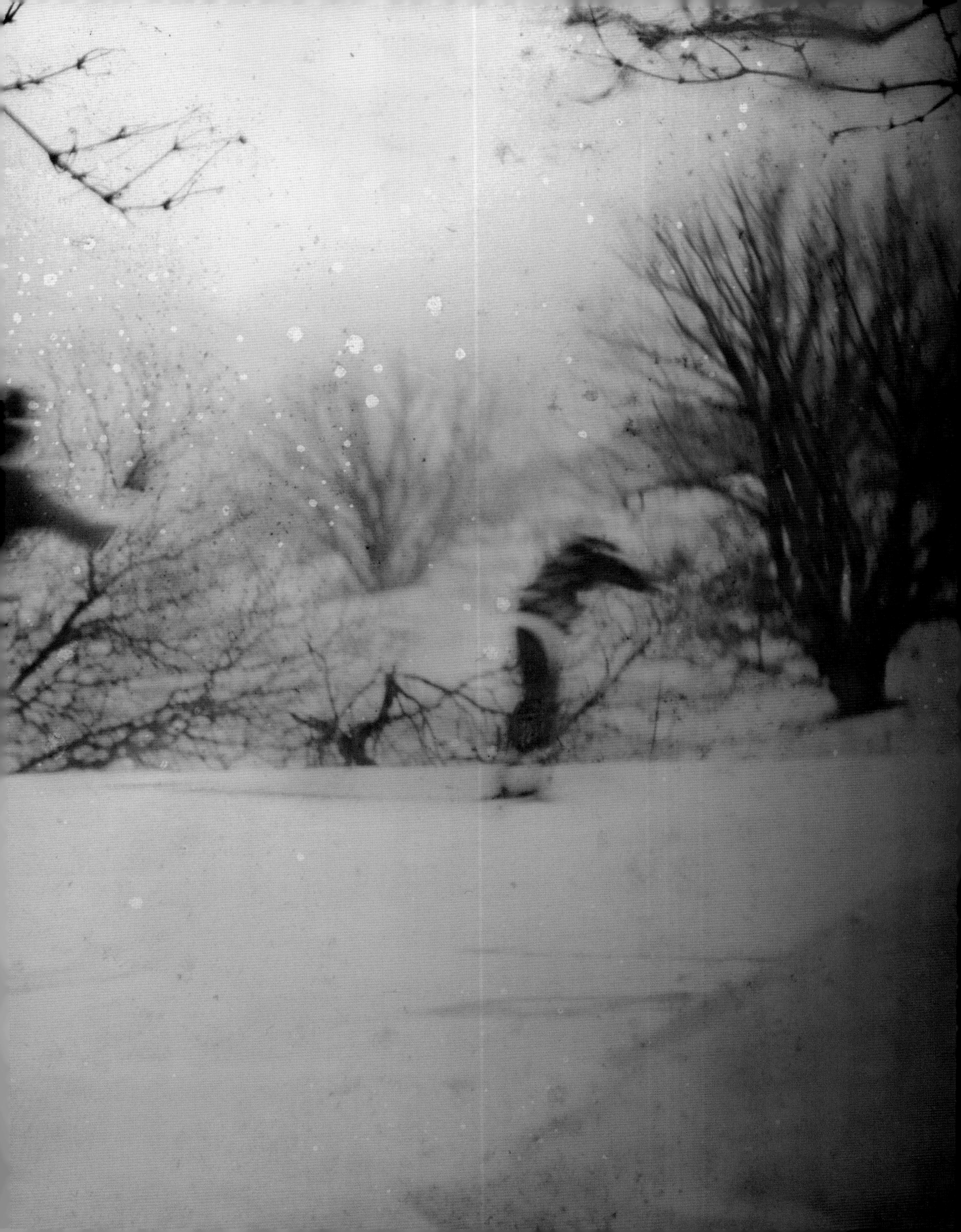

295. GEORGE PITTS

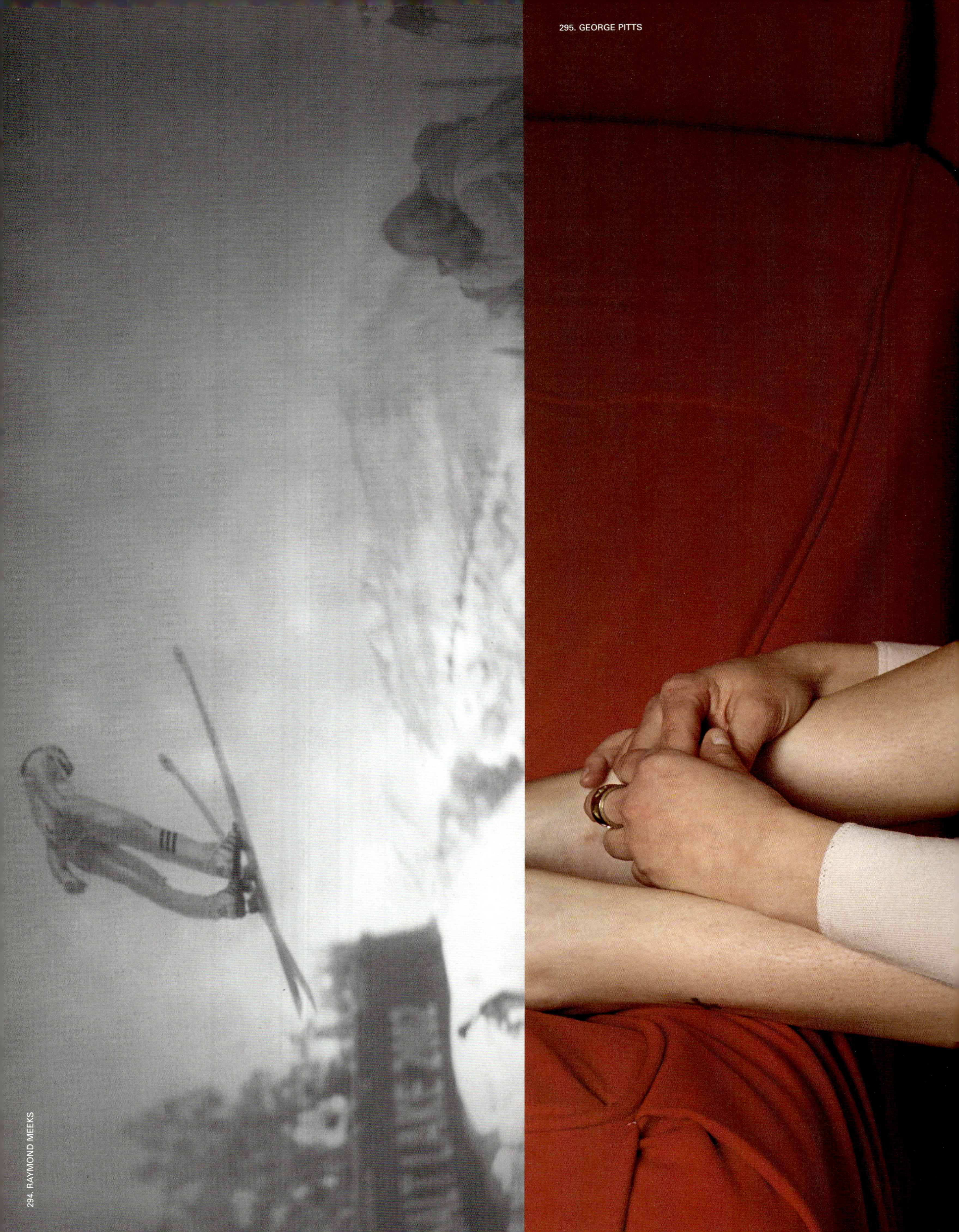

294. RAYMOND MEEKS

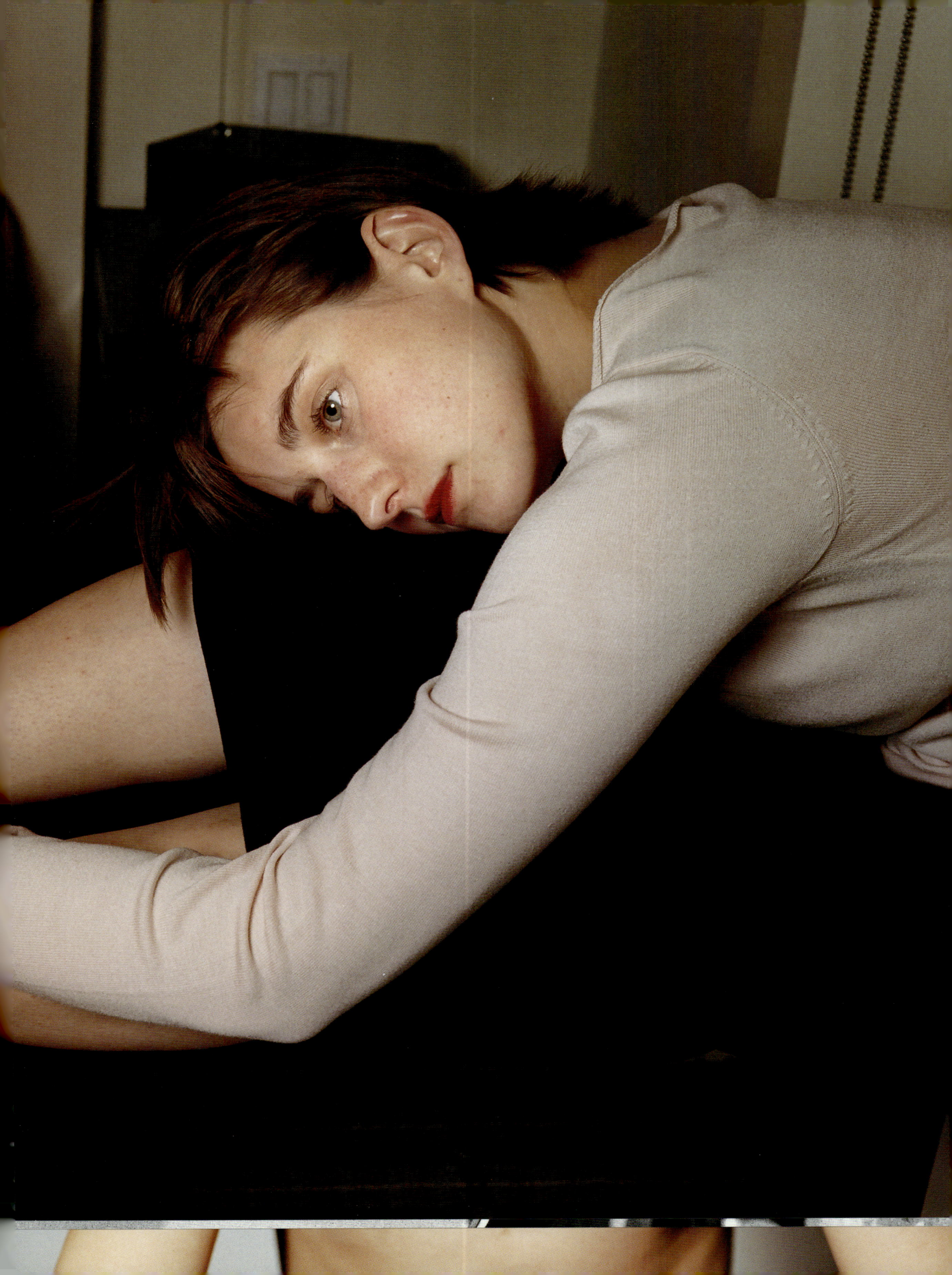

301. JULIANA SOHN

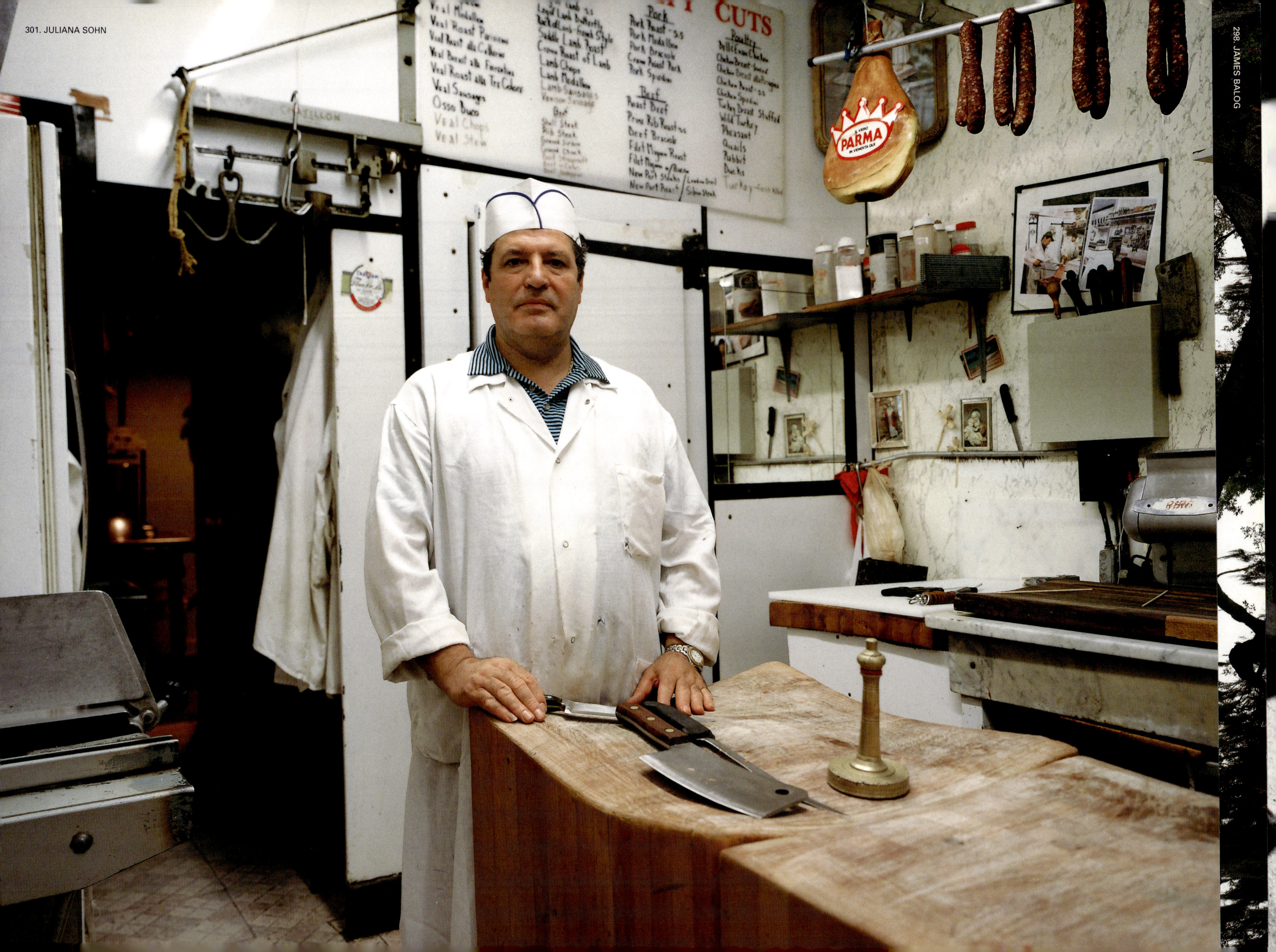

298. JAMES BALOG

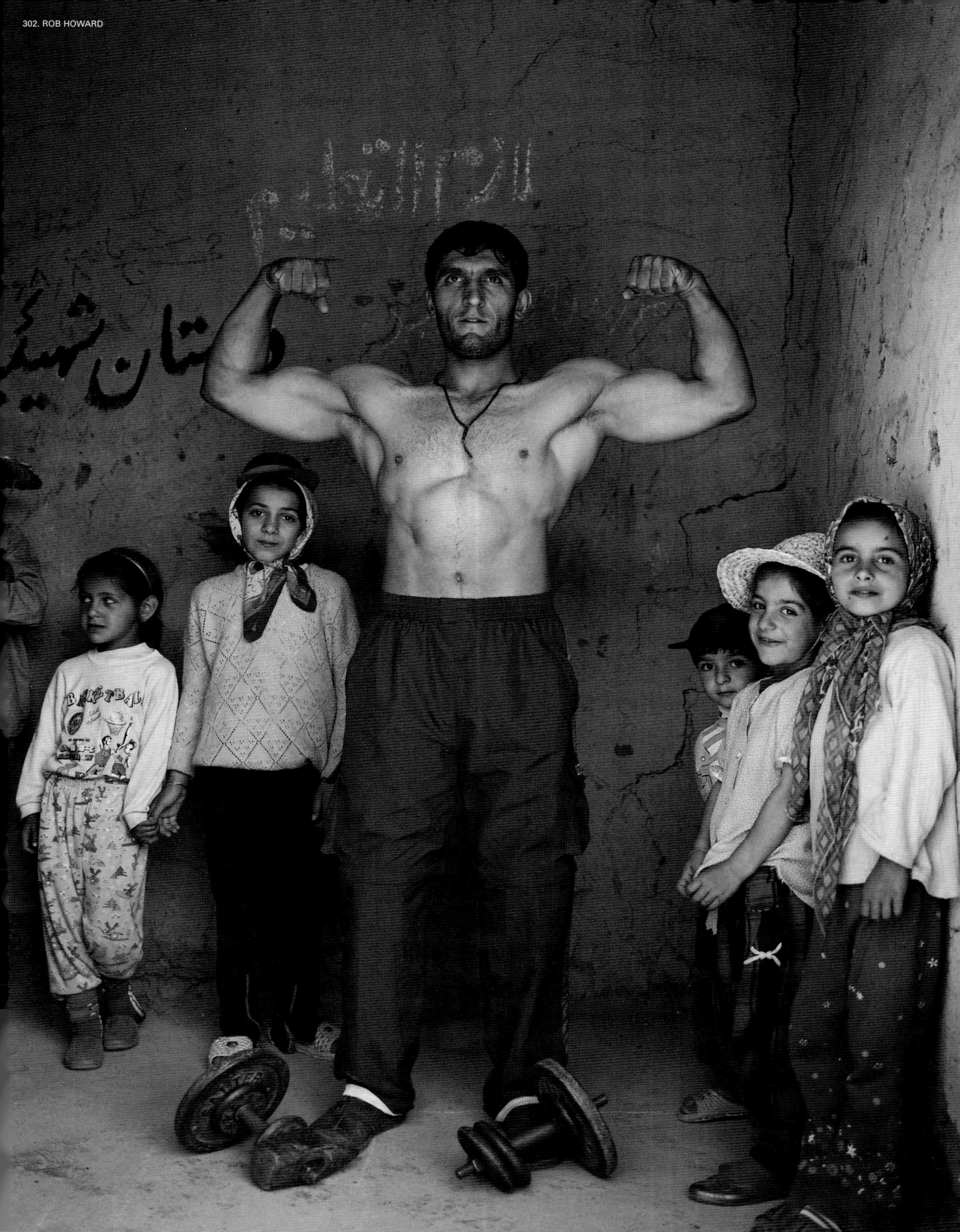

302. ROB HOWARD

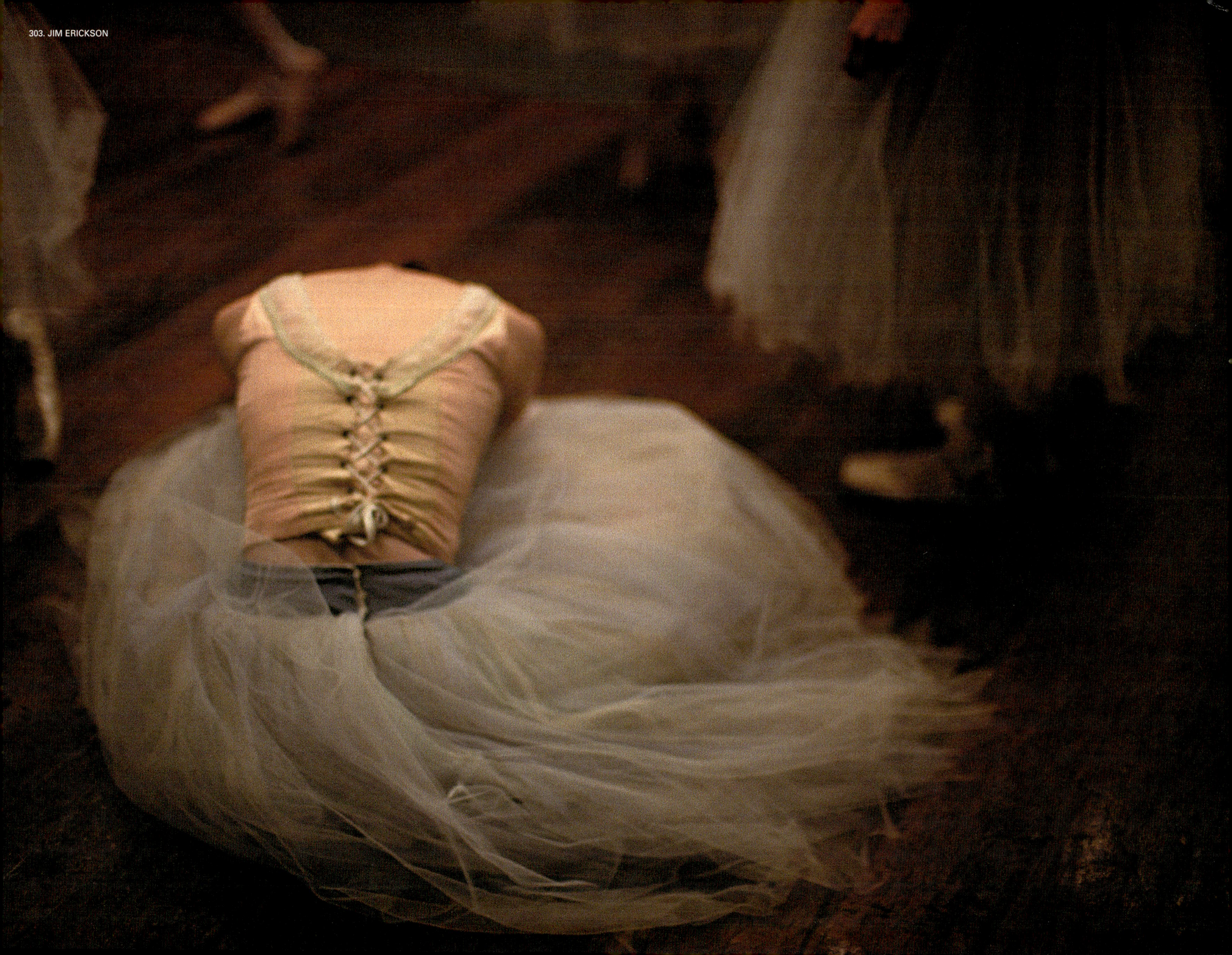

303. JIM ERICKSON

304. HENRY HORENSTEIN

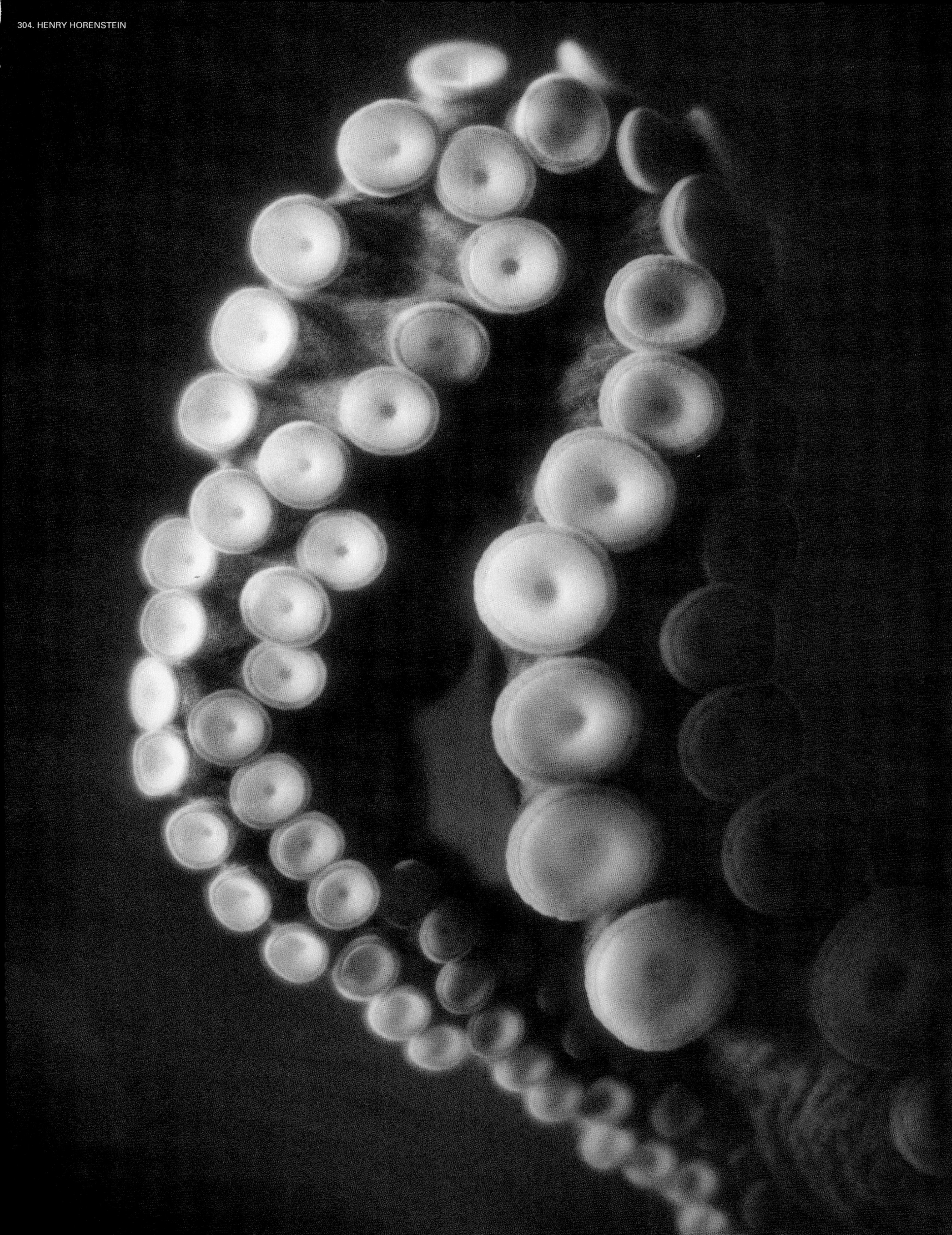

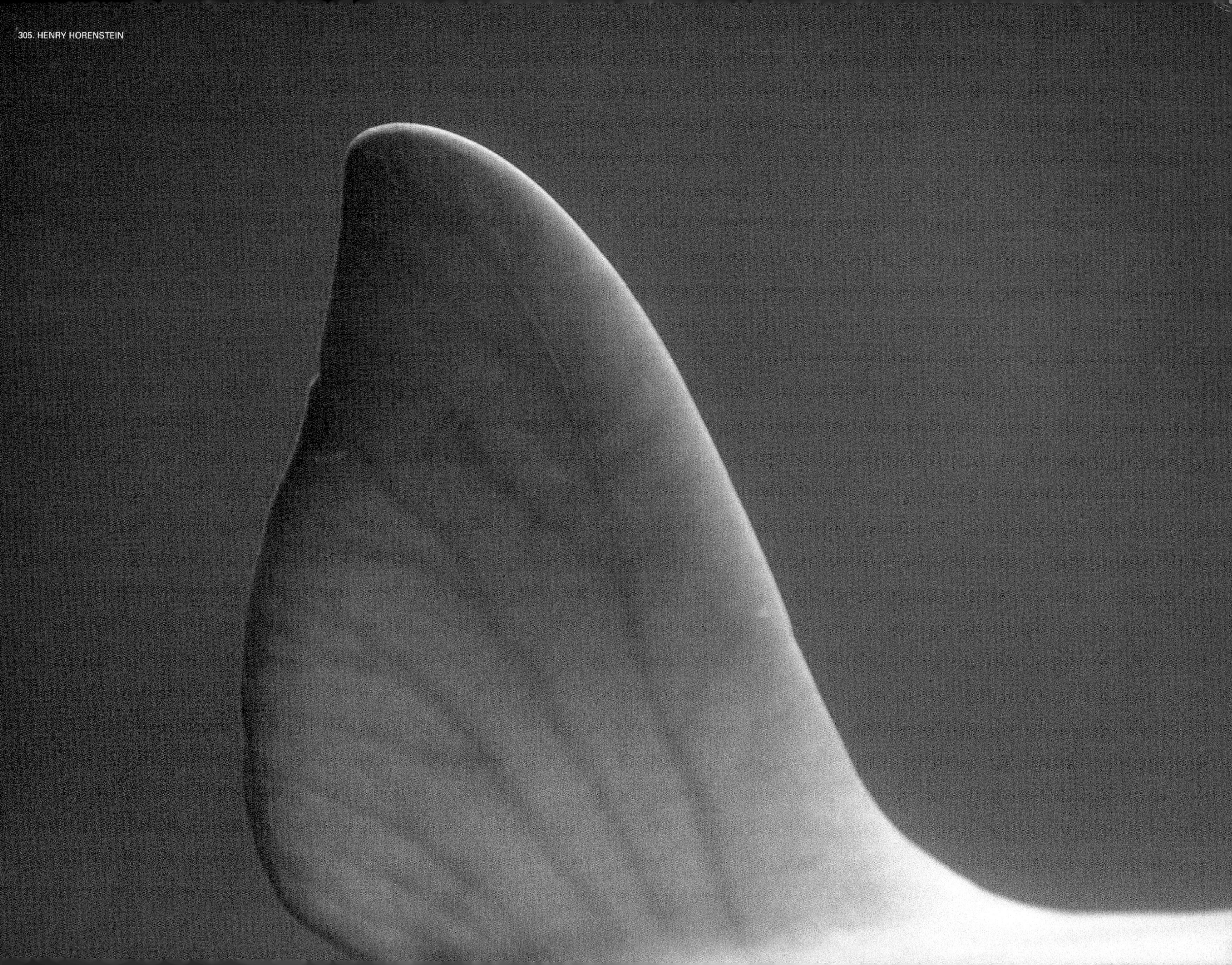

305. HENRY HORENSTEIN

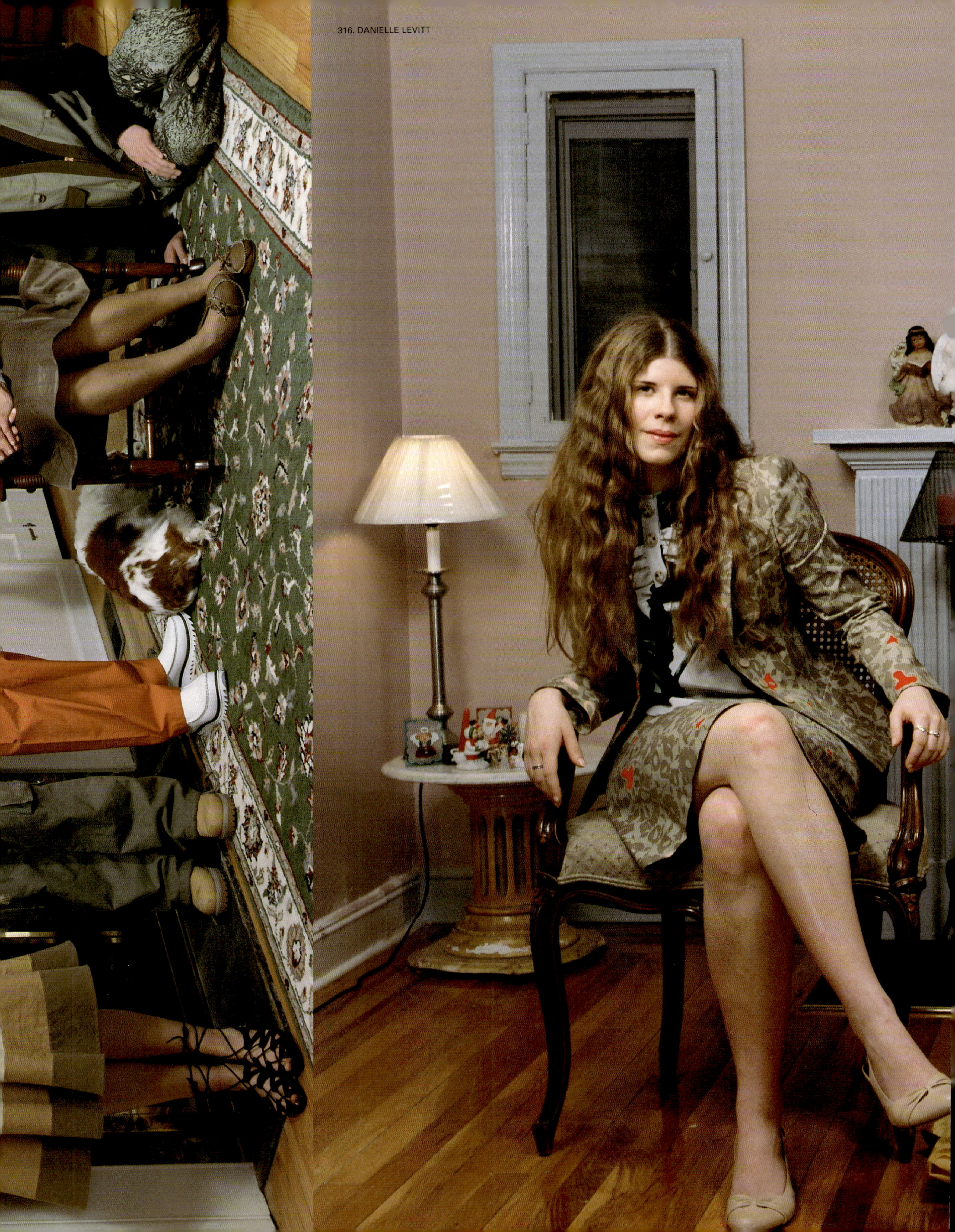

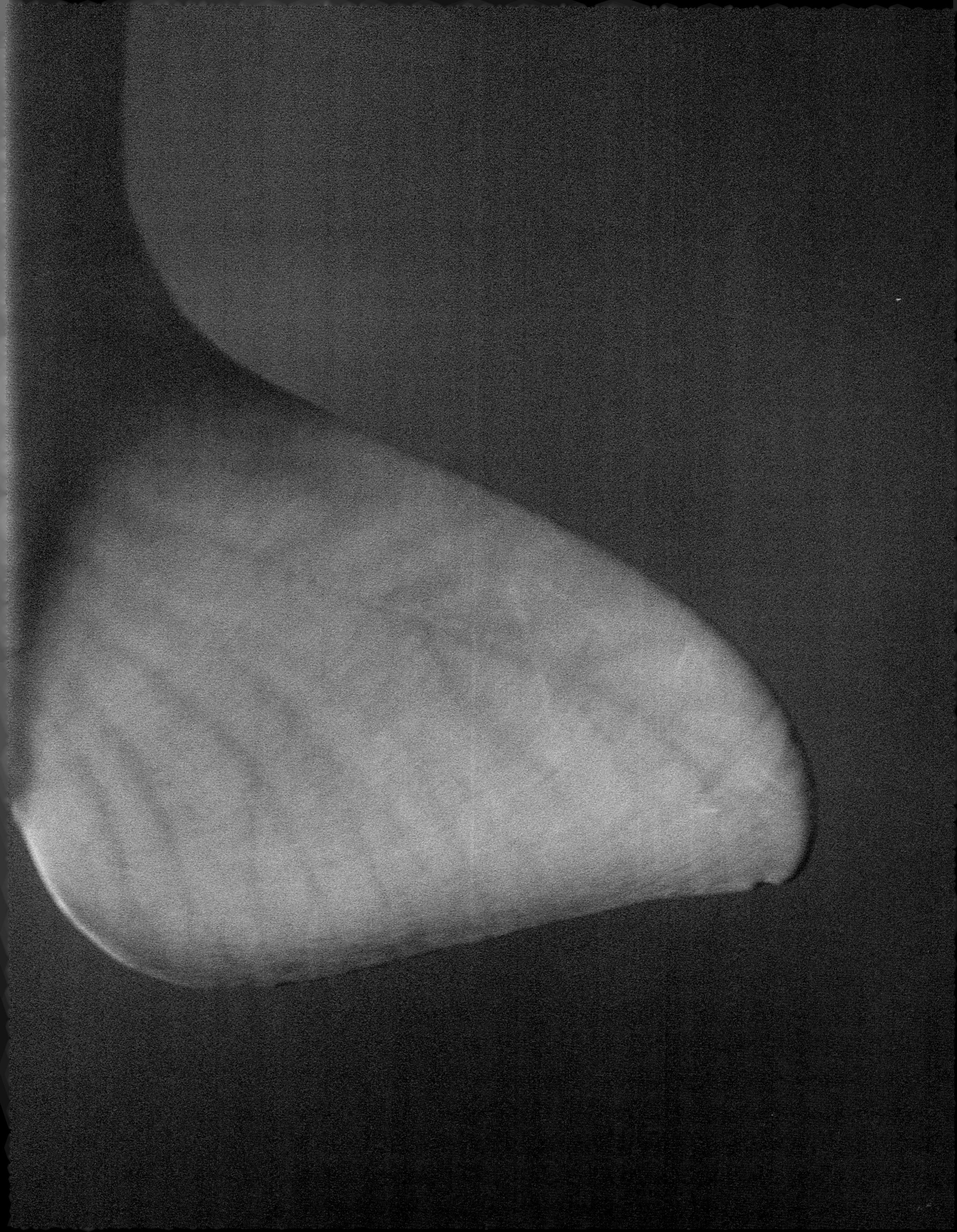

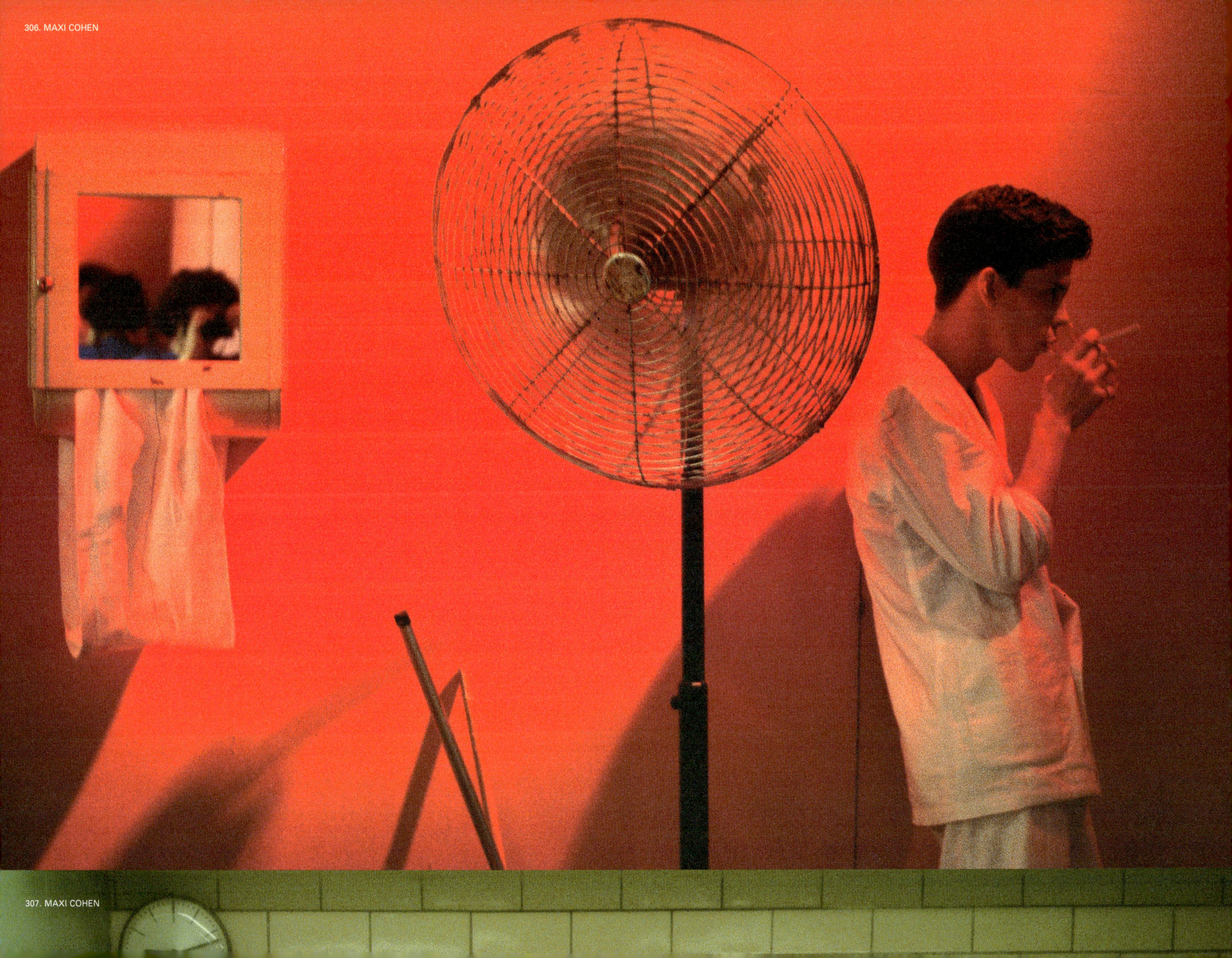

306. MAXI COHEN

307. MAXI COHEN

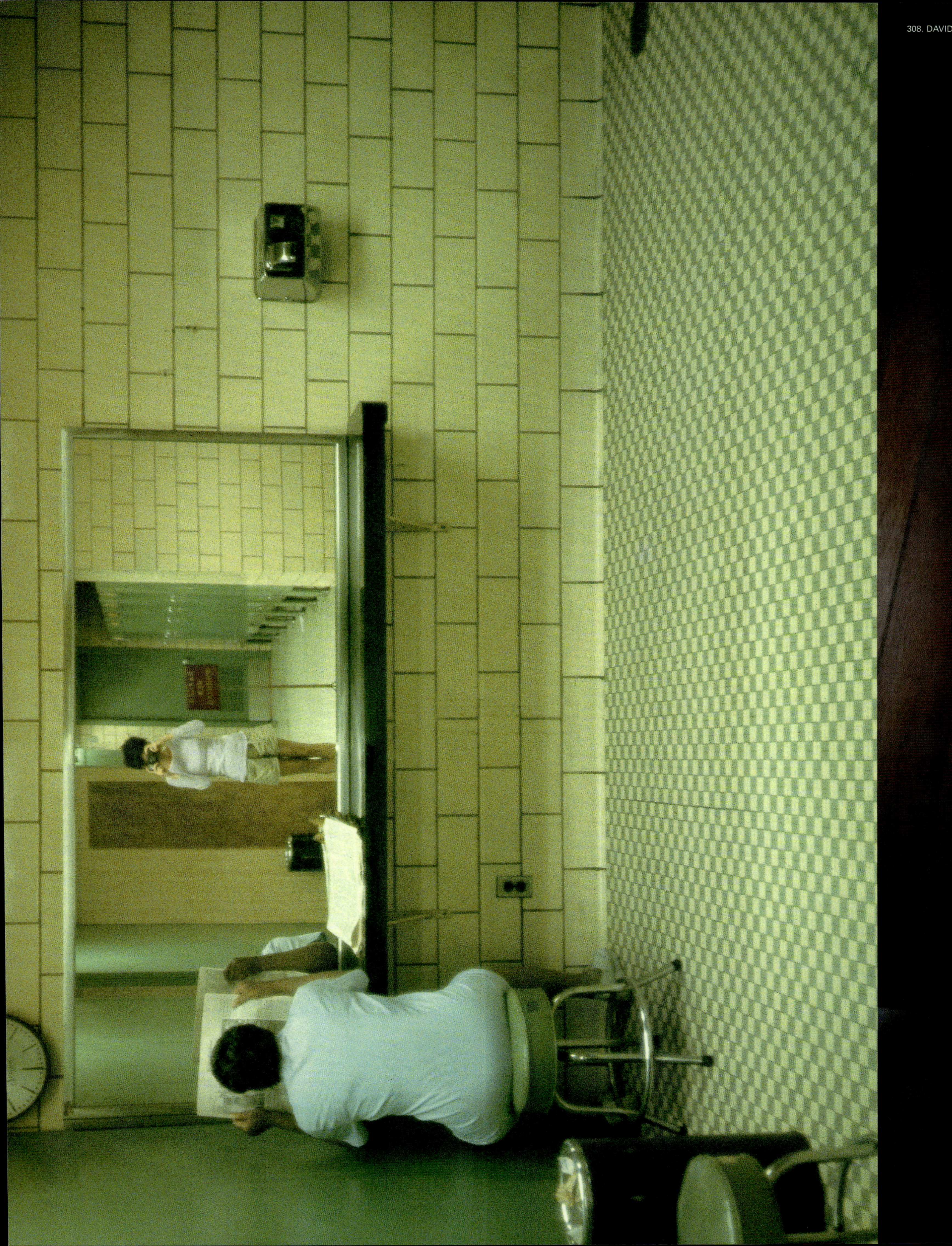

308. DAVID

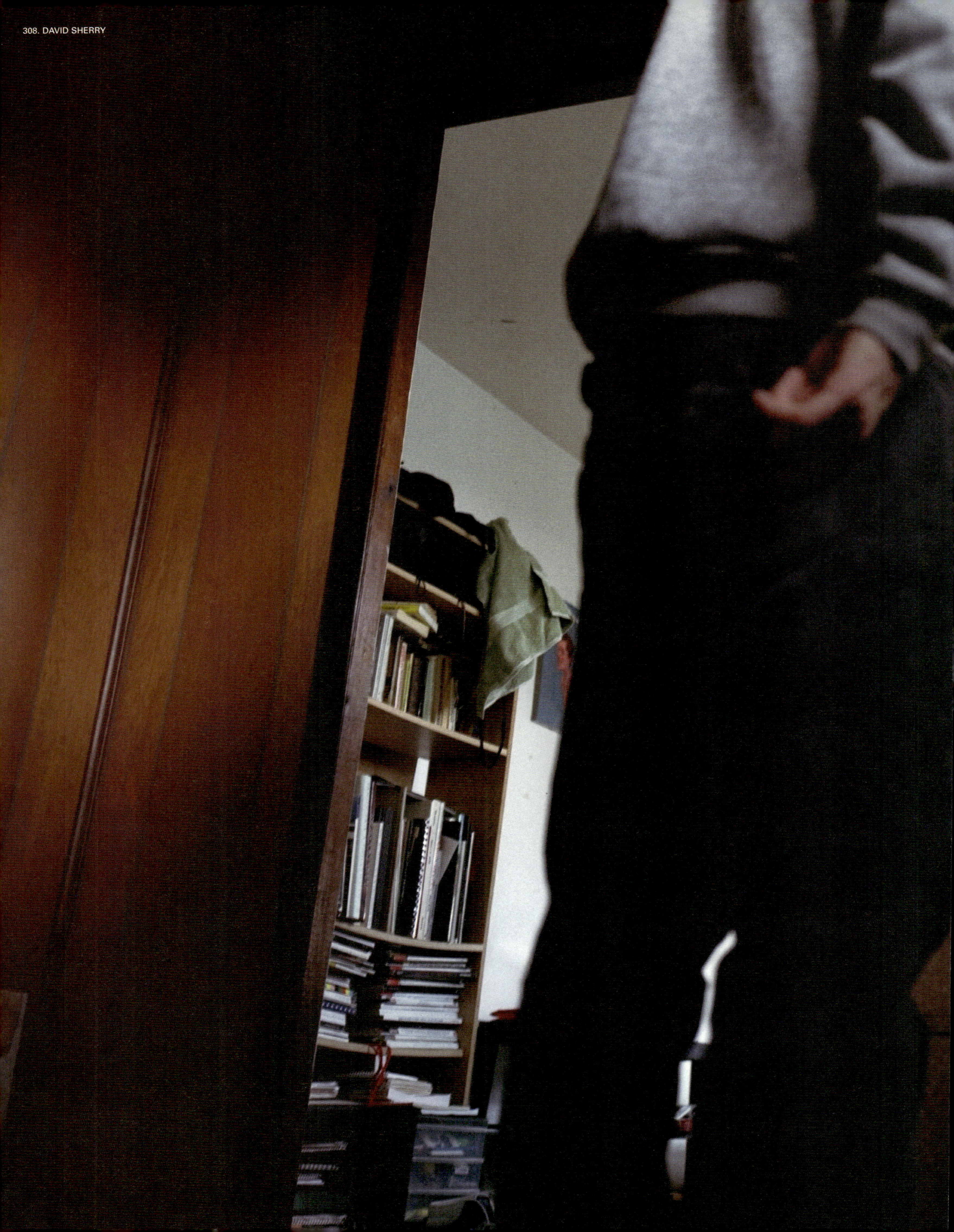

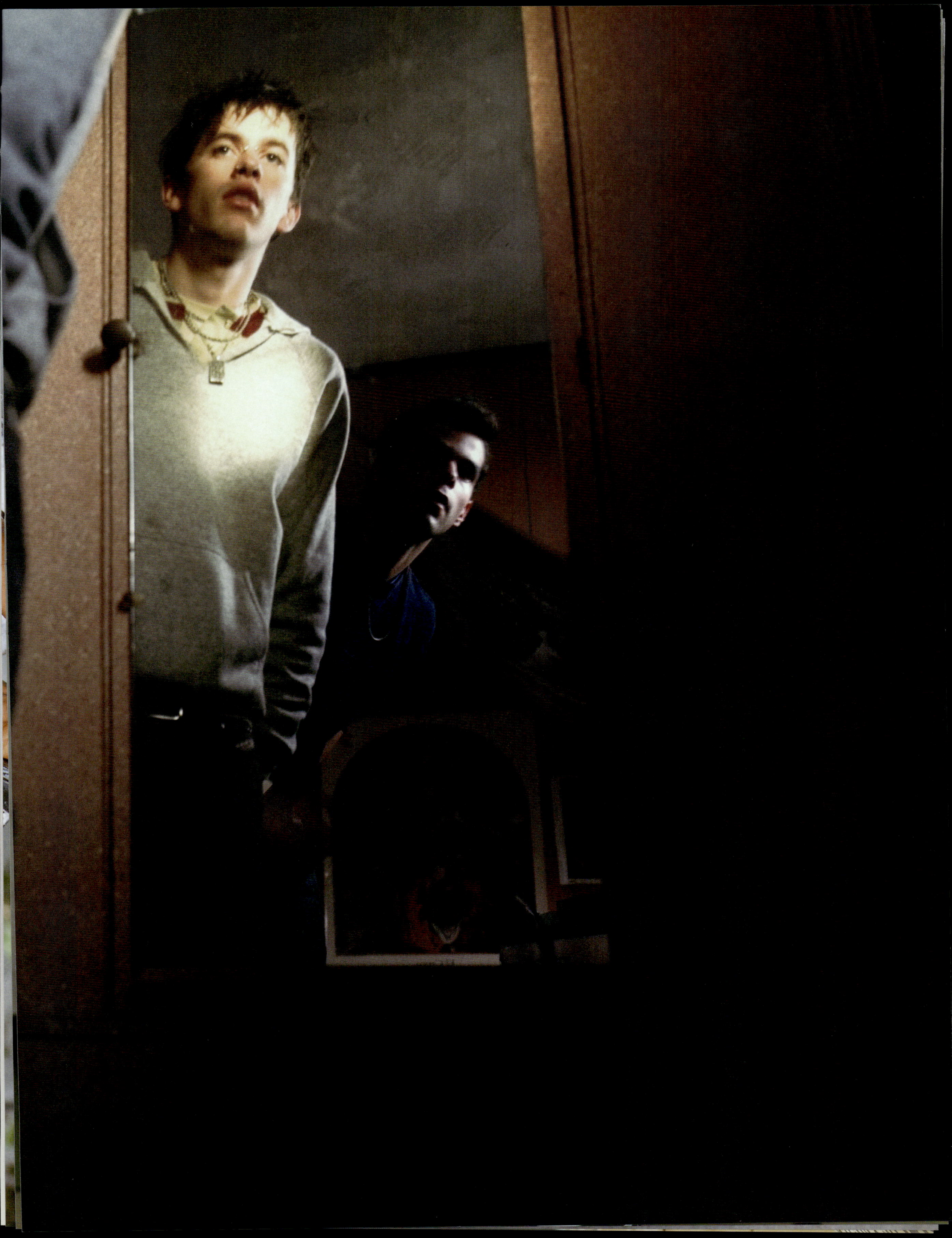

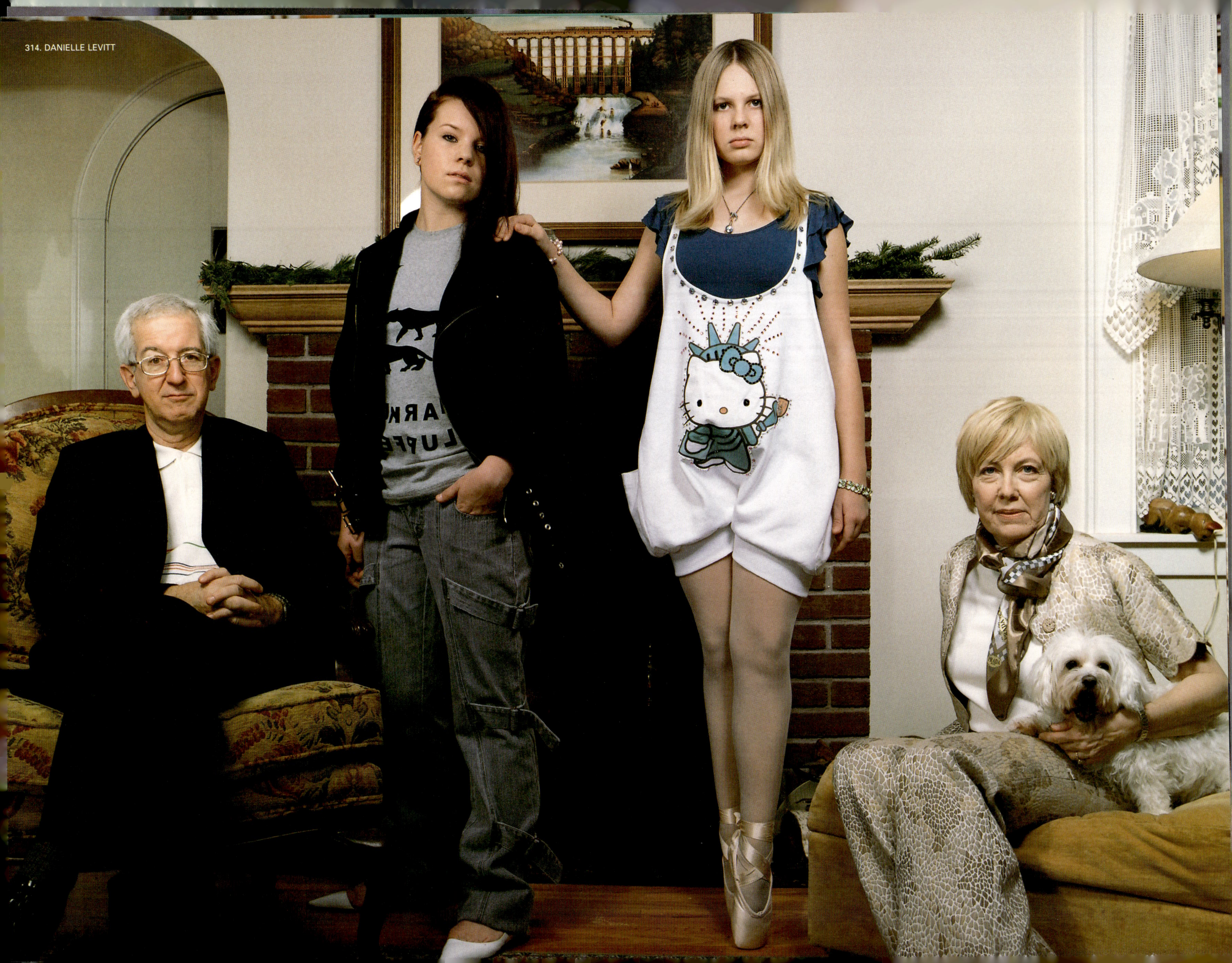

314. DANIELLE LEVITT

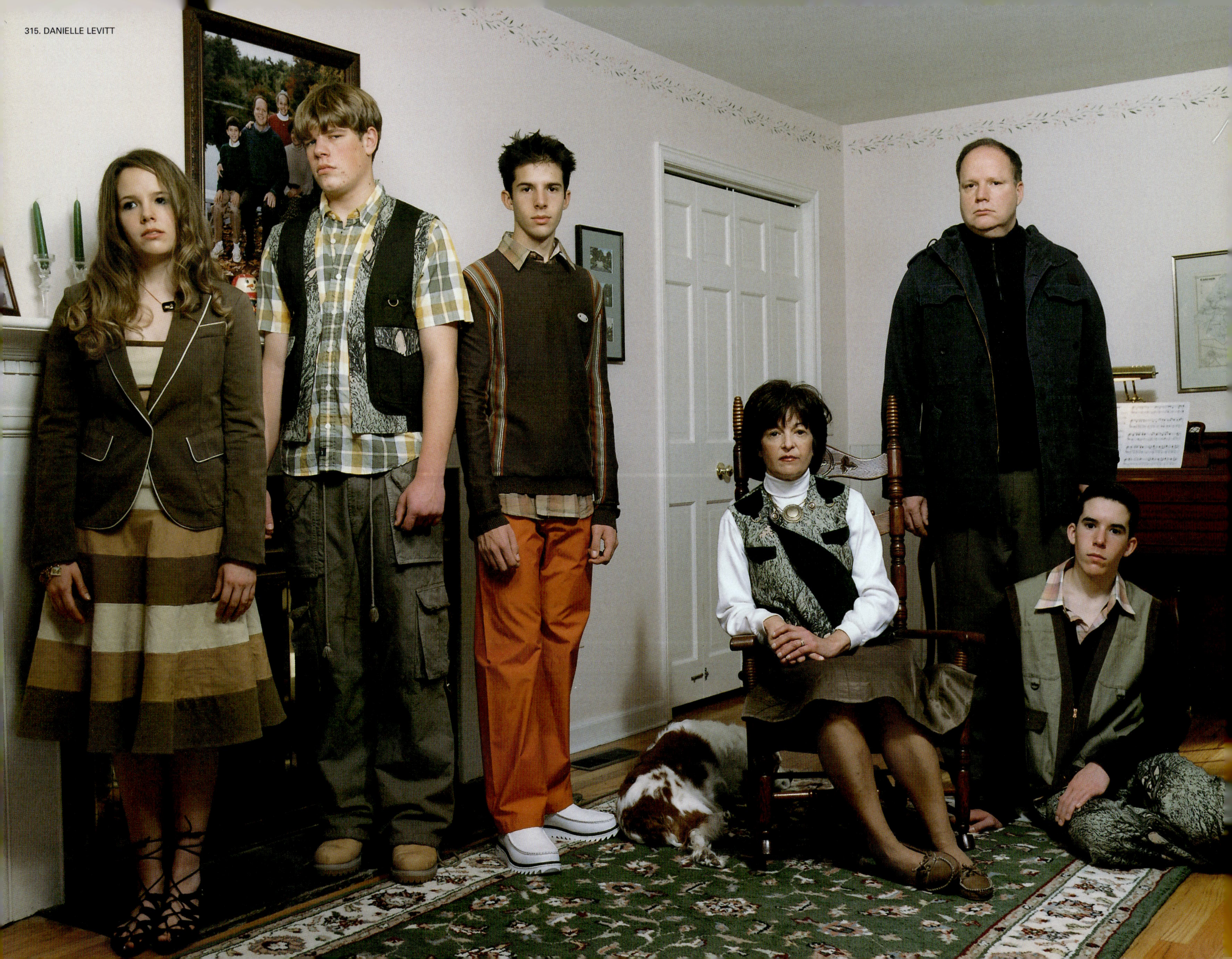

315. DANIELLE LEVITT

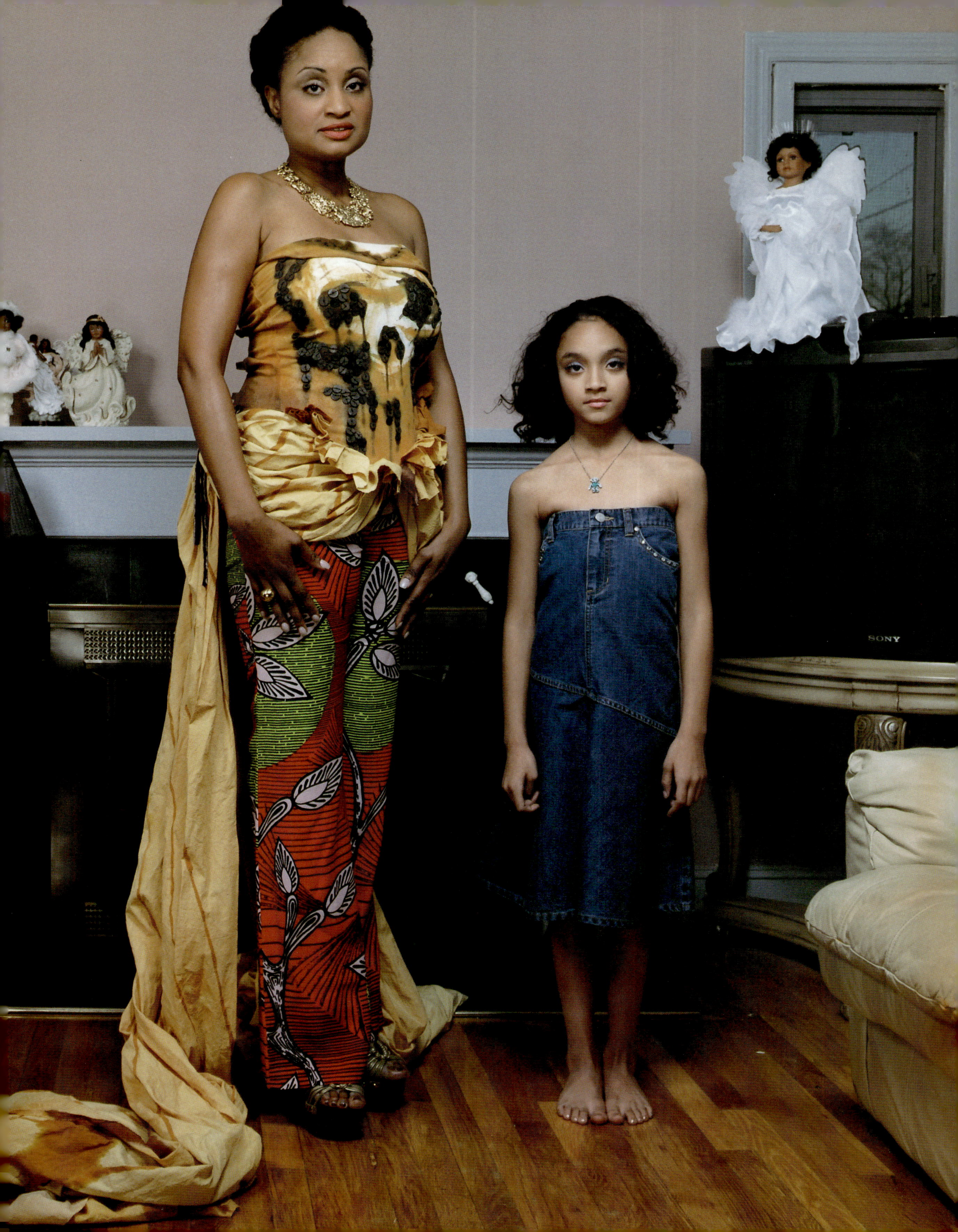
SONY

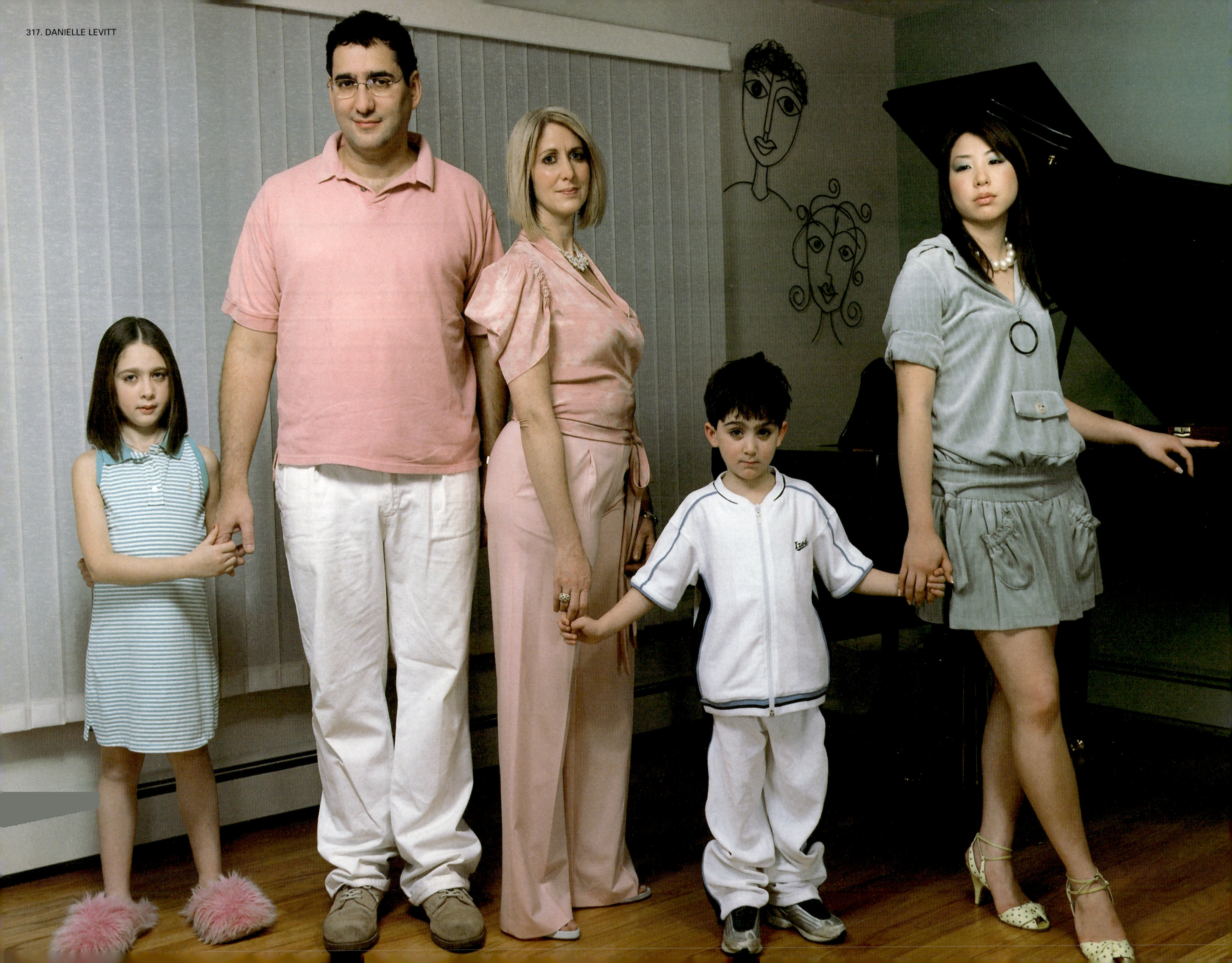

317. DANIELLE LEVITT

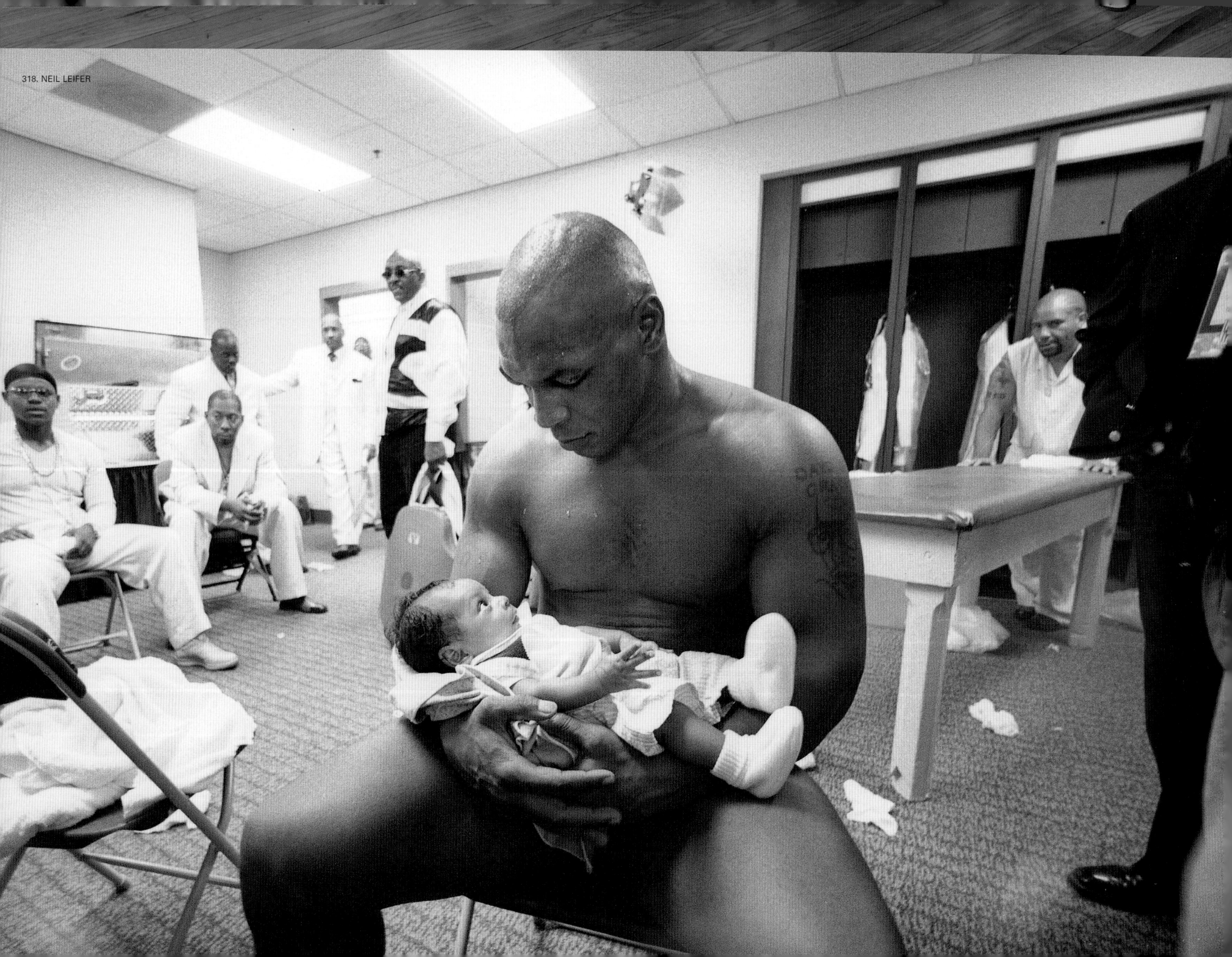

318. NEIL LEIFER

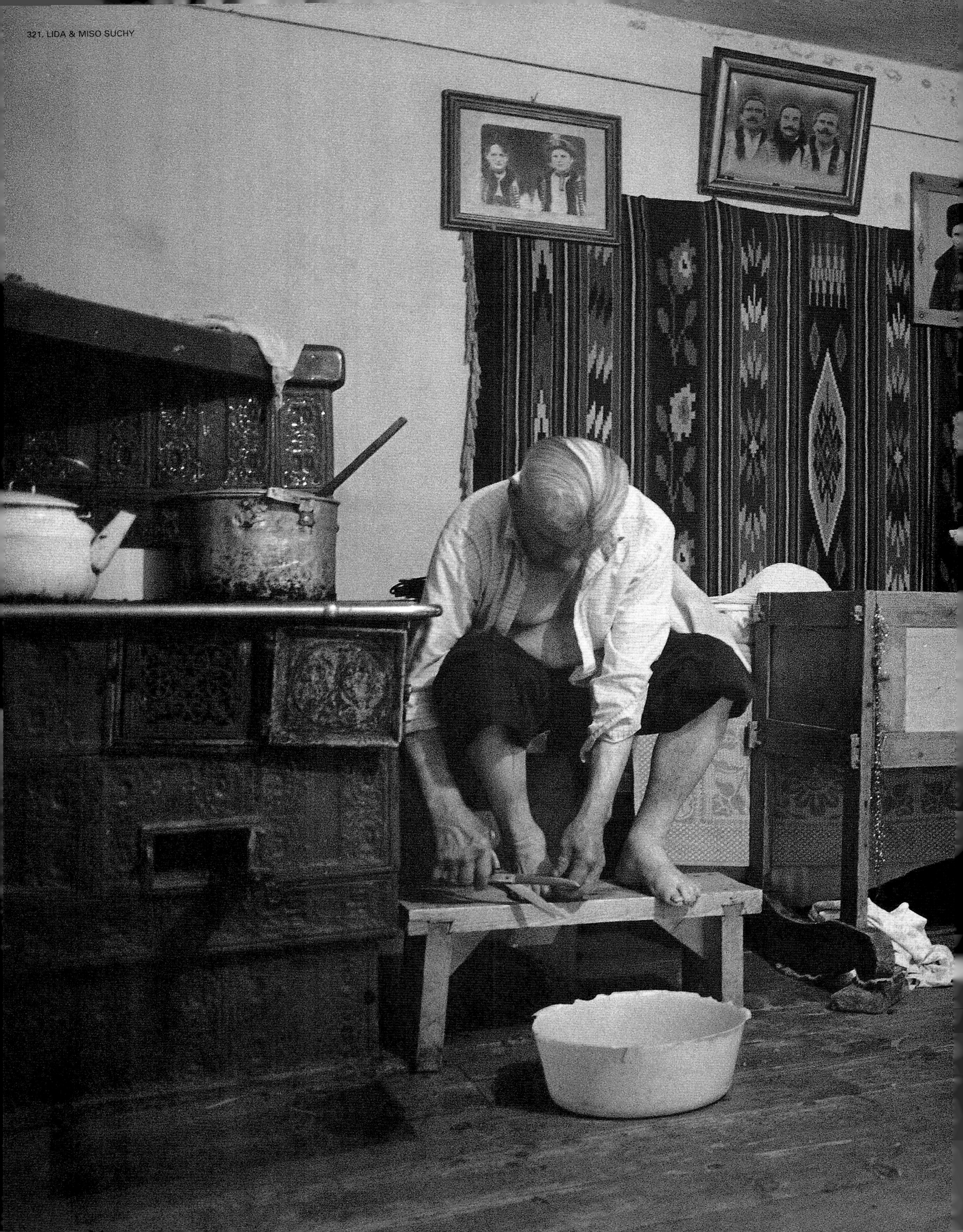

321. LIDA & MISO SUCHY

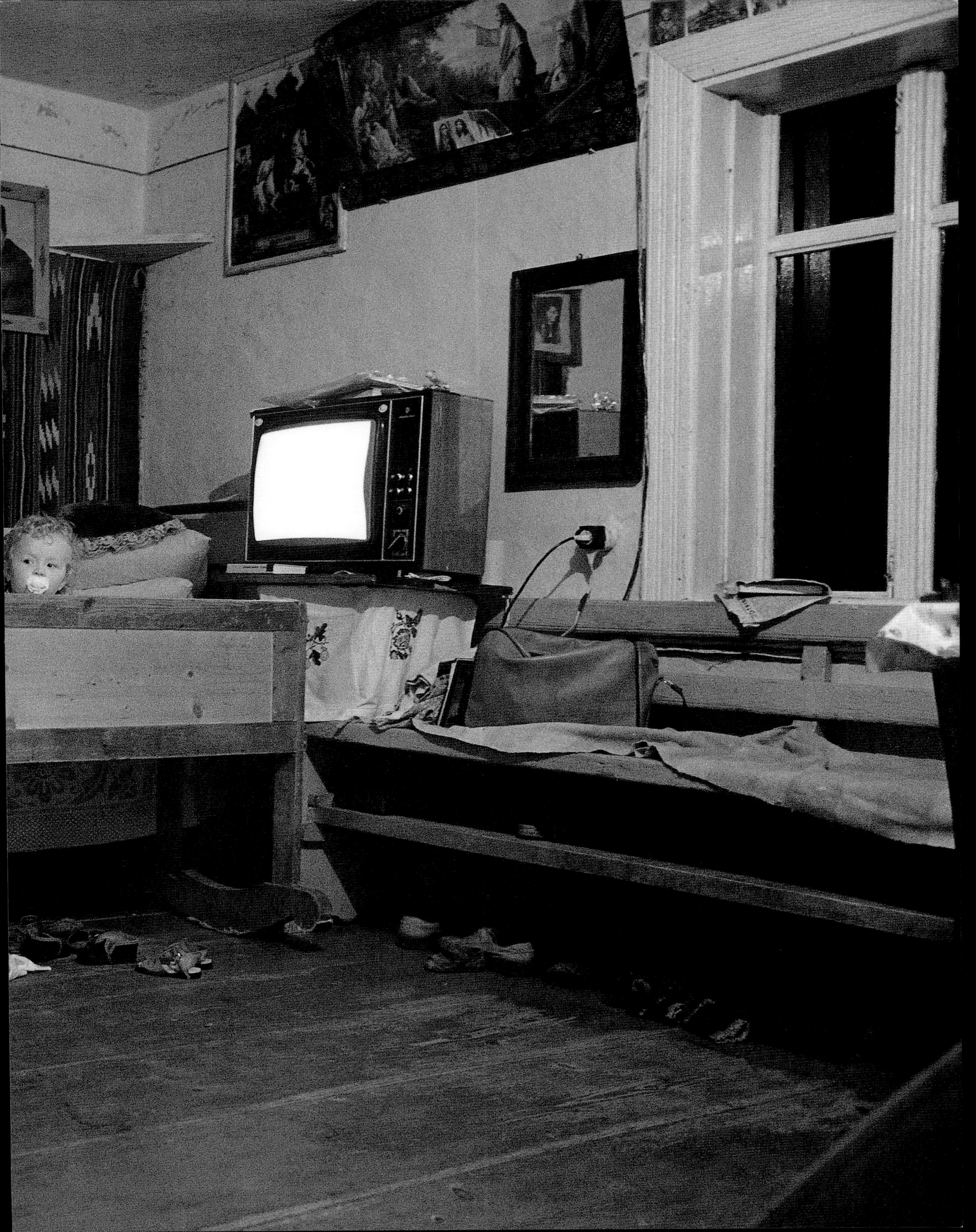

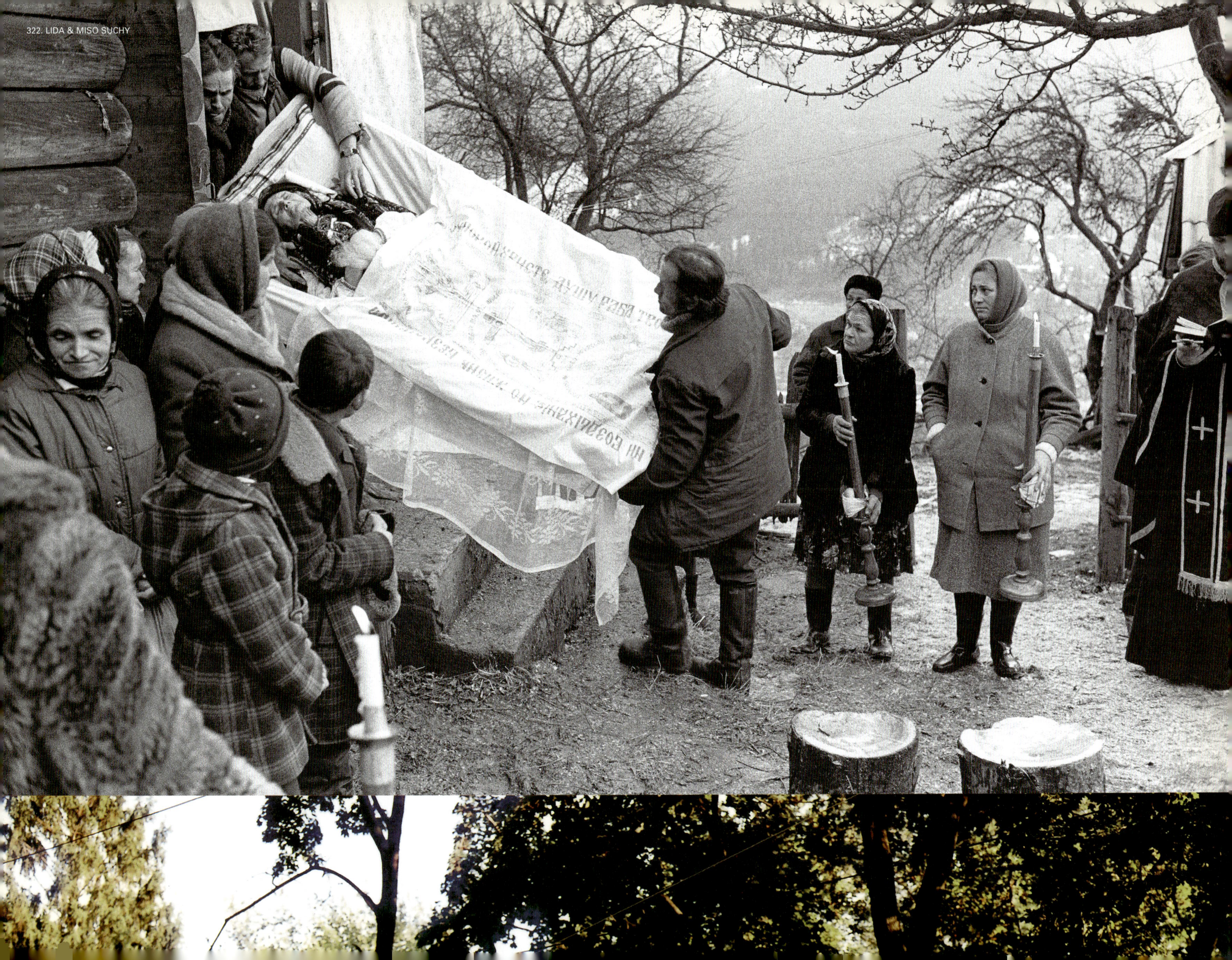

322. LIDA & MISO SUCHY

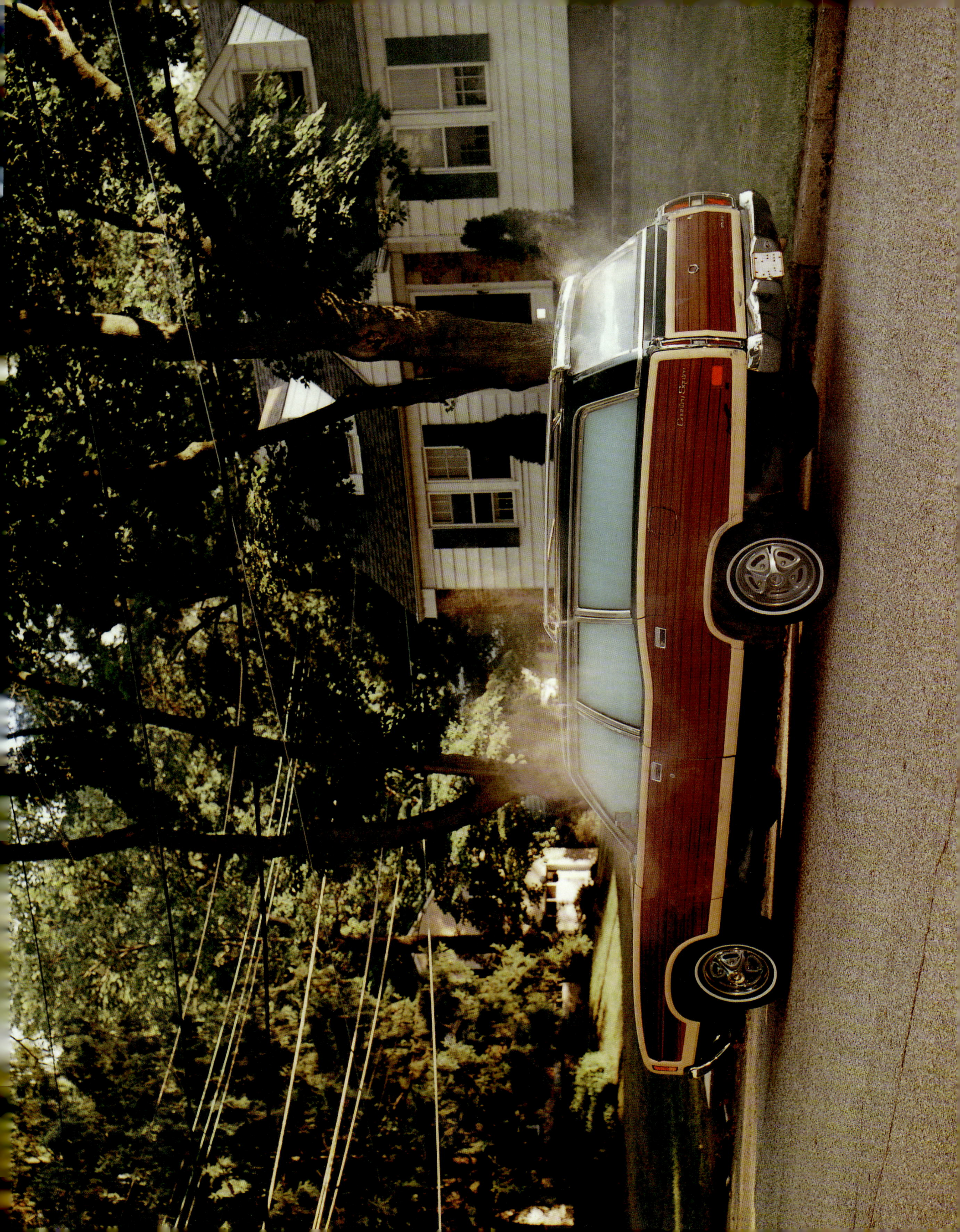

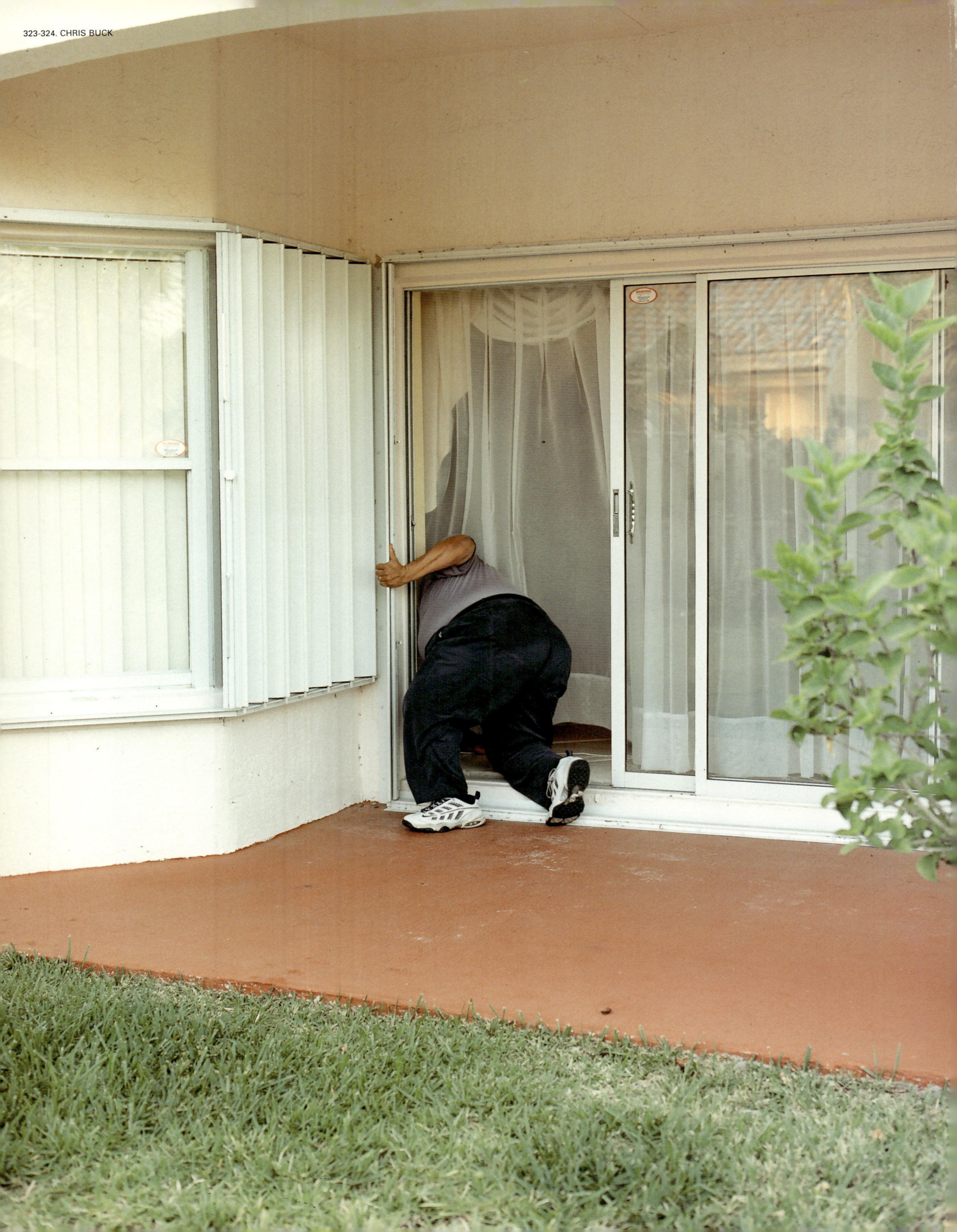

AMERICAN PHOTOGRAPHY 19

FOR ALMOST TWO DECADES, AMERICAN PHOTOGRAPHY HAS PRESENTED "THE YEAR IN PICTURES"— A COLLECTION OF IMAGES THAT REVEALS THE STATE OF THE MEDIUM, THE STATE OF THE WORLD, EVEN A STATE OF MIND. SELECTED BY A JURY OF OUTSTANDING PUBLISHING AND DESIGN PROFESSIONALS, THESE PHOTOS, IN A SENSE, CHARACTERIZE THE PREVAILING MOOD OF THE COUNTRY AND OF THE PHOTOGRAPHERS WHO CAPTURED THAT TIME.

THIS YEAR'S SELECTION MARKS A TURNING POINT FOR PHOTOGRAPHY IN THE AGE OF TERRORISM. THE IMMEDIACY WITH WHICH STILL IMAGES NARRATE THE WORLD WE INHABIT, AND THE FREQUENCY WITH WHICH THEY ARE RECEIVED AND DEMANDED BY THE PUBLIC, HAVE CREATED AN URGENT NEED FOR PICTURES THAT OPERATE ON THE VIEWER'S PSYCHE AT HEIGHTENED LEVELS. AND THE WAYS IN WHICH TRUTHFUL PICTURES ARE BEING PRESENTED IN ALL KINDS OF MEDIA — FROM MAGAZINES, NEWSPAPERS, AND BOOKS TO ADVERTISING AND EVERYTHING IN BETWEEN — SUGGESTS THAT WE LIVE ON A FAULT LINE AS CLEARLY RECOGNIZED BY THE PUBLIC AS BY MEDIA PROFESSIONALS.

ANXIETY,
PATRIOTI
SM, TERR
ORISM

URISM,
MEMORI
ALS, WAR,
PLASTIC

SURGERY, FEAR, HIP HOP.

FROM WAR ZONES IN THE WEST BANK AND AFGHANISTAN AS WITNESSED BY CHRIS ANDERSON, KATE BROOKS, AND CHIEN-MIN CHUNG TO THE UNPREDICTABLE IMPLICATIONS OF THE MUNDANE

WORLD AS PORTRAYED BY WILLIAM EGGLESTON, LARRY FINK, AND CHRIS BUCK, THIS YEAR'S COLLECTION BRINGS TOGETHER SOME OF THE MOST RESPECTED NAMES IN PHOTOGRAPHY. IT ALSO INCLUDES A HOST OF EMERGING ARTISTS, SUCH AS DAVID S. ALLEE, DANIELLE LEAVITT, AND MOLLIE LAURIENZO, EACH OF WHOM PRESENTS A HIGHLY ARTICULATED POINT OF VIEW.

WHETHER THE PHOTOGRAPHER IS NARRATING A STORY THROUGH ITS SUBJECT MATTER — OR THROUGH THE CAMERA'S CAPACITY FOR EXPLORATION OUTSIDE THE BOX — THIS YEAR'S COLLECTION DEMONSTRATES THE POWER OF PHOTOGRAPHY AS AN ART FORM, AS A COMMUNICATOR, AS A PERSUADER. FROM LARGE-FORMAT LANDSCAPES BY WILL WENDT TO 19TH-CENTURY PROCESSES BEING PRACTICED AGAIN TODAY BY JOHN DUGDALE, AMANDA MEANS, AND OTHERS TO DIGITAL FORMATS THAT ALLOW NEARLY SIMULTANEOUS CONNECTIONS BETWEEN PHOTOJOURNALISTS AND MEDIA OUTLETS, THE RANGE OF IMAGE-MAKING TECHNIQUES, STYLES, AND DEVICES IS EXTRAORDINARY. WHETHER EDITORIAL OR JOURNALISTIC OR PROMOTIONAL OR PERSONAL, MANY OF THESE IMAGES CONVEY THE NOTION THAT A NECESSARY CORRECTION HAS OCCURRED IN THE WAY WE APPREHEND VISUAL INFORMATION. AND THAT A HUNGER FOR PHOTOGRAPHIC TRUTH IS IN THE WIND.

THIS VOLUME OF AMERICAN PHOTOGRAPHY PRESENTS THE SELECTED IMAGES (THOSE THAT RECEIVED A MAJORITY VOTE OR BETTER) FROM OUR ANNUAL COMPETITION HELD IN JANUARY 2003. THE CHOSEN PHOTOGRAPHERS (THOSE WHOSE IMAGES RECEIVED AT LEAST TWO VOTES) ARE LISTED IN THE BACK OF THE BOOK. THEIR CHOSEN IMAGES, ALONG WITH THE SELECTED IMAGES IN THIS BOOK, CAN BE FOUND ON OUR WEBSITE: AI-AP.COM.

THE PHOTOGRAPHS IN THIS BOOK WERE ORIGINALLY PUBLISHED IN CONSUMER, TRADE, AND TECHNICAL MAGAZINES, PERIODICALS, NEWSPAPERS, AND THEIR SUPPLEMENTS. OTHERS WERE CREATED FOR ADVERTISEMENTS, PROMOTIONAL DESIGN, ANNUAL REPORTS, BOOKS, CD COVERS, CATALOGS, DIRECT MAIL, SELF-PROMOTION, OR WERE PERSONAL WORKS.

CAPTIONS AND ARTWORK HAVE BEEN SUPPLIED BY THE ENTRANTS. WHILE EVERY EFFORT HAS BEEN MADE TO ENSURE ACCURACY, AMERICAN PHOTOGRAPHY DOES NOT UNDER ANY CIRCUMSTANCES ACCEPT ANY RESPONSIBILITY FOR ERRORS OR OMISSIONS.

AMERICAN PHOTOGRAPHY IS INDEXED BY IMAGE NUMBER WITH ALL CREATIVE PERSONNEL INVOLVED WITH THE CREATION AND UTILIZATION OF THE WINNING IMAGES AND BY PHOTOGRAPHER IN ALPHABETICAL ORDER WITH CONTACT INFORMATION.

IF YOU ARE A PHOTOGRAPHER, ART DIRECTOR, DESIGNER, ARTIST REP., STUDENT, OR EDUCATOR AND WOULD LIKE TO SUBMIT WORK TO THE NEXT ANNUAL COMPETITION OR IF YOU WOULD LIKE ADDITIONAL COPIES OR BACK ISSUES, WRITE OR CALL:
AMERICAN PHOTOGRAPHY, 126 FIFTH AVENUE, ROOM 14B, NEW YORK, NY 10011 TELEPHONE: 212-243-5262 FAX: 212-243-5201 EMAIL: AIAP@SKYWEB.NET OR GO TO OUR WEBSITE: AI-AP.COM

IMAGE NUMBER INDEX

REALITY SERIES "THE OSBOURNES," FOR THE ARTICLE "OSBOURNE TO BE WILD," NOVEMBER 2002.

CREATIVE DIRECTOR: JILL ARMUS. DIRECTOR OF PHOTOGRAPHY: DORIS BRAUTIGAN. DESIGNER: NAZAN AKYAVAS. EDITOR: LORI BERGER. PUBLICATION: TEEN PEOPLE. PUBLISHING COMPANY: TIME INC. WRITER: DAVID KEEPS.

15. KWAKU ALSTON

ACTOR ADRIEN BRODY AS HIS BREAK-THROUGH FILM "THE PIANIST" OPENED, FOR THE FEATURE "A MINOR SYMPHONY," FEBRUARY 2002.

EXECUTIVE EDITOR: SARAH J.M. TUFF. BOOK TITLE: THE FIRE WITHIN. PUBLISHING COMPANY: HALLMARK

30. GREG MILLER

UNTITLED, 2001, ONE FROM A PERSONAL SERIES "ASH WEDNESDAY."

31. KT AULETA

"BALLOONS, BIRTHDAY PARTY, CENTRAL PARK, NYC," ONE FROM A SERIES FOR THE STORY "BEFORE THE PARTY."

ARTRICLE "ABANDON IT, AND THEY WILL COME," OCTOBER 6, 2002.

ART DIRECTOR: JANET FROELICH. PHOTO EDITOR: CAVAN FARRELL. DESIGNER: JOELE CUYLER. EDITOR: ADAM MOSS. PUBLICATION: THE NEW YORK TIMES MAGAZINE. PUBLISHING COMPANY: THE NEW YORK TIMES. INTERVIEW BY: AMY BARRETT.

40. JOSEPH MAIDA

"JJ," 2002, ONE FROM THE SERIES "INTERIOR PORTRAITS," PERSONAL WORK.

DEPUTY DIRECTOR OF PHOTOGRAPHY: SIMON BARNETT. ASSOCIATE PICTURE EDITOR: CARRIE LEVY. DIRECTOR OF PHOTOGRAPHY: SARAH HARBUTT. PUBLICATION: NEWSWEEK. PUBLISHING COMPANY: NEWSWEEK, INC.

55. MARK HEITHOFF

PHOTOGRAPH OF A GIRL AS SHE WEIGHS IN AT THE OBESITY CLINIC OF THE BOSTON CHILDREN'S HOSPITAL, FOR THE ARTICLE "IT'S NOT THE CARBS, STUPID," PUBLISHED IN NEWSWEEK AUGUST 5, 2002.

ART DIRECTOR: PETER YATES. PHOTO DIRECTOR: NIK KLEINBERG. DESIGNER: HENRY LEE. EDITOR: STEVE WOLF. PUBLICATION: ESPN THE MAGAZINE. PUBLISHING COMPANY: ESPN, INC. WRITER: TIM KEOWN.

68-69. JOHN HUET

TWO FROM A SERIES TAKEN AT THE 2002 SALT LAKE CITY WINTER OLYMPICS, FOR THE BOOK "THE FIRE WITHIN, " FEBRUARY 2002. PLATE 68: MEN'S 50 KM CROSS-COUNTRY SKIING. PLATE 69: UTAH OLYMPIC PARK'S SKI JUMP SITE.

1-6. ANTHONY GORDON

SIX KEY FRAMES FROM THE VIDEO "NEW YORK HEALS," PORTRAITS OF PEOPLE REACTING TO GROUND ZERO WORLD TRADE CENTER SITE OF THE 911 TERRORIST ATTACKS, ALL FILMED FROM THE SAME VANTAGE POINT FROM SEPTEMBER 2001 – FEBRUARY 2002.

DIRECTOR OF PHOTOGRAPHY: ANTHONY GORDON. EDITOR: ANTHONY GORDON. PRODUCER: ANTHONY GORDON. COPYWRITER: ANTHONY GORDON. SOUND DESIGN: ANTHONY GORDON.

7. KATE BROOKS

INTERIM GOVERNMENT LEADER MEETS WITH TRIBAL ELDERS FROM THE SOUTHERN PROVINCE OF PAKTIA IN A BID TO RESOLVE A CLAN DISPUTE BETWEEN TWO RIVAL ETHNIC PASHTUN CLANS IN AFGHANISTAN, MARCH 4, 2002.

ART DIRECTOR: ARTHUR HOCHSTEIN. ASSOCIATE ART DIRECTOR: CHRISTINE DUNLEAVY. DIRECTOR OF PHOTOGRAPHY: MICHELE STEPHENSON. ASSOCIATE PICTURE EDITOR: ROBERT B. STEVENS. PUBLICATION: TIME. PUBLISHING COMPANY: TIME INC.

8. KATE BROOKS

PHOTO OF AFGHANI CHILDREN FOR THE STORY "MY RETURN TO KABUL," SEPTEMBER 8, 2002.

PHOTO EDITOR: MIRIAM LORENTZEN. DESIGNER: NATALIE PRIOR. PUBLICATION: PARADE. PUBLISHING COMPANY: CONDÉ NAST PUBLICATIONS, INC. WRITER: TAMIM ANSARY.

9-10. JUDY WALGREN

TWO FROM A SERIES FOR THE ARTICLE "MEANWHILE BACK AT THE RANCH," NOVEMBER 2002, A STORY ON CRAWFORD, TX, HOME OF PRESIDENT GEORGE W. BUSH. PLATE 9: VISITOR GARRET BROWN GETS HIS PICTURE TAKEN WITH PRESIDENTIAL CUT-OUT AT THE COFFEE STATION. PLATE 10: BILLBOARD WELCOMING MOTORISTS TO CRAWFORD.

ART DIRECTOR: SCOTT DADICH. DESIGNER: SCOTT DADICH. EDITOR: EVAN SMITH. PUBLICATION: TEXAS MONTHLY. PUBLISHING COMPANY: EMMIS. WRITER: PAM COLLOFF.

11. HARRY BENSON

CREW ABOARD THE AIRCRAFT CARRIER USS THEODORE ROSSEVELT IN THE ARABIAN SEA, FOR THE ARTICLE "THE BIG GUNS," FEBRUARY 2002. THE PHOTOGRAPHER, HOVERING IN A HELICOPTER ABOVE, ASKED THE CAPTAIN TO TURN THE SHIP SO THE SUN WAS IN THE GROUP'S EYES.

ART DIRECTOR: DAVID HARRIS. PHOTO PRODUCER: RICHARD VILLANI. PHOTO EDITOR: LISA BERMAN. DESIGNER: DAVID HARRIS. DIRECTOR OF PHOTOGRAPHY: SUSAN WHITE. EDITOR-IN-CHIEF: GRAYDON CARTER. PUBLICATION: VANITY FAIR. PUBLISHING COMPANY: CONDÉ NAST PUBLICATIONS, INC.

12. DAVID HARRY STEWART

RAPPER EMINEM FOR THE FEATURE "MR. AMBASSADOR."

ART DIRECTOR: JANET FROELICH. PHOTO EDITOR: CAVAN FERREL. PUBLICATION: THE NEW YORK TIMES MAGAZINE. PUBLISHING COMPANY: THE NEW YORK TIMES. WRITER: FRANK RICH.

13-14. KWAKU ALSTON

JACK AND KELLY OSBOURNE, OFF-SPRINGS OF ROCKER OZZIE OSBOURNE, FROM THE MTV

DESIGN DIRECTOR: AREM DUPLESSIS. PHOTO EDITOR: PRIM CHUENSUMRAN. ASSISTANT ART DIRECTOR: MAILI HOLIMAN. EDITOR: DAVID ITZKOFF. PUBLICATION: SPIN. PUBLISHING COMPANY: VIBE/SPIN VENTURES LLC. WRITER: PAUL ZIMMERMAN.

16. KYOKO HAMADA

MALTESE DOGS TAKING A WALK IN CAPE TOWN, SOUTH AFRICA, PERSONAL PIECE.

17. KYOKO HAMADA

A COUPLE ON A GOLF COURSE IN KANSAS CITY, MO, OUTTAKE FROM AN ASSIGNMENT FOR KIPLINGER'S MAGAZINE.

18-21. ELINOR CARUCCI

FOUR PHOTOGRAPHS FROM A SERIES OF FAMILY PORTRAITS, SELF-PORTRAITS AND ABSTRACTIONS FOR THE BOOK "CLOSER," JUNE 2002. PLATE 18: MOTHER IS WORRIED, 1996. PLATE 19: MASKS, 1996. PLATE 20: WEDDING PICTURE, 1995. PLATE 21: HAIRCUT, 1994.

EDITOR: ALAN RAPP. BOOK TITLE: CLOSER. PUBLISHING COMPANY: CHRONICLE BOOKS. AUTHOR: ELINOR CARUCCI.

22-23. AMANDA MEANS

TWO PHOTOGRAPHS FROM A COLLECTION FOR THE BOOK "PHOTOGRAPHY'S ANTIQUARIAN AVANT-GARDE: THE NEW WAVE IN OLD PROCESSES," 2002. PLATE 22: LIGHT BULB 00010C, 2001, COLOR POLAROID. PLATE 23: LIGHT BULB 1, 1998-2000, GELATIN SILVER PRINT-PHOTOGRAM.

VP, CREATIVE DIRECTOR: MICHAEL J. WALSH JR. PHOTO EDITORS: LYLE REXER AND DEBORAH AARONSON. DESIGNER: BRANKICA KOVRLIJA. EDITOR: DEBORAH AARONSON. BOOK TITLE: PHOTOGRAPHY'S ANTQUARIAN AVANT-GARDE: THE NEW WAVE IN OLD PROCESSES. PUBLISHING COMPANY: HARRY N. ABRAMS, INC. AUTHOR: LYLE REXER.

24. MYRIAM BABIN

"ALAMOSA SNOW," ONE FROM AN ONGOING PERSONAL SERIES ON MOTELS.

25. RYAN MCGINLEY

UNTITLED, PERSONAL, FINE ART PIECE. COURTESY PETER HAY HALPERT FINE ART, NY.

26. ALLAN PENN

UNTITLED PERSONAL WORK.

27-28. ANDY ANDERSON

TWO FROM A SERIES TAKEN AT THE 2002 SALT LAKE CITY WINTER OLYMPICS FOR THE BOOK "THE FIRE WITHIN," FEBRUARY 2002. PLATE 27: MEN'S 120 METER SKI JUMP. PLATE 28: WOMEN'S LUGE.

DIRECTOR: LIBBY HYLAND. EXECUTIVE PHOTO PRODUCER: PAULINE PLOQUIN. PHOTO EDITOR: JOHN HUET. DESIGN MANAGER: RON STUCKI. EXECUTIVE EDITOR: SARAH J.M. TUFF. BOOK TITLE: THE FIRE WITHIN. PUBLISHING COMPANY: HALLMARK

29. TIBOR NEMETH

LUGE, FROM THE 2002 SALT LAKE CITY WINTER OLYMPICS, FOR THE BOOK "THE FIRE WITHIN," FEBRUARY 2002.

DIRECTOR: LIBBY HYLAND. EXECUTIVE PHOTO PRODUCER: PAULINE PLOQUIN. PHOTO EDITOR: JOHN HUET. DESIGN MANAGER: RON STUCKI.

ART DIRECTOR: MARK JUBBER. EDITOR: STEPHEN TONER. PUBLICATION: EXIT. PUBLISHING COMPANY: ENTER LTD.

32. CHRISTIAN WEBBER

"BECOMING: HERNAN," ONE FROM SERIES FOR THE EXHIBITION "WAR."

33. ALEXANDRA BOULAT

TRAGIC WEDDING PARTY IN KABUL, AFGHANISTAN. THE BRIDE'S MOTHER COLLAPSES FROM A HEART ATTACK AFTER HEARING THE GROOM FAILED TO BUY THE BRIDE THE PROMISED NECKLACE, MAY 2002.

ART DIRECTOR: ARTHUR HOCHSTEIN.DEPUTY ART DIRECTOR: CYNTHIA HOFFMAN. DIRECTOR OF PHOTOGRAPHY: MICHELE STEPHENSON. ASSOCIATE PICTURE EDITOR: JAY COLTON. PICTURE EDITOR OF TIME.COM: KARL SCHATZ. PUBLICATION: TIME/TIME.COM PUBLISHING COMPANY: TIME INC.

34-35. SIMON NORFOLK

TWO FROM A SERIES OF THE RACK AND RUIN SHOT AFTER THE BOMBINGS IN AFGHANISTAN, FOR THE ARTICLE "WHAT'S LEFT OF KABUL," JANUARY 6, 2002. PLATE 34: TEA HOUSE, THE EXHIBITION OF ECONOMIC AND SOCIAL ACHIEVEMENTS FAIRGROUNDS. PLATE 34: AQA ALI-KHUJA WITH HALO TRUST, A NON-PROFIT BOMB-CLEARING OPERATION.

ART DIRECTOR: JANET FROELICH. PHOTO EDITOR: KATHY RYAN. EDITOR: ADAM MOSS. PUBLICATION: THE NEW YORK TIMES MAGAZINE. PUBLISHING COMPANY: THE NEW YORK TIMES.

36. CHRISTOPHER MORRIS

U.S. SPECIAL FORCES SOLDIER FIRES ROUNDS WHILE PRACTICING A BREAKING CONTACT MANEUVER IN AFGHANISTAN.

ART DIRECTOR: ARTHUR HOCHSTEIN. DIRECTOR OF PHOTOGRAPHY: MICHELE STEPHENSON. ASSOCIATE PICTURE EDITOR: ROBERT B. STEVENS PICTURE EDITOR FOR TIME.COM: KARL SCHATZ. PUBLICATION: TIME. PUBLISHING COMPANY: TIME INC.

37. JAMES NACHTWEY

NEIGHBORS AND RELATIVES CONSOLE A GIRL IN BALATA CAMP OUTSIDE NABLUS AS SHE LEARNS A FAMILY MEMBER WAS KILLED IN AN EXPLOSION, AUGUST 19, 2002

ART DIRECTOR: ARTHUR HOCHSTEIN. DEPUTY ART DIRECTOR: CYNTHIA A. HOFFMAN. DIRECTOR OF PHOTOGRAPHY: MICHELE STEPHENSON. ASSOCIATE PICTURE EDITOR: ROBERT B. STEVENS. PUBLCATION: TIME. PUBLISHING COMPANY: TIME INC.

38. ILKKA UIMONEN

BEDROLLS, WATER BOTTLES AND OTHER DETRITUS SCATTERED AMID THE CORINTHIAN COLUMNS OF A CHURCH, FOR THE ARTICLE "INSIDE THE SIEGE OF BETHLEHEM," MAY 20, 2002.

DESIGN DIRECTOR: LYNN STALEY. DIRECTOR OF PHOTOGRAPHY: SARAH HARBUTT. PHOTO EDITOR: JAMES WELLFORD. ASSISTANT MANAGING EDITOR: LYNN STALEY. EDITOR: MARK WHITAKER. PUBLICATION: NEWSWEEK. PUBLISHING COMPANY: NEWSWEEK, INC.

39. JOSEPH MAIDA

SIOBHAN MEOW, 21-23 AVENUE C, ONE OF SEVERAL SQUATTERS ON THE LOWER EAST SIDE WHO WON THE RIGHT TO THEIR HOMES, ONE FOR THE

41. AMY ECKERT

HAMPTONS BEACH HOUSE OFFERING ALMOST INVISIBLE BARRIER BETWEEN LANDSCAPE AND HOME, FOR THE ARTICLE "THE PERFECT BEACH SHACK," AUGUST 2002.

ART DIRECTOR: JEANETTE HODGE ABBINK. PHOTO EDITOR: MAREN LEVINSON. DESIGNER: JEANETTE HODGE ABBINK. EDITOR: ALLISON ARIEFF. PUBLICATION: DWELL. PUBLISHING COMPANY: DWELL, LLC. WRITER: VICTORIA MILNE.

42-43. DAVID S. ALLEE

FROM A PERSONAL PROJECT ENTITLED "WHITE NIGHTS," PUBLISHED IN METROPOLIS MAGAZINE MAY 2003. PLATE 42: "RED ROOSTER PICNIC," A 1950'S STYLE FAST FOOD DRIVE-IN ON RT. 22 IN BREWSTER, NY. PLATE 43: "STADIUM LIGHTS," YANKEE STADIUM SHOT FROM THE ROOF OF A BOWING ALLEY WITH CAR THAT APPEARED IN THE FRAME HALFWAY THROUGH THE EXPOSURE.

ART DIRECTOR: CRISWELL LAPPIN. PHOTO EDITOR: SARA BARRETT. WRITER: PETER HALL.

44-47. TONY D'ORIO

FOUR FROM A SERIES OF PORTRAITS OF AWKWARD TEENS AT PUBERTY, FOR THE "ALTOIDS SOURS TEASER AD CAMPAIGN."

ART DIRECTOR: NOEL HAAN. AGENCY: LEO BURNETT USA, CHICAGO, IL. COPYWRITER: G. ANDREW MEYER.

48-49. CHRISTINE SCHIAVO

TWO FROM A COLLECTION FOR THE BOOK "PHOTOGRAPHY'S ANTIQUARIAN AVANT-GARDE: THE NEW WAVE IN OLD PROCESSES," 2002 PLATE 48: DAISY BOYS, 1999, TINTYPE. PLATE 49: UNTITLED LANDSCAPE, 1997, TINTYPE.

VP, CREATIVE DIRECTOR: MICHAEL J. WALSH JR. PHOTO EDITORS: LYLE REXER AND DEBORAH AARONSON. DESIGNER: BRANKICA KOVRLIJA. EDITOR: DEBORAH AARONSON. BOOK TITLE: PHOTOGRAPHY'S ANTIQUARIAN AVANT-GARDE: THE NEW WAVE IN OLD PROCESSES. PUBLISHING COMPANY: HARRY N. ABRAMS, INC. AUTHOR: LYLE REXER.

50-51. CRAIG CUTLER

TWO FOR THE ARTICLE "THE MEAT OF THE MATTER," DECEMBER 2002. PLATE 50: STEAKS AGING UNDER IDEAL CONDITIONS AT SMITH AND WOLLENSKY, NEW YORK CITY. PLATE 51: STILL-LIFE STUDY, THREE PRIME AGED STEAK CUTS.

PHOTO EDITOR: MARY SHEA. DESIGNER: FRANK TAGARIELLO. EDITOR: MALACHY DUFFY. PUBLICATION: BLOOMBERG-PERSONAL FINANCE. PUBLISHING COMPANY: BLOOMBERG L.P. WRITER: WILLIAM RICE.

52-53. JOHN DUGDALE

TWO FROM A SERIES FOR THE STORY "FLINT GLASS," FEBRUARY 2002.

ART DIRECTOR: SCOT SCHY. DESIGNER: SCOT SCHY. EDITOR: DOUGLAS BRENNER. PUBLICATION: MARTHA STEWART LIVING. PUBLISHING COMPANY: MARTHA STEWART LIVING OMNIMEDIA. WRITER: CAROL PRISANT.

54. MARK HEITHOFF

TOLL BROTHERS' REALTY AGENT DARLENE DIVONA STYLES THE CHILDREN'S SUITE OF THE SOMERSET CHATEAU MODEL HOME, RICHBORO, PA, FOR THE ARTICLE "BETTING AGAINST A HOUSING BUST," AUGUST 26, 2002.

DEPUTY DIRECTOR OF PHOTOGRAPHY: SIMON BARNETT. ASSOCIATE PICTURE EDITOR: CARRIE LEVY. DIRECTOR OF PHOTOGRAPHY: SARAH HARBUTT. PUBLICATION: NEWSWEEK..PUBLISHING COMPANY: NEWSWEEK, INC. WRITER: ELLEN. RUPPEL SHELL.

56-58. HOWARD SCHATZ

FROM THE BOOK "ATHLETES," ALSO FEATURED IN THE "LEADING OFF" SECTION, OCTOBER 14, 2002.

CREATIVE DIRECTOR: STEVEN HOFFMAN. PHOTOGRAPHY EDITOR: JAMES K. COLTON. PUBLICATION: SPORTS ILLUSTRATED.

59-60. KAI REGAN

TWO FOR THE FASHION STORY "VARSITY."

DESIGN DIRECTOR: AREM DUPLESSIS. PHOTO EDITOR: PRIM CHUENSUMRAN. FASHION EDITOR: DANILEA JUNG. PUBLICATION: SPIN. PUBLISHING COMPANY: VIBE/SPIN VENTURES.

61. BOB MARTIN

SERENA WILLIAMS AT THE FRENCH OPEN, FOR "INSIDE-THE WEEK IN SPORTS." JUNE 10, 2002.

CREATIVE DIRECTOR: STEVEN HOFFMAN. PHOTO EDITOR: JAMES K. COLTON. PUBLICATION: SPORTS ILLUSTRATED.

62. WYATT TILLOTSON

ROCHELLE BALLARD, PRO-SURFER, CHARGING BACKDOOR IN OAHU, AUGUST 26, 2002.

ART DIRECTOR: ARTHUR HOCHSTEIN. ASSOCIATE ART DIRECTOR: JANET MICHAUD. DIRECTOR OF PHOTOGRAPHY: MICHELE STEPHENSON. ASSISTANT EDITORS: MARIE TOBIAS, JESSICA TAYLOR TARASKI.

63. HENRIK KNUDSEN

"POOL," PERSONAL WORK FROM ICELAND.

64. LOGAN & LOGAN PHOTOGRAPHY

SNOWBOARDER, TOMMY CZESCHIN AT THE 2002 SALT LAKE CITY WINTER OLYMPICS FOR THE BOOK "THE FIRE WITHIN," FEBRUARY 2002.

DIRECTOR: LIBBY HYLAND. EXECUTIVE PHOTO PRODUCER: PAULINE PLOQUIN. PHOTO EDITOR: JOHN HUET. DESIGN MANAGER: RON STUCKI. EXECUTIVE EDITOR: SARAH J.M. TUFF. BOOK TITLE: THE FIRE WITHIN. PUBLISHING COMPANY: HALLMARK

65. BRYCE DUFFY

EVENING SURFERS UNDER THE GOLDEN GATE BRIDGE AT FORT POINT, SAN FRANCISCO, CA, FOR THE ARTICLE "EXPOSURE," JULY 2002.

CREATIVE DIRECTOR: HANNAH MCCAUGHEY. PHOTO EDITOR: ROB HAGGART. PUBLICATION: OUTSIDE. PUBLISHING COMPANY: MARIAH MEDIA

66. ANDY ANDERSON

ANNE ABERNATHEY, OLDEST OLYMPIAN AT 48, VISUALIZES THE COURSE AT THE 2002 SALT LAKE CITY WINTER GAMES, FOR THE FEATURE "RINGERS," MARCH 4, 2002.

ART DIRECTOR: PETER YATES. PHOTO DIRECTOR: NIK KLEINBERG. DESIGNER: HENRY LEE. EDITOR: STEVE WOLF. PUBLICATION: ESPN THE MAGAZINE. PUBLISHING COMPANY: ESPN, INC. WRITER: TIM KEOWN.

67. DAVID BURNETT

A SKI JUMPER TAKES FLIGHT AT THE SALT LAKE CITY 2002 WINTER OLYMPICS, FOR THE ARTICLE "RINGERS," MARCH 4, 2002.

DIRECTOR: LIBBY HYLAND. EXECUTIVE PHOTO PRODUCER: PAULINE PLOQUIN. PHOTO EDITOR: JOHN HUET. DESIGN MANAGER: RON STUCKI. EXECUTIVE EDITOR: SARAH J.M. TUFF. BOOK TITLE: THE FIRE WITHIN. PUBLISHING COMPANY: HALLMARK

70. JOHN HUET

CLEVELAND CAVALIER DARIUS MILES FOR THE FEATURE "DUNKER," NOVEMBER 2002.

ART DIRECTOR: PETER YATES. PHOTO DIRECTOR: NIK KLEINBERG. DESIGNER: HENRY LEE. EDITOR: JON PESSAH. PUBLICATION: ESPN THE MAGAZINE. PUBLISHING COMPANY: ESPN, INC. WRITER: BILL WALTON.

71. JOHN HUET

ONE FROM "THE TOUCH OF THE WILD," JANUARY/FEBRUARY 2002, A SERIES FROM A FAMILY VACATION IN MAINE.

DESIGN DIRECTOR: KEVIN FISHER. PHOTO EDITOR: KIM HUBBARD. DESIGNER: KEVIN FISHER. EDITOR: JENNIFER BOGO. PUBLICATION: AUDUBON. PUBLISHING COMPANY: AUDUBON. WRITER: TED LEVIN.

72. JANA LEON

SPLIT PHOTO-ILLUSTRATION OF A PREGNANT BELLY WITH THE HANDS OF A 20-YEAR-OLD AND 40-YEAR-OLD WOMAN, FOR THE ARTICLE "PREGNANCY IN YOUR 20'S, 30'S & 40'S," AUGUST/SEPTEMBER 2002.

ART DIRECTOR: STEPHANIE K. BIRDSONG. ASSOCIATE PHOTO EDITOR: VIRGINIA VINCENT-ORTH. DESIGNER: STEPHANIE K. BIRDSONG. PUBLICATION: FIT PREGNANCY. PUBLISHING COMPANY: WEIDER PUBLICATIONS.

73. NORMAN JEAN ROY

ACTOR SAMUEL L. JACKSON VOTED MOST STYLISH IN THE ANNUAL "GQ-MEN OF THE YEAR" ISSUE, NOVEMBER 2002.

DESIGN DIRECTOR: FRED WOODWARD. DIRECTOR OF PHOTOGRAPHY: JENNIFER CRANDALL. DESIGNER: MATTHEW LENNING. PUBLICATION: GQ. PUBLISHING COMPANY: CONDÉ NAST PUBLICATIONS, INC. WRITER: MAXIMILLIAN POTTER

74. NORMAN JEAN ROY

TOBY MAGUIRE, STAR OF THE MOVIE "SPIDERMAN," FOR THE FEATURE "THE IMMACULATE ASCENSION OF TOBY MAGUIRE," MARCH 2002.

DESIGN DIRECTOR: FRED WOODWARD. DIRECTOR OF PHOTOGRAPHY: JENNIFER CRANDALL. DESIGNER: PAUL MARTINEZ. EDITOR: MICHAEL HAINEY. PUBLICATION: GQ. PUBLISHING COMPANY: CONDÉ NAST PUBLICATIONS, INC. WRITER: JOHN BRODIE.

75. MELANIE WILLHIDE

"SUBMISSION HOLD," PERSONAL WORK.

76. JOHN B. CARNETT

SHOOT HOUSE AT THE FEDERAL AIR MARSHALL TRAINING FACILITY IN ALTANTIC CITY, NJ DURING THE ENACTMENT OF IN-FLIGHT THREAT SCENARIOS, ONE FROM A SERIES FOR "FALL OUT: PICTURES FROM THE YEAR AFTER 911", SEPTEMBER 2002.

DESIGN DIRECTOR: DIRK BARNETT. DESIGNERS: DIRK BARNETT AND HYLAH HILL. EDITOR: SCOTT

MOWBRAY. PUBLICATION: POPULAR SCIENCE. PUBLISHING COMPANY: TIME4 MEDIA.

77-80. BRENDA ANN KENNEALLY

FOUR PHOTOGRAPHS FROM A SERIES THAT WAS SHOT OVER A FIVE YEAR PERIOD SPENT WITH DREW AND HIS DRUG-ADDICTED AND DRUG-DEALING MOTHER, BUSHWICK, BROOKLYN, FOR THE PHOTO ESSAY "DRUGS IN THE BLOOD," OCTOBER 6, 2002.

ART DIRECTOR: JANET FROELICH. PHOTO EDITOR: KATHY RYAN. DESIGNER: JOELE CUYLER. EDITOR: ADAM MOSS. PUBLICATION: THE NEW YORK TIMES MAGAZINE. PUBLISHING COMPANY: THE NEW YORK TIMES. WRITER: ADRIAN NICOLE LEBLANC.

81. HUGH KRETSCHMER

CONCEPTUAL PHOTOGRAPH ILLUSTRATING THE PREMISE OF THE ARTICLE "THE FEMALE CEO CA. 2002," AUGUST 2002.

DESIGN DIRECTOR: PATRICK MITCHELL. PHOTO EDITOR: ALICIA JYLKKA. DESIGNER: JULIA MOBURG. PUBLICATION: FAST COMPANY. PUBLISHING COMPANY: GRUNER + JAHR USA. WRITER: MARGARET HEFFERNAN.

82. HUGH KRETSCHMER

PHOTOGRAPH FOR THE ARTICLE "HOW TO PICK A MECHANIC," SEPTEMBER 2002, AN ARTICLE ON HOW TO BEST EQUIP YOURSELF WHEN CHOOSING A MECHANIC.

DESIGN DIRECTOR: FRED WOODWARD. PHOTO EDITOR: CATHERINE TALESE. PUBLICATION: GQ. PUBLISHING COMPANY: CONDÉ NAST PUBLICATIONS, INC.

83. MICHAEL LEWIS

"NANCY," PERSONAL WORK.

84. MATT MAHURIN

PHOTO-ILLUSTRATION FOR "THE BEAST IN ME," MAY 2002, AN ARTICLE ON THE OVER-SEXUALIZED EFFECTS AND THOUGHTS THAT COME AS THE RESULT OF A SYNTHETIC TESTOSTERONE INJECTION.

DESIGN DIRECTOR: FRED WOODWARD. DIRECTOR OF PHOTOGRAPHY: JENNIFER CRANDALL. DESIGNER: MATTHEW LENNING. EDITOR: JIM NELSON. PUBLICATION: GQ. PUBLISHING COMPANY: CONDÉ NAST PUBLICATIONS, INC. WRITER: ANONYMOUS.

85. DAN WINTERS & GARY TANHAUSER

"SCHRÖDINGER'S CAT," ERWIN SCHRÖDINGER, FOUNDING FATHER OF QUANTUM MECHANICS, ASKED WHAT WOULD HAPPEN TO A CAT LOCKED IN A BOX WITH A RADIOACTIVE ELEMENT, FOR THE ARTICLE "DOES THE UNIVERSE EXIST IF WE'RE NOT LOOKING?" JUNE 2002

DESIGN DIRECTOR: MICHAEL MRAK. DIRECTOR OF PHOTOGRAPHY: MAISIE TODD. DESIGNER: MICHAEL MRAK. EDITOR: STEPHEN L. PETRANEK. PUBLICATION: DISCOVER. PUBLISHING COMPANY: DISNEY PUBLISHING WORLDWIDE. WRITER: TIM FOLGER.

86. DAN WINTERS

ACTOR DENNIS QUAID FOR THE FEATURE "UNBREAKABLE," APRIL 2002.

ART DIRECTOR: RICHARD BAKER. DIRECTOR OF PHOTOGRAPHY: DORIS BRAUTIGAN. EDITOR: KATHY HEINTZELMAN. PUBLICATION: PREMIERE. PUBLISHING COMPANY: HACHETTE FILIPACCHI MEDIA U.S., INC. WRITER: DAVID HOCHMAN.

BODY WEIGHT IS LINKED TO THE RATE OF HUMAN DECOMPOSITION, ONE FROM A SERIES FOR THE ARTICLE "THE BODY FARM," JUNE 2002.

DESIGN DIRECTOR: FRED WOODWARD. DIRECTOR OF PHOTOGRAPHY: JENNIFER CRANDALL. PHOTO EDITOR: CATHERINE TALESE. DESIGNER: KEN DELAGO. PUBLICATION: GQ. PUBLISHING COMPANY: CONDÉ NAST PUBLICATIONS, INC. WRITER: MAXIMILLIAN POTTER

97. GLEN ERLER

ACTRESS THANDIE NEWTON FOR THE PROFILE "BELOVED," NOVEMBER 2002.

DESIGN DIRECTOR: ROCKWELL HARWOOD. DIRECTOR OF PHOTOGRAPHY: AMY STEIGBIGEL. ASSOCIATE ART DIRECTOR: NATHALIE KIRSHEH. PUBLICATION: DETAILS. PUBLISHING COMPANY: FAIRCHILD PUBLICATIONS. WRITER: NICK COMPTON

98-99. BHARAT SIKKA

TWO FROM A SERIES FOR THE AMERICAN PREVIEW FALL FASHION STORY "PLAYING SOLITAIRE," AUGUST 2002.

DESIGN DIRECTOR: ROCKWELL HARWOOD. DIRECTOR OF PHOTOGRAPHY: AMY STEIGBIGEL. ASSOCIATE ART DIRECTOR: NATHALIE KIRSHEH. PUBLICATION: DETAILS. PUBLISHING COMPANY: FAIRCHILD PUBLICATIONS.

100. MAGNUS WINTER

DESIGNER D'URBANO'S SHIRT DIGITALLY PRINTED WITH IMAGES OF HER NAKED BODY, PART OF AN EXHIBIT AT NEW YORK'S COOPER-HEWITT NATIONAL DESIGN MUSEUM, FOR THE FEATURE "SECOND SKIN," MAY 2002.

CREATIVE DIRECTOR: DARRIN PERRY. PHOTO EDITOR: CAROLYN RAUCH. DESIGN DIRECTOR: SUSANA RODRIGUEZ DE TEMBLEQUE. EDITOR: JESSIE SCANLON. PUBLICATION: WIRED. PUBLISHING COMPANY: CONDÉ NAST PUBLICATIONS, INC. WRITER: SHONQUIS MORENO.

101. SEAN ELLIS

ANDREW W.K., FOR A FEATURE ON THE METAL-HEAD ROCKER, MAY 2002.

ART DIRECTOR: LISA STEINMEYER. PHOTO DIRECTOR: CORY JACOBS. EDITOR: GIA MICHEL. PUBLICATION: SPIN. PUBLISHING COMPANY: VIBE/SPIN VENTURES. WRITER: CRAIG MCLEAN

102-103. CHRISTOPHER BEIRNE

TWO FROM A SERIES FOR "JAWBREAKER," FEBRUARY 2002, A STORY ABOUT THE WRITER'S, ANDREW ESSEX, COSMETIC SURGERY.

DESIGN DIRECTOR: ROCKWELL HARWOOD. DIRECTOR OF PHOTOGRAPHY: AMY STEIGBIGEL. ASSOCIATE ART DIRECTOR: NATHALIE KIRSHEH. PUBLICATION: DETAILS. PUBLISHING COMPANY: FAIRCHILD PUBLICATIONS. WRITER: ANDREW ESSEX.

104-105. KIKE ARNAL

TWO FROM A PERSONAL SERIES ON THE VICTIMS OF THE WAR IN AFGHANISTAN.

106-109. LYNSEY ADDARIO

FOUR FROM A PERSONAL SERIES ON BOTCHED PLASTIC SURGERIES IN MEXICO.

110-111. HANS NELEMAN

TWO FROM THE BOOK "BODY TRANSFORMED," A STUDY ON BODY MODIFICATION.

NEW YORK APARTMENT, ONE FROM A COLLECTION OF PHOTOGRAPHS FOR THE BOOK "SCHATTENLICHT/SHADOW LIGHT," 2002.

DIRECTOR OF PHOTOGRAPHY: RUTH EICHHORN. PHOTO EDITORS: NADJA MASRI, MARKUS SEEWALD. DESIGNER: MELANIE WOLTER. EDITORS: ULRIKE MOSER, TORBEN MUELLER, JENS SCHROEDER. BOOK TITLE: SCHATTENLICHT / SHADOW LIGHT. PUBLISHING COMPANY: GEO, GRUNER + JAHR. GERMANY PUBLISHER: PETER-MATTHIAS GAEDE.

126. MARK KLETT

THE PHOTOGRAPHER'S LEGS DANGLING OVER THE GOOSENECKS OF THE SAN JUAN RIVER IN UTAH, FOR THE ARTICLE "LOVING THE LAND," JANUARY/FEBRUARY 2002.

DESIGN DIRECTOR: KEVIN FISHER. PHOTO EDITOR: KIM HUBBARD. DESIGNER: KEVIN FISHER. EDITOR: MARY-POWEL THOMAS. PUBLICATION: AUDUBON. PUBLISHING COMPANY: AUDUBON. WRITER: SCOTT RUSSELL SANDERS.

127. MOLLIE LAURIENZO

"CUPS, NEW JERSEY," ONE FROM A SENIOR DEGREE PROJECT ENTITLED "ULTERIOR OBJECT: A SERIES ON MOTEL INTERIORS," STUDENT WORK.

SCHOOL: MASSACHUSETTS COLLEGE OF ART.

128. MARTIN SCHOELLER

MAGICIAN DAVID BLAINE FOR THE FEATURE "DAVID BLAINE WANTS TO FREAK YOU OUT! IN THE DARK WORLD OF AMERICA'S STRANGEST MAGICIAN, NOTHING IS REAL BUT THE PAIN," MAY 23, 2002.

ART DIRECTOR: ANDY COWLES. DIRECTOR OF PHOTOGRAPHY: FIONA MCDONAGH. EDITOR: JANN S. WENNER. PUBLICATION: ROLLING STONE. PUBLISHING COMPANY: WENNER MEDIA, WRITER: ERIK HEDEGAARD.

129. MARTIN SCHOELLER

ACTOR JACK NICHOLSON FOR THE FEATURE "JACK ON JACK," JANUARY 3, 2003.

PHOTO EDITOR: MICHAEL KOCHMAN. DIRECTOR OF PHOTOGRAPHY: SARAH ROZEN. EDITOR: RICK TETZELI. PUBLICATION: ENTERTAINMENT WEEKLY. PUBLISHING COMPANY: TIME INC. PUBLISHER: DAVID MORRIS. WRITER: BENJAMIN SVETKEY.

130. MARTIN SCHOELLER

COUNTRY MUSIC LEGEND JOHNNY CASH FOR THE FEATURE "THE DAY IN THE LIFE OF JOHNNY CASH," DECEMBER 12, 2002.

ART DIRECTOR: ANDY COWLES. DIRECTOR OF PHOTOGRAPHY: JODI PECKMAN. EDITOR: JANN S. WENNER. PUBLICATION: ROLLING STONE. PUBLISHING COMPANY: WENNER MEDIA. WRITER: JASON FINE.

131. PEGGY SIROTA

CHILD ACTORS GROWN-UP ASHLEY AND MARY-KATE OLSEN FOR THE ARTICLE "AREN'T I ADORABLE?" MARCH 2002.

DESIGN DIRECTOR: FRED WOODWARD. DIRECTOR OF PHOTOGRAPHY: JENNIFER CRANDALL. PHOTO EDITOR: KRISTEN SCHAEFER. DESIGNER: MATTHEW LENNING. EDITOR: MARTIN BEISER. PUBLICATION: GQ. PUBLISHING COMPANY: CONDÉ NAST PUBLICATIONS, INC. WRITER: JIM NELSON.

132. ANDREW ZUCKERMAN

SOFIA THE DAY AFTER HER BIRTH, ONE FROM A SET OF TRIPLETS BORN PREMATURELY, FOR "OPEN

ART DIRECTOR: TOM BROWN. DESIGN FIRM: TBA+D.

148. FREDRIK BRODEN

PHOTOGRAPH ILLUSTRATING THE ARTICLE "VENTURING TO VOTE ONLINE," NOVEMBER 2002.

ART DIRECTOR: ERIC MONGEON. DESIGNER: JAMIE KELLEHER. EDITOR: ROBERT BUDERI. PUBLICATION: TECHNOLOGY REVIEW. PUBLISHING COMPANY: MASSACHUSETTS INSTITUTE OF TECHNOLOGY. WRITER: JULIE CLAIRE DIOP.

149. DIRK ANSCHÜTZ

PHOTOGRAPH OF TOM RYAN AND EDGAR RODRIGUEZ, ONE FROM A SERIES ON GAY NEW YORK CITY FIREFIGHTERS AND POLICE OFFICERS INVOLVED IN THE 911 WORLD TRADE CENTER RESCUE AND RECOVERY, FOR THE FEATURE "STORY OF THE YEAR: GAY HEROES-WE WERE THERE," JANUARY 2002.

ART DIRECTOR: MARK HARVEY. PHOTO EDITOR: MICHELE FLEURY. PUBLICATION: THE ADVOCATE. PUBLISHING COMPANY: LPI MEDIA. WRITER: JESSICA DULONG.

150-151. MARTIN BRADING

GANGES, YAMUNA AND SARASWATI RIVER CONFLUENCE, INDIA, TWO FROM A SERIES FROM THE KUMBHA MELA FESTIVAL, ALLAHABAD, INDIA, SPRING/SUMMER 2002.

CREATIVE DIRECTOR: GLENN HUNT. DESIGNER: AMANDA BROWN. PUBLICATION: WISH U WERE HERE XXX #4. PUBLISHING COMPANY: WISH U WERE HERE XXX MAGAZINE.

152. JOSHUA PAUL

PHOTOGRAPH OF OLDHAM FARM, VASHON ISLAND, WA, PERSONAL WORK.

153-156. PLATON

FOUR FROM A SERIES FOR "RITRATTO DI FAMIGLIA," JULY 2002, A FASHION STORY USING ITALIAN FAMILY MEMBERS FROM BROOKLYN.

ART DIRECTOR: JOHN KORPICS. PHOTO EDITOR: CATRIONA NIAOLAIN. DESIGNER: JOHN KORPICS. PUBLICATION: ESQUIRE. PUBLISHING COMPANY: HEARST MAGAZINES.

157. PLATON

PORTRAIT OF AL PACINO, FOR A FEATURE ON THE ACTOR, JULY 2002.

ART DIRECTOR: JOHN KORPICS. DIRECTOR OF PHOTOGRAPHY: NANCY JO IACOI. PUBLICATION: ESQUIRE. PUBLISHING COMPANY: HEARST MAGAZINES. WRITER: CARL FUSSMAN.

158-162. LAUREN GREENFIELD

FIVE FROM A COLLECTION FOR THE BOOK "GIRL CULTURE," DECEMBER 2002. PLATE 158: ALLI, ANNIE, HANNAH AND BERIT, ALL 13, BEFORE THE FIRST BIG PARTY OF THE SEVENTH GRADE, EDINA, MN. PLATE 159: LAUREN, 23, EXOTIC DANCER, BLEACHES HER STAINED OUTFIT BACKSTAGE AT LITTLE DARLINGS, LAS VEGAS, NV. PLATE 160: A DANCER HIDES HER TAMPON BACKSTAGE AT LITTLE DARLINGS, LAS VEGAS, NV. PLATE 161: JENNIFER, 18, AT AN EATING DISORDER CLINIC, COCONUT CREEK. FL. PLATE 162: AMELIA, 15, AT A WEIGHT-LOSS CAMP, CATSKILLS, NY.

DESIGNER: LORRAINE WILD DESIGNS. EDITOR: CHARLES MELCHER. PUBLICATION: GIRL CULTURE. PUBLISHING COMPANY: CHRONICLE BOOKS. WRITER: LAUREN GREENFIELD.

PHOTOGRAPHS BORN OUT OF THE GRIEF AND CONFUSION SURROUNDING THE EVENT OF 911, COMMUNICATING THE VISION AND FEELINGS OF ONE PHOTOGRAPHER AS A RECONCILIATORY DOCUMENT TO THE GREATER WHOLE OF SOCIETY.

ART DIRECTOR: LYLE OWERKO. PHOTO EDITOR: LYLE OWERKO. DESIGNERS: LYLE OWERKO, MIKI ARAKI. EDITOR: LYLE OWERKO. BOOK TITLE: AND NO BIRDS SANG. PUBLISHING COMPANY: WONDERLUST INDUSTRIES, INC. AUTHOR: LYLE OWERKO.

178. JERRY SPAGNOLI

UNTITLED, SEPTEMBER 11, 2001, WHOLE PLATE DAGUERREOTYPE, ONE FROM A COLLECTION FOR THE BOOK "PHOTOGRAPHY'S ANTIQUARIAN AVANT-GARDE: THE NEW WAVE IN OLD PROCESSES," 2002.

VP, CREATIVE DIRECTOR: MICHAEL J. WALSH JR. PHOTO EDITORS: LYLE REXER AND DEBORAH AARONSON. DESIGNER: BRANKICA KOVRLIJA. EDITOR: DEBORAH AARONSON. BOOK TITLE: PHOTOGRAPHY'S ANTIQUARIAN AVANT-GARDE: THE NEW WAVE IN OLD PROCESSES. PUBLISHING COMPANY: HARRY N. ABRAMS, INC. AUTHOR: LYLE REXER.

179. WILL NUÑEZ

UNITED FLIGHT 175 GOING INTO WORLD TRADE CENTER TOWER TWO, SEPTEMBER 11, 2001, PART OF THE EXHIBIT "HERE IS NEW YORK, A DEMOCRACY OF PHOTOGRAPHS."

CONCEIVED AND ORGANIZED BY: ALICE ROSE GEORGE, GILLES PERESS, MICHAEL SHULAN AND CHARLES TRAUB.

180. ANDREA BOOHER/FEMA

"FIREFIGHTERS IN THE FEMA-911 RUBBLE PILE NIGHT SHOT," ALL SEVEN MEMBERS ARE FROM THE FEMA USAR CA-TF8 FROM SAN DIEGO COUNTY (FEDERAL EMERGENCY MANAGEMENT AGENCY-URBAN SEARCH AND RESCUE-CALIFORNIA TASK FORCE EIGHT). ONE FROM A SERIES FOR THE ARTICLE "AMERICAN GROUND: UNBUILDING THE WORLD TRADE CENTER."

ART DIRECTOR: MARY PARSONS. EDITOR: MICHAEL KELLY. PUBLICATION: THE ATLANTIC MONTHLY. PUBLISHING COMPANY: THE ATLANITC MONTHLY. GROUP WRITER: WILLIAM LANGEWIESCHE.

181-184. PAOLO VENTURA

FOUR IN A SERIES OF MUMMIES DATING FROM THE 18TH AND 19TH CENTURIES MYSTERIOUSLY PRESERVED AND DRESSED IN THE ORIGINAL CLOTHING, FOUND IN THE CAPPUCINI CATACOMBS IN SICILY, FOR THE ARTICLE "FIGURES FROM THE PAST," DECEMBER 2002.

ART DIRECTOR: ITALO LUPI. PUBLICATION: ABITARE. PUBLISHING COMPANY: ABITARE SEGESTA. WRITER: FERDINANDO SCIANNA.

185. ALEXANDER TSIARAS

HUMAN EMBRYO, ONE FROM THE BOOK "FROM CONCEPTION TO BIRTH – A LIFE UNFOLDS," 2002.

BOOK TITLE: FROM CONCEPTION TO BIRTH. PUBLISHING COMPANY: DOUBLEDAY.

186. NIGEL PARRY

LISA BEAMER, WHOSE HUSBAND DIED ONBOARD FLIGHT 93 IN THE 911 TERRORIST ATTACKS, WITH HER KIDS DAVID, MORGAN AND DREW, FOR THE ARTICLE "ONE YEAR LATER: THEIR FAITH AND FEARS," SEPTEMBER 11, 2002.

ANOTHER COME-BACK AND NEW MARRIAGE TO PRODUCER DAVID GEST, FOR THE ARTICLE "LOOKING FOR THE RAINBOW," MARCH 2002.

ART DIRECTOR: DAVID HARRIS. PHOTO EDITOR: LISA BERMAN. PHOTO PRODUCER: LISA BERMAN. DESIGNER: CHRIS ISRAEL. EDITOR: SUSAN WHITE. EDITOR-IN-CHIEF: GRAYDON CARTER. PUBLICATION: VANITY FAIR. PUBLISHING COMPANY: CONDÉ NAST PUBLICATIONS, INC. WRITER: JONATHAN VAN METER.

199. ROBERT MAXWELL

DANCER ALEXANDRA BELLER, ONE FROM A SERIES FOR THE ARTICLE "AMAZING GRACE."

PHOTO EDITOR: KATHY RYAN. PUBLICATION: THE NEW YORK TIMES MAGAZINE. PUBLISHING COMPANY: THE NEW YORK TIMES.

200-201. ROBERT MAXWELL

TWO FROM A SERIES ON ATHLETES FOR "FOCUS-AWAY FROM THE GAME, MINDS IN MOTION," DECEMBER 8, 2002. PLATE 200: LAFFIT PINCA JR., JOCKEY. PLATE 201: KELLY SLATER, SURFER.

PHOTO EDITOR: KATHY RYAN. PUBLICATION: THE NEW YORK TIMES MAGAZINE. PUBLISHING COMPANY: THE NEW YORK TIMES.

202. MAX AGUILERA-HELLWEG

HEAD OF YOUNG SPERM WHALE THAT HAD BEEN SEPARATED FROM HIS MOTHER AND HERD, FOR THE ARTICLE "DO WE KILL WHALES WITH SOUND?" APRIL 2002.

DESIGN DIRECTOR: MICHAEL MRAK. DIRECTOR OF PHOTOGRAPHY: MAISIE TODD. ART DIRECTOR: JOHN SEEGER GILMAN. EDITOR: STEPHEN L. PETRANEK. PUBLICATION: DISCOVER. PUBLISHING COMPANY: DISNEY PUBLISHING WORLDWIDE. WRITER: SUSAN MCCARTHY.

203. DANA LIXENBERG

ACTOR/DIRECTOR PHILIP SEYMOUR HOFFMAN, FOR THE FEATURE "CLASS ACTS-HOLIDAY MOVIE PREVIEW," DECEMBER 2002.

ART DIRECTOR: RICHARD BAKER. DIRECTOR OF PHOTOGRAPHY: CATRIONA NIAOLAIN DESIGNER: LUCIANA. EDITORS: KATHY HEINTZELMAN, RACHEL CLARKE. PUBLICATION: PREMIERE. PUBLISHING COMPANY: HACHETTE FILIPACCHI MEDIA U.S., INC. WRITER: TOM ROSTON.

204-207. DANA LIXENBERG

FOUR FROM A SERIES FOR "THE AGGRESSIVES," JANUARY 2003, A STORY ON LESBIAN COUPLES OF COLOR KNOWN IN URBAN COMMUNITIES AS "AGGRESSIVES."

DESIGN DIRECTOR: FLORIAN BACHLEDA. DIRECTOR OF PHOTOGRAPHY: GEORGE PITTS. PHOTO EDITOR: DORA SOMOSI. MANAGING ART DIRECTOR: WYATT MITCHELL. EDITOR: EMIL WILBEKIN. PUBLICATION: VIBE. PUBLISHING COMPANY: MILLER PUBLISHING. WRITER: KATHY DOBIE.

208. PAOLO PELLEGRIN

THE BLOOD SOAKED BED OF ISRAELI SETTLERS SHOT BY PALESTINIAN GUNMEN NEAR HEBRON, FOR THE ARTICLE "IN THE NAME OF GOD," MAY 20, 2002.

ASSISTANT MANAGING EDITOR/DESIGN: LYNN STALEY. DIRECTOR OF PHOTOGRAPHY: SARAH HARBUTT. PHOTO EDITOR: JAMES WELLFORD. EDITOR: MARK WHITAKER. PUBLICATION: NEWSWEEK. PUBLISHING COMPANY: NEWSWEEK, INC.

87. DAN WINTERS

AGUSTIN DE MELLO WITH HIS SON JAMES, WHO AT ELEVEN WAS THE YOUNGEST COLLEGE GRADUATE IN HISTORY, FOR THE ARTICLE "JUST ANOTHER FATHER-SON STORY," NOVEMBER 2002.

ART DIRECTOR: JOHN KORPICS. PHOTO EDITOR: NANCY JO IACOI. DESIGNER: TODD ALBERTSON. PUBLICATION: ESQUIRE. PUBLISHING COMPANY: HEARST MAGAZINES. WRITER: ROBERT KURSON.

88. DAN WINTERS

PORTRAIT OF BECK FOR THE FEATURE "THE MASTER OF EVERYTHING (AND NOTHING AT ALL)," NOVEMBER 2002.

ART DIRECTOR: JOHN KORPICS. PHOTO EDITOR: NANCY JO IACOI. DESIGNER: JOHN KORPICS. PUBLICATION: ESQUIRE. PUBLISHING COMPANY: HEARST MAGAZINES. WRITER: WIL S. HYLTON.

89. DAN WINTERS

ACTOR LEONARDO DICAPRIO FOR THE FEATURE "LEONARDO DICAPRIO'S SEVENTH ACT," NOVEMBER 24, 2002.

PHOTO EDITOR: KATHY RYAN. PUBLICATION: THE NEW YORK TIMES MAGAZINE. PUBLISHING COMPANY: THE NEW YORK TIMES.

90. WILLIAM WEGMAN

ANIMAL RIGHTS ADVOCATES PRESENT A COMPELLING VISION OF A MORE MORAL WORLD, BUT THIS VISION IS ECOLOGICALLY FOOLHARDY – AND BASED ON A NAÏVE DEFINITION OF ANIMAL HAPPINESS, ONE FROM THE ARTICLE "AN ANIMAL'S PLACE," NOVEMBER 10, 2002

ART DIRECTOR: JANET FROELICH. PHOTO EDITORS: KATHY RYAN, EVAN KRISS. EDITOR: ADAM MOSS. PUBLICATION: THE NEW YORK TIMES MAGAZINE. PUBLISHING COMPANY: THE NEW YORK TIMES. WRITER: MICHAEL POLLAN.

91-92. LISA KERESZI

TWO FROM A SERIES FOR "TRUNK SHOW," JUNE/JULY 2002, A FASHION STORY ON MEN'S BATHING SUITS.

DESIGN DIRECTOR: ROCKWELL HARWOOD. DIRECTOR OF PHOTOGRAPHY: AMY STEIGBIGEL. ASSOCIATE ART DIRECTOR: NATHALIE KIRSHEH. PUBLICATION: DETAILS. PUBLISHING COMPANY: FAIRCHILD PUBLICATIONS. WRITER: HORACIO SILVA.

93. SACHA WALDMAN

DAVID BOWIE AND MOBY FOR THE FEATURE "LOVING THE ALIENS," MAY 31, 2002.

PHOTO EDITOR: SARAH ROZEN. PUBLICATION: ENTERTAINMENT WEEKLY. PUBLISHING COMPANY: TIME INC.

94-95. TARYN SIMON

TWO FROM "DOWNTOWN GIRLS," MARCH 17, 2002 A SERIES ON WOMEN WHO MAKE LOWER MANHATTAN THE CENTER OF FEMALE MUSIC MAKING. PLATE 94: CHAN MARSHALL, AKA CAT POWER. PLATE 95: SUZANNE VEGA.

ART DIRECTOR: JANET FROELICH. PHOTO EDITOR: KATHY RYAN. DESIGNER: CLAUDE MARTEL. EDITOR: ADAM MOSS. PUBLICATION: THE NEW YORK TIMES MAGAZINE. PUBLISHING COMPANY: THE NEW YORK TIMES. INTERVIEWS BY: CAMILLE SWEENEY.

96. TARYN SIMON

RESEARCHERS AT THE UNIVERSITY OF TENNESSEE ANTHROPOLOGY RESEARCH FACILITY STUDY HOW

112-113. ERIN PATRICE O'BRIEN

TWO FROM THE SERIES "POET'S PARADISE," SEPTEMBER 2002, A STORY ON NYC POETS. PLATE 113: MUMS. PLATE 112: TISH BENSON.

ART DIRECTOR: TONY PAUL. PICTURE EDITOR: MARK GUTHRIE. DESIGNER: TONY PAUL EDITOR: PETER AKINTI. PUBLICATION: UNTOLD. PUBLISHER: PETER AKINTI. WRITER: MIRANDA PYNE.

114. LUCY LEVENE

"UNTITLED," ONE FROM A DOCUMENTARY SERIES ON NIGHTCLUBS, STUDENT WORK.

SCHOOL: ROYAL COLLEGE OF ART, LONDON.

115. LAUREN FLEISHMAN

"VIEW," ONE FROM A SERIES SHOT FOR A NURSING HOME CATALOGUE. HERE THE ENERGY OF THE PLACE CAME ALIVE WHEN THE GAME USING A NET, A BALLOON AND PADDLES COVERED WITH PANTY HOSE BEGAN.

116-117. CATHERINE LEDNER

TWO FROM A SERIES FOR "IT TELEVISION-IT TORTURED TEEN II," JUNE 28-JULY 5, 2002. PLATE 116: ACTRESS EVAN RACHEL WOOD. PLATE 117: ACTRESS LAUREN AMBROSE,

PHOTO EDITOR: DENISE SFRAGA. PUBLICATION: ENTERTAINMENT WEEKLY. PUBLISHING COMPANY: TIME INC.

118-119. VICTOR SCHRAGER

TWO FOR PHOTO ESSAY "A BIRD IN THE HAND," SEPTEMBER 2002. PLATE 118: COMMON GRACKLE, OYSTER BAY, NEW YORK. PLATE 119: CAROLINA CHICKADEES, CHARLOTTE, NORTH CAROLINA.

DESIGN DIRECTOR: KEVIN FISHER. PHOTO EDITOR: KIM HUBBARD. DESIGNER: KEVIN FISHER. EDITOR: DAVID SEIDEMAN. PUBLICATION: AUDUBON. PUBLISHING COMPANY: AUDUBON. WRITER: CAROLYN SHEA.

120-121. CHIEN-MIN CHUNG

TWO FROM A SERIES FOR "CHILDHOOD BURDENS," JULY/AUGUST 2002, AN ARTICLE ON THE RISING NUMBER OF CHILD LABORERS WORKING FULL TIME IN AFGHANISTAN.

DESIGN DIRECTOR: JANE PALECEK. PHOTO EDITOR: SARAH KEHOE. DESIGNER: AMY SHROADS. EDITOR: ROGER COHN. PUBLICATION: MOTHER JONES. PUBLISHING COMPANY: FOUNDATION FOR NATIONAL PROGRESS. WRITER: SCOTT CARRIER.

122. JAMIL GS

"MISS HONEY" IS 'HOOD RICH IN HER GHETTO FABULOUS FANTASY OF HIGH-END LUXURY, FROM A SERIES FOR THE FASHION STORY "BOURGEOIS GHETTO," DECEMBER 2002.

DESIGN DIRECTOR: FLORIAN BACHLEDA. DIRECTOR OF PHOTOGRAPHY: GEORGE PITTS. PHOTO EDITOR: DORA SOMOSI. EDITOR: EMIL WILBEKIN. PULBICATION: VIBE. PUBLISHING COMPANY: MILLER PUBLISHING.

123. OLIVIER LAUDE

"COLD WAR DIARIES," PERSONAL WORK.

124. OLIVIER LAUDE

"JEANETTE," FROM "THE DANES" SERIES.

125. CHIEN-CHI CHANG

ILLEGAL CHINESE IMMIGRANT ESCAPES THE UNBEARABLE HEAT AND STENCH OF HIS CRAMPED

WOUND," MARCH 2002, AN ARTICLE ON THE FRAGILITY OF LIFE AND THE EXTREME ADVANCEMENT OF TECHNOLOGY.

ART DIRECTOR: ANDREW ZUCKERMAN. PHOTO EDITOR: JOHN CLANG. DESIGNER: THESEUS CHAN. PUBLICATION: WORK. PUBLISHING COMPANY: WERK.

133-134. STEPHEN SHORE

TWO FROM A SERIES SHOT IN SAN CLEMENTE, CA, FOR THE ARTICLE "WILDING AMERICA," SEPTEMBER 2002.

DESIGN DIRECTOR: MICHAEL MRAK. DIRECTOR OF PHOTOGRAPHY: MAISIE TODD. ART DIRECTOR: JOHN SEEGER GILMAN. EDITOR: STEPHEN L. PETRANEK. PUBLICATION: DISCOVER. PUBLISHING COMPANY: DISNEY PUBLISHING WORLDWIDE. WRITER: ELIZABETH ROYTE.

135. MICHAEL WARING

"MAX," PERSONAL PIECE SHOT ON TOUR WITH THE BAND EVE 6.

136-138. JOSEPH RAFFERTY

THREE FROM A SERIES OF STUDENT WORK. PLATE 136: "A DAY IN THE LIFE OF A STARVING PERFORMANCE ARTIST," PLATE 137: "THE MODERN DAY CORPORATE FAT CAT," FORTUNE MAGAZINE MOCK COVER. PLATE 138: "WORKERS' COMP," ONE FROM A SERIES EXPLORING THE HUMAN CONDITION THROUGH HUMOR.

SCHOOL: ART CENTER COLLEGE OF DESIGN.

139-142. ROBERT PARKEHARRISON

FOUR PHOTO-ILLUSTRATIONS FROM A SERIES FOR "ABOVE AND BEYOND-THE PROGRESSIVE CORPORATION 2001 ANNUAL REPORT," MARCH 2002, COURTESY BONNI BENRUBI GALLERY. PLATE 139: THE SOWER 2002. PLATE 140: TREE SONATA 2002. PLATE 141: POLLINATION 2002. PLATE 142: FORESTBED 2002.

ART DIRECTORS: JOYCE NESNADNY, MARK SCHWARTZ. DESIGNERS: JOYCE NESNADNY, MICHELLE MOEHLER. PUBLICATION: THE PROGRESSIVE CORPORATION 2001 ANNUAL REPORT. AUTHOR: GLENN RENWICK.

143-144. WILLIAM EGGLESTON

TWO FROM A SERIES FOR "PORTFOLIO: IN COUNTRY," OCTOBER 20, 2002, NEWLY RECOVERED PHOTOGRAPHS OF THE AMERICAN SOUTH FROM 1965 TO 1974. COURTESY CHEIM & READ, NY.

ART DIRECTOR: JANET FROELICH. PHOTO EDITOR: KATHY RYAN. DESIGNER: JOELE CUYLER. EDITOR: ADAM MOSS. PUBLICATION: THE NEW YORK TIMES MAGAZINE. PUBLISHING COMPANY: THE NEW YORK TIMES.

145. LORI ADAMSKI-PEEK

"MAX AND MOMS," PERSONAL WORK.

146. FREDRIK BRODEN

PHOTOGRAPH ILLUSTRATING THE ARTICLE "SUPER WARRIOR," AUGUST 2003, A STORY ABOUT THE TECHNOLOGICAL ADVANCEMENTS BEING DEVELOPED TO ENHANCE THE FUTURE SOLDIER.

ART DIRECTOR: DIRK BARNETT. EDITOR: SCOTT MOWBRAY. PUBLICATION: POPULAR SCIENCE. PUBLISHING COMPANY: TIME4 MEDIA. WRITER: DAWN STOVE.

147. FREDRIK BRODEN

UNPUBLISHED PHOTOGRAPH FOR A BOOK COVER ON THE SUBJECT OF OFFICE INFIDELITY.

163-164. ZUBIN SHROFF

TWO PHOTOGRAPHS FROM A SERIES FOLLOWING A BURN CREW USING CONTROLLED BURNING TO PROTECT AND RESTORE THE PREVIOUS BIODIVERSE ECOSYSTEM, FOR THE ARTICLE "FIRE STARTER," FALL 2002.

ART DIRECTOR: LORI ENDE. PHOTO EDITOR: LORI ENDE. DESIGNER: JUNE PARK. EDITOR: COLLEEN MARZEC. PUBLICATION: THE NATURE CONSERVANCY. PUBLISHING COMPANY: THE NATURE CONSERVANCY.

165-166. JONAS KARLSSON

TWO FROM "THE EXPLORER'S HEART," MAY 2002, A SERIES ON 10 OF THE GREATEST LIVING EXPLORERS. PLATE 165: SIR RANULPH FIENNES, 58, VANCOUVER, BRITISH COLOMBIA. PLATE 166: NORMAN VAUGHN, 96, COOPER LANDING, ALASKA.

ART DIRECTOR: DAVID HARRIS. PHOTO EDITOR: LISA BERMAN. PHOTO PRODUCER: RON BEINNER. DESIGNER: JULIE WEISS. DIRECTOR OF PHOTOGRAPHY: SUSAN WHITE. EDITOR-IN-CHIEF: GRAYDON CARTER. PUBLICATION: VANITY FAIR. PUBLISHING COMPANY: CONDÉ NAST PUBLICATIONS, INC. WRITER: SCOTT GUMMER.

167. STEPHEN JACOBS

WWII RE-ENACTOR, GERMAN STAFF AIDE, ONE FROM A SERIES FOR THE ARTICLE "ATTACK OF THE CLONES."

ART DIRECTORS: STACIE REISTETTER AND SANDRA SCHNEIDER. PHOTO EDITOR: KEITH JENKINS. DESIGNER: SANDRA SCHNEIDER. EDITOR: DAVID ROWELL. PUBLICATION: THE WASHINGTON POST MAGAZINE. PUBLISHING COMPANY: THE WASHINGTON POST. WRITER: RICHARD B. WOODWARD.

168. JUSTIN SUTCLIFFE

FREED HOSTAGE, STUNNED BY THE GAS RUSSIAN SPECIAL FORCES USED TO FLOOD A THEATER CHECHEN REBELS HELD HOSTAGE IN MOSCOW, FOR THE ARTICLE "NIGHTMARE IN MOSCOW," DECEMBER 30, 2002.

ASSISTANT MANAGING EDITOR/DESIGN: LYNN STALEY. DIRECTOR OF PHOTOGRAPHY: SARAH HARBUTT. PHOTO EDITOR: STEPHANIE HEIMANN. EDITOR: MARK WHITAKER. PUBLICATION: NEWSWEEK. PUBLISHING COMPANY: NEWSWEEK, INC.

169. JASON FULFORD

STAIRCASE IN THE NILGIRI MOUNTAINS OF SOUTHERN INDIA, USED ON HANGTAGS FOR JACK SPADE, NOVEMBER 2002.

ART DIRECTOR: MATT SINGER. CLIENT: JACK SPADE.

170-173. EUGENE RICHARDS

FOUR FROM A SERIES FOR THE BOOK "STEPPING THROUGH THE ASHES," AUGUST 2002, A COLLECTION OF IMAGES FROM THE AFTERMATH OF THE 911 TERRORIST ATTACKS.

DESIGNER: EUGENE RICHARDS. EDITORS: EUGENE RICHARDS, MELISSA HARRIS. BOOK TITLE: STEPPING THROUGH THE ASHES. PUBLISHING COMPANY: APERTURE. AUTHORS: EUGENE RICHARDS, JANINE ALTONGY.

174-177. LYLE OWERKO

FOUR PHOTOGRAPHS FROM THE BOOK "AND NO BIRDS SANG," AUGUST 2002, A COLLECTION OF

ASSISTANT MANAGING EDITOR/DESIGN: LYNN STALEY. DIRECTOR OF PHOTOGRAPHY: SARAH HARBUTT. PHOTO EDITOR: SIMON BARNETT. EDITOR: MARK WHITAKER. PUBLICATION: NEWSWEEK. PUBLISHING COMPANY: NEWSWEEK, INC.

187. NIGEL PARRY

ARTIST WALTON FORD IN HIS STUDIO, FOR THE ARTICLE "NATURE BOY," OCTOBER 21, 2002.

DESIGN DIRECTOR: DAVID MATT. PHOTO DIRECTOR: CHRIS DOUGHERTY. EDITOR: CAROLINE MILLER. PUBLICATION: NEW YORK MAGAZINE. PUBLISHING COMPANY: PRIMEDIA. WRITER: MARK JACOBSON.

188. DONNA FERRATO

"I HATE YOU FOR HAVING BEATEN MY MOM AND I HOPE YOU ARE NEVER COMING BACK," A BOY YELLS AT HIS FATHER AS MINNEAPOLIS POLICE ARREST HIM, ONE FROM A COLLECTION OF PHOTOGRAPHS FOR THE BOOK "SCHATTENLICHT/SHADOW LIGHT," 2002.

DIRECTOR OF PHOTOGRAPHY: RUTH EICHHORN. PHOTO EDITORS: NADJA MASRI, MARKUS SEEWALD. DESIGNER: MELANIE WOLTER. EDITORS: ULRIKE MOSER, TORBEN MUELLER, JENS SCHROEDER. BOOK TITLE: SCHATTENLICHT / SHADOW LIGHT. PUBLISHING COMPANY: GEO, GRUNER + JAHR. GERMANY PUBLISHER: PETER-MATTHIAS GAEDE.

189-192. DANNY CLINCH

FOUR FROM A SERIES USED IN A SPECIAL PACKAGING BOOKLET FOR THE BRUCE SPRINGSTEEN CD "THE RISING."

ART DIRECTORS: CHRIS AUSTOPCHUK, DAVE BETT. DESIGNERS: DAVE BETT, MICHELLE HOLME.

193-194. DANNY CLINCH

TWO FROM A SERIES ON ELECTRONIC MUSIC SUPERSTAR MOBY FOR THE FEATURE "MOBY," MAY 2002.

CREATIVE DIRECTOR: DARRIN PERRY. PHOTOGRAPHY DIRECTOR: BRENNA BRITTON. DESIGNER: FEDERICO GUTIERREZ-SCHOTT. EDITOR: THOMAS GOETZ. PUBLICATION: WIRED. PUBLISHING COMPANY: CONDÉ NAST PUBLICATIONS, INC. WRITER: ETHAN SMITH.

195-196. COLLIER SCHORR

ACTRESS SHANNYN SOSSAMON, TWO FROM A SERIES FOR THE CELEBRITY PROFILE "ORIGINAL SIN," DECEMBER 2002.

DESIGN DIRECTOR: ROCKWELL HARWOOD. DIRECTOR OF PHOTOGRAPHY: AMY STEIGBIGEL. PUBLICATION: DETAILS. PUBLISHING COMPANY: FAIRCHILD PUBLICATIONS. WRITER: BART BLASENGAME.

197. MARY ELLEN MARK

ACTRESS LACHANZE SAPP-GOODING, WITH HER CHILDREN CELIA AND ZAYA, WAS PREGNANT ON SEPTEMBER 11 WHEN HER HUSBAND WAS KILLED IN THE TERRORIST ATTACKS, FOR THE ARTICLE "THE LIVES LEFT BEHIND," OCTOBER 16, 2002.

DESIGN DIRECTOR: DAVID MATT. PHOTO DIRECTOR: CHRIS DOUGHERTY. DEPUTY PHOTO EDITOR: ARMIN HARRIS. DESIGNER: MICHELE PARRELLA. EDITOR: CAROLINE MILLER. PUBLICATION: NEW YORK MAGAZINE. PUBLISHING COMPANY: PRIMEDIA. WRITER: MERYL GORDON.

198. MARY ELLEN MARK

LIZA MINNELLI, PORTRAIT FROM A SERIES ON THE ACTRESS/PERFORMER AS SHE EMBARKS ON

209-212. PAOLO PELLEGRIN

BEHIND ENEMY LINES WITH A PLATOON OF ELITE ISRAELI COMMANDOS IN A WAR THEY BELIEVE THEY MUST FIGHT BUT KNOW THEY CAN'T WIN, FOUR FROM A SERIES FOR THE ARTICLE "AN IMPOSSIBLE OCCUPATION," MAY 12, 2002

PHOTO EDITOR: KATHY RYAN. EDITOR: ADAM MOSS. PUBLICATION: THE NEW YORK TIMES MAGAZINE. PUBLISHING COMPANY: THE NEW YORK TIMES. WRITER: SCOTT ANDERSON.

213. GREGORY CREWDSON

UNTITLED, 2001, ONE FROM A COLLECTION OF 40 FOR THE BOOK "TWILIGHT," 2002.

VP, CREATIVE DIRECTOR: MICHAEL J. WALSH, JR. DESIGNERS: GARY TOOTH AND CARRIE HAMILTON. DESIGN FIRM: EMPIRE DESIGN STUDIO NYC. EDITOR: DEBORAH AARONSON. BOOK TITLE: TWILIGHT. PUBLISHING COMPANY: HARRY N. ABRAMS, INC. ESSAY BY: RICK MOODY.

214-217. GREGORY CREWDSON

FOUR FROM A SERIES FOR "PORTFOLIO: DREAM HOUSE," OCTOBER, 10, 2002. THE PHOTOGRAPHER INVITED A NUMBER OF CELEBRITIES TO PORTRAY THE ANONYMOUS FIGURES WHO PLAY OUT THE NARRATIVES. PLATE 214: JULIANNE MOORE, "IT'S PLAYING OFF HER BIOGRAPHY; AT THE SAME TIME, IT TRANSCENDS THAT." PLATE 215: DYLAN BAKER AND FAMILY, "THE WIFE IS DRAWN TO THE LIGHT COMING THROUGH THE SHAFT AS A WAY OUT." PLATE 216: GWYNETH PLATROW, "I WANTED IT TO BE SHAMEFUL IN A SENSE." PLATE 217: WILLIAM H. MACY, "IT'S A PERFECT WORLD THAT'S A FAILED MOMENT, TOO."

ART DIRECTOR: JANET FROELICH. PHOTO EDITOR: KATHY RYAN. DESIGNER: JOELE CUYLER. EDITOR: ADAM MOSS. PUBLICATION: THE NEW YORK TIMES MAGAZINE. PUBLISHING COMPANY: THE NEW YORK TIMES.

218-219. DAVID MAISEL

TWO FROM "THE LAKE PROJECT," AN AERIAL SERIES OF ENVIRONMENTALLY IMPACTED LANDSCAPES. PICTURED HERE, OWENS LAKE, WHERE WATER BEING DIVERTED TO LOS ANGELES IS CREATING AN ENVIRONMENTAL DISASTER

220-221. WILLIAM HOWARD

"CYCLIST #1" AND "CYCLIST #2," TWO FROM A SELF-PROMOTIONAL SERIES.

222. MICHAEL KELLEY

CRAIG STANFORD, DIRECTOR OF THE JANE GOODALL RESEARCH CENTER, IN HIS LAB, FOR THE ARTICLE "THE GREAT APE DEBATE," JUNE 2, 2002.

ART DIRECTOR: NAN OSHIN. PUBLICATION: LOS ANGELES TIMES MAGAZINE. PUBLISHING COMPANY: TRIBUNE.

223. MICHAEL KELLEY

BARRY DILLER ON A SOUND STAGE AT UNIVERSAL STUDIOS WHERE HE IS CHAIRMAN, FOR THE ARTICLE "THE PART TIME MOGUL," MARCH 24, 2002.

ART DIRECTOR: NAN OSHIN. PUBLICATION: LOS ANGELES TIMES MAGAZINE. PUBLISHING COMPANY: TRIBUNE.

224. ILAN WOLFF

NOTRE-DAME, 1997, STÉNOGRAMME, ONE FROM A COLLECTION FOR THE BOOK "PHOTOGRAPHY'S ANTIQUARIAN AVANT-GARDE: THE NEW WAVE IN OLD PROCESSES," 2002.

VP, CREATIVE DIRECTOR: MICHAEL J. WALSH JR. PHOTO EDITORS: LYLE REXER AND DEBORAH AARONSON. DESIGNER: BRANKICA KOVRLIJA. EDITOR: DEBORAH AARONSON. BOOK TITLE: PHOTOGRAPHY'S ANTIQUARIAN AVANT-GARDE: THE NEW WAVE IN OLD PROCESSES. PUBLISHING COMPANY: HARRY N. ABRAMS, INC. AUTHOR: LYLE REXER.

225-226. ANTONIN KRATOCHVIL

TWO FROM A SERIES FOR "BUBBLE IN THE HEARTLAND," NOVEMBER 25, 2002, AN ARTICLE ON THE TROUBLE FARMERS ARE FACING IN THE PLAIN STATES WITH A DROUGHT THAT RIVALS THE DUST BOWL OF THE 1930'S.

ART DIRECTOR: BLAKE TAYLOR. PHOTO EDITORS: SCOTT THODE, MICHELE MCNALLY. DESIGNER: LINDA RUBES. EDITOR: CLIFTON LEAF. PUBLICATION: FORTUNE. PUBLISHING COMPANY: TIME INC. WRITER: GRAINGER DAVID.

227-228. ANTONIN KRATOCHVIL

TWO FROM A SERIES FOR "9/11: "UNFINISHED BUSINESS/ARE WE SAFE YET?" SEPTEMBER 16, 2002. PLATE 227: COMMUTERS PONDER THE ALTERED SKYLINE FROM THE STATEN ISLAND FERRY. PLATE 228: DUAL-REACTOR NUCLEAR GENERATING STATION IN PENNSYLVANIA.

ART DIRECTOR: BLAKE TAYLOR. PHOTO EDITORS: SCOTT THODE, MICHELE MCNALLY. DESIGNER: MARIA KEEHAN. EDITOR: JIM IMPOCO. PUBLICATION: FORTUNE. PUBLISHING COMPANY: TIME INC. WRITER: BILL POWELL.

229-230. ANTONIN KRATOCHVIL

TWO PORTRAITS PHOTOGRAPHED IN MOSCOW FOR "THE SPY WHO SOLD OUR SECRETS," JANUARY 2002, A SERIES BASED ON COLD WAR ERA ESPIONAGE BETWEEN AMERICAN AND RUSSIAN SPIES.

DESIGN DIRECTOR: HANNU LAAKSO. DIRECTOR OF PHOTOGRAPHY: BILL BLACK. DESIGNER: VICTORIA NIGHTINGALE. EDITOR-IN-CHIEF: JACQUELINE LEO. PUBLICATION: READER'S DIGEST. PUBLISHING COMPANY: READER'S DIGEST ASSOCIATION, INC. AUTHOR: DAVID WISE.

231. NANCY WOLF

"UNTITLED," ONE FROM THE "PINK GLAM" SERIES.

232-233. RODNEY SMITH

TWO FROM A SERIES FOR "THE YEAR IN IDEAS" SPECIAL ISSUE, DECEMBER 15, 2002. PLATE 232: EVEN THE BLIND PEOPLE CAN DRAW. PLATE 233: BOTOX PARTY.

ART DIRECTOR: JANET FROELICH. PHOTO EDITOR: KIRA POLLACK. DESIGNER: EMILY CRAWFORD. EDITOR: ADAM MOSS. PUBLICATION: THE NEW YORK TIMES MAGAZINE. PUBLISHING COMPANY: THE NEW YORK TIMES.

234. WILL WENDT

"SCENIC VEIW," NEW MEXICO INTERSTATE 25.

235P. LARRY SULTAN

OPENING PHOTOGRAPH FOR "BREAST MEN," SEPTEMBER 2002, AN ARTICLE ON MEN WITH GYNECOMASTIA WHO FEEL THEIR ENLARGED BREASTS ARE A SOURCE OF PRIDE.

DESIGN DIRECTOR: ROCKWELL HARWOOD. DIRECTOR OF PHOTOGRAPHY: AMY STEIGBIGEL. ASSOCIATE ART DIRECTOR: NATHALIE KIRSHEH.

242. MATT HENRY GUNTHER

CHEF PAUL LIEBRANDT OF THE RESTAURANT PAPILLION IN NEW YORK CALLS HIMSELF "THE DAMIEN HIRST OF CULINARY," FOR THE FEATURE "TASTE SENSATION," OCTOBER 2002.

ART DIRECTOR: MATT HENRY GUNTHER. PHOTO DIRECTOR: LAURA CARLILE. PUBLICATION: ARENA.

243-244. SARAH HOSKINS

"LET GO PIGGY, LET GO," A GENTLE VOICE COAXES A HOG TO DIE, FOURTH GENERATION RESIDENTS FOLLOW TRADITIONAL METHODS IN HOG KILLING, TWO FROM A PERSONAL SERIES FROM A LARGER PROJECT ENTITLED "THE AFRICAN-AMERICAN HAMLETS OF KENTUCKY'S BLUEGRASS REGION"

245. LARRY FINK

CELEBRITY LOOKALIKE REENACTS THE REAL-LIFE TEMPER TANTRUM OF JACK NICHOLSON, ONE FROM A SERIES FOR THE FASHION PORTFOLIO "ACTORS GONE BAD," MARCH 2002.

DESIGN DIRECTOR: FRED WOODWARD. DIRECTOR OF PHOTOGRAPHY: JENNIFER CRANDALL. DESIGNER: PAUL MARTINEZ. PUBLICATION: GQ. PUBLISHING COMPANY: CONDÉ NAST PUBLICATIONS, INC.

246. LARRY FINK

ONE FROM A SERIES ENTITLED "PARTY ANIMALS," NOVEMBER 2002.

ART DIRECTOR: PERCY CHUNG.
DIRECTOR OF PHOTOGRAPHY: JENNIFER SPENCER. KENTRUP DESIGNER: HOWARD LEVING. EDITOR: STUART LAWRENCE. PUBLICATION: DISCOVERY. PUBLISHING COMPANY: EMPHASIS MEDIA LTD.

247. LARRY FINK

CELEBRITY LOOKALIKE REENACTS THE REAL-LIFE TEMPER TANTRUM OF JOHNNY DEPP, ONE FROM A SERIES FOR THE FASHION PORTFOLIO "ACTORS GONE BAD," MARCH 2002.

DESIGN DIRECTOR: FRED WOODWARD. DIRECTOR OF PHOTOGRAPHY: JENNIFER CRANDALL. DESIGNER: PAUL MARTINEZ. PUBLICATION: GQ. PUBLISHING COMPANY: CONDÉ NAST PUBLICATIONS, INC.

248. JULIUS SHULMAN / DAVID GLOMB

ANNE FRIEDBERG IN THE REDESIGNED FRONT ENTRYWAY OF HER LOS ANGELES HOME, ORIGINALLY DESIGNED BY JOHN LAUTNER. THE HOME WAS ORIGINALLY PHOTOGRAPHED IN 1957 BY SHULMAN, WHO REVISITS IT HERE, FOR THE ARTICLE "LAUTNER VS. LAUTNER," FEBRUARY 2002.

ART DIRECTOR: JEANETTE HODGE ABBINK. PHOTO EDITOR: MAREN LEVINSON. DESIGNER: JEANETTE HODGE ABBINK. EDITOR: ANDREW WAGNER. PUBLICATION: DWELL. PUBLISHING COMPANY: DWELL LLC. WRITER: MARC KRISTAL.

249. MARK SELIGER

JA RULE, VOTED BEST SOLO MUSICIAN IN THE ANNUAL "GQ MEN OF THE YEAR" ISSUE, NOVEMBER 2002.

DESIGN DIRECTOR: FRED WOODWARD. DIRECTOR OF PHOTOGRAPHY: JENNIFER CRANDALL. SENIOR ASSOCIATE PHOTO EDITOR: KRISTEN SCHAEFER. DESIGNER: MATTHEW LENNING. PUBLICATION: GQ. PUBLISHING COMPANY: CONDÉ NAST PUBLICATIONS, INC. WRITER: PETER RUBIN.

DOUGHERTY. EDITOR: CAROLINE MILLER. PUBLICATION: NEW YORK MAGAZINE. WRITER: JOHN HAMANS. PUBLISHING COMPANY: PRIMEDIA.

254. MARK PETERSON

INTERNATIONAL DEBUTANTE BALL AT THE WALDORF ASTORIA, 2002, PERSONAL WORK.

255-256. SHAUL SCHWARZ

THE TRANSVESTITES OF JUCHITAN, MEXICO, TWO FROM A PERSONAL SERIES.

257. CANDACE DICARLO

"UNTITLED" FROM THE MÜTTER SERIES, FOETUS APPROXIMATELY TWELVE-WEEKS, CLEARED AND STAINED WITH ALIZARIN, PRESERVED IN GLYCERIN, FOR THE BOOK "MÜTTER MUSEUM," OCTOBER 2002.

ART DIRECTOR: LAURA LINDGREN. PHOTO EDITOR: LAURA LINDGREN. DESIGNER: LAURA LINDGREN. EDITOR: LAURA LINDGREN. BOOK TITLE: MÜTTER MUSEUM. PUBLISHING COMPANY: BLAST BOOKS. AUTHOR: GRETCHEN WORDEN.

258. DALE GUNNOE

"UNTITLED," LATE NINETEENTH-CENTURY DRIED PREPARATION OF THE HAND DEMONSTRATING THE CIRCULATORY AND NERVOUS SYSTEMS, FOR THE BOOK "MÜTTER MUSEUM," OCTOBER 2002.

ART DIRECTOR: LAURA LINDGREN. PHOTO EDITOR: LAURA LINDGREN. DESIGNER: LAURA LINDGREN. EDITOR: LAURA LINDGREN. BOOK TITLE: MÜTTER MUSEUM. PUBLISHING COMPANY: BLAST BOOKS. AUTHOR: GRETCHEN WORDEN.

259. MARK KESSELL

"THE ZERO AT THE BONE," SKULL OF LEOPOLINE SOLAR, TWENTY-FIVE, BOHEMIAN DESCENT, FROM THE BOOK "MÜTTER MUSEUM," OCTOBER 2002

ART DIRECTOR: LAURA LINDGREN PHOTO EDITOR: LAURA LINDGREN DESIGNER: LAURA LINDGREN EDITOR: LAURA LINDGREN BOOK TITLE: MÜTTER MUSEUM PUBLISHING COMPANY: BLAST BOOKS AUTHOR: GRETCHEN WORDEN

260-261. OLIVIA BEASLEY

TWO FROM A SERIES FOR THE HEAL'S FURNITURE AD CAMPAIGN ENTITLED "HEAD OVER HEAL'S." PLATE 260: PETER REDDY, NARROWLY ESCAPED HOUSE FIRE. PLATE 261: PATRICK TRIMBLE, BANKRUPT AFTER HIGH PROFILE LIBEL ACTION.

ART DIRECTOR: GRANT PARKER. AGENCY: BMP DDB LTD. CLIENT: HEAL'S. COPYWRITER: PATRICK MCCLELLAND.

262. ANDREA BAKACS

"UNTITLED," FROM THE PHOTO DISTRICT NEWS "PHOTO ANNUAL 2002."

263. MARK RICHARDS

CAMPER AT CAMP KINGSMONT, WEST STOCKBRIDGE, MA, A SUMMER CAMP FOR OVERWEIGHT KIDS, FOR THE ARTICLE "EVERYTHING TO LOSE," NOVEMBER 4, 2002.

ART DIRECTOR: PHIL SIMONE. PHOTO EDITORS: CHRISTINE RAMAGE, MAURA FOLEY. PUBLICATION: PEOPLE. PUBLISHING COMPANY: TIME INC. WRITER: JILL SNOLOWE.

264. TOM MURPHY

CAMPSITE AT THE BASE OF COLTER PEAK IN THE RARELY VISITED AREA OF YELLOWSTONE

DESIGN DIRECTOR: ROCKWELL HARWOOD. DIRECTOR OF PHOTOGRAPHY: AMY STEIGBIGEL. ASSOCIATE ART DIRECTOR: NATHALIE KIRSHEH. PUBLICATION: DETAILS. PUBLISHING COMPANY: FAIRCHILD PUBLICATIONS. WRITER: BART BLASENGAME.

270. DAVID STRICK

MADE TO LOOK LIKE AN OLD MAN, 28-YEAR-OLD CHRIS PONTIUS, A.K.A. "PARTY BOY," ON THE SET OF THE MOVIE "JACKASS," FOR THE FEATURE "DAVID STRICK'S HOLLYWOOD," NOVEMBER 2002.

ART DIRECTOR: RICHARD BAKER. DIRECTOR OF PHOTOGRAPHY CATRIONA NIAOLAIN. DESIGNER: CHRISTINE CUCUZZA. PUBLICATION: PREMIERE. PUBLISHING COMPANY: HACHETTE FILIPACCHI MEDIA U.S., INC.

271. JEFFERY NEWBURY

MEMBERS OF THE PROJECT BANDALOOP AS THEY PERFORM OFF THE DE DOMENICO BUILDING IN OAKLAND, CA, FOR THE ARTICLE "FLYING WOMEN," MARCH 2002.

ART DIRECTOR: JAMES LAMBERTUS. DESIGNER: JAMES LAMBERTUS. EDITOR: K.C. PATRICK. PUBLICATION: DANCE MAGAZINE. PUBLISHING COMPANY: MACFADDEN DANCE MAGAZINE, L.L.C. WRITER: MARCIA SANDERSON.

272-275. CHRISTOPHER ANDERSON

FOUR FROM A SERIES FOR "DESTRUCTION OF JENIN," APRIL 7, 2002, A PHOTO ESSAY ON THE ISRAELI ARMY'S INVASION OF THE WEST BANK TOWN OF JENIN.

ART DIRECTOR: BRONWER LATIMER. PHOTO EDITOR: OLIVIER PICARD. PUBLICATION: US NEWS & WORLD REPORT.

276. RICHARD ROSS

"A SLICED HEAD," ONE IN A SERIES OF CORONAL SECTIONS OF THE HEAD, FOR THE BOOK "MÜTTER MUSEUM," OCTOBER 2002

ART DIRECTOR: LAURA LINDGREN. PHOTO EDITOR: LAURA LINDGREN. DESIGNER: LAURA LINDGREN. EDITOR: LAURA LINDGREN. BOOK TITLE: MÜTTER MUSEUM. PUBLISHING COMPANY: BLAST BOOKS. AUTHOR: GRETCHEN WORDEN.

277-278. SEBASTIÃO SALGADO

TWO PHOTOGRAPHS FROM "PLANET SALGADO," MAY 2002, A SERIES ON THE POLIO EPIDEMIC IN CALCUTTA, INDIA.

ART DIRECTOR: DAVID HARRIS. PHOTO EDITOR: LISA BERMAN. PHOTO PRODUCER: RON BEINNER. DESIGNER: CHRIS ISRAEL. DIRECTOR OF PHOTOGRAPHY: SUSAN WHITE. EDITOR-IN-CHIEF: GRAYDON CARTER. PUBLICATION: VANITY FAIR. PUBLISHING COMPANY: CONDÉ NAST PUBLICATIONS, INC. WRITER: CHRISTOPHER HITCHENS.

279-280. NELSON BAKERMAN

TWO FROM A SERIES ENTITLED "TEEN SCENE."

281. DEREK SHAPTON

HIERVE EL AGUA MINERAL SPRINGS, MEXICO.

282. PETER RAD

"SAID THE CHAIR," 2000, IMAGE FOR THE FICTION EXCERPT OF DANIEL PINCHBECK'S MEMOIR "BREAKING OPEN THE HEAD," FOR "FALL BOOK

ART DIRECTOR: JANET FROELICH. PHOTO EDITOR: CAVAN FARRELL. EDITOR: ADAM MOSS. PUBLICATION: THE NEW YORK TIMES MAGAZINE. PUBLISHING COMPANY: THE NEW YORK TIMES. INTERVIEWS BY: CATHERINE SAINT LOUIS.

289. KURSTEN BRACCHI

UNTITLED, PERSONAL WORK.

290. NINA BERMAN

UNITED AIRLINE FLIGHT ATTENDANTS HOLD A PRAYER VIGIL AT THE CRASH SITE IN PENNSYLVANIA TO MARK THE FIRST ANNIVERSARY OF THE 911 TERRORIST ATTACKS, SEPTEMBER 11, 2002.

ART DIRECTOR: ARTHUR HOCHSTEIN. DEPUTY ART DIRECTOR: CYNTHIA A. HOFFMAN. PHOTO EDITOR: MICHELE STEPHENSON. ASSOCIATE PICTURE EDITOR: JAY COLTON. PUBLICATION: TIME. PUBLISHING COMPANY: TIME INC.

291. ERIC WEEKS

PHOTOGRAPH OF AUTHOR ANDREW SOLOMON, ASSIGNED OUTTAKE FOR NEWSWEEK.

PHOTO EDITOR: NICKI GOSTIN.

292. RAYMOND MEEKS

POWDER RIVER, ONE FROM A SERIES FOR THE ARTICLE "POWDER KEG," DECEMBER 2002, A STORY ON METHANE DRILLING IN THE WEST.

DESIGN DIRECTOR: KEVIN FISHER. PHOTO EDITOR: KIM HUBBARD. DESIGNER: KEVIN FISHER. EDITOR: DAVID SEIDEMAN. PUBLICATION: AUDUBON. PUBLISHING COMPANY: AUDUBON. WRITER: KEITH KLOOR.

293-294. RAYMOND MEEKS

TWO FROM A SERIES TAKEN AT THE 2002 SALT LAKE CITY WINTER OLYMPICS FOR THE BOOK "THE FIRE WITHIN," FEBRUARY 2002. PLATE 293: CROSS-COUNTRY SKIING. PLATE 294: SKI JUMPING.

DIRECTOR: LIBBY HYLAND. EXECUTIVE PHOTO PRODUCER: PAULINE PLOQUIN. PHOTO EDITOR: JOHN HUET. DESIGN MANAGER: RON STUCKI. EXECUTIVE EDITOR: SARAH J.M. TUFF. BOOK TITLE: THE FIRE WITHIN. PUBLISHING COMPANY: HALLMARK.

295. GEORGE PITTS

PHOTOGRAPH ENTITLED "STEFFIE," PERSONAL WORK FOR AN UPCOMING BOOK.

296-267. LARS TOPELMANN

TWO IMAGES FOR THE "SWAT" VIDEO GAME AD CAMPAIGN. PLATE 296: SORRY WE SHOT YOU IN THE STOMACH, BUT YOU ARE A FUGITIVE COP KILLER. PLATE 297: HAPPY HONEYMOON.

ART DIRECTOR: JASON BLACK. CREATIVE DIRECTOR: TRACY WONG. AGENCY: WONGDOODY. CLIENT: SIERRA ENTERTAINMENT/SWAT VIDEO GAMES. COPYWRITER: MATT MCCAIN.

298. JAMES BALOG

PHOTOGRAPH OF A "MIDDLETON PLANTATION OAK," MORE THAN 1000 YEARS OLD IS ONE OF THE LARGEST TREES IN THE SOUTHEAST U.S., ONE FROM A SERIES FOR THE ARTICLE "TALL STORIES," SUMMER 2002.

ART DIRECTOR: EVA LEE. EDITOR: BARRY TANENBAUM. PUBLICATION: NIKON WORLD. PUBLISHING COMPANY: NIKON, INC. WRITER: BARRY TANENBAUM.

DESIGN DIRECTOR: KEVIN FISHER. PHOTO EDITOR: KIM HUBBARD. DESIGNER: KEVIN FISHER. EDITOR: DAVID SEIDEMAN. PUBLICATION: AUDUBON. PUBLISHING COMPANY: AUDUBON. WRITER: MARY-POWEL THOMAS.

306-307. MAXI COHEN

TWO IN A SERIES FROM THE PERSONAL PROJECT "LADIES ROOMS AROUND THE WORLD." PLATE 306: "AREA, NYC" PLATE 307: "EAST SIDE AIR TERMINAL, NYC"

308. DAVID SHERRY

"TERRY AND ME," ONE FROM A SERIES EXPLORING THE COMPLEXITIES OF THE HUMAN PSYCHE, STUDENT WORK.

SCHOOL: RHODE ISLAND SCHOOL OF DESIGN.

309-310. DANIELLE LEVITT

TWO FROM A SERIES FOR THE FASHION STORY "JOCK GOTHS."

EDITOR: GAVIN MCINNES. PUBLICATION: VICE.

311. DANIELLE LEVITT

RICHARD SANDRAK, AGE 9, FOR THE ARTICLE "THE STRONGEST BOY ON EARTH," JUNE/JULY 2002.

ART DIRECTOR: ROCKWELL HARWOOD. PHOTO EDITOR: AMY STEIGBIGEL. PUBLICATION: DETAILS. PUBLISHING COMPANY: FAIRCHILD PUBLICATIONS. WRITER: CARL SWANSON.

312. DANIELLE LEVITT

RALPH WITTINGTON, PORN ARCHIVIST ON FETISH PHONE WATCHING A PORN VIDEO OF HIMSELF, FOR THE ARTICLE "THE LIBRARIAN OF SLEAZE," SEPTEMBER 2002.

ART DIRECTOR: ROCKWELL HARWOOD. PHOTO EDITOR: AMY STEIGBIGEL. PUBLICATION: DETAILS. PUBLISHING COMPANY: FAIRCHILD PUBLICATIONS. WRITER: KAREEM SAHIN.

313. DANIELLE LEVITT

LIL TROY JR. SITS ON HIS BED IN SUGARLAND, TEXAS, PERSONAL WORK.

314-317. DANIELLE LEVITT

FOUR FROM A SERIES OF FOREIGN EXCHANGE STUDENTS WITH THEIR HOST FAMILIES, FEBRUARY 2003.

PUBLICATION: NEO 2.

318. NEIL LEIFER

"KID GLOVES," MIKE TYSON HOLDS HIS TWO-MONTH-OLD SON, MIGUEL, AFTER BEING DEFEATED BY LENNOX LEWIS FOR THE HEAVYWEIGHT CHAMPIONSHIP, FOR THE FEATURE "LEADING OFF," JUNE 17, 2002.

CREATIVE DIRECTOR: STEVEN HOFFMAN. PHOTO EDITOR: JAMES K. COLTON. PUBLICATION: SPORTS ILLUSTRATED.

319. ROBBIE MCCLARAN

EDDIE, CHARLIE, LAURA AND JOSHUA MCDOWELL. THEIR MOTHER, WHEN PREGNANT WITH JOSHUA SUFFERED A MASSIVE CEREBRA ANEURYSM AND WAS KEPT ON LIFE SUPPORT UNTIL THE BABY WAS DELIVERED BY CESARIAN SECTION, ONE FROM THE SELF-PUBLISHED BOOK "ORDINARY PEOPLE," DECEMBER 2002.

ART DIRECTOR: ROBBIE MCCLARAN. DESIGNER: LYDIA HESS. BOOK TITLE: ORDINARY PEOPLE.

PUBLICATION: DETAILS. PUBLISHING COMPANY: FAIRCHILD PUBLCATIONS. WRITER: T.Z. PARSA.

236. VERA HARTMANN

TWO MEMBERS AT THE MARS SOCIETY DESERT RESEARCH STATION IN UTAH, FOR THE ARTICLE "LOST IN SPACE-A TIGHTROPE WALK BETWEEN FAITH AND SCIENCE," PUBLISHED IN "FACTS" MAY 2002.

PHOTO DIRECTOR: JÜRG KLOTZ. PUBLICATION: FACTS. PUBLISHING COMPANY: TA MEDIA AG, ZURICH, SWITZERLAND. WRITER: RAINER KLOSE.

237. VERA HARTMANN

PHOTOGRAPH ON-SET WITH SIN CITY PRODUCTIONS IN MALIBU, CA, FOR THE ARTICLE "BODY WORK," OCTOBER 2002.

PHOTO DIRECTOR: JÜRG KLOTZ. PUBLICATION: FACTS. PUBLISHING COMPANY: TA MEDIA AG, ZURICH, SWITZERLAND. WRITER: STEFAN BARMETTLER.

238-239. CLAUDIO EDINGER

TWO PHOTOGRAPHS FROM A PERSONAL PROJECT ON THE BEACHES OF BRAZIL.

240. LLOYD ZIFF

"SARAH," DECEMBER 27, 2002, ONE FROM AN UPCOMING BOOK "MY FRIENDS' CHILDREN."

241. JOSEF ASTOR

ONE FROM A SERIES FOR "THE MAN WHO MISTOOK HIS WIFE FOR A DEER...AND OTHER TALES FROM THE NEW SCIENCE OF EXTREME SLEEP," FEBRUARY 2, 2003, A FEATURE ON A RARE SLEEP DISORDER.

ART DIRECTOR: JANET FROELICH. PHOTO EDITORS: KATHY RYAN, CAVAN FARRELL. DESIGNER: JOELE CUYLER. EDITOR: ADAM MOSS. PUBLICATION: ZTHE NEW YORK TIMES MAGAZINE. PUBLISHING COMPANY: THE NEW YORK TIMES. WRITER: CHIP BROWN.

250. MARK SELIGER

MODEL HEIDI KLUM AS SHE REENACTS A FAMOUS HOLLYWOOD MOMENT BETWEEN SOPHIA LOREN AND JAYNE MANSFIELD, ONE FROM A SERIES FOR "THE SEX GODDESSES," SEPTEMBER 2002.

DESIGN DIRECTOR: FRED WOODWARD. DIRECTOR OF PHOTOGRAPHY: JENNIFER CRANDALL. DESIGNER: PAUL MARTINEZ. PUBLICATION: GQ. PUBLISHING COMPANY: CONDÉ NAST PUBLICATIONS, INC.

251. JOHN MIDGLEY

HRITHIK ROSHAN, ONE OF INDIA'S BIGGEST MOVIE STARS, RUNNING THROUGH THE STREETS OF BOMBAY'S FILM CITY, FOR THE FEATURE "ESCAPE FROM PLANET BOLLYWOOD," MARCH 2002.

DESIGN DIRECTOR: FRED WOODWARD. DIRECTOR OF PHOTOGRAPHY: JENNIFER CRANDALL. PHOTO EDITOR: CATHERINE TALESE. DESIGNER: MATTHEW LENNING. EDITOR: JIM NELSON. PUBLICATION: GQ. PUBLISHING COMPANY: CONDÉ NAST PUBLICATIONS, INC. WRITER: GUY LAWSON.

252. CHRIS SHIPMAN

ARTIST ANDREA ZITTEL SOAKS IN HER RE-APPROPRIATED COW-TROUGH TUB IN HER JOSHUA TREE HOME CALLED A-Z WEST (THERE'S ALSO THE BROOKLYN HOME CALLED A-Z EAST), ONE FROM A SERIES FOR THE ARTICLE "LIVING A TO Z," DECEMBER 2002.

ART DIRECTOR: JEANETTE HODGE ABBINK. PHOTO EDITOR: MAREN LEVINSON. DESIGNER: JEANETTE HODGE ABBINK. EDITOR: ALLISON ARIEFF. PUBLICATION: DWELL. PUBLISHING COMPANY: DWELL LLC. WRITER: MIMI ZEIGER.

253. FRANK W. OCKENFELS 3

PHOTOGRAPH OF SATURDAY NIGHT LIVE CAST MEMBER TINA FEY AS DOROTHY PARKER, FOR THE NEW YORK AWARDS 2002.

DESIGN DIRECTOR: DAVID MATT. DESIGNER: RANDALL LEERS. PHOTO DIRECTOR: CHRIS NATIONAL PARK CALLED THE THOROFARE, FOR THE ARTICLE "HIDDEN YELLOWSTONE-THE MOONBOW CHRONICLES," MAY 2002.

ART DIRECTOR: JULIE CURTIS. PHOTO EDITOR: SABINE MEYER. DESIGNER: JULIE CURTIS. EDITOR: STEVE BYERS. PUBLICATION: NATIONAL GEOGRAPHIC ADVENTURE. PUBLISHING COMPANY: NATIONAL GEOGRAPHIC SOCIETY. WRITER: TIM CAHILL.

265. JAMES WHITE

WRITER AND AVID CYCLIST MIKE MAGNUSON FOR THE ARTICLE "HEFT ON WHEELS," MAY 2002.

DESIGN DIRECTOR: FRED WOODWARD. DIRECTOR OF PHOTOGRAPHY: JENNIFER CRANDALL. PHOTO EDITOR: CATHERINE TALESE. EDITOR: MARK HEALY. PUBLICATION: GQ. PUBLISHING COMPANY: CONDÉ NAST PUBLICATIONS, INC. WRITER: MIKE MAGNUSON.

266. JAMES WHITE

ACTRESS JULIANNE MOORE FOR THE FEATURE "MAKING HER OWN RULES," DECEMBER 13, 2002.

PHOTO EDITOR: SARAH ROZEN. PUBLICATION: ENTERTAINMENT WEEKLY. PUBLISHING COMPANY: TIME INC.

267. KATY GRANNAN

PORTRAIT OF SINGER/SONGWRITER BILLYJOEL.

PHOTO EDITOR: KATHY RYAN. PUBLICATION: THE NEW YORK TIMES MAGAZINE. PUBLISHING COMPANY: THE NEW YORK TIMES.

268. KATY GRANNAN

THE SUELTZ FAMILY FOR "HOUSE HUSBANDS."

PHOTO EDITOR: COURTNEY DOLAN. PUBLICATION: NEWSWEEK. PUBLISHING COMPANY: NEWSWEEK INC.

269. JENNY GAGE & TOM BETTERTON

ACTRESS JESSICA BIEL FOR THE PROFILE "HEAVEN SENT," SEPTEMBER 2002.

PREVIEW: NOT FOR HUMAN CONSUMPTION," SEPTEMBER 2002.

DESIGN DIRECTOR: ROCKWELL HARWOOD. DIRECTOR OF PHOTOGRAPHY: AMY STEIGBIGEL. ASSOCIATE ART DIRECTOR: NATHALIE KIRSHEH. PUBLICATION: DETAILS. PUBLISHING COMPANY: FAIRCHILD PUBLICATIONS. AUTHOR: DANIEL PINCHBECK.

283-284. DIDIER RUEF

TWO FROM A SERIES FOR "MOUNTAIN PROBLEMS," NOVEMBER 2002,SHOT IN THE SWISS ALPS.

ART DIRECTOR: PERCY CHUNG. DIRECTOR OF PHOTOGRAPHY: JENNIFER SPENCER KENTRUP. DESIGNER: HOWARD LEUNG. EDITOR: STUART LAWRENCE. PUBLICATION: DISCOVERY. PUBLISHING COMPANY: EMPHASIS MEDIA LTD.

285. ALEX MAJOLI

THE SOMALI BANTUS HAVE BEEN PERSECUTED AND EXILED AND WILL SOON FIND REFUGE IN AMERICA, FOR THE ARTICLE "FOLLOWING FREEDOM'S TRAIL," SEPTEMBER 2, 2002.

ASSISTANT MANAGING EDITOR/DESIGN: LYNN STALEY. DIRECTOR OF PHOTOGRAPHY: SARAH HARBUTT. PHOTO EDITOR: JAMES WELLFORD. EDITOR: MARK WHITAKER. PUBLICATION: NEWSWEEK. PUBLISHING COMPANY: NEWSWEEK, INC.

286-287. ALEX MAJOLI

TWO FROM A SERIES FOR "A DEADLY PASSAGE TO INDIA," OCTOBER 25, 2002, AN ARTICLE ON THE GROWING NUMBER OF AIDS CASES.

ASSISTANT MANAGING EDITOR/DESIGN: LYNN STALEY. DIRECTOR OF PHOTOGRAPHY: SARAH HARBUTT. EDITOR: MARK WHITAKER. PUBLICATION: NEWSWEEK. PUBLISHING COMPANY: NEWSWEEK, INC.

288. SAGE SOHIER

WESLEY MORGAN, WATERTOWN, MA, WITH HIS MODEL OF KANDAHAR, AFGHANISTAN, FOR "WHAT THEY WERE THINKING," DECEMBER 1. 2001

299-300. BRIGITTE LACOMBE

ACTOR RORY CULKIN, IN THE HANDS OF A LEADING MAKE-UP ARTIST, GOES FROM AGE 13 TO 30 FOR THE ARTICLE "COMING OF AGE IN HOLLYWOOD." NOVEMBER 3, 2002.

ART DIRECTOR: JANET FROELICH. PHOTO EDITOR: KIRA POLLACK. DESIGNER: NANCY HARRIS. EDITOR: ADAM MOSS. PUBLICATION: THE NEW YORK TIMES MAGAZINE. PUBLISHING COMPANY: THE NEW YORK TIMES.

301. JULIANA SOHN

PINO CINQUEMANI STANDING IN HIS CENTURY-OLD NEW YORK BUTCHER SHOP, FOR THE ARTICLE "IN THE WORKS...PRIME TIME," DECEMBER 2002.

DESIGN DIRECTOR: ROCKWELL HARWOOD. DIRECTOR OF PHOTOGRAPHY: AMY STEIGBIGEL. ASSOCIATE ART DIRECTOR: NATHALIE KIRSHEH. PUBLICATION: DETAILS. PUBLISHING COMPANY: FAIRCHILD PUBLICATIONS. WRITER: BRETT MARTIN.

302. ROB HOWARD

WRESTLER PARVIS KIAI FLEXES FOR HIS FAN CLUB, FOR THE ARTICLE "EVERYBODY LOVES THE ASSASSINS," OCTOBER 2002.

CREATIVE DIRECTOR: HANNAH MCCAUGHEY. PHOTO EDITOR: ROB HAGGART. PUBLICATION: OUTSIDE. PUBLISHING COMPANY: MARIAH MEDIA, INC.

303. JIM ERICKSON

"HEADLESS CORSET," OUTTAKE FOR A MAKE-A-WISH FOUNDATION OF AMERICA CAMPAIGN SHOOT.

AGENCY: MARC USA. CLIENT: MAKE-A-WISH FOUNDATION. ASSOCIATE CREATIVE DIRECTOR: STEVE LOWRY. VP, CREATIVE DIRECTOR: KRIS KNIEREIM. PRINT PRODUCTION SUPERVISOR: BETH HURLEY. COLOR RETOUCHING: FATCAT DIGITAL.

304-305. HENRY HORENSTEIN

TWO FROM A SERIES OF AQUATIC CREATURES FOR THE ARTICLE "WATER WORLD," MAY/JUNE 2002. COURTESY OF PHOTONICA.

320. MAURA MCEVOY

LAMB JUST AFTER HIS TAIL HAD BEEN "RINGED," FRASIER FAMILY FARM IN MT. BENGER, NEW ZEALAND.

PHOTO EDITOR: MAYA KAIMAL. PUBLICATION: SAVEUR. PUBLISHING COMPANY: WORLD PUBLICATIONS. WRITER: MEGAN WETHERALL.

321-322. LIDA & MISO SUCHY

TWO PHOTOGRAPHS FROM A COLLECTION FOR THE BOOK "SCHATTENLICHT/SHADOW LIGHT," 2002. PLATE 321: WASSYL POTJAK TAKES HIS ONE DAY OFF FROM WORKING THE FIELDS FOR A PEDICURE. PLATE 322: ANNA TSCHARUK, IN HER WEDDING GOWN, LEAVES HER HOME FOR THE LAST TIME.

DIRECTOR OF PHOTOGRAPHY: RUTH EICHHORN. PHOTO EDITORS: NADJA MASRI, MARKUS SEEWALD. DESIGNER: MELANIE WOLTER. EDITORS: ULRIKE MOSER, TORBEN MUELLER, JENS SCHROEDER. BOOK TITLE: SCHATTENLICHT - SHADOW LIGHT. PUBLISHING COMPANY: GEO, GRUNER + JAHR. GERMANY PUBLISHER: PETER-MATTHIAS GAEDE.

323. CHRIS BUCK

OPENING PHOTOGRAPH FOR THE ARTICLE "THE SECRET LIVES OF SUBURBAN STONERS," FEBRUARY 2002.

ART DIRECTOR: JOHN KORPICS. PHOTO EDITOR: NANCY JO IACOI. DESIGNER: JOHN KORPICS. PUBLICATION: ESQUIRE. PUBLISHING COMPANY: HEARST MAGAZINES. WRITER: ANONYMOUS.

324. CHRIS BUCK

"BEFORE" PHOTOGRAPH OF A MAN ABOUT TO GET GASTRIC BYPASS (STOMACH REDUCTION) SURGERY, FOR THE ARTICLE "THE DIET OF LAST RESORT," JUNE 10, 2002.

PHOTO EDITORS: CARRIE LEVY, SIMON BARNETT. PUBLICATION: NEWSWEEK. PUBLISHING COMPANY: NEWSWEEK, INC.

PHOTOGRAPHER CONTACT INDEX

LORI ADAMSKI-PEEK 145
435-649-0259
ADAMSKIPEEK.COM
LAPCAM.NET

LYNSEY ADDARIO 106-109
C/O CORBIS
212-375-7749
CHRISTINAC@CORBIS.COM

MAX AGUILERA-HELLWEG 202
C/O BILL CHARLES
212-965-1465
MAILBOX@BILLCHARLES.COM
BILLCHARLES.COM

DAVID S. ALLEE 42-43
917-923-9774
DAVID@DAVIDALLEE.COM
DAVIDALLEE.COM

KWAKU ALSTON 13-15
310-392-9957
KWAKUALSTON@ATTBI.COM
KWAKUALSTON.COM

ANDY ANDERSON 27-28, 66
208-587-3161
STUDIO@ANDYANDERSONPHOTO.COM
ANDYANDERSONPHOTO.COM

CHRISTOPHER ANDERSON 272-275
011-33-679-679055
ANDERSON@VIIPHOTO.COM
VIIPHOTO.COM

DIRK ANSCHÜTZ 149
212-475-4715
DIRK@KNIPSER.COM
KNIPSER.COM

KIKE ARNAL 104-105
C/O CORBIS
212-375-7749
CHRISTINAC@CORBIS.COM

JOSEF ASTOR 240
212-307-5588
ART-DEPT.COM

KT AULETA 31
917-907-3415
KTAULETA@EARTHLINK.NET
KTKT.ORG

MYRIAM BABIN 24
917-488-7198
MYRIAM.BABIN@VERIZON.NET

ANDREA BAKACS 262
917-968-6415
ANDREA_BAKACS@HOTMAIL.COM

NELSON BAKERMAN 279-280
718-596-3696
NELSON@
NELSONBAKERMAN.COM

JAMES BALOG 298
JAMESBALOG.COM

OLIVIA BEASLEY 260-261
011-44-207-831-6361
OLIVIA@OLIVIABEASLEY.COM
BURNHAM-NIKER.COM

CHRISTOPHER BEIRNE 102-103

HARRY BENSON 11
212-249-0284
INFO@
HARRYBENSON.COM

NINA BERMAN 290

TOM BETTERTON 269

ANDREA BOOHER 180
970-925-7447
ABPHOTOG@AOL.COM

ALEXANDRA BOULAT 33
C/O VII
011-33-1-4348-4540

KURSTEN BRACCHI 289

MARTIN BRADING 150-151
212-255-6171
SSEYFRIED@THEAGENCYREPS.COM
THEAGENCYREPS.COM

FREDRIK BRODEN 146-148
214-748-7397
RENEERHYNER.COM

KATE BROOKS 7
C/O CORBIS
212-375-7749
CHRISTINAC@CORBIS.COM

CHRIS BUCK 323-324
212-219-1269
CHRIS@CHRISBUCK.COM
CHRISBUCK.COM

DAVID BURNETT 67
C/O CONTACT PRESS IMAGES
212-695-7750

JOHN B. CARNETT 76
201-323-9053
CARNETTPHOTO.COM

ELINOR CARUCCI 18-21
C/O SIMON CROCKER,
LIGHT INDUSTRY LTD.
011 44 (0) 207 713 8337
SIMON@LIGHTINDUSTRY.INFO
ELINORCARUCCI.COM

CHIEN-CHI CHANG 125

CHIEN-MIN CHUNG 125
CHINSTER@YAHOO.COM
CHINA-PIX.COM

DANNY CLINCH 189-194
212-244-8548
DCLINCH@EARTHLINK.NET
DANNYCLINCH.COM

MAXI COHEN 306-307
212-925-0295
MAXICOHEN@AOL.COM

GREGORY CREWDSON 213-217

CRAIG CUTLER 50-51
212-779-9755
CRAIG@CRAIGCUTLER.COM
CRAIGCUTLER.COM

CANDACE DICARLO 257
215-468-8000
CARAMELLA@EARTHLINK.NET

TONY D'ORIO 44-47
312-421-5532
TD1147@AOL.COM
HUREWITZ.COM

BRYCE DUFFY 65
888-226-4151
BRYCE@PICTUREALITY.COM
PICTUREALITY.COM

JOHN DUGDALE 52-53

AMY ECKERT 41
917-945-7494
AMY@ECHONYC.COM

CLAUDIO EDINGER 238-239
C/O CORBIS
212-375-7749
CHRISTINAC@CORBIS.COM

WILLIAM EGGLESTON 143-144
C/O CHEIM & READ, NEW YORK
212-242-7727

SEAN ELLIS 101
KAYTE@THEOFFICE.COM
SEAN-ELLIS.COM

JIM ERICKSON 303
707-789-0405
INFO@ERICKSONSTOCK.COM
ERICKSONSTOCK.COM

GLEN ERLER 97

DONNA FERRATO 188

LARRY FINK 245-247
C/O BILL CHARLES
212-965-1465
MAILBOX@BILLCHARLES.COM
BILLCHARLES.COM

LAUREN FLEISHMAN 115
917-692-0035
LAURENJ1978@AOL.COM

JASON FULFORD 169
570-430-0712
MAIL@JASONFULFORD.COM
JASONFULFORD.COM

JENNY GAGE 269

DAVID GLOMB 248
760-340-4455
D.GLOMB@WORLDNET.ATT.NET

ANTHONY GORDON 1-6
917-912-3497
ANTHONYGORDON@
EARTHLINK.NET

KATY GRANNAN 267-268
C/O BILL CHARLES
212-965-1465
MAILBOX@BILLCHARLES.COM
BILLCHARLES.COM

LAUREN GREENFIELD 158-162
310-822-3545
LAUREN@LAURENGREENFIELD.COM
GIRLCULTURE.COM

JAMIL GS 122

DALE GUNNOE 258
917-803-7988
DGUNNOE@OPENUNIVERSE.COM

MATT HENRY GUNTHER 242
212-780-5754
BEG8@EARTHLINK.NET

KYOKO HAMADA 16-17
212-777-1472
KYOKONEXTDOOR@
EARTHLINK.NET
DSREPS.COM

VERA HARTMANN 236-237
213-713-0976
323-666-3818
VERAHARTMANN@SBCGLOBAL.NET
INFO@VERAHARTMANN.COM
VERAHARTMANN.COM

MARK HEITHOFF 54-55
212-941-1549
MHEITHOFF@EARTHLINK.NET
MZPHOTO.COM

HENRY HORENSTEIN 304-305
617-426-4222

SARAH HOSKINS 243-244
847-573-8122
SHOSKINSPHOTO@EARTHLINK.NET
SARAHHOSKINS.COM

ROB HOWARD 302
C/O DS REPS
626-441-2224
DEBORAH@DSREPS.COM
DSREPS.COM

WILLIAM HOWARD 220-221
626-441-5483
WILLIAM@WILLIAMHOWARD.NET
WILLIAMHOWARD.NET

JOHN HUET 69-71
C/O MARILYN CADENBACH
617-868-2004
JOHNHUET.COM

STEPHAN JACOBS 167
617-780-9763
STEPHANWJACOBS@
HOTMAIL.COM

JONAS KARLSSON 165-166
C/O WALTER SCHUPFER
212-366-4675
SCHUPFER.COM

MICHAEL KELLEY 222-223
626-405-1965
MKELLEYPHOTOS@
EARTHLINK.NET

BRENDA ANN KENNEALLY
718-574-7022
MSBIGMOPHO@MSN.COM

LISA KERESZI 91-92
LISA.KERESZI.ART.00@AYA.YALE.EDU
RHIZOMESTUDIOS.COM/ARTISTS/
LISA_KERESZI.HTML

MARK KESSELL 259

MARK KLETT 126
480-968-1281
MKLETT@ASU.EDU

HENRIK KNUDSEN 63
212-219-1269
HENRIK@HENRIKKNUDSEN.COM
JULIANRICHARDS.COM

ANTONIN KRATOCHVIL 225-230
C/O VII
212-947-1589
K.KNYC@VERIZON.NET

HUGH KRETSCHMER 81-82
718-237-2602
HUGH.STUDIO@VERIZON.NET
SHARPEONLINE.COM

BRIGITTE LACOMBE 299-300
C/O JANET JOHNSON
212-929-9660
JANET@LACOMBENW.COM

OLIVIER LAUDE 123-124
415-753-2662
OLIVIER@OLIVIERLAUDE.COM
OLIVIERLAUDE.COM

MOLLIE LAURIENZO 127
617-792-0531
MOLLIE5@EARTHLINK.NET

CATHERINE LEDNER 116-117

NEIL LEIFER 318
212-315-2957
NEILLEIFER.COM

JANA LEON 72
212-966-2050
JANA@JANALEON.COM
JANALEON.COM

LUCY LEVENE 114
C/O MILLER/GEISLER GALLERY
212-255-2885

DANIELLE LEVITT 309-317
917-749-5114
DANIELLELEVITT@HOTMAIL.COM
DANIELLELEVITT.COM

MICHAEL LEWIS 83
917-589-1277
MICHAELLEWIS88@
EARTHLINK.NET

DANA LIXENBERG 203-207
212-431-9466

LOGAN & LOGAN PHOTOGRAPHY 64
310-318-3920
LOGAN-LOGAN.COM

MATT MAHURIN 84

JOSEPH MAIDA 39-40
212-531-1814
INFO@JOSEPHMAIDA.COM
JOSEPHMAIDA.COM

DAVID MAISEL 218-219
415-331-8383
DAVID@DAVIDMAISEL.COM
DAVIDMAISEL.COM

ALEX MAJOLI 285-287
C/O MAGNUM PHOTOS
212-929-6000

MARY ELLEN MARK 197-198
212-925-2770

BOB MARTIN 61
212-522-3131
BOB@BOBMARTIN.COM

ROBERT MAXWELL 199-201
212-925-4222
ART-DEPT.COM

ROBBIE MCCLARAN 319
503-234-6588
ROBBIE@MCCLARAN.COM
MCCLARAN.COM

MAURA MCEVOY 320
646-279-6317
MCEVOYPHOTO@
EARTHLINK.NET

RYAN MCGINLEY 25
C/O PETER HAY HALPERT FINE ART
212-988-3662
PHHFINEART.COM

AMANDA MEANS 22-23
212-477-4935
AMEANS9933@AOL.COM
C/O RICCO/MARESCA GALLERY
212-627-4819

RAYMOND MEEKS 292-294
406-363-2773
RAYMONDMEEKS@
EARTHLINK.NET

JOHN MIDGLEY 251

GREG MILLER 30
718-625-8938
GREG@GREGMILLER.COM
GREGMILLER.COM

CHRISTOPHER MORRIS 36
C/O VII
MORRISVII@MAC.COM

TOM MURPHY 264
406-222-2986
TOM@MURPHYWILD.COM

JAMES NACHTWEY 37
C/O VII

HANS NELEMAN 110-11
212-274-1000
HANS@NELEMAN.COM
NELEMAN.COM

TIBOR NEMETH 29
978-741-2555
TIBOR3@ATTBI.COM
TIBORNEMETH.COM

JEFFERY NEWBURY 271

SIMON NORFOLK 35
011-44-207-254-9620
SIMON.NORFOLK@GROWBAG.COM

WILL NUÑEZ 179
212-908-0871
WILLIAM.NUNEZ@
FITCHRATINGS.COM

ERIN PATRICE O'BRIEN 112-113
718-783-8635
ERINPATRICEOBRIEN.COM

FRANK W. OCKENFELS3 253

LYLE OWERKO 174-177
212-349-3600
LYLE@WONDERLUST.COM
WONDERLUST.COM
POLARISIMAGES.COM

ROBERT PARKEHARRISON 139-142

NIGEL PARRY 186-187
C/O CREATIVE
PHOTOGRAPHERS INC.
212-683-1455

JOSHUA PAUL 152
718-855-2040
JOSH@JOSHUAPAUL.COM
JOSHUAPAUL.COM

PAOLO PELLEGRIN 208-212
C/O MAGNUM PHOTOS
212-929-6000
MAGNUMPHOTOS.COM

ALLAN PENN 26
617-423-1776
PENN@ALLANPENN.COM
ALLANPENN.COM

MARK PETERSON 251
C/O CORBIS
212-375-7749
CHRISTINAC@CORBIS.COM

GEORGE PITTS 269
212-448-7437
GPITTS@VIBE.COM

PLATON 153-157
C/O ART DEPARTMENT
212-925-4222
PLATONPHOTO.COM

PETER RAD 282

JOSEPH RAFFERTY 136-138
213-380-3933
INFO@HAMILTONGRAY.COM
HAMILTONGRAY.COM

KAI REGAN 59-60
C/O (SIC)
212-352-8247
WAKEFIELD@SICUSA.NET
SICUSA.NET

EUGENE RICHARDS 170-173
718-788-5342
RICHARDSEUGENE@AOL.COM

MARK RICHARDS 263
415-389-8253
MARK@MARKRICHARDS.COM

RICHARD ROSS 276
805-965-0486
805-452-1933
RICHARDROSS.NET

NORMAN JEAN ROY 73-74

DIDIER RUEF 283-284
41-79-691-2070
DRUEF@PIXSIL.COM
PIXSIL.COM

SEBASTIÃO SALGADO 277-278
C/O JEFFREY SMITH
CONTACT PRESS IMAGES
212-695-7750
CONTACTPRESSIMAGES.COM

HOWARD SCHATZ
212-334-6667
HOWARDSCHATZ.COM

CHRISTINE SCHIAVO 56-58
917-647-5736
RIVETGIRL@EARTHLINK.NET
CHRISSCHIAVO.COM

MARTIN SCHOELLER 128-130
C/O CORBIS
212-375-7749
CHRISTINAC@CORBIS.COM

COLLIER SCHORR 195-196

VICTOR SCHRAGER 118-119
212-925-3028

SHAUL SCHWARZ 255
C/O CORBIS
212-375-7749
CHRISTINAC@CORBIS.COM

MARK SELIGER 249-250

DEREK SHAPTON 281
416-588-7924
DEREK@DEREKSHAPTON.COM
DEREKSHAPTON.COM

DAVID SHERRY 308
917-273-8983
DAVIDSHERRY@HOTMAIL.COM
DAVIDSHERRY.NET

CHRIS SHIPMAN 252
C/O GENERAL & SPECIFIC
212-219-9919
CHRIS@GENERALANDSPECIFIC.COM
GENERALANDSPECIFIC.COM

STEPHEN SHORE 133-134
C/O BILL CHARLES
212-965-1465
MAILBOX@BILLCHARLES.COM
BILLCHARLES.COM

ZUBIN SHROFF 163
646-638-4022
ZUBIN@MINDSPRING.COM

JULIUS SHULMAN 248
323-654-0877
MCKEE@MAIL.SILCOM.COM

BHARAT SIKKA 98-99

TARYN SIMON 94-95
C/O ART & COMMERCE
212-206-0737

PEGGY SIROTA 131

RODNEY SMITH 232-233
845-359-3814
RODNEY@RODNEYSMITH.COM
RODNEYSMITH.COM

SAGE SOHIER 288
617-277-3530

JULIANA SOHN 301

JERRY SPAGNOLI 178

DAVID HARRY STEWART 12
212-242-0457
STUDIO@DHSTEWART.COM
DHSTEWART.COM

DAVID STRICK 270
310-473-5349
DAVID@DAVIDSTRICK.COM
DAVIDSTRICK.COM

LIDA & MISO SUCHY 321-322

LARRY SULTAN 235

JUSTIN SUTCLIFFE 168
C/O ISF 011-44-1628-54255

GARY TANHAUSER 85

WYATT TILLOTSON 62
808-277-4004

LARS TOPELMANN 296-297
503-288-6013
STUDIO@LARSMANN.COM
LARSTOPELMANN.COM

ALEXANDER TSIARAS 185

ILKKA UIMONEN 38

PAOLO VENTURA 181-184
718-221-8171
PAOLOVENTURA@YAHOO.COM

SACHA WALDMAN 93

JUDY WALGREN 9-10
214-282-5422
JWALGREN@EARTHLINK.NET

MICHAEL WARING 135
917-225-1540
INFO@TROOPER-CA.COM

CHRISTIAN WEBER 32
212-655-6500
INFO@CHRISTIANWEBER.NET
CHRISTIANWEBER.NET

ERIC WEEKS 291
917-701-1965
ERICWEEKSPHOTO@EARTHLINK.NET

WILLIAM WEGMAN 90
WEGMANWORLD.COM

WILL WENDT 234
413-446-9492
WILLIAMWENDT01230@YAHOO.COM

JAMES WHITE 265-266
C/O ART MIX THE AGENCY
310-473-0770

MELANIE WILLHIDE 75
MELANIEWILLHIDE.COM

MAGNUS WINTER 100
BRANSCH.NET

DAN WINTERS 85-89
323-957-5699

NANCY WOLF 231
415-971-0336
NANCYWOLFPHOTOGRAHY.COM

ILAN WOLFF 2224
212-864-4960
PARIS2NY@EARTHLINK.NET
CHARLESNESPHOTOGRAPHY.COM

LLOYD ZIFF 241
631-323-0121
LZIFF@OPTONLINE.NET
LLOYDZIFFPHOTOGRAPHY.COM

ANDREW ZUCKERMAN 132
212-727-3988
ANDREWZUCKERMAN.COM